THE PRESIDENTS AND THE PASTIME

The Presidents and the Pastime

The History of Baseball and the White House

CURT SMITH

University of Nebraska Press
Lincoln and London

Small portions of this book originally appeared in *Windows on the White House* (South Bend IN: Diamond Communications, 1997), also by Curt Smith.

Library of Congress Cataloging-in-Publication Data
Names: Smith, Curt, author.
Title: The presidents and the pastime: the history of baseball and the White House / Curt Smith.
Description: Lincoln: University of Nebraska Press, 2018. | Includes bibliographical references and index.
Identifiers: LCCN 2017045455
ISBN 9780803288096 (cloth: alk. paper)
ISBN 9781496207395 (epub)
ISBN 9781496207401 (mobi)
ISBN 9781496207418 (pdf)
Subjects: LCSH: Baseball—United States—History—Anecdotes. | Presidents—United States—History—Anecdotes. | BISAC: SPORTS & RECREATION / Baseball / History.
Classification: LCC GV867.3 .S63 2018 | DDC 796.3570973—dc23 LC record available at https://lccn.loc.gov/2017045455

Set in Minion Pro by E. Cuddy.

Cover caption: President Franklin D. Roosevelt throws out the first ball on April 24, 1934, to inaugurate the home season of the defending American League champion Washington Senators before a crowd of twenty-five thousand at Griffith Stadium in the nation's capital. FDR tossed the traditional presidential first pitch of the season a record eight times. The visiting Boston Red Sox won this game, 5–0. Shown at right are DC's owner and manager respectively: Clark Griffith (*left, standing, in suit*) and Joe Cronin (*right, in uniform*).

For my parents
Howard and Guendolen Smith
The best teacher is example

CONTENTS

ILLUSTRATIONS

Following page 232

ACKNOWLEDGMENTS

A t one time or another, almost every American will express a view on two institutions that are *ours*—the presidency of the United States and the national pastime of baseball. *The Presidents and the Pastime: The History of Baseball and the White House* is the first book to explore in detail this only-in-America twinning of the heart.

A father may not know the color of his children's eyes but can explain why he feels a certain president is or was a failure or success. Aunt Maude long ago forgot her favorite nephew's birthday but not what Carl Yastrzemski hit in Boston's forever magic place of 1967.

In 1950 Lawrence Peter "Yogi" Berra was honored by his hometown of St. Louis. Six decades later he exceeds William Shakespeare as the man most quoted by American public speakers. "I'd like to thank all the people who made this day *necessary*," Yogi had told his home people. *The Presidents and the Pastime* shows how most presidents have found baseball to be necessary.

In 1943 many believed broadcaster Bill Stern's specious admonition that president Abraham Lincoln, on his deathbed, was said to have told General Abner Doubleday, the game's fictitious founder: "Save baseball for the kids. Don't let it die." As a child, my armies of the interior were baseball and the presidency. This book suggests why most presidents have regarded baseball as the Great American Game, tied inexorably to the Great American Dream.

xi

Begun during president Barack Obama's second term, *The Presidents* was written for release in his successor's—surprisingly, Donald Trump's—first term. After writing speeches for president George H. W. Bush in 1989–93, I informally headed his volunteer speech staff when he and I left the White House. The number 41, to signify his forty-first presidency, distinguished Bush from son George W. Bush's 43, as in forty-third. I have used nicknames for some presidents that they originated, encouraged, or had attached to them by others.

The Presidents and the Pastime tells of the official, political, and personal relationship between America's most mythical office and mythological game. It begins with future presidents before America became a nation; wends to Martin Van Buren in 1839 at Cooperstown, New York, a century before the birth there of the National Baseball Hall of Fame and Library (now Museum); and segues to the first trek to the Hall by a president in office. Obama writes in its 2014 guest register his ode to Chicago's Pale Hose: "Go [White] Sox!" In 2005 they finally had, taking the World Series after an eighty-eight-year title lull, apparently not wishing to peak too soon.

Herein are events told by and about presidents and other major-party nominees with whom I have been privileged to speak, including George H. W. Bush and George W. Bush, Michael Dukakis, Gerald Ford, George McGovern, Walter Mondale, Richard Nixon, and Ronald Reagan. Some are gone now. I thank all for their time. Several writers merit special note. TIME magazine's late columnist and White House correspondent Hugh Sidey was John F. Kennedy's favorite journalist. Many of Hugh's best stories timelessly reference honor. Tom DeFrank, *Newsweek magazine* White House correspondent and long-time student of Bush 41, was Ford's favorite White House contributor. Peggy Noonan's *Wall Street Journal* column is must weekend reading. I am glad here to employ at least a sample of her art.

I specifically want to thank William B. Mead and Paul Dickson for the splendid research they provided a quarter century ago with their 1993 work, *Baseball: The Presidents' Game.* I have referenced every distinguished journalist and his or her invaluable work throughout. I am indebted to L. Robert Davids, founder of the Society for American Baseball Research (SABR), for the list of the majority of games attended by each U.S. president. Thomas B. Koetting's superb *Wichita Eagle* story of May 3, 1992, reported Dwight Eisenhower's strange baseball odyssey. The Nixon Presidential Library and Museum supplied the late president's 1972 and 1992 "Nixon Dream Team." The late Ron Menchine, whom I came to know in the last several years of his life, spun one Senators baseball tale after another. (Incidentally, these pages interchangeably use the names "Senators," "Nationals," and "Nats" for Washington's historic baseball franchise, as their teams and fans have since the early 1900s.)

I wish to thank numerous baseball and other electronic and print journalists: David Barron, Greg Brown, Joe Castiglione, Fred Dicker, Doug Gamble, Hank Greenwald, Bob Grim, Ken Harrelson, Pat Hughes, Peter King, Ken Korach, Jon Miller, Phil Mushnick, Bill Nowlin, Mary Ann Peters, Ben Platt, Ed Randall, Richard Sandomir, Charlie Steiner, George Vecsey, and the late and great Dick Enberg and Bob Wolff. I am especially grateful to Sean McGrory, executive editor, Messenger Post Media, a member of GateHouse Media, for helping my column to coexist with this book's travel and research.

Winston Churchill said, "To jaw-jaw is always better than wah-wah." (Whatever the situation, Churchill almost invariably coined a quote that pertained.) Many of those listed above, playing baseball in their youth, later wrote or talked—jaw-jawed—about it. The late Nixon writer William F. Gavin grew up a working-class Giants fan yet was stirred by the exalted Yankees' Mel Allen. His *Speechwright: An Insider's Take on Political Rhetoric*, inspired this work. It had "heart," a trait that Nixon often attributed to Bill and that is necessary to success in both the presidency and baseball.

The University of Nebraska Press senior acquisitions editor Rob Taylor adeptly oversaw the project from first pitch to final out. Associate acquisitions editor Courtney Ochsner skillfully answered questions and thwarted roadblocks. Associate project editor Elizabeth Zaleski superbly kept the book intact and on schedule. Let me also thank the invaluable Tish Fobben and Rosemary Sekora. The historian Thaddeus Romansky and archivist Hanna Soltys scrupulously fact-checked. I could not have attempted this without my wife Sarah and our children Olivia and Travis. Longtime friends John Zogby and Bruce DuMont kindly read the text. Phil Hochberg has been a friend and counselor since the book *Voices of The Game*. I wrote where I am privileged to teach: the University of Rochester in Upstate New York. Finally, I am grateful to students in my presidential rhetoric class, who each year share insight about presidents in this book from Franklin Roosevelt to Donald Trump.

Leadership bubbles from the top. Each year nearly two million people visit the thirteen presidential libraries, from FDR's to George W. Bush's. The fourteenth, Barack Obama's, will be in Chicago, the city he chose to call home and where he community organized and practiced law and which he left to represent in Washington. Most former presidents have spent substantial time at their libraries since the first was dedicated in 1941. Among the officials I wish to thank are directors R. Duke Blackwood, William J. Bosanko, Elaine Didier, Michael D. Ellzey, Meredith Evans, Warren Finch, Terri Garner, Kurt Graham, Alan C. Lowe, Patrick X. Mordente, Thomas P. Putnam, Timothy D. Rives, Thomas F. Schwartz, Paul Sparrow, Mark K. Updegrove, and Karl Weissenbach. Their library websites and other superb archives vastly aid research.

The Presidents and the Pastime candidly explores how each president has treated baseball, how it reciprocated, and what the public has intuited. Many chapters invoke a key team or player, events on and off the field, and how a president viewed—even changed—the culture of his time. For instance, a great number of citizens saw the 1960s as an age of American diminution. They pined for Dwight Eisenhower's 1953–61 presidency, Ike often phoning Senators owner Clark Griffith and then his successor, nephew Calvin Griffith. "The missus is out of town tonight," he would say. "How's about I come out to the park tonight?"

Question: Why didn't this self-styled "great baseball fan" lift a finger to keep the Senators, of DC since 1901, from moving to Minnesota in late 1960 or to keep the even longer ensconced Giants of New York and Dodgers of Brooklyn from fleeing to California in late 1957?

Answer: Eisenhower felt a government that acted least acted best, unwilling to make business act honorably, here even consciably.

Among other things, Ike, who had led history's greatest wartime invasion to free imprisoned Europe, could have yanked baseball's antitrust exemption and had his Justice Department sue the game under the Interstate Commerce Clause. Instead, he did nothing when something was required.

If Ike wanted to avoid the specter of Big Brother, he might have urged Major League team owners to sell the Senators, Dodgers, and Giants *locally*. In return, they would have gotten rights to new teams in virginal Minneapolis–St. Paul, Los Angeles, and San Francisco respectively, when baseball soon expanded, except the owners wouldn't wait and Ike wouldn't act. Those who wrongly call him a do-nothing president this time were right.

As we shall see, as injurious to baseball's future was the way in which this late 1950s Westward-Ho shaped a media void in New York City that the then unsung National Football League (NFL) began to fill. "Professional football had been nothing but a bunch of pot-bellied longshoremen," the twentieth century's preeminent sports announcer, Vin Scully, said. The NFL had rivaled pro wrestling—except that wrestling had a niche.

With three big-league teams, baseball had monopolized New York's crucial print and air time. The Dodgers' and Giants' exit gave the football Giants entrée to Manhattan's network, finance, and ad men. This book will trace the rivalry, even hostility, *since then* between baseball and media-intuitive pro football—moreover, what happened when the pastime failed to protect the game itself, in the 1950s greater than any body in the republic.

Despite this, it astounds—baseball always flaunts a saving grace—that except for soccer the sole game to tout its climax as worthy of the globe remains the *World Series*, still evoking the sense of coming home to an America where we *belong*. Baseball can be biographical, a subject of television, book, and film. It can eclipse the factional, as great a symbol of assimilation as Ellis Island. It is cultural, knitting the values of family, work, and freedom. It is *us*.

In certain parts of this country, including author James Fenimore Cooper's Upstate New York, where I live and teach, with its changing seasons and wooded glens of oak, pine, and maple and broad lawns and brick and white clapboard homes, you can still find—*feel*—what the historian Allan Nevins called this "story of an America now so far lost in time and change that it is hard to believe it ever existed. But it did exist," he said, "and some memory of it, in our all too artificial day, ought to be cherished by the Nation."

In Cooperstown, perhaps Upstate's heart, you cherish being "lost in time." This is particularly true at its Hall of Fame and Museum. Let me thank members of its wonderful staff: the president, Jeff Idelson; vice president of communications and education, Jon Shestakofsky; coordinator of rights and reproductions, John Horne; communications director, Craig Mulder; librarian, Jim Gates; reference librarian, Cassidy Lent; manager of the Giamatti Research Center, Matt Rothenberg; photo archivist, Kelli Bogdan; and senior library associate and senior researcher, Bill Francis, whose incalculable help on this book, like that of his colleagues, makes doing research there a delight.

At the Hall of Fame, a young and restless child can become aware of a world beyond his earliest imaginings. With luck perhaps he can do that later at the White House too. I have loved writing this book about two institutions that help forge America. I hope that you enjoy as well.

ONE

Beginnings

1700s to Theodore Roosevelt, 1901–1909

Envision American presidents as friends around a table—giants, mediocrities, each a household word. Depending on your choice, their lives trace defeat and even tragedy—also triumph and statecraft, evoking a sort of childlike faith. Each dons hats worn in and beyond the Oval Office: politician, captain, chaplain, commander in chief. Harry Truman called the White House a prison. Most have liked it. "I have a nice job," said John F. Kennedy. "The office is close by"—fifty yards from the residence—"and the pay is good."

"Presidents, like great French restaurants," said the writer and educator S. Douglass Cater, "have an ambiance all their own." Like a Rorschach test, their image depends on us. Presidents have been elitist, redolent of the middle class, and/or pitchfork populist. What they have in common is that even before Paradise Found—Dodger Stadium, its original 1962 address 1000 Elysian Park Avenue, "Elysian" being Greek for "paradise"—most presidents have found in baseball *joy*. (In 2016, the address was renamed for retiring announcer Vin Scully, whose genius behind a microphone had brought joy to America for sixty-seven years.)

Growing up in mid-eighteenth-century Massachusetts, one Founding Father, John Adams, played "one old cat," a variant of baseball played in England and numerous other nations. Adams described a typical boyhood day, in a letter written to Dr. Benjamin West of Philadelphia, as "mornings, noons and nights, making and sailing boats, in swimming, in skating, flying kites and shooting, in marbles, ninepins, bat and ball, football, quoits, and wrestling." How did he later have time to fit in a revolution?

Before the terrible winter of 1777–78 at Valley Forge, Pennsylvania, troops of General George Washington, the most famous Founding Father, are thought to have played "rounders," another baseball antecedent from Great Britain. On April 7, 1778, a Revolutionary War soldier, George Ewing, wrote that during free time he "played base"— the first written reference in the colonies to the sport. Of Washington himself, another American soldier wrote, "He sometimes throws and catches a ball for hours with his aide-de-camp"—again, baseball as an import. Not all liked the game's blue-collar cast. Princeton College banned "baste ball," popular among students, saying that it was "in itself low and unbecoming."

From "one old cat" to "rounders," the balance between offense and defense could change as quickly as a move from a pitcher's canyon to a hitter's bandbox now. Basics, though, endured. Each variant involved a ball "pitched by one player and hit by another, who ran to or around bases," wrote William B. Mead and Paul Dickson in *Baseball: The Presidents' Game*, "while the pitcher's teammates tried to catch the ball or otherwise put the batter out." Four bases moored a diamond, as in baseball. A "feeder" tossed a ball to a "striker," who "tried to hit the ball to score runs." The striker could be out by missing three pitches, having his batted ball caught, or being "hit by a thrown ball while running the bases," the latter a feature of "the so-called Massachusetts game."

Jack Redding, 1968–82 National Baseball Hall of Fame and Museum librarian, compared baseball's past styles of play: "New York's [triangular mode] reflected the rules of Alexander Cartwright," thought by many to be the real inventor of the modern game. "Massachusetts's was rectangular, like British cricket." Most early U.S. presidents played at least one alleged British progenitor, aware of America's decided English tilt in the early to mid-nineteenth century. Henry Chadwick, the inventor of the box score, led those saying that baseball's mother was born in the "mother country."

Later, baseball was judged to have been born in Cooperstown—the American fable goes yard. Pre–Civil War newspapers fused truth and myth to liven narrative and swell circulation. In 1861 Union general Abner Doubleday fired the war's first shot of defense at Fort Sumter. A later century revered him more for allegedly creating baseball. More truth and myth: Doubleday, twenty in 1839, somehow birthed baseball at West Point after stealing or borrowing a horse to ride to Cooperstown. The yarn was and is irresistible: baseball invented here, in this Rockwellian village, a 1939 centennial celebrating Doubleday for finding the first baseball in an attic in 1839!

To a crowd five times Cooperstown's population, baseball's first commissioner, Federal Judge Kenesaw Mountain Landis, stated, "Since for a hundred years this game has lived and thrived and spread all over this country, I should like to dedicate this museum to all America." A parade soon sashayed from the nascent Hall of Fame to Doubleday Field, the supposed site of the original 1839 diamond where Doubleday is said to have marked out baselines with a walking stick. Thousands cheered. The *New York Times* ran a long story on page one.

As noted in the acknowledgments, in 1839 Martin Van Buren became the first president to visit Cooperstown, finding, as James Fenimore Cooper wrote in *The Deerslayer*, that "here all was unchanged." It is a feeling that almost all who frequent its bewitching Main Street share—a sense that here lies baseball's Brigadoon. As early as 1856 the game itself was commonly termed the "National Pastime," its lure spreading in the Civil War until the Blue and the Gray opposed each other as allegedly neutral sentries stood guard. Each team often played rudiments of the game behind its own line until action resumed against the other.

By 1859 amateur teams met on the White Lot, the area in the District of Columbia between the South Lawn of the White House and the then incomplete Washington Monument, which stood 152 of its current 555 feet tall. Now called the Ellipse or, officially, President's Park South, the site houses the National Christmas Tree, the highest in-play obstacle of any pitch-and-catch December exhibition. Baseball's growth had become exponential, a vehicle for the ordinary and towering, the self-assured and unself-confident, the devious and honest, and most of all, as any successor would attest, the great sixteenth president of the United States.

In 1860 Abraham Lincoln was among four leading Republican Party candidates contending for president. Founded on, above all, opposition to slavery, the Grand Old Party (GOP) would choose its second nominee (John C. Frémont was first in 1856) in his political stronghold, Chicago. The new *Sport* magazine, a sports and political megaphone, printed a widely circulated story during the campaign about the Republican field. According to *Sport*, friends of Lincoln arrived at his home in Springfield, Illinois, to report that Abe had enough votes to be nominated. "I am glad to hear of their coming," he said while playing in a town game. "But they will have to wait a few minutes while I have another turn at bat." It should not surprise that many believed the tale. It seemed to etch Lincoln's core—humility, irony, and equality.

The day of his nomination, Lincoln camped at Springfield's Great Western Railway Station, ear cocked to voting on the telegraph line from Chicago. Nominated, he began a multi-party general election campaign. A Currier and Ives illustration, in which the four candidates hoist bats, uses baseball to illustrate the futility of the other three.

"It appears to me," says John Bell, the Union Club nominee, "very singular that we three should strike 'foul' and be 'put out' while old Abe made such a 'good lick.'"

"That's because he had that confounded rail, to strike with," the "Little Giant," Stephen Douglas, the Democratic Party choice, huffs. "I thought our fusion would be a 'short stop' to his career."

John Breckinridge, the National Democratic Club candidate, says, "I guess I'd better leave for Kentucky, for I smell something strong around here, and begin to think, that we're completely 'skunk'd.'"

Lincoln stands apart, holding a ball in his right hand and a giant stick in the left. "Gentlemen, if any of you should ever take a hand in another match at this game," he observes, "remember that you must have a 'good bat' and strike a 'fair ball' to make a 'clean score' and do a 'home run.'"

Inaugurated in 1861, Lincoln played hooky to view games on the Ellipse, even playing baseball *in* the White House. A friend, Francis

Preston Blair, owned Blair House, a residence that now houses presidential guests across Pennsylvania Avenue from the Executive Mansion, as the White House was then named. He wrote a grandson: "We boys hailed his [Lincoln's] coming with delight because he would always join us . . . on the lawn. I remember how vividly he ran, how long were his strides, how far his coattails stuck out behind."

Baseball intrigued Lincoln. It obsessed successor Andrew Johnson, once "so caught up with the prospect of a two-inter-city match between the Washington Nationals [official name: the National Club of Washington], Philadelphia Athletics, and Brooklyn Atlantics" that he gave government clerks and employees "time off to watch," wrote I. Kirk Sale of *Sport*. Joining the *Washington Post* at eighteen in 1923, future longtime sports editor Shirley Povich knew of nineteenth-century teams playing by Washington regional rules: "no outfield fences, and a batter could *recircle* the bases till the cows came home. A ball eludes the fielder, and you might get two home runs on a single hit." Batters loved being almost certain to stay permanently in the black.

Anxious to attend an August 1866 Nationals–A's game, Johnson was kept by business on Capitol Hill. Instead, on September 18, he became America's first president to even briefly attend a baseball game: "Brooklyn Excelsiors thirty-three, Washington Nationals twenty-eight," wrote the *Washington National Republican*. Another game that year on the White Lot totaled four hundred runs. Baseball groups yearned for Johnson's blessing. The Enterprise Baseball Club of Philadelphia wrote: "We hope you will not scorn this humble offer of a membership in our National Game, but accept it as a token of our esteem for you as a man, our generation as a patriot, and our admiration as a statesman"—premature, given that Johnson was impeached less than two years later by the House of Representatives and barely acquitted by the Senate.

Perhaps aptly, the District's teams—the National Association Olympians, Nationals, Unions, and Washingtons—were also impeached and convicted, out of business within proximity of postwar baseball's end. Especially bleak was the 1872 Nationals' same-*year* birth and burial. In 1876 DC vainly romanced the National League (NL). The 1884

American Association (AA) rented tiny Atlantic Park. In 1891 the re-named AA Senators opened National Park, also known as Boundary Field, at the Boundary at Seventh Street and Florida Avenue. A year later the entire *league* went kaput. In the nation's capital, nothing in baseball seemed to last.

Few presidents have matched Johnson's baseball zeal. Ulysses S. Grant, the Union's larger-than-life general in the Civil War, might have had he lived longer. The victor of, among other battles, Vicksburg, Chattanooga, and the Overland Campaign rose from the U.S. Army to the 1869–77 Executive Mansion. In his two-term administration, Grant walked around the District, chanced on pickup games, and was "almost certainly the first president to witness a professional [as opposed to Johnson's amateur] game," said Hall of Fame historian Lee Allen.

"When the first professional team, the 1869 undefeated Cincinnati Red Stockings, visited Washington to play the Nationals, Grant's carriage made an appearance on the outfield grass," Allen said. "No one saw him, so his presence is not confirmed." What is: after leaving office, Grant often saw Giants home games at the original Polo Grounds in New York, his new home. On May 1, 1883, the National League's and Giants' first game there wooed the city's then largest baseball crowd—fifteen thousand. Grant "sat in the rear of the main grandstand," wrote the *New York Times*, "and enjoyed the game as he at times took part in the applause accorded the players" like Roger Connor, Mickey Welch, and John Montgomery Ward.

Fighting throat cancer, penury, and business fraud, Grant spent his last year valiantly writing arguably America's greatest presidential memoir: the *Personal Memoirs of Ulysses S. Grant*. Publisher Samuel Clemens (Mark Twain) was a close friend and baseball zealot. Grant's memoir scored, critically and financially, saving his family from bankruptcy. The ex-president never knew, dying near the book's 1885 release. By then Rutherford B. Hayes had won a contested 1876 election in the House of Representatives, part of the Oval Office's 1865–1901 Long Gray Line.

Thomas Wolfe called presidents between Lincoln and Theodore Roosevelt "the Lost Americans: their ... faces mixed, melted, swam together. Which had the whiskers, which the burnsides, which was which?" It was hard to tell. Cities swelled in the postwar industrial boom, national income quadrupling by 1901, the slickers' influx upping the value of a big-league team. Still, most people lived in rural America, the game's spiritual home, where prospects bloomed, like *The Natural's* fictive Roy Hobbs, hoping to be "the best there ever was."

Hayes stepped on too many toes—his *own*, and the GOP's—to run again in 1880, declaring himself "ineligible." James Garfield was elected, was shot, and died September 19, 1881, new president Chester A. Arthur becoming the first to greet a Major League team at the White House on April 13, 1883: the National League Cleveland Blues. A year later Grover Cleveland continued the post-Lincoln score of musical chairs, beating Republican James Blaine of Maine in a campaign soiled by bigotry (Blaine attacked Catholicism), illegitimacy (Cleveland was accused of fathering a child), and other 24/7 muck. Much later Cleveland greeted Cap Anson, skipper of 1885's great 87-25 Chicago White Stockings, asking "How's my old friend Jimmy ["Pud"] Galvin?" He continued, "You know, he and I were good friends when I was a sheriff and mayor of Buffalo." Baseball was different then, more personal, players known by a first name or moniker, often paid per month. Millions could identify—and did.

Pud Galvin, also known as "the Little Steam Engine," managed twenty-four games for Buffalo in 1885, won 308 games pitching for its NL Bisons and Pittsburgh Pirates, and like another pitcher—Cleveland's namesake, Grover Cleveland Alexander—made the Hall of Fame. Years earlier Anson had told the president that Galvin was "doing great." Cleveland was too, until Cap's high-powered handshake made the 250-pounder feel like a 98-pound weakling. Mike "King" Kelly, like Galvin, at high noon of *his* Hall of Fame career, then approached the president, later writing, "There wasn't a man in the crowd that wasn't six feet in height and they were all in lovely condition. Their hands were as hard as iron. The president's hand was fat and soft." Sensing Cleveland's vulnerability, Kelly "squeezed so hard that he winced."

Speaker of the House Thomas P. "Tip" O'Neill famously remarked that all politics are local. Usually Cleveland showed that all politics are individual—one by one. Now, though, Kelly wrote, Cleveland's right hand was so swollen that "he would rather shake hands with 1,000 people than a bad nine after that day," neglecting to shake players' hands when they left. Exiting, Anson asked if Cleveland would like to see a White Stockings game in person. "What do you imagine the American people would think of me if I wasted my time going to the *ballgame*?" the president barbed, knowing the stern age's emphasis on church work and Sunday sanctity and how the country would applaud him spurning pleasure. Victorian America liked Cleveland's commitment to duty. He also knew enough not to qualify the term "ballgame"; people knew that it meant *baseball*.

Cleveland is still the sole president to serve two nonconsecutive terms: 1885–89 and 1893–97. He is not, however, as some suggest, the only president to be the major subject of a sports motion picture. On January 20, 1981, Ronald Reagan became America's fortieth president. After giving his inaugural address, the new chief executive used the speaker of the house's lounge and men's room to change from formal to business clothes. Speaker O'Neill told him that he was sitting near a desk that once belonged to President Cleveland. According to Tip, the story made Reagan glow.

"Hey, Grover Cleveland!" the new president is said to have exclaimed. "I played him in the movies!"—1952's *The Winning Team*.

"No, no, Mr. President," O'Neill replied. "You played Grover Cleveland *Alexander*, the baseball player." It was then, he said, that "I knew the Nation was in tough shape. But still [Reagan was] a good, lovable guy."

On June 6, 1892, Benjamin Harrison, reserved, lighter than Cleveland, to some a "human iceberg" floating between the two Cleveland terms, became the first president to see an official Major League game. Washington bowed to Cincinnati, 7–4, in eleven innings, the District a loser even then. Harrison next saw the Senators (a.k.a. the Nationals or Nats, names used synonymously for more than a century) lose to Philadelphia, 9–2. "So much for the Bully Pulpit," said Morris Siegel, a columnist for four Washington papers, including the *Post* and *Star*. "Hail to the Chief" put few backsides in the seats.

Late-century presidents rivaled table-game pieces, yanked from, then returned to, the board. After Cleveland's second term, Ohio governor William McKinley was elected. On April 17, 1897, he was first to greet a big-league team—the Senators—in the Oval Office. (Arthur had hosted elsewhere in the Mansion.) *Sporting Life*, a baseball weekly, headlined: "M'Kinley on Ball / The President a Lover of the National Game / The Washington Team Presented to the Nation's Chief Executive / He Speaks Encouragingly of the Sport and Will Attend Many Games." McKinley more or less vowed to throw out the first ball at the April 22 home opener, after which a presidential box was built with flags and bunting. More than a hundred members of the House and Senate appeared, as contrasted to McKinley, who did not, "disappoint[ing] the 7,000 spectators at the opening game . . . [whom] the Senators [also] disappointed . . . by losing to Brooklyn 5 to 4," wrote the *Washington Star*.

The fallout all but felled McKinley. Spalding sporting goods couldn't change a national ad that ran a day *after* the game: "It seems very appropriate for the American game of Base Ball to be formally opened by the President of the United States," its text read, "as was done yesterday by President William McKinley, in breaking the seal and tossing to the umpire the Spalding Official League Ball." The Associated Press (AP) let McKinley have it: "It was expected that President McKinley would favor the Senators with his presence, having promised the Washington players if his duties did not prevent he would toss the first baseball to the umpire, but he evidently was too busy entertaining office-seekers"—ouch—"and [for that] reason players and spectators alike were greatly disappointed."

Ironically, said the Hall of Fame's Lee Allen, McKinley liked the sport much more than the row over its roots. As noted, early "rounders" had laid a claim as baseball's paterfamilias. Now new evidence called America the forebear. The movement's architect was Albert Goodwill Spalding, founder of the National League, 1871–78 Chicago White Stockings pitcher-turned-president, then father and head of the company that still bears his name. Like the British support of "rounders," Spalding's pro-USA campaign felt "profit" a patriotic word. NL head A. G. Mills got congregants chanting, "No rounders! No rounders!" as if the Brits had again burned the White House. Had audio and video film existed then, Mills might have produced shorts of the War of 1812.

As an aging child looks increasingly like a parent, baseball came to resemble the United States. The more you peered, the more it seemed homegrown. Some saw a game of grand hauteur—Joe DiMaggio, Roberto Clemente; some, grand rhetoric—announcer Red Barber; others, heroism writ large—Jackie Robinson, defying, and Lou Gehrig, dying. Many saw a mental map of veterans from Pearl Harbor to the Bulge: Bob Feller, Hank Greenberg, Jerry Coleman, Teddy Ballgame (a.k.a. Ted Williams). Some sang of a feel-good age: Bing Crosby's "Accentuate the Positive" could mean Stan Musial on harmonica. Depending on the season, others reminded you of *South Pacific*, evoking "Something Wonderful": Brooklyn's 1955, the 1969 Mets, the "Impossible Dream" Red Sox. Almost all sensed baseball poetry's flesh and blood: Willie Mays in center field, Josh Gibson going long, Ozzie Smith in the hole. The historically astute recalled Churchill's "We shape our buildings and afterwards our buildings shape us"—Ebbets Field; Fenway Park; Oriole Park at Camden Yards, forging two dozen other new parks since its 1992 debut—*each* shaping the game. All lay ahead.

Spalding beseeched the names and places of his time to help "discover" baseball's place of birth, the commission he formed in truth more stacked than a loaded deck. In 1907, its chairman, Mills, reported after three years of study: "The first scheme for playing baseball, according to the best evidence obtainable to date, was devised by Abner Doubleday at Cooperstown, New York, in 1839," the same year of Van Buren's visit. To agree, you would have to explain how this West Point plebe not allowed to leave the plains of the military academy high above the Hudson could ride to Cooperstown at night, invent this ingenious game with no one seeing him, then beat a path back to West Point without being glimpsed or punished—not even a demerit! Only a child could believe such fantasy, which was surely the point.

Arriving at Cooperstown, any visitor still finds youth entrusted to his heart. Why *wouldn't* you believe in Abner Doubleday or *Peter Pan*,

Baby Boomers yearly watching NBC-TV in the early 1960s as Mary Martin sang "I Won't Grow Up"? Tens of millions did. Others, disproportionately enamored of the Chicago Cubs, became an example of children hallucinating badly as adults—at least until the centennial of the Cubs' opening year, 1916, at Wrigley Field.

In 1939, as noted, Doubleday was posthumously honored at the Hall of Fame for allegedly having originated baseball a century earlier. Today, Everyman has helped baseball make Cooperstown an ATM, loving the myth as much as the game.

Even more than baseball, railroads came to link the country in the nineteenth century, especially its economy. By 1880 the United States brandished 93,262 miles of line, despite worker riots against profit hoarding in Baltimore, St. Louis, Pittsburgh, Chicago, and San Francisco. "It is wrong to call this a strike," one newspaper critiqued. "It is a labor revolution." It was neither, only workers slowly stirring, like a still stream shedding ice.

Of the nearly 20 percent of the population that was foreign-born, a majority was foreign-speaking. To succeed they had to learn English. The best way was to read. Rail carried newspapers, magazines, and books to a print-reliant public. For those keeping score near the turn of the century, the geometry of the diamond lured exposure in such journals as the *Saturday Evening Post, Collier's,* and *Baseball Magazine.* The *Sporting Life* and St. Louis-based *The Sporting News* (also TSN) took a fractured game and somehow made it whole. The reader then returned to daily coverage, there being much to return to. Each big-league city had at least one morning and evening paper, teams eager to buy writers food, drink, and dames. Coverage was quid pro quo, reporters covering up, not covering, a player's fast-lane life. Gradually it cleansed and changed.

As the Founding Fathers' "Grand Experiment" turned one hundred in 1876, *The Nation* wrote, "People here are far less raw and provincial than their fathers," yet primitive baseball parks and grounds tied cow dung, a single deck, no bleachers, and fences at a property's edge. If Washington's road to a Major League niche was potholed, New York's flowed from Alexander Cartwright's first town team of amateur gentlemen—the Knickerbockers, knitting historic firsts: an organized team (1845), a uniform (high collars and long pants, circa 1849), and a dynasty (between them, New York and Brooklyn won nine amateur titles in thirteen years from 1858 to 1870). The Knickerbockers began in Manhattan, then moved to Elysian Fields in Hoboken, New Jersey. In 1852 ultimately baseball's grandest borough joined the fray, Brooklyn forging its first organized team.

By 1858 New York and Brooklyn hatched an all-star series next door to the future Shea Stadium, home of the Metropolitan Baseball Club of New York—the Mets. "Clearly God had a design," laughed Bob Murphy, their great 1962-2003 announcer. "Think of it—baseball and New York joined umbilically from the start!" From Jamaica to Staten Island, town ball adopted the Cartwright-ruled "New York" style of play. By 1862 businessman William Cammeyer opened the first enclosed field in Brooklyn's unregal Williamsburg: Union Grounds, a horseshoed park with a one-story building *inside* a fence. It forecast a franchise dicier than most.

When President Johnson left office in 1869, impeached but not convicted after radical Republicans charged him with creating policies they felt overly lenient toward a prostrate South, he took solace in having more time to watch the first solely professional team—his Cincinnati Red Stockings. In 1866 the Brooklyn Atlantics, part of a group of twenty-four teams from New York and New Jersey, were said to have paid three players. On June 14, 1870, in the most famous game of the time, they beat Cincinnati, which began the day having won seventy-eight straight games without a tie. Afterward other management slowly embraced pay-for-play.

"Stopping that trend was like King Canute trying to stop the tide," said Jim Gates, Jack Redding's successor twice removed as Hall of Fame librarian. "With pros, you paid them. That meant getting people to watch, which demanded wooden parks," including bleachers. By 1871 the new National Association enclosed eight parks, fields flanked or intersected by passenger or freight lines. Born in Raleigh, North Carolina, Johnson, now former president, used train and horse to travel the rural South, as he had for decades, especially North and South Carolina, Alabama, and Tennessee.

In 1875 Johnson was elected to the U.S. Senate, called it "vindication," had a stroke, and died, missing the National League of *Professional* Baseball *Clubs*, which, unlike prior amateur leagues, inked players to a contract. It debuted in 1876, the Boston club becoming the Red Stockings, Beaneaters, and eventually Braves and taking the NL title in 1877–78, 1883, and five times from 1891 to 1898. Rutherford B. Hayes once said, "If Napoleon ever became president, he could make the office whatever he wished to make it." Three would-be Major Leagues folded between 1884 and 1990, leaving a surviving Western League of Detroit, Milwaukee, and Minneapolis–St. Paul. Executive Ban Johnson renamed it (American League), became president (through 1927), and put a club in Chicago (White Sox). Born in 1901, the new league wished to dent the National.

Ban moved the Grand Rapids club to Cleveland, bought National League parks in Baltimore and St. Louis, and set about to build AL fields in Chicago, DC, and Philadelphia. Finding that the NL wanted to revive the American Association, make *it* a second big league, and put a club in Boston, he moved the AL charter franchise from Buffalo to the Hub, named it the Americans (a.k.a. Pilgrims or Somersets; the future Red Sox), and added it to new owner Charles Somers's three other teams. In 1901 the Americans opened Huntington Avenue Grounds with its in-play tool shed and signature surrealistic 635 feet to dead center field, only to flunk the first division in 1906–08 and 1911. An exception to early bust was pitcher Denton True Young, or Cyclone (Cy), a nickname alluding to his heater.

Each Hub team was reluctant to pay players much. Unlike the future Braves, the future Red Sox were at least willing to pay better. In 1903 they made the first World Series. "We can beat Pittsburgh no matter *how* good [Honus] Wagner is," patrons shrilled at Boston's McGreevey's 3rd Base Saloon. "Enough said," railed bar boss Michael McGreevey, renamed Nuf Ced, who danced atop the Sox dugout and whose Royal Rooters fan club drank alone, with strangers, and with friends. "Honus, why do you hit so badly?" Rooters jeered to the tune of "Tessie," a then popular song. "Take a back seat and sit down. Honus, at bat you look so sadly. Hey, why don't you get out of town?" Wagner is felt to be the best ever at his position, shortstop. Young, best at his, took Game Five, 11–2, to pivot the then best-of-nine Classic, winning, five games to three—given later Sox history, saving the best for first.

In 1904 the *Boston Globe* owner, General Charles Taylor, bought the Pilgrims to keep his son John busy. On Closing Day, the Yankees' née Highlanders' Jack Chesbro wild-pitched Lou Cigar home with the Hub's flag-waving run. Such a year deserved a glorious World Series postscript—except that "We don't play minor leaguers," said National League pennant-winning Giants skipper John McGraw, killing the Fall Classic. Meantime, the NL Boston team kept changing names, settling on "Braves" in 1903 after a Tammany Hall politician—"a brave"—bought them. The league had juggled franchises as dizzily: thirty-one in 1876–1900.

In 1907 the AL Americans stole a nickname from the other league: "From now on, we'll wear red stockings and I'm grabbing that name Red Sox," John Taylor said, planning a new home on the property of the Fenway Realty Company. Huntington Avenue Grounds closed in 1911. Today a plaque at Northeastern University marks the former pitcher-friendly park. A statue stands above old home plate: "Cy Young. At this site in October 1903 baseball's winningest pitcher led Boston to victory in the first World Series." The Series Exhibit Room, in the Cabot Cage, recalled an age in which "Bully!" was Theodore Roosevelt's catchword for something that "delighted" him. TR was busy living what he called "the strenuous life." It did not include every sport.

America's twenty-sixth president was born October 27, 1858, in New York City, a sickly second of four children to glass businessman and philanthropist Theodore Roosevelt Sr. and socialite Martha Stewart "Mittie" Bulloch. Home schooled, TR—Roosevelt hated the name "Teddy"—found early that physical exercise could build his body, check bullies, and curb childhood asthma. He took boxing lessons and went skiing in the Alps. Often bed-bound, he was not a courageous child but read about and lived through courageous men. "I was nervous and timid," agreed Roosevelt, "but I felt a great admiration for men who were fearless and who could hold their own in the world." In the end, he more than held *his*.

Graduating from Harvard College in 1880, Roosevelt attended Columbia Law School; published a classic book, *The Naval War of 1812*; and was elected to the New York State legislature. At twenty-two he married socialite Alice Hathaway, who bore a daughter, Alice Lee, in 1884, but died of an undiagnosed case of kidney failure, then named Bright's disease. Two days later TR drew an "X" over the date of her death on its page in his diary. He left daughter Alice Lee with his sister Bamie, braved another shock with his mother's death, and in a black hole trekked west, operated a cattle ranch in the Dakotas, wrote three books on the wilderness, and sought what Quakers deemed "peace at the center."

In 1886 TR married childhood friend Edith Carow, with whom he had five children, four of them boys. He anchored the U.S. Civil Service Commission, became president of the board of the New York City Police Commissioners, and in 1897 was named assistant secretary of the navy by President McKinley. In 1898 Roosevelt enlisted in the American army of the Spanish-American War, leading the Rough Riders, or First U.S. Volunteer Cavalry Regiment, part of the cavalry division led by former Confederate general Joseph Wheeler. Landing in Cuba, TR led troops in the battle of San Juan Hill.

Lacking written orders, he led regulars up Kettle Hill, commanding on horseback until barbed wire trapped his mount and he advanced on foot. Heavy U.S. casualties—more than two hundred men killed, three hundred wounded—taught a lesson: "The only way to get them [troops] to do it in the way it had to be done was to lead them myself," TR said, aware that casualties would be forgiven if the Rough Riders won. As war fever heightened, Colonel Roosevelt—his preferred title even to "Mr. President"—returned home a hero, even the Oval Office in reach.

For the rest of his life, perhaps America's best-read and most outsized president gloried in his image, calling the charge up San Juan Hill "the best day of my life" or "my crowded hour," even as crowding became a rule. Back in New York, Roosevelt was asked by the state GOP to run for governor in 1898. He won by 1 percent, using it as a steppingstone to the 1900 vice presidency. Reelected, McKinley skipped baseball's 1901 Opening Day, still ashamed at ignoring the first-game crowd in 1897. He never got another chance, being shot in Buffalo on September 6, 1901, by an anarchist. (McKinley died eight days later.) At forty-two Roosevelt took the oath as president, the nation's youngest chief executive, and soon invited Booker T. Washington to dinner at the White House, prompting vicious backlash. This might be a different kind of leader.

As president, Teddy busted the trusts, regulated railroads, and touted the environment before it was called "conservation." His "Square Deal" provided 5 new national parks, 18 national monuments, and 150 national forests—a dowry president George H. W. Bush admired almost a century later, worshiping at what Bush called our "cathedral of the outdoors." TR helped build the Panama Canal, expand the navy, and send the Great White Fleet around the world, his foreign policy dubbed "America First" a century before Donald Trump's quite different vision. Many saw him as the British writer and statesman John Morley did: a cross of "St. Vitus and St. Paul."

Before and after his presidency, TR explored the Amazon River, backed purer food and drugs, hunted big game, wrote eighteen books, and quoted poetry to Robert Frost. He urged any president to "speak softly, and carry a big stick," winning the Nobel Peace Prize in 1906 for ending the Russo-Japanese War. In 1910 Roosevelt spoke about "Citizenship in a Republic" at the Sorbonne in Paris: "The credit belongs to the man who is actually in the arena . . . who spends himself in a worthy cause . . . whose place shall never be with those cold and timid souls who know neither victory nor defeat."

TR hoped to mold strong, self-reliant American youth, believing what his father had told him upon entering Harvard: "Take care of your *morals* first, your *health* next, and finally your *studies*." At heart Roosevelt preferred a sameness in which players must advance ten yards in four tries, one that "can exist anywhere a hundred yards of flat ground rests," as the *New York Times'* George Vecsey wrote of football. Roosevelt was a Renaissance Man—above all, an American. His conundrum was that since childhood he had treated baseball like castor oil. "Father and all of us regard[ed] baseball as a mollycoddle game," said daughter Alice Lee Roosevelt Longworth. "Tennis, football, lacrosse, boxing, polo, yes: They are *violent*, which appealed to us. But *baseball*? Father wouldn't watch it, not even at Harvard!" How could a baseball-hating president brave an increasingly baseball-loving land? Discreetly, which could mean disingenuously. Lauding baseball, TR didn't mean a word.

One May day in 1907 a delegation from the National Association of Professional Base Ball Leagues arrived at the White House to give TR a season pass "made in fourteen-karat gold and doubl[ing] in two so that it may be carried in the vest pocket," according to its press release. Roosevelt's face on the pass was beautifully enameled in gold. The card, dated April 1, was an accidental April Fool's joke—free entry to the association's 256 professional baseball parks. (TR did not intend to use it, a baseball visit his private root canal.) "The sport of this country, above and beyond all others, is base ball," said association secretary John H. Farrell. "It is rightly called the national game and its right to be so called is undisputed." Roosevelt said nothing. Farrell droned on: "There is nothing more gratifying than the fact that the present executive head of this great nation is an ardent champion of the national game." TR nodded, wishing he were elsewhere. Oval Office rhetoric was taking a surrealistic turn.

The delegation wished, said Farrell, to hail the president's support of "a game that nourishes no 'mollycoddlers'"; Teddy was being strangled with his own prose. Moreover, Farrell quoted TR about how "base ball was the typical American outdoor sport"; Roosevelt liked it because "men of middle-age could still engage in it"; and the pastime had his "good wishes." There you have it: TR thought baseball *typical*, which it *wasn't*; and wished it *well*, which he *didn't*. "He was a popular president renowned for his rough-and-tumble physical prowess," observed *Baseball: The Presidents' Game*, "a former war hero who boxed for exercise. He publicly scorned non-bruising sports. . . . But baseball was the national game," wanting "to embrace" him, "to make him part of the mystique." The president it wanted, merely wanted it to go away.

Roosevelt had rejoiced on election night 1908, thinking William Howard Taft a protégé, but soon was disabused of his Republican successor's intent. TR found him less an activist than a mossback pining to reclaim the late-nineteenth-century GOP of small government and smaller vision. Irate, he headed a progressive third party in 1912. By that October, Roosevelt had conquered childhood timidity, New York City police corruption, Standard Oil abuse, and any hint of misconduct in his 1901–09 presidency when a bullet from an onlooker struck TR's chest as he began a ninety-minute speech in Milwaukee. Blood seeped into his shirt, yet Roosevelt completed the speech without medical aid.

"Ladies and gentlemen," he thundered, "I don't know whether you fully understand that I have just been shot, but it takes more than that to kill a Bull Moose!"—his party's name and emblem. TR finished a distant second to Democrat Woodrow Wilson but improbably ahead of the GOP major-party Taft, then returned to a riddle he couldn't solve. Why couldn't the hero of San Juan Hill beat this girly sport? Even sons Kermit and Quentin played and studied it, Kermit's youth team mauling the P Street Boys, 23–4, on the White House grounds—a great home field edge. No wonder Dad recoiled. The enemy was within.

In time Roosevelt confronted the inevitable, proud that Quentin knew the players and their averages. "I like to see Quentin practicing baseball," he wrote Kermit. "It gives me hope that one of my boys will not take after his father in this respect, and will prove able to play the national game." In a letter to third son Archie, he wrote, "Quentin really seems to be getting on pretty well with his baseball. In each of the last two games he made a base hit and a run." Resigned to defeat, the Harvard middle-weight boxer still felt that being "manly" meant violence. "I am glad you play football," he wrote Kermit, and "that you box and ride and shoot and walk and row as well as you do."

In May 1908 TR invited manager Clark Griffith's New York Highlanders (in 1913 named the Yankees) and the Cleveland Naps (for 1902–14 star Napoleon Lajoie, in 1915 named the Indians) to the White House. Griffith soon became Senators manager, then owner. TR later opposed President Wilson's reluctance to intervene in World War I and considered running for the 1920 GOP nomination. Quentin was shot down behind German lines and killed. On January 6, 1919, TR died in his sleep. Baseball went its way, and Roosevelt went his.

Years later, on the day that he resigned as president, Richard Nixon told his staff and millions of viewers the story of TR's wife's death in her early twenties, invoking how Roosevelt had said, "And when my heart's dearest died, the light went from my life forever." Nixon then added, poignantly: "The greatness comes . . . when you take some knocks, some disappointments, when sadness comes, because only if you have been in the deepest valley can you ever know how magnificent it is to be on the highest mountain." TR had been to each, and emerged unforgettable from both.

TWO

Power of Two

William Howard Taft and Woodrow Wilson, 1909–1921

I t would be hard to find a president less like William Howard Taft than Thomas Woodrow Wilson. America's 1909–13 chief executive was conservative, obese, and droll—at three hundred pounds, our heaviest president. Taft's 1913–21 successor was ascetic, rail thin, and a don of the Progressive movement. Taft found rhetoric something to take or leave. Wilson found it synonymous with policy, renewing the *spoken* State of the Union address last used in 1801. Taft's presidency accented domestic affairs. Wilson looked abroad. He knew, like British foreign secretary Sir Edward Grey, that the world was getting smaller, auguring World War I. "The lamps are going out all over Europe," Grey said. "We shall not see them lit again in our lifetime." As desperately as any world leader, Wilson strove to light them.

What linked almost each American was the hope to avoid war— also, as the *Boston Globe* columnist William A. Henry III wrote, the wonder that almost every citizen found in "purple mountain majesties, amber waves of grain, small-town school marms, the cavalry to the rescue, Norman Rockwell Thanksgivings, the [later] flag-raising at Iwo Jima, the World Series, and [much later] astronauts landing on the moon." All seemed entwined, he said, "because they, in turn, evoked a swelling sense of personal participation in national purpose." Opening Day would too, its presidential bandstand playing nostalgia, hope, and myth.

A felicitous word or phrase attaches itself to each U.S. president. Washington suggests father, as of a country; Jefferson, renaissance; Lincoln, wisdom; Hoover, the man that luck forgot; FDR, redeemer; Ike, the 1950s; Kennedy, stillborn hope. Among some others, Lyndon Johnson implies consequence; Ronald Reagan, language; George H. W. Bush, character; Bill Clinton, charm; Barack Obama, pioneer; Richard Nixon, defiance. Such personae help occupy America's psychic attic. Perhaps "missionary" defined Wilson. "First Fan" might describe the bulbous Taft, the popular originator of throwing out the first ball, who loved baseball to a degree that few predecessors or successors equaled. He would have echoed future broadcaster Harry Caray's "You can't beat fun at the old ballpark."

In 1857 Taft was born into politics near Cincinnati in an upscale Republican clan. Father Alphonso became secretary of war and attorney general under Ulysses S. Grant. William graduated from Yale University and was named first to varied judicial posts, then civilian governor of the Philippines in 1901 and secretary of war by President Roosevelt in 1904. Hoping to one day become chief justice of the U.S. Supreme Court, Taft felt duty-bound to stay in politics. The 1908 GOP presidential candidate was easily elected, rewarded for bringing needed change and limited self-government to the Philippines—then a U.S. protectorate—and was inaugurated at fifty-one.

Hapless politically, Taft mocked public relations for not being "result-oriented." Unlike Roosevelt, he spoke little ill of business. In the end, the media spoke much ill of him. When a reporter snapped, "You are no Teddy," Taft replied that he aimed "to accomplish just as much without any noise." He proposed the Sixteenth Amendment to authorize the federal income tax, helped create the U.S. Chamber of Commerce, and fostered Asian and Latin America development and Panama Canal security—"Dollar Diplomacy." Moreover, TR's successor handled the Mexican Revolution with skill, not "noise," sending troops to the border, upping his prestige, and keeping combat at a length.

Taft's early schedule was so hectic that Archie Butt, his and Roosevelt's military aide, worried about the new president's weight, writing, "I thought it would be just as necessary to get his [Taft's] mind off business as it was to exercise." How to exercise mind and body was a large question in every way. On April 19, 1909, Butt and Senators owner Thomas C. Noyes left home early to remove a box seat from American League Park II at Seventh Street and Florida Avenue and substitute a massive man's chair. Many people then and in the second third of the twentieth century grew up in an age when fat was thought funny: envision the fictive Reginald van Gleason III pitching from the mound on CBS-TV's 1960s *Jackie Gleason Show*.

"One loves him at first sight," said TR of his successor, enviously. Taft's late arrival at his first baseball game that April at the DC site known as National Park and Boundary Field proved Teddy prescient, the match interrupted, according to the *Washington Post*, by "a great wave [of] cheering" as the throng spotted the president in top hat and formal wear. Inning after inning, Falstaff from the Oval Office gulped candy, dodged fouls, and wowed the crowd. Meanwhile, vice president James A. Sherman worried about the crowd booing the umpires. Butt told him not to sweat it: "They never kill the ump before the seventh inning."

The game ended, Boston winning, 8–4, Hall of Fame pitcher Walter Johnson later explaining why in a 1925 *Washington Times* serialized memoir: "Our players got so excited [by Taft's presence] that we booted the game away." Taft feared being a jinx: "I hope I am not a 'hoodoo.'" In 1901, surely hating every second, then Vice President Roosevelt had become the first to throw an Opening Day pitch for the Senators. April 14, 1910, continued the evolution. William Mead and Paul Dickson describe Taft rising "from the broad, sturdy chair that had been installed to accommodate his corpulent frame [to hurl] a ceremonial sphere"—the first president to toss the Opening Day "official" ball in the capital, a yearly rite through baseball's 1971 exit to Texas and since its 2005 return to Washington.

Before a sellout crowd of 12,226, a then big-league record, the president's wife, Helen, held the ball until Taft took it and threw a low wobbler that Opening Day starter Johnson barely caught on the fly. In his book *The Washington Senators*, Morris A. Bealle wrote, "President Taft, in spite of a big bay window, threw the ball with the finesse and grace of an accomplished ball player." Aptly the April 14 opening game was the first at which movies were made. The *1910 Reach Official American League Guide* added, "The immense crowd . . . jumped to their feet as they made out the President and gave him a thundering round of cheers." The Big Train (i.e., Johnson) blanked the A's, 3–0, missing a no-hitter due to DC's early-century sellout practice of stringing outfield ropes for people to stand behind. A foul by Frank "Home Run" Baker glanced off the head of secretary of the senate Charles G. Bennett, landing for a double.

Taft created the old-school way of throwing to an individual. Later presidents from Franklin Roosevelt through Lyndon Johnson stood, poised, while both teams' players, coaches, and skippers stood near the presidential box, jostling for their throw. (More recently old-school has returned.) Next-day April 15, 1910, papers showed Taft in his ample glory: gesturing, mugging, winding up, not grasping why some treated baseball with the solemnity of a bar exam. "To Walter Johnson," Taft signed a baseball, "with the hope that he may continue to be as formidable as in yesterday's game." A formidable first-game presidential rite had itself been born.

For most of the twentieth century, each big-league team dotted America's Northeast quadrant, St. Louis its southern- and westernmost extremity. Picture the nation as a clock: the Majors ran from twelve to three. The White House kept time at the latter. "You'd think Washington would draw—but it didn't," a writer noted. Familiar culprits loomed: too many transients, too few longtime denizens to develop an abiding clientele. After decades of leagues that thrived and died, DC's niche finally crystalized when the National League put four of twelve teams, including the eleventh-place Nationals, out of their misery in 1899. Irrespective, in 1901 the new eight-club American League gave Washington a new team with the same name.

In 1904 the Senators left original American League Park at 14th Street and Bladensburg, NE. At its new home, previously cited American League Park II, DC finished in the second division every year through 1911. Like other parks of the age, an idiosyncratic nature made it an adventure. Grounds help stored the flag between games in a dog-house near the outfield flagpole. One day, after removing Old Glory, the groundskeeper forgot to close the door. "A Senator hit a drive over the head of the A's center fielder [Socks Seybold]," wrote the *Post's* Morris Siegel, whereupon the ball rolled inside the house, at which point the outfielder put his head and shoulders there and couldn't get them out. "When his teammates rescued him, the batter completed the only inside-the-dog-house homer."

As unusual was Taft's maniacal passion to see the sport. On May 4, 1910, the year of six of his fourteen in-person games—second only to Harry Truman's sixteen—he became the only president to visit a same-day game in *each* Major League. In St. Louis Taft eyed the first two innings at National League Park, leaving with the Cardinals leading his hometown Reds, 9–3. He then raced to Sportsman's Park, where Cleveland's Cy Young faced the local Browns, the final score three-all in fourteen innings—"one of the most amazing days the home team has ever seen before," *The Sporting News* exclaimed. Unsurprisingly the *1911 Spalding's Official Baseball Guide* hymned: "President Taft believes in Base Ball. . . . He [says] that it is a pastime worth every man's while and advises them to banish the blues by going to a ball game." The *Post's* J. B. Grillo added that the Tigers never came to town without Ty Cobb visiting the White House, the mansion increasingly a bullhorn for his sport.

On March 17, 1911, Taft needed a fire hose for a different house when wooden American League Park II's stands caught fire from a plumber's blow lamp and burned to the ground. Improbably, in eighteen days, a single tier of seats, many temporary, rose from first to third base to replace them. On Opening Day, a crowd of about 16,000 saw the president throw out the first ball at the steel and concrete grandstand at the same site between Georgia Avenue and 5th Street and between W Street and Florida Avenue, NW. The only box seats ready were the presidential party's as the Senators unveiled Washington's most abiding baseball shrine. In 1920 AL Park II was officially renamed Griffith Stadium. Like each park built through the 1940s and even 1950s, it differed from every other. "My house, my house, though thou art small," George Herbert said, "thou art to me the Escurial."

In 1910 vaudevillian Jack Norworth wrote what remains baseball's full-throated anthem: "Take Me Out to the Ballgame." Its first two steel-and-concrete ballparks, Shibe Park and Forbes Field, in Philadelphia and Pittsburgh respectively, had opened a year earlier. By 1923 fourteen other parks, most fitting on an urban parcel, rose from the grid of city streets. Ebbets Field could rival a pinball machine. A berm flanked Cincinnati's left-field wall. Current "new old parks," like Oriole Park at Camden Yards in Baltimore and Nationals Park in Washington, owe much to Griffith, as they do to Wrigley Field, the Polo Grounds, and Briggs Stadium in Detroit, among others. For a century and more, such classic parks were the street where your team lived.

On April 15, 1912, the ocean liner *Titanic* sank after striking an iceberg, taking an estimated fifteen hundred passengers and crew to the bottom of the Atlantic, including Archie Butt, who had first convinced Taft to attend a baseball game. Distraught, the president sent Vice President Sherman in his place to pinch-toss at the opener four days later. By then Clark Griffith had had a thought. "[Griffith]'d been a turn-of-the-century pitching star," wrote Morris Siegel, "and was a showman determined to create a ritual of presidents." Just named Senators skipper, Clark would later own them, hoping to be as luminous there as on the mound, his 237-146 record mostly from 1893–1906. Finding, as T. S. Eliot said, that this April *had* been "the cruelest month," Griffith suddenly announced Opening Day to be ex post facto June 18. Taft arrived to see the team's world turned upside down.

For a year the Nationals had no longer been woebegone, leaping from seventh place to second and currently having won sixteen straight games. A record 15,516 invaded Griffith for the two-month-late opener. Congress adjourned early. Ticket scalpers got fifty dollars for a box seat. According to the *Washington Post*, the crowd blew a cork when Taft and Sherman arrived, the president waving his hat on the first pitch, the VP upon the last. It saw the club "make one of those 'story book' ninth-inning finishes and defeat the Athletics by a score of 5 to 4 bringing their string of successive victories up to 17 replete with sensations," noted the *Post*. In baseball the law of averages usually prevails.

The 1912 Senators shattered it. President Taft, unhorsed from without and within his party, would have settled for a drip-drab of their luck.

Instead the GOP, split in 1912 by TR challenging his one-time protégé, imploded, starting a toxic liberal-conservative Roosevelt/William Howard Taft schism that devolved into Thomas Dewey/Robert Taft (1948), Ike/Robert Taft (1952), Nelson Rockefeller/Barry Goldwater (1964), and Gerald Ford/Ronald Reagan (1976) before largely ending with Reagan's 1981–89 presidency. By contrast, serendipity garbed Griffith, whom Taft called "the Old Fox" and who in 1912 got AL head Ban Johnson to let Washington be the first team to open its season at home, in the nation's capital, forgetting that *Taft*, not he, had begun the first-ball rite while Griffith was managing at Cincinnati, not even the capital of Ohio! "Clark liked the visibility it gave the game," said longtime Senators announcer Bob Wolff. Buying the team in 1920, Griffith claimed to have scripted the opening game liturgy. In 1955 Griffith wrote a *This Week* newspaper supplement, its title mocking modesty, even honesty: "Presidents Who Have Pitched for Me."

To some, whether Griffith had "started the opening-pitch custom back [in 1910]," as one writer said, was academic as opposed to how to reach his park, "with [its] confusions of traffic patterns." A 1915 cab jaunt from the White House cost twenty-five cents. It took the Majors' longest trolley ride of 402 feet from home plate to clear left field. Right field was 326 feet away. Five houses and a giant tree stood beyond center field near the bullhorn. The wall jutted in, then back at a right angle around them to 457 feet. Two tiers encircled the plate from first to third base. In 1920 Griffith stretched seating to each pole, the roof of the new stands inexplicably higher than the old, as though, said Shirley Povich, "some damn carpenter [had] worked with a bottle—not a saw!" The addition presaged fences and capacity that rose and shrank. Only in 1946 did attendance top a million, at 1,027,216. "Try something," said FDR, with whom the Old Fox often played poker. "If it doesn't work, try something else." The Senators czar agreed.

Taft died in 1930, Griffith 1955. One myth outlived their passing. The president was said to have attended a 1910 game in Pittsburgh. "In the seventh," Mead and Dickson write, "he got up to move his large body.

The crowd, thinking Taft was leaving, rose to its feet in respect." He and the crowd then sat, allegedly ending the seventh-inning stretch. Fact was less adorned. Harry Wright, manager of baseball's first all-professional team, the 1869–70 Cincinnati Red Stockings, explained an old local custom: "The spectators rise between halves of the seventh . . . and sometimes walk about. In so doing they enjoy relief afforded by relaxation from a long posture on hard benches." In the 1970s Harry Caray sang "Take Me Out to the Ballgame" and twinned it to the seventh-inning stretch, a riveting combination. By the time he died, most Americans likely thought the announcer had invented each.

Truth, slow to spread, rarely dims perception. By contrast, presidents are often judged more fairly after leaving office, as if retrospect lessens bile. Taft's reappraisal involved baseball. In 2002, "Baseball as America," a first-ever national touring exhibition, began in Cooperstown, carrying 520 historic artifacts around the land, including Taft's ceremonial 1910 Opening Day ball caught by Walter Johnson. Forty years earlier, *The Sporting News* (*TSN*) headlined: TAFT RATED TOP FAN AMONG PRESIDENTS. The story began: "Soon, the cry of 'Play Ball' will be heard again across the land," rousing "many anecdotes." Taft liked trading stories at the park, he said, "because I enjoy it and because I thought my presence as a temporary chief magistrate"—in 1921-30, he *did* become the only president to be a Supreme Court chief justice—might spur baseball participation and lift "a city's mental and physical state."

Evidence of Taft's *TSN* "top fan" status was a September 16, 1909, visit to West Side Park in Chicago. A photo shows a scorecard in his right hand and cigar in his left, the latter used to gesture: the president is seen shouting toward the field. A caption explained: "When the committee in charge of arrangements for his entertainment during his visit of last week wired him for suggestions, [Taft] insisted on seeing the game of September 16 between the Cubs and Giants, won by the latter, 2 to 1, in a pitching duel between [Christy] Mathewson and [Mordecai "Three Fingers"] Brown." President Taft was attentive and "exhibited enthusiasm over plays out of the ordinary." The headline, REAL ROOTER IN WHITE HOUSE! tells why millions fondly remembered him, then and now.

Today each game at Washington's Nationals Park presents "The Presidential," a race between halves of the fourth inning by twelve-foot mascots of historic U.S. presidents. Since the race's 2006 start, mascots of Washington, Jefferson, Lincoln, and Theodore Roosevelt have been contestants. In January 2013 the club disclosed that William Howard Taft would regularly join them, given his historic first-pitch niche. Sadly, his running gait has usually kept Taft from winning, like the Senators of old.

Both Taft and Woodrow Wilson often left the capital for "the City of the Big Shoulders," as poet Carl Sandburg called Chicago, whose blue-collar workers and Eastern Europeans worked in stockyards and slaughterhouses, braved epithets, and cheered the White Sox at Comiskey Park, which opened in 1910, wrapped double-decked from the plate to the outfield, and was owned by Charles Comiskey, the Old Roman. Arch windows enhanced a classical look. Interest in the White Sox's new empyrean became so intense as to temporarily make the Cubs feel second in the Second City.

The baseball of Taft's and especially Wilson's age cannot be grasped without invoking the pastime's darkest, history-changing 1919–20 "Black Sox" scandal to throw the 1919 World Series. Its prologue was the last White Sox world title until 2005. In June 1917 Americans began arriving at Saint-Nazaire, France, a major World War I point of entry. That October the Sox beat the Giants in six games, even as most Chicago players, given the tightwad Old Roman, panted for a living wage. Then, in 1919, Joe Jackson hit .351, Lefty Williams had 27 complete games, and Eddie Cicotte had a 29-7 record, despite baseball's lowest salary structure. Chicago won another AL pennant; its Fall Classic foe, Cincinnati, having joined the National League in 1890. Later the Reds' Edd Roush said, "I knew that some finagling was going on."

In Game One of the Series, Cicotte hit the first batter, sending a prearranged sign to gamblers: the fix was on. Ignorant of the scandal, the country expected the heavily favored Pale Hose to rout the Reds—until Chicago lost four of the first five games in a then best-of-nine. Desperate, White Sox fixers, innocents in a hoodlums' world, waited for payola for their play. Eight players had conspired to lose the Classic. "They'd done *their* part," wrote author Richard Lindberg. "Now they expected [gambler] Arnold Rothstein to do his." Ignored, they seethed. Chicago won Games Six and Seven. It was too late. October 9's eighth match ended the ignominy: 10–5, Reds.

In 1920 Cicotte and Williams won forty-three games as Jackson hit .382—each a fixer. That September several confessed their 1919 Series guilt, Comiskey suspending all of the now Black Sox. On October 22, a Chicago grand jury struck: eight indicted! A small boy outside the court is alleged to have approached Jackson and said, "Say it isn't so, Joe." In November baseball named its first all-empowered commissioner, Kenesaw Mountain Landis (a.k.a. the Judge, introduced in chapter 1), whose force and integrity made him the Excalibur of any trial.

Prior to the 1921 season, Landis placed each defendant on the "ineligible" list. "Regardless of the verdict," he boomed, "no player who throws a ball game, no player that undertakes or promises to throw a ball game, *no player that sits in conference with a bunch of crooked players and gamblers* where the ways and means of throwing a game are discussed and *does not promptly tell his club about it, will ever play professional baseball*" (author's emphasis). The language was final, clear, and fatal.

On August 2, 1921, the jury rendered a not guilty verdict, jurors partying with defendants. Next day Landis's first major decision as commissioner shook baseball and beyond, banning all eight accused players for life, the sound of his hammer landing with almost biblical effect. "Baseball is something more than a game," he said. "Destroy . . . [an American boy's] faith in its squareness and honesty, and you have planted suspicion of all things in his heart." Landis was a severe prosecutor and pastime-loving arbiter who "got his job," pricked Will Rogers, not, as ads hyped, through the *New York Times*. Rather, "Somebody said, 'Get that old boy who sits behind first base all the time. He's out there every day anyhow.' So they offered him a season's pass and he jumped at it."

The Judge tried to treat all defendants equally—slice, dice, and threaten. Once he recalled a case in which he meted out fifteen years in jail for robbery. "Your Honor," replied the defendant, "I'm seventy-five years old. I can't serve that long." Landis paused in his retelling. "Well," he told the robber, "do the best you can."

Landis was a populist, not a businessman, and a rock, as he proved after the Black Sox verdict, when it seemed that the jury must have worn ear plugs as the judge instructed its members on what "not guilty" meant. Buck Weaver was a fine third baseman, a member of the Chicago Eight, and a good citizen who made a bad mistake. He played in each Series game, hit .324, and had known of the scandal but neither participated in nor profited from it. Six times Buck pled with Landis to reinstate him, but the commissioner refused: anyone aware of fixing who did not come clean was as guilty as the rest. "Buck, you can't play ball with us again," Landis said.

Baseball got what it wanted—a hanging judge who found that illegal gambling, bank robbery, wartime treason, and a monopoly against the little guy were on the same moral plane. It sought someone who exuded trust—and got lucky. It also got a hero.

The hero was Babe Ruth. He did what no insider solely could: lift baseball from the canvas, helping it to start to earn back its name. Together Landis and Ruth helped make the pastime paid in full—despite what many felt an undue taste for money. The taste of William Howard Taft's successor, it was widely agreed, was higher in almost every way.

Woodrow Wilson's taste ran more toward classical and Christmas music, apt since he was a Christmas week baby, born in Staunton, Virginia, on December 28, 1856, of Scotch-Irish descent. His father, a Presbyterian minister, cared for wounded Civil War soldiers at church and briefly served as a chaplain in the Confederate Army. Woodrow recalled learning at the age of three that Lincoln had been elected and that war was probable. He also remembered standing for a moment at General Robert E. Lee's side and being at one with the lifeblood of the South.

After Appomattox, Dixie given up for dead, Wilson tried to navigate through the region's disarray. Perhaps slowed by dyslexia, he began reading at ten, later blaming inadequate schooling in the South. Teaching himself the Graham shorthand system, he used it to compensate. The latecomer attended Davidson College at seventeen and after a year transferred to Princeton University, where his father began teaching. Wilson studied political philosophy and history, made Phi Beta Kappa fraternity, and got his BA in 1879. He attended law school at the University of Virginia for a year, headed the Jefferson Literary and Debating Society, and entered Johns Hopkins University to study history, political science, and German. In 1886 Wilson received his PhD, completing his doctoral dissertation, "Congressional Government: A Study in American Politics." Already, he had shown what the actress, studio head, and television legend Lucille Ball—Lucy—would one day say: "If you want something done, ask a busy person."

Like Franklin Roosevelt, Wilson loved to drive, as president favoring a 1919 Pierce-Arrow. He absorbed baseball more deeply too than all but a few in the Oval Office who preceded or succeeded him. A page from a Wilson boyhood geometry notebook, titled "Base Ball Ground," shows a hand-scribbled diagram of a baseball diamond. The future president was later Davidson's varsity center fielder and Princeton's assistant manager. In his twenties he added another interest, dating and ultimately marrying Ellen Louise Axson, a Georgian with whom he had two daughters. To support them, Wilson taught at Bryn Mawr, Cornell, and New York Law School. In 1890 he was elected by the Princeton University board to the Chair of Jurisprudence and Political Economy. The student newspaper, *Argus*, later wrote, "His work has been an inspiration."

In 1896 Wilson shook up Princeton's sesquicentennial celebration by saying the school hadn't fulfilled the words of its motto, "Princeton in the Nation's Service." Agreeing, in 1902 the board of trustees made the professor university president, asking him to transform "Gentlemen C" students just performing tasks into "thinking men"—like himself. Wilson made biblical studies academic, created core requirements, and hired faculty based on their record. Always fragile, he awoke one day in 1906 blind in the left eye, the cause a blood clot and hypertension. Doctors now suggest a stroke—the result of hardening of the arteries. Yet when politics beckoned, the academic was intrigued.

Wilson's 1910 bid for governor of New Jersey was uncommonly compressed. He met party elites in July, was nominated in September, resigned from Princeton October 20, and on election day became the state's thirty-fourth governor by more than 650,000 votes over Republican Vivian M. Lewis. The presidency now seemed within grasp—especially with the GOP increasingly a two-headed Janus. In 1912 either William Howard Taft or Theodore Roosevelt might have beaten the Democratic nominee mano a mano. Instead the division of the Republican vote ended the campaign before it began. Wilson dismissed the opposition, mocking TR's Bull Moose Party as "the irregular Republicans, the variegated Republicans." On November 8, he defeated every stripe of Republican, receiving 41.8 percent of the vote to Roosevelt's 27 and Taft's 23 (the balance to minor candidates): 435 electoral votes to the GOP's abysmal 8.

In his 1913 inaugural address, Wilson repeated the agenda vowed in his presidential campaign: lower tariffs and banking reform, more intrepid trust and labor legislation, and contempt for luxury and frills. He canceled the inaugural ball, pioneered twice-weekly press sessions, forbade the media from quoting him, and prohibited office seekers from visiting the White House. Wilson signed the Federal Reserve Act, Federal Trade Commission Act, Clayton Antitrust Act, and Federal Farm Loan Act. A special session of Congress passed the Revenue Act of 1913, a federal income tax, and the Adamson Act to impose an eight-hour railroad workday and avert a railroad strike. Like FDR to come, this Democratic president had his *own* First Hundred Days.

Less then than now, Wilson was scored on civil rights, though how much opprobrium stemmed from the location of his birth is still debated. Legitimate criticism includes his using economic criteria to oppose slavery; drafting African Americans into the army but keeping them in all-black units under white higher-ups; backing segregation in the federal civil service; and saying that "Segregation is not a humiliation but a benefit." He wrote of a "great Ku Klux Klan"—a racist statement from a racist time. It is also true that Wilson balanced private conscience and public opinion; some even felt him radical, and America was more insensitive than today. Of note is that in an age when blacks loved baseball despite past and present cruelty, his affinity took up where Taft's left off.

Wilson began his first term by seeing four games in April, the most that month for any president. In 1912 the Red Sox won their first World Series of four in seven years through 1918. Even before the April 10, 1913, Senators-Sox opener, Wilson told *The Sporting News* that he would visit the popularly referenced but not yet officially renamed Griffith Stadium as a "paying fan," not "dead head," retiring his free presidential pass. By now the Opening Day throng almost expected to see a president. "Every neck was craned to glimpse the 'first American' as he rose to toss the ball to Walter Johnson, by every true Washingtonian thought to be the 'first pitcher,'" wrote TSN. As Johnson "caught the ball from the President's hand men and women arose that they might make even more vociferous their tribute to the hero of the diamond."

A famed epigram called Washington "First in War, First in Peace, and Last in the American League." Wilson's first Opening Day briefly made it *first*. In April the president saw the Senators play three games against the Red Sox. On Memorial Day, May 29, Wilson rode back to Griffith Stadium to again see the Olde Towne Team. For the next century—even in 1972–2004, when DC lacked a club—soldiers of Red Sox Nation have heavily populated Boston games on the Washington or nearby Baltimore home schedule. "We travel well," the esteemed Red Sox 1983– radio voice Joe Castiglione said of the diaspora. In 1913 Wilson did too, radio not yet available to help follow his Sox.

On August 2, 1913, "Walter Johnson Day," Boston beat the Senators, 3–2, the president's last first toss of the year caught aptly by the Big Train. Unlike Wilson, many took the rail to Washington's Union Station and then got a cab or rode the trolley to the park. Any seat offered a view of the honoree, about whom Shakespeare might have said, "Why, man, he doth bestride the narrow world like a colossus." Something about Johnson lured warmth and adulation, especially from the working press.

In 1906 Walter had been plucked from Idaho's Snake River Valley League for a $100 bonus, $350 monthly salary, and train fare to the nation's capital. A year later he won his first of 417 games against 279 defeats for Washington from 1907 to 1927—astonishing, given the sheer God-awfulness of many of the clubs for which he played. The year 1910 *made* Johnson's niche, his Opening Day one-hitter the first of eight first-day shutouts. Thirty-eight complete games and twenty-five wins *changed* his niche. Boys named Walter Johnson began studding the area. A Bethesda, Maryland, high school bears his name.

The major cause of Walter's once-in-a lifetime popularity was his once-in-a-lifetime skill. Johnson sidearmed 3,509 strikeouts, had a record 110 shutouts, ten times won twenty or more games, and won his first (1913) MVP award. Another factor was Walter's nice-guy air. Once a year young Jimmy Dudley came to Griffith from southwest Virginia. "It'd be a Sunday and dad would bring us thirteen kids," said the 1948–67 voice of the Indians, whose pop worked for the Southern Railroad, so fare was free. "He used him [Walter] as a standard if I got out of hand. 'Walter Johnson would never do a thing like that!'"

Dudley's father was most impressed by Johnson's kindness. Only once did he see the Big Train mad. "A little black boy named Snowball would hang around the clubhouse," said Jimmy, "just wanting to be around his heroes." Objecting, a policeman prepared to bounce him from the park. Quickly Walter shoved the cop against the wall: "Don't *ever* lay hands on this boy again! Dadgum your soul, I *mean* it!" Dudley formed a smile. "Washington was segregated until the sixties," he said, "and remember too that 'dadgum' was the strongest language anyone heard Johnson use."

The officer got with the program, having little choice. On a good day, even in a popular administration like Wilson's first term, a president of the United States would be lucky to command as much reverence among men of a certain generation in the nation's capital as could a man dead since 1946, the incomparable Big Train.

By 1914 kidney failure had withered the health of Wilson's wife, Ellen Axson. "My dear one . . . grows weaker and weaker, with a pathetic patience and sweetness," her husband wrote. "Oh, my God, what am I to do?" She died on August 6, the president crying, "God has stricken me almost beyond what I can bear." Wilson sank into a labyrinth of gloom, surfacing finally in January 1915 to give a speech, saying, "The trouble with the Republican Party is that it has not had a new idea for thirty years . . . The Republican Party is still a covert and a refuge for those who are afraid." Rarely afraid, the president was briefly alone.

A month later Wilson met Edith Bolling Galt, a Southern widow and jeweler with whom he fell in love and to whom he became secretly engaged that fall. They wed December 18, 1915, a more proper distance in that time and context between one marriage and another. After World War I began in 1914, Wilson maintained neutrality, letting his 1916 campaign against former New York governor Charles Evans Hughes sail under the slogan "He kept us out of war." The outcome hung on California, Minnesota, and New Hampshire, Wilson winning by only 3,773 (California), 393 (Minnesota), and 54 (New Hampshire) popular votes and 277 electoral votes to Hughes's 254. A year earlier German submarines had torpedoed and sunk the British ocean liner RMS *Lusitania*, killing many Americans. Wilson reacted passively. Now, in early 1917, Germany reacted to America's strict neutrality by resuming unrestricted submarine warfare. What would Wilson do?

Again he temporized, even after learning of an extraordinary German offer. In Wilson's first term fighting had erupted at the U.S.-Mexican border, killing 126 Mexicans and 19 Americans. Germany now pledged that if Mexico backed it against the United States, a grateful victor would help Mexico regain the states of Texas, New Mexico, and Arizona. Wilson threatened to break diplomatic relations. When Germany sank several American ships, Theodore Roosevelt stormed, "If he [Wilson] does not go to war I shall skin him alive!" Finally, on April 2 Wilson addressed Congress, saying that Germany had rendered his "armed neutrality" untenable, the German government had "stir[red] up enemies against us at our very door," and that "the world must be made safe for democracy." Congress easily endorsed Wilson's declaration of war.

Wilson gave help to allies Britain and France; sent troops to Europe; nationalized the rails; created the War Industries Board; and wisely left strategy to the military, especially General John J. "Black Jack" Pershing," who emerged from the war almost as prominent as the president. Wilson also used the mistrust of anarchists, Communists, and other suspect groups, backing the Espionage Act of 1917 and Sedition Act of 1918. At heart he worked to democratize the world, issuing principles for peace—the "Fourteen Points"—which included diplomacy, freedom of the seas, and a new League of Nations. After the 1918 Armistice, he brooked influenza to conclude the Treaty of Versailles, which created a new League and urged a harsh treatment of Germany, "seek[ing] to punish one of the greatest wrongs ever done in history, the wrong which Germany sought to do to the world and to civilization." Wilson even received the 1919 Nobel Prize for Peace. Yet increasingly, work, travel, and exhaustion changed the man in the Oval Office.

In 1914 Wilson had missed the baseball opener, Speaker of the House Champ Clark performing the first-pitch rite. That July 14 the president saw the Tigers blank the Nationals. On Opening Day 1915 Wilson tossed the first ball to Johnson, who beat the Yanks, 7–0. Then, on October 9 he accompanied his fiancé in their public coming-out at Red Sox-Phils Game Two: the first president to attend a World Series and uncork a first pitch. The couple looked in the pink. The Sox looked even healthier, taking each game by one run and winning their second Fall Classic in four years. In April 1916 a ruddy president seemed supremely happy on the eve of his reelection bid, throwing out another Opening Day pitch and later watching the visiting Yankees bow, 12–4. For the ultimately seventh-place Senators, it was the Everest of their year.

By April 1917, with war just declared, the president missed the opener, vice president Thomas R. Marshall tossing in his stead. Marshall was neither well known nor long remembered. His motto was: "What this country really needs is a good five-cent cigar." Griffith also hosted a flag ceremony with a man worth recalling: assistant secretary of the navy Franklin Delano Roosevelt. In 1918 Wilson threw out the first ball for the annual congressional game, braving the 19–5 GOP romp, and attended his final game May 24, for charity. The *Washington Post* bannered: PRESIDENT, AT HIS FIRST BALL GAME IN 2 YEARS, SEES GRIFFS AND TIGES IN TIE (2-all). The subhead: "President Throwing Out Ball to Start Red Cross Benefit Game." A picture showed him flanked by his physician—Admiral Dr. Cary Grayson—Edith, and Clark Griffith. He seemed to have aged twenty years in two.

Increasingly, Wilson's frail health in effect made the new First Lady president. The two-time elected president left alone an issue that would have normally absorbed him: baseball's wartime status. Workers in certain fields—singers, actors, producers—were exempted because the government deemed them "essential" to the welfare of the war. Baseball was felt nonessential. In *Baseball Magazine*, on May 23, 1918, the provost marshal of the army in charge of conscription, General Enoch Crowder, issued an order that by July 1 young men should find essential work or be drafted by a branch of the armed forces. Headline writers called it "work or fight." It took more than two years for baseball to finally hire a commissioner to provide crisis guidance or at least knock heads.

Normally Wilson might have done both. His leverage dulled, much of baseball's hierarchy cracked. AL president Ban Johnson said he wanted America to close "every theater, ballpark, and place of recreation in the country and make people realize that they were in the most terrible war in the history of the world." Erratically, he then declared that baseball should be exempted as "essential." Governor of Pennsylvania-turned-NL head John Tener thought even that obeisance minimized baseball's role. It was "a moral and spiritual production . . . Simply because what baseball produces is intangible I do not think it can be called non-essential or not productive." His case was hurt by players having left clubs to farm again or work in a war factory, some hired to play on a company *baseball* team.

That summer Senators catcher Eddie Ainsmith, twenty-six, a career .232 hitter, appealed the loss of his draft exemption—to him, baseball essential. On July 19, 1918, secretary of war Newton Baker said that Ainsmith would be drafted unless he found a job. In turn, Ban Johnson, losing leverage, said the season would end after games on July 21. He had not even asked the teams, which kept playing even as players left. Rarely had baseball seemed so unhinged. "If the [draft] order is made effective, this large and respectable business will be ruined," Tener telegrammed Wilson, saying he needed to see him. The president wrote an aide: "How am I to escape this? There is no earthly use in my discussing the baseball situation" with Tener. Tangentially he did.

On July 27, 1918, the White House made public a letter to the editor of *Spalding's Baseball Guide*. "The President asked me to acknowledge receipt of your letter of July 26th," wrote the Wilson aide, "and to add that he sees no necessity at all for stopping or curtailing the baseball schedule." The First Fan wasn't needed since Crowder and Baker already worked for Wilson. They, in turn, let the season end the first weekend of September and the World Series a week later. Returns increasingly favored the owners: a season thirty days shorter meant a month in which players weren't paid.

The war ended November 11, 1918—Armistice Day (renamed Veterans Day)—freeing owners to return by 1919 to normalcy. Otherwise Wilson would have had to endure an entire year bereft of baseball, just when he needed it most.

A weary Wilson returned in 1919 from Europe to begin a cross-country pilgrimage. His goal: gain two-thirds of Senate approval for the Treaty of Versailles, including the League of Nations. If Congress wouldn't see the light, he would make it feel the heat through brilliant public speaking, as of old. Weaker with every speech, he refused to rest, feeling too much left undone—the Fourteen Points; global democracy; the League, a lasting means, he was sure, of peace. The War to End All Wars would be verified by a treaty he had helped to draft.

"At last," Wilson exulted, barnstorming by train, "the world knows America as the savior of the world." On September 25 he collapsed giving a speech on the League of Nations in Pueblo, Colorado, and never fully recovered. The trip ended a day later, Wilson returning to the White House, where on October 2 he had a serious stroke that left him paralyzed on his left side, with only partial vision in his right eye. For the rest of his life, wife Edith insulated and protected him. The public did not know that it had an invalid as president.

Wilson was confined to bed for weeks and kept from everyone except his wife and Dr. Grayson. He used a wheelchair, then cane. Edith chose which issues and personnel deserved his time and energy. Aides and Cabinet members did the rest. Yet work and duty were so ingrained in Wilson that somehow he found strength to shepherd what became the Nineteenth Amendment, passed in 1919 and ratified a year later, giving women the right to vote. In February 1920 the nation learned of his condition, many anxious about his fitness to serve. No one would certify, as required by the Constitution, that Wilson was unable "to discharge the powers and duties of the said office." This contributed to the Twenty-Fifth Amendment, ratified in 1967, about presidential succession.

The Senate rejected the Treaty of Versailles, Senate Majority Leader Henry Cabot Lodge ensuring that America would spurn the League of Nations, which sputtered before the birth of the United Nations in 1945. In 1920 Wilson, the treaty, and liberalism, among other things, were rejected in the then greatest Republican landslide. Ohio senator Warren G. Harding demolished James M. Cox for president with more than 60 percent of the popular vote. The House and Senate GOP gained more than a two-to-one and almost a three-to-two majority respectively. It is hard to grasp how desolate the Peacemaker must have felt. Redemption came later, long after Wilson's death. Admiration for his courage and martyrdom won loyalty from politicians as disparate as Richard Nixon and Adlai Stevenson. There was depth here, and character.

Many saw this ultimately. Until then baseball saved Wilson: a strong verb, but no other word will do. A semi-recluse, reluctant even to see old friends, he sought refuge in a game whose inner world was never out of season. At his DC home, where Wilson remained upon leaving the presidency March 4, 1921, a downstairs room was called "the dugout." Every morning the ex-president and his secretary, Randolph Bolling, met to review each prior day's big-league scores. In the afternoon, by arrangement with Senators owner Clark Griffith, he was driven to Griffith Stadium to see his team play. Wilson's auto entered through a special gate, then parked by the home bullpen. From there the president watched, top down, the Secret Service—helped by players—protecting him from foul balls. Whatever the score, he stayed to the end.

Before his illness, Wilson had avidly opened each season. Healthy, the Virginian, like William Howard Taft, might have become baseball's first commissioner. Instead, Judge Landis was named the sport's first czar before Wilson left office. Two of the great presidential fanatics (*Webster's* defining "fan," derived from the Greek "fanatic," as "a person whose extreme zeal, piety, etc. goes beyond what is reasonable") were left to celebrate their game. For Taft, Opening Day became each year's red-letter date, a paean to tradition. Sadly he fell to Shakespeare's "sea of troubles" in the 1912 election, as Wilson did in his second term, compounded by several strokes.

In his office Clark Griffith framed a photo of a jarringly aged former president sitting in his car beyond the outfield at Griffith Stadium. It showed Wilson's fidelity to the sport, a pastime that returned his love, giving him something to live for, about which to feel alive. In the end each kept the faith. In 1970 Stan Musial, among the greatest hitters of the second third of the American Century, and wife Lil visited the Woodrow Wilson House, a National Trust of Historic Preservation property in Washington. From 1964–67 Stan had been President Johnson's physical fitness adviser, helping children in a way that Wilson would have hailed.

On display at the Wilson House was an exhibit, "President Wilson, Athlete and Sports Fan," showing such a revolutionary coach that Wilson merits being titled a founder of modern football, from using college football gate receipts to finance other athletic department sports to introducing "chalk talk," whereby plays outlined on a blackboard let a series of six or seven plays be run without a signal on the field. The exhibit featured the tennis racquet, golf clubs, and knapsack of a president who liked to hike and bike through hilly Scotland, play billiards, and ride horseback.

Always Wilson returned to baseball. High school notes list the lineup for the Light Foot Baseball Club of 1870, which he organized and managed. A prized baseball bearing the autograph of King George V of Great Britain was among his sports memorabilia on exhibit. Wilson found that discussing the national game never went out of vogue. You could hardly say less of him.

THREE

Triple Play

Warren Harding, Calvin Coolidge, and
Herbert Hoover, 1921–1933

Franklin Delano Roosevelt, inaugurated a first time in 1933, is commonly thought of as America's first radio president. To reference *Porgy and Bess*, "It ain't necessarily so." The wireless became commercially available on November 2, 1920, election night, over Westinghouse-owned then one-hundred-watt KDKA in Pittsburgh, the nation's first radio station. Republican presidential nominee Warren Gamaliel Harding won a landslide over Democrat and Ohio governor James M. Cox, the loser's running mate being—FDR! For the next quarter century each major party, including 1921–33's presidential triple play of Harding to Calvin Coolidge to Herbert Hoover, made radio the primary medium.

Roosevelt became the first president to *master* radio. Harding was the first president to *use* radio. Alice Roosevelt Longworth once said, "Harding was not a bad man. He was just a slob." Others felt him ready for Mt. Rushmore—fine chin, full hair, seeming gravitas. Whatever the 1921–23 president's condition, radio let him reach twenty million Americans for a twenty-minute speech. No newspaper of the infant decade could even begin to vie.

Born in 1865 in Corsica (now Blooming Grove), Ohio, a young Harding moved to nearby Marion, playing the baseball game of pepper with a friend, Bob Allen. For each, that small city became the center of his boyhood universe. Shortstop Allen batted .241 with 306 runs batted in for the National League (NL) 1890–94 Phillies, 1897 Braves (née Beaneaters), and 1900 Reds. In addition, he managed 1890 Philadelphia and 1900 Cincinnati and later owned four Southern Association (SA) franchises, including Nashville, then a flagship franchise of the game.

In his twenties Harding owned part of Marion's town team, the Diggers, in the Ohio State League. The ex officio scout also eyed two players who became Major League regulars. In 1912–26 pitcher Wilbur Cooper forged a 216-167 record for the Pirates, Cubs, and Tigers. The future president's other find was first baseman Jake Daubert, who twice led the NL with a .350 and .329 average, hitting .303 for the 1910–18 Dodgers and 1919–24 Reds. Perhaps the best-ever left-handed pitcher was even named in Harding's honor. Born in 1921, Warren Spahn retired in 1965 with a 363-245 record, a 3.09 ERA, and the consensus greatest pickoff move. Once Spahn is said to have picked a runner off first base—and the batter swung.

Presidents vary in ease of transition between politics and baseball. Harding preferred talking ball to dull issues with duller people. As the 1920 GOP nominee, he staged a parade evocative of William McKinley's 1896 "front-porch" campaign. One by one, special interests—a developer here, a lawyer there—arrived in Marion with political, policy, and other counsel. Finally, after sessions that bored the object of veneration, Harding was quizzed by *Brooklyn Eagle* baseball writer Thomas S. Rice, who put the candidate at ease—and considerably behind schedule.

For a long time they talked of Allen, Daubert, and Cooper; of "Brooklyn USA" as a big-league town without peer; and of the great also-ran team of the 1910s. In the three years after 1910, Christy Mathewson and Rube Marquard won seventy-four and seventy-three regular-season games respectively for John McGraw's Giants. Yet New York lost each of its four Series that decade—a total matched only by the Red Sox, who won all four of theirs. In 1911 A's pitching stopped the Giants. In 1913 A's hitting did the trick. In 1912 a muffed fly by Fred Snodgrass saved the Red Sox. In 1917 the White Sox's Urban Faber dispatched New York. "The team that loses gracefully loses easily," said McGraw, doing neither.

Talking to Rice, Warren Harding was soon surprised: he was *enjoying* himself. Not wishing to impose, the baseball writer excused himself and prepared to leave—except that Harding wouldn't bite. Perhaps debate turned to the game's then cynosure: the fox taken as a naif who ends up taking the taker. In 1998 the Cubs' Sammy Sosa, engaged in a homerthon with St. Louis's Mark McGwire, said, "Baseball has been very, very good to me." Harding's early 1920s were very good to George Herman (Babe) Ruth, as he would be to baseball.

In a sense the Babe had seemed misplaced on the 1910s Red Sox. For one thing, he embodied power. The decade's Olde Towne Team accented pitching, defense, and speed. For another, Ruth was a high school dropout. The Red Sox had the most college men in the league. Duffy Lewis said, "Look at that big ignorant ape, making all that money." Larry Gardner thought ignorance a plus: "We're all making more because of Babe."

In 1918 Sox manager Ed Barrow asked, "Babe, how would you like to play left field?" (He had pitched exclusively since 1914.) Boston took its fifth world title, Ruth hit .300, and his Fall Classic record reached twenty-nine and two-thirds straight scoreless innings. In 1919 Babe's twenty-nine home runs—the rest of the Sox had *four*—broke Ned Williamson's all-time record of twenty-seven in 1884, making Ruth wonder if they pitched Ned underhanded.

In early 1920 Boston owner and financier Harry Frazee sold Babe to New York for $100,000 and a $300,000 loan secured by a mortgage on Fenway Park for would-be Broadway hits, including *My Lady Friends*—a farce, like that decade's Red Sox. The early Yankees née Highlanders played at tiny Hilltop Park until a 1911 fire damaged the Polo Grounds, home of the Giants. For the next two months McGraw slummed at Hilltop before returning to a new double-decked horseshoe in a hollow below Coogan's Bluff. Outgrowing Hilltop, the Yankees became a Giants tenant, staying as Ruth, hitting .376 in 1920, made McGraw feel small in his own home park. In 1921 the Yanks won their first of forty pennants. Few now minded Ruth's lack of a diploma.

In 1922 the Giants won a second straight Series, then kicked the Yanks off Manhattan Isle. "They'll have to move to Long Island, or the

Bronx," puffed McGraw, "and nobody'll ever hear from them again." That year construction of the first baseball field to be called a *stadium* rose in 284 working days one-quarter mile from the Polo Grounds. The new joint initially had the most seats of any park—82,000 in 1927; 67,000 by World War II—and postwar wall numbers that would change when one plus one equaled three: 301 feet (left-field pole); 402 feet (left side, left-center bullpen gate); 457 feet (left-center, a.k.a. Death Valley); 407 feet (right-center); 344 feet (right side, right-center bullpen gate); and 296 feet (right-field pole). Center field was 461 feet away. The three-tier grandstand wrapped home plate beyond the bases. Bleachers trimmed the fence. At the new Yankee Stadium, soon known as The Stadium, the shape affected the game within.

Harding saw more games at Griffith Stadium than at any other park but felt the Big Ballpark in the Bronx "the last word in ball parks," wrote *Literary Digest*. Yankee Stadium was meant to utilize Ruth's pull hitting—"the House That Ruth Built"—and helped make him a sunny-dark hero, "not so much mortal as part of our native mythology," as Ron Fimrite wrote of the Babe's whopping bat and massive girth. Like Ruth's, Harding's baseball was more intuitive than intellectual, the Ohioan growing up playing more than watching the local team. His habits were also more than faintly redolent. Ruth drank before and after games and at any time available. Bourbon at its best arrived at the White House even as lawmen elsewhere tended to Prohibition. Harding relished hosting Babe when the Bronx Bombers played in Washington—the teams met there eleven times a year—as much as he enjoyed tossing the first ball at each Nationals home opener. Like Ruth, he was careless about ethics, a fatal flaw. Yet his knowledge of baseball made even a routine conversation about it caring.

In the July 12, 1999, *Sports Illustrated*, Richard Hoffer put the Babe in focus as "like rock-and-roll and the Model T . . . a seminal American invention. Be it his power at the plate, his popularity or his various appetites, the Babe was huge." Ruth burst upon baseball before Harding's 1921 inauguration. Graham McNamee crashed through later. In 1923 the opera student-turned-radio-tyro broadcast his first of thirteen straight Series, the Yankees taking their first of a U.S. professional record twenty-seven world titles. Graham got seventeen hundred letters, which, as a broadcaster said in 2010, is "like a zillion now." In 1924, he aired the 103-ballot Democratic National Convention; 1925, covered President Coolidge's address to Congress; 1927, broadcast Charles Lindbergh's flight from New York to Paris. Each solo began, "How do you do, ladies and gentlemen of the radio audience?" and closed like a séance: "This is Graham McNamee speaking. Good night, all."

As we will see, Harding died in the year of McNamee's debut. The day of the president's funeral, Walter Johnson recalled the prior year when his son, Walter Jr., played in front of the dugout at Griffith Stadium. Harding had called the boy over and put him on his lap, where he sat for the first inning. "This is a mighty fine boy you have here," the president said.

In 1923, Harding had been eager to savor Johnson's high, hard one. He also looked forward to hearing McNamee describe Ruth on more Series wireless, seeing him at parks in DC and elsewhere, and having the Babe return to the White House, where baseball talk, like Prohibition booze, was free and always flowed.

Harding was the oldest of eight children born to a doctor, George, a.k.a. Tryon, and a state-licensed midwife, Phoebe, also deemed a doctor under Ohio state law. Except for his stay in Columbus as state senator and lieutenant governor and his time in Washington as U.S. senator and later president, the future chief executive spent his fifty-seven-year life entirely in rural Ohio. The small town was Harding's touchstone, as for much of the America that elected him, touting what Margaret Thatcher, raised in a similar milieu in Great Britain, later called "the things [she] and millions like [her] were brought up with: an honest day's work for an honest day's pay; liv[ing] within your means; put[ting] by a nest egg for a rainy day; pay[ing] your bills on time; support[ing] the police." Harding could have said every word. Living by them could be something else.

His family moved when he was eleven to Caledonia, Ohio, where Dad bought a small weekly newspaper, the *Argus*. At fourteen Harding enrolled at Ohio Central College in Iberia, he and a friend publishing another small paper, the *Iberia Spectator*. In Warren's final year of school, his clan moved to Marion, six miles from Caledonia, where he joined them after graduation. In 1884, Harding, nineteen, raised $300 to help buy the failing *Marion Star*. By 1923, long revived, it hailed the former Major Leaguer and now businessman Bob Allen as "that sort of supporter of the national game that every town of thirty or forty thousand knows and for the lack of whom minor league baseball would die out."

At the time, Harding was widely respected and liked. His public lay among the Grange and Elks Club and Chamber of Commerce, not among those destined by lineage or other privilege to rule. In 1891 he married Florence Kling, a divorcee with a young son, Marshall. She became Harding's personnel director and business manager, some calling her more ambitious for her husband than he was for himself. In 1899 Warren was elected Republican state senator, periodically hospitalized for "fatigue, overstrain, and nervous illnesses," a prophecy of heart trouble. In 1901 and 1904 he overcame it to be reelected senator and lieutenant governor respectively, lost a 1910 bid for governor, but at President Taft's request gave a speech nominating his fellow Buckeye for reelection at the 1912 GOP national convention.

In 1914 Harding became U.S. senator from Ohio. Increasingly at his side: Harry M. Daugherty, a Columbus lobbyist who oohed after meeting him, "Gee, what a great-looking president he'd make." In 1916 Warren gave the convention keynote speech. Two years later, the GOP regained the U.S. Senate, putting him on its Foreign Relations Committee. Still, Harding neared the 1920 Republican convention in Chicago feeling himself more a spectator than participant. The crowded GOP field included a general (Leonard Wood), governor (Frank Lowden, Illinois), and senator (Hiram Johnson, California) joined by Massachusetts governor Calvin Coolidge, World War I humanitarian Herbert Hoover, and the Great War's General Pershing.

Harding pined for Senate reelection, had little thought of becoming president, but was acceptable to the party's center-right base. On April 27 he barely won his Ohio Senate primary, was leveled next door in Indiana's presidential primary, and needed to file for the general election in one state or the other.

Torn, talking with Daugherty, now campaign manager, Warren was interrupted by his wife. "Warren Harding, what are you doing?" Florence yanked away the phone, correctly fearing that he was about to file nomination papers for the Senate. "Give up [the presidency]? Not until the convention is over! Think of your friends in Ohio!"

Harding said that Daugherty had just left the line to avoid her. "Well," she stormed, "you tell Harry Daugherty for me that we're in this fight until Hell freezes over!"—which they were, until death came instead.

Harding was next spotted May 15 at Boston's Home Market Club, giving the speech that improbably pivoted the campaign. "America's present need is not heroics, but healing," he said, and then, "Not nostrums, but normalcy; not revolution, but restoration." A sentence caught the mood. "Return [a.k.a. Back] to Normalcy" became *the* campaign line of that year and many more.

One month later, on June 8–12, Republicans held their quadrennial national convention in the Chicago Coliseum. It began terribly divided, ended somewhat united, and crested on June 11–12 in the now legendary "smoke-filled room" at the Blackstone Hotel. For most of two days and an entire evening and its morn, Republican leading and lesser lights caucused and cajoled on behalf of one candidate or another on one ballot after another. At last Harding was chosen on the tenth ballot as GOP nominee for president. Coolidge became the imminent VP.

Harding used his remodeled front porch, referred to above, to resemble McKinley's 1896 campaign, getting a record 60.2 percent of the popular vote and 404 electoral votes against James Cox's 34.0 and 127 respectively. Third-party Socialist Eugene Debs received 3 percent campaigning from a federal prison, serving time for opposing World War I. "For the Republicans," the PBS documentary, *FDR: The American Experience*, declared, "the victory was more than a landslide, it was an earthquake." The first sitting U.S. senator elected president moved quickly to pick up the pieces.

First, Harding appointed an all-star cabinet, including Hoover at the Department of Commerce; future chief justice of the U.S. Supreme Court Charles Evans Hughes at the Department of State; and financier Andrew Mellon at the Treasury Department. Next, he moved to cut income taxes; end the railroad strike of 1921; and reject, with the Senate, the Treaty of Versailles, denuding the League of Nations. The Washington Naval Conference froze American, British, and Japanese naval expansion, in time limiting Japan's navy to 60 percent of the others' fleets. Ironically, since the United States and UK deployed globally, Japan could focus regionally—and would, for a decade and beyond.

America was trying to buy time and turn distance into security to avoid an Armageddon in Harding's time—another world war. Maybe he was not "a slob," many got to thinking. Perhaps the Ohioan was not a "bad" man at all.

Many presidents bond with a hometown team: Woodrow Wilson's Senators, Barack Obama's White Sox, George H. W. Bush's Astros, long prior to their Cinderella 2017. Before he found the Yanks, Warren Harding followed the Midwestern Cubs, whose early franchise ancestor a.k.a. the Colts, Orphans, and White Stockings helped to make baseball Chicago's kind of game. A sixth-century Greek philosopher said a man cannot stand in the same river twice. The future Cubs thought they could ford any stream as often as they wished.

Twenty-Third Street Grounds or Park came first in 1876–77. Lake Front Park followed, flaunting a home field edge of ashes, boulders, broken bottles, and glass. In 1883 the Cubs-to-be moved to Lake Front II Park, also playing at South Side Park II, West Side Park, and West Side Grounds. The latter was Chicago's first double-decked ark and had a huge center field—560 feet from the plate—for tykes and teens to stand near fielders and "Keystone cops" to patrol. "That's where the name 'Cubs' is said to come from," said popular 1996– radio voice Pat Hughes. "All the kids in the outfield." The team later shaped a glorious half-decade: pennants in 1906, 1907, 1908, and 1910 and a 1908 world title. "Tinkers to Evers to Chance" became immersed in verse and on the field. It sustained a century—by circumstance, not choice.

"Baseball was so exciting, I thought I'd own the [1914–15] Whales for years," said Charles Weeghman after the Federal League died and he bought the 1916 Cubs and moved them to Weeghman Park. He was the first owner to let a patron keep a foul ball and to put a mascot (Joa, a real bear) in a cage (on Addison Street, at the park). Did Joa feel confined? We know only that this became the Friendly Confines. By 1918 William Wrigley bought the park and team, lowered the field, double-decked the single tier, and renamed it Wrigley Field. "For the first time, Wrigley's shell resembled today's," noted Bill Veeck, baseball's most fan-friendly owner.

From 1929 the Cubs won the pennant every third year through 1938. "[Announcer] Jack Brickhouse told me every kid on the block knew about the three-year itch," said Hughes. The most memorable game dotted 1932. Two years earlier the Yankees had dealt popular Mark Koenig to Detroit, which sent him to Chicago, where in 1932 he hit .353 and helped the Cubs win the pennant. Chicago then proceeded to deny Koenig a full World Series share, inflaming that year's Fall Classic rival, Mark's ex-teammate Yanks.

The Bombers won the first two Series matches. A pre-Game Three photo shows Franklin Roosevelt, Yanks skipper Joe McCarthy, and Chicago's wary Charlie Grimm. In the fifth inning, the score was tied four-all at Wrigley: the Stripes at bat, Charlie Root pitching. The Cubs righty threw a strike, then a ball. The Yankees bayed "Cheapskates," the home dugout responding "Flatfoot" and tossing liniment.

Root threw ball two. Babe Ruth raised two fingers: a 2-2 count. Did Babe then point to a bleacher spot to deposit the next pitch? "Hell, he never called it," Root later sneered. "If he had, next time up I'd have stuck the pitch in his rear."

Babe walloped the pitch to the center-field seats, a writer later asking about Babe "calling" the homer. Frank Crosetti said that Ruth harangued each mate in the postgame clubhouse: "If anybody asks the greatest day in the Babe's life, it's today when I pointed where I'd homer."

At the park at the junction of West Addison and North Clark, a pitcher could inherit the wind. A breeze blowing in from Lake Michigan could lower an ERA by a run or two a game. Blowing out, as in Game Three, a gale might lead to schizophrenia—and a fan to the area of Wrigleyville, often easier to find relief from a bar or speakeasy than from the latest shell-shocked hurler.

Wrigley Field's blue grass and animal-cracker size are still precious. The ivy and full bleachers have been added since the ballpark's birth. The neighborhood remains, albeit more high rise than in the past. You can still toast the Cubs fan—and an irrepressible plat.

Almost prophetically in early 1923 the president sold his hometown *Marion Star* newspaper and wrote a new will. Harding brooked influenza, his heart condition worse due to stress, but in June began a "voyage of understanding" that rivaled FDR's later tours in length and intensity. Speaking almost daily, he would entrain cross country, go north to the Alaska Territory, turn south along the West Coast, navigate through the Panama Canal to Puerto Rico, and be scheduled to return to Washington DC by the end of August. On July 26, Harding toured Vancouver, British Columbia, the first U.S. president in office to visit Canada. A day later he spoke to twenty-five thousand at the University of Washington in Seattle, predicting statehood for Alaska thirty-five years before its time.

Exhausted, Harding sped through his speech, not waiting for applause, then rushed to San Francisco, where doctors thought him better, thus letting their patient sit up in bed. On August 2 Florence was reading a *Saturday Evening Post* paean to him, "A Calm Review of a Calm Man." She paused to fluff his pillows, the president saying, "That's good. Read some more." Suddenly her husband began to twist convulsively, then collapsed. His body soon lay in a casket in a cross-continental train from San Francisco to DC for services, nine million people lining tracks across the country, shocked by Harding's death at fifty-seven of a cerebral hemorrhage caused by heart disease. He was taken to Marion for burial, then among the more beloved presidents since Lincoln.

In one sense death cheated Harding of a later chance to explain his private conduct, which began to publicly emerge not long after his heart attack. Surely, as America hailed him in August 1923, many thought of Harding's "front-porch" campaign of 1920 and his vow, apparently kept while alive, to retrieve normalcy. In office he opposed the League of Nations, fueled peace and also prosperity, and endorsed the Eighteenth and Nineteenth Amendments, the former forbidding the use or sale of alcohol and backed by Harding even as barrels rinsed the White House. As hypocritical was the Teapot Dome scandal, of which the nation had been more or less forgiving until the unethical scent of the administration began to rock Harding's name.

In 1963 the Ohio Historical Society released many of his papers. "He spoke his mind candidly," maintained Edwin K. Gross in the *Buffalo Evening News*. "Harding demolished the idea that he was everyone's pal," making distinctions between and among people as individuals. "He dissects himself, peers, aides, and officials of every age, determined to show he was a tough if not a hanging judge." Teapot hearings had intensified in 1923, Harding's hope of being such a "judge" in the public mind dying amid disgust at the license of his closest aides. The head of the Veterans' Bureau went to prison for corruption. Harry Daugherty's factotum at the Justice Department committed suicide. The attorney general was indicted for defrauding the government. Teapot Dome made the secretary of the interior the first Cabinet member to go to prison for crimes committed in office—here, for taking bribes during negotiations for naval oil reserves.

Worst for his constituency, which trusted Harding to defend Christian culture and convention, other disclosures showed the president not to be the man it believed while alive. Letters from Harding to Carrie Fulton Phillips of Marion attested to an extramarital affair of fifteen years that conveniently ended in 1920, the year he was elected. In 1927 Nan Britton, also of Marion, published a best-selling book *The President's Daughter*, alleging an affair with Harding that included having sex in a White House closet while Secret Service agents stood guard outside. It also charged the president with being the father of her child, Elizabeth Ann Blaesing.

For a long while Britton's claim was suspect, showing only that Elizabeth Ann likely stemmed from Nan, not that Harding was the father. In 2015, however, DNA tests confirmed both. Not suspect is the emotion expressed upon Harding's death by Charles Evans Hughes, who greatly admired and so capably served him in the Cabinet and who said, "I cannot realize that our beloved chief is no longer with us." At the time it was a sentiment that most of the country shared. Harding's various scandals devalued a social stratum: the innate virtue of a hail-fellow-well-met member of, say, a Masonic Lodge. On one hand, it could be said that successor Calvin Coolidge restored the presidency's moral rubric. On the other, as a Washington hostess barbed, Coolidge looked "like he had been weaned on a pickle."

Senators owner Clark Griffith described the man known as "Silent Cal" as "a calculating, unexcitable man who showed nothing." Knowing almost nothing of the game that Griffith and Harding loved, Coolidge possessed a politician's sense of grasping what the public wanted. An April 15, 1924, picture shows photographers standing on the Nationals dugout as Calvin primps to throw. He looks clueless, but belatedly willing to be clued. In 1920 Griffith mortgaged his ranch to buy the team. The Senators had or would finish second in 1912–13, third in 1914 and 1918, and fourth three times from 1915 to 1923. In 1917, the first full year of U.S. participation in World War I, annual attendance slumped to 89,682, lowest in franchise history. By 1924 it hit a level—584,310—once thought as impossible as a talking film.

Mark Twain said, "There are lies, damn lies . . . and statistics." Statistics about the 1924 Washington nine tell the truth. Offensively the club was built for its yawning power-alley park. The Senators were last in AL homers, 22, but first in triples, 88, and second in team batting average, .294, and stolen bases, 116. Flapping his arms while awaiting a fly ball—thus the nickname—Goose Goslin starred in much of what there was to gander at: first, runs batted in, 129; second, triples, 17; and fourth, total bases, 299. Historically, pitching, defense, and speed contend. The Nationals' 171 errors trailed only the Yanks' 156. Above all, pitching paid the freight.

At thirty-six, Walter Johnson belied his age with 23 victories, 6 shutouts, and a 2.72 ERA, the lowest in the league. As in 1913 the Big Train was voted AL Most Valuable Player. Led by "Boy Wonder" player/manager Bucky Harris, twenty-seven, the Nats took first place in June, clinched Washington's first pennant on September 29, and returned from Boston by train October 1, where thousands greeted them at Union Station. Ahead lay an official salute by the capital, especially a certain tightwad in the Oval Office. Previously baseball had been as offensive to Calvin Coolidge as an overdrawn check or misspent dime. Now, in fall 1924, the pastime overnight became the president's pal. Officially his campaign slogan was "Keep Cool with Coolidge." By election day it could have been "Coolidge: A Baseball Life."

The stratagem arose from letters to the White House from worried GOP donors, many cool indeed toward a president who could be legendarily terse. A woman at a White House dinner once gushed, "You must talk to me, Mr. Coolidge. I made a bet today that I could get more than two words out of you." Cal told her: "You lose." Reticence was one thing, frigidity another. How to humanize a man whose degrees of body temperature seemed measured in Celsius, not Fahrenheit? One morning, recalled *Baseball Magazine*, White House adviser Frank Stearns read a telegram: INDUCE PRESIDENT TO TENDER RECEPTION AND BANNER TO JOHNSON AND WASHINGTON TEAM OUR AMERICAN PRINCES FEEL IT HIGHLY DESERVED AND FURTHERMORE WOULD BE ONE OF FINEST POLITICAL STROKES IN HISTORY. The telegram made sense, often frowned upon in politics. Stearns showed it to colleagues, who gave a thumbs-up: tether Cal to ball.

The brainchild became tangible as Senators players began a motorcade from Union Station to meet the president: twin the Senators' unlikely pennant and an election not in the bag, equating Coolidge with a pastime in glow. Thousands cheered them on either side of Pennsylvania Avenue, each player riding in a new convertible, following a police escort to the White House. Arriving, players traipsed to the Ellipse, where Abraham Lincoln played town ball in the 1860s. His baseball makeover less extreme than political, Cal peered down from the flag-draped platform and gave, for him, a tub-thumping talk—the kind of speech that the president had rarely given and rarely gave again.

"They are a great band, these armored knights of the bat and ball," Not So Silent Cal began. "They are held up to a high standard of honor on the field, which they have seldom betrayed. While baseball remains our national game, our national taxes will be on a higher level and our national ideals on a finer foundation. By bringing the baseball pennant to Washington you have made the National Capital more truly the center of worthy and honorable aspirations." In the crowd, cheering, was another Coolidge aide, Edward T. Clark, who shortly wrote, "I believe that the speech to the Washington team has been immensely valuable as showing an entirely new side of his [Cal's] character." Coolidge vowed to attend the Series, predicted the Nationals would beat John McGraw's NL Giants, and urged Congress to adjourn so that members could attend. Thankfully no one asked him the difference between a sacrifice bunt and a Baltimore chop.

To reporters this was a new Coolidge: language-savvy and baseball-cool. Who could have known? The *real* baseball Coolidge was his wife. Grace Coolidge had followed the game since youth; stayed at Griffith Stadium on Opening Day after Cal returned to the White House; and gone to games on her own, keeping a perfect scorecard. Spotting it, Clark Griffith was amazed. "Where did you *learn* that?" the owner said. "At college"—University of Vermont—"I was the official scorer for our baseball team," Grace said, inhaling the game, as much a baseball fanatic as her husband, Mr. President, was not.

In the next three days ticket requests for Republican donors deluged the White House. On October 4, diplomats, a military band, the Cabinet, and the Coolidges traveled to Griffith Stadium. Cal became the first president to attend a Series opener, the game evocative of the home team's bad old days, the commander-in-chief's cigar expiring with the Senators, 4–3, in twelve innings.

Harry Clatfelter, an advertising executive, wrote to Coolidge: "Thank God for a president who is human enough to chuck the whole United States inside his roll top and slam the lid down while he goes out to see his hometown team play a World's Series baseball team." Many agreed, despite how Coolidge had hardly seen a game. *The Sporting News* was among them, styling Cal baseball's "great and sincere friend." The "friend" knew that without wife Grace his baseball rowboat lacked an oar.

Earlier that year players of the visiting Yankees had formed a straight line to greet the president. At last the Sultan of Swat came face-to-face with Coolidge.

First Fan: "Mr. Ruth."

Ruth wiped his forehead with a handkerchief: "Hot as hell, ain't it, Prez?" he said.

The First Lady's response is unknown.

From the start the Series stirred. After Johnson lost the opener, yielding fourteen hits, the Senators scored in the last of the ninth inning to win Game Two by the same 4–3 score. At the Polo Grounds 47,608 filled the rectangular tub, the Giants clubbing twelve hits: home team, 6–4. A day later Goslin's three-run homer keyed a 7–4 DC assault, again tying things, two games apiece. On October 8, 49,211 packed Coogan's Bluff to see the Big Train lose, 6–2. In Walter's first World Series—and John McGraw's last—the all-time greatest Senator's record was 0-2. The Giants skipper returned to the Potomac on the cusp of his fourth Series title.

Back at Griffith, where offense often took a hike, Tom Zachary's 2–1 complete game kept Washington alive. Game Seven became the coda of arguably the most memorable World Series yet played. Bucky Harris's fourth-inning blast built a 1–0 Nats lead. Two sixth-inning Senators errors scored three Giants runs, the home crowd as silent as Congress on recess. In the eighth inning the game, like the Series, *again* dramatically U-turned. Harris hit a bases-full two-out grounder to eighteen-year-old Freddie Lindstrom. It hit a pebble, careened over the third baseman's head, and tied the score at three. A city of sublime American history sensed that for the first time baseball's was being written there.

In the ninth inning, still three-all, Harris beckoned baseball's Grand Old Man. Battered all Series, Johnson rallied. "Time and again as tense moments tumbled after each other in the thrilling battle President Coolidge fell into the spirit which held the throng, sitting rigidly on the edge of his seat," wrote the *Post*. "He pounded his hands heavily as Walter returned four times from the box with the Giants still at his mercy!" In the last of the twelfth inning Muddy Ruel popped behind the plate, Giants catcher Hank Gowdy tripping on his mask. Reprieved, Muddy doubled. Johnson reached when shortstop Travis Jackson bobbled his grounder. Earl McNeely then bounced to Lindstrom, the ball *again* hitting a stone and bouncing over the teen's head. Washington won its first World Series, Ruel plating its fourth one-run decision, each 4–3 at Griffith Stadium.

McGraw mourned another Series lost. Students and working men and bureaucrats circled the Senators, collectively and ecstatically. Grace Coolidge was again a college official scorer. "She jumped up and down on both feet, waved her arms, yelled, called out to Walter Johnson," wrote *The Sporting News*. "The picture of sedateness on her arrival, she left as rumpled, as tired, and as happy as the thousands of other fans." Johnson found Coolidge, who shook his hand and later wrote a baroque letter of congratulation. Meeting the Big Train, Cal had sounded more himself: "Nice work. I am glad you won."

The White House was too. "No New England man ever was born who does not know baseball," TSN proclaimed. Few campaigns on any level have so shrewdly tied politics to culture. On election day 1924 Calvin Coolidge won every state in the presidential contest but the solid South, taken by Democratic nominee John W. Davis, and Wisconsin, home state of U.S. senator and Progressive candidate Robert La Follette. Few credited his victory directly to Cal's embrace of baseball. (Peace and prosperity helped more.) Many *did* think it made him seem more human, thus acceptable. The popular and electoral vote read Coolidge, 15,723,789 and 382; Davis, 8,386,242 and 136; La Follette, 4,831,706 and 13 respectively. On March 4, 1925, Coolidge was inaugurated. Commissioner Landis should have been his guest but wasn't, political loyalty obscenely brief. Instead Washington's most nascent fan rode in the Opening Day parade.

If the 1925 Nationals had been a board game, they would have been "Monopoly," the Big Train dominating first through fifth place in *fourteen* AL pitching categories. Johnson took that fall's Series opener, beating the Pirates, 4–1. Pittsburgh then countered, 4–3. Game Three showed why Coolidge, less gripped by baseball than when he needed a new lease on the Oval Office, was still intrigued. In the Bucs' eighth inning, Nats up, 4–3, Earl Smith drove deep to right-center field. Sam Rice sped over, leaped, and dove out of sight into temporary Griffith seating. Seconds later he reemerged, ball in glove. The umpire called Smith out, some crying that a DC denizen had found and given Rice a ball. In 1974 the outfielder said that a sealed envelope would be opened when he died. "At no time," it read, "did I lose possession of the ball."

Game Four proved that Johnson still possessed a blazer, blanking Pittsburgh, 4–0, to give the Senators a 3–1 match lock. No club had lost such a Series edge before the Bucs won twice to force Game Seven, this battle, like 1924's, ricocheting from day to day. The final seesawed: one team scored, then another. In the first, seventh, and eighth inning, Washington shortstop Roger Peckinpaugh drove in a run, dropped a pop to score a Pirates tally, and homered respectively, for a 7–6 DC edge. Already the game's history was *largely* his. In the eighth inning it became his *irretrievably*. First his wild throw tied the score. With two out, bases full, Kiki Cuyler doubled for the last two of the four un-earned runs: 9–7, Pittsburgh. Peckinpaugh's eight errors broke Honus Wagner's 1903 Series record six. "I tell people that I once broke one of Wagner's records," he laughed later. "But I don't tell them what it was."

"It's been a long time coming," sang Crosby, Stills, Nash, and Young in the early 1970s. The Bucs' 1925 world title was their first since 1909 and last till 1960. As for the Senators, they have not won another Se-ries since 1924, finding that success was going to be a "long time gone."

Like Ann Landers and George M. Cohan, Rube Goldberg and George Steinbrenner, Stephen Foster and Nathaniel Hawthorne, John Calvin Coolidge was born on July 4—in his case, 1872. To those sympathetic to his time in office, Silent Cal had a star-spangled background based less on style than substance, feeling that government was the problem, not solution, as Ronald Reagan said. To the disaffected, Coolidge was a minimalist leader, capable of more than he achieved or tried. Few denied that Cal revived the office after its bloodied nose with Hard-ing. Wrote biographer Donald McCoy, "He embodied the spirit and hopes of the middle class, could interpret their longings, and express their opinions. That he did represent the genius of the average [per-son] is the most convincing part of his strength."

In the 1630s Coolidge's ancestors arrived from Great Britain to settle in Plymouth Notch, Windsor County, Vermont. As a teen, Cal attend-ed Black Rock Academy and Amherst University, excelling in debate.

After graduation he was admitted to the bar, became a country lawyer, and married Grace Goodhue, about whom he wrote, "For almost a quarter-century she has borne with my infirmities and I have rejoiced in her graces." A similar time of local flavor preceded his campaign for president. Cal gradually entered politics, finding it hospitable in Northampton, Massachusetts. Often Coolidge won a following by touting women's suffrage, elsewhere backing higher teaching salaries.

In 1912 each GOP member of the Massachusetts Senate, to which Cal had been elected, stayed put to back President Taft against TR—a triumph of loyalty over ideology. In 1914 Coolidge was elected Senate president; in 1915, he became lieutenant governor, halting his practice of law; in 1919, he edged Richard Long for governor, having backed America's role in World War I and upheld the rule of law. When, in 1919, Boston police threatened to join a union, their police head, Edwin Curtis, said such an act would harm the public. The American Federation of Labor (AFL) then set a date to strike. Curtis called the bosses insubordinate, said the union would be suspended, but added he would revoke the suspension if the union dissolved. Instead 75 percent of it struck. Coolidge at first demurred. Let thugs self-destruct: only lawbreaking would make the middle-class demand that police never strike. Then, adapting, he called in the militia, which clashed with strikers. Cal felt sure that the public equated rioting with communism.

"People are terrified of revolution," said Herbert Hoover. Coolidge ordained: "There is no right to strike against the public safety by anyone, anywhere, any time." More than anything, Coolidge's rhetoric made him vice president. As Harding's 1920 running mate, he gave hard, concise speeches—a shy, stern official who, like the Greek Heraclitus, believed that "a man's character is his fate." Cal became the first VP to attend Cabinet meetings. He also utilized the first presidential speechwriter, Judson Welliver, whom Harding had hired as "literary clerk" because the volume of material needed for a head of state had swollen even then beyond one man's capacity to respond.

An aloof, frosty mien—asked why he graced so many dinner parties, Cal said, "Got to eat somewhere"—unhinged the DC commentariat. Not content to lash Harding, Alice Longworth said, "When he wished he were elsewhere, [Coolidge] pursed his lips, folded his arms, and said nothing." Cal knew of his reputation: "I think the American people want a solemn ass as a President," he told actress Ethel Barrymore, "and I think I will go along with them." He did by necessity on August 3, 1923.

The vice president was in Plymouth Notch, Vermont, visiting his family home lacking electricity and telephone when the solemn man got solemn news from a solitary messenger: Harding was dead. Coolidge dressed, said a prayer, and went forth to greet reporters. His dad, a notary public, administered the oath of office at 2:47 a.m. in the family parlor, lit by a kerosene lamp. Becoming president through an event not fit for celebration, Coolidge went back to bed, returning next day to Washington, sworn in by a Supreme Court justice to preclude any question of legality. Coolidge kept Harding's Cabinet intact through the 1924 election, except for Harry M. Daugherty, who refused to cooperate with a congressional probe of Teapot Dome and whom Coolidge made resign as attorney general.

On December 6, 1923, Cal addressed Congress after it reconvened. The first presidential speech broadcast on radio backed most of Harding's agenda, including the enforcement of immigration laws, which excluded, to his anger, immigrants from Japan. He touted the Washington Naval Treaty, vainly vetoed a World War I veterans' "bonus bill," but named as his 1924 VP Brigadier General Charles G. Dawes. A victory margin of 2.5 million more votes than all other candidates combined was dimmed by son Calvin's fatal poisoning, leaving his father even more withdrawn than usual. "When he [Jr.] died," said Cal, "the power and the glory of the presidency went with him."

Elected, Coolidge scalded regulation, famously telling the American Society of Newspaper Editors, "The chief business of the American people is business." Foiling the opposition was his skill as an open-field runner: ideologically, Cal was hard to pigeonhole, thus attack. He called for legislation to prohibit lynching—"a hideous crime"—chiding a man who wrote that blacks should not be allowed to hold elective office, publicizing his reply: "I was amazed to receive such a letter." The president was not silent about "Indian citizenship," "race hatred," or "religious intolerance." Like TR, he was a conservationist, making Custer State Park in the Black Hills of South Dakota his "summer White House." Here Cal said he would not run for president in 1928, later adding, "The Presidential office takes a heavy toll on those who occupy it and those who are dear to them." Given Coolidge's 1933 fatal heart attack, you sense his time running out.

As president, Cal was available to the working press, giving 520 radio press conferences, delivering the first presidential inaugural address on the wireless, and signing the Radio Act of 1927, assigning radio regulation to the newly created Federal Radio Commission. In August 1924 Theodore W. Case, using the sound-on-film process he developed for famed producer Lee de Forest, filmed Coolidge on the White House lawn—another first, a president appearing in a sound film. Its title was *President Coolidge, Taken on the White House Grounds.* The theme was Cal on the economy, wearing well: any Republican could give his talk today. In 1927 de Forest shot Coolidge welcoming Charles Lindbergh arriving in Washington on a U.S. Navy ship after his 1927 transatlantic flight. A sound-on-film record exists.

Two years later the thirtieth president repaired to Northampton. The New Englander wrote his memoir, *The Autobiography of Calvin Coolidge*, published in 1929. In 1930–31 he crafted a syndicated newspaper column, "Calvin Coolidge Says," leaving a broad oral/video library. Five decades later Ronald Reagan put his portrait in the Cabinet Room of the White House, calling Coolidge his favorite president. Reagan admired Cal's integrity, sane tax and spending dicta, limited government, self-reliance, traditional faith, and belief in American exceptionalism. Before he died, Coolidge said, "I feel I no longer fit in with these times." He would be pleased to know that to many his values still do.

Like Andrew Johnson and Woodrow Wilson, Herbert Hoover liked baseball's familiarity. Like William Howard Taft, he dreamt of playing the sport at its highest level. Like Lincoln, he had played baseball as a boy—at shortstop—then for Stanford's freshman team in 1893, challenging "the San Francisco professional team to play us on campus," Hoover said good-naturedly. The team accepted, but, he continued, "When the score was something like thirty to *nothing* at the end of the fifth inning and getting dark, we called it off. In time, my colleagues decided I would make a better manager than shortstop," having dislocated a finger. Hoover took a job promoting Stanford baseball and football as a student in a post now known as "business manager," which helped him pay his way through college.

Hoover endorsed boys' baseball leagues on every level, tossed out the first pitch at an American Legion title game, and signed and gave dozens of baseballs for use as awards to young players. A photo of the 1921–29 secretary of commerce shows him opening Washington's sandlot baseball season by throwing out the first ball. "The rigid volunteer rules of right and wrong in sports," Hoover said, "are second only to religious faith in moral training—and baseball is the greatest of American sports." Prior to their 1970 move to Riverfront Stadium, the Cincinnati Reds displayed his quote on a tablet at Crosley Field.

By 1928 Hoover seemed the prototypal poor boy who made good—born 1874 in West Branch, Iowa (pop. 350), orphaned at three, and raised by various aunts and uncles. His family birthplace cottage was self-contained: fourteen by twenty feet, built largely by father Jesse in 1871. Other places that filled his youth included a Quaker meeting house, one-room schoolhouse, and blacksmith shop operated by his dad. Close your eyes, Hoover said when his presidential library opened in 1962, "and think of Iowa as I saw it through the eyes of a ten-year-old boy—and the eyes of all ten-year-old Iowa boys . . . filled with the wonders of Iowa's streams and woods, of the mystery of growing crops."

Hoover's rhythm jarred with, say, Babe Ruth's strikingly urban youth, yet mimed Ronald Reagan's remembrance of *his* boyhood home. Once Hoover said of West Branch, "If you want to know me, go there," as Reagan would say of Dixon, Illinois; and Richard Nixon of Whittier, California; and Lyndon Johnson of the Texas Hill Country; and Jimmy Carter of Plains, Georgia, their air of freedom and discovery and neighbor helping neighbor. Hoover's compass was tenacity, pointed at a new, tuition-free university in 1891 founded by California U.S. senator Leland Stanford. He majored in geology, took odd jobs, and "practically lived in the lab," a classmate said. One reason was another would-be geologist—his future wife, Lou Henry.

The 1895 graduate pushed ore cars in Nevada; managed mines and became China representative and junior partner for the British firm of Bewick, Moreing, and Co.; and found the silver and zinc deposits in Burma that made him rich, saying, "If a man has not made a million dollars by the time he is not forty, he is not worth much." Yet he was raised to be a Samaritan, so Hoover left engineering in World War I to head the Commission for Belgian Relief and oversee America's wartime food supply, "sav[ing] more humans from starvation," wrote journalist and Hoover historian Raymond Henle, "than any man who walked the earth."

Hoover returned home to serve Harding and Coolidge, aiding flood recovery in 1920s Mississippi. On August 2, 1927, a note on the White House press board affirmed Coolidge's decision "not . . . to run for reelection in nineteen twenty-eight." By now Hoover was so popular that many Democrats wanted to draft him for president. Instead he became the 1928 GOP nominee. Hoover was rural, small town, and Protestant. The Democrats chose New York governor Alfred E. Smith—Tammany Hall, urban, and Catholic. Most of America empathized with Hoover. The world champion Yankees did not.

New York's 1928 regular lineup, pitcher Waite Hoyt, and batboy posed for a photo, each carrying a bat with a letter attached. Collectively the bats read "For Al Smith." The Bombers had little company, few finding malice in Smith's rival. The photo of the Yankees hailing Smith appeared in many papers, one claiming that Ruth somehow favored Hoover. Babe made another campaign photo wearing a suit, top hat, and sign that read, "I'm for Al Smith." That seemed to end the matter, except that a few days later a publicity flack asked if Ruth would pose with Hoover, visiting Yankee Stadium. "No sir," said Babe. "Tell him I'll be glad to talk to him if he wants to meet me under the stands."

RUTH REFUSES TO POSE FOR HOOVER! papers screamed, some vowing to cancel Babe's syndicated column. The contretemps almost became a crisis, each version inconsistent with the others. Soon a picture of the principals surfaced: an armistice, if not Ruth's support. The Republican won every state but one outside the South. Smith got fifteen million to Hoover's twenty-one million votes and just 87 electoral votes to the Iowan's 444, even losing his own New York. Wall Street meant wealth, which spurred jobs, which propelled the economy. Nothing had prepared the new president for an equation turned upside down.

By Inauguration Day, March 4, 1929, the average of common stock prices on the New York Stock Exchange had risen 123 percent in the last thirty-nine months. "We in America," Hoover had said, "are nearer the final triumph over poverty than ever before in the history of any land." He ignored calamity's midwife—fear. By October 24—Black Thursday—stock sales had soared. Investors tried to protect securities by putting up cash as collateral. On October 29, 16,410,030 shares were traded. Thousands of speculators threw their holdings in the pit. That winter Ruth was told that his $80,000 salary topped Hoover's $75,000. "I know," Babe belched, "but I had a better year than he did!" The offshoot was an America that had seemed impossible to conceive of when 1929 began.

Mocking "the Great Humanitarian," new names were abruptly seen and heard. Urban shantytowns of the jobless down by rivers became "Hoovervilles." Rusted cars became Great Depression tents ("Hoover hovels"). At night men asleep in parks ("Hoover hotels") lay covered by newspapers ("Hoover blankets"). Jackrabbits became "Hoover dogs"; pockets turned inside out, "Hoover flags." Bread lines dotted city blocks. Soup kitchens were endemic, like pleas for one meal a day and billboards declaring, "I will share."

Hoover subsidized airmail, backed the Boulder and Grand Coulee Dams, reorganized the Federal Bureau of Investigation, and reordered the federal conservation program. He jawboned—the economy was "on a sound and prosperous basis"—hoping to help those unemployed. He prized sheer merit. The Depression demanded traits— oration, inspiration—alien to his core. The president spoke like an engineer when America needed an evangelist. The job description had turned on him overnight.

By 1932 the running mate of Democratic presidential nominee Franklin Delano Roosevelt, John Nance Garner, said that all FDR had to do to win was live until election day. Editor William Allen White backed Hoover but saw the writing on the wall: "A fool who can lead is better than a wise man who fumbles." It is true that "apart from the Roosevelt measures of reform," wrote columnist Walter Lippmann, "all the major features of the Roosevelt program were anticipated" by Hoover. It is also true that just as the president cast for trout in California, post–Black Thursday, millions went fishing over the man whom both parties had once cheered.

Hoover spent the rest of his days living a good life of good works. After World War II he went to Europe to feed refugees. It was a job in which he could be said to have more experience than anyone, placing "prime responsibility upon the individual for the welfare of his neighbor." He became the GOP's Grand Old Man, addressed ten national conventions from 1924 through 1960, and helped found the Boys Clubs of America.

Hoover outlasted setbacks that would have crushed a lesser man, turning inward but not bitter and relying on faith in God. Few presidents had more cause to rely upon it, or less reason to doubt its worth.

The team whose public most humiliated Hoover during his presidency reached its apex under the Philadelphia Athletics president, owner, and manager. Envision Connie Mack, tall and gaunt, in suit and tie, a scorecard in one hand, signaling to the field from the dugout. He used a weathervane to direct hitters, holding opera glasses to steal signs from a building beyond right-center field. Seven of the nine big-league games that Hoover saw in person as president involved Mack's Athletics. The First Fan attended each 1929 through 1932 Opening Day, Philadelphia twice the visitor, and saw the A's twice more visit Griffith Stadium in 1930–31. In addition, the president tossed out the first ball at an A's World Series against the Cubs in 1929 and Cardinals in 1930–31 in Philadelphia. Barely two hours by train from Washington, the Athletics were the Senators' natural geographic rival. They also monopolized Hoover's first-ball rites as baseball's then royalty.

In 1910 the A's "$100,000 infield"—the four infielders' purported combined market value—put Mack in the money with his first Series title. Philly won its third Classic in 1913, next year taking a fifth pennant in ten years. Needing cash, Mack then began largely selling pitchers, most moving elsewhere in the Major or Federal Leagues. It took a while, but Connie got back where he belonged. On April 17, 1929, Hoover threw out his first ball as president. A pattern started—Athletics 13, DC 4—but what about October? What A's pitcher would start the Series against the Cubs? Shockingly Mack chose Red Sox retread Howard Ehmke, thirty-five, for a game where only the nerveless need apply. "Ehmke hadn't pitched much," A's outfielder Al Simmons said, "so Connie had him spend the last month trailing the Cubs around." Philly won, 3–1, Ehmke fanning a then Series record thirteen.

After a two-game split, the A's trailed, 8–0, in Game Four's seventh inning. Simmons then homered to launch another Series-record ten-run assault to beat the Cubs, 10–8. Afterward Judge Landis called Mack and Cubs manager Joe McCarthy to his room, deploring unprintable language in their dugouts and on the field. "If these vulgarities continue," the commissioner said, "I'll fine the culprits a Series share." Prior to Game Five catcher Mickey Cochrane mocked the Cubs: "After the game we'll serve *tea* in the clubhouse!" Mack winced: Landis might impose a fine.

Instead, decorum restored, Hoover closed the season as it had begun: throwing out the first ball in the final Series game and liking a pitcher's duel he otherwise would have loathed. "I want more runs in baseball," he told a dinner of baseball writers, foretelling FDR. "When you were raised on a sandlot, where the scores ran twenty-three to sixty-one, you yearn for something more than two to two." Excitement spiked "when a runner reached base. It reached ecstasy when somebody ma[de] a run." By that criterion he would have snored before the game turned official. In the ninth inning, down, 2–0, the A's scored thrice to win the Classic. Afterward starter Ehmke, already a Series legend, shook Cochrane's hand. Said Landis, not without a sense of humor, "Where's the tea?"

In 1930 Mack's Athletics beat the Cardinals in the Series. Then in 1931 they staged a grand reunion, Temple, Oklahoma's down and grungy Pepper Martin making the Redbirds for good after six years in the

Minors. In the first two games Martin got four hits and scored twice, the second run leaving Cochrane leaping near the plate like the victim of a hot foot upon umpire Dick Nallin's ruling, "*Safe!*" "What is he hitting?" Mack asked, thinking he might change how to pitch Martin. "Everything," A's pitcher George Earnshaw said. Final: Martin 2, Athletics 0, tying the World Series. Three days later, after each club's train trip to Philadelphia from the Mississippi, the teams played Game Three, where a larger verdict loomed.

U.S. presidents normally receive a decent measure of respect. The Depression made people less concerned with propriety than housing, clothing, food—a *job*. In 1931 alone, more than 2,200 banks closed, often robbing families of life savings since deposits weren't insured till 1933. On October 4, 1931, the president met banking and insurance leaders to get them to support his plan to rescue their industries, who passed the buck to "a proposal that the government do it," Hoover said. After midnight he returned to the White House, so depressed that—*this* was a first—he rued attending that afternoon's Series game in Philadelphia, finally going to reassure "a country suffering from a case of jitters." Hoover, feeling that he could reassure any crowd, had shown a certain delusion. Still, keeping his word, he and Mrs. Hoover entered Shibe Park to their ground-level box. Lefty Grove and Burleigh Grimes stopped warming up in deference, but deference was the last thing of import to most of the people there.

Hoover waved to those who by now filled much of Shibe—papers had promoted his presence—and from whom sparse applause could be heard. A few boos followed, then more, then a chant—taunting, furious—in the twelfth year of National Prohibition, by people unable legally to drown their sorrow. Few there ever forgot: "We want beer! We want beer!" The president's wife Lou appeared stunned. Guests peered down, trying to ignore the din. Hoover's face remained stoic, in denial. Taunting and booing worsened: "We want beer!"

No one could recall such a scene. Joe Williams of the *New York World-Telegram and Sun* was shocked: "This must be the first time a president ever has been booed in public, and at a ballgame, of all places."

After eight innings, St. Louis ahead, 4–0, the public address (PA) voice announced the Hoovers' departure. "Silence. Silence, please," the voice said, asking the crowd to remain seated. The Hoovers walked onto the field past the A's dugout toward the exit. Boos resumed, as did the chant: "We want beer! We want beer!" The Depression overwhelmed.

Even Hoover's favorite sanctuary, save the church, had been violated—the president, "who had taken a day off to relax at a ball game, a privilege at the command of even the most obscure citizen," Williams wrote, greeted by "a shocking manifestation of bad manners and lack of respect." Perhaps he should have followed his instinct to stay home: Hoover backed Prohibition, but a commission he appointed had early in 1931 dubbed enforcement a bust. In Game Seven the Cardinals repaid Mack for the year before, winning the Series. Pepper Martin left a hero: twelve hits, a .500 average, a symbol of grit and dash and anything to pay the bills. "The Wild Horse of the Osage," whom luck once had left behind, became that American specialty: an overnight success.

Beyond the A's, several teams—as noted above, the Cubs, Tigers, Yankees, and notably the Cardinals—seized a pennant or Series beachhead in the time from directly *before* to *after* Hoover's term. St. Louis waved its first flag in 1926, both sides of a Grand Avenue parade suggestive of why it has always been a one-game town (by late 1953, one-team too; the Browns moved to Baltimore). In the Classic the Cardinals led the Yanks, 3–2, three on, two out in the seventh inning of the seventh game. Player/manager Rogers Hornsby had alcoholic and epileptic pitcher Grover Cleveland Alexander trudge from the pen. New York's Tony Lazzeri swung and missed. The rally died—and the Series ended with Ruth out trying to steal second base. Two years later general manager (GM) Branch Rickey's brain child—the farm system—built another pennant, among five between 1926 and 1934.

As former president, Hoover often saw the Redbirds in the first half of the century—and two stars as polar in attitude as Joe Louis and Muhammad Ali. One was modest: Stan "the Man" Musial. The other, born in a shack to Arkansas sharecroppers, was the brash son of a migratory cotton picker. Jay Hanna "Dizzy" Dean's education ended in the second grade—"and," he jibed, "I wasn't so good in first grade, either." Ol' Diz won eighteen games as a 1932 rookie, treating discipline, as Ring Lardner said, like a side dish he declined to order. In 1933 Frank Frisch became player/manager. A year later Diz vowed that "Me 'n' [younger brother] Paul will win forty-five games." They won forty-nine, the older brother taking thirty. After Diz spliced three hits to open a doubleheader, Paul no-hit Brooklyn. "Daw-gonnit," Diz blared. "If I'd knowed Paul was gonna' throw a no-hitter, I'd a' throwed one too."

In 1934 the Cardinals' "Gas House Gang" beat Detroit in a seven-game classic Classic. Named for tough-luck kids from seedy precincts, the Gang dirtied uniforms, dropped water bags from windows, and disrupted lobbies with workmen's tools. Willard Mullin's cartoon etched gas tanks on the shabby side of railroad tracks with players hoisting clubs, not bats, on their shoulders and entering the good part of town. Their band—the Mississippi Mudcats—used fiddles, harmonicas, washboards, and guitars to play "Rock Island Line" and "The Wreck of the Old '97" on trains to Cincinnati and points east. "I am possibly the only manager that carried an orchestra," Frisch said. "We traveled with more instruments than we did shirts or anything else." Unlike ballplaying, the Gang's musical playing was not always in accord.

The Cardinals found special resonance in Depression America's most down-and-out corners. More haughtily and almost unnecessarily, Yankees president Ed Barrow said, "The Yankees mean baseball in every corner of the land." In 1928 a huge reason for New York's world champion prepotency was Babe Ruth and Lou Gehrig. Next year, Hoover's first in office, the Bronx Bombers joined the Indians as the first to put numbers on uniforms, based on the batting order. Ruth was assigned No. 3; Gehrig, 4, in cleanup. They set a model for each team in the Majors.

Hoover and Indian prime minister Jawaharlal Nehru were once introduced at a Series game at Yankee Stadium. The ovation given catcher Yogi Berra, No. 8, dwarfed both. A day later Yogi's childhood friend and broadcaster Joe Garagiola said, "You amaze me, Yog. You've now become such a world figure that you draw more applause than either a prime minister or former prez. Can you explain it?" Berra could:

"Certainly. I'm a better hitter." His claim could be made by every pin-striped member of the Yankees' 1927 "Murderer's Row."

Babe and Gehrig hit a record 107 homers, the Bombers' 158 were 102 more than the runner-up A's, and their 110-44 record franchise was a best till 1998. In Buffalo, Ruth wrestled kids on the field. Convicts watched as the club played at Sing Sing prison. To fete July 4 New York crushed the then contending Senators, 12–1 and 21–1, before 72,641 at Yankee Stadium. On September 30 Ruth smacked homer No. 60 off Tom Zachary. At age eight future Mets voice Lindsey Nelson heard the Yanks sweep Pittsburgh in the Series, sound carried by radio from a nearby class. As his teacher discussed Caesar, Nelson focused on hearing Gehrig double. Referencing Julius, she asked, "Lindsey, who was that?" Nelson: "Gehrig—doubled to right!"

For Hoover, baseball was something to read, hear, and talk about: conversation, a haven, somewhere to retool. Selective coverage of the time was less cynical than today's. Once Yankees pitcher Waite Hoyt drank so much that he entered a hospital to dry out. Papers explained it by dubbing Waite an amnesiac, Babe telegramming his critique: "Read about your case of amnesia. Must be a new brand." Despite Ruth's animus, Hoover esteemed his play, even as the 1929–31 sans pennant Yanks marked their driest patch between 1921 and 1964. The A's, Cardinals, and 1932 Stripes won the World Series in his presidency. Much later Brooklyn won too. For some reason—empathy with Dem Bums as underdogs, a guess—Hoover became a rabid Dodgers fan in his last quarter century. "Our spirits go up and down with the Dodgers' wins and losses," he told boss Walter O'Malley after the Bums lost the 1952 Fall Classic.

In 1916 and 1920 Brooklyn took a pennant but lost both Series, braving the event's first and only unassisted triple play. In 1941 a then-NL-record 1,214,910 attendance hailed another flag. The borough then mourned another Series loss, still without a title. For the next two decades the Classic meant autumn in New York, Hoover linked by radio, TV, or at the park. The ferocity of Stripes versus (usually) Brooks became more real than acting's feigned Bob Hope versus Bing Crosby. "Salaries were so low that every player had a winter job," Dodgers captain Pee Wee Reese noted. "The difference between a Series' winning and losing share meant a mink for your wife." Friendship vanished as a Fall Classic reached its height.

Hoover, "the Chief" to friends, often spoke with his adopted team about playing in Brooklyn. "Just being there was amazing," Pee Wee said of Ebbets Field, the Dodgers' 1913–57 arabesque, and Flatbush, its neighborhood, through which regulars and reserves walked or took the subway to work. "The park was like entering a bar and saying, 'How are you doing, Joe?' Everybody knew everybody else." Housewife Hilda Chester became famous for waving a cowbell. The Dodger Sym-Phony was a vaguely musical group. Until 1898 the borough was an independent city. Incorporated into New York, it still felt like a nation-state.

To see a game, Hoover—shy, instantly identifiable—took a limousine. The bandbox's cement wall / scoreboard / wire screen had twenty-nine different angles and yelped a clothier's message: "Hit Sign! Win Suit!" A barrier linked the left-field line to center field, whose wall went from fifteen feet via nineteen to thirteen at a screen. Protruding five feet at an angle, the concave wall and board wed center field to the right-field line. Scant turf aided Ebbets Field's hitter's edge, as evinced by 1950s distances: left field, 343 feet from the plate; left-center, 351 feet; left-center at a bend of the wall, 395 feet; center field, 393 feet; right side of grandstand, 376 feet; right-center scoreboard, 344 and 318 feet (left to right side); right field, 297 feet. Brooklyn's largest bar had thirty-five thousand stools.

In World War II Hoover raised money for Allies, including a Baseball Writers' Association of America (BBWAA) dinner for the Finnish Relief Fund. One June, Dodgers flagship station WOR interrupted a game to present Hoover's Republican National Convention address, angering club head Larry MacPhail. Later Hoover attended many Old Timers' Days at Yankee Stadium, including tossing out the first ball at eighty-six, greeted by Joe DiMaggio, Bob Feller, and Red Ruffing. Telling are photos of him, in and for a long time after office, wearing a coat and tie while fishing—antithetical to today's mantra of "feel, don't think." He was never too old to follow baseball—and did so until the end.

When his wife died in 1944, Hoover moved to the Waldorf-Astoria Hotel in Manhattan. Having created a rural presidential retreat, "Camp Hoover," in the Blue Ridge Mountains of Virginia, near what is now Shenandoah National Park, he eventually no longer fished, a pastime he liked almost as much as baseball. Like the Yankees dynasty, Hoover died in 1964, at ninety. A U.S. memorial postage stamp carried the epitaph, "Engineer, President, Humanitarian." Near the end Hoover said of his enemies, "I outlived the bastards."

He also saw Brooklyn's sole Series title after it had lost seven in a row, beating the Yankees, 2–0, in the seventh game in 1955. If a picture is worth a thousand words, The Stadium's eruption on the final out wrote a glossary. Next day Willard Mullin's gap-toothed "Brooklyn Bum" cartoon filled the *Daily News* front page. "We dood it! We beat 'em!" the Bum began. "We beat dem Yankees. We spot 'em th' first two games . . . an' we beat 'em! . . . Woil Cham-peens! Me!"

To Hoover, Brooklyn's millennium in the morn explained why he loved the game—the sense of community in a West Branch or Corsica, Ohio, or Flatbush; the engineer's precision of a finely tuned double play; the joy of a wind-lofted blast helping any dog that was under; the feel of baseball's rhythm, especially on radio. The affair can last a lifetime, and here with God's grace did.

FOUR

"The Champ"

Franklin D. Roosevelt, 1933–1945

As much as any president, Franklin Delano Roosevelt is recalled largely by what he left—in part, his presidential library and museum ninety miles north of New York City at Hyde Park, where he grew up and where he is buried, along the Hudson River. The original structure was conceived of by FDR on April 12, 1937, and resembled today's site, still visited by the children and grandchildren of those who heard or saw Roosevelt lay its cornerstone on November 19, 1939, when work on the library officially began.

With much of the world at or nearing war, FDR spoke at the ceremony about a globe at peace—the universe of his late-nineteenth-century boyhood. The president loved to reminisce about his youth and did so then. "Half-a-century ago a small boy took especial delight in climbing an old tree, now unhappily gone, to pick and eat ripe sickle pears," he commenced. "That was one hundred feet to the west of where I am standing now. . . . In the spring of the year, in hip rubber boots, he sailed his first toy boats in the surface water formed by the melting snow. In the summer with his dogs he dug into the woodchuck holes in this same field. . . . Indeed, the descendants of those same woodchucks still inhabit this field, and I hope that . . . they will continue to for all time."

Roosevelt delivered the library cornerstone dedication and other speeches on such networks as the Columbia Broadcasting System

(CBS); Mutual Broadcasting System (MBS); and National Broadcasting Company (NBC) "Blue" for news. Its "Red" network aired entertainment. He often spoke from the White House to sixty million or more listeners, text sired by a speechwriting Murderer's Row of poet Archibald MacLeish, playwright Robert Sherwood, economists Raymond Moley and Rexford Tugwell, and aide Harry Hopkins, among others.

Each helped their boss with almost every type of speech, most notably the "Fireside Chat," FDR conversing with each American, a simple talk among friends. In the end *his* work reflected *his* mind and prose. My favorite line—"No man can tame a tiger into a kitten by stroking it"—scorned the folly of appeasing fascism. Roosevelt led America through its two great twentieth-century crises, neither victory ever sure: the early and mid-1930s global Depression and 1941–45 World War II fight-to-the-death against Germany, Italy, and Japan. FDR rallied a nation when often all looked lost, as it must have when polio struck him in August 1921.

Poignantly and paradoxically, paralysis—FDR, at thirty-nine, never walked again—and family dysfunction meant that his personal life would end neither serenely nor fulfilled. Roosevelt's response was to try to relive his boyhood life of charity of heart and fullness of body—a time when all things seemed possible—by secretly returning to Hyde Park time and again during the war. "He always felt that this was his home. He loved the house and the view, the woods, special trees," said his wife, Eleanor, about what Hyde Park evoked: his mother, Sara Roosevelt, and FDR sliding down a snowy hill before polio, unimpaired.

The First Lady died on November 6, 1962, eighteen years to the day after FDR's final election speech. In 1972 the library was completed with the north and south wings—the Eleanor Roosevelt Addition. FDR dedicated this library in 1941 to "the spirit of peace—peace for the United States and soon, we hope, peace for the world." Of the twenty-nine Fireside Chats Roosevelt gave as president, four originated from his Hyde Park study.

Many of his speeches recorded there and in Washington can be heard at the library, including his famed 1944 riposte, where FDR denied that he had left his dog behind on the Aleutian Islands and sent a destroyer back to get him. "These Republican leaders have not been content with attacks on me, or my wife, or on my sons," he said. "No, not content with that, they now include my little dog Fala." Walking his estate, it is easy to see why that year he briefly deferred a fourth term in office. "All that is within me cries out to go back to my home on the Hudson River."

In the end Roosevelt—"the good soldier," as he called himself; "the Champ," as styled by 1940 Republican opponent Wendell Willkie— succumbed to reelection. How could he not, given the colossal stakes? By now most of America *did* believe, to quote the partisan mantra, that he *was* its "indispensable man." Watching a newsreel, you see why Roosevelt once privately told actor Orson Welles, "Mr. Welles, there are two great actors in the United States, and you're the other one." The world is a different place because of the actor who was not Orson Welles.

Despair was king and isolation first minister as the first Democrat to become president since Woodrow Wilson took the oath of office March 4, 1933. Said outgoing President Hoover, "We are at the end of our string." Roosevelt's view differed, even as the nation seemed more Dogpatch than New Jerusalem. "First of all," FDR began, "let me assert my firm belief that the only thing we have to fear is fear itself— nameless, unreasoning, unjustified terror." The seas didn't part, but curtains opened. Today Roosevelt suggests the greatest president of his century. Then we knew only that he could hardly be worse than Hoover—Harvard '03 graduate, New York State senator, assistant secretary of the navy, 1920 Democratic vice-presidential candidate, and 1929–33 governor of New York. Four times he was chosen president, serving longer than anyone had or will. Even crippled, vacationing at his summer home at Campobello, a Canadian island off the coast of Maine, he would not abide being pygmy in any way. A younger Roosevelt had often crossed a line between jaunty and arrogant. Polio softened him, made FDR aware of what it meant to suffer.

In 1928 Roosevelt nominated his state's governor, Alfred E. Smith— "the Happy Warrior"—for president. In 1932, nominated for the top job himself, he vowed, "I pledge you, I pledge myself, to a New Deal for the American people." Its hub was what worked. "Give me a laundry list," said a composer, "and I'll set it to music." Give Roosevelt politics, and he set about to try anything. If it didn't fly, he tried something else. "Anything" began the day after his first inaugural. The new president stopped gold transactions, called a national bank holiday, and hauled Congress into special session. On March 9, 1933, Congress passed a blitz of presidential powers over banking. Would they work? Few knew.

Politics' fuel is trust. FDR ran on America's. He knew that if good conversation was fine, animate rhetoric was better, and that radio was in harmony with each—and his full-register tenor. "My friends" . . . "you and I" . . . "we neighbors" drew a listener to him. (Segue to Ronald Reagan on 1980s TV: same intent and end.) Hoover received about four hundred letters a week at the White House. Five hundred thousand wrote Roosevelt in the wake of the inaugural. Six hundred banks had closed when his chat termed it safe to save. A day later, some doors opening, deposits mauled withdrawals. "The country needs and, unless I mistake its temper," he said, "the country demands persistent experimentation." The improviser parried advice, pitted aides against one another, and touted public over private interest. Hits came quickly. Runs took longer.

By June 15, 1933, as it adjourned, Congress had passed each of Roosevelt's fifteen separate proposals. Critics bemoaned a "welfare state." The Champ replied, "Government has a final responsibility for the well-being of its citizenship." Slowly America began to heal, its leader "all grin and gusto," wrote Arthur Schlesinger Jr., "but terribly hard inside . . . [a man] who had been close enough to death to understand the frailty of human striving but who remained loyal enough to life to do his best in the sight of God." FDR realized that each president needed a real or fancied foil: us against them. His was "economic royalists": "I have earned the hatred of entrenched greed, and I welcome their hatred."

All decade FDR fought unemployment, business monopoly, and wind and drought sowing farms into sand. Just when the worst seemed over, mankind's worst world war appeared. The 1933 inaugural address devoted one paragraph to foreign policy. In 1937 Roosevelt said that if he were to give that speech then, it would dwell on events abroad. The president's second term doubled the budget, tried to swell the Supreme Court—FDR's goal: reverse New Deal acts that had been ruled unconstitutional—and sought to purge party rightists. History stops elsewhere. FDR is thought a superb war leader. Perhaps he was an even greater *prewar* leader.

Like most Americans, bitter over World War I, FDR at first opposed U.S. intervention. "I have seen war," Roosevelt told the Chautauqua Institute in 1936, adding, "I hate war" to prolonged applause. Hitler thereafter seized Austria, Britain's Neville Chamberlain chose appeasement, and the Third Reich devoured Czechoslovakia. FDR changed, sensing that America must fight a war the Axis had made inevitable. On August 22, 1939, Hitler and Joseph Stalin signed the Nazi German-Soviet Pact of Nonaggression, our distance from Europe shrinking by the day. Move: ten days later the Nazi military crossed the Polish frontier. Countermove: FDR began the greatest naval construction program since World War I. America was militarily impotent. Roosevelt's cross was that most citizens didn't care.

From 1933 to 1945 the average American oscillated between following the Depression and the War on one hand—unemployment, say, and the fight for Stalingrad—and everyday activity, especially baseball, on the other—the batting average of the Pirates' Paul Waner. He or she cared less that FDR could be cynical—"cold at the core," wrote Peggy Noonan in 2017—than that he enjoyed baseball like a child. At the Groton School, New England's academy prep factory, Roosevelt had shed his dream of making the team since, according to his diary, he did "not play well." Practical even then, the future president joined a vagabond team named the "Bum Base Ball Boys," composed, he said, "of about the worst players in the school." FDR became team manager, a picture of the baseball club showing a straw-hatted youth. "He enjoys himself at a ballgame as much as a kid on Christmas morning," wrote Harold Burr in *Baseball Magazine* in 1939. Watching, "the president believes again that there is a Santa Claus," cheering good plays and "chuck[ling] over bad."

From youth FDR was the "kind of fan who want[ed] to get plenty of action for my money," he chortled. "I get the biggest kick out of the biggest score—a game in which the hitters poke the ball into the far corners of the field, the outfielders scramble, and men run the bases." He differed from the norm only in sublimating home runs to other extra-base hits boomed around the yard, for which Washington's Griffith Stadium was made. As noted earlier, its left-field pole was baseball's longest: now 405 feet from home plate. Left-center field was 391 feet away, third-deepest of eight American League teams. A center fielder played deep because acreage ran to 421 feet. A tall wall in right-center field stood 373 feet away. Griffith's right-field pole now read 320 feet. The yawning lengths regularly spawned inside-the-park "round-trippers," scribes would say, to FDR's "far corners of the field."

The *1934 Spalding Official Base Ball Guide* observed that most presidents, describing baseball "in a complex, arcane manner, [had not] been in the habit of recognizing the national game in their speeches." Roosevelt differed, borrowing "from the vernacular of the game some of its terms to better illustrate his meaning before the public." A May 7, 1933, Fireside Chat showed FDR's baseball state of mind. "I have no expectation of making a hit every time I come to bat," he said. "What I seek is the highest possible batting average, not only for myself but for the team." Roosevelt likened a batter sacrificing for the team's good to a citizen sacrificing for the nation's good—a good point. Moreover, he used baseball to make it.

FDR grasped education, telling listeners, like a play-by-play man, relevant facts and yarns. On May 24, 1935, he threw a White House switch to light another precedent: baseball's first official big-league night game. By luck it featured the Dodgers and the Reds from Cincinnati's Crosley Field in the first match aired on nascent MBS radio: its voice, Red Barber, already a broadcast model for objectively collecting and dispersing truth. Another part of many lives, including Roosevelt's, was stamp collecting, the president sending Postmaster General James A. Farley to Cooperstown to debut an official U.S. postage stamp hailing the Hall of Fame and Library's (later Museum's) dedication.

From 1933 through 1941 FDR threw out the first ball every year but one with his unorthodox, overhand lob. The entirety of the president's regular-season slate consisted of opening and savoring baseball's inaugural—his record 5-3. It began with the Nats spanking the Athletics, 4–1, led to Boston's 5–0 shutout in 1934, and reverted to a 4–2 encore against Philly in 1935, box guests including wife Eleanor, 1933 rookie player/manager Joe Cronin, earlier/later skipper Bucky Harris, Senators owner Clark Griffith, and AL head William Harridge. By then two teams' openers preceded Major League Baseball's other fourteen: Cincinnati's, in the home of baseball's oldest professional franchise, and Washington's, in the park of the presidential coming out. Given the score in 1936—Senators 1, Yanks 0—FDR could be excused for feeling put out, lamenting the more pomp than runs.

Instead the next day's headline, A HIGH, WIDE AND HANDSOME SEASON OPENING GAME, showed Roosevelt's right arm with the ball at its apex, in his box near Harris and smiling Yankees manager Joe McCarthy. "The President acted like a man on a picnic," reported the Associated Press. "He took his hat off and munched peanuts with the avidity of a youngster at a circus." In 1937–38 the visiting A's won, 4–3, and lost, 12–8, respectively. Then, in 1940–41, the Senators unwittingly dimmed the commander-in-chief's last two first pitches, losing to Boston and New York, 1–0 and 3–0, respectively. On one hand, the brief streak inverted FDR's relationship with baseball that was, if nothing else, victorious. On the other, to use pitching terminology, it preceded his greatest "save" of all.

In 1933, Roosevelt's first year in office, the Senators won the pennant and lost the World Series. In 1945, FDR's last year alive, Washington almost won another pennant, losing on the final weekend. It seemed strange for the 1933 Fall Classic not to involve manager John McGraw, since, after all, New York played Washington. As ironic was that the first Giants team in forty-four years *not* led by baseball's then leading but recently retired skipper boasted pitching almost as evocative as McGraw's World Series titlist of 1905, 1921, and 1922.

Carl Hubbell ranked from first to fifth place in nineteen National League categories, leading in victories (23) and earned run average (1.66), among others. Hal Schumacher won nineteen games and had a 2.16 ERA. Washington's American League category-firsters included Joe Cronin's 45 doubles and Heinie Manush's 221 hits. The 1924 Senators' "Boy Wonder" Bucky Harris had won a pennant. In 1930 another DC precocity, Joe Cronin, twenty-three, began five straight years driving in more than one hundred runs. In 1933 he replaced Walter Johnson as manager, July ending a 23-3 run to boost the Nats record to 61-35. They finished seven games ahead of the defending champion Yankees—the final winning percentage, .651, still a franchise high.

Before the Series opener, the voice Barber termed "the greatest announcer we ever had" began his last Classic play-by-play. Graham McNamee thought the Senators and Giants equal, making them tectonic on a network, NBC, whose symbol was a peacock, like "the King," wings spread wide. McNamee long ago had become shorthand for "America's greatest sports spectacle," the World Series: his presence proof of an "Event," not "event." The Giants took the first two Series games at the Polo Grounds, the teams then moving to the capital, where Depression crowds smaller than Washington's in 1924 watched 1933's *denouement*.

FDR attended Game Three, greeted royally in a manner contrary to that which insulted Hoover. Inevitably he wanted more runs than scored in a 4–0 masterwork by the Senators' Earl Whitehill. At the same time, the verdict gave DC a 2-0 record in games Roosevelt attended, evoking applause the pol in him loved. Some vainly hoped his contagion might permanently rub off on Washington, the Nats a day later again yearning for offense in a 2–1 Giants victory ensured in the eleventh inning when player/skipper Bill Terry ordered an intentional walk to fill the bases, followed by what announcers call "a pitcher's best friend": a Game Four–ending 6–4–3 double play that brought New York one *W* from a title.

October 7, 1933, scripted the last World Series game to date played on the Potomac. The Giants led, 3–0, before the Senators' Fred Schulte's sixth-inning Game Five-tying blast. Mel Ott, homering, had begun

Series scoring in the first inning of the first game. Now he ended it by going yard in the tenth inning of the last. New York reliever Dolf Luque promptly shut the home team door, 4–3, it staying shut through twelve U.S. presidencies, including and beyond Barack Obama's. Ott led both clubs with a .389 average, topping the Giants' exquisitely named Kiddo Davis at .368. Hubbell yielded no earned runs in twenty innings. DC flat-worlders were sure that 1934 would bring recovery. Instead it began near ruin, the Senators ending seventh.

In the next/last quarter century of Washington's original franchise, the Nationals resided in or near the cellar. Roosevelt's next Autumn Occasion, in 1936, was fortuitous for him and writers covering it, since each game was played in the little more than half-mile that separated Yankee Stadium and Coogan's Bluff. The Giants' former tenants at the Polo Grounds beat their ex-landlord in six games, the Stripes' first Series title since 1932. Two of the games befit the term "Bronx Bombers," the Yankees winning, 13–5 and 18–4, and rendering the kind of slugfest the one-time Groton team manager loved.

On July 7, 1937, FDR, Clark Griffith, and baseball in Washington forged among the great points of its past. For most of Griffith Stadium's 31,391, the All-Star Game began with Roosevelt entering the park and riding from right field in an open car, giving his clasped-hands salute. As celebrities go, the presidential box's went far: FDR, in a light suit and hat; Griffith, nattily attired in summer white; Bill Terry, seven years after hitting .401; and the Bombers' McCarthy, "Marse Joe," such a household name at the time that he looked ready for presidential box time-sharing.

McCarthy used only twelve players, including four Yankees, to down the National League, 8–3, the score secondary to a third-inning event. Lou Gehrig blasted a two-run homer off the Cardinals' Dizzy Dean, "the stunning comic heroic," wrote *Chicago Daily News* sports editor Lloyd Lewis, "most famous of all living pitchers."

Irate, Ol' Diz threw a fastball to the next batter, Earl Averill, whose drive struck a glancing blow off Dean's left toe. "Your big toe is fractured," a doctor soon told him.

"No, it ain't," said Diz. "It's broke."

Dean tried to return prematurely as a pitcher but altered his motion, leading to a sore arm and ending his career in the early 1940s.

In 1938, Hugh Mulcahy, pitching for the hopelessly comatose Philadelphia Phillies, lost twenty games. He dropped twenty-two more in 1940, earning the creative nickname "Losing Pitcher." Mulcahy then became the first big leaguer to be drafted into the armed forces for World War II, responding unforgettably for those who knew that we would have to fight: "My losing streak is over. I'm on the winning team now."

By 1940 isolationist America had still not adopted Mulcahy's view. The Nazis devoured Norway and Denmark, the Low Countries, and France. Only Britain remained to deprive Hitler of "the abyss of a new Dark Age," said new prime minister Winston Churchill, needing America to become accomplice, then lead actor. Congress approved the sale of surplus war materiel to Britain, FDR transferred fifty overage destroyers, and as pitcher Mulcahy could tell you, the House of Representatives resumed the draft. Meanwhile, seeking a third term, Roosevelt ran as much against time as 1940 GOP nominee Willkie. Scales had partly begun to fall from Americans' eyes.

For freedom to survive Roosevelt had to aid Britain with everything short of war. In late 1940 he lent arms and equipment on Britain's agreement that it would return or replace them at war's end. Lend-Lease helped save the island nation: America's pre–December 7, 1941, shield. That Sunday U.S. sailors were readying for the 8 a.m. flag-raising at the naval base at Pearl Harbor in Hawaii when enemy fire began. A day later Roosevelt gave an unforgettable speech to Congress decrying Japan's "unprovoked and dastardly attack" on Pearl's installation, planes, ships, and defenders and reporting that "very many American lives have been lost"—2,403. The president then asked for a declaration of war between "America and the Japanese Empire." For decades Americans marked their lives by how and where they learned of the "date which w[ould] live in infamy."

On Opening Day 1940 FDR had been asked to aim "One more, Mr. President!" by the *Washington Post* photographer Irving Schlossenberg. He obliged, smashing the *Post* employee's eyeglasses with an errant throw. In 1941 Roosevelt warned those nearby to beware, laughing, "Last year I almost killed a photographer." Until then he presided at the congressional baseball game between Democrats and Republicans. "As a four- or five-year-old, I'd sit on his knee," said broadcaster Jay Randolph, son of U.S. senator Jennings Randolph (D-wv), "and I'd feel those steel braces, five to ten pounds on each leg. A great father figure." World War II canceled the congressional game until 1946.

Early on, Clark Griffith erected a ramp to let FDR reach his box. His friend was grateful but embarrassed, noting his Secret Service detail. "I'd come out more often, Clark," Roosevelt said, "but I'm such a nuisance." At the park paralysis was not always or easily obscured. "If I didn't have to hobble up those steps [uncovered by the ramp] in front of all those people," he told Griffith, "I'd be out there at the park every day." FDR spun a parallel world by betting on games with aides and Cabinet officials, phoning Clark for advice. "Griff, tell me about these pitchers," he would say, immune from inside trading. After Pearl Harbor almost no one was immune from saying one way or the other whether professional baseball could or should exist in 1942—or again.

That January Pacific Coast League (PCL) president W. C. Tuttle wrote club heads that in two weeks the PCL would meet to ask: (a) Would the league operate in 1942? (b) Could it play at night? (c) Under "present circumstances" on the West Coast, would fans deride baseball players as "slackers" and refuse to attend a game? and (d) Was it worth risking financial loss to presume that a wartime public even wanted baseball as a safety valve? On January 14 W. G. Bramham, president of the National Association of Professional Baseball Leagues, wrote Tuttle, urging patience. All awaited FDR, Griffith ensuring that pro-play opinion by large and small bylines reached his desk.

Wendell Willkie, whom Roosevelt greatly respected, penned, "If the American way of life is to survive, let baseball survive. And, too, if the game should perish, then in my opinion, the larger part of what we are fighting for to protect will end." New York mayor Fiorello H.

La Guardia wrote, "The one great tie with home for men in Africa, Australia, the Pacific or Europe, aside from family letters, is baseball scores." An army private, John Stevenson, replying to a poll by *The Sporting News*, said, "Baseball is part of the American way of life. Remove it and you remove something from the lives of American citizens, soldiers, and sailors." Startling is the mom-and-apple-pie niche that baseball filled in the sanctum of the nation, accepted unquestionably, without a modicum of doubt.

With post–Pearl Harbor morale key to winning a worldwide war, Kenesaw Mountain Landis wrote a January 14, 1942, letter to FDR asking guidance. "The time is approaching when, in ordinary conditions, our teams would be heading for spring training camps," the Judge stated. "However, inasmuch as these are not ordinary times, I venture to ask what you have in mind as to whether professional baseball should continue to operate." A day later, January 15, Roosevelt read his reply aloud at a press conference, telling the commissioner that it was vital to the national interest to keep the pastime alive. "I honestly feel that it would be best for the country to keep baseball going."

Writing speeches for President Reagan's Cabinet, then for President George H. W. Bush, I saw how aides both inside the White House and out affect policy. Landis, a conservative, and Roosevelt, a liberal, despised each another. Clark Griffith was baseball's unofficial DC lobbyist, somehow keeping that secret from the commissioner, who hated FDR's agenda and refused even to meet the president. Eleanor and Franklin Roosevelt's dislike of Landis was personal. Each rued how a game they liked was led by a man they felt a segregationist. It astounds that Roosevelt's letter, which, to the public, was his and Landis's official rapprochement, survived their mutual contempt.

In secrecy, Landis's and especially the president's letters were largely arranged by Griffith and close Roosevelt ally and future Democratic Party national chairman Robert E. Hannegan. "Without them," wrote the *New York Times*' Arthur Daley, "baseball might have disappeared in the war." Griffith and Hannegan helped compose the public exchange of letters to suggest a warmth that did not exist—in particular, what became known as "the Green Light Letter":

The White House
Washington

January 15, 1942

My dear Judge:

Thank you for yours of January fourteenth. As you will, of course, realize the final decision about the baseball season must rest with you and the Baseball Club owners—so what I am going to say is solely a personal and not an official point of view.

I honestly feel that it would be best for the country to keep baseball going. There will be fewer people unemployed and everybody will work longer hours and harder than ever before.

And that means that they ought to have a chance for recreation and for taking their minds off their work even more than before.

Baseball provides a recreation which does not last over two hours or two hours and a half, and which can be got for very little cost. And, incidentally, I hope that night games can be extended because it gives an opportunity to the day shift to see a game occasionally.

As to the players themselves, I know you agree with me that individual players who are of active military or naval age should go, without question, into the services. Even if the actual quality of the teams is lowered by the greater use of older players, this will not dampen the popularity of the sport. Of course, if an individual has some particular aptitude in a trade or profession, he ought to serve the Government. That, however, is a matter which I know you can handle with complete justice.

Here is another way of looking at it—if 300 teams use 5,000 or 6,000 players, these players are a definite recreational asset to at least 20,000,000 of their fellow citizens—and that in my judgment is thoroughly worthwhile.

With every best wish,
Very sincerely yours,
Franklin D. Roosevelt

Hon. Kenesaw M. Landis,
333 North Michigan Avenue,
Chicago,
Illinois.

FDR's letter earned a Burma Road of gratitude. *Baseball Magazine* likened it to "the shot that was fired at Lexington in 1775." Columnist Warren Brown called "the Green Light Letter" the "most important document baseball has had since the original code of rules was written," noting its January 15 date. "The President," Brown observed, "in the midst of activity the like of which no Chief Executive before him ever had to contend with"—the attack on Pearl Harbor; his declarations of war against Japan, Germany, and Italy; almost instant two-front global conflict, its early weeks at best harrowing for the Allies; the stupendous difficulty of transforming American business into a war-making machine—"turned his attention to baseball's future in less than 24 hours after it had been brought to his attention." We cannot know what would have happened had Roosevelt not intervened. We *do* know that baseball survived because he *did*.

Coverage everywhere typified baseball's manifest destiny, then almost a synonym for the republic. LANDIS DELIGHTED BY PRESIDENT'S LETTER, wrote the *New York Times*. Other headlines added GRIFFITH, MACK PRAISE FDR'S BASEBALL STAND and GIANTS, YANK, DODGER OFFICIALS ELATED. St. Louis *Star-Times* columnist Sid Keener wrote an open letter to organized baseball, recommending an annual President Roosevelt Night at each Major and Minor League park, receipts to benefit the Red Cross, war relief organizations, and the Infantile Paralysis Fund, "in which the President [wa]s so deeply interested." Keener did not mention that FDR was paralyzed, both the president and columnist understated, like the age. Keener died in 1981, at ninety-two. Alive, he would probably still be awaiting organized baseball's reply.

Hard-line on the war, Landis shared the view that players of eligible age qualified to serve without exception should. Ewell Blackwell, Tommy Henrich, and Johnny Pesky, among many, gallantly traded one uniform for another. Some players remained in the United States to work.

Others rose from the Minors. The offshoot, as FDR saw, was "a recreation . . . which c[ould] be got for very little cost." On the home front, towns formed organized local teams, gasoline and rubber rationing keeping almost every family close to home. Baseball held fundraisers to benefit the uso, American Red Cross, and other service groups. Military personnel played "pickup" games. More night matches were slated as FDR had asked so that "the day shift . . . [could] see a game." Abuzz with wartime workers, dc got twenty-one night sets yearly from baseball through 1944. When Griffith wrote a memo stating that more than four million military had been admitted gratis to a big-league game since Pearl Harbor, Roosevelt intimated in a March 1945 press conference that the pastime should be played that year too. He could not have waved a more baseball-friendly flag.

Freeze-frame this time. Baseball's cachet was so overwhelming that FDR did not consider obliging another sport. When others, including bowling and horse racing, slowed or closed, they asked for a statement similar to "the Green Light Letter." Roosevelt ignored them or refused. Fifty-five to sixty million troops and civilians would die from World War II, including FDR himself. Polio had taught him to prioritize. The priority here was the war, which baseball could help win. Polio also had taught him to take things as they came—a difficult lesson, given how driven and impatient he had been. Disabled overnight, Roosevelt learned to value an outer world that forged his and America's 1930s and 1940s. Films blared Jimmy Stewart and John Wayne and Claudette Colbert. Radio flaunted Kate Smith and Ethel Merman, voices not necessarily needing a microphone, and Frank Sinatra, Fred Allen, and Jack Benny, as well as boxing, the Triple Crown, and college football—baseball above all. If ever an age screamed American exceptionalism on the field, set, and screen, it was Roosevelt's.

Moreover, polio forced FDR to adjust his life, unable to golf, say, or exercise or live a normal man's routine. Until the war this gave him more time to read. Increasingly, the wireless occupied more of his and millions of other Americans' time. In 1923 10 percent of families owned a radio. Almost all did by the war. In baseball, "Most coverage was local," said Mel Allen, debuting on late 1930s Yankees radio. It was also away, since pricey road play-by-play was apparently impossible to air without *being* there. Solution: wireless telegraphy, enabling coverage, wrote *The Sporting News*, "within seconds of the action." An operator at Braves Field might send code to a radio station in Pittsburgh. "B1L" meant ball one, low; "S2C," strike two, called. Eureka! The announcer then described—*recreated*—a game unseen.

Arriving in the capital just after FDR, Arch McDonald, Washington's baseball Barnum, became heard almost as often as the man with a Hyde Park postmark. Like clockwork, you heard "Right down Broadway" (strike), "Ducks on the pond" (runners), and "There she goes, Mrs. Murphy" (home run). Upon a save, key hit, or circus catch, McDonald unfurled a hillbilly ballad, "They Cut Down the Old Pine Tree." Arch recreated in a People's Drug Store three blocks from the White House. "He'd stand beside a second-floor window with these homey sayings," said 1962–68 Senators PA voice and leading sports cable lawyer Phil Hochberg. "People on the sidewalk roared."

The Arkansan then moved to a studio in the basement, where the baseball Senators elsewhere dwelled. As Bill Veeck said in another context, McDonald achieved what Roosevelt did in each campaign: make each game a carnival, each day a Mardi Gras, and each fan a king. "Small wonder," Hochberg said, "that Arch became known as the 'Rembrandt of the Recreation.'"

It was no coincidence that the people from among whom McDonald came—from Arkansas and Oklahoma and the Carolinas and Tennessee—forged baseball's arguably then widest public. Until 1958, when the Dodgers and Giants moved to California, the Cardinals were baseball's southern- and westernmost team—said writer Bob Broeg, "their spiritual following enormous." As Herbert Hoover perceived watching baseball after leaving office, many aligned with "Ol' Diz"(zy Dean) and Enos "Country" Slaughter and Joe "Ducky Wucky" Medwick in the 1930s. No team was glad to lose stars or substitutes to World War II, but as big leaguers in a new uniform abroad read *Stars and Stripes* and listened to the new Armed Forces Radio, those 1942 Cardinals left at home formed a team still good enough to beat the first club (Brooklyn) to win more than a hundred games (104) and *not* win a pennant.

Behind by ten and a half games in August, St. Louis ended 43-8 to finish 106-48 and meet the Yankees in the World Series. "That team," said Slaughter of his twenty-two-year career, "was the best I ever saw." More than ever, the Fall Classic meant America's grand affair, vital to the home front and especially the troops, wholesome in a swelling of the heart "White Christmas" way. It began with a Redbirds' split at home and moved to Yankee Stadium, where St. Louis swept a trifecta, ending on third baseman Whitey Kurowski's Game Five ninth-inning blast.

In 1944 teammate Marty Marion, who had a gold glove at shortstop before the award began in 1957, was voted MVP as both St. Louis teams won the pennant, most shockingly the Browns. The Cards then took the Streetcar Series—the first Classic held west of the Mississippi. By 1946 Brooklyn's Preacher Roe said he had found how to retire Stan Musial: "I'd throw him four wide ones, then try to pick him off." It didn't work, the Man that year hitting .365. Yet if you wore your Red Sox with pride, you approached Game Seven of that World Series against St. Louis—ironically, given the next half century of Sox self-immolation—with history on your side.

Boston had never lost in five prior Series. The score tied at three in Game Seven, Slaughter singled to start the eighth inning at Sportsman's Park. What happened next turned dogma to cliché. With two out, Cardinals skipper Eddie Dyer ordered a hit and run. Harry Walker hit to left-center field, weak-armed Leon Culberson fielded the ball, and Enos spied third base. Culberson relayed to shortstop Johnny Pesky, who—at this point, accounts cleave—turned toward the plate and was or was not stunned to see Country running and did or did not pause before throwing up the third-base line as Slaughter scored the 4–3 Series-winning run.

"Holding" the ball hovered like a northeasterly over the rest of Pesky's life. "Culberson lobbed the ball to me," he said. "I'd have needed a rifle to nail Slaughter." Five times the 1940s Redbirds placed second, their deficit as puny as a game, positioned to have won eight pennants in 1941–50—potentially the greatest-ever NL reign. As it was, the Cardinals waved nine flags from 1926 through Slaughter's mad dash for home. Their next World Series graced 1964. After pennants in 1967 and 1968 St. Louis waited till 1982 for another. What it really needed was to clone the Man.

Like twelve other big-league teams, the Depression Cardinals could be followed from sites far from your living room. Only New York's three teams abstained, the Dodgers, Giants, and Yankees inking a five-year radio ban in 1934 to protect attendance, fearing that few would pay to see a product they could hear for free. They got it wrong. In 1939 Larry MacPhail arrived from Cincinnati as executive VP to let Brooklyn use the wireless, Red Barber wooing the committed and intrigued. Ironically that year a new medium began haltingly to carry ball.

At the end of a Fireside Chat, FDR redid its best lines, giving the film to a firm making the newsreel soon seen at cinema nationwide. Two facts suggest Roosevelt in a full fourth term. First, he seemed at ease moving from radio to picture. Second, the technology needed to telecast had improved. Had FDR lived, he might have begun a regular series of *television* chats. Baseball's greater bind was twofold: its diamond shape was foreign to a rectangular screen, and "it was [often] not possible to pick up the ball," TSN wrote of professional baseball's video debut on August 26, 1939: Cincinnati visiting Ebbets Field.

Barber on play-by-play had only two cameras, having to guess when each was on and where it pointed. Eventually few had to guess baseball's direction. In 1946 fifty-six million radios in thirty million U.S. homes dwarfed television's seventeen thousand sets. By 1948 the number of TVs reached three million. It had been a quarter century since superscout Paul Krichell returned to Yankee Stadium after seeing Columbia's Lou Gehrig play Rutgers in 1923. "I think," he told then GM Ed Barrow, "I saw another Ruth today."

The year prior to TV's big-league baptism had been Gehrig's worst since 1925: a .295 average, 29 homers, and 114 RBIS. "Just a slump," said Yankees skipper Joe McCarthy of 1938. "We figured Lou'd get over it"— or hoped. As 1939 spring training ended, he may have turned to prayer.

That April baseball's Sparta and Athens made history at Yankee Stadium—the sole regular-season game in which the Bombers' Gehrig and Boston's Ted Williams played. Gehrig made a boot, hit into two double plays, and swung like still frames of film. One day a ball was hit between first base and the mound. "Lou muffed it, all thumbs, no coordination," McCarthy added. "Something was wrong."

The Yankees' first brief home stand ended Sunday, April 30. "I knew I ought to get out," said Gehrig later. "I came up four times with men on base, and a hit any time would have won the game. But I left [five] on." That night, at home in New Rochelle, he mulled the enemy within: amyotrophic lateral sclerosis, a fatal hardening and collapsing of the spinal cord.

The next day a Yankees road trip began. In Detroit Lou waited for McCarthy in the lobby of the Book-Cadillac Hotel. "You'd better take me out," the captain said. "Oh, Lou, you'll get over it," said Joe, heart breaking. "Come on, let me put you in." Gehrig refused: It was over. "I can't go on like this." Shuffling, he took the lineup card to home plate—the date, May 2, 1939.

That July 4, the Yankees retired No. 4 between games of a doubleheader at The Stadium. Gehrig had set a games-played streak that lasted until 1995. Now, knowing that he was dying, Lou proceeded to give baseball's Gettysburg Address. I have taught public speaking for the last two decades at the University of Rochester. To me, Gehrig's speech ranks among the finest given by an American in the past century—honest, moving, and brave.

"For the past two weeks you have been reading about the bad break I got," he began. "Yet today I consider myself the luckiest man on the face of the earth." Lou explained why, thanking everyone from grounds help to late Yanks owner Jacob Ruppert to McCarthy to his parents and, above all, his wife Eleanor who had "been a tower of strength and shown more courage than you dreamed existed—that's the finest I know."

The man a.k.a. the Iron Horse concluded: "So I close in saying that I may have had a tough break, but I have an awful lot to live for." His address was selfless, sans self-pity of any kind, and showed the kind of character Shakespeare attributed to "nature's nobleman."

In 1940 Gehrig took a job with New York City, on occasion taking a limousine to the park. Word spread among the players: "Lou, Lou, the Captain's coming," their hero on and off the field.

Gehrig sat alone on the bench with Mel Allen during infield practice. Turning, he patted the announcer's knee. "You know, I never got a chance to hear you broadcasting 'cause I was always playing," he said. "But I got to tell you, it's the only thing that kinda' keeps me going." Mel excused himself, found a runway, and sobbed. Lou remains among the few, living or dead, to warrant the term *legendary*, like his speech.

Gehrig died June 2, 1941, eighteen days after Joe DiMaggio singled at Comiskey Park to begin a hitting streak that shattered Wee Willie Keeler's big-league game skein of forty-four, set in 1896–97. Soon every radio, corner bar, and paper sang Joe's name. On July 17 in Cleveland, DiMag's record ended at a still-Olympian fifty-six straight games.

In 1936 Joe, a rookie, wed a .323 average, twenty-nine homers, and artistry in center field. "I get credit," laughed pitching mate Lefty Gomez. "Before me, they never knew he could go back on a ball." By coincidence, Yankee Stadium staged the 1939 All-Star Game a week after Gehrig's ode. Six Bronx Bombers started, DiMaggio homering. Joe's season tethered 30 homers, 126 RBIs, and a .381 average—the last AL righty to clear .380. Was there ever a more hull-up baseball man?

"You're beating the A's, 21–0. Why are you out there running around like it's a one-run game?" DiMag was asked. "Because," he replied, "there may be someone here who never saw me play before."

Between 1932 and 1964 the Yankees won twenty-two pennants and sixteen world titles—to HBO's *When It Was a Game*, "without a doubt, the most successful and recognizable team in all of sports." *The Sporting News* named McCarthy "baseball's greatest-ever manager," his .615 career winning percentage the best in baseball history. He won eight big-league pennants, took a record seven world titles, and as 1931–46 skipper was crucial to Yanks' success.

Marse Joe never played in the Majors but by reputation mentally outplayed any managerial peer in strategy and intuition. His players made few mistakes, won on defense, and knew baseball rules. One day a two-men-on-base pop neared the mound. Frank Crosetti whistled, Joe Gordon slowed, and Tommy Henrich trapped it. By delaying the infield fly call, New York got a double play.

"What's the score?" McCarthy fixed one player in the dugout. The player was speechless. Another, sitting, stretched his arms. The next sound he heard was his manager's disdain: "Where the hell do you think you are, a canoe?" Marse Joe's Stripes commonly reached port first if not always with smooth sailing.

By mid-1941 naval imagery seemed at high tide. The Japanese had a design on every island in the southwest Pacific. To America, Pearl Harbor seemed safe, farther east. German U-boats patrolled the Atlantic, sinking U.S. ships full of foodstuffs and trying to starve Britain into waving a white flag. In September Germany attacked the uss destroyer *Greer*. The next month FDR missed the first modern Subway Series. It started in the Bronx, the Dodgers and Yankees each winning a 3–2 game.

Yankee Stadium had been full-throated, pulsing from the first pitch, as if the crowd, fearing a war that few wanted but many sensed inevitable, was holding onto baseball preciously, refusing to let go. Ebbets Field was as raucous in Game Three, New York winning by a 2–1 score to lead by that much in games. The next match crossed into infamy, the Bums ahead, 4–3, in the visitors' ninth inning. By now actor William Bendix had only to say Brooklyn's name on film to prompt a state of wackiness. Few laughed after reliever Hugh Casey got two Yanks, went to a 3–2 count on Tommy Henrich, then threw the pitch that to Flatbush benevolence forgot.

"The ball gets away from Mickey Owen!" Allen roared of strike three eluding Henrich, umpire Larry Goetz, and the Dodgers' catcher. "It's rolling back to the screen! Tommy Henrich races down toward first base! He reaches it safely! And the Yankees are still alive with Joe DiMaggio coming up to bat!" No. 5 singled. Charlie Keller doubled off the right-field wall, scoring Henrich. Bill Dickey walked. Joe Gordon doubled: 7–4, New York. Tom Meany wrote of Owen's muff: "The condemned jumped out of the chair and electrocuted the warden." A day later New York won its fifth world title since 1936, missing only in 1940. "Wait till next year" seemed too cruel to even utter.

For much of 1941 public consciousness careened, in no special order, among DiMag's streak, the London Blitz, Gehrig's death, Hitler's invasion of the Soviet Union, and Ted Williams's rise. Boston's part-Gibraltar and part-child pined to have others say, "There goes the greatest hitter who ever lived." By September, the Yanks clinching early, pressure on Ted had turned interior: become the first since Bill Terry in 1930 to get four hits each ten at-bats. Daily No. 9 became a peaceful tour de force followed by those readying for war.

Williams entered the last day of the year hitting .3995, rounded to .400 in the record book. Red Sox manager Joe Cronin pleaded with The Kid to skip the season-ending twin bill at Philadelphia. "You got your .400. Sit it out," said Joe, who could have been speaking Sanskrit.

"No, I don't want it that way. I'll play," said the supernova who wouldn't crash. Ted, twenty-three, and clubhouse attendant Johnny Orlando walked city streets for hours, thinking. In the first game Williams whacked a home run and a single, then added two second-game hits, one breaking the loudspeaker horn. He ended six-for-eight for a .406 average, reality becoming myth.

A World War II Marine Corps aviator, Williams admired his commander-in-chief. Exhausted but inexhaustible, FDR bestrode what we *still* dub "The War." On D-Day, June 6, 1944, he gave a moving prayer over network radio: Americans as congregants and Roosevelt as parish minister. In October, seeking a fourth term, he visited Ebbets Field for the first time, despite carrying Brooklyn in each previous campaign for president by a greater percentage than in any borough. "I've followed the Dodgers," Roosevelt told the crowd, clearly enjoying himself, as beloved as any regular, "and now I hope to come back and see 'em play."

The president's first visit to Ebbets Field on Opening Day 1945—the Depression long over, a world war almost won—would have been a grand occasion even for a Republican: baseball's public face throughout the land. FDR often said, "I love it!" America would have. Another pet phrase fit: "How wonderful!" The last baseball game Roosevelt saw in the flesh, as opposed to heard on radio or saw by newsreel, was at Griffith Stadium on April 14, 1941. Thereafter his time spent on baseball dwindled—the exception "the Green Light Letter"—as he focused exclusively on winning the war.

In early 1945 the president reported to Congress upon dividing the postwar world at the Yalta summit. For years a gentleman's agreement had banned newsreels from showing him in a wheelchair. Too weary to pretend, FDR now sat in a chair, face creased, eyes pools of black. He looked like death—but death was unthinkable, for few could separate the office and the man. In a cable he wrote, "It is fun to be in the same decade with you [Winston Churchill]." It was also necessary if we were not to plunge into the lowest meridian of hell. Eventually he helped build a United Nations in his vision, which had also been Woodrow Wilson's: the triumph of freedom, not just the absence of war.

Detroit long ago had changed to a wartime economy; American commerce boasted a huge female workforce; and more recently Allied leaders triumphed around the globe: MacArthur, Nimitz, Bradley, Patton, Marshall, Britain's Bernard Montgomery ("Monty"), and especially Churchill, who, with FDR, regularly rank in polling as the two greatest persons of the century. It took both to preserve what the British lion called "all that we have known and loved." Even then, "It was a damn close-run thing," as the Duke of Wellington supposedly said at Waterloo.

To revive his spirit FDR returned to Hyde Park one last time on March 28, 1945. To try to restore his health President Roosevelt then went to his vacation home in Warm Springs, Georgia, where on Friday, April 12, he suffered a fatal cerebral hemorrhage. Later that afternoon vice president Harry Truman ended a dry day presiding over the Senate by joining speaker of the house Sam Rayburn for a drink. At 5:12 p.m. the White House switchboard located Roosevelt's successor and ordered him across town.

Like many, Truman had not yet heard the news. Arriving, he heard Eleanor Roosevelt say, "Harry, the president is dead." Was there anything he could do for her? the vice president asked. The First Lady replied, "Is there anything we can do for *you*? For *you* are the one in trouble *now*."

On Capitol Hill GOP Senate Leader Robert Taft forever caught the mood: "Franklin Roosevelt literally worked himself to death on behalf of the American people," sixteen to eighteen hours a day, beset by heart disease and other illness, pressure so intense as to kill a healthier and younger man, never complaining, bravely soldiering, carrying the Roosevelt code of stoicism to the grave. The fate of democracy lay upon him. Abroad soldiers had confronted places they had only heard or read about. Now they faced a change few had envisaged: the president was dead.

Roosevelt died twenty-five days before Nazi Germany surrendered: an indescribable irony. Many evoked his rhetoric, enlisting the American people to "win through" in "their righteous might" to "absolute victory" as "the great arsenal of democracy" for our "Four Freedoms" of "speech, worship, and against want and fear" toward "our rendezvous with destiny." Almost everyone felt a private memory: FDR's first inaugural, a tear at Pearl Harbor, his D-Day prayer, "my little dog, Fala," all the notes of emotion played by friendship or something more.

In a period eulogy columnist Samuel Grafton wrote, "One remembers Roosevelt as a kind of smiling bus driver, with cigarette holder pointed upward, listening to the uproar from behind as he took the sharp turns." He heard that "he had not loaded his vehicle right for all eternity. But he knew he had it stacked well enough to round the next corner and he knew when the yells were false and when they were real, and he loved the passengers."

Some recall how for many the term "president" still means FDR, others how he changed America so fiercely that thirteen successors—many trying—have not changed it back. Roosevelt left what he had sought. His America never felt puny or afraid.

President Roosevelt's life, like his death, stirred emotion—still does, almost three-quarters of a century later. Hearing the Friday afternoon wire bulletin, tens of millions wept as they would for a loved one, inner turmoil cresting, as battle in Europe ebbed. The next morning the train carrying FDR's body headed north from Warm Springs to Washington. Hundreds of thousands, perhaps millions, of Americans of every stripe flanked the tracks. In the nation's capital the procession attracted hundreds of thousands more. Never, Truman said, had he seen so many people, a wall of woe block after block, silent except for sobs, some crying uncontrollably: women waving handkerchiefs at the cortege; a young girl, gazing between spokes of a White House gate; men in suits or service garb, some recently discharged; the photo of a woman, perhaps fifty, face set in pain, floral hat as gay as the day was somber—a symphony of grief.

Late that Friday the Brooklyn Dodgers president and GM, the brawling and combative Colonel Larry MacPhail, issued a valentine of the heart:

> During my stay in the War Department I had many opportunities to learn about the President's love for sport. He swam every day he could—it was this which helped keep him in shape during long hard years. It was the President who twice gave the green light to baseball. It was he who stressed the fact that sport provided relaxation from worry and strain in war time.
>
> Franklin Roosevelt was not only a great sports fan—he was, in my book, the greatest sports man of all time—and was the Commander in Chief of thousands of other great sportsmen—the boys who have given their lives on distant battle-fields. He was tried by the same tests of loyalty and devotion as the least of them—was proved by these same tests—the most heroic and faithful.
>
> There is grief and sorrow tonight in the hearts of the boys on all the seas, in the air, in the foxholes on every front. They liked the warmth of his personality—his cheerful smile—the courage with which he overcame long physical pain and suffering. They have lost a buddy—a buddy who gave his life for his country. They will write his epitaph in two words—VICTORY—PEACE.

MacPhail was not alone in grasping how Roosevelt preserved the then-only national game. On March 16, 1945, nearly four weeks *before* FDR's death, J. G. Taylor Spink, the incorrigible, often volcanic 1914–62 publisher of *The Sporting News*, baseball's then weekly "Bible of

Baseball" and last-word authority on the sport, sent a Western Union telegram from *TSN* offices in St. Louis to Hall of Fame president, Stephen C. Clark; Hall treasurer, Paul S. Kerr; Yankees president, Ed Barrow; A's owner and manager, Connie Mack; New York sportswriter Sid Mercer; Braves president, Bob Quinn; and Boston sportswriter Mel Webb—the seven members of the National Baseball Hall of Fame and Library Old-Timers Committee, sired a year earlier to help the Baseball Writers' Association of America (BBWAA) increase the number of players and others inducted at Cooperstown. His 1945 telegram read:

IN VIEW OF FRANKLIN D. ROOSEVELTS GREAT SERVICES TO BASEBALL, I RESPECTFULLY SUGGEST THAT HIS NAME BE ENSHRINED IN THE HALL OF FAME AT COOPERSTOWN AS A FITTING TRIBUTE BY THE GAME. NO OTHER PRESIDENT HAS DISPLAYED SUCH WARM INTEREST IN BASEBALL OR GIVEN SO MUCH ENCOURAGEMENT TO THE GAME. HIS LETTER TO COMMISSIONER LANDIS IN JANUARY 1942 SAVED BASEBALL FROM WARTIME SUSPENSION. ON OTHER OCCASIONS MR. ROOSEVELT REITERATED HIS INTEREST AND HIS SUPPORT. HE PRESERVED THE LIFE OF THE GAME AT A CRITICAL JUNCTURE: HE DESERVES RECOGNITION IN THE HALL OF FAME AMONG THOSE WHO HAVE MADE NOTABLE CONTRIBUTIONS TO THE WELFARE OF THE SPORT.

J. G. TAYLOR SPINK, PUBLISHER, *THE SPORTING NEWS*

You might think that putting FDR in a hall of fame enshrining baseball would be a given—even for such a motley maze as big-league mandarins—if for no other purpose than as a thank-you. Surely the arch-conservative Spink did—the political antithesis of the liberal Roosevelt. Below: the record and, given research and lack of *any* other reason to block approval, a probable cause as to why more than seventy years have passed without the former president's induction.

That Saturday, April 13, the day after the Champ's death, a Western Union telegram from Major League Baseball secretary Leslie M. O'Connor bearing the mantra "FOR VICTORY BUY WAR BONDS TODAY" was sent to all Major and Minor League presidents. It read: "Major-Minor Advisory Council recommends and asks that no games be played Saturday, and that flags be half-masted for thirty days in respect to late President Roosevelt." A same-day telegram from AL president William Harridge was sent to ensure that nothing harmed baseball's FDR tribute. It read: "Since burial of President Roosevelt is to take place at Hyde Park, New York, ten o'clock, Sunday morning, games scheduled for Sunday afternoon may be played."

Before and at the time of FDR's death, the Old-Timers Committee and others familiar with his relationship with baseball spoke benignly with one another about his admission. Paul Kerr contacted several owners about exhibiting Roosevelt's letter to Judge Landis, asking Clark Griffith if he had an autographed photo of FDR to display. Then: silence. Plainly some committee members were having second thoughts. On April 17, Spink, his month-earlier telegram unanswered, again wrote a member to say: "[Roosevelt] preserved the life of the game at a critical juncture." Ten days later Stephen Clark replied that FDR had been considered, adding, "I wish to inform you that he was not elected." No explanation was provided. What gave?

A day later, April 28, Spink wrote back: "In view of President Roosevelt's great services to baseball which are a matter of record, I am amazed that no consideration was given to his recognition of a place in [the] Hall of Fame." To Kerr, he lamented FDR's rebuff: "It is difficult to figure out how such men [voting] as Connie Mack, Ed Barrow, and Bob Quinn can ignore the great effect the late President had upon the history of baseball." Spink noted that commissioner-elect Albert B. "Happy" Chandler, U.S. senator from Kentucky, would replace Judge Landis, who had recently died. "I hope that under [his] . . . administration greater consideration will be paid to the Hall of Fame and what it represents to baseball." From baseball came not a peep, Roosevelt shelved, as it happened, to this day.

Ten days later the "Bible of Baseball" publisher, usually viewed as wise, even Delphic, by the pastime—in this case barely able to get a hearing, let alone a rationale, from those who had most benefited from his support—wrote an open letter to each member of the Hall committee and each reader in TSN's May 10, 1945, issue. Below is J. G. Taylor Spink's testimony on behalf of Franklin Roosevelt for admittance to the Hall of Fame.

Spink's letter to *The Sporting News* readers and the Hall of Fame committee began as follows: "But for the late Franklin Delano Roosevelt's . . . support, encouragement, and active espousal of the game in Washington, professional baseball would have been shut down as early as the immediate aftermath of Pearl Harbor"; in short, he kept baseball from going out of business. Spink cited FDR's historic January 15, 1942, missive—"the first definite, emphatic notice to those who would have meddled with the workings of our national pastime that he wanted 'hands off.'" The publisher continued:

> From time to time thereafter, Mr. Roosevelt reiterated his stand in support of wartime baseball. From time to time, those who delight in kicking over the apple cart made ready to take body blows at baseball, in the guise of moves for the national war economy. But just when these meddlers thought the late President wasn't looking, when they believed he was too greatly engrossed with vastly more vital problems, he invariably forestalled them with still another warning. "Hands off. I want this game to go on. It's good for our people at home. It's a benefit to millions of our men overseas."
>
> However, gentlemen, you know the story as I do. You know precisely what the support of the late President meant to our game. Yes, what it still means, for President Harry S. Truman has indicated he will pursue a similar policy and help baseball in every possible way. He gave assurances to that effect when Commissioner-Elect Albert B. Chandler visited him in the White House a fortnight ago.
>
> It is reported that some of you might be inclined to name Mr. Roosevelt to the Hall of Fame at your next meeting in the Hall if you were convinced that you had that jurisdiction in the matter. It appears that some of you do not believe it is within your power to elect a man who was not a player, umpire, writer, club presi-

dent, manager, commissioner, or league head. *Gentlemen, from Pearl Harbor until his recent death, Mr. Roosevelt in his attitude toward baseball really combined the contacts of all of these diamond functionaries, figures, and liaison officers* [author's emphasis].

Let me emphasize that but for Franklin Delano Roosevelt, you would have had no baseball these past four seasons [author's emphasis]. Your parks would have been padlocked, your overhead would have eaten into your reserves with dangerous insistence, your players would have gone from you into the limbo of the forgotten and, in many cases, out of the game to stay. However, here again I need paint no picture for any of the things that would have happened, had baseball been forced to suspend.

Of all our sports activities, baseball alone gained the support of Mr. Roosevelt [author's emphasis]. When, last January, War Mobilizer James F. Byrnes interdicted horse racing, and those interested in that sport turned appealing eyes toward the White House, there was no response. But within ten days after the banishment of horse racing, Mr. Roosevelt came out with a rare— and, I am sorry to say, his final—appeal for baseball.

Gentlemen, you have the right and power to elect Mr. Roosevelt to baseball's Hall of Fame. You not only enjoy the right and the power, but you have the commission, from baseball itself, from its fans, from its past and its present, from its bright destinies, to name Mr. Roosevelt at your next meeting.

Let there be a stated occasion for our game to make its obeisance to the man who saved it, and kept saving it, and who gave to it the charter of life which today keeps our national pastime alive and vibrant in the wartime scene.

With thanks for your consideration, and the belief that action should not be delayed long, I am,

Very sincerely yours,

J. G. Taylor Spink

Roosevelt's "Green Light Letter" made the bond between baseball and America personal and official—a "special relationship" unique among American sports. Yet his absence from the Hall of Fame reflects his special clash with baseball's boss. Kenesaw Mountain Landis practiced one-man government, owners acquiescing after the Black Sox Scandal. "Don't kid yourself that that old judicial bird isn't going to make those baseball birds walk the chalk line," Will Rogers observed in the early 1920s. By World War II almost a quarter century in office had made his popularity, thus power, replete.

As commissioner, Landis was striking, a made-from-central-casting jurist for a would-be czar: handsome, theatric, white-maned, a well-pitched voice. Like baseball's ruling class, he was in tune with 1930s American Gothic: deemed upright by the middle class, a billy club by the Left. Jackie Robinson cracked the color line only after Landis's death, some feeling the Judge a Neanderthal if not worse. Like Spink, his attitude toward political liberalism was of a oneness with the Old-Timers Committee, which became the Veterans Committee in 1953 and a revised Veterans Committee in 2001.

Baseball's first empowered leader cleansed the game of sin, apotheosized a more innocent time, and helped give the pastime a cachet dreamt of by every U.S. institution. It is likely that had it been possible for Landis and Roosevelt to have remained in office forever, most Americans would have voted yes. In 1944, the last full-time year for both in office, the commissioner probably would have outpolled FDR's 53.5 percent of the vote.

The irony of their public union was private disdain. One cause was ego: no room was large enough for both. Ego aside, Spink's fury rose from FDR's perceived ostracism. As his open letter said, the Old-Timers Committee had at one time worried about a lack of jurisdiction to elect someone not "a player, umpire, writer, club president, manager, commissioner, or league head"—an obstacle to induction. For many, Spink's May 10, 1945, earthquake erased that rationale, noting how FDR yoked *each* role to complete a historic mission—the salvation of the country and the game.

The Sporting News publisher was as or more rightist than Landis, any committee member, and baseball's then conservative power structure— as chapter 5 will show, Branch Rickey an exception. At the same time,

Spink prized fact over ideology, as did the American people, who loudly urged the committee to induct the deceased president. With reason to act, it declined. Spink's letter revealed the nature of the opposition to Roosevelt, whose death stunned the game, which knew how he had saved it.

A writer cannot say with surety that FDR's rejection stemmed from animus toward his liberal policies and persona. The committee principals are dead. Most decision-making was verbal, by telephone and/or in private. Records have been lost, or never made. A writer *can* say that records that do exist, as we have seen, suggest a probable cause of bias—a conclusion bolstered by the absence of any other cause put forth since Spink's letter. The verdict ignored how without Roosevelt baseball could not have survived the war.

Peculiarly paradoxical was spurning the commander in chief of the sixteen million Americans who served in the armed forces in World War II and for whom baseball was by far the favorite sport. Who can doubt that if asked, they, like the home front, would have cried "Yes!" to FDR's admission to Cooperstown? To honor them—to posthumously and finally induct the thirty-second president—would be a great and good thing for the Hall of Fame's current Veterans Committee to do.

In late 1944 Commissioner Landis caught a severe cold, entered the hospital, had a major heart attack, was given a new seven-year contract, turned seventy-eight on November 20, died five days later, and was presently elected to the Hall. The end of the world's worst-ever conflagration in 1945 left America as history's supreme force. Even within baseball, what mattered was that the boys were coming home, not merely that some would again play ball.

To Eleanor Roosevelt, ever the pragmatist, the extraordinary age of her husband ended with his death. Taking the train to her Washington Square apartment in New York, she found a group of reporters waiting at the door. The former First Lady said simply that she had nothing to say. "The story," she explained, "is over."

FIVE

The Accidental President

Harry S. Truman, 1945–1953

As Franklin Roosevelt passed into mythology, he was succeeded by a man of whom most of America knew nothing. Harry Truman had been chosen FDR's third vice president in 1944 because incumbent Henry Wallace was too liberal for the electorate. The president and Truman barely knew each other, having met alone only twice after the latter took office. Harry and wife Bess were said to pray regularly. Becoming president, he told reporters, "Boys, if you ever pray, pray for me now." Fifteen years after another death, Theodore H. White conceded, "I still have difficulty seeing John F. Kennedy clear." By comparison Truman left almost nothing to the imagination. The thirty-third president was a bespectacled, five-foot-nine machine protégé with poor sight and, as it happened, great vision. House speaker Sam Rayburn termed him "right on all the big things, wrong on most of the little ones." Color Harry pugnacious, hyperbolic, petty, and huge.

John Dos Passos called Roosevelt's "the patroon voice, the headmaster's admonition, the bedside doctor's voice that spoke to . . . all of us"—a voice that seemed almost musical. Truman's was flat and high, a would-have-been audition dropout. FDR was dressed to the manor born. Harry wore double-breasted suits with two-toned wingtip shoes. Roosevelt scent of Major League. Truman could seem out of his. "To err is Truman," jibed sophists. "I'm just mild about Harry." It was said that FDR saved capitalism for the capitalists. Who foretold Churchill's saw, "No one more saved western civilization" than Truman?

Returning after World War I to his Missouri hometown of Independence, Truman married fifth-grade sweetheart Elizabeth "Bess" Wallace and became a Kansas City clothier. His partner was Eddie Jacobson, with whom he had run an army post canteen. Sadly, their new threads turned bare. Olympian, FDR fought disability. Rotarian, Harry fought a history of going broke. At thirty-eight, Truman, born in 1882, was in debt. To his rescue came Kansas City political boss Tom Pendergast, helping elect Harry to a 1922 district judgeship. Truman became a Missouri U.S. senator and vice president in 1935 and 1945 respectively.

"Who the hell is Harry Truman!?" White House chief of staff Admiral William D. Leahy asked FDR in summer 1944. Truman had been a World War I artillery captain in France, was a Shriner and member of the Baptist Church, merited the terms "self-confident," "plain," and "plain-spoken," and was viewed as a Middle America singsong speaker.

"We chose Truman," an FDR aide confessed, "because he was from a Border state and all of us were tired." He could also laugh at himself and hated phonies. So what if Truman seemed unpresidential? The president was FDR. Only as commander-in-chief did Harry learn of the atomic bomb—Roosevelt had not informed him of the Ultimate Weapon—and how dropping it on Japan might cost untold casualties as well as save lives later by avoiding an invasion.

Eventually Truman told Japan to surrender or face ruin. Ignored, he ordered a B-29—the *Enola Gay* and *Bockscar* respectively—to drop a first, then second, atomic bomb. Earlier General Dwight Eisenhower had signed the Axis surrender in the European theater. On September 2, 1945, General Douglas MacArthur signed Japan's surrender in the Pacific theater, ending World War II. MacArthur's basso voice, even apart from the event, made his formal signing aboard the USS *Missouri* in Tokyo Bay unforgettable. "Let us pray that peace now be restored to the world," said the general, whom Truman would come to detest, "and that God will preserve it always."

v-J Day started the long-sought transition from a war to a peacetime front. Before long the new president found that peace, like war, had its price. Truman's domestic policy closely resembled what Roosevelt's would have bannered: civil rights, national health insurance, and a decent standard of living. America bestrode the world. So where were housing and domestic goods? After the 1946 Senators home opener, it was found that ten members of the team were temporarily living in the clubhouse. Live together, lose together. The first postwar year brooked shortages, price controls, rising prices, the black market, and 102,476 man-hours lost to strikes. The first task of Truman's "Fair Deal" was to meet pent-up demand.

Abroad, at first liking Stalin—to Truman, "Uncle Joe"—Harry soon chafed at war-allied Soviet armies that occupied Poland and much of Europe. He was helpless, hating it: "I'm tired of babying the Soviets." Churchill hadn't tried, saying, "From Stettin in the Baltic to Trieste in the Adriatic an Iron Curtain has descended across the continent." Later Herbert Agar wrote of Truman, "During the next few years this strange little man—lively and pert to the verge of bumptiousness; more widely read in history than any President since John Quincy Adams; more willful than any President since James K. Polk—would make and enforce a series of decisions upon which, for better or worse, our world now rests, or shakes."

Truman came to Opening Day like the boy falling off the turnip truck, asking townspeople, "Fellahs, what's it all about?" The first pitch tradition had endured during the war, Harry not involved. John Nance Garner tossed the first ball at Griffith Stadium in 1939. In 1943 wartime manpower chief Paul McNutt threw another. Twice Henry Wallace hurled the ball. (He also *had* one in his free spirit way, portending a wild 1948 presidential bid.) In 1942 Wallace's pitch inexplicably reached an unoccupied zone in center field. In 1944 FDR's second VP deliberately threw to Washington pitcher Alex Carrasquel, saying a group of Venezuelans, including Alex, had asked him to hype the "Good Neighbor" policy toward Latin America. Opening Day 1945 came eight days after Truman succeeded Roosevelt, Sam Rayburn subbing. That September 8 Harry became the first presi-

dent to attend a big-league game since 1941, the Senators on best behavior, beating the Browns, 4–1.

Southpaw Truman was the first to throw the ball right- and left-
handed from the presidential box. As a boy, he had followed but rarely
played baseball, "afraid of the rough-and-tumble of the schoolyard, and
because of his glasses, fe[eling] incapable of any sport that involved a
moving ball," wrote biographer David McCullough. Truman read Homer's *Ulysses*; Lytton's *The Last Days of Pompeii*; and about the civiliza-
tions of Egypt, Greece, and Mesopotamia. He touted everything U.S.
in business, World War I service, and politics, American exceptionalism extending to cards. Of playing Churchill, Truman told aides, "The
reputation of American poker is at stake, and I expect every man to
do his duty." He thought it an index of character, ordered chips em-
bossed with the presidential seal, and kept a sign with a poker phrase
scripted "The buck stops here" on his Oval Office desk.

On April 16, 1946, a chilly day in the East, Truman performed *his*
symbolic presidential duty of inaugurating the baseball season's opening game by throwing out the first ball for the first time since before
America had joined the war. Few gestures could have more precisely
signaled normalcy, a sense that the horror that took humanity to the
cliff and back was over. A week earlier Captain Clark Griffith and NL
head Ford Frick visited Harry in the White House to present his season passes. Later Griffith termed Truman in "rare form," saying the
president had given the two visitors a "preview" of his first-ball form.
On Opening Day Truman lunched with some U.S. senators, greeted wounded veterans, then drove to Griffith Stadium, wearing, said
Frederick W. Turner in *When the Boys Came Back: Baseball and 1946*,
"a buff-colored fedora and blue-gray topcoat to his flag-draped box."

With him were Bess, daughter Margaret, and a friend. Waiting
was a panoply of names—Truman's presidential party—that had and
would help America steady the globe: chief of staff Leahy; Admiral
Chester Nimitz, icon of the Pacific theater; attorney general Tom
Clark; and political adviser Clark Clifford, one day to become secretary of defense and a legal pillar of the DC elite. The managers
flanked the party: Washington's Ossie Bluege and Boston's Joe Cro-

nin, the prewar Senators star. The sixty-five-piece army band began to play "Hail to the Chief." The band, led by Clark Griffith, Nimitz, and two squads, shuffled to the flagpole in deep center field. An overflow 30,372 stood for the national anthem. Truman became the first left-hander to inaugurate the season, firing the ceremonial first pitch into a maze of players, each grasping for the ball. Boston's Dom DiMaggio then stepped into the batter's box, waiting for Roger Wolff's first-of-the-season pitch.

As was their bent, the Senators lost, 6–2, the real moment hailing baseball's return from war a 440-foot leviathan by Ted Williams to the seats in dead center field. According to Turner, "No ball, the writers agreed, had been hit that far in Griffith Stadium." Williams was often called John Wayne in baseball garb. Even the Duke was said to admire The Kid's extempore sense of style.

Like Roosevelt, Truman as president began the long and still incomplete task of creating a color-blind America, not an America blind to justice. Truman desegregated the American armed forces—a striking American success story two-thirds of a century later. On August 13, 1945, a group headed by Branch Rickey bought 50 percent of the Ebbets estate—in effect, the Brooklyn Dodgers—for $750,000. Perhaps only a visionary—as stated, Rickey founded baseball's farm system—could see its future around the corner.

Jack Roosevelt "Jackie" Robinson was a lion at the plate, a tiger in the field, and "had wounds," Rickey said, "[that] you could not feel or share." On October 23, seventy-one days after buying the Dodgers, Branch inked Robinson, breaking baseball's color line. A week later Jackie joined Montreal, Brooklyn's Triple-A affiliate in the International League. Professional baseball's first black player debuted April 18, 1946, with a home run and three singles. On April 15, 1947, Robinson played in his Major League opener at Ebbets Field. "I was there," said television host Larry King. "Jackie just seemed to glide." Among other teams, the Cardinals were more interested in a boycott. Even mates petitioned Robinson's return to Montreal. What would the team captain do?

Pee Wee Reese was from Kentucky. "Growing up," he said, "I didn't come into contact with black people. I was taught that Negroes were to ride in the back of streetcars." Pee Wee refused to sign a petition. In Atlanta a writer vowed to shoot Robinson if he played. Hearing about the threat, Reese sidled over in warm-up, drolly joking, "Don't stand so damn close. Move away, will you?"—as if Jackie's proximity might risk Reese's life. Pee Wee was using humor, one player to another, to relax the rookie. Robinson started laughing, the two soon lifelong friends. FDR's rendezvous with history entailed destroying men bent on destroying us. Rickey's began by signing Robinson. Truman's involved a moral tone that made Jackie's success personal, yet national.

If you lived in "the States," as visitors still term America, you almost certainly followed 1947's second chapter of the Dodgers-Yankees odyssey. Mutual radio featured Mel Allen and Red Barber, like John Gielgud and Laurence Olivier sharing a gilded stage. The World Series began with the Yankees winning twice. Game Three spun a 185-minute 9–8 Dodgers parody. In its successor, the Stripes led, 2–1, after eight and two-thirds innings in Brooklyn, starter Floyd "Bill" Bevens improbably ceding ten walks and no hits.

Even in our technological age, a quaint or antique broadcast custom persists that an in-process no-hitter should not be mentioned, lest a pitcher's fate be determined by an announcer's voice. "Some guys think you jinx a no-hitter by mentioning it," said radio's W. Earnest "Ernie" Harwell. "So a few broadcasters don't mention it. [Ernie did.] They dub it tradition, making baseball special." Allen called the first four and a half innings, respecting the tradition. Inheriting the mike, Barber, a self-described "reporter, not a dealer in superstition," did not.

Allen gasped as Red leaked the fact that Brooklyn had "no hits." The Bums still were hitless as, a run behind, they put a second man on base in the ninth inning, Cookie Lavagetto pinch-hitting. Bill Bevens threw. "Swung on, there's a drive hit out toward the right-field corner!" said Barber. "It's off the wall for a base hit! Here comes the tying run and here comes the winning [3–2] run!" Box seat: eight dollars. Sensation: priceless. Many blamed Barber for jinxing his own team. Few were surprised by a next-match letdown: Yankees, 2–1.

Back in the Bronx, Game Six wed a record Series crowd (74,065), the longest Classic regulation time (3:19), and a robbery of Joe DiMaggio. Brooklyn led, 8–5, when the game-saving catch by journeyman outfielder Al Gionfriddo of DiMag's long drive led Joe to kick dirt near second base—the only time mates ever saw him show emotion on the field. Both teams spent, the Series schlepped to a 5–2 Yanks clincher. One statistic augured: Robinson and Reese led the Dodgers with seven hits apiece.

That winter a man who had backed FDR four times would ordinarily have endorsed Truman too. Sadly, Babe Ruth's life had begun to run out just as Harry's reached its peak. In 1946 Ruth was diagnosed with throat cancer, caused by a lifetime of smoking. By April 27, 1947—*his* Day at The Stadium—Babe, in and out of the hospital, could barely talk. Allen, emceeing, stood behind Ruth's trademark camel hair coat and matching cap. The ovation volleyed, rolled beyond the outfield, and crashed against the tiers.

"Babe, do you want to try and say something?" said Mel, hands cupped. Ruth croaked, "I must." Quavering, he hailed "the boys represented here today in [our] national pastime—the only real game . . . in the world, baseball," then shuffled toward the bench.

"Good luck, Babe," offered Francis Cardinal Spellman, Roman Catholic archbishop of New York. "I just wanted you to know that any time you want me to come to your house for Holy Communion, I'd be glad to do it." Ruth smiled. "Thanks, Your Eminence. That's just great, but I'd rather come to *your* place."

As a player, said Yankees shortstop Phil Rizzuto, "Babe'd sit there with that big cigar. When he wasn't going to bat he'd stay in the outfield and talk to people in the stands and eat hot dogs." Broken, Ruth's shell resembled his old body in nothing more than name.

In 1947 the Stripes forgot to retire Babe's number. Red-faced, they held ceremony in June 1948, Ruth so weak, said Rizzuto, that it took two men to lift him. In uniform, he leaned on the Indians' Bob Feller's bat like a cane.

Again emceeing, Allen once more asked if Ruth wished to speak. Babe didn't, couldn't. Much later Mel told CBS broadcaster Edward R.

Murrow, "I shall never forget it [Ruth's farewell], nor shall I ever forget him."

Truman was more Ruth than Gehrig: flawed, impulsive, the center of any scene; the presidential gambler who most often bet the ranch, second-guessed himself the least, and won more than he lost the pot. In 1947 a bankrupt Britain ended aid to Greece and Turkey. That March 12 Truman asked Congress for $400 million in aid to back their shaky pro-Western governments—indeed, any like imperiled body—citing the need to support "free people who are resisting attempted subjugation by armed minorities or by outside pressures." The Truman Doctrine benefited from secretary of state George Marshall's economic Marshall Plan to help nations rebuild Western Europe. Spurning it, Stalin halted Western traffic into Berlin, 110 miles behind the Iron Curtain, and blockaded railways to starve its non-Russian sectors. Would the United States respond? An airlift fed Berlin for 321 days before the Russians caved.

"Had enough?" Republicans had asked, in 1946 taking control of the House and Senate. Forget Rayburn's "big things." Truman at first seemed to invite being patronized. Near Fulton, Missouri, where Churchill gave his "Iron Curtain" speech, he donned an engineer's cap and drove the locomotive. In Kansas City Harry visited a barbershop, saying, "None of that fancy stuff. I don't want anything that smells." He dubbed Bess "the boss" and Margaret "the boss who bosses the boss," termed White House visitors "the customers," and took his daily "constitutional." "If you can't stand the heat," he said, "get out of the kitchen." Truman felt he could and rarely left.

In 1945 a reporter first called him "Mr. President." Harry said, "I wish you didn't have to call me that." By 1948 most agreed, a Gallup Poll reporting that Truman would lose to any Republican—MacArthur, Harold Stassen, Arthur Vandenberg, or Thomas Dewey. Harry's already bad odds seemed even worse when the Progressive and States' Rights (Dixiecrat) Parties threatened to erode support. The presumed inheritor—"an authentic colossus," announcer Lowell Thomas called New York governor and ultimate GOP nominee Dewey—began campaigning as if already coronated.

Somehow the incumbent—"Give 'em Hell, Harry"—believed he could win with a Tooth Fairy type of certitude. The GOP Congress spurned Social Security and minimum wage legislation and passed the Taft-Hartley Act, which labor detested. Truman saw a wedge: was Congress the guardian of your purse or a tribune of privilege? He exploded: "If you send another Republican Congress to Washington, you're a bigger bunch of suckers than I think you are." Dewey was a fascist "front man" endorsing Hitler, Tojo, and Mussolini; the GOP, a.k.a. "gluttons of privilege," "stuck a pitch fork in the farmers' back." Was Harry spunky or hysterical? He often seemed more the latter. Odds against him rose to 15–1.

The October 11 issue of *Newsweek* stated, "Fifty political experts unanimously predict a Dewey victory." Truman told aides, "Oh, those damned fellows, they're always wrong, anyway." Dewey cautioned aides: "Remember, when you're ahead, don't talk." On election day Harry was asleep by 8 p.m. In the outside world an early *Chicago Tribune* headline screamed: DEWEY DEFEATS TRUMAN. Then came the shock. Minute by minute the headline seemed more and more askew. Like Pearl Harbor, FDR's death, and Bobby Thomson's homer, at least a generation (or more) knew where it was when Truman upset Dewey. At midnight Harry awoke, turned on the radio, and heard commentator H. V. Kaltenborn say that while Truman was ahead by 1.2 million votes, he was "undoubtedly beaten." Harry went back to sleep.

The farm vote, Republican since McKinley, was going Democratic—in the end, Dewey improbably carried only seven states between the Alleghenies and the Pacific. Slowly, the Associated Press would write, the GOP mood changed from "surety to surprise, surprise to doubt, doubt to disbelief, and then on to stunned fear and panic." Truman dined for a long time on steak, while top pollsters digested crow.

"Unlike the current White House tenant, whose lease at 1600 Pennsylvania Avenue was extended recently for four [curbed to two] more years," the *Washington Post*'s Morris Siegel wrote of Richard Nixon in early 1973, "Harry Truman was not a sports nut." In Missouri he was deemed a decent horseshoe pitcher, "but if he had any other sports interest, it was confined to whipping the daylights out of Republicans, whom he considered his natural rivals." Ask Dewey.

The irony is that Truman probably enjoyed Opening Day—hell's bells, he had a ball—more than any other president. To begin, Senators owner Clark Griffith was a rancher's son from Clear Creek, Missouri, a natural for any conversation with Harry, and a yellow dog Democrat, denoting a party member so loyal he would back any Dem, human or yellow canine. Unlike even Mrs. Truman and Margaret, Griffith was sure that Harry would win in 1948, making him that rare bird to raise money for Truman—and bet his own.

"Everyone is against Harry except the people," said Griffith, evangelizing the old-time Democratic campaign message of Wall Street elitism against Truman's "little man" populism. Harry's campaign, wildly outspent by Dewey, was to the last reliant on labor unions and friends like Clark. Election night—a stunning over-the-moon rabbit out of the hat—was even more of a pip than Truman's yearly sojourn on Opening Day, a surprise as to what he had in mind—or up one or the other sleeves.

Griffith brought perspective to his friend. Three weeks before FDR's death, Truman visited Clark's office, lined with mostly Opening Day photographs of every president dating back to Taft. As authors William B. Mead and Paul Dickson render the scene in *The Presidents' Game*, Griffith went from one to another describing them to Harry.

Two photos of Roosevelt put contrast in relief: FDR in his prime, from 1933; and from March 1945, FDR accepting a season pass from Clark, barely more alive than dead. "Look at the differences in the two men," Griffith said. "That job you got is a killing one, Harry. Don't let that happen to you."

Truman eyed his host. "Don't worry, Clark," he replied. "I walked into the White House and I aim to walk out of it. They won't carry me out of there in a box."

Truman threw the opening pitch about every way you can: one year right-handed, one year left-handed, the next both arms successively, another with both arms cupping the same pitch. According to Griffith, no president threw a spitball—"the Great Expectoration," he termed it—at his park on Opening Day, nor ostensibly did any pitcher after the spitter was outlawed before the 1921 season. "When they banned the pitch they let those boys who threw the spitter spit out their natural lives. [Burleigh Grimes was the last to throw it, retiring in 1934.] Of course, those rules don't apply to Harry Truman. He can throw it any way he wants to at my park"—and did.

From 1945 to 1952 Truman forged a 4-3 Opening Day and 8-8 overall record, his sixteen games at Griffith Stadium a presidential high. As noted, Harry's initial "first ball" serviced September 8, 1945. In 1946 Truman went one for two, beating Detroit, 5–3, June 1 after losing Opening Day. A year later the president again saw a .500 nine. The 1947 Nats lost a 7–0 opener to New York. Then, on June 21—Senators 5, Browns 4—Griffith unveiled a monument to Walter Johnson, dead the prior December at fifty-nine. Truman endured two 1948 Stripes shellackings: a 12–4 opener and an 8–1 pasting on August 18, the night game a presidential first. First in War, First in Peace, and Last against the Yankees.

The tide flowed toward Washington in 1949, Harry seeing the Nats win twice. April 18, 1950: good, bad, or indifferent, he kept 'em guessing, tossing a first ball with each arm—DC, 8–7. After a next-year 5–3 Opening Day capital decision over the Yankees, their winning skein now five, Truman saw three losses: September 1, 1951, to New York, 4–0; April 15, 1952, to Boston, 3–0; and July 4, again to the Yanks, 9–4, Harry the first president to see a game on Independence Day. The next day, aware that this was likely his final game in office, he stayed for each pitch. It was worth his wait: Senators 4, Red Sox 3.

Meantime, the greatest baseball student to be First Lady since Grace Coolidge watched, scored, and listened to as many games as possible even before her favorite spot was completed in 1948—the second-floor Truman Balcony, overlooking the South Lawn of the White House. "The boss is the real fan," Harry said of his tomboy crush, having met Bess in Sunday School, begun carrying her books to school, been wowed by her golden locks, blue eyes, and ability to whistle through her teeth—and seen her play baseball as a child with her brothers and their friends, the sole girl on an all-boys team.

Bess's childhood position was third base—baseball's "hot corner," perhaps an augury of her husband's fiery rhetoric. As First Lady, Mrs. Truman often went to Griffith Stadium on her own or with Margaret and/or friends, using her scorebook every game. A picture shows her casting a fan ballot for the annual All-Star Game. In 1947 Bess began appointment baseball hearing and viewing the lead voice of Senators wireless and television in the postwar capital—a navy veteran, Duke University Phi Beta Kappa, and the nation's first TV sportscaster. Each season Bob Wolff strove to keep the Nats from being the Atlantis of the American League.

From 1947 to 1960 Wolff's baseball tenure in the capital coincided with the rest of Truman's and all of Eisenhower's presidencies. Each Opening Day a select audience, including White House, navy, army, and other federal officials, followed him by radio, often aired across the land. Once a letter arrived from the Federal Bureau of Investigation. Not knowing whether to open or return to sender, Bob gambled. It was a fan missive from FBI director J. Edgar Hoover. By contrast, an army colonel called him the morning after one Opening Day seeking a more dubious kind of praise.

"Bob, yesterday, third inning, foul behind the first-base dugout," the colonel said. Wolff knew what lay ahead. "I made that catch," the colonel said, wanting Bob to acknowledge him on air. "Tell you what," said the Senators play-by-play man. "Keep me posted on your future baseball exploits." The man never called again.

Wolff's Opening Day record was 8-6, improbable given the Nationals' normal blunderbuss on the field. "With everyone watching," he gulped, "I couldn't afford a muff." Before the game players stood near the presidential box, hustling for the first-ball lob. Invariably Bob asked his audience, "Which player will get it?" feeling pressure "like the president's to throw a strike."

"A rare win," Wolff recalled, led to this first-day on-air toast: "To the Senators! Amazing! *Washington leads the league!*" Mostly the Senators were so bad that Bob is alleged to have omitted saying who was ahead—his team or the opposition. "I didn't need to," he said, tongue in cheek. "Folks tuning in heard me say, '5–3,' '10–5,' '4–2.'" People already knew who was winning, and it wasn't the Senators.

Raised in New York, Wolff had hit .583 at Woodmore Academy, entered Duke on a baseball scholarship, then broken his leg as a sophomore. In a cast, he tried radio, caught the bug, and asked Duke coach Jack Coombs if he should play or talk. "I've never seen an arm or a pair of legs outlast a voice," Coombs said. In 1942, Bob graduated. A naval commission led to Harvard Business School, the Seabees, and the Solomon Islands, where, finding Navy Base Supply Corps officer procedures flawed, Wolff wrote a World War II manual revising them. Transferred to Washington, he scripted official Supply Corps books and films, then segued into media behind the mic.

In 1946 Bob became a radio host and DC's first telecaster a year after the wartime Senators almost won the pennant, "Hank Greenberg crashing a last-day 1945 homer to give Detroit the flag," he rued. Fatal was a power shortage: one Nats homer in seventy-seven home games—a modern big-league low. In 1947 Wolff began airing his team with insight and anecdote yet found it hard with the Senators to make a network splash. Finally, in 1956 Mutual radio gave him the All-Star Game and World Series: a good year to break through. Half a century later, George W. Bush disclosed his reading: "three Shakespeares and a Camus." Wolff's 1956 World Series coda may still be replayed as frequently as *King Lear* is read.

"I'll guarantee that nobody—but nobody—has left this ball park," Bob intoned of Dodgers-Yankees Game Five. "And if somebody did manage to leave early—man, he's missing the greatest! Two strikes and a ball! . . . [Dale] Mitchell waiting, stands deep, feet close together. Larsen is ready, gets the sign. Two strikes, ball one. Here comes the pitch. Strike three! A no-hitter! A perfect game for Don Larsen!"— the first and still sole Fall Classic no-no. A day later Jackie Robinson worked overtime in the tenth inning against the Bombers' Bob Turley: "[Enos] Slaughter's after it, he leaps! It's over his head against the wall! . . . Jackie Robinson is being pummeled!"—his last big-league hit scoring Brooklyn's last World Series run to give the Bums their last Classic triumph, 1–0.

Back at Griffith Stadium, Wolff worked on and off air with the local Nats Knothole Gang, "fan in the stand" interviews, and celebrity in the booth—he founded each—anything to distract from the maladroits on the field. Bob did not, unlike Truman, put down a buck or two on games he saw in person. As mentioned, poker regular Clark Griffith bonded with Harry even more than with FDR: feisty, pugnacious, and inclined to risk. In 1879 his clan had taken a covered wagon for the Oklahoma Territory, settling in Missouri. In 1886, at seventeen, Clark made $10 pitching in a game in Illinois; in 1901, with Ban Johnson, he formed the American League; in 1906, he won his 237th and last victory. Griffith later became White Sox player/manager, skippered three other teams, and owned the Senators from 1920 to his 1955 death.

Clark became as close to Wolff as he had been to Truman, the older man regarding Bob, twenty-seven when they met, like a son. Wolff prized how Griffith, "a man who meant baseball for the entire first half-century," remained unchanged from a time when culture was less cynical and coarse. At Griffith Stadium, Clark—"Griff" to friends—worked from 9 a.m. to 1 p.m., played pinochle, then shooed friends away. "All day he'd have family, groundskeepers, wall sign-makers around," said Wolff. "At 4 o'clock he wanted privacy." Alone, he heard or watched *The Lone Ranger*. Radio, then television, took Clark back to another time. TV's Lone Ranger, Clayton Moore, once sent a birthday telegram, Griff telling Wolff, "You can't imagine the memories this brings back." Cash-poor, he rarely postponed a game due to weather, sympathetic to people who traveled a long distance to watch. Self-interest factored too, Griffith one morning phoning Bob to say, "We're going on, 'cause I want to see a game."

Griff and Wolff shared the Nats' misery that loved company—also a 1949 exception to misery's rule. Washington was so starved for decent baseball that after a nine-game winning streak it held a parade down Pennsylvania Avenue as if the Senators had won a pennant. Signs read, "We'll Win Plenty with Sam Dente" and "Drink a Toast with Eddie Yost"—the regular shortstop and third baseman respectively. Bob got used to losing—and calling records *against* his team. In 1953 Mickey Mantle hit the first "tape-measure" homer at Griffith Stadium, to be described in chapter 6. In 1956 the Switcher's blast against Washington almost became the first big-league home run to leave the Big Ballpark in the Bronx.

In 2017, a month before his death at ninety-six, Bob still recalled "Mr. Griffith's" wisdom. Rain had pelted the field, leading a visiting player to bunt a few feet into a puddle. Knuckleball pitcher Mickey Haefner came in, stepping gingerly so he didn't slip, and threw late to first base. *Safe!* Irate, Griff felt Haefner should have raced to the ball irrespective of the weather. He stewed awhile, then told the press that Mickey could take his knuckler and ginger elsewhere, having just been released.

Assuming victory in what became its calamitous November 1948 election, the GOP Congress appropriated a record $100,000 for the January 1949 inaugural. Truman was glad to spend it. Divining his 1953 exit from the White House and the 1956 Broadway hit *The Most Happy Fella*, he threw out 1949's first ball with a homey cast: friend Connie Mack; Bucky Harris, in his third tenure as Senators manager; VP Alben Barkley; and Bess and Margaret. Each witnessed a very merry Truman at his most creative, again tossing the ball with his left, then right, arm.

August 29 of his second term's first year was far less cheery, the Soviets' explosion of an A-bomb starting a fall of dominoes that for Truman made 1949–53 a political no-man's land. In June 1950 he took to television to announce a "police action," a.k.a. the Korean War. Former State Department official Alger Hiss was charged with giving secret documents to the Soviet Union, found guilty of perjury, and sentenced to five years in jail. Harry called the case a "red herring." In fact, Hiss was a spy.

Who lost China to the Communists? Truman, said Republicans. George Marshall's successor as secretary of state, Dean Acheson, replied: "The Nationalist [Chinese] Armies did not have to be defeated; they disintegrated." U.S. atomic scientist Klaus Fuchs was arrested for giving the Soviets atomic secrets. "Fuchs and Acheson and Hiss and hydrogen bombs threatening outside and New Dealism eating away the vitals of the nation," scalded senator Homer Capehart. "In the name of Heaven, is this the best America can do?" United Nations commander Douglas MacArthur asked too. On March 24, 1951, he issued a statement urging Truman to attack Communist China's "coastal areas and interior bases" in the Korean War. Wanting a truce, the president refused.

MacArthur, wanting China's demise, mocked Truman in an April letter to the House GOP. It was the last straw, Harry sacking him for insubordination. Truman was burned in effigy, the American flag flown at half-staff or upside down. On April 19 MacArthur returned from abroad to give a gilt-edged speech to Congress, recalling a ballad of his youth "that proclaimed most proudly that 'old soldiers never die, they just fade away.'" Men cried in the aisles; one congressman said he had seen "the face of God"; elsewhere, response turned defiant; impeachment was in the air. A day later the Senators opened at Griffith Stadium. Truman threw out the first ball. Boos rose above the field, crashed against the wall, and wafted beyond the bleachers.

"I am sorry to reach a parting of the way with the big man in Asia," Truman wrote of MacArthur to General Eisenhower, "but he asked for it and I had to give it to him." Avenging Truman's 1948 no prisoners taken assault on Dewey, the congressional GOP went for his jugular— K1C2, shorthand for Korea, corruption, and communism. In 1952 Truman's Gallup Poll approval rating dropped to 23 percent. A case can be made that he was right on the Marshall Plan, Berlin, Korea, and MacArthur, given the presidential authority granted by the Constitution. He floundered on the personal. Ike was "a phony." Richard Nixon was a "no good lying ——." When Dewey died in 1971, Truman refused even to issue a condolence.

Trenching himself in fiat, Harry's view of politics was unforgiving and unself-conscious. Of daughter Margaret's debut as a professional singer at Constitutional Hall, the *Washington Post* music critic wrote that she "communicates almost nothing of the music." Truman hit the roof. "Someday I hope to meet you," he wrote in a letter. "You'll need a new nose, a lot of beefsteak for black eyes, and perhaps a supporter below."

Equanimity surfaced as the street fighter left office. "I have tried my best to give the Nation everything I have in me," Harry said. "There are a great many people—I suppose a million in this country—who could have done the job better than I did it. But I had the job and I had to do it." The political statesman, not partisan, was more attractive, then and now. That was especially true as the Trumans returned to a land and people from whose character and codes they had never wandered far away.

On April 12, 1955, the former Philadelphia Athletics, having moved to Kansas City, opened their first season at Municipal Stadium: A's 6, Tigers 2, before a standing-room crowd of 32,844. Flanked by franchise parent Connie Mack, Truman tossed the transplanted team's first ball in Missouri's first AL opener. Pitchers loved the A's sprawling new home. Local chroniclers did also, the ex–ash heap and swimming hole frog pond having opened in 1923 as Muehlebach Field, been renamed Ruppert Stadium in 1937 and Blues Stadium in 1943, and housed the Negro League Kansas City Monarchs and AA Blues through 1950 and 1954 respectively.

"For years we had a great Negro League tradition and Yankees farm club," said Kansas City Royals 1969– announcer Denny Matthews. In 1945 Del Webb and Dan Topping bought the Yankees. In the early 1950s *Kansas City Star* sports editor Ernie Mehl persuaded Blues owner Arnold Johnson that the city merited a big-league team. Johnson, owning Blues Stadium and Yankee Stadium, bought the A's from Mack in November 1954 and moved them from Philly, Webb and Topping greasing the league's okay. Kansas City bought Blues Stadium, renamed it Municipal, and leased it back to the new A's owner. In twenty-two weeks the city rebuilt and double-decked the park to a capacity of 30,611.

Less than a month after the A's debut, on May 8, Harry's seventy-first birthday, the Truman Library and Museum in Independence, an hour away, broke ground. Mrs. Truman dusted off her scorebook for Missouri's 1955 first-year team. It placed sixth (in thirteen years the Athletics never made the first division) while luring 1,393,054 (quadrupling the total of their last year in the East). In 1956 attendance barely hit one million for the final time. Earlier Bess had attended a game at Yankee Stadium, by coincidence seated three rows in back of former First Lady Grace Coolidge. All decade Johnson kept trading fine players to his old Yankees benefactor who then starred in the

Bronx—Art Ditmar, Bobby Shantz, Ralph Terry, Roger Maris. The relationship soon resembled its former vassal state—Major League Kansas City still the Stripes' valet.

In December 1960 Chicago insurance broker Charles O. Finley bought the A's. Cruel and stingy, he nonetheless grasped baseball like a farmer senses rain. Catfish Hunter and John "Blue Moon" Odom got a bonus. Bert Campaneris arrived from Venezuela. Sal Bando, Reggie Jackson, and Rick Monday launched free agency. "Charlie was his own scouting system," said Monday, keying a 1972–74 title dynasty in Oakland, the A's moving again in 1968. In 1963 the Trumans left Independence on Opening Day to sit with Finley and his wife, the men wearing ten-gallon hats vaunting the A's new color scheme of Kelly green and gold—each an iconoclast, although Harry out of Charlie's league. Finley even built a children's zoo with a mule named Charlie O and monkeys that ate Vodka-soaked oranges fed them by Tigers pitchers, likely based on the notion that A's ineptitude was best viewed through a bottle.

While health allowed, the Trumans frequented the Athletics and Cardinals in person, Harry saying memorably, "May the sun never set on American baseball." Regularly Bess turned to the A's four-state radio and TV network. After the Truman Library opened in 1957, a visitor arrived one day from Washington. To dent boredom on Senators road trips, Bob Wolff made a list of household names he wanted to meet in different places across the country. In Kansas City, he phoned Truman out of the blue. "We hadn't talked at length when he was president," Bob said, "but now that he was out of office, lived in Missouri, and was at his library a lot, he had much more time to talk."

"What was he up to date on?" I asked.

"What *wasn't* he?" Wolff laughed. "He talked politics, partisan, but in a good-natured way." Yearly he kept up with his true interest, books, becoming probably our best-read president. Truman's private collection, acquired since boyhood, showed why historian Stephen Ambrose termed reading presidential biographies "the best possible training a . . . [would-be] president can have." America's last president to lack a college degree substituted a library for a classroom, the volume of Truman's life-long love revealed by the sheer number of books catalogued—more than thirty thousand, the most of any president. Countless other thousands fill bookcases not catalogued.

Married in 1919, Harry and Bess lived in the same fourteen-room house until each died, in 1972 and 1982 respectively. HST's later life passed quietly, an exception 1964, when, turning eighty, Truman returned to Washington for a week of reunion and farewell. A great admirer, president Lyndon Johnson, attended a dinner in Truman's honor, as did "about 300 other good friends," Harry wrote in the *Saturday Evening Post*. "The greatest event was my return to the Senate to listen to the nice things twenty-seven different senators—Republicans as well as Democrats—had to say about me. When they finished, I found that a response simply wasn't in me—and it's a rare day when I can't talk." The *Congressional Record* for May 8, 1964, recorded Truman's response: "Thank you. If I have many more happy birthdays I shall never have another one like this."

Truman rightfully took pride in his visit to the U.S. Senate: the first time a former American president had appeared on the floor as a participating member, as provided under a resolution passed the prior year. He addressed history—the real thing never got old—and old age, with Harry an oxymoron. "All my life I've been relatively free from worry, and maybe that's the best formula for long life," Truman said. "Long ago I learned to gather all the facts and the best opinions, then to make my decision. If I made a wrong decision, I made another one to correct it. But a man can nag himself to death with regrets and self-doubts. I've been one of the worst customers the sleeping-pill manufacturers ever had."

The Truman Library echoes Harry's homily: get the facts, be objective in your decision, let nothing cow you, move on. The edifice, a six-hundred-foot-long structure, overlooks U.S. Highway 24. Inside, near a reproduction of the White House office, is an auditorium where Truman met with and was quizzed by mostly children of pre-voting age. Surprising some adults who knew him as a partisan, the former president vaunted old-world grace. He came almost every working day, prepared speeches, answered letters, welcomed guests, and saw old friends. A museum staffer would call Truman in a meeting and say, "'Some kids are here, and they want you to speak to them.' No problem. He spoke to them always with the same message—'Study your history.'"

By now, Truman had arguably become America's greatest twentieth-century example of studying, then making, history. Perhaps his proudest library artifact was a framed map of the 1948 whistle-stop campaign: 31,739 miles and 355 speeches oozing "Give 'em Hell." Here also hung a framed letter of December 19, 1962, from Herbert Hoover, with whom Truman had developed a heartfelt friendship. It refers in part to Hoover's perceived treatment by a third president, Franklin Roosevelt. "Yours has been a friendship which has reached deeper into my life than you know," Hoover's unsolicited letter began. It continues:

> I gave up a successful profession in 1914 to enter public service. I served through the First World War and after for a total of about 18 years.
>
> When the attack on Pearl Harbor came, I at once supported the President and offered to serve in any useful capacity. Because of my varied experience during the First World War [helping to save millions from starvation], I thought my services might again be useful; however, there was no response. . . . When you came to the White House within a month you opened the door to me to the only profession I knew, public service, and you undid some disgraceful action that had been taken in the prior years. I am deeply grateful.

Truman reciprocated, one small-town boy to another. In his three hundredth news conference as president, Harry quoted an epitaph in the cemetery at Tombstone, Arizona. "It says: 'Here lies Jack Williams. He done his damnedest.'" More than most, Truman's damnedest was enough.

Like Hoover, Bess Truman heard and/or watched an extraordinary period of immediate postwar baseball—a last-weekend tussle for the AL pennant in 1949, a last-weekend duel for the NL title in 1950, and the towering "Shot Heard 'Round the World" on October 3, 1951. The density of coverage reflected the intensity of feeling. It almost always does.

October 1948. Truman's solitary campaign rolls on. In New York, laughter fills the press room if not in the way Yankees officials hoped. Apparently the team has hired a comic as manager. Baseball's gold standard is being laughed *at*, not *with*. Only twice in nine big-league years has Casey Stengel placed even fifth. The ex-NL manager now explains having seemed a buffoon. Clowning around is all right in the second division, he says. "But you don't have to always leave them laughing when you're up there—and I mean to be up there." Casey was, managing the Stripes through 1960, coining the language "Stengelese," and becoming baseball's dominant 1950s character.

In Ernest Hemingway's *The Old Man and the Sea*, Santiago says to Manolin, "Have faith in the Yankees, my son. Think of the great DiMaggio." On April 10, 1949, Joe limped off a Texas field after three innings of an exhibition. The great DiMaggio—with a heel spur; he could barely walk—missed the season's first sixty-five games. In late June the Red Sox and Yankees gathered for a three-game series at Fenway Park. Joe, last having faced real pitching in 1948, hoped for a loud foul. Instead he crashed a first-game homer. Next day DiMag twice went deep. The Yanks then swept the series. No. 5 made *Life* magazine's cover. The race seesawed, Boston finally taking a one-game edge. Ahead: in the Bronx, a two-match last weekend. Angst hung like cicadas on a screen.

The penultimate game was Saturday, October 1, Joe DiMaggio Day, the Yankee Clipper telling 69,551, "I'd like to thank God for making me a Yankee." The Red Sox built a 4–0 lead, New York scoring twice in the fourth, then fifth, inning. Johnny Lindell's homer broke the tie: Yanks, 5–4. In Sunday's pennant-deciding final before 68,055, Phil Rizzuto's first-inning leadoff drive bounced like Silly Putty in the left-field corner for a triple, Tommy Henrich's grounder plating the first run. In the eighth inning, the Bombers ahead, 2–0, Jerry Coleman batted with the bases full. "A little blooper into short right field!" Mel Allen roared. "[Al] Zarilla comes fast and he can't get it!" Three runs scored, the frame ending 5–0. A ninth-inning Sox three-spot teased; final, Stripes 5–3.

Later the sore rubbed raw. "[Ted] Williams never forgot that eighth—two [*sic*] guys get on and I knock 'em in," Coleman said, adding that The Kid never stopped fuming. "What got him were all [the Boston] superstars, and little Phil and I beat him. I said, 'Scooter, we're carrying this club, it's just that nobody knows it.'"

Before 1950 ended, even those not immersed in baseball knew how that season's Phillies, their sole prior flag thirty-five years old, had become the Whiz Kids, the starting lineup an average age of twenty-six. By early September they topped the Dodgers by nine games. With ten days left, the lead was seven and a half and shrinking. Series tickets were printed, even as Brooklyn surged. The National Guard called up Phils starting pitcher Curt Simmons, making Robin Roberts start thrice in the last five games. On Saturday, September 30, the Quakers trekked to Flatbush, the Bums needing to win two games to force a best-of-three NL playoff. Would Philly youth serve or be served?

That afternoon Brooklyn won a 7–3 opener. On Sunday the Phils led, 1–0, when Pee Wee Reese lashed a drive in the sixth inning that stuck on the right-field wall ledge as he completed an inside-the-park game-tying homer. In the ninth inning two Dodgers reached base leading off. Duke Snider then hit a "line drive to center field," reported Phillies voice Gene Kelly. Fielding it, Richie Ashburn "thr[ew] from center" toward the potential winning run. "He is . . . *out!* A beautiful throw by Ashburn!" Next Roberts got Carl Furillo and Gil Hodges with the bases full—the inning painful to hear or watch, impossible not to. The Whiz Kids' tenth inning began with Roberts's hit. Eddie Waitkus singled, and Ashburn made out, bringing Dick Sisler up, who hit deep to left field. "Moving back, [Cal] Abrams, way, way back, he can't get it!" Kelly called. "*It's a home run! A home run for Dick Sisler!* The Phillies lead, 4 to 1. One out and Dick gets an opposite-field homer! . . . Pandemonium is unloosed at Ebbets Field!"

Another half-inning put Philly on the eve of a wholly upside-down event. Its prior frame of reference had starred Murphy's Law: if things could go wrong, they would. Now Dodgers reserve Tommy Brown swung at a bottom-of-the-tenth-inning pitch. "[Lofted] first-base side!

Waitkus under it! The Phils win the pennant!" In Center City, along the Main Line, in nearby states, many viewed store window TV. "With afternoon games, life stopped," Kelly said. More heard by radio, like a chain letter passed pitch by pitch. World Series coverage matched the wireless's unbeaten champion against television's new kid on the block. CBS's Fall Classic telecast west to Omaha; thirty-eight million watched. Most of America still preferred radio, Mutual telling how New York ran the Series table. It is unknown which medium Bess Truman used to follow. It is certain that she did.

This amazing postwar interregnum of theater peaked in 1951. The Giants and Dodgers were scheduled to play each other twenty-two times, radio and TV coursing baseball's greatest rivalry through New York. In April Douglas MacArthur invaded Flatbush. "I have been told," said the general, recently axed by Truman, "that one hasn't really lived until he has been to Ebbets Field." He became a regular, although Brooklyn was 0-13 when America's then most popular man visited home and away. On August 11 the Dodgers led by thirteen and a half games. What happened next wrote wonderwork. By September 20 the Giants trailed by six games with seven left. Urban myth claims that Brooklyn folded. In fact, said Bums voice Vin Scully, then twenty-three and living with his parents, "The Dodgers finished well enough [24-20], but we recall the end"—a playoff miracle capping the Giants' 37-7 *finis*. The Dodgers-Giants playoff became the then most widely covered event in radio and television history.

The best-of-three opus began at Ebbets Field: Giants, 3–1. Game Two changed place (Coogan's Bluff) and score (Bums, 10–0). The Polo Grounds also hosted the timeless next-day Game Three. Bobby Thomson batted at 3:58 p.m.: the Dodgers ahead, 4–2, home half of the ninth inning. For decades any red-blooded U.S. schoolboy knew the script. Brooklyn reliever Ralph Branca threw a two-on, one-out pitch. "There's a long drive!" began Giants voice Russ Hodges. "It's going to be, I believe! . . . The Giants win the pennant! [5–4] The Giants win the pennant! The Giants win the pennant! The Giants win the pennant! Bobby Thomson hits into the lower deck of the left-field stands!

The Giants win the pennant! And they're going crazy! They are going crazy! Oh-oh!" The bulletin spread instantly, invading the nearest bar, bowling alley, a diner, even library, where some had retreated for study or inner peace.

At the Polo Grounds confetti swirled like snow. The Dodgers staggered to their clubhouse, less hurt than numb. A picture by Brooklyn team photographer Barney Stein showed Branca, on his stool, disbelieving, stunned. Meanwhile, Hodges ate noise thick enough to chew. "I don't believe it!" Russ yelped. "I do not believe it! Bobby Thomson hit a line drive into the lower deck of the left-field stands, and the whole place is going crazy!" The Giants were "picking Bobby Thomson up and carrying him off the field!"

Two-thirds of a century later, Thomson's Rock of Ages blast remains arguably baseball's greatest moment. Dodgers-Giants was at high meridian. Ours was the world's postwar colossus. Possibly America never believed more totally in itself. Perhaps baseball never meant more to America. It is not hard to see why.

SIX

"From the Heart of America"

Dwight D. Eisenhower, 1953–1961

For most of the twentieth century Hollywood's existential memory involved heroes—stoic but not unfeeling, more similar to than different from their country, sharing its joys, worries, and confessions of the heart. In 1952 Truman's successor, Dwight David Eisenhower, relying less on rhetoric than such a grasp, was elected—born in Texas, raised in Kansas, rural and lower middle class, Protestant, and conservative, as formal as a West Point drill yet informal enough to make golf a national belly laugh—the greatest military hero of America's greatest war. Leaving office at seventy, Eisenhower was then our oldest president.

As chapter 7 will discuss, Ike was succeeded by John Fitzgerald Kennedy, an elegant, liberal, Harvard-educated, distinctly urban man, our first Catholic and youngest elected president at forty-three: imagery still alight of sailing off Cape Cod, touch football at Hyannis Port, and a clan large enough to staff both teams. Ike, then JFK, governed America in 1953–61 and 1961–63 respectively. Each had a different concept of the presidency, how it could be used, and what it meant around the world. Both were similar in the values that endure.

First, each loved America—totally and unashamedly—and believed in American exceptionalism—proudly and unapologetically. Both had served in war and peace, presiding over a golden time, based on fact, not nostalgia. A 1954 Gallup Poll reported that 84 percent of all Americans could not name *one* thing Ike had done wrong in his first near-ly two years as president. Kennedy was a Good War hero, aides proud of wearing a button, PT-109, named for his boat in the Pacific theater. Ike oversaw Operation Overlord, the D-Day Allied assault at Norman-dy to rescue the European continent: the seminal day of the twenti-eth century. Both would have deemed political correctness—a willful diminution of one's own country—to be unpatriotic, even warped.

Ike grew up to be a West Point football running back, class of '15, and the only man trained as a speech*writer* (for Douglas MacArthur) before becoming POTUS (President of the United States). Kennedy was much better at *giving* speeches. A final tie was the reverence Ameri-ca had for their office and its occupant. I was weaned on Eisenhower, raised in a GOP family with Democratic friends who—this was true across the land—respected the Republican five-star general. Similar-ly, my family was crushed when Kennedy edged Ike's vice president, Richard Nixon, in the 1960 election, but gave him a chance, thought JFK growing as a person and in office.

When Eisenhower or Kennedy went abroad, they were wildly cheered as the blue sky of America, Democrats here proud of a GOP president, and vice versa. *Our country mattered most.* Growing up in Iowa, TIME magazine columnist Hugh Sidey later evoked nation-first among the people of rural and small-town, which was Ike's, America. "They come from different places, with a common goal," he wrote. "They want to give birth and grow and love and laugh and die, bonded and sustained by the land, which is the oldest way of life Americans know."

For more than two centuries the presidency has written much of their and the rest of America's daybook. Churchill was said to have jibed, "An empty cab drove up and [political foil] Clement Attlee got out." The U.S. president most cardinal to my 1950s youth was not an empty cab. In 1955, when I was four, 60 percent of *Democrats*, according to Gal-lup, wanted *Ike* as their 1956 nominee. "Everybody ought to be happy every day," Eisenhower said. "Play hard, have fun doing it, and despise wickedness"—what his mother had taught him growing up. Ike's Main Street persona—a day at the ballpark, steak in the backyard, Sunday in a pew, family all around—almost *became* the 1950s. Many miss it still.

The first extended act of political TV theater I recall was Eisenhower at the 1960 GOP convention in Chicago, deplaning, waving in a confetti motorcade, later speaking. In liberal writer Richard Cohen's words, Ike was "a buoyant and humane man, encircled by a captivating grin." You see Ike's grin at his library and museum, opening at Abilene in 1954. Twelve years later a Place of Meditation chapel was dedicated on its campus. When Eisenhower died in March 1969, he was buried with his first-born son, Doud Dwight, who had died at age three of scarlet fever. Wife Mamie joined them in 1979.

Eventually Stephen Ambrose became Ike's closest biographer, calling him "a great and good man" as well as president, who linked peace and prosperity, the Interstate Highway System, St. Lawrence Seaway, the first civil rights bill in eighty-two years, and domestic unity. Another historian, Theodore H. White, beamed, "Never did the sun shine fairer across a great Nation than it did in the age of Eisenhower." At the same time, we often forget its cloud of being slow to enter space and even slower to forcefully address race.

America's forty-first president, George H. W. Bush (Bush 41) often spoke of predecessors he admired. They included Lincoln, who abolished slavery and saved the Union; Theodore Roosevelt, the conserver of lands and wildlife for unborn generations; and the U.S. Military Academy graduate who became general of the army, chief of the Allied Expeditionary Force, president of Columbia University, first Supreme Commander of the North American Treaty Organization (NATO), and thirty-fourth president. Ike became to Bush what Andrew Jackson was to Truman, Truman to Gerald Ford, and FDR to Ronald Reagan—a presidential frame of reference.

Eisenhower governed as president, not partisan, through text of a plaque on his Oval Office desk: "Gently in manner, strong in deed." He was not, however, a benign father knew best. Reserved, Ike was mercurial. Only intimates saw his temper. Most despair over separation or death. Eisenhower exploded over a lousy seven iron. He could be cold. Journalist Hedley Donovan shocked people by terming him smarter than two-time Democratic nominee Adlai Stevenson but not as nice. Nixon recalled how general Bedell Smith, Ike's wartime chief of staff, tearfully told him, "I was only Ike's prat boy. Ike always had to a have a prat boy." It didn't matter. Leaders can be loved in their own countries or others. Why was Ike loved *globally* as America's *sine qua non*?

Publicly he prized good will. At home he felt that "the road to success must be down the middle." Its Wall Street wing supplied most of the GOP money. The Main Street wing supplied most of the party's votes. Both liked Ike. Having dispatched Hitler, he left political quibbling to mortals. Abroad, knowing war, Eisenhower hated it, launching the age of summitry at Geneva in 1955. He was also beloved for manifesting the age and place, as Ike's favorite movie showed—*Angels in the Outfield*, released in 1951, set on location in Pittsburgh, mainly Forbes Field, the Pirates' idyll of a suburban park.

Starring Paul Douglas as Aloyius X. "Guffy" McGovern, the Pirates foul-mouthed skipper, and Janet Leigh, Keenan Wynn, and the great Spring Byington, *Angels* showed McGovern hearing an angel's voice, intoned by James Whitmore, vowing to help the Bucs if Guffy stops profaning. It embodied 1950s escapism, like Ike's Zane Grey novels, TV Westerns, and his favorite band, Fred Waring and the Pennsylvanians. Eisenhower loved to fish, hunt, and golf, installing a putting green outside the Oval Office. His place in forging golf's middle-class lure is still not grasped more than half a century later.

In 1953 Ike missed the Senators' opener to play at the famed Augusta National Golf Club. Luckily for him, the game was rained out. Knocked in print for ignoring the presidential first pitch, Eisenhower scurried back to DC for the next day's rescheduled opener, so panned—said TSN, "He has aroused an outcry"—that the only other opener he missed was while out of the country in 1959. Nixon subbed, prompting Truman to send a telegram to Senators owner Calvin Griffith: BEST OF LUCK TO YOU ON OPENING DAY AND EVERY DAY. WATCH OUT FOR THAT NIXON. DON'T LET HIM THROW YOU A CURVE. YOUR FRIEND, HARRY TRUMAN. For Eisenhower, the whole episode was a rare misstep.

Finally, Ike was beloved because he behaved as a president should. Other men had a splendid resume running for president—but it didn't include "he preserved civilization." Eisenhower's did. In a 1945 ceremony in Britain's ancient Guildhall, he was made a "Freeman of the

City of London." Ike gave a warm, moving, plain as the plains speech, mesmerizing the British, whom he had come to love. "I am not a native of this land. I come from the heart of America," he said. "To those people I am proud to belong." To preserve liberty, Eisenhower said, "a Londoner will fight. So will a citizen of Abilene." Today the only streets in London named for an American are those for FDR—and Ike.

Eisenhower's, JFK's, and their presidencies' relationship with baseball began in a time of the Salk vaccine, 3-D film, Marilyn Monroe's movie *Niagara*, and later Chubby Checker's "The Twist." It ended on a Friday afternoon in Texas. To this day, something remains, if but a vague recollection, of circa 1953–63's sober poise. Some wrongly tar the age as pale and dull. In fact, its baseball mimed Ronald Reagan's later snapshot of America: "hopeful, big-hearted, idealistic, daring, decent, and [finally, after Jackie Robinson, at least starting to be] fair."

Baseball was without question the national sport: no other game was close. Even strangers traded big-league talk, increasingly fixated on an opiate some jeeringly called an idiot box. In 1950 only four million U.S. homes owned at least one TV set. By 1960 forty-four million homes—88 percent of families—did. "For the first time," Theodore White said, "it was possible to tell a foreigner what Americans do after dinner. . . . They watch television." Ahead lay slow motion, stop-action, and instant replay. At the time, television's presence was enough.

By the late 1940s New York's WPIX and WOR put base runner and close-up cameras near each dugout and above first and third base. Color TV began August 11, 1951: Brooklyn at Braves Field on WCBS New York. The 1952 World Series sired the split-screen: left side, the Yankees' Vic Raschi, pitching; right side, the Dodgers' Pee Wee Reese, off first base. Soon Charles P. Ginsburg of Ampex developed videotape, allowing replay. Each year the screen turned more viewer-friendly. WGN Chicago began using a camera beyond the outfield fence to show each pitch to the plate—the "center-field" shot. "A guy at a school prep game, seeing the scoreboard, thought, 'It'll focus the batter, pitcher, catcher, and ump,'" said Second City voice Jack Brickhouse. WPIX and NBC soon adopted it, Yanks GM George

Weiss raging, "The other team'll steal our signs. Worse, it's showing too much. People'll stay at home."

Many had on April 17, 1953, only 4,206 seeing the Bombers bop the Senators, 7–3, in a non-televised game at Griffith Stadium. Those there also saw baseball's first "tape-measure" homer. "Mantle swings [off Chuck Stobbs].... There's a tremendous drive going into deep left field!" said Mel Allen, recreating. "It's going, going, it's going over the bleachers and over the sign atop the bleachers into the yards of hous-es across the street!"—Perry L. Cool's at 434 Oakdale Street. "It's got to be one of the longest home runs I've ever seen hit! How about that!" Lacking a tape measure, Yankees publicist Arthur "Red" Patterson be-gan walking off the blast, estimating how far the ball went—about 391 feet to the bleachers; another 69 to the outer wall; then, bonking the sixty-foot-high National Bohemian Beer scoreboard, 105 feet across Fifth Street: 565 feet total. National Bo painted an "X" where the ball hit the board. Irked, Clark Griffith erased it.

That fall the 1953 Yankees neared their fifth straight World Series ti-tle, some musing that players might resent skipper Casey Stengel us-ing several—"platooning"—at one position. Hank Bauer would have none of it, saying, "When you get that World Series check every No-vember, you don't want to leave. There were no Yankees saying play me or trade me." Leading Brooklyn in games, 3–2, and in the sixth game, 3–1, the Stripes survived Brooklyn's Carl Furillo's score-tying ninth-inning homer, which preceded Billy Martin's last-of-the-frame Series-winning hit.

From 1951 to 1956 the Yanks five times made the Classic, Cleveland interrupting only in 1954—the season Douglass Wallop aptly wrote the fictional *The Year the Yankees Lost the Pennant*. That September 12, before 86,563, the Tribe, ending the year a then AL best-ever 111-43, twice spanked Stengel at its lakeside bowl. The Bombers' train re-treated to Manhattan via Upstate New York, Casey heckled by drunks at each station stop.

"Stengel never forgot it to the last day of his life," said Red Patter-son of the Perfessor. Publicly the manager kept calm, playing Mantle and Yogi Berra at third base and shortstop respectively, the last day of the season. "My power lineup," Casey smirked, confident that Yankees power would reemerge next spring.

In addition to the tape measure, Chuck Stobbs also threw baseball's longest wild pitch, said the Senators' Bob Wolff. It wildly hopped, leapfrogged Griffith's backstop screen, landed in a concession stand, and spilled mustard on a fan. Three years later, on May 30, 1956, the switch-hitting Mantle—DiMaggio's center-field successor, a golden-haired drop-dead blue-eyed handsome man—almost hit a fair ball out of Yankee Stadium against the Nats' Pedro Ramos, rising when it hit the right-field copper frieze above the third deck. "Otherwise," Wolff said, "it would have been the first big-league ball to leave the park." Twelve days earlier the Switcher homered a record third time left- and right-handed in a game. Said Berra, "I think you'd call him *amphibious*."

Mantle spoke to and for much of a generation—the Baby Boomers, born between 1946 and 1964—who shared Teresa Brewer's song, "I Love Mickey." His 536 home runs, twenty All-Star teams, and twelve World Series peaked with 52 homers, 130 RBIS, and a .353 average in 1956. Bombers Hall of Fame catcher Bill Dickey later dubbed No. 7 "healthy, the best [he] ever saw": "Who else could drag a bunt, then hit a 600-foot homer?" Mantle could reach first base in just over three seconds but swung to go yard. His father had died young. Thinking he would too, Mickey, who had osteomyelitis, a degenerative bone disease, caroused, said Dickey, a Yankees coach. "But that's not what broke him down. It came from Mantle pushing himself so hard on the field."

Ike empathized both with Mantle's drive and pain, having found it hard to stay healthy in high school—in particular, a freshman class knee injury—yet making his baseball team as a senior and becoming president of the Abilene High School Athletic Association. Graduating in 1909, Dwight then made a deal. In 1911 brother Edgar attended the University of Michigan, Ike working in a creamery to help him. A year later Edgar was to bankroll Dwight, at that or another college. Instead in 1911 Eisenhower won a tuition-free appointment to the U.S. Military Academy, ending Edgar's obligation and changing the future president's life.

Albeit briefly, Ike continued athletically at West Point where in high school he left off. In freshman baseball, mates included Omar Bradley, another World War II general. Later the varsity team rejected him, Eisenhower admitting that "not making the baseball team at West Point was one of the greatest disappointments of [his] life, maybe the greatest." He turned to football, where as a right end in high school the Kansan had been named by the *New York Times* "one of the most promising backs in Eastern football," injury not yet a permanent disabler. In November 1912 Army opposed the Carlisle Indian School, its legendary Jim Thorpe having won that year's individual competition in the Summer Olympic decathlon and pentathlon. The Cadets fell to Carlisle, 27–6, then played Tufts, a lineman again wrenching Eisenhower's knee. A horseback riding accident then *again* damaged it, ending football and pivoting Ike toward golf.

In 1945 the ballplayer-turned-spectator returned from Europe, having written to George Marshall, the army chief of staff: "I have no general suggestions . . . regarding [my] entire trip, but secretly I hope that New York has that ball game." Marshall agreed. As Eisenhower hoped, he rode into the Polo Grounds, where he met Giants and Braves skippers Mel Ott and Bob Coleman respectively before their regularly scheduled big-league game. Ott unexpectedly asked if "it was true that [Ike] had once played semi-pro baseball," wrote the *Times*.

"The general admitted that as a youth he had done so, under the assumed name of Wilson [the brand name of Ike's glove]," the paper continued. In another story it added that Eisenhower told the two managers what he termed "the one secret of [his] life": as a student, Ike had played professional ball in the Kansas State League, bridging as many did the early-century income gulf between the lower working and/or middle class and the upper class. He was playing ball for cash, not to make it a career, and told the Associated Press: "I wanted to go to college that fall, and we didn't have much money. I took any job that offered me more money, because I needed money. But I wasn't a very good center fielder, and didn't do too well at it." At that point he stopped talking. It was wise that he did.

Ike had more to worry about than his quality of play. Like now, the National Collegiate Athletic Association (NCAA) barred anyone from staining amateur status by having played professionally—rules so thorough that even Thorpe, arguably the greatest athlete of all time, was stripped of his Olympic medals for playing baseball in the 1909–10 Eastern Carolina League. Did Thorpe know its rules? Did Ike? "No student shall represent a college or university in any intercollegiate game," read the NCAA rule, "who has at any time received, either directly or indirectly, money, or any other consideration . . . [or] has competed for any prize against a professional." Student athletes also had to complete an eligibility card with fifteen questions about playing professionally. On its bottom they had to sign a pledge: "On my honor I state that the above answers contain the whole truth, without any mental reservations."

Without question Ike had been a professional. Moreover, he may have denied it on a West Point application, ironic for one so lauded for his integrity. Worse, signing the pledge would have been a lie, violating the West Point honor code. Eisenhower would have been expelled. Yet the code was not finalized until 1920, five years after he graduated. Ike lived with this confusion for the last fifty years of his life—hero of the civilized globe, two-time landslide president, author of the best-selling book *Crusade in Europe*, subject of the mantra "I Like Ike," Gallup's Most Admired American during and after World War II, even in 1968, his last full year alive. Eisenhower never forgot the issue, as a memo among presidential papers at his library (written by an aide, Colonel Robert Schulz) shows: "As of August 1961, DDE [Ike, author] indicated inquiries should not be answered concerning his participation in professional baseball—as it would necessarily become too complicated."

Ike often told of how he and a young friend sat on a Midwest river bank one summer afternoon and talked of what some day they'd like to be. Ike as a poor boy who made good validated the American Dream. He enjoyed baseball, keeping score, rising to dispute a play, or cheering a hit-and-run as well as a triple up the alley; Ike knew the game's fine points better than, for instance, FDR. He also liked its camaraderie, as Roosevelt had at Groton and as observed in the acknowledgments section of this book. In 1957 Eisenhower phoned the Nationals owner to say, "Calvin [Griffith], the wife is away. How about me coming to the ball game?"

Each Opening Day Ike played a role he was good at and liked: baseball's avuncular and egalitarian host. One April outfielder Jim Piersall, whose life already included mental breakdown, shock treatment, isolation, and resilience if not recovery, watched the president's toss before giving Ike another ball. "Mr. President," he said, "would you sign *this* ball while those idiots scramble for *that* one?" About this time Eisenhower told a friend, "[As a boy] I wanted to be a real Major League baseball player, a genuine professional like Honus Wagner. My friend said that he'd like to be president of the United States." Neither got his wish.

In 1953 the would-have-been big-leaguer-turned-new-president held a White House lunch for athletes, including Joe DiMaggio, Lefty Grove, Tris Speaker, and ex-Senator Sam Rice. From then through 1960, his Senators teams won 506 games, lost 724, never made the first division, and ended a collective 278½ games behind first place. It was baseball, but what kind? Few Nats failed more grandly than utility infielder Herbie Plews. Some said Plews's license plate should read, "E-4–5–6." Others charged he had no license to play. One day hits and errors ricocheted off Herbie's body as if he were target practice. Finally, manager Charlie Dressen left the dugout and called Plews to the mound. If Plews were removed, his ego might suffer. If he remained in the game, the team might lose. Herbie stayed in. "If there'd been a crowd," Bob Wolff mused, "it would have roared." The next batter hit to Plews, who bobbled, snatched the ball, and nipped the runner. The Senators still trailed in the ninth when Mr. Plews slayed in Washington, bombing a two-run triple. Senators win. Players sob. "Herbie Plews!" canted Wolff. "Tell me there weren't giants in the land."

In one sense, Clark Griffith had preceded 1947's big-league integration—Cleveland's Larry Doby was second to crack the black-white color line—by scouting minority players in Cuba since before World War II. The Nats '50s roster of Cuban stars Camilo Pascual and

Pedro Ramos and others like Julio Becquer, Carlos Paula, and Jose Valdivielso enhanced what there was of a franchise nucleus: Mickey Vernon, taking a second batting title in 1953; Eddie Yost, "the Walking Man," five times leading the league in walks; and Roy Sievers, team MVP by fan ballot, pacing DC in home runs and RBIS from 1955 through 1958 and the AL with 42 and 114 respectively in 1957. Another upside was the last All-Star Game at Griffith Stadium, in 1956, Vice President Nixon dedicating a statue to Clark Griffith outside the main entrance on the first-base side. Still another: the 1958 film *Damn Yankees*, using footage of Griffith, the lead character selling his soul for a Neverland Senators flag.

Wolff's aria was less commercial: "The [late 1950s] Singing Senators." Albie Pearson, Russ Kemmerer, Truman "Tex" Clevenger, Jim Lemon, and Sievers tuned melody. Howie Devron played accordion. Wolff strummed ukulele. "People liked us, anyway," he jibed. Their greatest stage was NBC's 1959 *The Today Show*. Was the age kinder, gentler? "Let's suppose I went to the Senators of today and said, 'Fellahs, you want to join me for free in a singing group?' Can you imagine? You couldn't print their answer in a book." Had the club stayed in Washington, its record book would belong to Harmon Killebrew, who ended his career with a then fifth all-time-high 573 home runs.

Killebrew joined the Senators from Fayette, Idaho, a week before turning eighteen in 1954. The phenom's power and reticence made him almost a Garbo of the game. One day Wolff hatched a scheme. "I said to Killebrew, 'I'll bring you to a father and son softball game and put you in the game as Mr. Smith. After you hit the ball ten miles, we'll say, 'That's Harmon Killebrew!' The crowd'll go wild." Wolff used the PA mike to introduce a pinch hitter—Harmon, anonymous in street garb. On Killebrew's first three swings he missed, tapped to the pitcher, then missed again, Bob growing desperate trying to explain Harmon's impotence. "Folks, the catcher tipped the bat," he explained. "Let's do that again." Washington's monument proceeded to barely tip the softball. Driving back, Wolff said, gently, "Harmon, a tip. Stick to the harder stuff."

Life magazine wanted Harmon to fixate on it too, telling Nats officials in 1959 about a planned feature. "They took adhesive tape and put it into every spot at Griffith where he'd homered," Wolff said. "Then they had a plane take a shot of where and how far the homers went." For days *Life* waited for the gentle, misnamed "Killer" to go long. On May 29 Ike came to a game on cue as Killebrew went yard. Sadly, that week Pittsburgh's Harvey Haddix hurled a twelve-inning perfect game against Milwaukee to KO the scripted cover. Perhaps the cynics were correct: if the Senators didn't have bad luck, they'd have no luck at all.

In 1956 Ike entered and exited the World Series opener through the center-field gate at Ebbets Field—the first president to appear at a Series since FDR in 1936. Eisenhower greeted each player, manager, and other officials of the Dodgers and Yankees on the field, stopping a moment to talk with each, especially Brooklyn's Gil Hodges, Roy Campanella, and Don Newcombe and New York's Yogi Berra and Enos Slaughter. Also on hand: New York governor Averell Harriman; New York City mayor Robert Wagner; former president Hoover; and the Duke of Windsor, formerly Edward VIII, the King of the United Kingdom. Game film was poignant, Ike kibitzing with Dodgers owner Walter O'Malley, who within a year, moving his team to California, reminded some of Thoreau: "Eastward I go only by force. Westward I go free." Others likened him to Hitler and Stalin.

In Game Seven Newcombe was hammered in what had become a Series rite, his coverage worse than that of Britain's former king, leaving office in 1936 for, he said, "the woman I love." Ike sympathized in a letter: "I think I know how much you wanted to win a World Series game," he wrote Newk, who never did. "I for one was pulling for you. I suggest that . . . you think of the twenty-seven [regular-season] games you won [against seven losses, with a 3.06 ERA] that were so important in bringing Brooklyn into the World Series." A year later Ike invited the Little League champions from Monterrey, Mexico, to the White House after an ABC documentary on the team.

Like the military, Eisenhower's putting, and "under God" added to the Pledge of Allegiance, the culture of the 1950s found room for announcers of a non-urban, non-elitist, non-Eastern Seaboard lilt. Convention had insisted that few would watch regular-season network TV baseball. "It was all local," said CBS Sports head Bill MacPhail. "Why would Omaha watch Red Sox–Tigers?" Dizzy Dean was why. In 1953 Ol' Diz's *Game of the Week* began on ABC each Saturday, moved to swankier CBS in 1955, and added a Sunday *Game* in 1957. To protect local coverage and attendance, baseball banned the series within fifty miles of any big-league city. Unvexed, *Game* astounded industry kingpins by luring a yearly 12 to 15 rating (one point: 1 percent of all homes with a television in America, more impressive than merely a TV in use). "More than thirty percent of the country was blacked out," said MacPhail. "In the rest, we had up to four of five sets in use!" To horsefeathers with New York or Boston. To Main Street, Ol' Diz fused Ma Kettle, Gabby Hayes, and Tennessee Ernie Ford.

At one time or another, Dean slept, ate a watermelon, and sang "Precious Memories" in the booth. He called the planet "pod-nuh"; cracked the mid-'50s Gallup Poll most admired top-ten list; and tied three hundred pounds, a string tie, and a Stetson—the whole rustic goods. "In Mid-America," said MacPhail, "watching him was an absolute religion." To media critic Ron Powers, "Dean was a mythologizing presence." In many towns businesses *literally* closed when he was "commentating." To Ol' Diz, a batter *swang*; a pitcher *throwed*; a runner *slud*. Fielders returned to their *respectable* positions. That "hitter stood *confidentially* at the plate." They had "to be my words," Dean said, "'cause no one else would have 'em."

"By the mid-1950s," said the grand stylist Lindsey Nelson, then of NBC, "Dean had passed Red Barber as baseball's biggest broadcast name except Allen," nuking English like no one had before or since. "Mel showed in the Series how baseball could work each fall. Ol' Diz was the first to show how it could work each week." Dean was an Ike-age phenomenon. Allen underplayed his voice and lilt. Broadcasting's fuel is wearability. Like Dean's, Mel's ran on charm.

Hearing Allen was to marvel at the voice—melodic, histrionic, and buoyed by unpredictability. If Mel sold fish, said critic Bud Furillo, "he could make it sound as if Puccini wrote the score." Cameramen on the roof drew an "uneven fringe of shadow." A shortstop was "an exponent of the art." Allen could make the infield fly rule seem as imposing as the Constitution—and take as long to explain it. He could also seem as artless as they come.

One day Mel spied two teenagers kissing at Yankee Stadium. "That's interesting," he said. "He's kissing her on the strikes, and she's kissing him on the balls." Colleague Phil Rizzuto shook his head. "Mel, this is just not your day." For a long time, most days were.

The childhood plowboy grew up in an Alabama Sinclair Lewis town. In 1932 he entered law school, began a five-dollar-a-week clerking job, graduated, vacationed in New York not intending to stay, did, and evolved into what *Sports Illustrated* termed "the most successful, best-known, highest-paid, most voluble figure" in sportscasting, making "How about That!" an institution. Everyone knew it—even my mother.

At one time or another Mel hosted or did play-by-play or voice-over of the Yankees (1940 through 1964), World Series (twenty-one in number), All-Star Games (twenty-four), Rose Bowls (fourteen), the *Mel Allen Sports Spot* (cbs-tv), *Monitor* (nbc Radio), and nearly three thousand Twentieth Century Fox film newsreels. Sixty million weekly heard Allen say, "This is your Movietone reporter." To Mel a home run became a "White Owl [cigar] Wallop" or a "Ballantine [beer] Blast." Many, liking the product, liked the trapping more.

The Southerner cowed New York. The Caucasian much later aired a rap hit. The Orthodox Jew wowed a predominantly Christian nation. Most fell for Mel's real life nice-guy air. Yankees sponsor Atlantic Refining Company once hyped "Red Ball Service," its theme, "Atlantic Keeps Your Car on the Go." To his death in 1996 Allen knew every word. It did not surprise, Mel having a word for any situation.

Author William Manchester once suggested that America's apogee "extended from the Korean Armistice of 1953 to the Russian *Sputnik* of 1957," the Soviets, as we shall see, stealing a step on us in space. "To those who cherished it, the 1953–57 breather would come to be remembered as an uncomplicated, golden time, mourned as lost childhoods are mourned and remembered, in nostalgia, as cloudless." Actually, it fit as well as lit the decade and its early 1960s continuum, baseball miming the mid-century's pulse in an altogether thorough way—in columnist George Will's phrase, the pastime being "perfectly congruent with an era." If America flowered soon after mid-century, so did the game.

Its heart pulsed through the "Subway Series between the Yankees and the Dodgers," said the ESPN documentary *Voices of The Game*. "The Duke of Flatbush versus No. 7. Sal the Barber Maglie and the Springfield Rifle, Vic Raschi. The Captain, Harold (Pee Wee) Reese, and the Scooter, Phil Rizzuto. Ultimately, the argument came down to the teams." As Leonard Koppett writes, "No other team generated a richer collection of memories, more closely held by so many people" than the 1950s Bums. Campy resembled Santa Claus in catching gear. The aging infield still turned doubles into slumps. Oisk, Preacher, and the Duke of Flatbush were a.k.a. Carl Erskine, Elvin Charles Roe, and Duke Snider, a center fielder so dazzling that on occasion he could eclipse Messrs. Mantle and Mays.

Entering October 1955, Brooklyn had crosshatched victory and misery: five postwar pennants but having lost a pennant or World Series the last game of each year but 1948 from 1946 to 1953. As Herbert Hoover could attest, they had dropped five straight Series to the hated Yanks—a single-team Series deficit sans peer. The Brooklyn team that finally won would knit the richest "collection of memories" of all. In 1952 director John Ford won an Oscar for the movie *The Quiet Man*. That fall 0-for-21 Gil Hodges heard a Classic leather-lung: "Here comes the quiet man!" Three years later, NBC's Vin Scully began play-by-play in the last of the fifth inning of Game Seven at Yankee Stadium, Brooklyn up, 2–0, on Gil's two RBIs. Said Vin, simply: "The Quiet Man finally made some noise."

In the sixth inning the Yankees' Billy Martin and Gil McDougald led off by reaching base safely. Yogi Berra, baseball's best clutch batter, then sliced down the left-field line. Sandy Amoros raced madly toward the spot and at the last moment "stuck out his glove hand," said McDougald, "and found that Easter egg." Amoros threw to shortstop Reese, who fired to first baseman Hodges. Double play! To starting pitcher Johnny Podres, twenty-three, who had vowed to blank the Yanks, it was "the greatest catch in the world."

Inning after inning the Dodgers' history held their borough hostage. With two out in the last of the ninth, Brooklyn held its breath. Podres threw a change-up to Elston Howard, who slapped to Reese, who threw to Hodges: Captain to Quiet Man. Time stopped on The Stadium clock—3:45 p.m., October 4, 1955. Millions said a prayer, leapt into one another's arms, or tried, tearing, not to cry. Scully uttered a timeless coda: "Ladies and gentlemen, the Brooklyn Dodgers are the champions of the world."

Today those words top a photo of Yankee Stadium that afternoon, exploding, at the entrance to Dodgers offices in Los Angeles. All winter, people asked how Scully remained so calm. "That was the happiest point of my career, because it meant everything," Vin said. "That's why I shut up when Pee Wee threw to Hodges. If I'd said another word at that very instant, I'd have broken down and cried."

Later the team bus entered the Brooklyn-Battery Tunnel. On one side Manhattan scent of winter absorbing fall. The other bared a springtime of possibility—dancing, block parties, disbelief above all. The next morning the *Times'* John Drebinger wrote: "Far into the night rang shouts of revelry in Flatbush. Brooklyn at long last has won the World Series and now let someone suggest moving the Dodgers elsewhere." In two years someone would.

That 1955–56 offseason the Yankees toured Japan, "even there," said an HBO-TV documentary, "instantly identifiable." *Sports Illustrated* dedicated its entire April 12, 1956, issue to "The Great American Game." Reading Robert Creamer, you remember life in Ike's America and how much you miss baseball's overwhelming presence and how wonderful it was. Creamer begins:

You feel this more in the North than you do in the sun country, but one day late in the winter you hear a voice over the radio. You may be driving a car through slush, with bags of groceries on the floor in front and a bunch of kids in mufflers and galoshes on the back seat. . . . Then the car radio, which you have turned on haphazardly, warms up and a familiar voice says, "Two away now. Musial down off third. Cards lead, 2–0. The pitch. It's in there! Strike one." It is the somewhat droning, somewhat nasal voice of your favorite baseball announcer, broadcasting a spring training game from Florida. Last summer you cursed him out when he failed for an inning and a half to mention the score of a game you had tuned in on late. [Now, in the slush,] you love him. His voice is the promised kiss of springtime . . . heralding the return of baseball to the land.

At that moment, Creamer states, "the baseball fan, like the crocus, pokes his head up, through the snow and starts to live again. It is hard to explain, to those who do not understand, how large a role baseball plays in the warm-weather life of the average American male." Dad playing catch with Junior, he wrote, "like the flag raising at Iwo Jima, is only a small part of the whole." Baseball's role was exponentially greater. Creamer continues:

It is something to read about, to talk about, to listen to on radio, to watch on television. It occupies an extraordinarily large part of [a fan's] time. [The average American male] listens to baseball over the radio while he works in the garden or lolls on the beach. He reads about it in the morning paper the next day. He talks about it at the office. He reads about it in the afternoon newspaper. He talks more about it that night. It does not interfere with his business or with his relations with his family or with his bowling or his church-going or his duties as a citizen. But it is always with him.

Why? Because baseball is a game of limitless dramatic possibility, an incredible melodrama, a constant theater of delight, the great American *divertissement*, a flamboyant and continuing drama bound by certain hard unities: nine innings, three outs, one pennant. Within these unities baseball presents a variety as endless as the waves of the ocean, as intricate as a fugue by Bach.

My dad taught and was in business; was a fine father, husband, and citizen; bowled; went to church; and found baseball "always with him."

Like Robert Creamer, he would have bet the Senators would win a pennant before the pastime's music died. "Think Ted Williams, Stan Musial, and Mickey Mantle," Creamer writes. "Their names tower over other sports." In the 1950s it would have taken fiction of a cosmic scale to imagine baseball's future names being challenged, let alone reduced. At no time did that seem more correct than in October 1956.

Having seen the Brooks win that Series opener in person, Ike saw Game Five of the Fall Classic, like most Americans, on NBC Television. The Dodgers had waved a last-weekend pennant, then won the first two games of the last pre-2000 Subway Series. Period footage shows Democratic presidential nominee Adlai Stevenson simultaneously wearing a Bums and a Yankees cap as New York's Don Larsen, a drinker and curfew-breaker, folded in Game Two, 13–8. On October 8 Larsen again faced Sal Maglie in Game Five. Bob Wolff's account on Mutual radio is described in chapter 5. Like 1953 and 1955, Allen and Scully divided 1956 play-by-play on NBC-TV.

In the fourth inning the Stripes' Golden Boy lashed a drive down Yankee Stadium's right-field line as if to punctuate his Triple Crown Golden Year. "There's one if it stays fair!" Allen chimed. "It is going, going, gone! Mickey Mantle achieves his third home run of the Series!" The Bombers led, 1–0, as Berra drove to left-center field. "The Duke on the run! He dives! He got it!" said Mel, granting Snider equal time. When Brooklyn batted in the fifth inning, Hodges too hit to Death Valley. "Mantle on the run! Going, going! He makes the catch! How about that!" Methodically Larsen set the Dodgers down. Only Reese went to a 3–2 count. Just three Bums neared a hit.

Succeeding Mel in the home half of the fifth inning, Scully grasped history: Yanks and Dodgers; mid-century's Grand Event; the World Series line score for Brooklyn: 0–0–0. "Can he [Larsen] do what no one . . . [in Series] history has ever done [throw a perfect game]?" Vin asked. "Overwhelming," he later described the pressure. "You remember Larsen's no-windup delivery. The skim of smoke across the field. Noise starting to build." New York added a sixth-inning 2–0 run. Scully's "heart was in [his] mouth." Allen sat, transfixed. A no-hitter's code of silence held. Vin, "younger and thoroughly intimidated, . . . followed

Mel's example," in time reversing it for all pending no-hitters through his 2016 retirement.

The MLB Network rebroadcast Larsen's game to inaugurate its 2009 birth. Watching, Vin marveled at the minimalism: "Ball one, strike one," in innings five through eight. Missing in the 1956 teleplay were instant replay, glitzy graphic, and a center-field and fan-reaction shot; "How primitive TV baseball was!" Scully said. More felicitous were the sixty-second network sponsor break and the game's two-hour, six-minute length. "Let's all take a deep breath as we go to the most dramatic ninth inning in the history of baseball," video shows Vin saying. "I'm going to sit back, light up, and hope I don't chew the cigarette to pieces."

Larsen got two out to begin the ninth. In the Yankees' dugout, Casey Stengel said, everyone became a manager. Even to the Ol' Perfessor— "I have been around so long, I can get along with anybody"—the day lacked reference. What was there to compare it to? With two out, Larsen worked the count on pinch hitter Dale Mitchell to one ball and two strikes.

"Got him!" Scully yelped of strike three, his suit as damp as a greenhouse, as Babe Pinelli, umpiring his final game, pointed skyward and Berra leapt into Larsen's arms. "The greatest game ever pitched in baseball history by Don Larsen!"

"I don't think you or I shall ever see such a thing again," said Allen, postgame. "I think we can both just go now," said Vin, later allowing to "feeling baked, wilted like a rose."

Afterward Berra spotted Yankees publicity director Jackie Farrell in the clubhouse and said, deliciously, "Hi, what's new?"

Larsen's World Series jewel was so surpassing it has never again been approached. Game Six at Ebbets Field, though, was abiding on its own: Brooklyn USA's last baseball moment in the sun. For one inning after another Clem Labine and Bob Turley matched zeroes. Finally, in the tenth inning, the Dodgers' Jim Gilliam reached second base and Robinson, as we saw earlier, made history too, singling for his last hit, Brooklyn's last Fall Classic run, and its last World Series victory, 1–0.

The Yankees took Game Seven, 9–0, bombing Ike's friend Don Newcombe, whose Series ERA soared to 21.21, "a sad way," wrote *New*

York Times columnist George Vecsey, "for him [and the Subway Series] to end." On October 4, 1957, the Russians put into space the first artificial satellite to orbit the Earth, Sputnik 1, named after the man-made object which meant "fellow traveler." It shocked the United States, which since World War II had felt unrivaled, even invulnerable.

Ike had greased a sense of America as God's chosen land. Now some thought him complacent in science and education. After Sputnik 1 our nation felt self-doubt if not yet the self-flagellation of the 1960s and since. In December 1956, Robinson, whose compass forbade doubt, had been dealt to—the Giants! Unable to brook such heresy, Jackie retired, entered business, became politically active, and touted minority voting and employment. In time, his legacy bloomed.

In 1954, the Supreme Court ruled segregation unconstitutional, even if many refused to make it extinct. Jackie's coming out let a slew of black players crash the '50s Majors: Henry Aaron, Ernie Banks, Elston Howard, Willie Mays, Frank Robinson, Willie McCovey, to cite a few. It augured the first true Hispanic wave, including Cuba's Minnie Minoso; Venezuela's Luis Aparicio and Chico Carrasquel; Mexico's Bobby Avila; Puerto Rico's Orlando Cepeda and Roberto Clemente; and the Dominican Republic's Felipe Alou, the first of three big-league brothers. The flood varied and cleansed the game.

Robinson died of diabetes in 1972, his biography becoming part of the American curriculum. Later his number was retired, never to belong to another. Each April 15, the anniversary of Robinson's 1947 big-league debut, baseball honors him by having each player wear No. 42. Jackie's number and legacy remain. Only his team, linked to both, is gone.

To recall author William Manchester, referenced earlier, baseball's, like America's, "uncomplicated, golden time" of the 1950s began to tarnish in the decade's last few years. "We weren't drawing," said Senators owner Calvin Griffith of Washington, "so we made our park more intimate." Center field remained 421 feet from home plate. Other distances shrank, to no avail. Carlos Paula led 1955 Nats outfielders with *six* homers for the *year*. In 1956 his team drew *460* customers for a *game*. Increasingly a cycle deadened. A bad club sired empty seats, forging a worse team, which lured a lower gate. Griffith Stadium braved four mid-to-late-fifties last-place years of league-low 425,238 to 475,288 attendance. Calvin's bills rose, a greater burden for him than for owners whose portfolios were more diverse. "For some, baseball was a hobby," said Bob Wolff. "For the Griffiths, it was the way to pay the bills."

Then, in 1959, duality began. Ticket payers sensed stirring from the corpse: a 63–91 record but gee-whiz feel even as old habits died hard—Baltimore turned an Opening Day triple play. Yet by season's end, Killebrew and Jim Lemon had forty-two and thirty-three home runs respectively. Pascual fused an electric fastball and the bigs' best curve into a league-high six shutouts. A best-since-1952 615,372 pilgrims trooped to Griffith, many hailing, said Wolff, "guys compared to previous years who were a lot younger and seemed a lot less bad."

Former Israeli statesman Abba Eban said, "The Palestinians never miss an opportunity to miss an opportunity." The Senators' last such opportunity came just as a productive farm system finally hinted of a finer crop. Griffith Stadium had the bigs' smallest capacity, oldest structure, most transient public, and tiniest season ticket list. Calvin Griffith lacked Clark's emotional tie to Washington. The hand-to-mouth Senators started talking to Minneapolis–St. Paul after the Dodgers and Giants had to Los Angeles and San Francisco respectively, baseball overnight shredding tradition, geography, and loyalty. After New York imploded, stiffing DC must have seemed a breeze.

It is fairer to blame Washington's city government for dysfunction and baseball itself for making no effort to keep the Senators than to solely blame the club for being tempted by Minnesota's bauble. Baseball's 1951–65 commissioner Ford Frick merits special censure for not meshing owners, businesses, and local pols to renovate the Nationals' aged yard or build a new park—and not plotting American League expansion to Minnesota, whose new club Griffith could have owned, and to Los Angeles, a prospective tenth AL team. Such a careful plan would have kept the Nats' name, roster, and history in DC; given Calvin the AL's virginal Upper Midwest market; and staffed expansion through a big-league draft. It never had a chance, being too fair to everyone.

Griffith's 1960 fifth-place crew lured 743,404, Washington's highest gate since 1949, before moving to Minnesota in 1961 as the renamed Twins. The Twin Cities deserved a team—but not the U.S. capital's. The piracy enraged the public, especially Congress, which threatened to revoke baseball's antitrust exemption, created in 1922. Not about to return to the Potomac, baseball expanded in 1961 largely to appease the Hill. Bad is that DC did not retrieve the flush Twins team and farm, only a barren draft-stocked club playing to 597,287 at Griffith Stadium. Worse is that in 1962 the new Nats moved into District of Columbia Stadium—"so cold," said a friend, "that if it were a president it would have been Calvin Coolidge"—making you ask why they ever left homey Griffith.

Disproportionate blame for this game of musical chairs lies with the man often falsely accused of a do-nothing presidency. In 1956 Dwight Eisenhower won his second landslide, greatest ever for a Republican before Richard Nixon's 1972 avalanche. Using power elsewhere, he husbanded, not leveraged, it here. In a 1958 news conference baseball's self-termed "great fan" was asked if a Senators move was justifiable. Ike's answer left an English-speaker speechless: "I would want to answer that one if. If the National, I mean if the Nationals here, the American League club here, would have a club that had a fighting chance on the average of getting into the first division. I, for one, would be down at a good number of their evening games to see them, and I would be one of their customers."

Ike paused, perhaps for translation. "Now, unfortunately, because of my present position, I am not a paying customer," he said, adding curiously, "and therefore, I can't help keeping this club here. But if we could only have that, I am practically certain this city would demand that they stay here, and I think they should. But I think they should have a little bit better ball club." The president put no pressure on the Nats to stay or to sell to a group or individual vowing to keep the club in Washington, saying only and incorrectly that a first-division club would always draw and a second-division team would not. By Ike's criteria baseball would have let the perennially awful but lovable Cubs move more than half a century before they won their first World Series in 108 years.

William Rogers, then U.S. attorney general, was a former gangbuster and protégé of New York governor and 1948 GOP nominee Thomas E. Dewey. He would have leapt at the chance to make himself and Ike look good, mediating among the Nats, Frick, Griffith, and other owners. Nixon, his close friend, in his second term as vice president, was ideally positioned to help: a lawyer and self-described "baseball nut" who later argued a case before the U.S. Supreme Court.

Nixon had already shown the needed patience and inside baseball knowledge to facilitate the plan above: keep the Senators in DC; give Griffith a green market and an expansion team; get the AL to expand to Los Angeles (it did in 1961); and if necessary, use the federal government's ultimate weapon, antitrust. This stance viewed baseball from the perspective that Franklin Roosevelt brought to "the Green Light Letter," treating the pastime as a "common good," linking and lifting the nation. Uncle Sam would play a special role, acting justly and honorably.

Ike had always shown a commitment to—indeed veneration of—the "common good." First, as general of the army, he helped crush Hitler and save liberty. Next, as president, he more than anyone helped secure peace and prosperity. Yet Eisenhower's refusal to demand baseball responsibility can only be explained by a parochial view that, as Coolidge stated (see chapter 3), "The chief business of the American people is business"—Ike excusing *uncommon greed*.

On October 27, 1960, Griffith said he could not elude the sheriff by keeping the Senators in the nation's capital. Ike made a statement but took no action. Without a hail to the chief, the once Washington Senators skipped town.

In retrospect it surprises how few people believed the Dodgers and Giants would trade Brooklyn and New York for a one-way ticket west. Eisenhower confessed that he thought of the Bums as Brooklyn's, presumably forever. He ignored the Dodgers' white base moving to suburbia. Also overlooked: Ebbets Field's small seats, few amenities, and the city grid and weak infrastructure that kept the park from expanding out or up.

Walter O'Malley and New York City Parks Commissioner Robert Moses both prized the real estate at Flatbush and Atlantic Avenues. Cynically Moses proposed a Dodgers stadium at two other sites. "One was next to the Battery Tunnel," said Walter. "The other was [on a seventy-eight-acre tract] in Flushing Meadows"—the Mets' future site. O'Malley declined, saying they would not be the Brooklyn Dodgers in Queens.

"Walter felt the discord was Brooklyn's doing," Vin Scully told the *New York Daily News*'s Bob Raissman. "Had Walter got what he wanted, the team would've never left. For him, it came down to either he got a place in Brooklyn where O'Malley could draw to compete," or he would move. The Dodgers' voice called O'Malley a "businessman," not thug. New York University president John Sexton differed, placing the Dodgers' owner "in the seventh ring of Dante's Hell on the list of the most vile people of the twentieth century."

A businessman needs profit. In 1957 Brooklyn's $750,000 TV revenue led the National League. O'Malley's rub was fewer bodies in the seats, his team's home schedule aired on WOR Channel 9 helping attendance drop by 779,268 in a decade. Still, "[I did] doggone well during the past few years," Walter later conceded to a Congressional probe, "with the best earnings record in baseball." If O'Malley "worried about the gate," wrote the *New York Post*'s Phil Mushnick, "all he had to do was stop giving away his product." Even as rumor swirled about Dodgers relocation, jet air travel having halved coast-to-coast flight time to enfranchise California, watching the team on Channel 9 didn't cost a dime.

In May 1957 the NL ruled that the Brooks could move west if another team also did by October 1. The *Daily News* screamed: GIANT-DODGER MOVE OKd. In August 1957 Giants owner Horace Stoneham yielded: "We're sorry to disappoint the kids of New York, but we didn't see many of their parents out there at the Polo Grounds in recent years." Unknown to almost anyone, O'Malley had viewed Chavez Ravine, two miles from center city Los Angeles, by helicopter in early 1956, next year verifying the elephant in the room: "The stockholders and directors of the Brooklyn Baseball Club have . . . unanimously agreed that the necessary steps be taken to draft the Los Angeles territory."

It is true that the Dodgers' overlord tried to get Brooklyn to build a new park—"what he wanted," to quote Scully—as early as 1951. Meanwhile, Stoneham tried to interest Manhattan and Queens, even as crime, mediocrity, and "giving away his product" on TV plunged Polo Grounds attendance to a league-worst 629,179 in 1956, down by two-thirds since 1947. It is also true that nearly two dozen cities in both leagues from Detroit to San Francisco between 1990 and 2010 successfully waited longer than the 1950s Dodgers and Giants for a park. "It's been a long wait," said Mets owner Fred Wilpon, baptizing Citi Field in 2009, "but worth it."

O'Malley and Stoneham would not wait. At least the Giants were losing money. O'Malley merely wanted to put to rout a team nine hundred miles away. On March 18, 1953, Milwaukee acquired the Braves, of Boston since 1876, proceeding to nearly kill its new team with love. Brewtown led baseball in 1953 through 1958 attendance. That first year O'Malley flew to County Stadium, saying of its full house, "We can't compete with this—not even a year." The '57 variety of Braves clinched their first flag September 23, then soldiered on to a magical Game Four tenth-inning 7–5 victory against the Stripes to tie the Series. "Cinderella," said pitcher Ernie Johnson. "We're dead, then the Classic's tied."

Game Seven at Yankee Stadium flagged: only 61,207 there, many irate at the two NL teams' impending exit. Milwaukee led, 5–0, in the ninth inning, Bob Neal on MBS play-by-play: "[Lew] Burdette's [bases-full] pitch. Swung on, lined, grabbed by [Eddie] Mathews who steps on third, and the World Series is over and the Milwaukee Braves are the new world champions of baseball!" The Braves were the first franchise to change sites since 1901. Their river of euphoria running through the Upper Midwest—however briefly, expiring before the 1960s did—ensured it would not be the last. Through 1959 Milwaukee won two pennants and missed two on the final day. The Los Angeles Dodgers likely would not exist had there not been the Milwaukee Braves.

New York governor Averell Harriman flummoxed fact and fiction: "The Dodgers won't move. Los Angeles smog won't let them play at night." Brooklyn didn't believe O'Malley would go—until he had. Baseball didn't seem to care. "Who said the National League *has* to have a team in New York?" league head Warren Giles bellowed, oblivious to the cost of deserting the republic's sports media capital. Baseball had been as American as doughboys at Verdun. Until now National Football League (NFL) anonymity had even smote its largest-market team. "When we won the 1956 title [against Chicago], the town was still all baseball," mused football Giants TV voice Chris Schenkel. Their bit players and glamour boys would now fill baseball's void: new game, our team on top.

Most New Yorkers stuck with baseball. Others went underground or found a new sport for a while or a life. If timing is all, the 1958 NFL title game linked everything: NBC-TV, Yankee Stadium, John Unitas, Giants DEE-fense, and Baltimore's 23–17 sudden-death victory—"the greatest game ever played." Nationally baseball's decline as Big-Game America began with its Split Apple. Network television, located in New York, simultaneously midwifed football's rise. Huddles spurred anticipation. Both teams appeared at once on screen. NFL higher-ups were more TV-savvy than baseball's. In 1959 owners named Rams GM Pete Rozelle commissioner, aware how the tube could establish trend. In 2016 pro football led baseball in a Harris Poll, 33–15 percent, as respondents' "favorite sport."

"Ask not for whom the bell tolls, baseball fans," SI wrote in 2013. It first tolled for them when the New York media needed something to cover—and the NFL raised its hand. Football had not expected such a gift. The baseball Giants needed only a new park in a safe area to stay. Brooklyn had drawn a million fans for a league-record thirteen straight years, making more money, as O'Malley said, than any other team. The Dodgers' CBS *Game of the Week* ratings topped each team but the Yanks'—and the Bombers were less a team than a *Wall Street Journal* entry. TV loved Ebbets Field, felt the Bums an idée fixe. The largely Eastern press reviled the immorality of maiming two franchises that meant so much to so many—in the Dodgers' case, deserting a borough a year after making the World Series and two years after winning it.

As baseball's non-California public mourned, many asked why Ike again refused, as with Calvin Griffith, to demand the "common good" of Stoneham and O'Malley. The Ike of World War II made even its cobra and mongoose, warring generals George Patton (America) and Bernard Montgomery (Britain), act responsibly—and more amazingly, with each other! Here the president failed to even note that government tax and land policy aid required civic accountability. Nixon, a Californian, likely would have backed a plan similar to Griffith's: O'Malley and Stoneham could sell to local parties in return for NL expansion teams in Los Angeles and San Francisco respectively. Otherwise he and Attorney General Rogers would pull the antitrust trigger; not doing so, they unintentionally enabled the NFL's rise.

"After all these years of great competition the Yanks had New York baseball to themselves," said NBC's Lindsey Nelson. "They thought they'd draw from everywhere"—except that as the 1958 Bombers won another flag, they drew their worst home attendance since 1945: 1,428,348. "Baseball didn't understand that with the Dodgers and Giants gone, other sports almost had a monopoly in New York." For the pastime, moving day had truly come.

In February 1957 the Dodgers dealt their Texas League franchise for the Cubs' PCL park, Wrigley Field, and team, Los Angeles Angels—insurance, should Brooklyn's attempt to keep them go unredeemed. When it did, a new Dodgers park in Los Angeles was scheduled to open by 1962. Until then California's Wrigley Field, with its ivied wall, trademark office tower with short lines and alleys, and twenty-two thousand capacity would house the transplanted Bums. If leaving New York hurt national baseball interest, wrote famed *Los Angeles Times* columnist Jim Murray, "you could never tell it here."

O'Malley deplaned October 23, 1957, in Los Angeles. *Vindication?* His reception rivaled secular *absolution.* By that December 4, ticket orders topped $1 million. Good: almost all of the intake was cash. Bad: "At that point," confessed O'Malley, "we knew we couldn't expand Wrigley enough by Opening Day [1958]." At sea, he eyed the one-hundred-thousand-seat Rose Bowl, then spurned Pasadena—"too little time, too much to renovate"—for a site making Ebbets Field look sane. Built for football and track and field, the Dodgers' 1958-61 temporary but memorable home, the Los Angeles Memorial Coliseum, needed a much different baseball footprint.

The Dodgers carved dugouts, a screen, and a tunnel behind the plate. A four-foot-high wall circled most of the field. It began with right field's 301-foot line, receded to an eight-foot-high right-center-field fence (440 feet from home), and waned to center field (425 feet), the last bleacher row *seven hundred feet* from the plate. Left field's 251-foot line hypnotized a visitor. To halt any home run blitz, O'Malley built a 40-by-140-foot screen, angling to the ground. Capacity was 94,600. Baseball seemed so foreign—the back bleachers needed binoculars to espy the plate—that many brought radios to hear Scully tell them what they couldn't see. Many sojourners to the Coliseum became so fixated by his prose that they took a transistor to the park *after* the team moved to Chavez Ravine in 1962.

"People were so far away they could just see images. Radio gave them a good connection," said Vin, interpreting baseball as pantomime. The Dodgers' New Frontier occurred even before it became the theme of John F. Kennedy's 1960 presidential campaign, most notably in the 1959 World Series: Dodgers over the White Sox, four games to two. NBC's television audience reached a then composite record 120 million, including the final's *90 million*. Three gigantic hordes jammed the Coliseum: 92,394; 92,650; and a still-record 92,706 on a Tuesday *afternoon* respectively. Brooklyn had waited fifty-five years for a happy Classic ending. The Golden State got one in Dodgers Year Two.

"The first World Series west of the Rockies," Scully introduced the 1959 official Series highlight film. "This is Los Angeles, where a long-time dream of big-league baseball came true two years ago." Film showed visors and binoculars, sunglasses and Hawaiian shirts. The California Republic flag flapped. Movie stars primped. In Game Three, the first at the Coliseum, Vin etched the decisive two-run single: "Pinch-hitter [Carl] Furillo rams one up the middle": 3–1, Dodgers. A day later another ex-Brook, Gil Hodges, broke an eighth-inning tie. "There it goes! Al Smith goes away back to the base of the fence! But she is gone! Here comes Gil! And the Dodgers are back in front, 5 to 4!"—3–1 in games. Vin prefaced Game Five: "The Dodgers need only one more victory." They got it in Game Six, thumping the White Sox in Chicago, 9–3.

Los Angeles's first world title was bookended by the last two World Series of baseball's oldest manager, watched by America's then-oldest president. Casey Stengel, like Ike sixty-eight in 1958, began that year with six Classic titles, behind only Joe McCarthy's seven. His Yankees made the Series but trailed Milwaukee, three games to one, when Stengel summoned pitcher Bob Turley, who won Game Five, 7–0, saved the next set, and relieved Don Larsen in the final. NBC-TV's Mel Allen recalled "the old man st[anding] on top of the dugout steps pumping his arms like a boxer, yelling at everyone all at once, the men on the field and the men on the bench, insistent as a fire engine, demanding that they go get them."

The Bombers' Bill "Moose" Skowron did, in the eighth inning of the seventh game. "Here's the pitch," Allen said of Braves starter Lew Burdette. "Moose swings. There's a long drive going out into deep left field! It's going, it's going, it is gone! A home run! And the Yankees lead, 6 to 2!" Straightaway Casey feted his last great—perhaps greatest—peak with sport's premier team, tying Marse Joe's record. "I guess," he jibed, "this shows we could play in the National League."

Paid by the word, the Ol' Perfessor might have owned the Stripes. In July 1958 he had testified before a U.S. Senate committee on baseball's antitrust exemption. For an hour Stengelese ricocheted around the Cannon Office Building, causing heads to shake and mouths to gape. Almost no one knew what Casey was talking about. The next witness famously abstained. "I don't got much to say," said Mickey Mantle, his next words bringing down the house: "My views are the same as Casey's."

Stengel's next/last Series may have been his hardest. The 1960 Bronx Bombers vaunted Roger Maris's league-high 112 RBIS, Mantle's AL-best 40 homers, and 193 times as a team going deep. The Pirates' hull had listed since a last pennant in 1927. It helped that Roberto Clemente now made right field his canvas. Shortstop Dick Groat won an NL batting title. Second baseman Bill Mazeroski was unequaled at two for the price of one. The Bucs-Yanks Fall Classic remains a Boomers' touchstone. Everywhere, people followed—even the cast of TV's hugely popular *Andy Griffith Show*, filming an episode in Hollywood. At break, they heard the Series on radio, played catch, and took batting practice. Don Knotts as Barney Fife aped the Mick.

The Series itself was otherworldly, its script redolent of Alfred Hitchcock presaging Stephen King. The Yankees outhit (.338–.256), outhomered (10–4), and outscored the Pirates, 55–27. New York won games by 16–3, 10–0, and 12–0 but couldn't deck the Bucs. Game Seven broke mild and bright at Forbes Field's in-play batting cage, taxi-cab alleys, and exquisite Schenley Park by the University of Pittsburgh. The Pirates jumped to a 4–0 lead, fell behind, 7–4, then scored twice in the eighth inning before an ex-Yanks catcher batted with two out and two on: "Hal Smith hits a drive to deep left field!" said NBC-TV's Allen. "That ball is way back out there! Going, going, gone!": 9–7, Pittsburgh. "And pandemonium breaks loose at Forbes Field!"

Tide preceded riptide. In the ninth inning the Stripes' Bobby Richardson and Dale Long reached base, Mantle plated a run to make the score 9–8, and Yogi Berra's sharp bounder triggered a play many had never seen before. "And there's a shot, grabbed by [Rocky] Nelson, [who] steps on first [erasing Yogi as a base runner and letting an instinctive Mick reclaim the bag], and Mantle gets back!" Mel blared. "He's safe, and [pinch runner Gil] McDougald scores the [nine-all] tying run on an amazing turn of events!" Yanks reliever Ralph Terry entered to throw Mazeroski a last-of-the-ninth slider. The left-center-field Timex clock read 3:36 p.m. "There's a drive deep into left field!" Allen cried. Yogi receded to the 406-foot sign. "Look out now! That ball is going, going, gone! And the World Series is over! Mazeroski hits it over the left-field fence for a home run! And the Pirates win it, 10 to 9, and win the World Series!"

In Upstate New York, this nine-year-old began crying at a Cub Scout meeting. In suburban Pittsburgh, thirteen-year-old Larry Lucchino, the future president of the Orioles, Padres, and Red Sox, was walking home from school. "[I] was a Pirates fan," Lucchino recalls, "and had a radio. When Maz homered, I threw it toward the sky." Aglow, he raced home, "really, walking on air." By contrast, six days later Stengel was grounded by the Yankees. "I'll never make the mistake," the Ol' Perfessor said of his dismissal, "of being seventy again."

This chapter has been critical of Eisenhower's attitude toward baseball. Like FDR, Ike knew it to be a "common good" of America. Yet he declined to ask the game to act *for* the common good—even when it could have helped to save baseball from itself. The pastime's present still pays a price. It is only fair to close with Ike's far larger niche as a great, even historic, leader.

After reading and writing millions of words about Eisenhower, biographer Stephen Ambrose concluded that the secret to his success was trust: "I never found him in a personal lie." It was a quality he shared with president George H. W. Bush, who in 1989 traveled to the Mediterranean island of Malta for his first meeting as president with Soviet leader Mikhail Gorbachev. Bush's address was to the five thousand sailors on the USS *Forrestal*. My first draft ended with the D-Day prayer Franklin Roosevelt had read over nationwide radio. Instead Bush asked for Ike's presidential model of leadership, and his December 1 remarks concluded so:

> Let me close with a moment that you are too young to remember, but which wrote a glorious page in American history. It occurred on D-Day as Dwight Eisenhower addressed the sailors, soldiers, and airmen of the Allied Expeditionary Force.
>
> "You are about to embark," he told them, "upon a great crusade. . . . The eyes of the world are upon you. The hopes and prayers of liberty-loving people everywhere march with you." Then Ike spoke this moving prayer: "Let us all beseech the blessing of Almighty God, upon this great and noble undertaking."
>
> Like the men of D-Day, you, too, are the hope of "liberty-loving people everywhere." As the Navy has been in wartime and in peacetime—keeping our hearts alight and our faith unyielding. Thank you for writing still-new pages in the history of America and her Navy. God bless you and our "great and noble undertaking." And God bless the United States of America.

Later Bush marveled: "It's amazing what occurred in a blink of history's eye." He meant the Cold War's end in 1989–91 but could have meant World War I or World War II or Korea or Vietnam—all wars in which Ike either served or observed.

Once, after a fit of temper, a ten-year-old Eisenhower was gently lectured by his mother: "He that conquereth his own soul is greater than he who taketh a city." Ike did. Lucky us.

SEVEN

"The First Irish Brahmin"

John F. Kennedy, 1961–1963

D wight Eisenhower read Louis L'Amour, hosted stag dinners at the White House, liked TV dinners in the personal quarters, and danced with Mamie to Guy Lombardo and the Royal Canadians. To many, the contrast with his successor seemed inspirational even more than generational. William Manchester termed John F. Kennedy's children, Caroline and John, "friendly but reserved with strangers, alert, bright, possessed of immense curiosity and fired by awesome energy." He was describing their father too.

JFK had brown hair, a perpetual tan, and a twist to his bite. Emphatic and sensitive by nature, he was not a hater, seeking to grasp other points of view. Kennedy synthesized the Gaelic mix of promise and foreboding. He saw humor almost everywhere—in life's absurdities, improbabilities, and cant. World War II was an exception, from which he emerged a hero. Once *TIME*'s Hugh Sidey asked what JFK recalled of the Depression. "Really nothing," said Kennedy, whose family worth ran far north of $200 million. "It didn't have an effect. But ask me about the war—that's what I remember."

The upper-class product had a middle-brow bent, enjoying Sinatra, Armstrong, Crosby. The commander-in-chief himself liked to sing loudly, if not always well; Mrs. Kennedy called his favorite tune "Hail to the Chief." Kennedy quoted the ancient Greeks' definition of happiness: "the full use of your powers along lines of excellence." In public, he tied irony, a graceful phrase, and perspective. "Last year more Americans went to symphonies than went to baseball games," JFK told one audience. "This may be viewed as an alarming statistic, but I think that baseball and the country will endure."

Born in Brookline, a Boston suburb, Kennedy grew up enjoying baseball's comity as well as strategy. Hy Hurwitz wrote in *The Sporting News* about JFK aide and friend Dave Powers, who "always amazed [the president] as he rattled off batting averages and pitching records of major league players." Like Joe Cronin, another family friend and Red Sox player, manager, and GM, Powers, a lifetime Soxaphile, would tell how a teenaged "Jack" asked his older brother, naval lieutenant Joseph Kennedy Jr., killed later in the war, for an autographed Red Sox team ball. The Olde Towne Team was for JFK always a family affair.

In 1957 he got his father, Joseph P. Kennedy Sr., onetime U.S. ambassador to the Court of St. James, to successfully approach the *London Sunday Express* about printing baseball scores for U.S. expatriates. It continued a political-baseball tie dating to Jack's maternal grandfather, John "Honey Fitz" Fitzgerald, a congressman (1895–1901 and 1919), Boston mayor (1906–08 and 1910–14), and chairman of the Royal Rooters, the Sox's most fanatic sect. "Honey Fitz" also helped plot his grandson's first campaign (congressional) in 1946, baseball and Hub politics like two shafts of silver gleaned from a common mine. On April 20, 1912, Fitzgerald tossed the first pitch at Fenway Park's inaugural.

The Kennedy clan settled in Massachusetts in the mid-nineteenth century, part of the Irish potato famine exodus, its ancestors sixty miles from County Cavan. Fitzgerald was largely unassimilated Irish, a trait JFK lauded after his 1961 inauguration, renaming the presidential yacht the *Honey Fitz*. Kennedy wished, however, a different image for himself—a "picture of total urbanity," a writer said. If JFK got another leg up from his father's money—the future president inherited $1 million at twenty-one—Joe Sr.'s fortune did not sire his son's lyric style. "Jack," said Massachusetts governor Paul Dever, "is the first Irish Brahmin."

JFK's biography includes Harvard '40 and service in World War II (1941–45), the U.S. House of Representatives (1947–53) and Senate (1953–61), and as thirty-fifth president (1961–63). Memory retrieves the manner that so gripped reporters. In the 1960 campaign a drunk tossed a glass in his face. Kennedy picked it up and said, "Here's your drink." History records how he changed the presidency: from an office held by businessmen to a job open to other fields; from a Protestant-only post to one of greater equal opportunity; from presidents equating success with legislation to a sense that chic could gird the legend that was Camelot.

Author Tom Wicker termed Kennedy "the most fascinating might-have-been in American history." At the time, many felt in JFK's Era of Good Feeling a leader who already was. As of 1960 no Catholic had been elected president. None had been a serious candidate since Al Smith in 1928. "I refuse to believe that I was denied the right to be president on the day I was baptized," Kennedy said in the 1960 West Virginia primary. Protestants could show tolerance only by backing Kennedy. Astute, he could be as hard as Ike.

In 1950 we largely conversed around the radio. A decade later television had become so dominant that "more than anything," said JFK, "[it] turned the tide." In 1960 Republican nominee Richard Nixon accepted Democrat Kennedy's gauntlet of four TV tussles. The first, before seventy million viewers, sent expectation reeling. Sweaty, whiskered, and slack from illness, Nixon addressed himself to Kennedy, like a pre-video debater. Addressing the camera, JFK took the kinetic tube—and the election by a popular vote margin of fewer than 113,000 votes of a record 68.8 million cast.

The new president sought a "ministry of talent" to fill his Cabinet and senior staff. The inaugural portended change. Black contralto Marian Anderson sang "The Star-Spangled Banner." Robert Frost prepared a preface to his poem, "The Gift Outright." Kennedy outshone each: "Let the word go forth from this time and place, to friend and foe alike, that the torch has been passed to a new generation of Americans." Elected by TV, JFK prepared to further use it. He was interviewed by network correspondents, profited by foreign footage flown back for nightly news, and held the first live TV press conference—soon the biggest show in town.

Slowly change *became* the 1960s. Race was one example. Another was our "remov[al] from the log cabin," a reporter wrote, the Kennedys inviting Pablo Casals, Igor Stravinsky, a ballet troupe, and a Shakespeare company to perform in the White House. Writers, musicians, artisans, and academics lauded JFK—and imagined an idealized version of themselves. Yet he made a hash of the Bay of Pigs in 1961, withholding air cover from a failed exile-led attack on Communist forces on Cuba's southern coast. Deeming him a bungler and provocateur, Soviet premier Nikita Khrushchev bullied Kennedy at the Vienna summit and smirked at his vow to land a man on the moon before the decade was over.

If, quoting JFK, the presidency was "the vital center of action," language was its core. To his inaugural, Kennedy added addresses on civil rights and nuclear disarmament, the latter called by Khrushchev "the greatest speech by an American President since Roosevelt." In another speech, on June 26, 1963, before hundreds of thousands of people in the divided city, JFK condemned the Soviets' concrete and barbed wire wall built in 1961 to split Berlin permanently and halt the refugee flow from the Communist East to the democratic West. He spoke briefly but unforgettably: "*Ich bin ein Berliner*" (I am a Berliner).

In a Gallup Poll taken after Kennedy began the Peace Corps and Alliance for Progress and which merited the phrase "white lie" or "faulty memory," 62 percent said they voted for Kennedy in 1960. (He got 49.7 percent.) Guesswork about what would have happened had he lived mimics darts thrown in the fog. Kennedy often mentioned how he loved his job. He would have fought fiercely to keep it. At one Army-Navy football game the Navy veteran sat on the Army side in the first half, crossing the field at halftime. The entire naval section rose to cheer, a chant erupting: "Welcome home!" The thirty-fifth president beamed.

In October 1962 troops went on high alert to counter Soviet offensive missiles in Cuba, JFK having seen from aerial photos that launching pads were being built for intermediate long-range missiles. Kennedy brooded. Should he strike by air? Try another alternative? In a historic speech, the president memorably called the Soviet deployment "a clandestine, reckless, and provocative threat to world peace," chose to "quarantine" shipments of military equipment to Cuba, and told Khrushchev that nuclear attack from there would mean "full retaliatory response upon the Soviet Union."

Secretly Kennedy vowed to dismantle American missile bases in Turkey at a later date, the withdrawal not to be linked to the Soviets' removal. The Communists removed their weapons. Beating Khrushchev in a turning point on earth, JFK's America later beat his nation to the moon. Many Americans under the age of sixty cannot recall a President Kennedy or his administration. An administration in waiting in academia, government, and much of the media seems forever present to reintroduce him.

Symmetrically, President Kennedy's first year of tossing out the first ball in 1961 was Griffith Stadium's last before moving to District of Columbia Stadium. As if the home team hadn't historically grieved enough, that year's expansion Senators failed to sell out their tiny (27,550 capacity) park. August 13 against the Yankees came closest: 27,368. Opening Day lured just 26,725. Even so, Kennedy, hating the second-rate in himself and others, practiced throwing thirty minutes a day the last week before the season started. "I want to do it [the first pitch] well," he told Dave Powers. "People expect it in a President." A photo shows them at the April 12 opener, reading *The Sporting News*.

Earlier that day, JFK became the first U.S. president interviewed on TV at a baseball game, on WGN Chicago's *Lead-off Man Show*:

WHITE SOX ANNOUNCER VINCE LLOYD: Mr. President, have you had an opportunity to do any warming up for this, sir?
KENNEDY: Well, we've just been getting ready here today.
LLOYD: Throwing nothing but strikes? Very good.
JFK: I feel it important that we . . . not be a nation of just spectators, even though that's what we are today, but also a nation of participants—particularly to make it possible for young men and women to participate actively in physical effort.

Lloyd then asked about Mrs. Kennedy. JFK smiled and said, "Well, it's Monday. She's home doing the wash." If she needed help, a large domestic staff stood by.

The White Sox voice had arrived on Opening Day to meet the already ubiquitous Charlie Brotman, the then Senators' promotions director, 1956–71 public address announcer, and voice of every presidential inaugural parade—fifteen in a row—from Eisenhower's in 1957 to Barack Obama's in 2013.

On Opening Day 1956 Ike had been impressed by Brotman on PA and asked him to announce the next year's inaugural parade. A staffer asked Charlie, "Will you charge a fee? Because our parade budget is very minimal." "No," said the son of Russian-Jewish immigrants. "As a matter of fact, I'd pay you for the honor." He became legendary in his public address and publicity field, inducted into eleven halls of fame.

In 1961, greeting a new White House party, Brotman introduced JFK to Washington and Chicago players in their dugout and clubhouse. "President Kennedy got such a kick out of it," Charlie said. "He already knew most of them by name." Brotman then asked him to stay near the dugout. "I'm going to get the baseball you'll be throwing out. Now don't go anywhere." "I won't, Charlie," Kennedy said reassuringly. "Don't worry."

Brotman returned in several moments with baseballs for JFK. The putative user, though, was missing, no one, including the Secret Service, knowing where he was. Charlie retook the tunnel from the dugout to the clubhouse: no president. Anxious about the time, he took a dark passageway that players often used, eyeing only a dim Bogart-like profile, outlined by a match.

"Mr. President," he said, haltingly, "is that you?"

"Charlie?" JFK said. "I thought I'd sneak off and smoke a cigar." He continued, puffing away contentedly. "I know we've got to leave."

"Yes, Mr. President," Brotman nodded.

"I just didn't think fans would like to see their president smoking a cigar," Kennedy said, relaxed, vigilant about his image. He enjoyed a last whiff of tobacco scent, put the cigar on a ledge, then traipsed to the presidential box near the home dugout.

Today the U.S. president usually tosses a warmup pitch to the home catcher or another player. JFK continued the practice of his time by throwing the first pitch to or over the heads of players en masse, who dispersed to nab a prized souvenir. Kennedy flung the first toss as far as he could—in this case near the previously cited Nationals outfielder Jim Rivera, who gobbled it, ran to JFK, and asked for his signature. The president complied, but Rivera, seldom known for class, dubbed it illegible, saying "What kind of garbage college is that Harvard, where they don't even teach you how to write?"

Nearby, Powers seethed at the disrespect for his friend, the office, and Kennedy's alma mater. Unfazed, the president signed again. Said Rivera, "You're all right." Sadly, the rookie Senators weren't, losing to Chicago, 4–3. Opening Day 1961 caught another picture of Kennedy and Powers, both suited with ties, in the presidential box. Dave carried JFK's baseball glove, as usual at the park. Kennedy, who almost never wore a hat, ribbed Powers that he, like Ike, did. It made Dave seem "nineteenth century overnight," jibed the president, aware that his example was killing the hat industry.

In 1961 Roger Maris belted a superhuman sixty-one home runs, including four at Griffith Stadium. In 1962 the media pilloried him for hitting a human thirty-three. Besieged, Maris visited the White House for a guided tour. "Roger," host Powers said, "the Cabinet met today and agreed that nobody would ask you how many home runs you expect to hit." Maris smiled, broadly. "That's the best news I've had in a long while."

Kennedy's New England past and Irish sensibility—"Dad taught me politics. Mother taught us history"—made him, as his inaugural address said of America, "proud of our ancient heritage." That love of history would have almost surely made JFK oppose the 1960s new generation of ballparks. Planners sought "super blocks" to flank freeways, abut parking, and spur ease, trying vainly to help baseball and football, like oil and water, coexist. Each pre–cookie cutter park had a different personality: Ebbets Field, Wrigley Field, Kennedy's Fenway Park.

In 2011 Michael Dukakis, like JFK a Democratic presidential nominee (1988), and wife Kitty were taking the usual twenty-minute walk to their suburban Brookline home from a game at Fenway. "How can you beat this?" Kitty asked her husband, Massachusetts's 1975–79 and 1983–91 governor. "The crowd, the team, the atmosphere?" Dukakis later said it stemmed from the park: "The Red Sox without Fenway would not be the Red Sox."

To him, each multipurpose stadium seemed a carbon copy—also to Richie Hebner, who played for five teams, notably Pittsburgh from 1968 to 1976, and loathed cookie cutters' vast foul turf, bad sightlines, identical yardage, and distant seating. "When I bat, I can't tell . . . if I'm in Cincinnati, Philadelphia, or St. Louis," he said. They were dull, duller, dullest, lacking, above all, grace—a word often attached to Kennedy. Reasons varied: few 1960s and 1970s parks were forged by a city grid. "Form followed function," added architect Ludwig Mies van der Rohe. "Less [symmetry of shape and length] was more."

Computers and steel design helped concrete better cantilever, build multiple tiers, and extend seating distance. Loge seats surfaced, often hanging beneath a deck. "The result," said architect Joseph Spear, "was to further push stands away."

Football's shape was rectangular, baseball's triangular. A final woe: "column-free" design made decks even farther off and limited the roof. "Welcome," said Spear, "to more rain and less cover," more banality and boredom.

Such sameness began, like many trends, in our nation's capital.

In April 1962 District of Columbia Stadium became just the second new AL park, with Minnesota's, since 1932's Cleveland Municipal Stadium. It opened in the city's southeast section, had a 43,500 capacity, was circular, and had a symmetry throughout: each foul line, 335 feet; alley, 385 feet; and center field, 410 feet. The wire outfield fence was seven feet high from pole to pole. "It had great football sightlines," said the *Washington Post*'s Shirley Povich, "and was formal, pretentious, and cold." An Opening Day crowd of 42,143 cheered the Senators over Detroit, 4–1. It didn't help. DC placed tenth.

Arkansas Democrat Oren Harris had introduced a bill to build the stadium with public funds. Publicly Kennedy hailed the park as "an enduring symbol of . . . the importance of physical fitness and of the contributions which athletic competition can make to our way of life." Privately he told Powers, "Boy, baseball can be a slow-moving sport," apparently having changed his mind from a year earlier at the Senators' 1911–61 empyrean.

Washington's Fine Arts Commission oversaw public sites like DC Stadium as being "on direct line with the United States Capitol and the Lincoln and . . . Jefferson Memorials," a 1962 release said. Light towers were therefore banned and arcs tacked on its curved, dipping roof, making it look "like a wet straw hat," one critic wrote—antipodal to its predecessor. Two decks circled the field from one foul line to another. Bullpens linked the fence and back concrete wall. "More remote and antiseptic than Griffith," said entertainer Maury Povich, son of *Post* columnist Shirley and former aide to Bob Wolff. "Griffith felt like baseball. Not this." It did feel new, like Kennedy, his new administration incorporating the contemporary. In another sense, new reigned because it was glitzy, like ornaments on a tree.

A presidential opener braves rain, snow, or gloom of night to avoid postponement. Thus 1962's first-inning twenty-two-minute rain delay gave JFK, who could be a chatterbox, the chance to leave his box, find the runway between the field and umpires dressing room, and probe them about their craft. "He talked baseball and football. He really knows his stuff," said Charlie Berry, shortly to retire as an AL umpire and NFL official. "Kennedy knew all about one of Detroit's catchers, Mike Roarke. He remembered Mike as a big [college] player in Boston." DC Stadium's first opener included Willie Tasby's popup, denting the dugout roof three feet from JFK's attempted catch, and a decision Kennedy made in the eighth inning to postpone a meeting with Laos's ambassador to the United States, Prince Tiao Khampao. It let him stay to the end, as the president did whenever he saw a big-league game, enamoring those who liked baseball, and that day avoid a region that already made him ill.

Entering the Nats' new home, a guest passed monuments on the north and south to Clark Griffith and Redskins owner George Preston Marshall respectively. In its first year six feet of leveling sank sections of left and left-center field. Pros: Tom Cheney struck out twenty-one Orioles in sixteen innings. The 1963 Senators beat Cleveland, 7–2, in the bigs' one hundred thousandth game. Con: Novelty faded, attendance falling to 535,605 from 729,775 in 1962. "A tightrope act," said Nats announcer Dan Daniels. "At the park were people from every state cheering for the visitor. I couldn't root, and yet a lot of fans pulled for Washington," usually in vain. The expansion Senators were almost as bad, if not quite as funny, as the NL expansion Mets, originally forged by a committee chaired by lawyer William Shea to get *another* New York team to replace the Dodgers and Giants. Spurned by the Reds, Phils, and Pirates, Shea and Branch Rickey combined eight cities into a third major—Continental—league. Said former official baseball historian Jerome Holtzman, "Threat of player raids and anti-trust suits made them [the NL] expand" in 1962.

In 1961 the New York State Senate okayed $55 million for the park that O'Malley had snubbed in Queens. The Mets' 1962–63 temporary home was the Polo Grounds, gussied up with $250,000 in funds. The NL expansion draft affirmed the symbiotic relationship among the Dodgers, the Giants, and the Metropolitan Baseball Club of New York. "Their uniform showed our parents," new announcer Lindsey Nelson said of Mets garb, tying Dodgers blue and Giants orange. The "Metsies," Casey Stengel's shorthand for his players, met in February 1962 in Florida. "We got to work on the little finesses," he told them. "Runners at first and second, the first baseman holding a runner, breaking in and back to take a pickoff throw." New York lost its first exhibition game, 17–1. "The little finesses," the Perfessor reconsidered, "ain't gonna be our problem." The 1962–63 Mets finished 91-231, somehow drawing 2,002,638 and making Stengel say, "If we can make losing popular, I'm for it." Daily they strove to please.

The question was how long losing would satisfy. Many thought Shea Stadium, christened April 16, 1964, with Dodgers Holy Water from Brooklyn's Gowanus Canal and Giants Holy Water from the Harlem River at the point it passed Coogan's Bluff, a long-term solution. "The early Mets played for fun," said Nelson. "They weren't capable of playing for anything else." The early first baseman, *Marvin Eugene Throneberry*—MET—"Marvelous Marv," voice Ralph Kiner said, "never made the same mistake twice. He always made different ones." A *New Yorker* cartoon showed several dejected Mets entering the dugout. A bystander says, "Cheer up. You can't lose them all." Many thought DC's impatience a difference between its and the Mets' expansion team, Washington having been let down much longer. Tasby rode by train when weather threatened. Pitcher Dick Donovan's mates learned not to sit where he laid his glove between innings. Eccentricity didn't translate into funny for a team *sans* pennant since 1933.

In 1963 a player still adored in Flatbush became Washington skipper. "Gil [Hodges] fretted quietly when his players threw to the wrong base," said the *Washington Post*'s Morris Siegel, "missed the cutoff man, screwed up rundown plays, and misran the bases." Frank Howard was 6-foot-7, 255 pounds, and that decade's most beloved Nat. He once went deep ten times in twenty at-bats, thrice hit forty-four or more homers, and retired in 1973 with 382, many of them ballistic. "That's where they landed," Hondo later said of his upper-deck seats painted white, "one of the few things that remind you there was baseball here." Ultimately the 1960s and early '70s Senators made 1930s through '50s Nats teams look World Serieux; a rare highlight the August 1, 1962, DC big-league record crowd of 48,147. Seven years later Ted Williams became manager, baseball's brightest star during almost all of John F. Kennedy's political career.

In 1969 the era begun under JFK of one new park or name replacing another reached a point no one had imagined: DC Stadium was renamed for his brother, Senator Robert F. Kennedy (D-NY), assassinated campaigning for president in June 1968. On July 19, 1982, a crowd of 29,196 attended the Cracker Jack Old-Timers Baseball Classic played there on its football configuration—Washington's first even unofficial big-league game since baseball left a second time in 1971. The left- and right-field poles stood 260 and 295 feet respectively from the plate. Former White Sox shortstop Luke Appling, seventy-five, homered off Warren Spahn. Exhibition events teased baseball's return. For the moment the nation's capital settled for one show game a year.

Two decades later Commissioner Bud Selig ordered a study: Would a Washington team hurt nearby Orioles attendance? It took Montreal's losing the Expos, DC gaining the renamed Nationals, a new ballpark less than four miles from the White House, and Baltimore's stab at baseball revival to at least tentatively answer *no*.

Like Jack Kennedy, as noted above, each early-century baseball site had personality. None was more individual than the Giants' oblong cafe at 157th and 159th Streets and Eighth Avenue, across the Harlem River from Yankee Stadium. "Man, I loved the Polo Grounds," said Willie Mays, its signature player. Built on a point, the team's next permanent home, Candlestick Park, was a 1960–99 site that Mays loathed; where he braved sub-freezing cold; and whose wind, he felt, cost him a chance to break Babe Ruth's home run record. "You'd hit it a mile," Willie said, "and it would blow a half-mile back."

The Stick hosted the 1961 All-Star Game: NL, 5–4, on tenth-inning hits by Hank Aaron, Mays, and Roberto Clemente. Starkest was reliever Stu Miller, balking. The papers blared: MILLER BLOWN OFF MOUND! The Giants blew off the Dodgers in a 1962 pennant playoff. Ahead: the Yankees in a Transcontinental (née Subway) World Series, Mays, the "Say Hey Kid," against No. 7, Mickey Mantle, batting .250 and .120 respectively and unexpectedly. Before 1958 their parks had been divided by a river; now three time zones and three thousand miles. Game Three at Yankee Stadium lured a standing-room-only 71,434. The next day Don Larsen, now a Giant, tied the Classic at two games apiece on the sixth anniversary of his perfect game. Rain thrice postponed the sixth set, the Series lasting a longest-since-1911 thirteen days. Finally, in Game Seven, the Yankees' Ralph Terry got a chance to rewrite an event gone wrong.

"I came into the Series with a bad record [0-3, especially his 1960 Series-losing blast to Mazeroski]," the righty pitcher said. "You rarely get a second chance." The Stripes led, 1–0, as Mays hit in the seventh inning. "[Tom] Tresh races over!" Mel Allen said. "Makes a spectacular one-handed running catch!" In the ninth inning Matty Alou pinch-bunt singled, brother Felipe Alou and Chuck Hiller struck out, and the Say Hey Kid doubled to the right-field corner. Matty, the tying run, stopped at third base. "My heart was in my throat," Terry said, his 1-1 pitch to the next batter, massive Willie McCovey, lined to the second baseman. "A foot either way," rued Willie, "we win." A third way blessed the Yankees: Bobby Richardson, catching the ball, never had to move.

A year later America's "greatest sports event," according to NBC-TV, struck a yearning for the ghosts of World Series past, pitting arguably the age's premier pitchers—the Dodgers' Sandy Koufax, nearing his peak, and Bombers' Whitey Ford, slightly past it. JFK prefaced the October 2 opening game by sending Yankees owners a letter hailing the 1963 Series—a White House first—then watching on color TV the first Dodgers-Stripes Fall Classic since 1956. Koufax won the opener, fanning a Series record fifteen. Johnny Podres and Don Drysdale took the next two games, the American Leaguers' dynasty breaking up, though few knew till their 1965 sixth-place thud. In role reversal, New York trailed, three games to none.

On Sunday, October 6, baseball's then-largest-ever TV audience, a record 25.6 million homes, watched in Game Four as Sandy threw a "hellacious curve that dropped out of the sky," according to his catcher, John Roseboro, who heard Mantle mutter, "How in the hell are you supposed to hit that shit?" In the fifth inning Frank Howard's homer reached the second deck: 1–0, Los Angeles. "The first man to hit it at Dodger Stadium!" caroled Vin Scully, on NBC with Allen. In the seventh inning Mantle's blast tied the score. Like the Classic generally, this duel of old rivals especially absorbed the culture. "Our national life used to practically stop [in the Series]," said TV's *Brooklyn Bridge* creator Gary David Goldberg. "The whole country came together—people on farms, factory workers, kids in school—everyone following the progress of the game." The Yankees—thirteen pennants in the last fifteen years, twenty Series titles since 1923, evil or righteous empire, sport's mightiest in the world—lost, 2–1, swept by the Dodgers. "Shock" is not too strong a word.

From rural America Eisenhower got support, a common background, and mistrust of fancy talk and fancy people. Kennedy's base was more contemporary. In 1962 the president told Senators brass that he was leaving them in first place after opening the new park. For a third of a century after baseball deserted the capital a second time in 1971, Washington feared it had left for good. For a National League fan, interest corked up the Eastern Seaboard through Philadelphia to the Mets' three digs—the Polo Grounds, 1964–2008 Shea Stadium, and since 2009 Citi Field—Stengel saying in 1971, "The craziness of that Polo's park made them people ever [since] fall in love." A chant of "Let's Go Mets!" having first shaken Coogan's Bluff, Metsomania forever became an allegory of the team.

It took little time after Casey's "Metsies" left the Polo Grounds for many to miss the joint's old-timey charm. This became a common post-1950s big-league theme. In 1965 Houston introduced less variance than promised in baseball's first covered structure, the faux grass Astrodome, an engineering marvel bereft of quirk. A year later the Braves left Milwaukee for Atlanta-Fulton County Stadium, the pastime a football afterthought. Baseball-crazed St. Louis dealt Busch Stadium for a same-name-more-sterile site. New ballparks stifled debate. Older unpredictable parks burnished it. A double to center field at Crosley Field might have been caught at Comiskey Park; "a can of corn" at Briggs Stadium was "long gone" at Ebbets Field. Even Ike and the Ol' Perfessor hailed old-style ballpark individuality in 1961, when the AL expansion Angels, in their only year at Los Angeles's Minor League toy shop Wrigley Field, built in the early '20s, enthralled *Sports Illustrated*.

In LA, it wrote, "Despite their obvious shortcomings and the Dodgers obvious strengths, the Angels have gained the edge in newspaper publicity and got equal time from . . . discussion groups." One day "from a shiny Cadillac stepped Dwight Eisenhower, [who] took his place discreetly in the stands. This was still being written about three days later." Another morning, "Casey Stengel . . . left his [nearby] Glendale bank to watch the new team and get his photograph in all the Los Angeles papers." By contrast, in 1968 the A's traded Kansas City for the huge foul ground of the Oakland Coliseum. The 1970 Reds and 1971 Phillies were sentenced to tomblike Riverfront Stadium and Veterans Stadium respectively. Seattle occupied the Kingdome, the Expos dealt Jarry Park for Olympic Stadium—the Big O, as in zero—and Minnesota inhabited the Metrodome. In time, personality returned to almost each big-league park.

Especially joyful will be to relive here how, using a favorite word of JFK's, a "terrific" park rose in the twenty-first century in the City of Presidents after Washington was deserted by baseball from 1972 to 2004. "Many parks [of that age]," recalled Hall of Famer Mike Schmidt, "had the charm of a parking garage." He did not wish the comparison to be unkind to a garage.

In John F. Kennedy's last year on earth he urged Congress to approve a Limited Nuclear Test-Ban Treaty, telling a friend, "It [nuclear fall-out] doesn't really matter as [far as] you and I are concerned. What really matters is the children." In 1960 he had said, "I think it's time that America started moving again." Like any elected politician, at some point he started moving toward reelection. Already in his bank were steady economic growth, a huge tax cut, and low inflation. JFK now asked Capitol Hill for deposits from aid to education to legislation against segregation. He wanted a landslide—thus the 1963 trip to Texas—to turn popularity to muscle.

Already Kennedy's pre-presidential and presidential personae conjured a composite of one image or another: his 1957 Pulitzer Prize-winning book for biography, *Profiles in Courage*; JFK's hatless, coatless health; the accent, made for mimicry. The 1960 campaign against Nixon still conjured fire in the blood. Kennedy meant to build on those beginnings. For us, memory still intrudes. It invokes JFK's rocking chair to ease back pain—and the natural athlete, playing golf as often as feasible. Like FDR, sailing was the outdoor activity Kennedy most enjoyed. At Hyannis Port he played touch football as if Saint Peter's verdict on admittance to heaven depended on the score. The last athletic event the president saw in person was Harvard-Columbia football at Harvard Stadium on October 19, 1963, the same night he keynoted a Democratic Party dinner in Boston. "What a perfect day for Jack," said Dave Powers. "His two loves—politics and sports." Son John became America's prototypal toddler. As a young girl, daughter Caroline entered the West Wing lobby in her mother Jacqueline's high heels. Asked about daddy, she said, "Oh, he's upstairs with his shoes and socks off, not doing anything."

In 1961 Jackie left him speechless on seeing her at Paris's first evening event on a trip to Europe. "Well," he finally said, "I'm dazzled."

Leaving, he addressed a luncheon, saying "I do not think it altogether inappropriate to introduce myself to this audience. I am the man who accompanied Jacqueline Kennedy to Paris, and I have enjoyed it." *TIME* wrote, "Hollywood would not have cast such a"—that word again—"dazzling pair." Less glamorous, fiction might at least have written a less horrifying end than crumpled roses in the back seat of the president's limousine outside Parkland Hospital.

For those then alive, memory's last act lies inside midnight's muddle: dried blood on Mrs. Kennedy's suit, Lee Harvey Oswald, Jack Ruby, and the swearing-in on Air Force One of Lyndon Johnson with the widow at his side. Where were you in November 1963? Doubtless watching John salute at age three. The riderless steed. The caisson's trek across the Potomac to Arlington Cemetery, where JFK had told a friend, "I could stay here forever." Ike's poetry was biographical. Kennedy's was personal, quoting from William Faulkner to Flannery O'Connor; literacy, it was said, no longer evidence of high treason. It is hard to imagine that thinking man's exchange on today's iPhone or DVD.

As he showed by daily honing his Opening Day pitch before the season, JFK was a disciple of self-improvement. The first president to master television worked hard to grasp its vernacular. He toiled with a speech coach to lower his voice. Kennedy was a voracious reader, building perhaps politics' largest vocabulary since Churchill. Before running for president, he often put on a smoking jacket, sat in his study, and played Winston on his phonograph to hear, among other jewels, "This was their finest hour" and "blood, toil, tears, and sweat" and "Give us the tools, and we will finish the job." Later, as president, JFK used chief speechwriter Theodore Sorensen to help draft his inaugural, Cuban Missile Crisis, and nuclear disarmament treaty texts. He absorbed Churchill well.

Kennedy grasped the difference between writing for the eye and ear: the latter was more informal, casual, yet still structured, with an opening, middle, and close. Before the inaugural, Sorensen reread the Gettysburg Address, finding that 71 percent of all its words were one syllable. "Let the word go forth," said JFK, each word monosyllabic. Over the years social media have conducted informal polls about the leading New Englander of the twentieth century. Subscribers often make Ted Williams runner-up. Invariably, Kennedy ranks number one, defining what F. Scott Fitzgerald called style or personality: "an unbroken series of successful gestures."

Kennedy evoked a dream boat home less of a fictional Camelot than that of quality and ambition. Williams was more volcanic: elegant as a stallion, long-limbed like a pelican, and jittery as a colt. Their fates flanked, overlapped, but seldom merged. "I didn't like the [Kennedy] family," said No. 9, a long-time Republican. "A lot of it was the old man [JFK's father]. Win at all cost. Bootlegging, prostitution." The Kid and JFK circled each other, warily, with respect, Williams through the 1950s larger than the clan. Kennedy's revenge was the support of elites who once abhorred his family and the joy of becoming president.

On May 30, 1961, the day after JFK's forty-fourth birthday, the Yankees, visiting his home city, previewed their 109-53 season of a big-league-record 240 homers, six players hitting 20 or more. Whitey Ford finished 25-4. Reliever Luis Arroyo was 15-5. The infield seemed as impregnable as Fort Knox. Kennedy greeted one group of Nobel Prize recipients by calling them "the most extraordinary collection of talent . . . that has ever been gathered together at the White House, with the possible exception of when Thomas Jefferson dined alone." The 1961 Yankees may have been the most extraordinary collection of baseball talent ever gathered at Fenway, with the possible exception of when Teddy Ballgame took batting practice. As proof, in that game they bashed a franchise-record seven homers, routing Boston, 12–3.

"A good mixture of Red Sox and Yankees fans," Mel Allen said of Governor Paul Dever and Democratic National Chairman John Bailey, among others meeting in the Hub to fete JFK. A year later actress Marilyn Monroe sang "Happy Birthday" to the president at Madison Square Garden. "Having been sung to in such a sweet, wholesome way," Kennedy said of Monroe, "I can now retire from politics." In another event, JFK hosted a dinner at 1600 Pennsylvania Avenue for distinguished Harvard alumni, most a generation or two older. "It is difficult to welcome you to the White House," he told them, "because at least two-thirds of you have attended more stag dinners here than I have."

Kennedy used age in a self-deprecatory fashion. Early in the 1960 season, the NL batting titan of his time, Stan Musial, was waiting for the Cardinals team bus outside the Schroeder Hotel in Milwaukee when a fellow Democrat came up and shook hands. "I'm Jack Kennedy," the forty-two-year-old told Stan the Man, thirty-nine. "They tell me you're too old to play baseball and I'm too young to be President, but maybe we'll fool them." Musial, who played twenty-two seasons for St. Louis, retired with 3,630 hits—1,815 at home and 1,815 on the road—like something out of Ripley's *Believe It or Not*. In 1960 baseball's Polish Pope also campaigned ardently for JFK, especially among key ethnic Democrats.

In 1962 age once more tied them. DC Stadium hosted the capital's second All-Star Game since the 1937 event chockablock with Dizzy Dean, Earl Averill, and FDR. Kennedy was delighted to see Stan, who recalled 1960 and added, "Mr. President, I guess we fooled 'em." They made some pair: JFK, forty-five, growing as a leader; the Man, almost forty-two, hitting an age-defying .330. Each attended a black-tie White House pre–All-Star Game event. The next afternoon the Irish Brahmin threw out the first pitch. Musial then got the loudest ovation of any player from the capacity 45,480 crowd, pinch-hitting in the sixth inning. "Wouldn't it be great if the old pro got a hit?" JFK asked Dave Powers, at which point the Man spanked a single, left for a pinch runner, and heeded Kennedy's wave to revisit his box. "I got a bigger kick out of the handshake before the game," Stan conceded. The throng, going bonkers, disagreed.

By then the president had named long-time muse Powers his "undersecretary of baseball," Dave joked, his job description including briefing JFK on the Red Sox. As for Musial, he retired with a single in his last at-bat in 1963 and was elected to the Hall of Fame in 1969, his first year of eligibility.

In 1989, Musial attended a seminar. "Stan," the moderator said, ".331 lifetime, what do you think you'd hit today—watered-down pitching, expansion?"

The Man replied, "Oh, .285, .290."

"Stan, you're a modest guy," the moderator jousted, "but what are you talking about, .285, .290?"

Musial said, "What the hell, I'm sixty-nine years old."

Stan shared Boston's adulatory tone toward the JFK Library and Museum, dedicated in 1979. Kennedy "loved [the] city with a patriot's love," said his brother, Senator Edward Kennedy, or "Eddie," as JFK called him. "He loved the sea with a sailor's love." The library lies adjacent to the University of Massachusetts, four miles from downtown Boston. Kennedy's twenty-six-foot sloop, the *Victura*, overlooks the entrance to Boston Harbor. Acquired by the family in the 1930s, the boat is named for a Greek word meaning "bound to win." Forever the Young Man and the Sea.

Kennedy called speechwriter Sorensen his "intellectual blood bank." In 1946 Powers, a Democratic strategist and JFK's *political* blood bank whom he met a year earlier, guided the then-shy twenty-nine-year-old navy war hero through stump speeches in strange Hub neighborhoods to a seat in Congress. That spring The Kid, twenty-seven, rejoined the Red Sox after World War II. In June Williams blasted Fenway's longest homer—502 feet, to a right-field bleacher seat in section 42, row 37, the seat still painted red—then went deep off Rip Sewell's blooper, or "Eephus" pitch, at the 1946 All-Star Game a month later in the Fens. Sewell threw the Eephus "like a softballer," said Williams. "And I swung as hard as I could and the wind was blowing out."

Cleveland player-manager Lou Boudreau shifted all but his left fielder to the right-field side of second base, trying to make Ted pay for thinking it illegal not to pull. In the 1946 World Series Cardinals skipper Eddie Dyer emulated the "Boudreau Shift." In response Williams bunted. St. Louis won a seven-game epoch. Ted spent the next decade and a half obsessed with winning the first Sox Series title since the last year of the first Great War, "more for Mr. [Sox owner Tom] Yawkey," he said, "than me." In 1952, Williams off to Korea, JFK upset U.S. senate incumbent Henry Cabot Lodge Jr. His staff readied for 1958 reelection, prologue to a bigger job in 1960.

In 1957 Williams, thirty-nine, averaged a stunning .388, the Yankees' Mantle doing what he did when Ted batted, "sit on the dugout step and study" the man with as many nicknames as batting titles (six): The Kid; the Thumper; the Splendid Splinter; No. 9; Teddy Ballgame; and, in Irish wards, using Gaelic, Himself. Journalist Murray Kempton wrote, "I don't think of myself as a Democrat as much as I am a fan of Adlai Stevenson." The *Boston Globe*'s Martin Nolan was first a fan of Williams, then baseball. Nolan said his "boyhood admiration of the graceful swing of No. 9 was not much upset by revelations that he cussed." Once Ted gave boo-birds what papers primly called "a French salute."

In 1966, entering the Hall of Fame, the 1939–42 and 1946–60 Sox signature gave a moving speech, written the night before in longhand, saying, "[I hope] that someday the names of Satchel Paige and Josh Gibson in some way can be added as a symbol of the great Negro players that are not here only because they were not given a chance." To Curt Gowdy, the 1951–65 voice of the Red Sox and a close friend of The Kid's, "this was just Ted doing what he thought was right." Williams could be prone to bully. Less known was his sensitivity to others' pain. His mother—"the Angel of Tijuana," preferring volunteering to parenting—left their home in San Diego a sty when he was young. Ashamed, Ted spent a life helping those who seemed alone.

In the 1950s he learned of a ten-year-old with leukemia who had made his Midwest hospital room a Williams shrine. Each day nurses sat the boy on the floor with a little bat, got on their hands and knees, and rolled a ball down the corridor. As he hit it, they yelled "Double!" or "Triple!" or "A homer was hit by Ted!" Listening, The Kid insisted on seeing him—he had his own plane—on two conditions: no media and no one would mention it. "The boy died, but met his hero," said Gowdy. "This happened all the time."

Later Ted became what *si* termed "the patron saint of Cooperstown"; he had an opinion on everything, less mellowed than matured. As a player, Williams gave new connotation to the term "perfectionist," often a pain in the patootie. "Our tie was hunting and fishing," said Wyoming-born Gowdy, "and only then baseball." Once Ted showed his friend why the Air Force rated his vision perfect, Curt disbelieving what he saw.

"There!" Williams boomed, hunting. "Watch two ducks coming at 3 o'clock."

Curt: "Where?"

"*There!*" In two minutes, ducks appeared.

In 1960 Ted helped his team draw more than 1.1 million, the last time it passed one million till 1967. Most came to bid an affectionate farewell. "For so long," said Curt, "he'd been too stubborn to meet Red Sox fans halfway." Only as New England belatedly eyed a future without The Kid did a white-hot affair become old-shoe love. On Wednesday, September 28, Gowdy arrived only thirty minutes before the year's last game at Fenway Park. Sox equipment manager Johnny Orlando revealed that Williams had a chest cold and would miss that weekend's final three-game series in New York.

"Listen, this is The Kid's last game," Orlando told Gowdy. "He's gonna retire after today."

Curt approached Williams: "Are you [retiring]?"

Ted said, "Yeah, don't mention it till the game starts."

Years later, Gowdy said, "Nobody knew."

In a pregame *salaam*, the Sox retired uniform No. 9, Curt emceeing. Warned that he didn't have a note of introduction, Gowdy ad-libbed, saying, "I don't need any [notes] about Williams." To the last, as Sox announcer Ned Martin dubbed Ted, the Big Guy was himself. He pricked reporters: "Despite some of the terrible things written about me by the knights of the keyboard up there . . . I'd like to forget them but I can't." He lauded "the greatest owner in baseball and the greatest fans in America." Gowdy understood. "You had to know Ted—he got mad at himself more than anybody. I think New England forgave him more than he did himself."

A game against Baltimore followed—meaningless and all-meaning. Williams walked and flied out twice. In the eighth inning he batted against Baltimore's Jack Fisher, half his age at twenty-one. It was raining, lights on, the ball not carrying. "And there's a long drive to deep right-center! It could be! It could be! It is!" said Curt—incredulous, tone rising, voice breaking. "It's a home run! Ted Williams has homered in his last time at bat in a Red Sox uniform! . . . At home plate, they're waiting for him!" Curt remembered being "choked up": "My heart was pounding—unbelievably emotional." A crowd of 10,454 had tonsils redder than Red Sox hose.

The Kid refused to tip his cap, John Updike observing that "God does not answer letters." (He last tipped it when some of the Fenway faithful, to No. 9 "fair-weather," booed Ted in his second year.) In 1958 a writer said: "Because of [Williams's hitting .388 a year earlier], Boston finished third. Without him, it is hard to say how far they could sink." The Athens of America was about to learn, wrote Ed Linn in 1960, "how England felt when it lost India."

Enamored of sports on TV, John F. Kennedy partook in America's early 1960s pro football spiral. Liking baseball, his restless nature made it hard for him at one time or another to endure the game in person or on the tube. He never complained publicly, realizing the pastime's appeal. Of greater threat to baseball was its invasion by football body snatchers—especially those deeming Fenway Park a dinosaur, not knowing what they had. Had JFK lived, his administration might have faced a pickle. "About twenty times," Yawkey said, he tried to close Lansdowne Street, moving back the left-field wall. Later he endorsed a commission's $87 million retractable roof stadium. Repeatedly the city of Boston and state legislature balked. What should officials do— renovate Fenway or build a Red Sox/pro football Patriots hub, only to later find, as Michael Dukakis said, that "the Red Sox without Fenway [were] not . . . the Red Sox"? The dilemma needed adult supervision, perhaps in a second Kennedy term.

JFK had grown up on the Olde Towne Team, in a time and area where baseball was ubiquitous. Now some spoke of the Sox moving if they failed to get what Washington, New York, Atlanta, and St. Louis, among others, had or would shortly have—a multi-sport clone. Leaving Boston would be heretical to a son who had followed Lefty Grove and Jimmie Foxx and Bobby Doerr while attending Harvard, being schooled in Britain, and serving in the Pacific. Kennedy loved the Fens, had attended days where the Sox honored each New England state, and expected the unexpected from The Kid. The 1961–66 Red

Sox placed sixth, eighth, and seventh before November 22, 1963, and eighth and ninth twice after. On one hand, much of Fenway's infrastructure was as old as the park's 1934 reconstruction. On the other, JFK knew from boyhood why Leonard Bernstein said that music—here, baseball's—"didn't have to pass the censor of the brain before it could reach the heart."

Politics being what it is, a solution seemed insolvable when, out of nowhere, 1967 reached the heart. Memory pictures JFK in love with the Sox again—had he had a chance. The year began with rookie skipper Dick Williams and outfielder Carl Yastrzemski, No. 8, who as a 1961 rookie had been somehow expected to replace No. 9. In a game at Yankee Stadium viewed by Jackie Kennedy and son John, Yaz's great ninth-inning catch briefly preserved rookie Billy Rohr's first-week near no-hit 3–0 victory. "The fans began to sense it," announcer Ken Coleman said later. "This year was not quite the same." It was not the same across America: Riot seared 159 cities; seventy-six died. Protestors fought police. Vietnam presaged today's Divided States. The Sox took a fractured time and magically made it better. The post–All-Star break Townies had a ten-game winning streak, returning in contention to Logan Airport. Ten thousand met their plane. One day the Sox twirled a triple play. Another, rookie Reggie Smith hit a scoreless tenth-inning triple, a driver, listening on car radio, refusing to enter the Sumner Tunnel until learning if the Sox had won. Hundreds of drivers backed up, not honking; they were listening too. By late summer two-and-a-half games divided five teams.

The lead kept changing, Boston winning once on last-out ballet: "A chopper. Over the mound. May be tough!" Ned Martin said. "Charged by [Rico] Petrocelli. Throws to first. He's out! The ball game is over!"—Red Sox, 12–11. A day later, the Townies trailed, 8–0, prompting Yaz to navigate the dugout. "'We're going to *win* this game!' he told each of us," said Petrocelli. "Man, by now we *believed*!" In the eighth inning, eight-all, an unsung Boston infielder smacked a fly ball deep into left-center field: "It is . . . a *home run*!" Coleman cried. "Jerry Adair has hit his second home run of the 1967 season and the Red Sox, who trailed, 8 to 0, are now leading in the eighth inning, 9 to 8!" Four miles away

Adair's poke prompted "a sound wave—one crescendo after another"—from one hundred thousand at Revere Beach, most listening to Sox radio from Fenway. The roar blanketed the beach; few believed what they were hearing. Faith fell back on the man with, as Gowdy said, "that unbelievable last name."

Dick Williams had played on the '50s Dodgers of Campanella, Hodges, Snider, and Robinson, having never seen a year like Yaz's 1967: a .326 average, 44 homers, 121 RBIs, and his third of seven Gold Gloves. By Thursday, September 28, Minnesota led Boston by a game, closing the season Saturday and Sunday in the Fens. Stores closed. Churches opened. Truth and consequence: Boston must sweep to win or force a playoff. It led on Saturday, 3–2, in the seventh inning. "Hit deep toward right field!" Martin said of Yaz. "This may be gone! It's outta' here!" Girders throbbed. Seconds later Ned tied precision, incredulity, and frame of reference: "If you've just turned your radio on"—pause—"*it's happened again*. Yastrzemski's hit a three-run homer, and it's now 6–2, Red Sox." Boston won, 6 to 4.

On Sunday Detroit had to take a doubleheader from California to tie the Sox or Twins. Minnesota led, 2–0, as pitcher Jim Lonborg, batting in the sixth inning, executed an older-than-Fenway play. "Lonborg bunts it down third! Tovar in, no play!" Boston scored five runs. "The Red Sox are out in the sixth," said Coleman. "But what a sixth inning it was!" Detroit won its first game. At Fenway Yaz threw out a runner to kill a Twins eighth-inning rally: Boston, 5–3. The next inning Minnesota's Rich Rollins batted. "The pitch . . . is looped toward shortstop. Petrocelli's back, he's got it! The Red Sox win!" Martin disbelieved. "And there's pandemonium on the field! Listen!"

Watching, Michael Dukakis feared for Lonborg's post-game safety, hundreds of bodies converging on him between the mound and dugout to form a tide carrying the starter for a frightful moment toward right field. "To me, he's the one who stands out about '67, even more than Yaz," the then State House Representative said of that year's 22-9 AL Cy Young honoree. "We hadn't had a great pitcher since before the Korean War. And here he is, a matinee idol, went to Stanford, would become a dentist" only to that winter hurt himself in a skiing accident. All that lay unknown, including the second game of the Tigers doubleheader.

After Boston's victory, radio in that different age tied its clubhouse and Tiger Stadium: Detroit had to lose for a Red Sox pennant. In the ninth inning the Angels led, 8–5, two Tigers on and one out. Dick McAuliffe promptly slapped into a game-ending double play. Petrocelli saw tears in Yawkey's eyes: "[He] loved the Sox so much, all those near-misses [five pennants or Series lost on the final day or in the seventh game respectively from 1946 to 1975, the year before his death], drinking champagne, more fan than owner." The next day's *Boston Record American* cover blared CHAMPS! above a drawing of two red socks. It was crewel, not cruel.

Ultimately the Cardinals won the World Series. Edward Kennedy threw out the first ball before the opener at Fenway. Many thought then of JFK, as writers and others had in the wake of Dallas, urging that DC Stadium be renamed in his honor. (The site of Philadelphia's Army-Navy game was instead.) At the time, terming John F. Kennedy "a true friend of sports . . . [who] left a magnificent mark on the sports world," *The Sporting News* noted that there was still "much doubt that the tradition of having the president throw out the first ball to open the Washington baseball season would continue." The Secret Service feared he would be a "sitting duck."

Churchill maintained that "courage is rightly esteemed the first of human qualities . . . because it is the quality which guarantees all others." Kennedy identified with that quotation because the English legend was his hero and because he lived so much of life on the edge. We know instinctively that JFK would have wanted the first-pitch tradition preserved. Knock on wood: it gloriously survives. Think of John Fitzgerald Kennedy each Opening Day and of how as president he would have loved the team that ennobled 1967, New England's Ozymandias year.

EIGHT

Larger Than Life

Lyndon B. Johnson, 1963–1969

In January 1965 the former home of the Washington Senators, then "a mass of tangled weeds and spectre-like stands," according to the *Washington Post*, yielded to a wrecking ball that savaged steel and cement but spared sweet memory. The prior fall local NBC-TV affiliate WRC had aired a documentary, *The Last Out*, about 1911–61 Griffith Stadium, now replaced by a Howard University hospital—"pretty apt," observed 1962–68 expansion Senators PA announcer Phil Hochberg, "when you think of how many broken hearts the ball club left behind." (To restate, the names "Senators" and "Nationals" are used interchangeably, as they were through franchise history.)

Hosted by network and local sportscaster Jim Simpson, *The Last Out* captured the household names and theatric plays of the yard's motley past, not exclusively but mostly baseball's. Alone stood the Nationals' Everest. "The gates of Troy never had to withstand a storm of humanity such as assailed the gates of Griffith Stadium," the program waxed of the Senators' first World Series title in 1924. As any Washingtonian worthy of the name knows, to this day they have not won another.

As he did in 1924, Nats outfielder Sam Rice absolved Giants third baseman Freddie Lindstrom of muffing a ground ball that was said to have caromed off a pebble and over Lindstrom to score Game Seven's 4–3 twelfth-inning Series-winning run. "It was just a slow bouncer," Rice told *The Last Out*. "Otherwise it would have been an easy out."

A year later more debate roiled another Fall Classic, Pittsburgh's Earl Smith lashing a third-game fly to deep right-center field. Did Rice catch the ball?

"You measured the distance to the fence at the crack of the bat, turned, ran back, leaped and pulled in the ball as you fell into the stands," Simpson asked of 1925. "Isn't that right?"

"The umpire said so," Rice said, tongue in cheek.

"Yes, but did you actually catch the ball?" Simpson asked.

As noted earlier, Rice vowed to tell all in a letter to be opened when he died, sowing doubt where none deserved to dwell. It said he never lost possession. Still, the Pirates won Game Three, 4–3, and that Series. *The Last Out* also aired pitcher Walter Johnson reporting to spring training in a derby, Babe Ruth in retirement bringing center stage—himself—to the seats, and the Bears nipping the Redskins, 73–0, in the December 8, 1940, NFL title game. On December 7, 1941, Pearl Harbor Day, the 'Skins led Philadelphia at home when the PA voice began ordering all admirals and generals to immediately report to duty.

The 1964 TV program showed broadcaster Arch McDonald visiting Griffith Stadium after Clark Griffith died in 1955. Archival film vaunted the Nats' owner helping form the American League, partly birthing the presidential liturgy of throwing out a first pitch, and listing Griffith's all-time DC team on a tableau outside its entrance: Clyde Milan, Sam Rice, Goose Goslin, Joe Cronin, Joe Judge, Bucky Harris, Ossie Bluege, Muddy Ruel, Walter Johnson, Earl Whitehill, and Fred "Firpo" Marberry. Even included on the program was a mock-sore fan looking for Fred Schulte after another Series loss in 1933: "I took your advice and bet fifty dollars on the Senators. How about lending me fifty dollars on my seven-jewel watch?"

Jim Simpson pointed at the sign crowning Griffith's left-center-field stands, nicked by Mickey Mantle's 565-foot home run in 1953 before the ball exited the park. "Did you ever see a longer hit here?" he said. Rice nodded: "Do you see that tree beyond the . . . stands? Well, Babe Ruth hit a ball into the top of that tree." As happens, one baseball story spins another. Yankee Stadium was not the only House That Ruth Built, Rice said: Griffith Stadium's predecessor had wooden stands, outfield ropes, and a capacity then of about fifteen thousand. Actually, a fire sired Griffith. Babe begot *other* parks, "so exciting that crowds increased around the league." Ruth hit as high as he did long, once lofting a pop so remote that he seemed to reach third base before the ball reached the ground.

As much as anything, *The Last Out* aired presidents enacting a first-ball script. You saw Wilson ablaze in white pants, blue blazer, and straw hat; Harding with Graham McNamee; and Coolidge keeping uncommonly warm in overcoat and homburg hat, wife Grace keeping score. Hoover was shown building Stanford University's sports program; FDR, with cigarette holder tilted upward; Truman, smiling, yawning; and Ike, recalling the diamond at West Point. JFK had been Griffith's last first-toss pitcher and apparently, said Simpson, "the president who threw the ball farther than any other president."

As poignant was the coda—a benediction, of sort. Across the street from the Senators' chapel stood the "Church of God." Griffith Stadium's last day of baseball was September 21, 1961, Washington eerily playing Minnesota, which had robbed DC of its pre-1961 team. Here the old Nats returned, before teens wanting souvenirs and old men misting and vendors peddling and a church carillon playing "Auld Lang Syne."

Griffith was demolished at a time when some in the nation for which John F. Kennedy had nearly died in World War II had already begun to worry about the America that had asked for their sacrifice. Raised on modesty, unity, and pride in our past, most of the 1961 Senators' final-game 4,460 attendees had grown up in such a land. They did not expect that the decade ahead would increasingly mouth, "Do your own thing," "If it feels good, do it," and other bromides attractive to a largely narcissistic upper class. As we look back, self-absorption in the 1960s enjoyed a triumph undreamed of under Ike or JFK.

Such a fate was not inevitable when two days after Dallas, Lyndon Johnson was in the Oval Office, having not yet moved into the White House. Aides at the vice presidential home were drafting his first speech to Congress, text passed back and forth. The object of such attention was known to have a healthy ego, once parodying an introduction that even he thought immodest. "I only wish my parents were alive to hear those words. My father would have enjoyed them. And my mother would have believed them." Fact or pose—who knew? Aides enjoyed repeating stories they knew might seem unbelievable but for the source. Johnson reportedly gave his secretary dictation while taking an enema, spoke to aides while on a bathroom stool, urinated off the front porch of the LBJ Ranch, and gulped food from the plate of the person next to him without asking. Show *that* to the nation.

In 1908 a baby had been born in the Hill Country of Texas, where Johnson soon heard train whistles in the night. They stirred "child's dreams," protégé and three-term Lone Star governor John Connally said in a poignant eulogy, "[that] could be as wide as the sky and [make] his future as green as winter oats because this, after all, was America." Later LBJ, a 1930 Southwest Texas State Teachers College (now Texas State University) graduate; 1930s teacher in Cotulla, Texas; and congressman first elected in 1936 mocked "Ivy Leaguers" and "Harvards," insecurity making him pine for their esteem. The stiletto lingers of a boy, walking barefoot behind a plow. To know Johnson meant fathoming Texas's impatience with limits of any kind.

America's first impression of him as president came on November 27, 1963: LBJ as Paul Bunyan out of Johnny Appleseed by way of Billy Graham. "Mr. Speaker, Mr. President . . . my fellow Americans," he told Congress the day before Thanksgiving, "all I have I would have given gladly not to be standing here today"—a brilliant first line written by Kennedy speechwriter Theodore Sorensen. JFK had said, "Let us begin." The new president urged, "Today, in this moment of new resolve . . . let us continue."

Likening FDR to his daddy, the son began to show his will. In that address Johnson said, "We have talked long enough in this country about equal rights. We have talked for one hundred years or more. It is time to write the next chapter, and to write it in the book of law." Congress's bill desegregated public facilities. Yet the "Great Society"—LBJ's domestic vista—was inchoate until a 1964 liberal landslide put the next Congress in Johnson's pocket. It passed aid to the poor, Medicare for the aged, federal aid to education, and the Voting Rights Act, among others. Ralph Ellison wrote that Johnson might have to settle for being the greatest president for the poor and black "for that, in itself, is a very great honor indeed."

At LBJ's peak he appeared invulnerable. It couldn't and didn't last. The 1949–61 U.S. senator and 1961–63 VP had little background abroad, fewer bona fides, and only a belief born of World War II that appeasement must not stand. He had inherited sixteen thousand advisers in South Vietnam, Dwight Eisenhower warning against matching troops "against the teeming millions of Asians." Ignoring him, the president introduced more than one hundred thousand American combat troops in 1965, a "gradual escalation" aimed at winning the war while building the Great Society. Connally said, "The economy can't sustain guns *and* butter." Johnson might have listened to him here too.

Ultimately the number of U.S. troops reached 543,000. Still LBJ dallied between what journalists termed "the hawks' more war" and "the doves' more peace." He hid the cost of the war abroad, fearing that Congress would cut the cost of his war at home. "We don't want American boys to do the fighting for Asian boys," he said in 1964, but let it happen while denying it. Many later ascribed Johnson's fall to jiggering Vietnam statistics. Or was it that he trusted no one to take the *real* LBJ?—masking what he was to *project* what he wasn't.

Privately LBJ would squeeze, caress, and nigh overwhelm a visitor— the famed "Johnson Treatment." Publicly he was by dizzying turn solemn and unctuous, then exuberant and effervescent, wearing glasses, then contact lenses—each a makeover. Which was he? What if the thirty-sixth president had seemed the same? He would have at least appeared *sincere*—as insiders knew, always trying to help "the weak and the meek," if he could only leave "that bitch of a war."

Johnson began choosing bombing targets for generals: a novice guiding experts. At night, haunted, he checked casualties in the Situation Room, an intelligence center in the White House basement created after the Bay of Pigs in 1961 to monitor and confront crises here and abroad. Hardliners felt he should leave the military alone. Others scorned U.S. intervention. On TV, university buildings burned and scholarly works were destroyed, inner-city riots torched firms and killed residents, and anti-war protestors clashed with club-swinging police. Middle America blamed LBJ. What part of right against left, hard hat against hippie, "counterculture" against law and order stemmed from Vietnam, who knew? In 1969 the Canadian group The Guess Who released the song "She's Come Undone." America did.

Outside students raged, "Hey! Hey! LBJ! How many kids did you kill today?" Hurt, he seemed lost: "I can't get out [of Vietnam]. I can't finish it with what I have," he told wife Lady Bird. "So what the hell can I do?" At the August 1968 Democratic Convention in Chicago, tear gas and broken glass affirmed that year's March 31 Johnson decision to spurn reelection and unite the country, suggestive of how he once distinguished politics. He left the White House the next January, obsessed over history's view, and died four years later at sixty-four "of a broken heart," Richard Nixon said.

Napoleon mused, "Ability is fine, but give me commanders who have luck." Johnson fused courage, intellect, and a raw feel for power—everything but luck. LBJ inherited a war mostly from Kennedy and also Ike. Aide Jack Valenti wrote that Johnson was "a classic Achilles figure, immensely human, often commanding in presence, and noble in aim . . . flawed by human error and a misperception of ultimate reality in a war seemingly without end." The war in Vietnam ended Lyndon Johnson's presidency. It should not dim the memory of what earlier he bequeathed.

LBJ once likened himself to baseball's colossus with a bat. "They booed Ted Williams too, remember?" he said. "They'll say about me I knocked the ball over the fence—but they don't like the way he stands at the plate." It was unusual for Johnson to use baseball as a metaphor since he had rarely had time for anything but politics. Father Sam, a member of the state legislature, took Lyndon as a youth to Austin to strategize and through the Hill Country to campaign. "I wish[ed] it would never end," Lyndon said. "I loved the feel, smell, everything about it." Later he and John Connally attended football games at the University of Texas. "He wouldn't even watch [the game]," said the person who, except for Lady Bird, knew Johnson best. "He'd look at the crowd, waving all over, look at everything but the field." His closest aide admitted to "never seeing Johnson read a book," even about politics. As a child LBJ played baseball along the Pedernales River, later not seeming to care about it. Ironically, like the summer game, Johnson as president was labeled "establishment" and "square."

Before the mid-1960s, with baseball clearly Big-Game America, LBJ's South was the sole region where (college) football was competitive. In a sense Johnson's baseball *dis*interest stemmed from politics being his *only* interest. If the pastime involved politics, he liked the pastime. As 1950s Senate majority leader, LBJ attended games at Griffith Stadium, finding old Texas pals like Red Sox skipper Mike "Pinky" Higgins. "Politics was people," said then Sox voice Curt Gowdy, "and Johnson related to that even in baseball, hoping to translate a relationship into legislation." In July 1962 Lyndon keynoted a luncheon to honor the new DC Stadium, hosting its first All-Star Game just after the Supreme Court outlawed prayer in public schools. "We cheer for the Senators, we pray for the Senators," Johnson quipped, "and we hope that the Supreme Court doesn't declare that unconstitutional." It was a safe and not unwitty mot.

In 1965 commissioner Ford Frick retired, succeeded by former Air Force lieutenant general William D. Eckert, who as baseball's "Unknown Soldier," jibed writer Larry Fox, remained its feeble commish through 1968. Ignorant of everything balls and strikes, Eckert made even LBJ appear a graduate scholar of the game. Not long ago, wrote the *Wall Street Journal*, "Baseball had ranked with apple pie, the flag, and motherhood as an American institution. Not now." A year after taking office, Eckert came to the White House to present the customary season pass. Unlike Ike or JFK, Johnson couldn't wait for the commissioner to leave. After sixty seconds to receive the gift and take photos, LBJ clapped his hands and snapped, "Let's go. We've got a lot of work to do." No questions, please, from reporters; Johnson virtually threw Eckert off the White House grounds.

To LBJ baseball only intrigued with a Texas twinge. In April 1965 he dedicated the Houston Astrodome, the 6-foot-4 president likely viewing baseball's first indoor stadium as a colossus, like himself.

At DC Stadium Johnson saw opening games in 1964, 1965, and 1967. Among those he missed: the September 26, 1965, union of town and teams, Minnesota edging the Nats, 2–1, to clinch a first pennant in its old home, Washington. Another: the April 11, 1966, big-league debut of Emmett Ashford, the Majors' first African American umpire, on DC's Opening Day. Vice president Hubert Humphrey threw out the first ball. Johnson could and should have. In April 1968 Martin Luther King Jr. was murdered, strife tore more than 250 cities, and Opening Day was twice postponed. The capital rioted. The Eighty-Second Airborne Division and National Guard patrolled its streets and parks. *Again* Humphrey handled the first pitch, saying incongruously, "This is the finest opening day I've ever experienced." *Again* LBJ was missing in action, due to business, wanting to avoid catcall, or hoping to cool the public temper—who can say? He should have attended, respecting the game and showing courage. The gulf between president and pastime had seldom loomed as wide.

To compound insult, a late 1968 Lou Harris Poll noted that for the first time "football [had] passed baseball as the favorite sport," 23 to 19 percent. "The problem is that baseball has become too dull." By two to one "fans agree that 'there are too many times during a baseball game when there is no action.'" Even its best teams now seemed to accent pitch and catch. Sandy Koufax threw a record fourth no-hitter, a perfect game in 1965. A year later he won a third Cy Young Award (after 1966, each league named one) and had a record of 27-9, 317 strikeouts, and 1.73 ERA. That fall, what was bad for the ex-Brooklyns was great for Baltimore: Los Angeles offensively set a World Series record for fewest runs, hits, total bases, lowest batting average, and most straight scoreless innings. On November 18, 1966, Koufax retired with an arthritic elbow, saying "I don't regret for one minute the twelve years I've spent with baseball, but I could regret one season too many."

For batters, one game against Bob Gibson was normally one game too many. In the 1967 World Series the Cardinals right-handed pitcher struck out twenty-six Red Sox in twenty-seven innings. In 1968 he arguably forged the greatest-ever season, best in complete games (28), shutouts (13), strikeouts (268), and lowest-ever ERA (1.12). That year's

NL Cy Young honoree and MVP retired 251-174, fanning 3,117 with 9 Gold Gloves, a warrior between the lines. In 1965 mate Bill White was traded to the Phillies. The next time they met, Gibbie threw at his head. Once, pitching like an egg timer, Bob was asked by his own catcher, Tim McCarver, to slow down. "What are you doing here?" Gibson barked when Tim neared the mound. "Go back behind the plate—the only thing you know about pitching is that it's hard to hit."

Democrat Humphrey and Republican Nixon, 1968's major-party nominees for president, enjoyed, unlike Franklin Roosevelt, good pitching as well as batting. This was fortunate since almost everyone that year forgot how to hit. Carl Yastrzemski's paltry .301 average won the AL batting title. The Dodgers' Don Drysdale threw a record fifty-eight-and-two-thirds scoreless innings. Most boppers had almost vanished. "Westward look, the land is bright," wrote the English poet Arthur Hugh Clough. For hope, baseball looked to Michigan, where Jim Northrup bombed four grand slams and the Tigers franchise smashed its all-time attendance record—2,031,847. After the season, baseball lowered the mound and reduced the strike zone from fifteen to ten inches to restore offense. "For the game, 1968 was a year to forget," said Tigers announcer Ernie Harwell. Detroit wanted to remember. "Every night there was a hero." The patient was baseball. Its placebo was Detroit.

If the 1968 Tigers helped rescue baseball, they could not save its ex-military-man-turned-commissioner, Eckert decommissioned, as noted, December 6. The *Los Angeles Times*' Bob Oates touted a successor. "[Vin] Scully has been with the [Dodgers] for many years on both coasts," he wrote. "He would bring . . . a first-class mind as well as the self-confidence to act when necessary and the self-control to abstain from action in other circumstances." Oates evoked Pete Rozelle, head of the post-1959 NFL. "Scully's knowledge of baseball now is at least as great as Rozelle's knowledge [then] and the problems are similar." Owners wanted a lawyer, eventually making NL counsel Bowie Kuhn commissioner through 1984, his sixteen-year skein the post's longest since Landis's. He was born in Washington, where in fall 1968 another election held sway.

Throughout, the view of LBJ treating baseball as take-it-or-leave-it was basically correct. Yet the famed testimonial of Parisian-born Columbia University professor Jacques Barzun, "Whoever wants to know the heart and mind of America had better learn baseball," ironically applied almost as much in Johnson's early presidency as when it first appeared in 1954. The sport's regular-season network television audience trounced rival programming. The World Series and All-Star Game were TV's first- and second-ranked sports events respectively. The age's baseball fostered period culture. In the film *One Flew over the Cuckoo's Nest*, Jack Nicholson played a schizophrenic trying to hear Harwell air 1963 Series radio play-by-play. By 1964 the Fall Classic had been a small boy's Thanksgiving, Christmas, and Fourth of July for more than a third of a century. Johnson was the last president under whom each Series game was played in daytime, a gift today's youth cannot fathom. A student smuggled the Classic into class by radio; hearing faint play-by-play, even a teacher craved the score.

By the age of ten, unaware of Thomas Wolfe, I knew why he said, "Almost everything I know of spring [also fall] is in it"—a child's game played with bat and ball. On black-and-white TV the Series' seeming home was Bob Costas's Emerald City: "I was so impressed with the monuments at Yankee Stadium that the first time I walked on the field I was careful not to disturb their [Babe Ruth's and Lou Gehrig's] plot," he said. George Will spent his October boyhood hallucinating in Illinois: "You'd hear the [Series sponsor] 'Gillette Blue Blades March' and then the camera'd pan Wrigley Field. The Cubs'd be in the Series." He dreamed of ivy, bleachers, gales off the lake, and perhaps their 2016 Classic triumph.

In 1971 NBC aired the first prime-time Series game for working people. A year later all weekday coverage repaired to night. Since 1985 virtually every minute has been prime time, aiming to swell viewership. Instead it shrank under the law of unintended consequences, making the Classic common prime-time programming, not something that "you'd talk about in the morning at school," then "listen to or watch on TV," said future TV host Larry King, growing up in Brooklyn. Afterward "the street corner replayed every play of every game."

In 1978 each World Series game *averaged* 44.28 million viewers. By 2012 a new average low watched of only 12.64 million. For the last thirty years the Fall Classic has lost an average of 775,000 viewers per annum. In 1980 a massive 130 million of 225 million saw all or part of the Series on NBC. Even in 2016 little more than *half* that number (75 million) watched America's Cubs triumph in a far *larger* public (325 million). The Classic's 22.85 million per-game average was *half*, in turn, of 1978's.

More glumly, in 2017 the kaleidoscopic seven-game Astros-Dodgers Series fell to an average of 18.71 million viewers. Largely missing is the feeling, especially among the young, that Costas expressed when asked what baseball meant to him and other Baby Boomers growing up. "Everything," he replied.

This feeling began to fade for those of Boomer age in the mid-1960s with four changes that heightened baseball's sad and unexpected fall: each disturbing—in total, shocking—to an average fan. The first involved the announcer most synonymous coast-to-coast with baseball, especially "America's greatest sports event." Mel Allen had aired his first Fall Classic in Roosevelt's second term, another in his third term, and seven under Truman. Reaching full flower under Ike, he did a maximum eight Series (1953–60) and maximum three (1961–63) under JFK—eleven in a row during baseball's last duration as America's undisputed sport. Allen's final Series game was at Dodger Stadium on October 6, 1963.

In 1964 the Yankees and NBC fired sportscasting's marquee name, a reason revealed decades later involving mistreatment by Allen's celebrity physician (who was also John F. Kennedy's). In his book *President Kennedy: Profile of Power*, journalist Richard Reeves relates Max Jacobson a.k.a. "Dr. Feelgood" prescribing for JFK a strange mix of vitamins, human placenta, and amphetamines for back pain, the president saying, "I don't care if it's horse piss, it works." Alarmed, Attorney General Robert Kennedy banned him from the White House. In 1975, Jacobson's license was revoked by the New York State Board of Regents, the physician dying in 1979.

As the 2007 book *The Voice: Mel Allen's Untold Story* says, by 1964 "Dr. Feelgood" had prescribed pills for Allen for several years to sustain his manic schedule, Mel's speech and thought devolving. He never grasped the change, even as it occurred. For a quarter century Allen had done virtually every major sports event; now, like *that*, he simply vanished. Better, he later staged a 1977–96 comeback on TV's *This Week in Baseball*. Until then, wrote *Newsday* in 1966, "Fans [were] still debating the merits of Allen, canned without public explanation. They . . . had a hard time making the adjustment. Who [could] forget . . . the boring game in Washington that Allen picked up by singing 'Yankee Doodle' between pitches?" There was no precedent for his disappearance and no parallel since.

The second shoe to drop hurt baseball's lure less than Allen's exit but perhaps its reputation more. In September 1966 a dreadful Yankees team drew 413 fans to The Stadium the day Michael Burke became president. On TV Red Barber, a Stripes voice since 1954, felt it "the perfect place for Burke to start, nowhere to go but up." Barber asked the director to pan the stands. No shot. He asked again. No go. He discovered a Yankees executive telling the director not to show the empty seats. "Report," Red recalled from old Dodgers teletype, saying, "I don't know what the paid attendance is, but whatever it is, it is the smallest crowd in the history of Yankee Stadium, and this crowd is the story, not the game." That month the man who quoted Carlyle and Thoreau was axed. Red's coda became to earn broadcasting's Pulitzer, the George Foster Peabody Award, for work on National Public Radio, before his death in 1992.

Like baseball, Allen, of Alabama, and Barber, of Florida and Mississippi, endured a third change for which many had ironically hoped and even a non-fan noted—the collapse of the twenty-four-karat franchise whose very name meant the game. In 1964, making their fourteenth World Series in the last sixteen years, the Yankees made their last Fall Classic until 1976. In 1965 New York flunked .500 in the regular season for the first time since 1925. Incredibly the 1966 Stripes placed last. The stereotypic insufferable Yankees fan had helped define the sport. Even Yankee-haters missed the team's peerless ability to gild big-league interest. To millions the worst baseball change of the mid-Johnson presidency involved another Southerner and favorite of LBJ's lifelong Sunbelt constituency—the pastime's most beloved network star.

As observed, Dizzy Dean had aired a CBS-TV *Game of the Week* each Saturday and Sunday since the mid-1950s. "The hinterlands and especially the South and West were his base," said CBS sports head Bill MacPhail—Johnson's too, when in 1960 he first ran for president, clientele overlapping. To protect local viewing, the series was blacked out near each Major League city, leaving Diz the entire nation west and south of St. Louis. Most *Game* viewers, like most Americans, were then small town or suburban, lower to middle class, identifying with *Grapes of Wrath* émigrés from the Dust Bowl and beyond. In 1958 *Game* was blacked out for the first time in Los Angeles and San Francisco. The down side of California's getting the Dodgers and Giants was losing Dean.

Some viewers drove to hotels beyond the fifty-mile blackout radius or bought roof antennas to see Diz. No solution existed when in 1966 NBC began a Saturday series whose exclusive coverage went everywhere. It wanted a more conventional play-by-play man, getting him in Curt Gowdy, only to have ratings drop. Diz was dispatched, having trounced NBC and ABC Saturday and Sunday baseball in his 1953–65 network spell by a Nielsen margin of three and four to one.

"Dean slaughtered guys like me, Joe Garagiola, Jack Buck, Bob Wolff," said NBC's Lindsey Nelson of sportscasters earning the Hall of Fame's Ford C. Frick broadcast award. (Diz's ongoing exclusion from that award is inexcusable). In two years, three of baseball's most luminous voices—Allen's, Barber's, and Dean's—had vanished from the sport, never to regularly broadcast it again.

By consensus this left Vin Scully, superstar, to embody baseball on the air through the last half century. Scully will revisit us when Ronald Reagan does, neighbors on the same street in Pacific Palisades, California, before taking their act national. Rick Reilly wrote, in the *Los Angeles Times*, "Flip on the car radio, and you can almost see him

[Vin] riding shotgun, swapping stories." The same could not be said of Lyndon Johnson, whose failure to communicate cost in peace and, above all, war.

Unlike the future president, LBJ's closest political friend for much of his time in Washington paid microscopic attention to big-league pillars on the field and behind the mike. Among the most respected and powerful members of the U.S. Senate from 1933 until his death in 1971, Richard Russell (D-GA) liked to study batting averages of not only his adopted hometown Senators but also of many players from the American League, preaching from the Book of Baseball for almost five decades on Capitol Hill.

A cherished tradition was Opening Day, which the political senators attended as a group. For Russell, finding friendship and affection hard to form, it was a command performance: a twin bill of his favorite sport and people. Later, asked what drew Johnson and him together, Russell said, "We both liked baseball. Right after Lyndon came to the Senate, for some reason we started going to the night baseball games together." Lady Bird might accompany them. "They would buy hot dogs and sit," she said, "and watch and talk about the prowess of this player or that player."

If no box seats were available, Russell and LBJ sat in the grandstand above them—two tall men in double-breasted suits and fedoras, sitting close together, talking informally and laughing. Johnson's abrupt love of baseball stunned those who had known him earlier. His aide John Connally, who in his twenties was even dubbed by author Robert Cairo "the only one . . . who dared to joke with him," once barbed that Lyndon hadn't been to a baseball game until learning that Russell loved the sport.

"Well, I see that you've become a baseball fan. Do you know the pitcher from the catcher?" Connally asked.

Johnson would smile, then say, "You know I've always loved baseball."

Connally said, "No, I've never been aware of that."

Actually Big Jawn was quite aware, saying, "Lyndon knew Dick Russell liked baseball games, so he went to games with Russell." Connally, who could quickly cross the river between candor and cynicism, was likely right in part, not whole. Russell and LBJ shared a Southern birth, rural leanings, and a yen for political immersion. Russell was a brilliant Senate majority leader intellectually. Johnson would be, personally, in 1955–61, his wider introduction to America. Many facts helped him reach that post, including Russell's friendship, which was reciprocal. Without it John F. Kennedy almost surely would not have named him vice president.

First curves first: on April 8, 1961, Johnson became America's first VP to toss out the first ball at a Minor League game, the Southern Association's Nashville Volunteers' home opener at Sulphur Dell, Tennessee. That night he spoke at the annual Jefferson-Jackson Day Dinner at Fairgrounds Coliseum. "I was just an average player," he said of his Austin high school team. "They had me at first base since I was the tallest on the team, but you might say I was good-field, no-hit, and not even too good in the field." The truth often hurts. Not here. *This* truth tied a future president to a room full of would-have-been big leaguers. What could be more American than meritocracy on the field? Flanking LBJ were Democratic U.S. senators Albert Gore and Estes Kefauver, as well as several teams of other elected and appointed officials. Johnson said, "I am an enthusiastic sports fan. Baseball is my favorite game." Friends turned to one another in wonder, learning so much overnight they hadn't known about this born-again big-leaguer.

The new student's baseball education continued in 1964 after he became president. According to the *New York Times'* Robert Lipsyte, on Opening Day "a military" phalanx of Angels and Senators was given an assault command, "jostling, pumping, and scrambling [for Johnson's first pitch] after it bounced off someone's glove and rolled free." Nats pitcher Dave Stenhouse threw himself briefly on top of it, endangering, if not his life, at least his right limb and career. The nobly named Salty Parker, a fifty-year-old Angels coach, then hurled himself toward the ball, snagging it for perpetuity. Next, DC bats died: Halos, 4–0. In July LBJ turned ambassador for Little League Baseball, pleasing more than a million boys by signing a bill granting a federal charter of incorporation to Little League Baseball Inc. putting it in the same select category as the Boy Scouts, Red Cross, Boys Clubs of America, and

4-H Clubs of America as agencies operating under federal charter. The thirty-sixth president's baseball conversion was "not left to accident," said a friend, but "right on track."

Johnson continued the ritual each predecessor had performed since William Howard Taft, Opening Day becoming less fraternal politically but more fractured regionally. In 1965 LBJ arrived at the Red Sox-Senators opener to greet speaker of the house John McCormack, postmaster general Larry O'Brien, AL head Joe Cronin (all from Massachusetts), and senator Edmund Muskie (from Maine). Fenway Park was second home to each. DC and Virginia officials tilted toward the Nationals; Maryland's were split. Snared by Vietnam, feeling each fatality, and spending more time in the Situation Room, Johnson increasingly found relief in baseball, where the worst thing to die was an opposition rally. The 1967 Yanks and Senators opened the year a record twenty-second time, an 8–0 Stripes rout giving them a 12–10 series lead. Johnson, briefed, told Cronin, "I've been reading where your league is going to have a hot race." If he had only known.

In 1954 the Nationals' Mickey Vernon swatted an Opening Day homer in the tenth inning to beat New York. Reliving his brief 1910s cachet as an Army broken-field runner, President Eisenhower rushed to a field box gate, grabbing Vernon's hand. "Nice going!" he said, bubbly as a schoolboy. "Wonderful! A wonderful home run!" Fast-forward to January 23, 1968, after a year in which the leader of the Free World's use of "wonderful" seemed understatement to a Red Soxaphile. That offseason, the capital's hardest ticket was for the annual Washington BBWAA dinner, hailing "the Impossible Dream" AL last-day titlist. Dick Williams was named miracle worker and American League manager of the year. Commissioner Eckert was feted for getting players to visit Vietnam that winter and show the 1967 World Series film. Other sports were so outnumbered that a non-baseball honoree almost had to be a waiter to reach the dais.

Carl Yastrzemski traded his Superman jersey for a formal suit, a talk with LBJ, and a *Sports Illustrated* issue naming him "Sportsman of the Year." Less than fifteen weeks earlier, Johnson had extended equal time to Yaz's opposite in the 1967 World Series, inviting the Cardinals chartered plane, flying from Boston to Missouri, to be diverted to the White House "for cocktails." It was filled with Redbirds players, coaches, the manager, and club officials after St. Louis beat the Red Sox, 7–2, in Game Seven in the Fens. Among those on board: President Kennedy's favorite Democrat, Stan Musial, just named head of the President's Physical Fitness Program.

August A. Busch Jr., Cardinals president and a close Johnson friend, declined the DC invite. "We have all our good St. Louis fans waiting for us," Busch replied to Johnson's telegram. He was, of course, correct. The Cardinals deserved their final home field advantage of the year.

For much of the century Houston helped berth the Cardinals farm system, begun by Branch Rickey before the Depression, its Minor League team the first to be affiliated with a Major League franchise. Growing up, Tom DeFrank watched the Double-A Houston Buffalos in the old Texas League, graduated from Texas A&M University, then became *Newsweek* magazine White House correspondent, chronicling six U.S. presidents from 1970 to 1995. When Tom returned home, he drove by the site of the Buffs' demolished park, Buffalo Stadium, site of a furniture store complex housing a shrine to the park inside, including home plate. Here, retrieving how as Roy Rogers sang, "Memories, like heroes . . . never grow old," Tom relived how his favorite team had remained the Cards partly because his father was from St. Louis and the Swifties were geographically their team—*his* club, like dad's.

Tom followed Stan Musial in the box scores, by Mutual radio's *Game of the Day* and through TV's *Game of the Week*. Once in an exhibition game in Houston, "Stan the Man launched a mighty shot over the right-field fence [of Buffalo Stadium, now] long gone everywhere but in my mind," said DeFrank. In 1962 the expansion Houston Colt .45s joined the National League just as Tom entered journalism. To know the team meant knowing Texas's boundless belief in size. There was nothing small about H. Roy Hofheinz: Houston mayor, county judge, and team head who in 1965 begot the Astrodome, the Eighth Wonder of the World. Its 1962 forebear was Colt Stadium, a.k.a. Mosquito Heaven. "Our grounds crew," vowed GM Paul Richards, "will spray between innings." Texas-size insects bombed the public like Stukas over Warsaw.

The Space City's futuristic space-age home was said to embody the end of more than a quarter of a century of post-Depression ballpark tradition. "The day the doors on this park open, every other park . . . will be antiquated," Branch Rickey said. A press release added, "The world's first air-conditioned, domed all-purpose stadium, sitting like a precious jewel in southwest Texas, was constructed by the citizens of Harris County" at a cost of $31.6 million for the entire project, becoming, Hofheinz added, "an emblem of the state."

The Harris County domed stadium had baseball's first covered roof, seventy-two degree temperature, and "baseball's [first] exclusive sky boxes," according to a video. "This is really some kind of baseball." Sky boxes suggested a *different* baseball. "People were there to socialize, make deals, not to watch the game," said Governor Connally. "The baseball was incidental." One VIP suite had a faux medieval chapel. "I'll pray for pitching," said Astros skipper Luman Harris, who soon prayed for calm.

In several exhibitions fielders missed or dropped flies masked by a ceiling of five thousand plastic windows and steel grate guides a foot and a half apart. The light and dark background obscured the ball. Day glare made fly balls clear to radar, not men. "We've had a billion dollars' worth of publicity and can't jeopardize it," Hofheinz told GM Richards. "If the game turns into a farce, refund the ticket purchase of any dissatisfied fans." The Astrodome officially opened with an NL game on April 12, 1965. Twenty-four of twenty-six U.S. astronauts got a lifetime big-league pass. First batter and hit: the Phillies' Tony Taylor. Homer: Richie (later Dick) Allen. Score: Astros lose, 2–0. Larger "farces" remained.

One was fielders' inability to see. A story detailed infielder Bob Lillis comparing a pair of sunglasses to see "which will cut back glare." Neither did. Hofheinz then applied a blue translucent acrylic to the roof. "This killed the problem of not seeing fly balls," said 'Stros announcer Gene Elston. "But daylight coming into the stadium was cut," killing the Tifway 419 Bermuda grass bred for indoor use. The offshoot can hardly be overblown: faux turf, a second "farce." In 1966 St. Louis's Monsanto Company birthed artificial grass—here, AstroTurf. At one point in the 1980s eleven of twenty-six big-league parks flaunted fake grass, compared to today's two in thirty.

"I don't want to play on no place my horse can't eat off of," said 1963–77 slugger Allen, speaking for a majority. The Astrodome kept false turf through its last 1999 season of baseball, taking refuge in a carousel of ground rules—proof that Texas did things big. On April 28, 1965, the Mets visited the Dome, Lindsey Nelson calling play-by-play in a gondola suspended over second base and improbably becoming a ground rule at skipper Casey Stengel's request. "Well, Case," said umpire Tom Gorman, "if the ball hits the roof, it's in play, so I guess if it hits Lindsey, it's in play too."

Originally the Eighth Wonder of the World and Johnson's presidency bannered how nothing was impossible. Texas did for baseball what NASA did for space: swell the borders of creativity. In 2000 the Astros—often "Lastros" to locals—enlarged them more, opening Minute Maid Park (née Enron Field), to *Sports Illustrated* "a ballpark with more nooks and crannies than an English muffin, with angles and wide spaces that will create doubles and triples, action everywhere." That muffin went down well.

On April 9, 1965, Johnson and a large presidential party arrived slightly after 6 p.m. in Air Force One at then Houston (now George H. W. Bush) Continental Airport for the Astrodome's unofficial first event: an exhibition with the Yankees. The party included current and former Cabinet officials, congressmen, and aides. Busy with business, LBJ got to the game late, he and Lady Bird watching from behind Hofheinz's glass-enclosed private box. The president sat in a plush gold swivel chair; ate hors d'oeuvres, fried chicken, and ice cream; and watched baseball under glass. He originally planned to stay several innings but stayed until near the end of regulation.

In his place Connally threw out the first ball. The governor stopped by LBJ's lower box in the second inning and promptly left the world's Eighth Wonder; the 47,878 capacity stayed to gape. Johnson also missed a single by Astrodome lead-off batter Mickey Mantle but was standing in his box high above center field when No. 7 smashed the Dome's first home run—a titanic blast over the 406-foot sign in the sixth inning to put New York ahead, 1–0. That inning Houston loaded the bases, fixing the president's focus on the field—not, as usual, on next-seat conversation.

Johnson hoped a fly ball would tie the score at one. Instead a force play did the trick. In the twelfth inning Nellie Fox singled to give Houston a 2–1 win and, with Mantle, cap a night of Golden Oldies. The president, leaving earlier, told Hofheinz, "You ought to be very proud of the stadium. It is massive, beautiful, and it will be a very great asset." Lady Bird, as always, added a grace endnote. "It is simply marvelous," she said. "It shows so much imagination."

An elevator took Johnson from Hofheinz's box above right-center field to a nearby box, the scoreboard flashing a profile of the president, beaming in lights, the message glowing, WELCOME, MR. PRESIDENT. The crowd roared, play briefly stopped, and players peered toward the box. It was the peak of his baseball career. He then gently said something for which he would be teased till leaving the presidency: "I wish Hofheinz worked for the government doing things like that." The Astrodome, built artfully and economically, was not always associated with the dubious efficiency of Uncle Sam.

By now few Americans would deny that Johnson was a workaholic and a patriot, knowing and learning from U.S. history: traits we like in a president. That epigraph fit a 1930s photo of LBJ towering over Lady Bird, the U.S. Capitol misty in the background, as well as a 1963 photo of Air Force One, the aircraft of two presidents returning to DC, one dead, the other taking the oath of office. Johnson, wrote the *New York Times*' Tom Wicker, "was beyond comparison the most dominant personality I have ever encountered" yet fated to seem a wheeler-dealer on Image TV.

Nonetheless, Johnson promoted the Great Society until almost everyone knew of it and no one was neutral. Later he wrote in his memoir, *The Vantage Point*, "I knew I had been there [the presidency]. And I knew also that I had given it everything that was in me." A 1965 *The Sporting News* cartoon about the Dodgers showed Johnson's vision already changing U.S. life by parading a partial list of injuries from

Tommy Davis's broken ankle and Sandy Koufax's injured finger to Don Drysdale's shoulder and Willie Davis's injured knees. The image brandished LBJ at the breakfast table, Lady Bird answering the phone and telling him, "It's long distance calling. . . . Someone in Los Angeles wants to know where he can soon apply for Medicare."

A day before Johnson visited the Astrodome, baseball brass made its annual pilgrimage to the White House to give the president his season pass. Hubert Humphrey, a Minnesotan and baseball student, predicted a 1965 Series between the Giants and his Twins, recalling that "Willie Mays used to play for the [Minor League] Minneapolis Millers." On cue the Twins' franchise won its first AL title since being the 1933 Senators. The Giants ended two games behind the Dodgers in a torrid pennant race, spoiling Mays's MVP year.

Johnson would presently decide to prosecute a war as well as pursue the Great Society. By and by his choice made America a house divided—and the president so polarizing that he feared he could not unite the country even if winning reelection in 1968. He returned to the LBJ Ranch, where Johnson died five days before a peace treaty was signed ending America's involvement in a war he had not wished to fight and did not know how to win.

On January 23, 1973, addressing the nation to announce the end of the Vietnam War and the return of U.S. prisoners of war, President Nixon praised the man who had died a day earlier of a heart attack. "In his life, President Johnson endured the vilification of those who sought to portray him as a man of war," Nixon said. "But there was nothing he cared about more deeply than achieving a lasting peace in the world."

The last time they talked was the day after New Year's, when Johnson spoke of building the right kind of peace, Nixon said. "No one would have welcomed this peace more than he. And I know he would join me in asking—for those who died and for those who live—to let us consecrate this moment."

Two days later, at a simple ceremony in Texas, John Connally memorably said goodbye to his friend and mentor. "He first saw light here. He last breathed life here. May he now find peace here."

NINE

Nixon's the One

Richard Nixon, 1969–1974

In early 1967 I wrote the Manhattan law firm of Nixon, Mudge, Rose, Guthrie, Alexander, and Mitchell to say that I would be in the City that August with a high school group. Was there a chance I could meet its senior partner—a Baby Boomer's cynosure of the post-war age? Secretary Rose Woods replied that Richard Milhous Nixon would be abroad, writing for *Reader's Digest*. However, schedules change, and would I phone upon arrival? I did, invited to Nixon's office at 20 Broad Street, off Wall. For half an hour we spoke of sports and college—my dad's alma mater was Cornell ("Good school," said the former vice president. "Thank God, the least Ivy of the Ivies")—and the financial, even psychic, need to work your way through school. Later I found this view typical not of the Old or New but the Real Nixon. Two years later I entered college as he took the oath of office, fusing person and president like no chief executive since FDR.

Post–Boomers still find it problematic to understand America's early 1970s secular passion play. Upheaval rent feminism, civil rights, drugs, and opinion as to whether police were pigs, love should be free, and this nation should—as 1972 Democratic nominee George McGovern said—"come home." In North Vietnam Jane Fonda railed against "those blue-eyed murderers—Nixon and the rest of those ethnocentric American white male chauvinists." On April 30, 1970, vowing we would not be "a pitiful helpless giant," the thirty-seventh president invaded Cambodia to thwart its use as an enemy sanctuary. Hundreds of colleges closed or went on strike after six students were killed at Kent State University and Jackson State College. Proportion took a hike. Peoria felt besieged, Nixon upholding it more via personality than domestic policy.

Foreign policy was another matter—to Nixon, the reason voters chose a president. Despite the Vietnam War, inherited from Lyndon Johnson, his diplomatic summitry helped end the bipolar world. In February 1972 the president ended a quarter century of U.S. estrangement from the Middle Kingdom by visiting the People's Republic of China. Television then meant ABC, CBS, NBC, and PBS, the prime-time coverage of each similar to America's 1969 Apollo 11 mission, still in the public mind. That July 20 Nixon had spoken by phone to astronauts Neil Armstrong and Colonel Edwin "Buzz" Aldrin on the moon, saying "This certainly has to be the most historic telephone call ever made from the White House!" Now, viewing the Great Wall, Shanghai, and the zoo from which China later gave the United States two rare pandas, even the most cynical here gawked like a college art major on a first pilgrimage to the Louvre.

That May, Nixon became the first president to visit Moscow, joining Communist Party leader Leonid Brezhnev in signing the Strategic Arms Limitation Treaty (SALT)—the first agreement to limit strategic nuclear arms. Television captured Red Square, the spires of the Kremlin, the cemetery holding some of World War II's dead—the Soviet Union had lost between twenty and twenty-seven million people, the most of any nation—and Nixon speaking directly to the average Russian, the first U.S. president using TV to reach a foreign audience. Nixon had been a late 1940s and early 1950s Cold War combatant. Presently he appeared as ready to fight America's cultural war. Boomers as a group liked the beat of rock. Said Thoroughly Modern Milhous at a White House event, "If the music's square, it's because I like it square."

Nixon had grown up poor, in the classic American way, working daily from 4 a.m. to 9 p.m. before and after high school, braving the death of two brothers, "trying," as his mother, Hannah, said, "to make up for his brothers' deaths by being the perfect son." She never had a new dress, nor did the family eat out, by the time the future president entered college. Later he thumbed his nose at the fashionable, had contempt for the idle rich, and, as he told me, "never had the wild times many trendies do. What we did have was a lot of fun. I, of course, and depending on the season, loved to sit down at the piano and belt out some Christmas carols."

Nixon's two boyhood towns in California were his birthplace, Yorba Linda, and nearby Whittier. Each was similar in ambiance, illumining a Norman Rockwell glow—fidelity to law; a belief in toil, God, and family; a fondness for the familiar; and a reverence for the everyday American. Nixon gave the working middle what elites withheld—respect for its nobility and injury. In return, it gave him support for being ready, indeed, eager, to defend those bullied by a ruling class antithetical to a democracy—those FDR had styled "the Forgotten American." Nixon became their post-war voice.

The *Washington Post*'s Meg Greenfield minted the phrase "Nixon Generation." She wrote, "Half of America spent its adult lives hoping every day that Nixon would become President. The other half spent it passionately hoping he would not." Aide Bryce Harlow likened him to a cork. Push him down, he resurfaced. His odyssey became our history before his presidency did. Born: 1913. Graduated: Whittier College and Duke Law School. Service: Pacific Theater. Politics: made Congress in 1946 (R-CA), joined the House Un-American Activities Committee (HUAC), and proved Alger Hiss a Kremlin spy. In 1952 the GOP vice presidential pick was accused of a "secret fund" by the then liberal *New York Post*. Nixon's rebuttal, TV's first network political address, was the triumphal "Checkers" speech. It saved his career—also likely Dwight Eisenhower's presidential campaign.

At nine, I knew little of this in 1960, only that each side expected victory in that year's supremely dramatic race. A 2016 CNN-TV *Race to the White House* critique of that election—a narrow John F. Kennedy victory—revealed Republicans as far less adroit at political guile. A press intrigued by Democratic chicanery might have fueled fury for a recount, except that such a media did not exist. "We'll win," JFK's father, Joseph P. Kennedy Sr., said of Chicago, "with the help of a few friends." Alleged skullduggery occurred there and in Texas: the names of deceased people were registered; the same people voted in different districts; more backed Kennedy than total ballots cast or people in a district. Such a catalogue of fraud began a series by the *Chicago Tribune*. Who halted it? *Nixon*, showing a side most snoots would not deign to see, telling reporter Willard Edwards, "Those are interesting stories you've been writing, but no one steals the presidency."

Worried about "chaos in the government," Nixon refused a recount of the living and the dead, amused thirty years later that "Mrs. Nixon has never stopped wanting [one]." In 1962 he lost to Edmund G. "Pat" Brown for governor of California, proclaiming the end of his elective life: "You won't have Nixon to kick around anymore." Mocked as a loser, a political ghost, *done*, like Dickens' fictional Jacob Marley from *A Christmas Carol*, Nixon then rose from the dead, serving the GOP in good times and bad, so that he again became leading man for the 1968 GOP nomination. Author and journalist Norman Mailer wrote at the convention: "It was his comeback which had made him a hero in their [Middle American] eyes, for America is the land which worships the Great Comeback [Nixon's remains the greatest return from nothingness in U.S. political history], and so he was Tricky Dick to them no more, but the finest gentleman in the land; they were proud to say hello."

There was nostalgia—akin to a gentle protectiveness—for the Nixon family, much-wounded but resolute, and wife Pat's cloth coat, referenced in the Checkers speech as a forever symbol of threadbare pride. What Nixon later christened the "Silent Majority" could accept what writer Raymond Price called his "dark side"—the Watergate "expletive deleted"—a view that the good outweighed the bad. "Nixon mobilized an immense, informal army of ordinary people," said biographer Conrad Black. A PBS documentary defined them as "people with an inbred respect for authority and an unyielding belief in the American Dream."

Duty towered. Vietnam was a test of character—whether as America conceded the limits of its power, adversaries would respect the power of its will. Religion mattered too. Nixon told aide Charles Colson, "You know, I could be a Catholic. I honestly could. It's beautiful to think about, that there is something you can really grab ahold of, something real and meaningful." Few politicians talk like that.

Even Nixon's awkwardness became an old virtue, endearingly unslick. On July 19, 1990, at the Nixon library dedication, George H. W. Bush told how one day at an airport Nixon heard a little girl shouting, "How is Smokey the Bear?"—then in the Washington National Zoo.

Nixon smiled as the girl kept repeating her question. Baffled, he finally turned to an aide for help. "Smokey the Bear, Mr. President," the aide whispered. "Washington National Zoo." In Bush's telling, Nixon walked over, took the girl's hand, and beamed, "How do you do, Miss Bear?"

Nixon had several goals, even as a child. One was "to be an orchestra leader and conduct a great symphony." Another became to teach and write a book or two a year, despite later believing that book writing was "the hardest work you can give your brain." Having it "to do over again," he said, "I'd love to write or announce sports." As president he revealed his heart—a rarity—by touting the boyhood "American sports" of baseball and football over "frilly sports" like squash and crew. Many recall Nixon's football bona fides, the Whittier team only taking him because he was the last man available. Later he was a close friend of many coaches, especially the pro football Washington Redskins' George Allen, a 1972 campaign near-surrogate, and Wayne Woodrow "Woody" Hayes, coach at Ohio State University and lineal heir of George S. Patton. "I'd want to talk football. Woody'd want to talk foreign policy," Nixon said of their relationship. "We'd compromise. We'd talk foreign policy." In 1987 he gave his friend's eulogy.

Nixon's favorite sport, though, was baseball, the future president playing sandlot ball as a boy among elementary school, homework, family (he drove daily to Los Angeles long before sunrise to buy vegetables for his parent's store), piano lessons (Hannah insisted he learn to play, which Nixon did expertly), and church (the family attended service four times on Sunday). Thereafter he watched, not played, baseball, due to a flaw shared by millions: the sport at a higher level required skill, not simply grit. Nixon followed the pastime more closely than any president by newspaper and magazine—reading a Depression staple—and later wireless and TV: the greatest baseball student to occupy the Oval Office.

Nixon saw his first ever professional game by taking a trolley downtown to see the Los Angeles Angels and Hollywood Stars in the 1920s Double-A PCL, a trek he repeated yearly. In 1936 he drove his first car cross-country to enter Duke Law School in North Carolina, having one priority beyond grade point average: at twenty-three, wanting to finally see "a big-league game." In fact, he saw two. "I don't remember much," Nixon mused, "except that the date was July 4, the Senators lost a double-header at Griffith Stadium to the Yankees, 4–3 and 5–0, and a rookie named DiMaggio put one in the bleachers." Each fact was correct. Joe's Rookie of the Year award hailed twenty-nine home runs against just thirty-nine strikeouts, a rare and lifetime trend.

Nixon's baseball ardor never ebbed. Like President Eisenhower, the two-term vice president frequently visited Griffith Stadium in 1953–60. In 1957 he took part in an on-field tribute to the Senators' Roy Sievers, who, overcome, broke down on his shoulder, Nixon putting an arm around No. 2 at home plate. Often, he attended unannounced, as that year for a doubleheader. Nats voice Bob Wolff asked him to appear on his between-games radio show, amending, "But let's play a game. Don't say your name until we've finished."

First Bob asked about the Senators' first-game victory. "Well, of course," Nixon replied, "being a Washington fan, I thought it was great." They ad-libbed for seven minutes, climaxing with Wolff's "Are you originally from Washington, sir?"

GUEST: No, I'm a Californian.
WOLFF: What do you do, sir?
GUEST: I work for the government.
WOLFF: Oh, for the government.
GUEST: Yes, yes, I work for the government.
WOLFF: What sort of work do you do, sir?
GUEST: Well, I'm the vice president.

Their interview led that week's *Sporting News* and sports, even news, sections in other daily and weekly papers.

In 1959 Nixon subbed for Eisenhower on Opening Day. On July 6, he was the main speaker at the All-Star baseball banquet for next day's All-Star Game at Forbes Field and Pittsburgh's celebratory bicentennial. The huge dais starred Stan Musial and Ted Williams, eight Hall of Famers, and all players on each team. Nixon signed autographs, enjoyed meeting celebrities, and talked for two hours with Casey Stengel. Planning to vote for a fellow Democrat in 1960, the Ol' Perfessor finally left, impressed by Nixon's baseball grasp: "I had to get out of there," he said, "before that boy made me a Republican." Ike's No. 2 manned the press room of the William Penn Hotel until it closed, Attorney General Bill Rogers tugging at his sleeve. The parade of baseball bigwigs augured his presidency.

When Nixon left the vice presidency in 1961, his financial status, if not Tobacco Road, was meager by DC measure. Joining New York's ultimately renamed law firm of Nixon, Mudge in early 1963 made him financially independent. Still, his interest remained in peace and in becoming president, not being a nouveau riche who "drank too much, partied too much, and thought too little." In 1953 pitcher Bob Feller had gotten the Major League Baseball Players Association to jump-start its pension program. Midway through Nixon's 1963–68 "wilderness years," the union had no office, no employees, one file cabinet, and $5,400. According to Wales-born writer Jack Henry, ex-Pirates pitcher Bob Friend, later to be controller of Pittsburgh's Allegheny County, and Phillies pitcher and stockbroker Jim Bunning, each a Nixon friend, discussed making him union head. Thinking him "retired to the law," Friend, Bunning, Robin Roberts, Rocky Colavito, and other members offered Nixon a salary of $50,000 a year, plus expenses, and flexibility to negotiate. His lure: stature in and beyond the game.

The ex-VP said he was flattered. Pat would love the stability, but, Nixon said, "It would have meant giving up politics. The job's ban on partisan speeches would have put an end to my hope" of winning the presidency in 1968. "Other things had come up," Nixon told the players, offering to still do their legal work. Instead they approached Marvin Miller, who wanted a full-fledged union, not an association, as they did. Players hired him anyway, still the strong-man-union archetype. Later in 1965, owners, enamored of the idea of Nixon as commissioner, pursued him independently. Ford Frick had been a stand-patter, pro football doing vast damage to baseball's image. Pittsburgh and Detroit owners, John Galbreath and John Fetzer respectively, offered Nixon $100,000 yearly plus expenses. Again he said no. The Yankees' Gabe Paul recalled his final words: "Don't tell Pat. She'd kill me for turning you down."

As described, baseball had already inked and axed William Eckert as Frick's heir when Nixon, now president-elect, received the football letter he never got at Whitter College from his coach, Wallace "Chief" Newman, at a January 2, 1969, testimonial dinner at the Anaheim Convention Center. Prizing his tenacity, Chief had used him as "cannon fodder" during weekly scrimmages with the varsity. Nixon reciprocated by thanking Chief for creating a "full-time spectator." For many writers, a lengthy love affair now began between Nixon and the sporting press, especially but not limited to baseball's. "This isn't a guy that shows up at season openers to take bows and get his pictures in the paper and has to have his secretary of state tell him where first base is," said Dick Young, then of the *New York Daily News*. "This man knows baseball."

As professional baseball turned one hundred in Nixon's first year as president, the man who knew his game planned an All-Star Gala at the White House for more than three dozen Hall of Famers, about sixty active players, and other members of baseball's family prior to that July's 1969 All-Star Game in Washington. Such a populist congregation—four hundred in all—had rarely worshipped in the People's House since Andrew Jackson opened the White House doors. The designated host and master of ceremonies could hardly wait.

"I'm proud to be in your company," Nixon would tell baseball's clan that summer. He meant it. The president tossed out the first ball at the All-Star Game in 1970. In 1972 he listed his all-time All-Star team. Before and even after the Watergate scandal forced him to resign in 1974, Nixon was the president to whom baseball mattered most and, except for FDR, who mattered most to *it* in office—and who most rooted in a Tom Mix–meets–Andy Hardy way. Shy, even asocial, Nixon used baseball to start a dialogue or be a point of reference, his vehicle to seeming one of the boys.

Toward the end of his life, as we shall see, he and grandson Christopher yoked over the pastime—as dads and sons and grandsons and others have for a century and more. Similarly, at the start of his presidency, Nixon looked forward to bonding with former and current players on Opening Day 1969—also old friend Charlie Brotman, whom Nixon had known since the inaugural parade announcer's debut in 1957.

"Mr. President, here's the ball to sign and use as the first pitch," said Brotman, also the Senators longtime public address announcer.

"Charlie, you've been so nice that I'm going to sign the first ball for you to keep," Nixon said. "Then I'll sign the second ball I throw to the players. Nobody'll know yours came first." The president signed, "To Charlie. Best wishes, Dick Nixon."

Nixon entered the presidential box to find an error on its seal— "Presidnt [*sic*] of the United States"—a relic of Lyndon Johnson's schedule, so frenetic that the presidential seal was misspelled. He then dropped Charlie's First Ball—according to the *New York Times*, "the first error in the 1969 season"—before tossing it. The *Times* and *Washington Post* displayed their peculiar brand of objectivity by devoting more space to the drop than to Nixon's longtime friendship with Ted Williams, making his celebrated Senators managerial debut. That year's "All-Star Baseball Centennial Program" cover featured an Opening Day photo of Nixon, Williams, and Griffith Stadium boyhood scoreboard operator-turned-rookie commissioner Bowie Kuhn, smiles all over. The Yankees laughed most, winning the first game, 8–4. For The Kid, losing to the Bombers had moved to the dugout from the field.

By any yardstick, July 22, 1969's, late-afternoon All-Star Gala remains the most memorable sports event of its type staged, meriting the definition of "perfect storm" before such a term existed—professional baseball's centennial anniversary; the capital of the United States; America's most famed building thrown open as it rarely has been, with names rarely better known; and the president of the United States, greeting every guest with facts and/or stories that moved one account to state, "The players, the old-timers, and the press all were astounded at Nixon's memory and his interest."

The president began: "For me, this is one of the most exciting receptions ever given in the White House." He spoke without notes for twelve minutes, first referencing the 1920s, when without a radio, he avidly read about his favorite team, Connie Mack's 1929–31 Athletics, who won three pennants and two World Series. Mack kept baseball in the dark about who would start the 1929 Series opener against the Cubs. "You remember. . . . He could have started with Lefty Grove or Rube Walberg, two great left-handers," Nixon said, "or George Earnshaw, who had won over twenty games with a right hand." Instead, surprise starter Howard Ehmke scouted the Cubs for the last month of the year, then beat them, fanning a Series-record thirteen. Game Three—Nixon's "first recollection as far as World Series were concerned . . . all . . . through sports pages in those days before . . . television"—taught him "never [to] leave in the middle" of a game. At Shibe Park—"I think it was October 12" (it was)—"the Cubs were ahead [8–0] going into the eighth [*sic*; the seventh] inning." The A's "then scored ten runs and won the game, 10 to 8." Pause. "I stayed all the way through every game after that experience."

Guests heard of Charlie Root, "a favorite" of Nixon's "because he came from Los Angeles back in the days when they [the Cubs' Double-A affiliate Angels] played at [a local park named after Chicago's] Wrigley Field"; and "Pepper Martin, going down to second base against . . . Mickey Cochrane"; and "Bobo Newsom . . . always lost, but . . . a hero" nonetheless; and "of course, Roy Sievers." The president especially read political née sports columnists: Bill Henry, Scotty Reston, and Bob Considine. "If I had to live my life over again, I would have liked to have ended up as a sports writer," became very probably the most popular line he ever said to journalists. Nixon also hailed the men in blue, saying umpires "have the toughest job of all." BBWAA president and Nixon admirer Dick Young then made the president an honorary member: association card "No. 1."

Kuhn injected that he had "planned" to detail "what a fine fan he [Nixon] is" but now he wasn't going to. Nothing more was needed, he said, "to demonstrate . . . that I have standing to my left America's number one baseball fan." Accepting the "No. 1 fan" award, the president said that he was relieved to finally make the team. For the next three hours one baseball celeb after another approached a man who, as one writer said, "often introduc[ed] players before they could introduce themselves."

In 1969 the Twins' Rod Carew would win his first batting title, averaging .332. Seeing his potential, Nixon said, "You have a chance to be the next .400 hitter." Carew came close, hitting .388 in 1977, his sixth of seven batting titles.

In 1958 Dodgers catcher Roy Campanella was disabled in a car accident. As a New Yorker in the mid-'60s, Nixon followed No. 39's road back, Roy helping others while trying to recover. "You're doing a great job with the youth in New York, Campy," the president greeted him.

Hank Aaron volunteered that Nixon "knows more about baseball than some of the people in the game." The would-be sportswriter spoke of Jackie Robinson not just as a baseball pioneer but also a "UCLA halfback, basketball player and broad jumper."

One guest had debated baseball with Nixon a decade earlier before another All-Star Game. "How's the banking business?" the president greeted Stengel, now the president of a Glendale, California, bank.

"Fine," replied the Perfessor.

"Even with those high interest rates?" Nixon prodded.

"If a banker can't make money in these times, he oughtn't be in the profession," said Casey, recently voted baseball's greatest living manager.

A year earlier Joe DiMaggio, baseball's greatest living player, had been named an Oakland A's coach. Shaking his hand, Nixon noted seeing a pupil hit several tape-measure homers in 1969. "You must be showing Reggie Jackson some of your hitting secrets," he said.

Soon after, a Detroit sports editor handed him a baseball covered with autographs and said, "Could you sign this for me, Mr. President. Right here, under Denny McLain?"

"*Nobody* should be above Denny McLain," he said, signing under the 1968 Tigers AL Cy Young and MVP.

Watching Nixon one-on-one at the gala, the *Boston Globe's* Harold Kaese wrote, "He charmed his four hundred visitors. Relaxed and truly enjoying himself." The Associated Press billed him "like a small boy with a new batch of bubble gum baseball cards as he greeted the game's great and near great."

Relative strangers or a topic about which he knew little could make Nixon uncommonly awkward—rock, modern art, and later hip-hop. By comparison, with people he knew well or a subject about which he was knowledgeable, Nixon could reveal warmth. Proof lay on a day when everybody who was anybody in the national game was uncommonly impressed.

After the reception, Nixon had planned to attend the White House dinner, join All-Star Game guests that night at RFK Stadium, then take Air Force One overnight for a Pacific Ocean rendezvous. Days earlier Apollo 11 astronauts had become the first humans to step on the moon and return safely. Nixon was to greet them, having left a message and his signature on the moon, except that a thunderstorm typical of Washington in July postponed the game, making it impossible for him to make it and the dinner. Two days later, aboard the USS *Hornet* off Guam, the president spoke through the space capsule's glass to ask the astronauts, "Were you told how the All-Star Game came out?"—NL, 9–3. Baseball toasted the rescheduled match, the All-Star Gala, and its host's reviews.

Like vines around a trellis, baseball encircled Nixon's life. In the 1940s he entered a restaurant to ask Babe Ruth for an autograph. Pre- and post-presidency, he usually spurned luxury boxes for a box seat, sitting among fans, keeping score, and signing autographs, saying, "If Ruth can sign, I can sign." Nixon won many, lost many, always came back, and wrote dozens of letters of congratulation, or more often condolence, to players, always siding with the underdog. At thirty-five, Pedro Ramos of the 1950s Senators rejoined his old team. Delighted, Nixon called. Luis Aparicio began 1971 with a forty-four at-bat hitless streak, then broke it. The president wrote: "In my career, I have experienced long periods when I couldn't seem to get a hit, regardless of how hard I tried, but in the end I was able to hit a home run. Best wishes, Richard Nixon."

As a Senators shortstop, great-field, no-hit Ed Brinkman was taught by skipper Ted Williams how to hit. Dealt to Detroit, he forgot, struggling to top .200. When Ed set a Major League record of seventy-two games without an error, Nixon wired, "Continued success both in the field and at bat." Tigers teammate Dick McAuliffe was incredulous. "Did you notice he mentioned the *bat*?" Dick said. Brinkman said, "He remembers when I hit .260 in Washington." In 1969 Nixon did more baseball watching than Lyndon Johnson had in his presidency, attending five Senators games and seeing a Detroit triple play—a presidential first. A June game lasted three hours and forty-two minutes, the president telling an aide to new owner Bob Short, "I'm amazed at this attendance [just 6,609]." Short was too, having outbid comedian Bob Hope to buy the Nats.

That March, Mickey Mantle retired. On June 8 the Bronx Bombers retired No. 7, emcee Mel Allen lauding his "playing despite enormous pain." Revisiting Yankee Stadium for the first time since his 1964 firing, Allen introduced "the magnificent Yankee, Mickey Mantle." The sound greeting him could be heard in Jersey City. Mick referenced another speech, saying, "I always wondered how someone who was dying could say he was the luckiest man on the face of the earth. Now I know how Lou Gehrig felt," the Stripes captain dying of amyotrophic lateral sclerosis in 1939 but saying, "I have an awful lot to live for."

It is true that for many, Nixon as president took a lot to get used to. Even harder to comprehend was what happened his first year in office: not just men on the moon, but the Mets in mid-air. The Amazins' 1969 cannot be fathomed without knowing what preceded it. Of their first-year 1962 expansion team, skipper Stengel asked not "how [they] lost 120" but how they "won forty." "Marvelous Marv" Throneberry was called out for missing second base on a triple. A coach told Casey not to argue: "He missed first base too." Team MVP Richie Ashburn took his prize, a boat, out on the Delaware River, where it sank. Five times the Mets finished last. Only America's slump that decade seemed worse.

In 1969 baseball split both big leagues into two six-team divisions, each titlist meeting in the best-of-five League Championship Series (LCS), the new gateway to the World Series. That August New York trailed the NL Eastern Division–leading Cubs by nine-and-one-half games, then closed 38-11, as Stengel said, "coming on *slow* but *fast*." In September, Nixon invited the anonymous 1969 Yankees to the White House, where he spoke most intently to catcher Jake Gibbs, ex–Ole Miss All-American quarterback. Meantime, a black cat hissed at the Cubs' dugout before a crucial game that month at Shea Stadium. A night later the Mets reached first place after seven years, four months, and twenty-nine days of franchise existence. The whole year mimed Don Larsen's 1956 World Series Perfect Game. You searched vainly for any frame of reference.

Since 1962 pilgrims had caroled, "Let's Go Mets!" A new chant now blared: "We're Number One!" At Forbes Field, the Metsies swept a September 12 doubleheader, the score 1–0 in each game, each starting pitcher knocking in his run. Three days later the Cardinals' Steve Carlton struck out a record nineteen Mets—and *lost*. On September 23 the magic number needed to win the East fell to one. A day later the New York Metropolitan Baseball Club clinched, a reporter asking Gil Hodges to "tell us what this proves." The Mets' manager sat back, spread his hands, and laughed, "Can't be done." They next swept Western Division titlist Atlanta in the LCS. The overwhelmingly favored 109-53 regular season AL champion Orioles looked on, neither bowed nor wowed. "We are here [at the Fall Classic]," said Baltimore's Brooks Robinson, "to prove there is no Santa Claus."

The one-hundred-to-oners split the first two games, 4–1 Birds and 2–1 Mets. Elves awoke. Mets outfielder Tommie Agee gift-wrapped Game Three, homering and making two catches, saving at least three, perhaps four, runs. In Game Four bad umpiring and outfielder Ron Swoboda's glove beat Baltimore, 2–1, in ten innings. The North Pole warmed. The next day, October 16, 1969, Santa called. The Birds led 3–0 in the sixth inning, before New York's Donn Clendenon homered. Al Weis encored in the seventh: three-all. The Metropolitans then scored two eighth-inning runs on two errors. In the ninth inning NBC's Curt

Gowdy chimed, voice full, "There's a fly ball out to left! The Mets are the world champions! Look at this scene!" Elves danced. Angels flew. In the clubhouse Mets voice Lindsey Nelson, having shared NBC play-by-play of each home game with Gowdy, inhaled the "miracle, the sheer enormity of the thing."

Afterward Lindsey, then almost as much as Stengel the Mets' apotheosis, drove into Manhattan, where "dancing in the streets [and] throwing confetti" ruled. The Mets' epigraph by head of the board M. Donald Grant is as perfect a half century later: "Our team finally caught up with our fans." Over time the club evolved into something much larger than the sport. Today a Little League or high school coach will cry, "You're worse than the '62 Mets," then moments later, "So what? Remember the *Amazin'* Mets!" Baseball will always have both, not likely to forget either.

The greatest Gallup Poll approval/disapproval disparity for an American First Lady occurred in 1969: nine to one for Pat Nixon (54 percent approved, 6 percent disapproved, and the balance had no opinion). Of pertinence to this work is that she was the greatest baseball fan among First Ladies since Bess Truman, watching on TV in the White House; the presidential retreat at Camp David; the Nixon home at Key Biscayne, Florida; and the Western White House at San Clemente, California. As U.S. Second Lady in 1953–61, she had accompanied Nixon to Griffith Stadium. At Robert F. Kennedy (RFK) Stadium, the park changed but not result: the 1969–71 Senators fourth, sixth, and fifth in a six-team division. Pat watched and threw out the first pitch of Game Two of the 1971 Orioles-Pirates Series—the first First Lady to do so at a big-league game—seeing Brooks Robinson single thrice, walk twice, and play a superb third base: a typical B. Robby day.

As a youth, Thelma "Pat" Ryan nursed two dying parents, was orphaned, yet kept house for two brothers and had five jobs to pay her way through the University of Southern California. Such an early life may explain Mrs. Nixon's populist fondness for two widely popular middle-class sports: baseball, to watch, and bowling, to do. For the latter, an alley was installed in the White House. For the former, the

Nixons visited RFK Stadium. Increasingly, they must have wondered if the Senators would be there when they arrived.

As stated, in 1968 Midwest businessman Bob Short purchased the long-losing franchise. He was reputed to be impatient and underfinanced. Short had once moved another professional franchise, basketball's Lakers, from Minneapolis to Los Angeles. Washington felt vulnerable, its transient populace fueling the prospect of baseball failing for the second time in a decade. Nixon didn't help, refusing to "discuss their [Senators'] future" in the city, aide Herbert Klein said. On one side, the president felt "it would be awful for the nation's capital to lose its team." On the other, Nixon, like Eisenhower, thought "it would be inappropriate to intercede in this business and financial matter." Eschewing happy talk, he practiced empty talk.

In 1970 the president arrived midway through the Nats' home opener after vainly entreating U.S. senators on the Hill to save the candidacy of G. Harrold Carswell as Supreme Court justice. That July he tossed out the first pitch at the All-Star Game, infamous for Pete Rose's twelfth-inning off-tackle demolition of catcher Ray Fosse: NL, 5–4. Nixon also saw DC win at RFK and lose at Anaheim. "I always root for the home team, but my home club—the Senators—are the *road* team" there, he explained his fix. Solution: cheer for both. The 1971 AL season-opening release about Nixon's first pitch gently twitted his career as a "much-traveled, right-handed spot starter and reliever." Sadly, he missed the second Nats franchise's last home opener, Master Sergeant David Pitzer, a former prisoner of war in Vietnam, subbing: Senators 8, A's 0.

August 15, 1971, ungently twitted another subject: the president's vow not to "intercede in . . . business and financ[e]." Without warning he froze wages and prices, devalued U.S. currency—"the most significant monetary agreement in the history of the world"—and severed the dollar's link to gold. Like activism—seeking a sale, waving baseball's antitrust exemption—might have slowed Short's move out of Dodge. In 1969 attendance hit 918,106, highest since 1946, for the fourth-place Senators. Soon the uptick vanished, 655,156 in 1971 watching them revert to form. Denny McLain arrived to go 10-22.

Curt Flood left after thirteen games for Denmark, vowing to "continue [his] suit" to challenge baseball's reserve clause binding a player in perpetuity to his team. Later its effect somersaulted baseball. At the time the suit greased DC's plunge. On September 29, 1971, the AL voted, 10–2, O's and White Sox dissenting, to let Short skip to Dallas-Ft. Worth as the Texas Rangers. Nixon was "distressed," called such a move "heartbreaking," and said he would back the Angels. At no time before or since did he so resemble Ike.

The next evening, Washington playing its last home game, Short conceded that he was leaving. Frank Howard homered in the sixth inning. "They thought it was my last time up," he said. "The ovation shook me when I batted." The rest shook the capital's baseball reputation into the twenty-first century. The Senators led the Yankees, 7–5, with two out in the ninth inning when thugs stormed and vandalized the field. Almost everything was taken, Short having taken the franchise's good name. At 10:11 p.m., head umpire Jim Honochick forfeited to New York, 9–0, by big-league rule, baseball's colony on the Potomac expelled to near-anonymity. In 1973 businessman Joseph Danzansky was said ready to buy the San Diego Padres and return a team to Washington, except that the Watergate scandal to be described here had by now caused Nixon's second term to implode. The incumbent was too weak to aid any sale. It took till 2005 for the Montreal Expos to move south as the Washington Nationals.

Nixon said that "history depends on who writes it." Baseball's depends largely on which team you watch and hear. The transcendent 1970 Orioles went 108-54, swept the LCS from Minnesota, and beat Cincinnati in the Series. Watching them on Baltimore TV, Nixon called the Birds "the best team since the 1961 Yankees," increasingly the pastime's all-time standard. Baseball is a nine- or ten-man game, depending on the designated hitter. Rarely is it one on one, except when men like Brooks Robinson and Roberto Clemente run like Secretariat, hit like Ali against Frazier, and/or "treat baseball," wrote Roger Angell, "like a form of punishment on the field." Each owned his early 1970s World Series. Over nearly half a century, both suggest a postcard from the past.

In 1954 then VP Nixon led the motorcade in downtown Baltimore as three hundred thousand cheered the arrival of the ex–St. Louis Browns. A year later Brooks Robinson made his transplanted Orioles debut. For two decades the PA announcement, "Batting [say] fifth and playing third base, Number 5, Brooks Robinson," was part of summer's soundtrack in and around the Chesapeake Bay, "the Human Vacuum Cleaner" inhaling a non-pitching record sixteen Gold Gloves. Shocked by the 1969 Mets, the 1970 Orioles sought redemption, which meant getting even, as they did in a five-game World Series where B. Robby hit .429 with two homers and enough diving stops in various positions to fill the Fall Classic highlight film. Abhorring 1969, Brooks became the 1970 Series MVP, winning a new car. Said the losing Reds' Johnny Bench, "If we'd known he wanted a car so badly, we'd have chipped in and bought him one."

Roberto Clemente's moniker was "the Great One" or "Arriba" in Spanish. In 1971 he became Series MVP in a Classic worthy of its name. No. 21 hit low outside pitches over the right-center-field fence, threw rifle shots to third base from the right-field corner, and made sliding catches in his more singular than showboat way. He linked three thousand hits, four batting titles, and a dozen Gold Gloves, his career climbing pinnacle after peak. One came in 1960: he hit safely in all seven Series games as the Bucs beat the Yankees. Another: in 1966 he hit .317, had 29 home runs, knocked in 119 runs, and won the MVP award. In 1967 Arriba hit a career-high .357. In 1971 Clemente climbed every mountain. He batted .414, again hit safely in each game of another seven-game Series over the favored O's, and led the Three Rivers Stadium organist to play "Jesus Christ Superstar."

On the evening of December 31, 1972, Nixon was phoned by Pittsburgh Pirates president Dan Galbreath, who told him that the soul of Pittsburgh and Latin baseball had apparently died that night in a plane crash, trying to help victims of a Nicaraguan earthquake. The president was stunned. He had long admired Clemente less for his statistics than for his artistry. The pianist who composed and memorized complex compositions was mesmerized by Roberto's élan and grace, traits Nixon feared he lacked.

The president asked if the Pirates were founding a fund. Told yes, he wrote a check to the Roberto Clemente Memorial Fund, asked aides to complement it, and sent the total to the Nicaraguan ambassador in Washington.

Nixon then asked, "Who can you get to fly down here to meet me as soon as possible?"

"I can come," said Galbreath, "plus Steve Blass [the Bucs' then leading pitcher] and Dave Giusti [a gifted reliever]."

"Fine," said the president, putting his legal office at Mrs. Clemente's use, especially the gentle and trusted White House special counsel Richard Moore. That week the Pirates party flew to DC, met Nixon and Moore, and traded thoughts on how to help the family.

Galbreath had watched Nixon steer baseball's 1969 centennial gala to the White House from Cincinnati, home of baseball's first professional team, and been impressed. His own franchise boasted a rich lineage, including Pie Traynor, Honus Wagner, and Ralph Kiner. He wanted players to give to the community, as very few like Clemente had.

Nixon's January 3, 1973, statement hailed "one of the greatest players of all time" and Clemente's "splendid qualities as a generous and kind human being," evinced by "sacrific[ing] his life on a mission of mercy." That summer the Hall of Fame inducted No. 21 posthumously, waiving the five-year waiting period. Only Babe Ruth's tops his as the Hall plaque most visited yearly. The Clemente Award for character is arguably baseball's most treasured off-field honor. Each year Latin players fill a higher percentage of the average big-league roster, all too young to recall the wonder of seeing Roberto play.

Outside of his family, the Pirates franchise brooked the greatest loss. Some teammates took refuge in recalling clubhouse humor. Blass, who peaked in 1972 with a 19-8 record, told Clemente once that he thought he had found the secret to getting him out. "If I ever get traded, I'm gonna pitch you inside because every pitcher throws you away and you hit .350," Blass said. Roberto eyed the pitcher. "Blass, I tell you one thing," he said. "You pitch me inside, *I hit the ball to Harrisburg!*" Said Blass, later, "That took care of that."

While Nixon mourned Clemente, rued the stealing of the Senators, and still basked in his trip to China, he shared the capital's devotion to the long-losing but finally contending football Redskins, who made Super Bowl VII in 1973 but lost to Miami, 14–7, the Dolphins still the NFL's only unbeaten team. The president exuberantly watched football on television, telephoned players and coaches afterward, prescribed a play for Miami coach Don Shula in the Super Bowl—it didn't work— even had a trophy made, and named Texas the 1969 national college champion, not endearing himself to unbeaten Penn State.

In 1971 Nixon spoke at the Pro Football Hall of Fame in Canton, Ohio, lauding the induction of Jim Brown, Bill Hewitt, Frank (Bruiser) Kinard, Vince Lombardi, Andy Robustelli, Y. A. Tittle, and Norm Van Brocklin. The football sage especially admired Lombardi, the Redskins coach who died of cancer in the president's second year in office. Later many tried to compartmentalize Nixon, viewing Watergate against the draft's end, the POWs coming home, and rapprochement with China. At the time Nixon's sports mania helped too. Some thought it overdone. In fact, it inspired and humanized, built a bridge to the middle and lower-middle class, and made affinity visible. Nixon as Walter Mitty was easier to grasp than his lonely, more cerebral side.

On November 24, 1972, the president visited the home team's camp. The *Washington Post* bannered: "Nixon Pays a Surprise Visit to Redskins and Gives Them a Pep Talk for Playoff Drive." In December, he invited Redskins and ironically former Whittier head coach George Allen and his family to the White House after DC beat Dallas, 26–3, to make the Super Bowl. "I'm a partial resident of Florida [Key Biscayne]," said Nixon, "and have a great deal of respect for" Shula. However, his residence was now in DC, and since "[he] always root[ed] for the home team, and [his] home team now [was] in Washington," he would root for the 'Skins. Nixon may have changed tax, spending, other domestic, and foreign policy—even his home team's name—but on rooting for the old home team, he was a rock.

As baseball deserted the capital, further accenting its national post mid-1960s fall, pro football rose, as it had over and again since Ike.

Nixon recognized the NFL's tumbleweed appeal, reveled in it, liking the sport since '50s Sundays spent at Griffith Stadium. Yet after what some felt a presidential dalliance, love of baseball reasserted itself, as the rest of his life proved. Like foreign policy, baseball was intellectual, Nixon consumed by each. In 1992 he mused, unforgettably, "The essence of diplomacy is to confuse the opposition. The opposition never knew what Casey Stengel was talking about. Casey always knew. If I had it to do over again, I'd name Casey Secretary of State." The very thought still staggers.

At the end of a Thursday, June 22, 1972, press conference, Nixon entertained a final question from the White House press: "Mr. President, as the Nation's Number One baseball fan, would you be willing to name your all-time baseball team?" That weekend he outlined his all-time All-Star team, with aid from David Eisenhower, more wed to baseball than even his father-in-law. The president split his Major League team into each league's early 1925–45 era and then modern 1945–70 era, chose names for each position, and named Jackie Robinson the best athlete, Ted Williams best hitter, Joe DiMaggio best outfielder, Brooks Robinson best infielder, and Sandy Koufax best pitcher.

On July 1 the Associated Press published a widely reprinted 2,800-word distillation of his remarks. Most found the roster potent, even if their lineup differed. In 1992 the Nixon Presidential Library and Birthplace (now Museum) staged an exhibit on presidents and baseball. Its namesake split his revised all-time team into players active before and including 1972 and 1992. Nixon divided the latter into the Yankee Era (1925–59), Expansion Era (1960–91), and Active Players (as of 1992) shortly before Mrs. Nixon's death and his own in 1993 and 1994 respectively. Note: In the "1992 Nixon Dream Team," the former president assigned each club in each era a designated hitter—this despite the NL never adopting the rule and the AL only approving it in 1973. All names are used as cited by Nixon.

No reaction to the original list topped Stengel's. "Well, it's so very nice the President is so well versed in sports with so many things he has in his sojourn as President and being international and all, he has to take care of so many countries, it's an honor that he chose me [as greatest living manager]," Casey said. "I'm gonna' be eighty-two July thirtieth [1972] and I've been in baseball since I was eight and that is the situation." Mr. Stengel is just one reason that while Nixon liked football, he loved baseball more.

The 1972 Nixon Dream Team

AMERICAN LEAGUE, EARLY ERA, 1925–45

First base: Lou Gehrig
Second base: Charlie Gehringer
Third base: Red Rolfe
Shortstop: Joe Cronin
Outfielders: Babe Ruth, Joe DiMaggio, and Al Simmons
Catchers: Mickey Cochrane and Bill Dickey
Pitchers: Satchel Paige, Herb Pennock, Lefty Grove,
    Red Ruffing, and Bobo Newsom
Reserve infielders: Jimmie Foxx, Hank Greenberg, and
    Luke Appling
Reserve outfielders: Goose Goslin and Harry Heilmann
Relief pitcher: Johnny Murphy
Manager: Connie Mack

NATIONAL LEAGUE, EARLY ERA, 1925–45

First base: Bill Terry
Second base: Rogers Hornsby
Third base: Pie Traynor
Shortstop: Arky Vaughan
Outfielders: Paul Waner, Mel Ott, and Hack Wilson
Catchers: Ernie Lombardi and Gabby Hartnett
Pitchers: Carl Hubbell, Dizzy Dean, Bucky Walters,
    Mort Cooper, and Burleigh Grimes
Reserve infielders: Frankie Frisch and Marty Marion

Reserve outfielders: Ducky Medwick, Chuck Klein, and
    Edd Roush
Relief pitcher: Mace Brown
Manager: Branch Rickey

First base: Harmon Killebrew
Second base: Nellie Fox
Third base: Brooks Robinson
Shortstop: Lou Boudreau
Outfielders: Ted Williams, Mickey Mantle, and
    Frank Robinson
Catchers: Yogi Berra and Elston Howard
Pitchers: Bob Lemon, Bob Feller, Early Wynn,
    Whitey Ford, and Dave McNally
Reserve infielders: Bobby Richardson and Luis Aparicio
Reserve outfielders: Al Kaline, Carl Yastrzemski, and
    Tony Oliva
Relief pitcher: Hoyt Wilhelm
Manager: Casey Stengel

First base: Stan Musial
Second base: Jackie Robinson
Third base: Eddie Mathews
Shortstop: Ernie Banks
Outfielders: Hank Aaron, Willie Mays, and
    Roberto Clemente
Catchers: Roy Campanella and Johnny Bench
Pitchers: Sandy Koufax, Warren Spahn, Juan Marichal,
    Bob Gibson, and Robin Roberts
Reserve infielders: Ken Boyer, Willie McCovey, Maury
    Wills, and Dick Groat

Reserve outfielder: Duke Snider
Relief pitcher: Roy Face
Manager: Walter Alston

The 1992 Nixon Dream Team

YANKEE ERA, AMERICAN LEAGUE, 1925–59

First base: Lou Gehrig
Second base: Charlie Gehringer
Third base: George Kell
Shortstop: Phil Rizzuto
Outfielders: Babe Ruth, Joe DiMaggio, and
    Ted Williams
Catcher: Mickey Cochrane
Designated hitter: Jimmie Foxx
Pitchers: Lefty Grove, Bobo Newsom, Bob Feller,
    Early Wynn, and Satchel Paige
Manager: Casey Stengel

YANKEE ERA, NATIONAL LEAGUE, 1925–59

First base: Johnny Mize
Second base: Jackie Robinson
Third base: Eddie Mathews
Shortstop: Ernie Banks
Outfielders: Stan Musial, Willie Mays, and Mel Ott
Catcher: Roy Campanella
Designated hitter: Rogers Hornsby
Pitchers: Carl Hubbell, Dizzy Dean, Warren Spahn,
    Robin Roberts, and Roy Face
Manager: Branch Rickey

EXPANSION ERA, AMERICAN LEAGUE, 1960–91

First base: Harmon Killebrew
Second base: Bobby Grich

Third base: Brooks Robinson
Shortstop: Luis Aparicio
Outfielders: Carl Yastrzemski, Mickey Mantle, and
    Reggie Jackson
Catcher: Thurman Munson
Designated hitter: Rod Carew
Pitchers: Whitey Ford, Catfish Hunter, Jim Palmer,
    Luis Tiant, and Rollie Fingers
Manager: Billy Martin

EXPANSION ERA, NATIONAL LEAGUE, 1960–91

First base: Willie McCovey
Second base: Joe Morgan
Third base: Mike Schmidt
Shortstop: Maury Wills
Outfielders: Henry Aaron, Roberto Clemente, and
    Lou Brock
Catcher: Johnny Bench
Designated hitter: Pete Rose
Pitchers: Sandy Koufax, Juan Marichal, Bob Gibson,
    Steve Carlton, and Tom Seaver
Manager: Walter Alston

ACTIVE PLAYERS AS OF 1992, AMERICAN LEAGUE

First base: Don Mattingly
Second base: Roberto Alomar
Third base: George Brett
Shortstop: Cal Ripken Jr.
Outfielders: Rickey Henderson, Ken Griffey Jr., and
    Kirby Puckett
Catcher: Carlton Fisk
Designated hitter: Jose Canseco

Pitchers: Nolan Ryan, Jack Morris, Roger Clemens,
   Goose Gossage, and Dennis Eckersley
Manager: Tony LaRussa

ACTIVE PLAYERS AS OF 1992, NATIONAL LEAGUE

First base: Will Clark
Second base: Ryne Sandberg
Third base: Howard Johnson
Shortstop: Ozzie Smith
Outfielders: Tony Gwynn, Darryl Strawberry, and
   Andre Dawson
Catcher: Gary Carter
Designated hitter: Bobby Bonilla
Pitchers: Dwight Gooden, Bret Saberhagen, David Cone,
   Rob Dibble, and Lee Smith
Manager: Tommy Lasorda

From late 1970 to mid-1972 John B. Connally was Richard Nixon's secretary of the treasury. The president greatly admired him, thinking Connally capable of any job, especially his own. Without Watergate, it is almost certain that Nixon would have endorsed Connally as the 1976 GOP nominee—indeed, likely that Big Jawn could have become the thirty-eighth president.

At a 1972 barbecue dinner at the Connally ranch in Floresville, Texas, Nixon was asked about A's pitcher Vida Blue, then holding out from Oakland owner Charles O. Finley. "He [Blue] has so much talent," Nixon said of his 24-8 record in 1971. "Maybe Finley ought to pay." He and Vida had first met in the Oval Office the prior September, with Nixon in the middle of a group photo, holding an A's cap and shaking the southpaw's hand. In 1972 Finley, a vain, cheap gasbag, had team colors changed to green or gold jerseys with white pants. Blue finished 6-10 but kept his money. Oakland began a dynasty, and Charlie kept the crown.

In the American League, prior to 1972 all three then-best-of-five League Championship Series under the split-league format begun in

1969 had ended in a limp sweep with acres of empty seats. Each National League playoff also lacked a fifth game. The lockout to start the 1972 season heightened the morass, siring an uneven schedule. Detroit took the AL East by winning two of its last three games before meeting the A's, their LCS as brassy as Chevrolet against Ford. In one game Lerrin LaGrow hit Oakland's Bert Campaneris, Campy flinging his bat toward the mound to stir a bench-clearing brawl. In another, Tiger Stadium shook *literally*. Oakland took a 2–1 fifth-game pennant, the first full-length LCS since its birth—or was that the day-earlier NL playoff, which also went the max? Pittsburgh led, 3–2, when Johnny Bench, batting at Cincinnati, hit a game-tying ninth-inning blast. Later Bob Moose bounced a two-out, man-on-third-base curve, George Foster scoring the Reds' flag-winning run—as Nixon loved to say, "an historic first," the first NL wild pitch to ever plate a pennant.

Would the Series be as tight? The Big Red Machine entered running on each cylinder. In the season Bench had gone long a league-high forty times. Joe Morgan had stolen fifty-eight bases. Shortstop Dave Conception turned two so quickly the ball seemed radioactive to his glove. Manager Sparky Anderson, a.k.a. Captain Hook, pulled starters preemptively for a brilliant pen. Joe Rudi had an AL-best 181 hits for the A's. Campy's fifty-two steals led the league for the sixth and final time. Catfish Hunter, Ken Holtzman, and Blue Moon Odom finished 55–24, Rollie Fingers adding twenty-one saves. Finley offered $500 to a player who grew a mustache by Father's Day, hoping some would apply. *All* did in that very different salary age, but none matched Fingers's handlebar mustache. Finley avoided a major pay hike by giving him a year's supply of wax. Cheap, he was creative.

Beyond baseball the Series acquired a cultural coloration. The counterculture A's fought like other teams played pre-game pepper. "So what else is new?" said Fingers of a Reggie Jackson–Billy North brawl in 1974. "Being on this club is like having a ringside seat for the Muhammad Ali–Joe Frazier fights." The clean-shaven Reds became a metaphor for the Silent Majority, Nixon's phrase appropriated in Donald Trump's 2016 campaign for president. Oakland's Gene Tenace had hit five homers all year. In the opener October's hero twice went yard his first two Series at-bats—another "historic first": 3–2, A's. Next day Rudi robbed Denis Menke of a potential game-tying homer at Cincy's Riverfront Stadium: A's, 2–1. Gone was the Reds' invincibility; Oakland led, two games to none.

The most indelible "first" graced Game Three. Bench had a 3-2 two-out and two-on base count when A's manager Dick Williams asked for time, went to the mound, talked to Fingers, Tenace, and Sal Bando, returned to the bench, and pointed to first base. The three other A's nodded: an intentional walk to load the bases. Set, Fingers looked at second base; Bench relaxed, sure that "they were putting me on." As Rollie kicked, catcher Tenace squatted and caught a slider on the outside corner—called strike three! Bench had been set up—conned.

In Game Seven Pete Rose batted in the ninth inning. "Fly ball, deep left field!" NBC's Jim Simpson said. "Rudi goes back near the warning track, is there. The World Series is over! The underdog Oakland Athletics win their first world championship [3–2] since they were in Philadelphia in 1930!" Series MVP Tenace had four homers, nine RBIS, and a .348 average. A last Series "first": six games were decided by one run.

On the roof of the A's dugout, Finley and Williams kissed their wives, the straw-hatted A's Swingers Band playing Charlie's favorite song, "Sugartime": "Sugar in the morning, sugar in the evening, sugar at supper time. Be my little sugar, and love me all the time." At that moment Oakland loved Charles O. Finley. One year later, resigning, Dick Williams strained to punch him in the nose.

A sentimental man, Nixon liked to reminisce about such distant events as being unable as a student to afford to go home to California for Thanksgiving 1936. A Duke Law School professor, finding that Nixon would be alone, invited him to spend the day with his family. Years later the president told his two daughters that he would never forget the teacher's kindness. Some events were too painful to recall. As a child he was very close to his mother, missing her terribly when she had to leave the family for several years to care for one dying son in drier Arizona. The same disease, tuberculosis, struck another, Nixon in each case falling into what Hannah called "an impenetrable silence."

Fig. 1. ABRAHAM LINCOLN. "The National Game" series of illustrations was published by Currier and Ives. This pro–Abraham Lincoln satire, "Three 'Outs' and One 'Run,'" casts him (*right*) as a political animal and more, running the 1860 field dizzy to become the Republican Party presidential nominee and ultimately America's sixteenth president. National Baseball Hall of Fame and Museum, Cooperstown, New York.

Fig. 2. WILLIAM HOWARD TAFT. (*above*) William Howard Taft (*right*) attending a game in the early 1910s. At three hundred pounds, the nation's 1909–13 chief executive was America's heaviest president. Named by one poll "Top Fan" among all occupants of the Oval Office, Taft made throwing out a season's first ball a long-running presidential rite. National Baseball Hall of Fame and Museum, Cooperstown, New York.

Fig. 3. THEODORE ROOSEVELT. (*opposite top*) Theodore Roosevelt, here in Spanish-American War "Rough Riders" garb, was the exception to baseball's rule. Virtually alone among U.S. presidents, he found the pastime dull. The total politician kept contempt to himself, knowing of baseball's popularity and wanting to keep his office in 1901–09. National Baseball Hall of Fame and Museum, Cooperstown, New York.

Fig. 4. WOODROW WILSON. (*opposite bottom*) From 1913–21 Woodrow Wilson heroically fought for the common man at home and peace abroad, strokes paralyzing him in a second term. Baseball, which he loved and once played at Davidson College, became a salvation during and after his presidency, trips to Washington's Griffith Stadium his lifeline. National Baseball Hall of Fame and Museum, Cooperstown, New York.

Fig. 5. WARREN HARDING. (*opposite top*) Since Taft, a president by tradition has thrown out each season's "first pitch." Few looked more presidential or loved baseball more than white-haired Warren Harding. A scandal involving women and corruption, which became public only after his death in August 1923, roiled the previously admired Ohioan's reputation. National Baseball Hall of Fame and Museum, Cooperstown, New York.

Fig. 6. CALVIN COOLIDGE. (*opposite bottom*) A woman bet that she could get taciturn 1923–29 president Calvin Coolidge to say more than two words. Said Silent Cal, deliciously: "You lose." The popular New Englander fused short speeches, a homespun bent, and wisdom not to run for reelection in 1928, thus skirting onus for the Depression. National Baseball Hall of Fame and Museum, Cooperstown, New York.

Fig. 7. HERBERT HOOVER. (*above*) Babe Ruth (*left*) blamed Herbert Hoover (*right*) for the Depression, explaining his salary, higher than the president's: "I had a better year than he did!" Seeking 1932 reelection, Republican Hoover sought the Democrat's support, Ruth declining to back him. Ultimately, Hoover vainly tried to purchase Babe's nod. National Baseball Hall of Fame and Museum, Cooperstown, New York.

Fig. 8. FRANKLIN D. ROOSEVELT. (*above*) America elected Franklin Roosevelt four times as president. Here he throws out the first ball in 1937, Connie Mack to the right of FDR. The greatest president of his century helped defeat the Depression and win World War II, his "Green Light Letter" of 1942 calling upon baseball to operate during the war. FDR's death in 1945 stunned the game, which knew how he had saved it. National Baseball Hall of Fame and Museum, Cooperstown, New York.

Fig. 9. HARRY TRUMAN. (*opposite top*) If Harry Truman symbolized U.S. post–World War II normalcy, nothing crystalized it on the field like the World Series and football's Army-Navy Game. Tossing out baseball's first ball, Truman, the only ambidextrous president, used both arms. He and Mrs. Truman are shown at the 1948 annual Army-Navy Classic in Philadelphia. Harry S. Truman Presidential Library and Museum.

Fig. 10. DWIGHT EISENHOWER. (*opposite bottom*) We recall Dwight Eisenhower, shown at Griffith Stadium in 1960, as a "great and good man" and president, said author Stephen Ambrose. The famed general of World War II knit eight years of peace, prosperity, and unity; was twice elected by landslide; and almost *became* his decade as 1953–61 president. National Baseball Hall of Fame and Museum, Cooperstown, New York.

Fig. 11. JOHN F. KENNEDY. (*opposite top*) Writer Tom Wicker terms John F. Kennedy "the most fascinating might-have-been in American history," tying prose, strength, and grace. His 1961–63 presidency was as memorable: a wall in Berlin, nuclear disarmament, the Cuban missile crisis. Here JFK rises for a foul at the 1962 All-Star Game at District of Columbia Stadium. National Baseball Hall of Fame and Museum, Cooperstown, New York.

Fig. 12. JOHN F. KENNEDY. (*opposite bottom*) "I need the . . . scent of the salt in my skin," said John F. Kennedy, here at twenty-nine, in memory always the young man and the sea. He is shown with younger brother Edward (*left*), aboard the family boat *Victura* at the Kennedy home at Hyannis Port, Massachusetts, circa 1946. John F. Kennedy Presidential Library and Museum.

Fig. 13. LYNDON JOHNSON. (*above*) Shown opening the 1964 season, Lyndon Johnson was a Shakespearean figure who looked larger than the office—Falstaff by way of Pecos Bill. His Great Society, including the Voting Rights Act, and policy in Vietnam dominated his 1960s presidency. In 1965, baseball's first indoor stadium, the Astrodome, debuted in LBJ's Texas. National Baseball Hall of Fame and Museum, Cooperstown, New York.

Fig. 14. LYNDON JOHNSON. (*above*) A consummate deal maker, Lyndon Johnson used every tool, including, as shown here, baseball bats, to wield his legislative will. Officials around him in the mid-60s Oval Office include (*right*) Senator Everett Dirksen (R-IL), a political foe and personal friend. National Baseball Hall of Fame and Museum, Cooperstown, New York.

Fig. 15. RICHARD NIXON. (*opposite top*) To many, vice president Richard Nixon meant the 1950s traditional middle class. As 1969–74 president, he artfully overlapped its working class, wrote Conrad Black, into an "overwhelming army of ordinary citizens." In 1958 (*left to right*) daughter Tricia, wife Pat, daughter Julie, and Nixon visited Griffith Stadium. National Baseball Hall of Fame and Museum, Cooperstown, New York.

Fig. 16. RICHARD NIXON. (*opposite bottom*) In 1972 Richard Nixon won a historic landslide, the Forgotten American forging the Silent Majority. Despite Watergate, he and Mrs. Nixon observed the 1973 Christmas season with a snowman built by White House staffers on the South Lawn. Richard Nixon Presidential Library and Museum, White House Photo Office Collection.

Fig. 17. GERALD FORD. (*opposite top*) Gerald Ford keyed two University of Michigan national football championship teams, was elected to Congress in 1948, became vice president in 1973, and was sworn in as president a year later on Richard Nixon's resignation, saying "our great Republic is a government of laws and not of men." With commissioner Bowie Kuhn (*right*) at the 1976 All-Star Game in Philadelphia. National Baseball Hall of Fame and Museum, Cooperstown, New York.

Fig. 18. JIMMY CARTER. (*opposite bottom*) Jimmy Carter became president by hard work and against all odds, a *Mr. Smith Goes to Washington*. His surpassing feat was forging peace between ancient foils Egypt and Israel. In 1978 Carter hailed Pete Rose (*left*) at the White House for a National League record forty-four game hitting streak. Later, he devoted his life to being a superb ex-president. National Baseball Hall of Fame and Museum, Cooperstown, New York.

Fig. 19. RONALD REAGAN. (*above*) In 1952 ex-baseball voice, movie star, and future president Ronald Reagan starred in the film *The Winning Team*, playing courageous epileptic/alcoholic pitcher Grover Cleveland Alexander. Here film hitting instructor Rogers Hornsby (*left*) suggests to Reagan, as Alexander (*right*), and another student how to hit. National Baseball Hall of Fame and Museum, Cooperstown, New York.

Fig. 20. RONALD REAGAN. (*above*) As 1981–89 president, Ronald Reagan launched America's longest peacetime boom. After he left office, the Berlin Wall fell, the Soviet Union dissolved, and Eastern Europe was freed, Marxism-Leninism ending, as he predicted," on "the ash-heap of history." A 2011 Gallup Poll called him America's greatest president. Here he addresses a crowd in Denver in 1981. Ronald Reagan Presidential Library and Museum.

Fig. 21. GEORGE H. W. BUSH. (*opposite top*) George H. W. Bush joined the navy in World War II, barely dodged death, and returned a hero. Lou Gehrig was his life-long idol; Bush, Yale's own "Iron Man" first baseman. In 1992, having helped remake much of the world, the great baseball fan and foreign policy president opened the first "new old park," Oriole Park at Camden Yards. Grandson George P. Bush is at right. National Baseball Hall of Fame and Museum, Cooperstown, New York.

Fig. 22. BILL CLINTON. (*opposite bottom*) Bill Clinton made the Democratic Party national again for the first time since the '60s, tying prosperity and peace. His popularity rose from 1993 to 2001—a political Virgil whose bonhomie evoked Harry Caray, who taught him baseball on the air. Here Clinton gets a cap from Joe Torre (*right*) at the White House to hail the Yankees' 1998 world title. National Baseball Hall of Fame and Museum, Cooperstown, New York.

Fig. 23. GEORGE W. BUSH. Mere weeks after 9/11, George W. Bush threw out the first pitch at Yankee Stadium before Game Three of the 2001 World Series. Vaunting poise and skill, he threw a perfect strike as the house erupted. Presidents face decisions that divide the nation. History affords the chance to unite. To Bush unity that night meant a heater down the middle. National Baseball Hall of Fame and Museum, Cooperstown, New York.

Fig. 24. BARACK OBAMA. In 2010 skilled speaker Barack Obama showed another trait: loyalty. About to open the Washington Nationals' season, Obama set to throw the home team's first ball. Hiding his home*town* White Sox cap in his glove, he revealed it on the mound, put on his chapeau, and pitched. Such tactical skill impressed even Republicans. National Baseball Hall of Fame and Museum, Cooperstown, New York.

Fig. 25. DONALD TRUMP. At New York Military Academy, 1964 senior captain Donald Trump (*center, first row*) was called by his coach, Colonel Ted Dobias, "the best baseball player I ever coached at first base, catching, and at the bat." The Phillies and Red Sox scouted, liking Trump's power, but he liked finance more. From the Wharton School, he moved to construction, media, and politics—Trump's peroration his stunning 2016 presidential victory. Seth Poppel Yearbook Library.

Nixon's ability to stir emotion, caused by his feeling it, spawned the address that, more than any other, made him president—the 1968 GOP convention acceptance, invoking his boyhood so wistfully that Jack London or John-Boy Walton could have spoken every word. "He hears the train go by at night and dreams of faraway places where he'd like to go," he said. "It seems like an impossible dream, but he is helped on his journey through life." As his speech—to television's Chris Matthews, "a masterpiece"—revealed, Nixon was moved by "faraway places." In February 1972 he visited China, which for a quarter century had been as alien as Jupiter or Mars, meeting President Mao Tse-Tung and Premier Chou En-lai and showing how *realpolitik* could further peace. "The week that changed the world," Nixon rhapsodized. That June 1, having gone to Iran and Poland from Moscow to sign the SALT pact, he returned to tell Congress, "The foundation has been laid for a new relationship between the two most powerful nations in the world."

Foreign policy gave the president a leg up on reelection. On November 7, 1972, NBC *Nightly News*'s anchorman John Chancellor stated, not liking it, "This is the most spectacular landslide election in the history of United States politics." Nixon trounced Democratic nominee George McGovern, taking more than one in three Democrats and a majority of the Catholic vote—the first Republican to do so. The Californian won forty-nine states, almost 60.8 percent of the turnout, and 47,149,841 votes to McGovern's 29,172,767—the greatest margin over a rival. Nixon even took half of the youth vote, said to be McGovern's via Vietnam, in the first election where eighteen-year-olds could cast a ballot. To complete his second-term "game plan"—aptly, a football phrase—the incumbent needed only to end the war.

Steadily Nixon withdrew the more than half a million troops from Vietnam that he had inherited from Johnson. Two weeks before the May 1972 Soviet summit, he mined North Vietnamese ports and bombed rail, road, and military targets to halt a Communist offensive. NBC's Chancellor claimed, "The summit is in jeopardy and a new phase of the war has begun." The Soviets said the summit had never been in doubt. That December Nixon renewed bombing the north, a decision that he thought begot "peace with honor." A month later he announced the Paris Peace Accords, ending U.S. involvement, a cease fire signed directly. With prisoners of war returning and Nixon's Gallup approval percentage higher than even his November rout of McGovern, he loomed, said *Newsweek*, as "a stern, sure, and uncompromising man who disdained to conciliate his critics." Ahead: reforming government to return to the middle class constitutional power "that elites ha[d] taken away," he said—among them, the media, Congress, the judiciary, interest groups, bureaucracy, and think tanks: each, the president believed, hostile to Mid-America.

Nixon felt that the courage of U.S. troops had made North Vietnam sue for peace—also, not anticipating Watergate, that the war was now behind him. General George C. Marshall once called America's secret weapon "the best damn kids in the world." As POWs came home, they volunteered how brave *Nixon* had been—"Richard the Lion-Heart," their favorite. His new team, the Angels, were to open their 1973 home season against Kansas City, Nixon throwing the initial presidential first pitch in any city outside of DC or Cincinnati. Almost overwhelmed by gratitude to the POWs, he wanted Major David Luna, enslaved for eight years by North Vietnam, to take his place. The Secret Service said, "Mr. President, they're ready to throw out the first ball. We'll bring Major Luna to you." Typical of his respect for the military, the former navy man said, "No, I'll go to *him*."

Nixon before the fall: optimism was in the saddle. For one thing, what could be worse than Vietnam? Moreover, Democrats were in disarray. He also seemed at long last to have fostered mass appeal. "Baseball finally has a real buff in the White House," wrote Jimmy Cannon in a column common at the time. "The game has a hold on Nixon"; crucial was that baseball had a hold on America. "Nixon . . . understands baseball and talks about it with the sentimental fervor of a true buff. It is not a small tribute that when a President goes to a ball game right off that it isn't [seen as] a corny political act. It [is] marvelous because . . . Dick Nixon is a true ball fan." Surely great innings lay ahead for the president and the fan.

As I left college in 1973, the president who said, "I am an introvert in an extrovert's profession," was also the tribune of people who never read the *New York Times*. Knowing what Nixon envisioned for a second term—peace in the Far East, a Middle East settlement—it reads like something out of Henry James to gauge how much one minor incident cost that he neither knew of nor approved. On June 17, 1972, five employees of the Committee to Re-Elect the President (CREEP) entered the Democratic National Committee at the Watergate Hotel complex in Washington. They were captured by police, who found that several of those arrested were employed by CREEP or the Republican National Committee (RNC). The story was investigated by the *Washington Post*, which set out to void what Nixon had done and hoped to do.

"It went right to our desk," said *Post* editor Ben Bradlee. "The notes, phone numbers, we had it within a day." The Miller Presidential Center at the University of Virginia likens Watergate to a loose string that unraveled a whole cloth of administration wrongs that Nixon attorney general John Mitchell called the "White House Horrors." They included: having the CIA tell the FBI to halt its Watergate inquiry; wiretapping officials and journalists; creating a presidential "Enemies List"; burglarizing the psychiatrist's office of Daniel Ellsberg for illegally releasing a secret Pentagon study of the Vietnam War; and covertly bombing Cambodia and Laos, in a war Nixon had not started and tried honorably to end. The president begot too many of these actions, was ignorant of others, and learned of the rest too late.

On August 5, 1974, two years after Nixon first sought a solution to Watergate's problem—those arrested, he feared, might be tied to his office, harming reelection—the White House released a June 23, 1972, tape of him ordering the CIA to stop an FBI probe of the break-in—an obstruction of justice. By then campaign and administration officials had been charged, pled guilt or innocence, and/or gone to prison. vice president Spiro Agnew, the seeming right-wing truth teller for the Republican base who made Nixon look liberal, resigned to avoid indictment for graft as 1967–69 governor of Maryland. The president's approval had plunged from 68 percent in February 1973 to 24 percent—Gallup's steepest-ever fall. Proclaiming "I am not a crook" was not the brightest thing to say. RNC chair George H. W. Bush phoned GOPers daily, cajoling them for time: *things will turn.* They didn't. For a long time Bush told callers that Nixon had been poorly served by aides.

A day after the 1974 release of the obstruction-of-justice tape, the Cabinet and aides attended a meeting where Nixon said he had committed no impeachable offense and would not resign. In an act of great courage or disloyalty, Bush spoke without being recognized, urging Nixon to resign. The next day he walked a letter to the president's office. It concluded, "If you do leave office history will properly record your achievements with a lasting respect." He was wrong, as Nixon knew, having said, "History depends on who writes it." One study after another shows historians leaning left. Loathing the president in life, they would hardly rehabilitate him in death. By contrast, Ronald Reagan was the last major Republican in office to ask Nixon to resign. "Some day," said California's then governor, "I think people will look back at Watergate and say, 'Now, what was that all about?'"

Reagan's question would not have satisfied the law, though it sustained many who voted for Nixon as many as *five* times for national office between 1952 and 1972—a record, tying FDR. On Thursday night, August 8, 1974, the thirty-seventh president said in his thirty-seventh Oval Office speech that he would resign his office. The next morning Nixon bid his staff a tender, defiant, haunting, and unforgettable farewell, his wife and family behind him in the East Room of the White House. He recalled his father; said "My mother was a saint"; thought defeat "only a beginning, always"; and sought lightness amid the dark—"Only if you have been in the deepest valley can you ever know how magnificent it is to be on the highest mountain." It traumatized. It mesmerized. Tens of millions sobbed. The rest were glad to see him go. It is how we remember him, even now.

Baseball stood by Nixon long after much of the republic had abandoned him, largely because he had stood by baseball in the late 1960s and early 1970s, when much of popular culture had abandoned *it. Fortune* magazine sacked "the beat-up national sport." New York's advertising firm of Kenyon and Eckhardt pricked a "game meant to be played before children, old men, and an occasional housewife watching." Against a tide of opinion that said watching paint dry was more exciting, at a time when baseball was being pummeled like a piñata, the president of the United States said unabashedly, over and again, that baseball was *the* American game. The pastime never forgot.

Their work was synergistic. Nixon engineered the White House site of the All-Star Gala for baseball's 1969 centennial. As writer Dick Young remarked, "It would not have happened in any manner close to what it did without him, and baseball knew it." Nixon ensured that the White House backed the yearly Hall of Fame induction day, calling induction "the highest honor anyone in baseball can receive, richer for [honorees'] contribution to a very important part of our way of life." In 1970, buoyed by Metsomania, Bowie Kuhn and league presidents Joe Cronin and Chub Feeney gave the president the Mets' World Series victory ring and a baseball autographed by all team members. The heavy ring was inscribed, "N.Y. Mets. World Champions 1969." Nixon told his guests, "This could be quite a weapon."

It took till spring 1973 for Watergate to emerge full blown, some alleging that baseball had asked the president to refrain from first pitches at any of the then twenty-four big league parks. Kuhn spokesman Joseph Reichler reset the record: "We'd be positively delighted and honored to have President Nixon attend any game, season opener or otherwise." Loyalty breeds loyalty. Nixon had also staged more comebacks than Henry VIII had wives. For a long while many refused to discount another. Finally, as Meg Greenfield wrote, "This traumatic clash of cultures"—Nixon as Grant Wood against the age's hip, camp, and art intelligentsia—had long ago cemented his rapport with America's working middle, to whom baseball was elemental.

A year later the Nixons landed in San Clemente, at the once Western White House, above steep cliffs to the Pacific. Despondent, Nixon moved as in shock, as if his heart lay outside his body. He almost died of phlebitis, operators at the hospital braving callers who hoped he did. Ruth Graham, Billy's wife, hired a small airplane to fly over the hospital with a sign: "God loves you, and so do we." Bob Hope's wife, Dolores, said, "Remember, Dick, one who loves you is worth ten who hate you." Pat, who often said, "I could be dying, and would never tell," brooked a severe stroke in 1976 and had to relearn functions "as if [she] were a child again." In 1978 her husband wrote the best-selling *RN: The Memoirs of Richard Nixon*. Eight more successful books followed, Nixon's last two decades fetching a man of letters back to his youth of the printed page.

In a larger sense Nixon returned to baseball, as he had since boyhood, watching the Angels secure their first title—the 1979 AL West. He often visited the Halos clubhouse, doused by players on clinching their division. Younger daughter Julie began working full time for the *Saturday Evening Post*, Pat missing her and sister Tricia in the East. In 1980 she and Dick moved to New York, then New Jersey, to be near family and on the "fast track," as Nixon said. In 1989 he sat next to Mickey Mantle and Yankees owner George Steinbrenner at St. Patrick's Cathedral for the funeral of mutual friend Billy Martin.

Steinbrenner regularly invited celebrities of all sort to his private box behind the plate at The Stadium, Nixon often eschewing his usual seat near the field to kibitz. Once the Yanks owner's most famous guest sent a note to the nearby booth of play-by-play and funny man Bob Uecker. "People even more famous than Bob want to meet him," said Pat Hughes, Uke's 1982–95 Brewers partner and Cubs 1996– radio voice. The note from the former president, "rather well-known himself, request[ed] Mr. Uecker's presence."

On the monitor Pat soon saw Nixon, Bob, and George, laughing at Uke's funnies. Afterward Hughes termed Nixon "the most memorable of all the people that Bob had met." On air he asked, "Bob, how'd it go?" Uecker replied: "Pat, you know what, Richie was a pretty good guy."

Richie!? "Richard Nixon was an incredibly controversial person who was called every name in the book," Hughes marveled, "Mr. President, Richard, Richard Milhous, Dick, by some, Tricky Dick, by others. But never Richie!"

At the 1968 Republican convention where Norman Mailer drew Nixon's bobbed-cork core, the novelist noted how the nominee "had taken punishment. There was an attentiveness in his eyes which gave offer of some knowledge of the abyss, even [a] gentleness" that found dignity in survival and survival in hope. We last saw Richard Nixon as a grandfather in the late 1980s and early '90s, when age and family helped "gentleness" transcend.

Living a few miles apart, Nixon and young grandson Christopher talked by phone while critiquing on their own TVs the same local Mets or Yankees or network game. "We talk about who was pitching, each team's batting order, a great fielding play," the ex-president said, "if the runner should try to steal second, a pitch was a ball or strike, talk strategy on the same phone line inning after inning."

This unique way to bond let grandpa and grandson share unspoken love by sharing what each truly loved. It also showed that what Dick Young had typed—"This man knows baseball"—remained, as Richard Nixon forever said, "perfectly clear."

TEN

"Friendship, a Perfect Blendship!"

Gerald Ford, 1974–1977

M any attended Gerald Ford's swearing-in as president in
the East Room on the August 1974 day where earlier Richard Nixon said, "Always remember, others may hate you,
but those who hate you don't win unless you hate them, and then
you destroy yourself." That night George H. W. Bush wrote in his diary of "indeed a new spirit, a new lift." Having joined Ford in the
House of Representatives in 1967, Bush felt the new president a friend—
paraphrasing Chuck Berry, a political "Jerry B. Goode." The sole U.S.
chief executive not elected president or vice president would tie autobiography and biography: think Ford's *A Time to Heal* and Frank
Capra's *It's a Wonderful Life* respectively.

Ford is said to have calmed America. In fact, he taught it. The former
congressman was impressed with policy, not himself. He was comfortable in the presidency, treating pomp like Billy Sunday did sin. James
Fenimore Cooper wrote, "Truth was the Deerslayer's polar star." It lit
Ford's first speech in his new office: "Honesty is always the best policy. . . . Truth is the glue that holds government together." Who would
not say right man, right time?

Born in Omaha on Bastille Day 1913, the unGallic Leslie Lynch King
Jr. was raised by mother Dorothy after his parents divorced. In 1916
Mom married Gerald Rudolff Ford in Grand Rapids, Michigan. The
boy took his stepfather's name, admiring him deeply. Jerry worked

odd jobs, was a lifetime Eagle Scout, and hoped to emulate legendary football running back Red Grange. As president, Ford endured several incidents, including inexplicably falling down stairs, that falsely evoked a stumblebum lacking coordination. Actually the center, linebacker, and line snapper on the University of Michigan's 1932–33 two-time national champion football team was a superb athlete who read the sports section first. He liked its lesson: "the value of team play."

Ford was colorblind, but not blind to justice. In his senior year, Georgia Tech refused to play a scheduled game if a black Michigan player, Willis Ward, took the field. Despite Ford's ire, including writing letters to officials, the administration decided to bench Willis— Jerry's best friend and roommate on the road. The future president threatened to quit. At Ford's funeral in 2007 president George W. Bush said, "He was furious at Georgia Tech for making the demand, and at the University of Michigan for caving in. He agreed to play only after Willis Ward personally asked him to." The episode augured a leader who, above all, was fair.

Ward became a probate court judge in Michigan, he and Ford remaining lifelong friends, speaking little of the incident but reuniting on a glorious 1970s weekday in the White House. Later Michigan retired Ford's jersey No. 48, the NCAA naming him among "the hundred most influential student-athletes" of the last century in 2006. In 2012 an Emmy Award–nominated documentary, *Black and Blue: The Story of Gerald Ford, Willis Ward, and the 1934 Michigan-Georgia Tech Football Game*, was released.

After college, Ford spurned pro football's Lions and Packers for Yale Law School, World War II, a law practice in Grand Rapids, and a fifty-eight-year marriage that only George H. W. and Barbara Bush have topped for presidential longevity. "I am indebted to no man," the new president said in his 1974 swearing-in address, "and only to one woman, my dear wife [Betty]." Ford soon proved that if a politician is reliable, electoral purchases will top returns.

For more than a century Michiganders beat a path to the corner of Detroit's Michigan and Trumbull Avenues, where the Tigers played ball at Navin Field (1912–38), renamed Briggs Stadium (1939–60), and Tiger Stadium (1961–99). They included Ford, who, at Grand Rapids, was 160 miles away. The park officially housed as many as 52,904, unofficially jammed thousands more, yet felt as intimate as a chapel. The towhead's saints included Hal Newhouser, Hank Greenberg, George Kell, and Norm Cash; pitcher Frank Lary; Charlie "Paw-Paw" Maxwell, disproportionately and perhaps divinely homering on Sunday; left-hander Dick McAuliffe, like Mel Ott right leg raised in the air; and, above all, Mickey Lolich, Denny McLain, and Ford's favorite player, Al Kaline, baseball's regal working man.

On September 24, 1974, Kaline doubled against Baltimore for the three thousandth hit of his 1953– career. A day later the Tigers fan in the Oval Office called the future Hall of Famer to hail a life built on the old-fashioned virtues—modesty, maturity, excellence. Presidential aide Warren Rustand had given Ford a word-for-word biographical telephone memo about what to say to his long-time friend as if they had barely met. Someone leaked it to sensation-seeking columnist Jack Anderson, a poor excuse for a poorer journalist. Instead, the president talked off-the-cuff.

"No one had to tell me about No. 6," Ford said, long after Kaline retired that fall. Losing the 1976 election, Jerry B. Goode himself was retired involuntarily in early 1977. He left the White House to, among other things, make speeches, play golf, chair conferences, watch sports, and reminisce with fellow Wolverines about events like the meeting Ford had held with Detroit native and Tigers ex-first baseman and general manager John McHale in the Oval Office to accept a big-league season pass.

As McHale recalled, he had decided to pose a question testing the depth of Ford's Tigers knowledge. "Do you remember Heinie Schuble, Mr. President?" he asked. "Sure," Ford said. "Wasn't he the Tigers shortstop just before Billy Rogell?" Schuble hit .233 in 1929 and .271 in 1932. Rogell never had fewer than five hundred at-bats in a season from 1932 to 1938. To Ford, Tigers trivia wasn't trivial. It is doubtful McHale ever tested him again.

Ford next imitated a submarine pitcher, recalling Elden Auker and his unusual 1930s underhand delivery. "Did you know," said McHale, each of them again a teen, "that Auker threw down under because he'd been a good football player who was hurt at Kansas State?" The president nodded. "I understand that Auker has done quite well for himself in Kansas."

Ford's grasp of most things Tiger helped make him a prism and progenitor of the state of Michigan. To paraphrase a favorite hymn of their beloved 1959–2002 announcer, W. Earnest Harwell, "Give [him] that old-time tradition, it's good enough for [him]." Ernie knew how in 1900 the minor Western League to which Detroit belonged renamed itself the American League. Two of its teams moved: the St. Paul Saints to Chicago and Ford's Grand Rapids Hustlers to Cleveland. A year later the now self-declared Major League AL placed charter stakes in eight cities, including Detroit. Tellingly, Harwell told me he was certain Ford knew this history too.

A man stuck in the mud with his car was once asked by a wayfarer whether he was really stuck. "Well, you could say I was stuck," said the man, "if I was really going anywhere." Having gone from one league to another, the un"stuck" 1901–02 Tigers played Sunday at Burns a.k.a. West End Park, then had Monday through Saturday dibs on Bennett Park, built on an old hay market's cobblestones, at Michigan and Trumbull Avenues—"the Corner" that Harwell christened. "Imagine!" said Arthur Brooks, whose grandfather owned Brooks Lumber beyond right field from the park's debut till its close a year before the new millennium. "Baseball, in the exact same place, for an entire century and more."

The site honored ex-Detroit catcher Charlie Bennett, who lost both legs in an 1894 train accident. Its archetype was 1891–1918 shortstop and 1907–20 manager Hughie Jennings, less martinet than sage. Connie Mack named him baseball's best-ever skipper, save John McGraw and Casey Stengel. "Never . . . scold . . . a man in anger," Jennings said. "Angry, your reasoning is not sound." "Ee-yah!" Jennings whooped from the coaching box upon a Tigers pennant in 1907, 1908, and 1909. "The city was blowing its top," added Ty Cobb a.k.a. the Georgia Peach. "Everyone in town seemed to own a tin whistle," imitating Hughie's piercing sound and lauding Sam Crawford and Germany Schaefer and, above all, Cobb. Each had flair—and a dilemma.

Home plate at Bennett Park stared at the afternoon sun. "Unfair!" Ty stormed. "With that plate, it's a miracle we survived!" Ralph Waldo Emerson wrote, "[Napoleon] was no Capuchin [i.e., saint], and he is no hero in the high sense." Cobb, no saint either, averaged .367, stole a then record 897 bases, had another record 4,189 hits, won a 1909 Triple Crown, and retired with a bumper crop of grudge. Some loathed the churlish deity. Others sighed to see him, like a young Arthur Brooks. Whenever it snowed, his grandfather hitched horses to a plow, then disposed of snow all around the stadium, getting four tickets to every game. Arthur got one, which seemed just right.

"That's what baseball does to people in Detroit," said writer Joe Falls, who covered the Tigers from 1956 to 1978. "Detroit [is] one of the great baseball towns. This is a town of three million managers—all of them right. And a town of beer drinkers—all of them thirsty. This is a town that has developed a true passion for a boy's game and love-hate relationship for the men who play it." Boy's game. Man's thirst. "Ee-yah!" then and now.

The wooden park where Ford first saw baseball at the Corner was re-built in concrete a year before his birth and renamed for Tigers owner Frank Navin. "When slugging teams came," Cobb wrote, "we'd put in temporary stands, turning triples and inside-the-parkers into ground-rule doubles. It balanced out," like skill. In 1922 Ty's .401 average trailed only George Sisler's .420, yet Detroit's post-1911 ERA never topped fourth in an eight-team league. A pattern formed. "Pitching!" flailed Cobb. "We never had enough!" In 1915 he led the AL in runs, hits, total bases, and steals—a then high ninety-six. His Tigers won a hundred games. No team had won as many and *not* won the pennant. The trend wended through the next nineteen years, four presidents, a world war, and the Depression. "I remember growing up," Ford laughed. "Each year they'd come up a little short and we'd say, 'Just wait till next year. It'll all be different.'"

Many years promised to be for the "Tiges" or "Detroits," as Harwell later coined. One year the Georgia Peach picked six-for-six at bat. Another, Johnny Neun turned an unassisted triple play. From 1921 through

1928 Harry Heilmann's four batting titles in odd years averaged between .393 and .403. The even years spanned .328 to .367. "Mr. Navin'd give me a two-year contract," he mused, "and I'd take it easy the second." In the early and mid-1920s Ruth and Cobb jousted like Romans and Maccabees. Ty ragged him in 1924: "Something around here really stinks. Like a polecat." Later they fought at home plate for half an hour before Detroit forfeited. Babe whacked an *eight-hundred-foot* home run that landed two blocks beyond center field. Navin huffed, "Maybe the sign above the door was for him: 'Visitors' Clubhouse— No Visits Allowed.'"

It is true that a quarter century earlier the Tigers earned a hat trick of AL titles—also that their public had grown tired of delayed déjà vu. Charlie Gehringer batted more than .300 in thirteen of sixteen full years, perfecting the image of the strong, silent type. Once roommate Chief Hogsett asked the Mechanical Man to pass the salt. Charlie ignored him. Chief said, "Did I say anything wrong?" Gehringer shook his head. Finally Hogsett sniffed, "You could have pointed." Hank Greenberg didn't make the 1934 All-Star team despite having already driven in 103 runs. Catcher Mickey Cochrane did, named league MVP. Greenberg became "Hankus Pancus"; Gehringer, "Mr. Tiger"; rookie pitcher Lynwood Rowe, "Schoolboy." That August he beat Washington, 4–2, for an AL-tying sixteenth straight decision. On September 24, Detroit finally waved a flag. "Hell, yes. We can win a Series," Cochrane assured a writer reciting its 1907–08–09 October of defeat. His team didn't listen: St. Louis, in seven.

In 1935 MVP Greenberg tied with a league-best thirty-six homers. Gehringer fanned only *sixteen* times in 610 at-bats. Their Series foe was Chicago, as in 1907–08. "We've lost four straight Series," said Charlie. "Who wonders why we worried?" Rowe lost the opener, 3–0. Lacking "Big Mo"—momentum, to parrot George H. W. Bush—the Tigers won three straight, then lost again at Wrigley Field. At Detroit, Game Six tied at three, Tommy Bridges stranded Stan Hack after that Cub led off the ninth inning with a triple.

Cochrane singled in the inning's home half of the ninth and took second on an out before Goose Goslin faced Larry French. "If they pitch this ball over the plate," Goose advised umpire Ernie Quigley, "you can take that monkey suit off." They and Quigley did, Goslin singling and Cochrane scoring. Wrote columnist Grantland Rice of Detroit's first Major League title, lending urbanity to an outcome some thought tied to destiny: "The leaning tower can now crumble and find its level with the Pisan plain." After forty-eight years "the Detroit Tigers at last are champions of the world."

By the time Ford graduated from Michigan that year, majoring in economics, Frank Navin had made his park a place where patrons and pullers liked to watch and slug respectively. In 1935 he double-decked the right-field pavilion, its upper deck ten feet wider than the lower: thus overhung, it made routine flies pop-gun homers, the distance to right field a mere 325 feet. That winter Navin, who liked to ride, fell fatally from a horse. The Tigers' owner had built a second deck from first base to third. Successor Walter Briggs extended it from the left-field pole to center field, lengths there 340 and 440 feet respectively. Seating capacity reached fifty-eight thousand, Briggs renaming Navin Field in his family's honor. Posts blocked ten thousand seats, but tens of thousands more sat within such a whisper of the turf that a difference of opinion between a batter and an umpire could seem as intimate as kitchen table dialogue.

In 1937, Gehringer became Detroit's third MVP in four years, though Greenberg drove in a career- and franchise-high 184 runs. Hank's 58 homers in 1938 came nearer Ruth's 60 than anyone's had or would until 1961. As noted, Gehrig's 2,130 straight-games streak ended May 2, 1939, in Detroit. Someone tossed a glove as Lou came out for batting practice, said usher Frank Price, behind the Yankees dugout. "He bobbled it, picked [it] up and started to walk back to the dugout. That was the last time he stepped on a field as a player." 1940: Detroit won another pennant, led the World Series, three games to two, then lost twice to Cincinnati. 1941: Briggs hosted the All-Star Game, Ted Williams's three-run last-inning game-winning belt preceding The Kid's kangarooing around the bases. 1945: Hal Newhouser became the only hurler named back-to-back MVP. Greenberg homered in his first game out of khaki. Liking symmetry, he dinged for a last-day pennant.

Ford was in the navy after enlisting post–Pearl Harbor and heard the 1945 Cubs-Tigers Series of castoffs and aged rookies and players spurned by the service. Asked to predict the outcome, Chicago columnist Warren Brown famously said, "I don't think either team is capable of winning." Detroit barely did in seven, hitting .223. The 1948 "Tiges" became the last club to play at night, before 54,480 against Philadelphia. Gates opened at 6 p.m, but lights took so long to work that "the game didn't start till 9:30," said the Bengals' Vic Wertz. In 1950 the Yanks and Tigers went long with eleven homers in a game, Detroit finished three games out of first, and attendance hit a record 1,951,474.

In 1951 the All-Star Game moved from Philadelphia to Detroit to fete the Motor City's 250th birthday, ex-Tigers star and then voice Harry Heilmann dying on its eve: NL, 8–3. In 1956 Mickey Mantle hit Briggs Stadium's roof. The next-day *Detroit Times* printed a mock photo of Al Kaline standing there, the caption reading, "Mantle Shift." Tigers GM-to-be John McHale called the paper to say, intently, "Don't take him up there [on the roof] again!" not fathoming that Al had never left the ground. A better sense of humor might have weathered the 1950s. The Bengals never placed above fourth, in 1960 finished sixth, and disposed of managers like diapers—six from 1952–60.

"A decade like this, most cities don't survive," said Harwell, incredulous that people still made a beeline for the Tigers park, talked baseball at the assembly plant, and turned to play-by-play on the radio. "Just enormous interest." Ford was far too modest and realistic to affix that phrase to himself, but despite that by 1948 he had become a self-described "moderate in domestic affairs, an internationalist in foreign affairs, and a conservative in fiscal policy"—a window onto his party. Umbilically tied to the Tigers, it might also be said of him what was claimed of George Washington—that he never told, at least never intended to tell, a lie.

In 1948 Gerald Ford was easily elected to the first of thirteen two-year terms in the House of Representatives from Michigan's Fifth District—in due time, his sobriquet became the "Congressman for Life" from heavily center-right Grand Rapids. In 1950 Ford joined the House Appropriations Committee and helped oversee defense spending, about which—his interest fueled by World War II—Ford became an expert. In 1953–61 President Eisenhower was the rare Republican who captivated then heavily unionized Michigan. The banal 1951–60 "Detroits" did too, drawing at least a then robust 884,658 a year. Said Ford, attending many games yearly: "The Tigers mean as much as any team to any State you can name."

On January 1, 1961, new Tigers owner John Fetzer renamed his park Tiger Stadium. Few guessed Detroit would draw 1,600,710, win 101 games, and almost edge the greatest team since Murderer's Row. Norm Cash's .361 led the league. Rocky Colavito had 45 homers. Kaline batted .324. "Yankee-killer" Frank Lary killed other clubs beside the Yankees to finish 23-9. "Mantle and Maris outhomered Ruth and Gehrig," said Harwell. "What's amazing is that we almost won." Lasting is the September 1–3 series at Yankee Stadium, Detroit only one and one-half games behind, hordes packing the triple tiers. Back home, baseball so thoroughly owned the public that the football Lions postponed an exhibition game scheduled to conflict with the Tigers televised opener from New York. For the Tiges it ended badly: 1–0, 7–2, and 8–5, Stripes. "Baseball at its best," said skipper Bob Scheffing. It was Ford's last sustained Tigers gaiety until the 1960s' next-to-final year.

June 24, 1962, tested durability more than joy. The Tigers and Yankees began at 1:30 p.m. Golf games commenced and ended. Barbecues were lit and doused. The match was seven-all after twenty-one innings, Jack Reed then hitting his sole career homer: 9–7, Bombers. The game maddened a madding Detroit crowd of 35,638: forty-three players, thirty-nine hits, more than six hundred pitches, and baseball's then longest length (seven hours). In the top of the twentieth inning an Ontario writer announced, "I've got to leave." "Where are you going?" another writer asked. "My visa just expired"—or was it hope?

By 1964 Tigers attendance plunged to 816,139 in a decade of mass migration from the city to suburbia. In 1967 a horrific riot scarred Detroit, forty-three dying in a burg so unsafe that three home games were moved to Baltimore. Earl Wilson and Denny McLain went 39-27. Kaline won his tenth and last Gold Glove for fielding. The Tigers lost their last game of the year at home, eliminated by the Angels to give Boston its improbable pennant and disperse the Detroit crowd to its muse. Later a crushed owner penned a note: "John Fetzer has just died. This is his ghost speaking."

Entering 1968, you were unsure if the Tigers would win the pennant—or Detroit would implode. From kinder, gentler Grand Rapids, Ford eyed a Motor City that, like Washington, seemed increasingly unhinged. Men bought firearms. Housewives bought triple locks. Would stores again be looted, smoke again blacken Tiger Stadium? As Martin Luther King Jr. and Robert Kennedy were murdered, urban life raged, and much of America appeared a carnage, no one knew. It is untrue that baseball mirrors life. It is true that it can soften life. "A strange thing happened [in Detroit during 1968]," Joe Falls wrote. "The ball club . . . started winning games. . . . Each game seemed to produce a new drama. People began staying in at night to listen to the games on radio. . . . And when the team was at home . . . there was a place to go. A place where it was exciting. A place where a guy could let off steam." Ford added: "The Tigers were very important in providing stability."

If the Year of the Pitcher strangled offense, Al Kaline was spared. In May 1968 No. 6 hit franchise record home run 307, ending his career with 3,007 hits, 399 homers, and 129 straight errorless games. Till his death in 2010, Harwell's favorite reverie remained Al chasing a hit into Tiger Stadium's right-field corner. "He'd catch it on two hops, turn, fire to second, and the guy'd be out or stay at first," he said in 2001. "I see it now—and he hasn't played since '74!" In 1968 Kaline (hitting .287 despite breaking an arm), Willie Horton (36 home runs), Bill Freehan and Norm Cash (25 homers each), Jim Northrup (90 RBIs), and Dick McAuliffe (95 runs), among others, buoyed Mickey Lolich (17-9), Wilson (13-12), and John Hiller, whose 2.39 ERA moored the pen.

Surpassing was McLain, an aspiring organist, later thrice suspended and sentenced to prison for racketeering, and in 1968 the first pitcher since Dizzy Dean in 1934 to win thirty games in a year—31-6. "In his own wild way," wrote Falls, "[Denny] created every bit [as much] of an impact as Cobb or Cochrane did in their greatest years." On September 14 Kaline pinch-hit to start the ninth inning, McLain down to

Oakland, 4–3, in Detroit. McAuliffe popped out, but after Mickey Stanley singled Al to third base, Northrup bounced to first, Kaline beating Danny Cater's throw to the plate: four-all. Horton then singled, Stanley scoring. Pleased: 33,688 in attendance, an NBC *Game of the Week* audience, and McLain, journalism's mark 30.

Ahead lay Detroit's first flag in twenty-three years. On September 17 a Tigers win or Orioles loss would clinch. At the Corner execs learned in the ninth inning of the latter but, fearing riot, kept it from the crowd. With Kaline on, Don Wert swung—"a line shot, base hit right field, the Tigers win it!" bayed Harwell. "Here comes Kaline in to score, and it's all over! . . . The fans are streaming on the field. And the Tigers have won their first pennant since 1945! Let's listen to the bedlam here at Tiger Stadium!" Kaline had waited sixteen years for a Series, manager Mayo Smith wanting his bat—but where? Stanley and Northrup patrolled center and right field respectively. Benching Ray Oyler, Mayo put Stanley at shortstop, Northrup in center, and Kaline in right—pure pluck, especially in October.

Straightaway St. Louis took a 3–1 game Series edge. Columnist Jimmy Cannon, who "told it like it is" long before anyone grasped what that term even meant, had seen enough of the Tigers: "They're stinking up the joint is what they're doing." Who could argue? Jose Feliciano sang the national anthem before Game Five in a folk-rock vogue. The Redbirds led, 3–2, when Horton threw out Lou Brock at the plate. Detroit then clawed from behind to win, 5–3. Kaline drove in the decisive run; Tiger Stadium was in an uproar. In Game Six McLain tied things at three games, 13–1, freeing Jimmy Cannon of the Tigers' stench.

Thursday, October 10, 1968: Game Seven. In the Year of the Pitcher, the ultimate big-gamer, Bob Gibson, faced Lolich, baseball's leading motorcyclist, driving daily to and from the Corner. In the sixth inning Mickey picked Curt Flood and Brock off base. An inning later Northrup lined to center field with two out and two runners on. The 1968 Gold-Gloved Flood moved in, back, and slipped, the ball clearing him and scoring Cash and Horton. By the ninth inning, a complete game then still constitutional, NBC's Jim Simpson said, "Lolich fires—

ball is hit high in the air. This should be the Series! Freehan, waving everybody away! Detroit Wins!"—4–1. Baseball's thank-yous began.

For a time Smith mimed a blur of Connie Mack, John McGraw, and the Ol' Perfessor. Unforgettable was his moving Stanley to shortstop to get Detroit's apotheosis in the lineup. In 1983, the Mayo Smith Society, an international club for Tigers fans, was formed in his memory, inspired, said co-founder Dale Petroskey, by "Smith's amazingly bold roll of the dice. Mayo gambled big-time, and won."

In 1968, savoring the team at the park and from afar, Congressman Ford returned to stump for himself and other candidates, including Richard Nixon's presidential campaign that fall in Michigan. "There've been other great years for the Tigers," said Jerry B. Goode, "but sixty-eight, cementing the city, was special." As almost any American then alive recalls, Ford found the 1970s special, in a way that no one could portend.

For the *Tigers*, the new decade really began in 1971. Lolich, Detroit's suddenly eminent pot-bellied left-hander, led the American League with a 25-14 record. "Finally, somebody knows who I am," said Mickey. We already knew Reggie Jackson, hitting Tiger Stadium's right-center-field light tower that July off Dock Ellis, his All-Star dinger matching Williams's Class of 1941. "When you think of this park, homers come to mind," said Gerald Ford, "like Reggie's." Also homering that Game were Aaron, Bench, Clemente, Harmon Killebrew, and Frank Robinson. The Americans won, 6–4, ending an eight-game NL streak.

For *Ford*, the 1970s had really begun earlier—his first brush with national repute, if not celebrity—when in 1964 President Johnson named the GOP Congressman for Life to the Warren Commission, named after Chief Justice of the Supreme Court Earl Warren. Its charge: determine how President Kennedy died in 1963, why he was killed, and who was responsible. Ford, respected for his objectivity, shared the findings of the final report: Lee Harvey Oswald had killed JFK, for reasons peculiar to a hater and loser, with a single bullet. A year later Ford became House minority leader, nearing "the ultimate achievement" he never reached—Speaker of the House. Instead, he joined Republican Senate dean Everett Dirksen on TV's quasi-camp *The Ev and Jerry Show*, addressing "the Question of the Week." Example: "Mr. President: Why is the War on Poverty being lost?" Ford backed LBJ in another war, Vietnam, but felt we pulled our punches.

Unlike Nixon, Spiro Agnew, later Reagan, and much later Donald Trump, Ford did not appear to know or especially care how to reach the working middle, whose voice was inchoate—not for nothing was it called the *Silent* Majority. Rather, he could be found advising a local banker, big businessman, or Democratic whip on the Hill. As minority leader, the old navy man was isolated by increasingly left-leaning House leadership, yet seemed content trying to navigate an institution toward consensus. Being the catcher on the Republican team in the annual congressional baseball game, which he headed and for which he once smashed an inside the park grand slam, showed Ford's yen for harmony. "Usually I play the outfield but everybody else [here] refuses to catch, so I'm stuck."

In 1964 LBJ signed legislation limiting Little League to boys. A decade later Ford, as president, inked a bill amending its charter to include girls. The Michigander liked to watch non-big-league ball too, courting Betty Bloomer before their 1948 marriage by taking her to see the Grand Rapids Chicks play in an All-American Girls Professional Baseball League. Much later, as the Atlanta Braves' Henry Aaron a.k.a. the Hammer neared sport's most famous record—Babe Ruth's career home run total of 714—and President Nixon, who would usually have reveled, was nowhere to be seen, Ford's watching took a different turn.

On October 10, 1973, Agnew, the grand purveyor of "vicars of vacillation," "nabobs of negativism," and "effete corps of impudent snobs," resigned as VP. Middle America's once-heartthrob—"Spiro's Our Hero" read a pet phrase and T-shirt—had been "the Robespierre of the Great Silent Majority," wrote then Nixon aide Patrick Buchanan. Battered by Watergate, needing help on the Hill, the president required his antithesis, nominating a conciliator, not ideologue; a tortoise, not hare. Ford was loyal, familiar, and—unlike Nixon's first choice, John Connally—sure to be confirmed by Congress. "They like you," the president stage-whispered to Ford, announced that October and confirmed December 6. Upon his nomination, *Newsweek* assigned Tom DeFrank, twenty-nine, to cover the future president.

For nine months they crossed the country in tiny Air Force Two, fencing warily, then bonding, like a younger and older brother. In 1991 DeFrank suggested taping Ford's views on policy, politics, and presidents—also, as it happened, on life and love and faith and aging. The Wolverine agreed, stipulating publication "only when [he was] dead." The former president died in December 2006, his book, with DeFrank, *Write It When I'm Gone: Remarkable Off-the-Record Conversations with Gerald R. Ford*, published a year later. Ford had prophesied his boss's resignation in April 1974, swearing DeFrank to secrecy, while terming Nixon a foreign policy virtuoso "who had not acted forthrightly."

By then, Nixon's successor-in-waiting was increasingly visible: waiting both to be president and for the Hammer to succeed. On September 29, 1973, Aaron had come within one home run of the Babe. All winter much of America fixed on 714, a number so revered as to grace the badge of Sergeant Joe Friday in TV's classic series *Dragnet*, starring Jack Webb. Each Baseball Hall of Fame Ford C. Frick Award honoree for broadcast excellence—forty-two through 2018—would have killed to air Hank's 715th record-breaker, which the Braves' future Frick inductee Milo Hamilton was sure to call. "From November on George Plimpton asked what I'd say when Aaron broke it," he said of the author of *One for the Book.* "I told him, 'I gotta be spontaneous,' but I kept preparing, planning what I could say."

Aaron's first swing on Opening Day 1974 at Cincinnati tied Ruth, Ford cheering in person. Then on Monday, April 8, a rainy night in Georgia, in the fourth inning at Atlanta–Fulton County Stadium, Dodgers starter Al Downing threw Hank a 1–0 pitch. "Sitting on 714. Swinging. . . . There's a drive into left-center field!" said Hamilton. "That ball is gonna be . . . outta here! It's gone! It's 715!" The ball cleared the fence into reliever Tom House's glove. "There's a new home-run champion of all time! And it's Henry Aaron! The fireworks are going! Henry Aaron's coming around third!" The noise would not abate. "His teammates are at home plate! Listen to this crowd!" The game was halted to honor the Right Honorable Mr. Aaron. Georgia governor Jimmy Carter, seated with wife Rosalynn and mother Lillian, rose to give No. 44 a special automobile tag: HR-715.

Without Watergate, Nixon would have stood "in tall cotton," as Red Barber liked to say, all over Aaron's 715th blast as baseball fanatic and choreographer—like FDR, polls showed, most popular in the South. With it, he brooked near-seclusion. Even Ford stayed away from Atlanta for fear of accenting it. Novelist Graham Greene referenced "the heart of the matter." To Nixon baseball's heart was composite study—the game even more than a favorite team like his Senators or Angels. To Ford it was his team—here, the Tigers—and being an athlete in the company of jocks.

That August Ford spoke to a White House audience, inheriting the presidency, hours after Nixon had, leaving it. "Our long national nightmare is over," he said, voice breaking, "May our former president, who brought peace to millions, find it for himself." The new president found crisis, which the old president had helped create. Unemployment hit 7.1 percent. Ford gave Nixon a "full, free, and absolute pardon" a month after taking office, siring a furor but freeing himself "to get on with the country's business." Two crazies, Lynette Alice "Squeaky" Fromme and Sara Jane Moore, pointed loaded pistols, each trying to kill him.

In November 1974 Ford met with Soviet leader Leonid Brezhnev in Vladivostok to sign a joint communique on the Strategic Arms Limitation Treaty II (SALT II). In late April 1975 U.S. civilians left Saigon as Communists, breaking the 1973 peace pact, seized control in South Vietnam. "To sit in the Oval Office and see Americans beaten," Ford said later, "was not a happy experience for the President of the United States." Fleeing troops were helicoptered from rooftops as TV showed the end of America's most prolonged military retreat. Ford said only that the war in Vietnam was over "as far as America is concerned," omitting formerly neutral Cambodia, just conquered by the Communist Khmer Rouge.

In May 1975, U.S. prestige crumbling, Ford ordered an assault on the Khmer Rouge, who, seizing the U.S. merchant ship ss *Mayaguez*, had refused to release it. Fifteen Americans were killed, another three presumed dead, and fifty wounded. The ship and crew were successfully released. In January 1975 Ford had said, "The State of the Union is not good." It seemed better by 1976. Inflation had dimmed. Ford and Brezhnev had signed the Helsinki accords to ensure sanctity of national boundaries, committing the Soviets to observe human rights in principle within Europe.

Skeptics hooted. In truth, the accords birthed the moral framework for Charter 77 and Solidarity in Czechoslovakia and Poland respectively, part of the movement toward democracy which eventually the Soviet state could not contain. Few grasped that then. In America, at least peace seemed the rule again, due largely to 1974's breath of fresh air who rose daily at 5:15 a.m., vowed "openness and candor," and seemed constitutionally unable to utter a nasty word.

In 1976 Ford, seeking a full term, got a standing ovation for donning a Rangers cap and tossing the season's first ball April 9 at Arlington Stadium. It augured little: Carter, the unforeseen Democratic presidential nominee, carried Texas in November. Meantime, Detroit rookie pitcher Mark Fidrych, named "the Bird," after the *Sesame Street* TV character, rose like a rocket launch, talking to the ball, prancing on the mound, patting it like a gardener, and begetting delirium in each start. Attendance at his eighteen home starts totaled more than 40 percent of Detroit's entire eighty-one-game 1,467,020. On June 28 the Tigers chickabiddy faced the Yankees on network TV—What a Made-in-the-USA storyline. "We were so delighted," said ABC announcer Warner Wolf. "The game was [nearly] sold out because of him. It's all you heard." Later injured, for a year Fidrych was a phenomenon, that night winning, 5–1, before 47,855 at the Corner.

The rookie acknowledged perhaps the first nationally televised sports curtain call. "Folks," Wolf exulted, "they're not going to stop clapping until the Bird comes from the dugout. . . . Fantastic! Mark Fidrych [final record: 19-9, league-best 24 complete games, and 2.34 ERA] is born tonight on coast-to-coast television." At July's All-Star Game in Philadelphia the Bird asked President Ford if son Steve, a then soap actor, could arrange a date for him with someone Hollywood. "A rumpled kid, so enthusiastic, with curly hair like Shirley Temple," Steve said of Mark, agreeing to help. More vitally, NBC broadcaster Joe Garagiola agreed to help Steve's dad, hosting half-hour telecasts with Ford and the first family in the last month of the campaign.

Phillies voice Richie Ashburn was a Philadelphia *Evening Bulletin* columnist. "The President doesn't come by himself," he wrote, amazed. "He brings a flock of security people, a host of White House staffers and a large contingent of media types"—also guests Garagiola, Aaron, and Ernie Banks, among others. Phillies VP Bill Giles told doubting pressies that "this is not a political trip for Mr. Ford. . . . He wants to see the whole show." Trailing Carter in the Gallup Poll, Ford wanted above all to be *seen*, walking on the field to shake hands with both managers and starting catchers at home plate and reserves before the game and after. The ABC telecast lured 36.3 million viewers, a jackpot quadrupling Fox's grab bag of 9.2 million in 2017. CBS Radio also had record ratings over 261 affiliated stations and the Armed Forces Network. Philadelphia columnist Bill Conlin was more impressed by the Bird, "a ready target for the electronic might of ABC-TV Sports," than Ford, who would toss the first pitch if he could "hold onto the ball long enough." Many overlooked a seeming has-been: ex-actor Ronald Reagan, still vying for the nomination, but "without a TV show tonight," jibed Conlin. "President Ford is here to win one *from* the Gipper."

None of this wowed the Right, which felt Ford a milquetoast moderate, causing Reagan to challenge him, almost take the nomination, and sap the president that fall. Ford offered a mixed bag: the Nixon pardon, a rebuilt economy, renewed détente, but defeat in Vietnam. He began the general election, said Gallup, thirty-three points behind. Then like a timer clicking, America recalled Jerry College. He nearly won despite Watergate, the pardon, and, bone tired, denying in the second debate that the Soviets "dominate Eastern Europe." On election night, Ford's voice spent, Betty read the concession. Garagiola watched returns, baring the close loss to Carter, with the president's family in the White House. "[He] took all the news very calmly," Joe said in his memoir. "I'd seen Enos Slaughter [his 1946–51 Cardinals teammate] get more upset about the umpire saying strike two than Gerald Ford did when he realized he wasn't going to win a presidential election."

Leaving Washington, Ford embroidered America's changing of the guard: "There are no soldiers marching except in the inaugural parade. No public demonstrations except for some of the dancers at the inaugural ball. The opposition party doesn't go underground, but goes on functioning; and a vigilant press goes right on probing and publishing our faults and our follies." In 2012 Nancy Gibbs and Michael Duffy wrote *The Presidents Club*, about the fraternity of former presidents, noting that George H. W. Bush and Gerald Ford admired each other. I was not surprised. In 1999 Bush asked me to write a quarter-century-later retrospective for *The American Enterprise* magazine on Ford's 1974 succession. Typically Bush mentioned that I had helped, and Ford wrote a thoughtful note. Politics did not preclude decency. That lesson was his life.

Jerry B. Goode was not a warrior, cultural or otherwise. Leaving the White House, he retired to Rancho Mirage, near Palm Springs, California, where good feeling rivaled godliness, civility equaled cleanliness, and green eclipsed black and white. Ford left DC as the Tigers ended a period so various as to make the Corner a keeper of baseball's faith. "Frank Lary killed the Yankees here," *Baseball Weekly*'s Bill Koenig wrote. "Reggie Jackson hit a roof-top light tower [1971]. Fred Lynn drove in ten runs in a [1975] game here." Once *Sports Illustrated* wrote, "Owners claim [Tiger] Stadium is the best park in baseball. Contented Detroit fans admit it probably is."

From the Sunbelt, Ford watched as second baseman Lou Whitaker and shortstop Alan Trammell joined the Tigers in 1978, retiring in 1995 and 1996 with three and four Gold Gloves respectively. "An institution," the former president said, much later, "like Hope and Crosby." Another institution began the day Harwell announced, "That foul's nabbed by a guy from Alma, Michigan." Whim turned ritual. Before a game bystanders pled, "Hey, Ernie, let a guy from Sarnia grab one"—or Puptown or Richfield Center. As a boy, I told Mom that Harwell must have a lot of friends.

For a long time after leaving office, Ford retained the friendly energy of a touring golf pro turning forty. He became president and chairman of the board of trustees of the Eisenhower Fellowships and distinguished fellow of the American Enterprise Institute. In 1979 he wrote the exquisitely titled memoir *A Time to Heal*, styled "serene, unruffled, like the author," by *Foreign Affairs*. That season Reds two-time champion skipper Sparky Anderson was hired to will himself and Detroit back to primacy. In 1980 Ford was nearly willed into a situation he soon thought better of. GOP nominee-to-be Reagan tentatively approached him about being VP, a post that to CBS-TV's Walter Cronkite, interviewing Ford, meant an unprecedented "co-presidency"—not exactly what the Gipper had in mind. Seeing Ford apparently agree, Reagan phoned him, met briefly, dissolved their union, and picked George Bush.

Unruffled, Ford became engaged in his presidential museum in Grand Rapids and library at the University of Michigan in Ann Arbor, each dedicated in 1981: the sole ex-president with a museum and library in different sites—also fourth to receive the presidential Medal of Freedom, America's highest civilian award. That September Reagan, now president, noted that on the night the Fords learned that Jerry would likely succeed Nixon, they recited a favorite prayer from the book of Proverbs—old, terse, and true: "Trust in the Lord with all thine heart; and lean not unto thine own understanding. In all thy ways acknowledge him, and he shall direct thy paths."

Increasingly, the Fords' path kept them in California most of every year. In 1984, little cable available, Ford used network TV to follow the Tigers, covered like the home team, their year-long anthem "Bless You, Boys." Motown began the season 35-5—only the fourth team to lead its league or division each day. Lance Parrish had thirty-three homers. Trammell hit .314. Willie Hernandez went 9-3, saved thirty-two games, and took Cy Young/MVP. An ancillary benefit: Detroit drew 2,704,792, breaking its attendance record. Kansas City braved an LCS sweep. Was Jack Morris, the most victorious (162-119) pitcher of the 1980s, arrogant? Yes, said Sparky, "but he's like a high-strung racehorse, a great thoroughbred who'll bite you if you come near him."

The Tigers and Padres split the first two games of the Series, moved east for a Game Three of thirteen combined walks and a 5–2 Bengals nod, before Morris threw his 4–2 second complete game. The next day, up, three games to one, Detroit led, 5–4, in the eighth inning: batting, Kirk Gibson, who had already homered; two on, one out. Anderson yelled from the dugout, "Five bucks you don't hit one out." Miffed, Kirk signaled to double the bet, then bashed Goose Gossage's fastball into the right-field upper deck. "It was ours," he said after dancing around the bases. "That's why it took so long [reaching home]. Everybody knew we had it." The 8–5 final brought the Tiges their fourth world title and last to the present. The vicinity afterward resembled less "Bless You, Boys" than an Augean stable. Thugs burned cars, smashed windows, and beat passersby on the final out. Locals rushed and crushed the field. Bottom-dwelling slugs threw mud at the press box. Looking for a culprit, some blamed the park.

In 1986 Motown mayor Coleman Young urged a new downtown dome. By 2–1 a *Detroit News* poll disagreed. The 1987 Tigers won the AL East, banged a second-best-ever team 225 home runs, and lost the LCS. In 1989 Tiger Stadium joined the National Register of Historic Places. Said Ford: "It's such a big outfield, guys can run there and on the bases all day, [so] that anything can happen." The Orioles' Frank Robinson and Paul Blair once led off from first and second base respectively. The batter lined to right-center field. "Way to the flagpole's right," said Robinson. "Nobody's going to get this." Blair wasn't sure. He stopped, saw the ball drop, then left for home, F. Robby nearly catching him. Both slid past Bill Freehan to the first and foul side of the plate to score at almost the same time.

With Fenway Park, the Corner became the oldest and longest continuously used site in professional sport. Should Tiger Stadium be renovated or torn down? Let Baltimore build an Oriole Park at Camden Yards—the first modern "retro" big-league site. *Here* was an original. The team retired its first four numbers: 2 (Gehringer), 5 (Greenberg), 6 (Kaline), and 16 (Newhouser). It could not forestall "new old" parks—a Coors Field in Denver, an AT&T Park in Baghdad by the Bay. On one hand, the creature comforts at Miami's Marlins Park dwarfed those at Michigan and Trumbull. On the other, no snap of the fingers there evoked Ernie Banks at Wrigley Field chiming, "Let's play two." Some said you couldn't buy tradition. Wiser heads knew you couldn't rent it.

A 1990s change in color scheme ended Detroit's age of all-green seats and walls. More wisely, the Tigers pleasance retained asymmetrical lines, a 125-foot center-field flagpole—baseball's highest-ever in-play curio—and a yawning outer garden. Steep-pitched stands placed a ticketholder right above the field. Ghosts traversed the turf. At third base Cobb's spikes cut a hapless fielder. See the plate: Freehan blocked Brock in the 1968 Series. Or right field: Gibson bombed Gossage in 1984. By rote, tableaux reemerged. Aromas blurred: hops and hot pretzels. Stores sold gloves and Tigers shirts. Infidels donned a Yankees cap. Slowly, by twos and threes, the old yard filled. "A grandfather might be there," said Ford. "He might have his son, and that father would have his."

In a new century of such exquisite new plots as PNC Park in Pittsburgh, the Tigers lair brooked a catch-up gloss. Eventually $289 million Comerica Park opened in 2000, north of town, east of Tiger Stadium. On September 26, 1999, the Tigers chose an all-time team. One day later they closed the joint down. Starters wore the numbers of the all-time Tiges team. Center fielder Gabe Kapler wore no number, like Cobb. Emotion was palpable. Grown men cried. The only Michigander more beloved than Ford stood at the house PA mic: "Farewell, old friend, Tiger Stadium," said Harwell, voice breaking, lights dimming, cabaret closing where Gehringer had dazzled, McLain thrown a heater, and Kaline simply played ball.

Later sixty-five Tigers formed a chronological line from the flagpole to home plate, the flag lowered and passed from one player to another. "Behind me stands over seventy years of Tigers history," said Elden Auker, the submarine pitcher whom Ford had instantly recalled a quarter century earlier, giving the flag to future Tigers manager Brad Ausmus. Born in nearby Pontiac, Kirk Gibson said, "This is the story of baseball in Detroit going down right here." A new chapter unfolded in 2006, the Tigers' first World Series since 1984, St. Louis avenging 1968, winning, four games to one. That December 26 Gerald Ford died of arteriosclerotic cerebrovascular disease—at ninety-three years and 165 days, the longest-living president.

The thirty-eighth president lay in state at the U.S. Capitol Rotunda, had a state funeral and memorial services at Washington's National Cathedral, and was interred in 2007 at the museum in Grand Rapids. The hometown boy was someone who embodied the joy of following and thoroughly rooting for the hometown team—with him, a club whose fandom was as rich as any in the game.

In 2011 a statue of Ford was unveiled in the Rotunda. On it are words from his August 9, 1974, swearing-in address: "Our constitution works; our great Republic is a government of laws and not of men. Here the people rule."

ELEVEN

From Softball to Hardball

Jimmy Carter, 1977–1981

Gerald Ford dreamt of being Speaker of the House of Representatives, but as with many dreams life intervened. He had retired by the time his Republican Party finally got a House majority in 1994. Meanwhile, President Nixon's choice of Ford as vice president in 1973, then his next-year farewell, left the Michigander with a consolation prize—the presidency. By comparison, the dream of his successor, James Earl "Jimmy" Carter Jr., was realized in an American schoolbook way: "the small-town man [a peanut farmer from the tiny burg of Plains, Georgia] who dreams of becoming president, and who by hard work and against incredible odds achieves his ambition," wrote *TIME* magazine columnist Hugh Sidey.

Carter came out of nowhere—indeed, *beyond* it—to win the presidency in 1976. Narrowly elected, he bred peace between Egypt and Israel with the Camp David Accords, created new departments of energy and education, and braved Islamic fanaticism that seized sixty-three hostages at the U.S. Embassy in Tehran. From 1977 through 1981 Carter's image mixed, among other things, Plains itself, a miniature Branson, Missouri; the Bible-carrying president teaching Sunday school; his mother, Miss Lillian, a character from Tennessee Williams's sunnier side; black sheep younger brother Billy, "like my mother," Jimmy wrote, "a walking encyclopedia of minutiae about . . . baseball"; the family peanut business; and softball, where a form of no-nonsense conduct reigned.

Billy had originally been the Carter clan's softball zealot, but Jimmy became its quintessence as president. "When I was on submarines," explained the older brother and Naval Academy graduate, "I was the pitcher of our ball team." In office, he logically became a hard-working hurler, with a Puritan distaste for sloth. At Plains and the presidential retreat at Camp David, Carter exerted his stern form of leisure, using softball to separate the weak and the strong. During the 1976 campaign the Democratic presidential nominee had forged a team of friends and Secret Service agents—the "News Makers"—against a group of reporters who called themselves the "News Twisters." Carter seldom confused the two. "They may play softball in Plains," Richard Nixon observed, "but they play hardball in the country."

The *Boston Globe* correspondent Curtis Wilkie told *Sports Illustrated* of Carter's no room for humor creed. "Someone hit a pop fly in my direction [third base]. It was out of my range, but I gave it a little chase anyway. When I got back . . . he [Carter] was standing there staring at me, and he said, 'You should have had that one, Curtis.' I never knew if he was serious." One player said Carter's teammates included "bionic Secret Service men," especially a former Triple-A Minor League shortstop. "The Secret Service guys were terrified that if they messed up they'd wind up stationed in Ohio." For most, Plains became their station, few mistaking it for Hyannis Port circa early 1960s.

By the 2010s Carter's boyhood home, a national historic site, hosted the annual Peanut Classic Softball Tournament to support the Carter Center, a nonprofit founded to back global health and democracy. Forty years earlier peanuts had been as crucial to the Carter persona as his easy, toothy smile. It was misleading: Jimmy could be as tough as Lyndon Johnson. The nation saw "the Grin," the press's moniker for the face Carter made at softball. According to *Baseball: The Presidents' Game*, in 1977 newsmen ensured that "the Grin w[ould] not win," realigning softball squads so that the Secret Service joined the media.

Sam Donaldson was then ABC-TV White House correspondent. "To us it was a grudge match," he said of softball. "Carter had always got the Service on his side, but now the agents got us bums in the media." Disliking their improvement, the Grin flashed a frown. For much of his life Carter enjoyed playing more than watching, many thinking that he disliked baseball, softball's more famous kin, or at least didn't know much about the game—ironic given his baseball-crazed clan.

This word spread like contagion through the sport. Used to Ford and especially Nixon, Bowie Kuhn asked what time he might give Carter his 1977 season ticket pass, a rite dating to Theodore Roosevelt. The new president was supposed to have said he would forgo it since he had campaigned on the novel, not traditional.

At last an appointment was made. The commissioner arrived at the White House, was taken to the basement, and was then summarily dispatched, having given a pass to Carter's son Chip in the president's name. The baseball–White House "Special Relationship," as precious to its realm as the United States–United Kingdom is to its, seemed less special than at any time since Miss Lillian was a child.

Born October 1, 1924, in Plains, Carter grew up with a Class D team in nearby Americus. Uncle Alton was a league director, always had tickets, "and never missed a home game." Each year's Zion for Jimmy's parents came in lay-by time, when the farm work load was lightest and Lillian and James Earl Sr. felt free to indulge their zeal. "My parents, my uncle Alton, and his wife would drive 'up north' to spend" up to ten days "immersed in major league baseball," Jimmy wrote. "To see the world," they chose one burg a year, rotating among the big leagues' sixteen teams in eleven cities. One year the Carters stayed in Boston for an entire Braves or Red Sox homestand; the next, Washington, for the Senators and several AL foils; another, Pittsburgh, for the Bucs series against the Cubs, Cards, and Reds. Travel was slower then, homestands longer. "It was clear to all," he wrote, "that these annual baseball excursions bridged gaps in the family and, in a strange way, even bound all of us younger Carters together. We children knew that these were the *best* experiences of our parents' lives, and they chose to share them. It was a lesson I never forgot."

Carter wrote the above in his book *Sharing Good Times*, published in 2004. I had never been impressed by his public rhetoric: the singsong voice, the cadence lacking rhythm. The president might accent the wrong word, run two sentences together, invert two paragraphs so that neither made sense. His written work was another kettle. *Sharing Good Times* evinced a fluid stylist, conversational throughout, baring one anecdote after another in a gentle, rural way. It was honest—about himself and his life. In 1953 James Earl Carter Sr. died, having "loved the game every bit as [much as] mama," Jimmy said. Miss Lillian added, "We [had] attended as many games as possible," visiting Minor League parks from the Midwest to Georgia; once at Yankee Stadium they saw Babe Ruth hit "two homers in a game." The Carters' family odyssey was and remains unmatched by any brood I have heard of—a baseball lover's dream.

Each year Miss Lillian had to see the Dodgers at Ebbets Field or on the road, for reasons not peculiar to her. She may have exceeded even Herbert Hoover's love for Brooklyn as an underdog. Bums voice Red Barber, was, like Mel Allen, a fellow Southerner—also, her favorite mikemen before Vin Scully in the 1950s. As we shall see, Jackie Robinson moved her deeply, culturally and morally. She especially liked Plains's shortest big-league trek to Crosley Field in Cincinnati, the Reds hosting Jackie and Roy Campanella and Gil Hodges and Duke Snider. All hit balls over Crosley's inviting left-field wall as if it were the nearest Putt Putt. As noted earlier, in 1974 Miss Lillian, Governor Carter, and wife Rosalynn sat in boxes at Atlanta–Fulton County Stadium to see Henry Aaron break the unbreakable against the Dodgers—the Babe's career home run record. Still, for a long time the president seemed not to inherit his mother's baseball mania or even DNA.

Carter became the first president not to see a regular-season game since Benjamin Harrison in 1892—as far as records date. A plausible cause for his sabbatical was the full plate of problems that made him consider *any* unwinding wrong. The sole game he saw in person was the final game of the 1979 Pirates-Orioles World Series, Carter riding the official presidential helicopter, Marine One, to Baltimore and landing near Memorial Stadium. Attended by son Chip and Speaker of the House Tip O'Neill, the president entered the O's clubhouse to be eyed by catcher Rick Dempsey, who, disgusted, told him, "Next time, get your ass here before the seventh game." Losing, 4–1, some Birds actually thought Carter a jinx. He left office in 1981 reputed to be arguably the president most hostile to baseball since Theodore Roosevelt—a criticism that has proved inane. Carter *was* very much his mother's son.

Born in 1898 in Richland, Georgia, the future Lillian Gordy Carter was a wonder woman more than half a century before the network TV show of that name began. She grew up "definitely a liberal," she said. "I've always been one"—a feminist in America's most traditional region, widowed at fifty-five, a single parent for her last thirty years, devoting those and prior decades to hard work and good works. At one time or another Mrs. Carter—to her country, "Miss Lillian"—was a registered nurse, physician's assistant, university housemother, Peace Corps volunteer in India, pecan grower, goodwill ambassador, inveterate reader, professional wrestling (!) patron, and—most relevant to this work— baseball connoisseur, imbibing by radio, video, print, and in person.

In another age, Miss Lillian said, "I might have been a doctor." Born a quarter century later, she might have owned a Major League team. On April 15, 1947, she attended baseball's most pivotal Opening Day— Dodgers and Phillies at Ebbets Field—in which Jackie Robinson, the pastime's first black player in his big-league debut, bent an American dividing line by breaking baseball's color line. To Lillian the day addressed history (especially the South's); affinity (Jackie was born ninety-two miles from Plains in Cairo, Georgia); equality (the game's integration began a path segregated America could not reverse); and the Faith of Our Fathers. Robinson and Dodgers head Branch Rickey of rural Ohio were Methodist; the Carters, Baptist. All were devout hymn-singing members of the overwhelmingly Protestant Bible Belt.

Robinson helped make the Bums a civic religion to Miss Lillian, his 1972 death mourned like that of a parish minister or adopted son. From 1941 to 1956 the Yankees and Dodgers played seven indelible "Subway Series." Their first bicoastal Fall Classic occurred in 1963. In 1977 the ancient foes were to meet again, bandleader Guy Lombardo's 1930s "Seems Like Old Times" a mental sound track for mid-century sorcery. To a teen the identity of such combatants meant little more than 1976's dull Yanks-Reds. For those who knew baseball and/or were thirty or over, wrote *Newsday* columnist Stan Isaacs, "their meetings were almost like adventure chapters in a serialized novel." Miss Lillian had seen, heard, or read about each Subway Classic, her knowledge encyclopedic. If you wanted to make this almost-octogenarian's existence, extend an invite to make this Series *hers*.

With son Jimmy a first-year president, stories brewing of brother Billy's favorite beverage, and the popularity of Mrs. Carter sky-high, the Dodgers asked her to throw out the first ball before Game Four at Chavez Ravine. After splitting the first two games in the Bronx, the Bombers took Game Three, 5–3. The next day New York fronted, 3–0; LA's Davey Lopes went yard; after which Reggie Jackson countered: Yanks win, 4–2. To some, the score was irrelevant. At an earlier game in Atlanta the Secret Service had told Dodgers manager Tommy Lasorda that Miss Lillian would like to talk. Not surprisingly, they hit it off. Before Game Four, he introduced her to members of his team—what Tommy called "Dodger Blue." He, Bowie Kuhn, and Dodgers owner Peter O'Malley treated her like a rock star: said Lasorda, "like my friend Sinatra." The capacity crowd of 55,995 did too.

The thirty-ninth president wrote a letter thanking O'Malley for the team's treatment of his mother, who hand-wrote a note calling the Series "the highlight of my life." On October 30, 1983, at eighty-five, she succumbed to breast, bone, and pancreatic cancer. Coincidence or not, at about this time the now *ex*-president (re)became the avid baseball spectator he had been *before* taking office, as if by celebrating time and place he could recall "the greatest influence on [his] life." In her final years Lillian lived at the family's "isolated Pond House," where Carter installed among the first satellite antennae to let her watch the Dodgers—Vin Scully on the air, friend Lasorda in the dugout, Dodger Stadium's palms swaying in the background; no wonder she appeared young. The sole down side affected a Dodgers visit South. Sitting in team owner Ted Turner's box, "[Miss Lillian] embarrassed all of us Braves fans," wrote Jimmy, "with her piercing voice urging the Dodgers on to victory."

With mama gone, the former president accepted many of the invitations that might have gone to her, like throwing out the 2008 San Diego Padres' season-opening first pitch. Carter could be seen more often with family members at Atlanta's Turner Field. In September 2015 he gave Rosalynn "a smooch," he said, as CAM kiss spotted them in their usual box seats near the home dugout. The crowd went berserk, Jimmy showing a side seldom seen. Carter too was diagnosed with cancer that year. Like Lillian, he believed in biblical miracles. Without wishing to seem sacrilegious, some thought his transition from softball to baseball, no-quarter player to fervid big-league fan, a small miracle of its own.

As a candidate who left rural Georgia to run for president, Carter said he would earn our trust, and for many did. Yet which epithet did his record earn: amateur hour or north star of liberty? What lingers is complex imagery: the pastor/politician who vowed to make government full of love; the master of detail who weighed the forest against the trees. What to make of his piety, smile, and ice blue eyes?

Look homeward, angel: the quandary stemmed from squaring Babylon on the Potomac with Plains's small shops, red clay, and witching power. Carter's town prized faith and fellow feeling. The capital's ruling class shared habits and predilections: networking, business cards, debating who's up and down. DC's aristocracy consisted, variously, of lawyers, lobbyists, and self-dubbed tastemakers. Jimmy felt them as shallow as a spoon. Round holes, meet oblong pegs. For four years Washington was where Carter worked. Plains was what he loved.

Miss Lillian would deflect praise for her eldest of four children, saying "Jimmy was just an ordinary little boy," adding with a twinkle, "his sister Gloria is the most intelligent child in the family [the other child was Ruth]." Few were fooled, especially those grasping his U.S. Naval Academy degree or the thirty-three books he wrote on such subjects as faith, climate change, and health care, including *An Hour Before Daylight, A Full Life: Reflections at Ninety*, and *Our Endangered Values: America's Moral Crisis*, the last winning a Grammy award for the best-spoken book.

"Jimmy was always the smartest in the class," a public schoolmate said long after Carter left Plains to study at the Georgia Southwestern College and Georgia Institute of Technology before entering Annapolis. At the academy, Carter fell in love with Ruth's friend Rosalynn Smith, whom he wed after graduating in 1946. The Southern Man then volunteered for submarine duty and joined an elite group of officers on the first nuclear-powered submarines. Jimmy's boss was Captain Hyman Rickover, who, he wrote, "had a [more] profound influence on my life than anyone except my own parents."

In 1951 Carter transferred from the Pacific Fleet back to duty in New London, Connecticut. A year later he and Rosalynn bought their first television, both temporarily becoming "avid Yankees fans." She knew the club better than he did, viewing their games while Jimmy was on duty. Back home she mentored him on the Stripes, the new couple together watching the Bombers win their fourth straight pennant.

When Carter Sr. died of pancreatic cancer, Jr. returned to Plains to manage the family business, his next business politics. He served in the Georgia Senate from 1963 to 1967, lost a bid for governor in 1966, and won a four-year term in 1970. His chief foe: the Georgia Constitution, which forbade reelection. If law closed doors, Carter might open others.

One day Miss Lillian asked what her eldest intended to do. "I'm going to run for president," he said. "President of what?" she wanted to know. "Mama, I'm going to run for President of the United States, and I'm going to win," Carter said. Miss Lillian hadn't realized her son had such a great sense of humor—except that Jimmy wasn't joking.

In December 1974 Carter announced for the Democratic nomination, forever changing the how-to first part of making a president. His guerilla race still evokes Mao Tse-Tung's 1940s combat against Chiang Kai-shek, the insurgent's weapons surprise, saturation, and living off the land in Iowa, the first caucus to elect delegates, and New Hampshire, site of the first primary. A reporter wrote, "The message was primarily Jimmy Carter, a man of warmth and decency. It won him the nomination."

From the start, populism clung to Carter like humidity does Georgia in July. He said grace, wore blue jeans, and carried his own bags—no imperial president. The Democratic Party was thought elitist, secular, and wastrel. Carter was a born-again, post-Watergate, military-trained moralist. How antipodal to Nixon! What a vision must exist in him—a ticket back to power.

Carter believed what the Bible taught: "principle" meant good will toward men. In turn that meant he must spend his life seeking peace. A high school teacher, Miss Julia Coleman, had told him, "We must adjust to changing times and still hold to unchanging principles." If he was elected, that creed would shape his inaugural—and first term.

As Carter readied for the 1976 quadrennial, baseball lauded Aaron's Ruth-busting feat, which even Franklin Roosevelt, who never got enough offense, would judge presidential. The Peach State summons No. 44, thin air, and the Braves' 1966–96 stadium, a.k.a. "the Launching Pad." A century ago it meant Ponce de Leon Park of the Southern Association Crackers. In 1923, wooden stands razed by fire, a concrete fifteen-thousand-seat fort arose. Ponce's scoreboard hovered 462 feet from home plate. Fronting it was a magnolia tree—to many, the insignia of the baseball South.

In 1934 Earl Mann became Crackers president, later planting a hedge from left field to center field. A fielder's catch in the hedge was ruled legal. A ball clearing it was ruled gone. In 1959 Mann gave the SA his franchise, Atlanta mayor Ivan Allen Jr. raising the bar in 1964: "I have the verbal commitment of a Major-League baseball club to move its franchise to Atlanta if we have a stadium available by 1966." Quickly the board of aldermen backed an $18 million stadium complex in a downtown urban renewal area one-quarter mile from the state capitol. Most grasped that the club was the Milwaukee (née Boston) Braves, parent club of a new 1965 Triple-A affiliate—the Crackers.

Atlanta–Fulton County Stadium hatched where famed Union general William Tecumseh Sherman had headquartered on his ridge during the Battle of Atlanta: ultimately, the junction of three interstates. "A judge ruled that the Braves had to play a final season of 1965 in Milwaukee—only then could they move here," wrote *Constitution* columnist Furman Bisher. "So the '65 Crackers inaugurated this park." Inside stood a dud. Distances were symmetrical: lines, 325 feet; alleys, 385 feet; center field, 402 feet. A six-foot (later ten-foot) fence linked the poles, paralleled by bullpens and an outer wall behind them. Foul turf was massive. Three levels of seats rimmed the yard, "Florida closer than the top tier," barked 1966–75 Braves radio/TV voice Milo Hamilton. The park seemed perfect—for the National Football League, giving Atlanta the 1966 expansion Falcons.

On April 12, 1966, the Braves debuted at home, losing to Pittsburgh, 3–2. In a preview of coming attractions, four batters homered. Tony Cloninger pitched all thirteen innings and lost. That July 3 he smashed two grand slams, had nine RBIS, was relieved, and won, 17–3. Go figure. "Anyone who says they know baseball is hallucinating," skipper Bobby Bragan said. Few were delusional about a neophyte big-league market. "One day there were about forty-five thousand people in the stands," said Braves catcher Joe Torre. "You could hear a pin drop. Fans just didn't know what to do at the game"—such a contrast to Milwaukee.

The Majors' newest region heard each game on the Braves' seven-state, thirty-six affiliate radio network. Eighteen games were telecast each year on baseball's largest (nineteen-outlet) single-team network in Alabama, Florida, Georgia, North and South Carolina, and Tennessee. On the road, Hamilton's poise and color linked Miss Lillian to the Braves. At Atlanta–Fulton, color meant red clay that splotched the infield, warning track, mound, and the area around the plate. The stadium also sported (American) Indian biases and deities, even borrowing Florida State University's "Tomahawk Chop," a mass movement of virtually each forearm forward and backward repetitively in concert, as in a rite.

Big Victor, the Braves' 1966 totem pole–styled model, preceded Atlanta–Fulton's first real Indian in tribal garb—Levi Walker Jr., a.k.a. Chief Noc-A-Homa, who camped in a tepee on a platform behind the inner fence. The 1978–82 Braves usurped 235 left-center-field seats to let him perform, dance upon each home team homer, and sign autographs. Later they benched, revived, and shelved the Chief again. Retiring in 1985, the man whose name clearly meant "Knock a Homer" attributed his success to altitude, the stadium more than a thousand feet above sea level—baseball's highest pre-1993 Denver site. From 1970 through 1973 the Launching Pad yearly led in NL homers, the 1971 Braves once popping four in an inning. In 1973 three players on a team hit forty for the first time—Davey Johnson (forty-three), Darrell Evans (forty-one), and Aaron (forty).

Later cable television penetration led Braves owner Ted Turner to dub his club "America's Team." Before the early '70s Atlanta was at least the Southeast's team. In 1969 Aaron hit forty-four homers for the fourth and final time. The Braves won the NL West, reached 1,458,320 in home attendance, and were swept in the LCS, obliging the Amazin' Mets. In 1970 Rico Carty led the league with a .366 average. In 1971 skipper Luman Harris was canned, succeeded by seven managers through 1978. On July 21, 1973, Aaron bashed his 700th homer. As seen earlier, he then prepared to cross a most Ruthian line.

Unlike the Babe, Henry never went yard sixty or even fifty times in a year. He did uncork more than thirty and forty homers fifteen and eight times respectively. "He thinks there's nothing he can't hit," said Stan Musial, intending praise of Aaron's equanimity, grace, and skill. There wasn't. Hank was third ever in games played and hits; second times at bat and runs scored; first RBIs, total bases, extra base hits, and until Barry Bonds, home runs. Aaron led the National League in batting twice and four times in homers and RBIs, won three Gold Gloves, and six times stole more than twenty bases. He made you think *eclectic* before you heard the word.

Without comparing their historic niche, it is not hyberbolic to say that Aaron became tied to Ruth as Franklin Roosevelt did to Lincoln. As Secretary of War Edwin Stanton is alleged to have said at the dying sixteenth president's bedside, "Now he belongs to the ages." After No. 715, the rest was anticlimax for the Braves, 1975 attendance even lower than for Wisconsin's lame-duck 1965 adieu. One night only 737 eyeballed a game in Georgia. Next year Turner purchased the team, upped its TV schedule, and renamed station WTCG. "This'll be the first step in our telecasts tying the Braves to the big-time," he predicted, even as the then small-time Braves finished last yearly through 1979.

Turner believed in cable television, even when few knew what it was—"a system of TV reception in which signals from distant stations are picked up by a master antenna and sent by cable to the individual receivers of paying subscribers," according to *Merriam*

Webster. At the time he sensed that cable TV would one day swell baseball's stage, even as baseball swelled cable TV's audience. It was hard to imagine when you could sit in Atlanta's mid-1970s press box and literally count the crowd.

The new Braves owner hyped camel relays, bathtubs on wheels, a home plate wedding, and an ostrich race. One day he and Tug McGraw rolled baseballs from home plate to first and third base respectively—with their noses. "Geez, look at your nose," a friend told Turner of the blood and dirt. "Yeah," Ted said, "but I won"— something that the most famous Southerner of the age did in the year Turner became an owner.

That November 2, 1976, Carter beat Ford by 297 to 240 electoral votes. Mandate or boydate? The new president had believed the former, in his inaugural address quoting the creed of his high school teacher, Julia Coleman, about "adjust[ing] to changing times and still hold[ing] to unchanging principles." A decade later the Jimmy Carter Library and Museum opened in suburban Atlanta on its namesake's sixty-second birthday, October 1, 1986. A visitor saw black-and-white photos of him shoveling peanuts; on a motorcycle; in his ensign's uniform with his new bride at his side; and in a 1976 campaign poster reading, "Hello. My name is Jimmy Carter. I'm running for President." He had run for president to redeem his 1971 inaugural address as governor: "I say to you quite frankly that the time for racial discrimination is over. . . . No poor, rural, weak, or black person should ever again have to bear the additional burden of being deprived of the opportunity for an education, a job, or simple justice."

At the library opening, successor Ronald Reagan said, "When Jimmy Carter was born on this date in 1924, many southerners knew only poverty, and millions lived lives that were separate and unequal because of the color of their skin," adding, "I want to express . . . that this celebration is in a sense a celebration of the South—the new South that Jimmy Carter helped to build." Like Atlanta–Fulton County Stadium, the library rose, he noted, where General Sherman had directed troops and strategy near the Battle of Atlanta, as the Old South died.

The New South, Reagan said, let a racial moderate like Carter unite the country racially and culturally.

Hearing Reagan convey the honoree's only-in-America life, Carter replied with equal grace: "If you'll permit me to inject a political note. . . . As I listened to you speak a few minutes ago, I understood more clearly than I ever have in my life, why you won in November 1980 and I lost." He hoped, too, that America would come to understand his presidency, having largely named Georgians to his White House staff—press secretary Jody Powell; political aide Hamilton Jordan; and others who cheered the Braves, shared Carter's slightly left-center creed, and, like their boss, were unfairly dubbed "provincial" by parochial official Washington. On Inauguration Day the new president walked down Pennsylvania Avenue—the populist and the people. Later he banned "Hail to the Chief," gave fireside chats in a sweater, and held picnics on the White House lawn.

Carter's first major act was to pardon nearly ten thousand Vietnam War draft evaders. He then said America would return the canal to Panama by 2000. Blitzing Capitol Hill, the new president proposed tax reform, electoral reform, and a new welfare system. Carter called the energy crisis "the moral equivalent of war," asking Congress to match *his* good will with *its* legislation. Popularity was key, resting on media coverage. Carter's problem was a DC culture of the elite, not middle, class. Miss Lillian's oldest son didn't fit, having not attended boarding school, skied in Aspen, or vacationed in Belize. Washington never got how Carter solved a moral dilemma in the Bible. Carter never got why to DC "moral dilemma" meant whether to eat at Dominique's or The Palm. How could Congress spurn a man who canceled chauffeur service, asked his staff not to live in sin, and that first year held more press conferences, saw more visitors, and talked to the "folks" more than any president since FDR? Many found it easy.

Carter was the first president to normalize relations with China, make human rights abroad a U.S. issue, and sign a nuclear non-proliferation pact with the USSR and thirteen other nations. His Thirteen Days richened September 1978, Carter nudging Israeli prime minister Menachem Begin and Egyptian president Anwar Sadat at Camp David.

Only Nixon could go to China. Only this man of faith could help Begin and Sadat end the Egypt-Israeli conflict. "It was not a friendly confab," said ex-library head Dr. Donald Schewe of the 1978 summit siring the Camp David Accords. "It was hammer and tong back and forth. At any point in thirteen days the whole thing could have gone 'kablooey.'"

Carter bred the presidential town meeting, coatless, in a common pose, playing to his strengths: good manners, a pleasant voice, and talking like a neighbor. At Camp David he used that tone to mediate two outsized egos, the Bible student helping to fashion pruning hooks from spears. In 1975 his autobiography, *Why Not the Best?*, plotted a road map of integrity. Taking the oath, he had 75 percent approval, plunging inevitably to 56. The Begin-Sadat accord gave the president a second chance to make a good impression, even as he said, "[The presidency] is much more complex than I anticipated."

Carter took office determined to "dismantle doors between the president and body politic," wrote *TIME* magazine. At the presidential getaway he dismantled a door blocking peace in the Middle East. Could he open others? Almost as inscrutable as Nixon, the navy man would try.

Except for Camp David—a historic exception, to be sure—Carter's presidency had peaked by the time his mother threw out the first ball at the 1977 World Series. Then, he said, "We have an inordinate fear of Communism." In 1979 the Soviets invaded Afghanistan. Carter conceded shock, embargoed sales of grain and technology, and boycotted Moscow's 1980 Summer Olympics. Meantime, he humanely let the deposed Shah of Iran, a longtime ally, enter the United States for medical treatment. On November 4, 1979, forces of Islamic leader Ayatollah Khomeini seized sixty-three Americans at the U.S. embassy in Tehran. Six months later eight soldiers died trying to rescue hostages there—to Carter, "the worst day of my presidency." At home U.S. power also flew the cage. A gas shortage occurred after Iran cut the flow of oil, among its offspring high prices, unemployment, and gas rationed by social security. "You couldn't go into a store with a 10-dollar bill," said economist Sylvia Porter, "and come out with much of a bag of groceries." Returning to Camp David, Carter queried aides, Cabinet members, governors, and solons.

Carter emerged to give a talk—to Ted Kennedy, the "Malaise" speech—that touted energy self-sufficiency, scored "a crisis of the spirit," and failed to lift his Gallup approval rating, the lowest for any president—17 percent. The office, he suggested, was too big for any man. Dogging him were a 15 percent inflation and 20 percent interest rate. Other ghosts refused to die. The candidate had conceded "lust in [his] heart" to *Playboy* magazine in 1976. A panicked swamp rabbit—the media termed it a "Killer Rabbit"—swam toward Carter's boat on a fishing trip. A *Washington Post* story headlined: "Bunny Goes Bugs: Rabbit Attacks President." Brother Billy used his family name to become a caricature of greed. Jimmy quoted daughter Amy in the 1980 debate against Reagan on nuclear weaponry. He did little better that year in a visit to Independence, Missouri.

As Carter stumped in that quintessential swing state, the Royals' George Brett, trying to become the first since Ted Williams in 1941 to bat .400, backed his reelection. (No. 5 finished with a stunning .390 average.) At Truman High School, the applause for Brett dwarfed that for the president. A wire photo showed Carter with a bumper sticker, "George Brett for President." George's sticker read, "Reelect President Carter." The president asked if the Royals would win the World Series and their third baseman would hit .400. The crowd's response, a bystander said, "carried all the way to Cooperstown." In 1999 the greatest player in Royals history made the Hall of Fame with a staggering 98.19 percent of the baseball writers' ballots. Carter's vote ended differently: 49 electoral votes to Reagan's 489 in 1980—the first incumbent president since Hoover to lose.

Peggy Lee sang, "Is that all there is?" Not with this indefatigable, quietly adamantine man. Leaving office, Carter built homes with Habitat for Humanity; emerged as ambassador without portfolio to Haiti, Korea, the Middle East, and Africa; and endured being called a freelancer less evocative of Mr. Smith than Citizen Genêt. Increasingly more judged him—and his worldview of curious tenderness—with respect, even admiration. As each year ended, baseball and political, the air grew cool, Carter acted as if time were running out, his schedule complex, priorities direct. Most germane to this book, without warning the former president once again became as maniacal a Braviac as his mother, seeing games in person and watching on renamed local station WTCG turned WTBS, which bred new cable Superstation TBS.

The influence of TBS, Braves owner Turner, and cable television on his team specifically and baseball generally, has been profound. The 1963 Dodgers had offered baseball's first pay-cable subscription, Tele-Vision (STV), a viewer paying for every game. By the late 1970s newly available satellites forged cable channels that charged a monthly fee to complement free programming. "It made TBS the first [and preeminent] Superstation," said Turner, wooing local cable operators. The satellite coverage sired "America's Team," its breakthrough year 1982. Phil Niekro went 17-4. The Braves lured a record 1,801,985. Outfielder Dale Murphy became cable's first poster boy by winning his first MVP award, another following in 1983. Atlanta won the West, was swept by St. Louis in the LCS, but swept TV buzz.

"Before '82, TBS was just one offering," said 1976–99 Braves voice and former pitcher Ernie Johnson. "Folks weren't aware how daily exposure could make a Braves fan of a guy in Nevada who'd never been near Georgia." The '82ers won a big-league record first thirteen games—and suddenly folks were aware. "One man said the streak was the 'two-by-four' which hit America between the eyes about cable." A Storm Lake, Iowa (pop. 8,814), billboard read, "The Atlanta Braves: Iowa's Team." In Valdez, Alaska, the Nanook Chapter of the Braves Fan Club pooled cash, bought a screen, and renamed its saloon the "Braves Lounge." Columnist Frank Dolson called it "the greatest thing to happen [to baseball] since Bat Day." Basic subscription is now available in almost every American home.

Picture early-1980s baseball on TV every night, coast to coast—if not a miracle, more welcome than an open bar. Cable would endure. Atlanta's success did not, by 1984 reduced to a world wrestling-style fight with San Diego on August 12, spiked by two bench-clearing brawls and nineteen ejections. July 4, 1985, was worse, the Mets scoring five to the Braves' two nineteenth-inning runs and winning, 16–13. The last out came at 3:14 a.m. Had 1982 just been three years ago? Yet as Jimmy Carter went back to Atlanta's 1976–79 last-place past with its equally awful 1987–90 last-place future, he still loved baseball's anecdotal lilt.

Ernie Johnson was a marine in World War II, arguably cable's first baseball broadcast star, and an announcer who yearned for a rain delay to tell one yarn, then another. A favorite referenced a home first baseman who was playing like a Little Leaguer. He struck out in the first inning. A blowhard behind the dugout started yelling. The same batter again fanned in the third. "Bum," said the fan, "you can't hit, go back to the minors!" The first baseman struck out again in the sixth, the troll now going bonkers. Sadly in the ninth inning the batter struck out one last time, the fan having lost his mind but not his mouth, unleashing every insult every police officer had ever told him not to say.

With that, the first baseman sprinted to the dugout, jumped on its roof, and looked down at the blabbermouth, now cowering. "When I was a boy, I was brought up on a farm and we had a jackass and I treated him horribly," said the player. "My dad used to tell me, 'Don't whip that jackass so bad. The way you're hitting him, someday his spirit will come back to haunt ya.'" Pause. "I never believed my daddy until today."

The Braves' God-awfulness of the late 1980s led one writer to proclaim the only thing worse than watching them drunk watching them sober. Yet as they swept the cellar, cable increasingly eyed Carter at the park. His conversion from Plains softball to hardball was natural, Miss Lillian having passed unto him its beauty as a boy. Yet recalling Carter's baseball-challenged presidency, the public must have thought him Saul on the Damascus Road, scales fallen from his eyes. This was most true in postseason, as viewing peaked and the Braves again became born-again. To Everyman, Carter seemed overnight to have come of age.

In 1991 the Braves soared from worst to first, winning the NL Western Division on the penultimate day and the LCS in the seventh game—their first pennant in Atlanta. The team had come out of the blue. The first part of the Series returned it there, Minnesota winning, 5–3 and 3–2, before Atlanta won thrice in Dixie, the Carters in their field box doing the "Tomahawk Chop." Back north, Kirby Puckett won Game Six, 4–3, with his glove and eleventh-inning homer. In the final, zeroes dueled. In the seventh inning Atlanta's Lonnie Smith singled. Terry Pendleton drove to the left-center-field wall. "Lonnie gets deked [by Chuck Knoblauch] that there's a play at second," recalled manager Bobby Cox. Fooled, Smith slowed, stopped at third base, and was stranded: Twins, 1–0, in ten frames, Jack Morris beating John Smoltz. Three games went extra innings. Five were decided by one run. The "Tomahawk Chop" looked exhausted. Sadly it revived.

On September 29, 1992, Atlanta's sorry past was recalled by Charlie Leibrandt's one thousandth strikeout. "I thought I'd keep the ball, so I rolled it back to the dugout," Leibrandt said, forgetting to call time as the runner on first base took second. Turner barbed, "S–it, like the bad old days." The present was a moment that no one who saw or heard will forget. The Braves began the home half of the ninth inning of the seventh game of that fall's LCS trailing Pittsburgh, 2–0. They scored a run, had two out and two on, and put in Francisco Cabrera to pinch-hit. Having batted only ten times all season, Cabrera lined a single to left field, scoring David Justice and the deciding run by lead-footed Sid Bream, for a stunning 3–2 victory and the pennant. As Bream slid, people in the booth began pounding radio play-by-play man Skip Caray on the back. He never knew it. "I didn't feel it, my concentration calling the play was total. All I knew was Frank's hit meant the pennant." Stick a fork in him. He's numb.

Most memorable was Carter, leaving his seat as Bream scored to clear the fence, sprint toward the plate, dodge police, and hug Cox, the players, and Cabrera like a teammate—not a front-runner but *fan*. Watching on television, the Orioles' Rick Dempsey, mocking Carter in the 1979 World Series and now ending a twenty-four-year career, must have been amazed. Again, the Braves coda left you bleary, Atlanta losing the 1992 Fall Classic to Toronto, 4–3, in the eleventh inning of Game Six. "Otis Nixon makes out bunting," a writer marveled, "with the tying run on *third!*" The next-year Braves drew a franchise-record 3,884,720—"more in a week," laughed Cox, "than we used to get in a month." They also lost a playoff to Philadelphia.

Good things come to those who suffer: in 1995 the Braves finally took a World Series, their first title since 1957—the first franchise south of the Mason-Dixon Line and first to win a Series in a third big-league city (Boston, Milwaukee, and Atlanta). Falling: Colorado in the new Division Series, Cincinnati in the LCS, and Cleveland in the Fall Classic. Said Skip Caray on the last out of Game Six, "Atlanta, you have your world championship!" Tom Glavine won twice, including his 1-0 Series-winning paradigm. Greg Maddux captured a fourth straight Cy Young award. A year later Smoltz led the league in, among other things, strikeouts, innings pitched, ERA, and victories (twenty-four). Daily they arrived at work to find a new park rising next door.

The Braves opened the 1996 World Series in the Bronx, clubbing the Yankees twice. They went home to lose three straight, the last 1-0 on the Stripes' Paul O'Neill's running, straining, ninth-inning catch. It marked Atlanta–Fulton's final game in a stadium many were glad to leave, the Braves then dropping the Series final in New York. In the end "the Team of the ['90s] Decade"—Atlanta—won a single Series in that time against the Yankees' three. Similar advance praise bathed the Braves' new home, Turner Field—"the Ted"—more theme park than baseball field, first used as the cynosure of Atlanta's 1996 Summer Olympic Games. Could it transition to a very different game?

"Turner was built with two things in mind," said John Schuerholz, Atlanta's GM at the time. "First, the Olympics. Then becoming our permanent home," which as it occurred, meant twenty years. If football and baseball sites denote oil and water, giant Olympic stadia and intimate baseball yards are, if possible, even more oxymoronic. To give Turner Field a baseball feel, statues greeted a visitor: Hank Aaron, Phil Niekro, Ty Cobb sliding into third. Each retired number of a Braves player was also hailed by a sculpture that fronted the brick and limestone site: Dale Murphy (No. 3), Cox (6), Chipper Jones (10), Warren Spahn (21), Smoltz (29), Maddux (31), Niekro (35), Eddie Mathews (41), Aaron (44), Glavine (47), and Jackie Robinson's No. 42 retired by the sport.

The Ted opened for ball on April 4, 1997, home team 5, Cubs 4, before 45,044. It linked tiny foul turf, a twenty-foot-below-street-level field, and the silhouette of a forty-two-foot-tall Coke bottle, a salute to Atlanta's hometown drink. A visitor eyed the skyline, tomahawk atop the scoreboard, Atlanta–Fulton's former out-of-town scoreboard, and center field's giant screen to show up-close pictures to the crowd. Alas, little translated to the tube. All heights were uniform, Turner Field's eight-foot fence lacking a Green Monster or Pittsburgh's twenty-one-foot-high right-field wall. Worse: "If the home-plate camera is a viewer's picture window," wrote *Baseball America*, "Turner's is the most remote."

The lens's distance from the field made players look like ants, helped ratings plunge, and sped TBS's decision to junk the Braves for generic, less frequent coverage, the Ted's TV baseball seeming to originate from somewhere in Alabama. Despite the letdown, Andruw Jones won the 1999 MVP award for a .319 average and forty-five homers. At Turner 20,024 unsold tickets marred the first two games of the LCS. In Game Six 52,335 finally packed the place, the Braves scoring the winning run on an eleventh-inning walk. New park, old script: Atlanta reached its fifth World Series of the decade, hitting .200 in a Yankees sweep.

New also was Braves relief pitcher John Rocker, perhaps off his, insulting gays, minorities, and New York City in an article by Jeff Pearlman in the December 27, 1999, issue of *Sports Illustrated*. Commissioner Bud Selig suspended him for part of the 2000 season. Some thought that Carter would have bounced him permanently had *he* been in charge. As it was, the former president's edition of any dictionary lacked the word "retirement."

In 2002 Carter presaged future president Barack Obama by visiting Cuba to see president Fidel Castro, watch an all-star baseball game that Jimmy dubbed "maybe the high point of my visit," and give a televised speech to the Cuban people. "I think the people of our countries share many things," said Carter. "Two of them are good music and baseball." Touring the island, talking with the poor, the self-described "fanatic follower of the Atlanta Braves" easily assimilated. Cuba's flow of big-league skill to the states continued through the time Obama visited in 2016.

Having mediated between Begin and Sadat, Carter had offered in 1994 to negotiate the labor dispute between players and owners. They politely declined, the strike ending only when District Court Judge Sonia Sotomayor, in 2009 elevated to the Supremes, found the owners guilty of committing unfair labor practices. (Her gavel adorns the Hall of Fame.) In 2002 players feared that if they didn't strike, owners would change work rules or lock them out after postseason. Carter hoped the parties could agree by themselves or be aided by a government negotiator, but, he said, "If all these options run out and baseball is endangered again, I would be glad personally to volunteer my services." He didn't think it would, though, and it wasn't, for a decade.

In August 1989 Commissioner A. Bartlett Giamatti, fifty-one, in his last major decision before a fatal heart attack a week later, banned Pete Rose from baseball for betting on the game. Rose's status split the country, some urging mercy, others wanting penance, not a few blaming him for Giamatti's death. On October 30, 1995, USA TODAY published Carter's opinion/editorial: "It's Time to Forgive Pete Rose: Make Him Eligible for Later Consideration."

Carter wrote: "Few players ever made greater use of their natural talents or brought more enthusiasm to the game." He ended, "I have never met or communicated with Pete Rose"—actually, Carter met him in the White House in 1978 to hail his forty-four-game hitting streak—"but would like to join with other Americans to help give him and the game of baseball his opportunity for redemption." Many agreed, feeling that Rose, who denied he had bet on baseball, had suffered enough. John Dowd, head of the investigation that found proof that Rose was a serial liar, did not.

As a player, Pete, a.k.a. Charlie Hustle, was the ultimate gamer. As a gambler, his nickname had an altogether scummier slant. Dowd wrote USA TODAY a withering response—"Rose Not Fit for Baseball Hall of Fame"—in which he called the former president's letter urging Rose to be reinstated by the commissioner so that he could be "considered into the Hall of Fame . . . wide of the mark on several points."

Dowd named seven, most tellingly that "*none* of the members of the Hall of Fame, save [ex-Phillies teammate] Mike Schmidt, wants Pete Rose in the Hall of Fame because he dishonored the game of baseball." Those who knew Rose best wanted his company least. In January 2015 Rob Manfred succeeded Selig. That December, after studying Rose's plea for reinstatement, he made it clear that, in Giamatti's phrase, Charlie

Hustle had not "reconfigured his life" and therefore would only make the Hall on a paid ticket or a visitor's pass.

At this point, except for the player lockout ending the 1994 season in August, Carter's Braves had made postseason each year from 1991 to 2015—2004's was cenceled—an unequaled streak. The Braves also won their division a record eleven straight years from 1995 to 2005, and in 2013. They took the World Series in 1995 and made other Series in 1991–92, 1996, and 1999, but lost the LCS in 1993, 1997–98, and 2001, the Division Series in 2000, 2002 to 2005, 2010, and 2013, and the Wild Card Game in 2012.

Carter saw countless games at Atlanta–Fulton County Stadium and Turner Field and untold more on the theater of the mind (radio) and radio plus pictures (TV). "We rarely miss a game [watching] mostly on television," the ex-president wrote in 2016 of the Carter family, "and my general well-being is strangely affected by the latest performance."

In 2017 the Braves opened suburban SunTrust Park, nearer their season-ticket base—not like Turner Field, as an afterthought to an Olympics. They hoped it would swell attendance and postseason interest, using lessons from Turner Field and Atlanta–Fulton on what to mimic and to avoid—a ballpark allegedly built to enhance the intimate and animate, on video and in person.

As always Carter was intellectually curious, intrigued by seeing SunTrust Park turn its opening page. Had Miss Lillian lived and been physically able, she too would have visited. Each prized the game more every year, thankful for their more than half a century together—as Paul Simon sang, a baseball "Mother and Child Reunion."

TWELVE

The Gipper

Ronald Reagan, 1981–1989

Some term language crucial to Ronald Reagan's presidency. They understate the truth. Language *was* his presidency, the spoken word its core. In the 2004 book *Ronald Reagan*, Dinesh D'Souza noted how many miss America's fortieth president. "He isn't returning," the author cautioned prior to the Gipper's death that year. "The truth is, we don't need another Reagan"—rather, to ask what he would say.

Even his first major job foretold the weight of language to Reagan's presidency. Franklin Roosevelt used 1930s radio to combat fear. Reagan used it to carry the Chicago Cubs over WHO Des Moines. Hugh Sidey would walk down a Depression street in the small town of Greenfield, Iowa. It was hot, windows open. From a hundred radios the future *TIME* columnist heard Reagan, speaking so winsomely that many felt him more seductive than the game.

"There was something in that voice," said Sidey, "that made Reagan seem like the happiest man around. This was an awful time, and his voice gave hope." As a baby, he was named the "Dutchman" by his father for a chubby countenance. In Des Moines, "Dutch" became Reagan's lifetime moniker, first employed over WHO, the only local outlet to "recreate" the actual goings-on of arguably Iowa's most popular big-league team.

As noted, recreation involved a wire operator sending code from Wrigley Field in Chicago to Reagan in WHO's distant studio: "B2O" meant ball two, outside; "s1s," strike one, swinging. The announcer then *recreated* a game he never saw. A batter singled. Rain threatened. A fight began. The broadcaster narrated—invented. If the wire was virtually an empty page, Dutch's imagination wrote the script.

One day the wire broke from Chicago. Reagan paused but didn't panic, knowing that three other Des Moines stations were airing the same game *live*. "I thought, if we have the studio put transcribed music on," he said, "people'll turn to another station doing the Cubs in person." What to do? Make a big *to*-do. Instantly Dutch recalled the one thing *not* to make the newspaper box scores. A batter can hit two million foul balls and still have two strikes. Thus in the next ten minutes he set a world record for calling fouls.

As Reagan told it, the Cubs' Augie Galan fouled to the left, right, and behind the plate; into the stands; and out of the park—anywhere a foul could go. A tornado neared. Cardinals pitcher Dizzy Dean thrice called time. Both managers were ejected. None of this happened, but at home it seemed real. Finally the wire revived, Dutch laughing. It read, "Galan popped out on first ball pitched." Years later Reagan said, "Making things up, mixing fact and fiction. [Pause] What great preparation for politics."

In 1936 an *Iowa Air Force* article hailed Reagan's "thorough knowledge of the game . . . gift for narrative, and . . . pleasant voice." Already his early places forged the footpath of a moral: born, February 6, 1911, Tampico, Illinois; raised, nearby Dixon and its Rock River, where as a lifeguard in high school he saved seventy-seven lives. Almost to his death, when Alzheimer's disease stole his memory, Dutch could recite that number he carved into a tree. Even then something remained, if but a vague recollection, of the oneness that he felt toward this time. "Everyone has to have a place to go back to," he said much later. "Dixon is that place for me."

After high school Reagan attended Eureka College, linked to the Disciples of Christ, the religion of his evangelical mother Nelle, to whom he confessed his hope to be a minister and who immersed him in her faith. As a bespectacled student Reagan "got poor marks, but . . . copped off the lead in most plays." About his time as an athlete, Dutch said, "I never cared for [baseball] . . . because I was ball-shy at batting. When I stood at the plate, the ball appeared out of nowhere about two feet in front of me." Football differed, Reagan winning three varsity letters: "No little invisible ball—just another guy to grab or knock down, and it didn't matter if his face was blurred." Graduating, he drove to Iowa, worked at small outlets, and joined WHO for University of Iowa football and the Cubs. At Wrigley, Dutch learned recreation, returning to Des Moines to find how well the tyro could master, say, a rundown play on the air. As Reagan said later, in his becoming way, "I guess I did okay."

Already he had done the Drake University relays. Scheduled to speak *after* the sixty-yard dash, Drake's president began his speech with runners still in the blocks. As they began racing, the president kept talking. When the speech ended, Dutch had to recreate "all the competition [they]'d missed." He joined the Cubs in their pennant-winning year of 1932. They won again in 1935, Billy Herman batting .341 and Gabby Hartnett named National League MVP. "In the first two [World Series] games," Commissioner Landis would write, "Cub bench jockeys were swearing at the Tigers and at [plate umpire] George Moriarty," English superfluous to profanity. "I must confess that I learned from these fellows some variations of the language even I didn't know existed." Landis said to stop cursing. The Cubs stopped winning, adding a 1935 Series loss to 1932 and 1929.

In 1937 the Cubs trained on South Catalina Island, a short hop from Warner Brothers Studios in Hollywood, a natural evolution for Reagan, who wanted "to get into pictures." Fortuitously, he knew the agent of a barn dance group, the Oklahoma Outlaws, which had a regular show on WHO and had been hired to play in a Gene Autry western. Dutch called, got an audition at Warner Brothers, and impressed the woman in charge of Warner selection. Seeing his takes, she said, "He's the greatest find since Robert Taylor [ironically Reagan's closest friend to be]—if he'll just get rid of those glasses and do something about that awful haircut." He did, feeling sad about perhaps covering spring training for the final time. "How could I tell him [Cubs skipper Charlie Grimm] that somewhere within myself was the knowledge I would no longer be a sports announcer?"

Soon Reagan evoked the same nation on film as John Wayne and Jimmy Stewart, among others, in which white hats won, honesty trumped irony, and courage endured all, abided all, conquered all. Dutch's fifty-four movies include *Kings Row*, his character's legs amputated by a sadistic doctor; *Knute Rockne All American*, Reagan as doomed Notre Dame football player George Gipp; thus "the Gipper," another lifetime moniker; and *Sante Fe Trail*, with screen idol Errol Flynn. Turkeys include 1951's *Bedtime for Bonzo*, a chimpanzee his co-star as the film career was ebbing. Portending Reagan's able negotiating in four summits with Soviet general secretary and president Mikhail Gorbachev was his eight-term presidency of the Screen Actors Guild. In the 1950s and early 1960s he hosted TV's *General Electric Theater* and *Death Valley Days*, filling living rooms each Sunday. As GE spokesman, Dutch crossed the land scoring the evil of big government red tape, tax, and spend.

By 1962 the lifelong Democrat who voted four times for FDR became a Republican, saying, "I didn't leave them [liberal Democrats]. They left me." Backing conservative GOP nominee Barry Goldwater in 1964, Reagan gave the most artful speech, "A Time for Choosing," of any Republican that year. In 1966 the self-described "citizen-politician" trounced Governor Edmund G. "Pat" Brown by a million votes. 1970: another Reagan rout. 1974: the law forbade a third Gipper term. 1976: Reagan ran valiantly against President Ford for the Republican nomination, barely losing and giving an impromptu speech that electrified the convention. 1980: Reagan overwhelmed another president, saying, "Recession is when your neighbor loses his job. Depression is when you lose yours. And recovery is when Jimmy Carter loses his." He soon faced the hardest job of all.

In a quarter century Reagan had spiraled from struggling film actor to president of the United States. He was elected because millions overcame doubt about his ability—and because of trust in the old verities, Dutch's character, America's remembered past, and unease about Carter. On Inauguration Day 1981 clouds yielded before the Gipper rose to speak. That March 30 vice president George H. W. Bush unveiled a historical marker at the Ft. Worth hotel in which John F. Kennedy had spent his last night in 1963 before being killed in Dallas. Early the next afternoon we learned that Reagan had just been shot.

That night America had expected to focus on the NCAA basketball title game (Indiana 63, North Carolina 50). Instead it rode a Ferris wheel of despair, uncertainty, then relief belied by the real condition of its president, turning seventy a month earlier. Leaving a midday speech in Washington, Reagan was hit by a bullet from the gun of a deranged would-be assassin, John Hinckley Jr., that lodged an inch from Dutch's heart. He was rushed to George Washington Hospital, the limousine crossing the divider on a congested multi-lane avenue, then was operated on and came close to dying, a fact most learned years later. "I didn't know I'd been shot when I heard that noise," Reagan said. "I thought it was firecrackers."

In Texas, Bush immediately ordered that his plane return to the nation's capital. Landing at Andrews Air Force Base, most of the vice president's party urged him to helicopter to the White House. It would be dramatic, pitch-perfect for television, showing the government intact and functioning. Instinctively Bush refused. "Only the president lands on the South Lawn," he said, doing what was right—a quality the president came to rely upon through the next eight years. When Reagan heard the story, he was impressed—better, touched. The helicopter flew to the VP's residence at 1 Observatory Circle. Bush then drove to the White House, went to the Situation Room, and joined the Cabinet meeting under way. Among issues discussed was the "Nuclear Football"—the button that could start a nuclear war.

In Bush's absence Secretary of State Alexander Haig told the country, "As of now, I am in charge here," lacking equanimity and severing credibility. By contrast, Reagan's composure reassured. "I hope you're all Republicans," the Gipper teased doctors in the operating room. "Honey, I forgot to duck," he told wife Nancy, using boxer Jack Dempsey's famous line when decked by Gene Tunney in 1926. He mimed W. C. Fields: "On the whole, I'd rather be in Philadelphia"—all while heavily sedated, the grim reaper real. Weak and underweight after surgery, Reagan left the hospital April 11 to pick up where he had left off before being so rudely interrupted. To many Lazarus had little on Dutch's bravura White House return.

In his 1993 book *President Kennedy: Profile of Power*, Richard Reeves wrote, "There was an astonishing density of event during the Kennedy years": the Bay of Pigs, Berlin, the space race, civil rights, the Cuban missile crisis. Reagan's first years as president had a similar feel. On April 28, 1981, the Gipper, still recovering, spoke on behalf of his economic program to Congress, like Caesar taking Gaul. The Economic Recovery Tax Act of 1981 lowered the marginal and lowest tax bracket from 70 to 50 and 14 to 11 percent respectively. In August Dutch signed it—"the most important economic law," he said, since FDR forged the New Deal. On August 5, 1981, Reagan fired 11,345 air traffic controllers, the largest union to back him in 1980, for violating a federal law forbidding a government union to strike. The Kremlin was stunned, U.S. intelligence later learned, to find a different president from the norm.

In Britain Reagan told Parliament that "the forward march of freedom and democracy will leave Marxism-Leninism on the ash-heap of history." Boldly or madly—there was little middle thought—he proposed a Zero Option in arms talks with the Kremlin. If the Soviets removed current ss-20 missile deployments, America would not install new missiles in West Germany. The USSR said no. Reagan went ahead, hailing the "Reagan Doctrine" to "roll back" communism and foreseeing a Strategic Defense Initiative (sDI)—to some, "Star Wars"—to protect America from nuclear ballistic system attack.

On October 23, 1983, American peacekeeping forces in Beirut, sent by the president during the Lebanese civil war, were attacked by a suicide truck bomber; 241 U.S. soldiers died. That week Reagan ordered American forces to invade the Caribbean nation of Grenada, where a 1979 coup d'état had formed a tenuous Marxist-Leninist government and a non-aligned military had just seized power, to protect several hundred American medical students at St. George's University, prevent another Iran hostage crisis, and thwart an alleged Soviet military buildup by Cubans on the isle.

Tangibly Reagan rebuilt hollowed-out U.S. armed forces. Symbolically he might sing "Amazing Grace" with troops abroad, eat in their mess, and beam when a soldier said he was from California. This different president felt armed by faith affirmed by near assassination. "[God] must have been sitting on my shoulder," he said. "Whatever time I've got left, it now belongs to someone else." You don't become president, he would tell a visitor. "The Presidency is an institution, and you have temporary custody of it." After March 30, 1981, America would view this custodian in both a harsh and a loving light.

That March 27 the new president hosted an East Room luncheon for thirty-two Hall of Famers, the grandest White House baseball event since Richard Nixon's centennial bash in 1969. Despite Reagan's baseball resume, he starred in only one baseball movie, *The Winning Team*, released in 1952. It profiled pitcher Grover Cleveland Alexander, Cooperstown '38, as an alcoholic, a condition that in that time and place was believed less shameful than Alex's epilepsy. "When he was arrested and picked up for being drunk in a gutter, as he once was," said Reagan, "he wasn't drunk at all." Epilepsy bore such a stigma that "he took [a status as a drunk] rather than admit the disease that plagued him all his life."

Indians pitcher Bob Lemon had helped Reagan imitate the pitching legend in the movie. As Dutch explained, Alex had a quirk to his motion, slightly hopping after releasing a pitch to be ready for any ball hit near him. "By the time filming started," said Lemon, "the President had that hop down pat. He was positioned for anything." Such reverie now positioned Reagan on memory lane. "Those were wonderful days," he told his audience. "The nostalgia is bubbling within me, and I may have to be dragged out of here. . . . I never had more fun or enjoyed anything more in my life than when we were making that picture." Certainly one reason was that he and Nancy were engaged and waiting for the picture to end to get married.

They met in 1949, at a time when Reagan's film career had begun to flag. He had also recently broken a leg in a charity softball game, been laid up for a year, and been divorced by actress Jane Wyman, who said politics now consumed him. When the Gipper learned of the marriage's end, he was stunned, saying, "Maybe I should have let someone else save the world and saved my own family."

About then actress Nancy Davis, mistaken for a Communist-leaning actress of the same name in the Blacklist era, sought help from Reagan, now the president of the Screen Actors Guild. Such a mix-up could wreck her career. Could he help? Yes, over dinner. "My life began when I met Ronnie," said Nancy, to which Ron added, "And then along came Nancy Davis, who saved my soul."

Without their 1952–2004 marriage, say many aides, Reagan would have never entered politics, let alone become president. Now, in 1981, his presidency's first year, Dutch told the Hall of Famers how during their engagement he had offered to get Nancy "a baseball autographed" by all the big-league extras on *The Winning Team*'s movie set in 1951—Johnny Berardino, Peanuts Lowrey, Gene Mauch, Bob Lemon, Jerry Priddy, Hank Sauer, and Chuck Stevens.

"And, oh, she thought that would be great," the Gipper noted in his East Room retelling, saying he then took a few steps, looked back at Nancy, and saw tears in her eyes. "And I said, 'What?' And she said," meaning the autographs, "'Can't I go get them?'" The Class of Cooperstown roared.

Nancy's regret was more momentary than that of the man behind Dutch's memorable role: Alexander, the 1911–30 big-league pitcher, whose suffering might have impressed Sisyphus or Job. Dutch related Alex being hit in the head by a catcher's throw, shelved for most of the 1918 season, having career-periling double vision, but "trying to find some way he could pitch." Finally, he asked for a tryout and went to the Minors, where the manager said, "Go to the mound and throw a few," then went behind the plate. The immortal's first pitch broke three of the skipper's ribs.

If Alexander's dry run was a flop, so was Dutch's as a hurler. Aiming to duplicate Grover's strike, he was told to close one eye and throw. Result: an exponentially wild first pitch. He tried again: same result. A friend asked what happened. Reagan said, "I closed the wrong eye."

After radio, film, and TV, being voted governor of California and just becoming president, the Gipper waited less than seventy days in office to honor baseball, especially center fielders, where klieg lights never dimmed. Reagan was seated between Duke Snider and Willie

Mays. Another center fielder, Joe DiMaggio, said, "[The] president enjoyed this visit even more than we did."

Three days later the Dutchman almost died in the assassination attempt. He had been scheduled to throw out the first ball in Cincinnati April 8. No one substituted, the crowd observing a moment of silence. During his recovery many recalled how Reagan liked telling baseball stories, and how baseball enjoyed stories about him.

One tale referenced the Athletics' first game at the Oakland Coliseum on April 17, 1968, the team just moved from Kansas City. As governor, Reagan threw out the first ball. "One thing I'm sure of," he said of Income Tax Day, "is that a lot of you paid your taxes." Boos rained down from the sellout crowd of 50,164. Dutch smiled. "Up to a few moments ago, I was happy to be here."

Another future story referenced the other coast. In September 1986 several friends in the Secret Service arranged lunch at the Reagan White House for a Red Sox party. "We're told no photos, above all, no recordings," Sox radio announcer Joe Castiglione said. "Someone forgot to tell [partner] Ken [Coleman]."

Vice President Bush entered the Roosevelt Room to recount his good-field, no-hit time at Yale: "I batted eighth—second cleanup." The president, Joe said, then entered "at his theatrical best," soon invoking film.

Beyond Reagan as Alexander, *The Winning Team*'s cast starred Doris Day as his wife and Frank Lovejoy as skipper Rogers Hornsby. "Knowing the script by heart," said Castiglione, Coleman, then sixty-one, "had a recorder, determined to tape the Gipper." At lunch questions start. "Ken's is a doozy: Like most Red Sox fans, he liked a time-warp fine."

In the movie, Coleman said, "[St. Louis's] Alex in relief strikes out the Yankees' Tony Lazzeri to save Game Seven" of the 1926 Series.

"Right," says the president.

"How did Doris Day take a cab all the way from mid-Manhattan to Yankee Stadium"—even then a lengthy ride—"while Alex trudges from the pen to the mound?"

"Well, ah," Reagan says. Next question. Lunch soon adjourns.

"It was amazing," Joe remembered. "The Secret Service must have seen the recorder, but didn't say anything." That night the tape of the president speaking at lunch was broadcast on Ken's pregame show. "With security, it could never happen today"—a difference you rue or hail, depending on your view.

In 1983 Reagan became the first GOP president since Dwight Eisenhower in 1956 to attend a World Series opener, traveling to Baltimore. Concern over safety led Dutch to a suite, not a box seat, spurning the first toss. With 1984 an election year, the Reagan staff asked that he throw the first pitch on Opening Day. After Dutch did, he sat in the Orioles dugout in their 5–2 loss to visiting Chicago. Each year "nostalgia [was] bubbling within" the Gipper as he measured today's baseball against the past's.

To America the 1980s wed television's delectably evil *Dallas*, the evil empire's collapse, and the former California governor-turned-U.S. president's "Shining City on a Hill." For another Californian, Vin Scully, the decade meant language, said *Scribner*, that almost never let his public down. In 1983 baseball's long-time TV partner, NBC, presented a new *Game of the Week* cast: Scully with Joe Garagiola, a fine and seasoned pair. By summer the *New York Times* opined, "That their duo is good, and even great, is no longer in dispute." The voice of the Dodgers almost instantly became the sound of baseball, calling not simply *Game* but also the World Series, LCS, and All-Star Game, Vin's wearability—"Pull up a chair"—as great as Reagan's.

That June Dutch named his all-time play-by-play men: "[WBBM Chicago's] Pat Flanagan," who invented the recreation, and "[CBS's] Ted Husing." He also said no list "of all-time greats would . . . be complete without Vin." Scully was often asked if he was a Dodgers fan. No, he had to be impartial. Was he always a southpaw? "Yes, very lefthanded," he said, despite the good Sisters at Vin's 175th Street parish school in New York. "Nuns would swat my left hand when I used it because back then people didn't think being left-handed was natural. They'd whack me with a ruler." His family doctor wrote them, saying that to make Vin right-handed might cause him to stutter, which would have cost the world a master linguist. The concluding sentence put their ruler to rout: "And besides, dear Sisters, why in the world would you want to change God's work?"

Scully was safer by the mid-1960s, when he and a neighbor began nightly returning to their homes in suburban Pacific Palisades in Los Angeles at about the same time from a Dodgers game and speech respectively. Seeing his car, Reagan waved him over: "How'd we do?" Vin answered regularly: "We [the Dodgers] won." Elected president, the Gipper gave Scully, then with CBS, a 1980 Thanksgiving interview: "You know, I'm the one who invented instant replay," Reagan said on air. "Really. Tell me about it," Vin gulped. Dutch then relived recreating the 1930 Drake University relays on WHO Des Moines. "No wonder," Scully observed, "he became President someday."

If some likened Dutch's and Scully's ad-lib art, others compared Reagan's and Nixon's baseball grasp. Nixon's insight was more detailed and au courant. Dutch would relate some long-ago extempore yarn. Deep down, he mimed his life-long hero. FDR would cry Offense! Give me runs! Reagan enjoyed the July 6, 1983, All-Star Game, the Americans sloshing to a 13–3 rout. "Know what this game reminds me of?" said Vin. "A fat man's softball game played for a keg of beer." It was the kind of jab the Gipper used.

A related Reagan parallel with FDR was the capacity of each to *sell*. Roosevelt promoted baseball before and during the war. The governor meshed at Dodger Stadium with movie/TV peers who still called Reagan "Ron." The president staged countless events for the game on and beyond the White House lawn. He was still a virtual rookie when the Cracker Jack Old-Timers Baseball Classic debuted in 1982 at RFK Stadium. That fall, said future Pirates voice Greg Brown, Dutch phoned Willie Stargell on his Day in Pittsburgh to bid the slugger adieu. "Now, get out there and play ball," he joked. "You're not retired yet!" After thirteen years of the ex-Senators deep in the heart of Texas, the Gipper's 1984 trek to Baltimore affirmed the Orioles as DC's adopted team. In 1986 Dutch, flanked by Commissioner Peter Ueberroth and O's owner Edward Bennett Williams, wound up for his first-ball variation of good old country hardball. He began the yearly rite of the Series title team being feted at the White House, Reagan funny on command. All kept interest alive in the Dark Ages of the capital after baseball had skipped town.

On September 30, 1988, stumping for his VP for president, Reagan segued to a turning point of his past: Wrigley Field's "Friendly Confines," with Harry Caray. Dutch did an inning and a half of play-by-play, the old play actor saying, "You know, in a few months I'm going to be out of work and I thought I might as well audition." Harry mused, "You could tell he was an old radio guy. He never once looked at the [TV] monitor." In 1989 Bush succeeded his boss, Reagan almost always making the complex simple. For the All-Star Game in Anaheim, Scully invited Dutch to the booth, wanting him to be himself. For some reason, the Gipper seemed a grind obsessing on statistics. "Somewhere along the way," said the *New York Post*'s Pete Coutros, "the man who loomed so invincible on celluloid had lost his stuff."

For one night Scully carried him—a task Vin was used to, having carried baseball since the Dodgers began in Los Angeles in 1958. Until then baseball there had meant the PCL and the CBS *Game of the Week*. "Now the Dodgers had to sell," wrote the *Los Angeles Times'* Jim Murray, "and Vinny did it" night after night, his value impossible to overstate. In the 1950s the portable transistor radio popularly appeared. "Before then," wrote Murray's colleague Larry Stewart, "forget radios at a game. And without that, Vin's craze doesn't happen." Instead "[even getting a Dodger Dog] at a concession stand you hear him on each pitch."

At an event in 2008 the crowd answered someone's question to Scully—When would he retire?—by roaring, "*No, no!*" Vin confessed having yearned for song and dance: "If I came back, I'd like to come back looking like Cary Grant, dancing like Gene Kelly, and singing like Bing Crosby." As it was, Scully retired in 2016 at eighty-six, the pastime's Homer, his last year baseball's celebration of its *uber*storyteller. Who would soon forget twilight's "little footsteps of sunshine" or "He catches the ball gingerly, like a baby chick falling from the tree"? Talk about your "all-time greats," as the former president said. With Vin the list began right here.

In 1981 Chief of Staff James Baker listed Reagan's trifecta: "Economic recovery. Economic recovery. Economic recovery." Like a fever, Reaganomics broke before reviving: "It's funny how they [critics] don't call it that anymore," said the Gipper in 1987, "now that it's working." The unemployment rate, peaking in December 1982 at 10.8 percent, highest since the Depression, dropped in 1983–84 to 9.5 and 7.4 percent respectively—and 5.4 percent by the time Reagan left office. At the same time 12.5 percent inflation at the end of 1980 dropped to 4.4 percent by 1988. Even with the 1981–82 recession, gross domestic growth increased yearly at 3.85 percent, including 8 percent in 1984, a fortuitous patch of election-year timing.

Reagan's TV campaign that year produced an oxymoron—a legendary *positive* political ad. "It's Morning in America," its voice-over began. The film shows hard hats building homes, ships trolling, weddings under way, people working farms, the flag being raised, tow-heads respecting it. "Today more men and women will go to work than at any time in our nation's history. With interest rates and inflation down, more people are buying new homes. And our families can take confidence in the new future. America today is prouder and stronger and better. Why would we want to return to where we were less than four short years ago?" The ad showed America coming home. Plus: The recovery became the longest peacetime boom in U.S. history—almost a quarter century. Minus: The federal debt exploded under Reagan from $987 billion to $3.85 trillion. It is arguably true that a budget deficit was necessary to rebuild a national defense largely ignored under Jimmy Carter. It also became the room you didn't show if you were trying to sell a house.,

On June 23, 1984, the house was full, as NBC's *Game of the Week* aired what became known as "the Sandberg Game," after the Cubs' Ryne Sandberg. At Wrigley Field, Chicago trailed the Cardinals, 9–3, then 9–8. In the bottom of the ninth inning Sandberg homered to left-center field: nine-all. Next inning Willie McGee dinged for St. Louis, 11–9. In their half the first two Cubs made out. After Bob Dernier's walk, Ryne, with four prior hits, incredibly homered again into the identical spot as his previous blast. "The same fan could have caught the ball!" said Bob Costas, on backup *Game* play-by-play. Thousands of Redbirders gasped. The rest of Wrigley shook. "That's the real Roy Hobbs, at least today, because this can't be happening!" Costas marveled, "It doesn't make any difference if it's 1984 or 1954—just freeze this and don't change a thing!"—beautifully put and still recalled. The Cubs won in the eleventh inning, 12–11. By mid-summer focus swiveled briefly back to politics, there being much on which to focus.

HERE COMES THE RECOVERY! bannered *TIME*. Then on July 12, 1984, U.S. Senator and about-to-be Democratic presidential nominee Walter Mondale (D-MN) made history and briefly rattled the GOP, picking America's first major party woman for VP: three-term U.S. representative Geraldine Ferraro. On one hand, she might swell the gender gap, Democrats already leading the GOP among women—and represented New York's Queens district of TV's *All in the Family*, its symbol Archie Bunker, who idolized "Richard E. Nixon." On the other, Ferraro had yet to hit big-league pitching. Reagan had led Mondale by sixteen points in the last Gallup Poll. Now the same firm showed them tied. At the GOP convention Bush posed not as Reagan's attack dog but as a would-be president, quoting Ike: "May the light of freedom . . . flame brightly, until at last the darkness is no more."

The Gipper's favorite club had been blacked out since 1945. Presently the Sandberg Game's namesake fused a .314 average, two hundred hits, and nineteen triples into the MVP award. On June 13 pitcher Rick Sutcliffe arrived by trade from Cleveland to amass a Cy Young 16-1 record in just 20 games. One day Caray bayed, "Cubs win! Cubs win! The good Lord wants the Cubs to win!" Their TV flagship, Superstation WGN, reached Cubs Power fan clubs in Idaho and the Costa Rica Key Largo bar, which flew the Cubs and City of Chicago flags. Night music buoyed September 24, 1984, at 8:49 p.m. Central Time. "One more, and it's over. The Chicago Cubs will be the new Eastern Division champs!" Harry crowed from Pittsburgh. "It's in there! Cubs are the champions! The Cubs are the champions! . . . The fans are getting on the field! . . . Now our lives are complete!" Reagan agreed: "I've believed in miracles all my life. And now after thirty-nine years it's happening."

The Cubs took a 2–0 game edge against San Diego in the then best-of-five roadway to the Series, including a 13–0 opener. Aware of history, they should have petitioned for best-of-three. The Padres countered, 7–1 (beating Dennis Eckersley), 7–5 (on Steve Garvey's ninth-inning poke), and 6–3 (blame Leon Durham's error), the Cubs becoming the Cubs again, as lovably damned as ever. They "are Reagan's kind of team," the *Washington Post*'s David Broder wrote. "They prefer not to work at night. They believe that three hours of labor in the afternoon are enough for any job. They know the old ways are best. God intended baseball to be played on grass and under the sun, so they play it that way. They appreciate baseball surroundings. There is no more gracious ball park than Wrigley Field."

The Cubs were dispatched the day of the first Mondale-Reagan debate, in Louisville. By its end Dutch had observed going to church "here in Washington," called military uniforms "costumes," and confused military salaries and pensions. Where was the *Gipper*? untold millions asked. A likely answer: the then oldest U.S. president was showing age. His debate staff had showered him with fact and statistic—to Dizzy Dean, *statics*—Dutch preferring anecdote to connect. The next debate, the president vowed, would let Reagan be Reagan. Four days later in their vice-presidential debate, Ferraro called Bush "patronizing" because he emphasized her inexperience. In its wake, Bush's wife Barbara was asked her opinion of the Democratic No. 2. "I can't say it," she said, "but it rhymes with rich"—a middle-class poseur.

The VP tussle reinforced, not changed, the race. On October 21 the Gipper and Mondale would meet again, in Kansas City. The president's age dominated the two weeks between debate set-tos, aides and writers deluging the Dutchman with one-liners and memoranda: advice to defuse fear that he had gone around the bend. Reagan gently assured them that he would neutralize the issue—not to worry. Most of the White House did.

Wall Street Journal panelist Hugh Trewhitt gave Reagan his chance, noting that President Kennedy had "very little sleep" during the 1962 Cuban Missile Crisis. He asked if Reagan, given his poor first debate, had any doubt that he could withstand the burden of the office, especially in a crisis. "Not at all, Mr. Trewhitt," said Dutch, "and I want you to know also that I will not make age an issue of this campaign. I am not going to exploit for political purposes my opponent's youth and inexperience." The crowd erupted.

In 2000, I interviewed Walter Mondale for ESPN TV's *SportsCentury* series, the then vice president having opened the 1980 Winter Olympics at Lake Placid, New York, and witnessed the American hockey team's stunning gold medal story—"The Miracle on Ice." Off camera, I asked about Reagan's 1984 debate stiletto, delivered with timing that would have made Jerry Seinfeld green.

"It was a great line and I laughed along with everyone else," remembered the 1984 Democratic nominee. "But the camera up closer would probably have caught some tears as well because I sort of sensed the damage," feeling his campaign was done. Reagan's reaction shot is telling, like the eighth take on the back lot at Warner Brothers: he is smiling, not boastfully, but contentedly, tongue faintly in cheek.

The rest was for history: Reagan, on the train from one small town through another, reliving his boyhood with an itinerant father and loving mother; Bush, touting his "friend and America's greatest President"; Mondale, knowing that defeat lay ahead, yet refusing to abandon liberalism; Ferraro, saying the Gipper would outlaw abortion, ignore the poor, and raise taxes—losing, yet proud of her precedent.

At every campaign stop Reagan used Al Jolson's line, "You ain't seen nothin' yet!" On election night he told the crowd, "You'll forgive me. I'm going to say it one more time!" Except for Nixon's tsunami in 1972, Dutch's was nonesuch: 58.8 percent of the vote, 525 electoral votes to Mondale's 13, and forty-nine states to the Democrat's Minnesota, plus Washington DC.

In late December 1984 President Reagan got to talking about what he would have liked for Christmas. He reportedly joked, "Well, Minnesota would have been nice."

Reagan was called "the Great Communicator" for his likability, skill at English, reassuring voice, rapport with our history, TV presence, and being a rarity in Washington—a politician who was funny on *purpose*.

He was proud of his former craft, aware what it meant today: "There've been times," he told aide Michael Deaver, "that I've wondered how you could do the job if you *hadn't* been an actor." He cared how a president should look and act, dressing formally but not ostentatiously. He rarely took his suit coat off in the formerly named Oval Room, respecting the office. Wherever Reagan was, he "had a habit of hitching his pants up to make sure they and the jacket fit just right," said Deaver. Even when just shot in 1981, a bullet an inch from his heart, Dutch "checked his pants, buttoned his suit" after leaving the limousine to enter George Washington Hospital, then collapsed after entering the hospital's revolving door.

Reagan had fine writers—Peggy Noonan, Tony Dolan, Ken Khachigian, Aram Bakshian, and Peter Robinson, to cite a few—but they would tell you the best writer delivered his speeches too. Reagan supplied the gift of knowing his own mind, writers never having to guess. He called the Soviet Union "an evil empire." In Berlin the Gipper directed his most famous line to the Soviets' general secretary and president: "Mr. Gorbachev, tear down this wall!" When the space shuttle *Challenger* exploded, killing a crew of seven, he vowed we would remember how they "slipped the surly bonds of earth" to "touch the face of God." On D-Day's fortieth anniversary the president spoke at the U.S. Ranger Monument at Normandy: "These are the boys of Pointe du Hoc. These are the men who took the cliffs." Why had they risked their lives—many no more than teens? "It was faith and belief; it was loyalty and love." Reagan's presidency wrote a long-playing score.

"Where do we find such men?" he asked Nancy, answering himself. "Where we've always found them—on the farms, in the shops, the stores, and the offices." His bond with their America evoked "a simpler place and a simpler time," said the pbs documentary *Reagan*— "small towns, patriotic values, family and community, an idealized America that no longer was, that perhaps never was," except that it *was* real for those who lived there. Reagan lived there, even as his dad bounced from one early-century place to another. George H. W. Bush lived there, even as he tried to volunteer at seventeen to avenge Pearl Harbor. Doubtless, most Americans lived there or hoped to from afar.

In July 1986 Reagan helped mark the centennial of the Statue of Liberty, given to America by France. It had been closed to the public, refurbished, and would be relit by the president, pushing a button to send a laser one mile to the statue in New York Harbor. Aboard the USS *John F. Kennedy*, Reagan hailed what Lady Liberty had promised for a century, musing, "The things that unite us—America's past, of which we're so proud; our hopes and aspirations for the future of the world and this much-loved country—these things far outweigh what little divides us." Then: "Tonight we pledge ourselves to each other and to the cause of human freedom— the cause that has given light to this land and hope to the world."

The historian Robert Dallek called Reagan "brilliant at creating a rapport with the country, appealing to its better angels." No other president could have so "found the American sweet spot," TIME wrote in a baseball reference to Liberty Weekend 1986, yet the Gipper was not immune to slump. In 1984 William F. Buckley, CIA station chief in Beirut, had been kidnapped by the terrorist group Hezbollah, tortured for fifteen months, and probably died of a heart attack June 3, 1985. Intent on thwarting terrorism, Dutch had vowed to spurn appeasement, not knowing of Buckley's murder. In 1985 national security adviser Robert "Bud" McFarlane proposed a plan to improve relations with alleged moderates in Iran, saying it might affect hostage takers in Beirut—and expedite the fall of the demonic Ayatollah Khomeini. The president okayed it, later saying he was unsure whether the plan included sending guns to anyone in Iran.

That November Reagan and Mikhail Gorbachev met in Geneva. British prime minister Margaret Thatcher had said, "This is a man we can do business with." Having opposed each arms treaty signed by a 1970s U.S. president, Reagan still hoped to do business on *his* terms with communism's newest boss. In their first meeting he lacerated the Soviet system yet managed to ingratiate himself personally. "Reagan had something which was so dear to Gorbachev, and that was sincerity," the Soviet Foreign Ministry's Alexander Bessmertnykh said. The president wanted to keep the Polish Solidarity movement alive, boot the Soviets out of Afghanistan, and sustain anti-Communist Contras in Nicaragua. Could "sincerity" neutralize Gorbachev's opposition?

By then Congress had ended all Contra funding. Publicly Dutch tied them to the Founding Fathers. Privately he told McFarlane, "I want you to do all you have to do to help those people keep body and soul together." At Geneva Reagan and Gorbachev agreed that "a nuclear war cannot be won and must never be fought." In October 1986 the reformist who preached *glasnost* and *perestroika* and knew that Reagan wished for his own nation's demise invited him to another summit, in Reykjavik, Iceland. What both almost achieved was enough to make each leader's aides gasp, and they did.

Reagan's foreign policy rested largely on his belief that America could spend the Soviets into irrelevance or oblivion. Gorbachev, unable to afford economic reform *and* arms competition, proposed ousting *all* nuclear weapons, contingent on the U.S. halting SDI. The Gipper, aware that America had no shield against incoming missiles, said no, cashiering Reykjavik. "We were *that* close," he said, putting his thumb and index finger less than an inch apart, "from eliminating all nuclear weapons." Dutch returned to a capital abuzz over a Middle East report that U.S. guns had been dealt for hostages released by Iran. He denied the swap, then amended his denial, saying that better relations explained the trade.

Whatever the cause, the exchange violated Reagan policy. Confused, Dutch could not justify why arms were shipped just before Iran released each hostage, asking Attorney General Edwin Meese to investigate. He reported a probable diversion of funds from Iran to the Contras in Nicaragua—a violation of the law. "What could have been going through their minds?" said Reagan, forgetting his having told Robert McFarlane to keep the Contras together body and soul. The president sent Meese to brief the press, a bloodbath devolving into Daniel in the lions' den. McFarlane had resigned a year earlier. Successor John Poindexter now followed. Reagan fired Oliver North, operations manager. To many it seemed superfluous. Talk raged of impeachment or resignation. Others merely shook their heads at a presidency disemboweled.

Reagan appointed an independent commission, headed by former senator John Tower. The Tower Commission found Dutch guilty of lazy management and trading arms for hostages. Shocked, the president belatedly agreed, giving a network address conceding that "what began as a strategic opening to Iran for hostages deteriorated in its implementation into trading arms for hostages." The Gipper then apologized, hating to do it, knowing he had to and perhaps should have done it earlier. "There are reasons that this happened, but no excuses. It was a mistake," he said, the apologia accepted. In time the Gipper's luster astoundingly reappeared.

In December 1987 Reagan and Gorbachev signed the Intermediate Nuclear Force (INF) Treaty, the first pact to cut the number, not just limit the rise, of nuclear missiles. The Soviets accepted Reagan's Zero Option, once scorned by *Pravda* as a fascist tool. "It is a simple proposal," said Reagan in the East Room as Gorbachev stood nearby. "One might say disarmingly simple." It was also a victory for a president whom Washington solon Clark Clifford once called an "amiable dunce."

In May 1988 Reagan spoke to Soviet dissidents at the U.S. Embassy in Moscow, about religious freedom at the Danilov Monastery, and of intellectual freedom at Moscow State University. He and Gorbachev walked through Red Square, like allies from World War II. Arms talks resumed, leading to the first Strategic Arms Reduction Treaty (START 1), signed in 1989 by Gorbachev and George H. W. Bush. In hindsight, like Truman's Marshall Plan, Nixon's Mideast initiative, and Carter's emphasis on human rights, more hailed Reagan's build up (arms) to build down (negotiate) as his own administration yielded to another.

On June 11, 2004, George H. W. Bush delivered a eulogy for Ronald Reagan at Washington National Cathedral. Voice catching, he told a story after deciding not to at several prior events, fearing he would break down: "Days after being shot, weak from wounds, [Reagan] spilled water from a sink. Entering the hospital room, aides saw him on his hands and knees wiping water from the floor. He worried that his nurse would get in trouble." Who, Bush asked, "could not cherish such a man?" At the time, most thought Dutch to be a good or above leader. By 2011, the Gallup Poll called him the greatest president in U.S. history. Why do many feel this to be true?

This text has discussed Reagan's ability to communicate, using rhetoric to inspire. Increasingly America also seemed to admire his qualities as a person. It sensed the kindness that Bush teared over in his eulogy: "thoughtful and sentimental, writing letters on yellow legal paper" to individuals in grief. People liked Reagan's modesty—a political oxymoron—deflecting credit for the Cold War's triumph. As with many presidents, you saw the mother in Dutch citing "the Man from Galilee" as the person he most admired. In the end Reagan's marriage touched millions, Nancy the partner and protector defining devotion to her husband. In the last decade of his life, she carried on, alone, caring for the one person she truly loved as that person disappeared.

America knew that Reagan could be errant, and ill-prepared. He said things he *shouldn't*. In 1984, forgetting a nearby radio mic, the Gipper muttered, "My fellow Americans, I am pleased to tell you that I've signed legislation that will outlaw Russia forever. We begin bombing in five minutes." It is also true—ask Gorbachev—that a sweetness let him say things others *couldn't*—Reagan's alleged "Teflon presidency." America forgave, Iran-Contra an example. Ceding that, Richard Nixon termed Dutch proof that "politics is poetry, not prose." Reagan termed himself simply an American. "Would you laugh," he asked reporter Lou Cannon, "if I said they look at me and see themselves?"

It didn't hurt that the Gipper was arguably our most humorous president. The fine actor began his cinematic career making movies in the B-division of Warner Brothers, where, he said, "they didn't want them good, they wanted them Thursday." Much of Dutch's wit was self-deprecatory, poking fun at himself. When Mondale accused him of government by amnesia, Reagan said, "I thought that remark accusing me of having amnesia was uncalled for. I just wish I could remember who said it." Another jab pricked a print opponent: "For the last four years, I've been urging the press to be more positive. Today I picked up the *Washington Post* and saw a story that said, 'We're positive the President will lose the election.'"

Reagan often targeted his seventy-something age, loving to quote the Founding Fathers, Thomas Jefferson in particular. "I know that's true," he said, "because Jefferson told me." It brought down the house.

By contrast Dutch never made fun *of* the people of his youth, deep-ly resenting those who did. In a fact far too little understood, Reagan sustained the continuum between Nixon's 1972 landslide and Donald Trump's 2016 shocker—the Silent Majority of the small town; sub-urbia; farmers; laborers; small businesses; retirees; and largely non-coastal Protestants, Catholics, and Orthodox Jews. Writer William A. Henry III defined his flock as "Main Street, and specifically, the people reviled in *Main Street* . . . for whom citizenship has more to do with loyalty than with ideology."

At the 1992 GOP convention Dutch gave his last major address, say-ing, "Whatever else history may say of me when I'm gone, I hope it will record that I appealed to your best hopes, not your worst fears, to your confidence rather than your doubts." His lure rested, among other things, on straight talk, courage, defying big government and a would-be assassin, and an itinerant's populist son becoming more Sam's Club than Skull and Bones. It also helped that Ronald Reagan rearranged the world, as became clear after he left office.

After the Dodgers moved to Los Angeles, the Reagans regularly trekked to Memorial Coliseum and then Chavez Ravine. At Frank Sinatra's home, they met Tom Lasorda, then a coach, when Dutch was gov-ernor. Nancy especially became a close friend, as Lillian Carter had, sending Lasorda a yearly birthday card. In 1988 the A's and Dodgers staged the Fall Classic, its opener still fictive. Lasorda, now manager, had proposed that Mrs. Reagan toss out the ceremonial first pitch. She pitched to Dodgers catcher Mike Scioscia, then graced the NBC booth with Vin Scully and Commissioner Peter Ueberroth to tout her "Just Say No" anti-illegal drug campaign. Such a stable of household names deserved a thoroughbred of a game.

Injury had benched LA's Kirk Gibson, soon to become league MVP. "He can't push off [with the back leg] and he can't land [on the front]," said Scully. The Dodgers began by forgetting the visiting A's record (104-58) and odds (2–1). "Fastball. Hit [by the home team's Mickey Hatcher] into left field and deep," said Scully. "It is gone!"—Dodgers, 2–0. Later Oakland's Jose Canseco hit a grand slam: A's, 4–2. The camera showed

Lasorda, arms crossed, "sitting quietly," added Vin, "and that's quite a trick." By the eighth inning postgame host Bob Costas was planning programming in a runway.

"Kirk is hurt . . . supposedly unable to pinch-hit," Bob said, seeing him in the trainer's room. Scully scanned the bench, asking, "Is Gibson in the dugout? And the answer would appear to be no." On cue NBC eyed the dugout for a Gibson sighting and "heightened the drama," said executive producer Michael Weisman. Icing a knee, Kirk heard Vin say, "The man the Dodgers need is Kirk Gibson, and he's not even in uniform. The man who [was] the spearhead of the Dodger offense throughout the year, who saved them in the League Championship Series, will not see any action tonight, for sure."

No. 23 rose, said "My ass," put on Dodger Blue, and momentarily began hitting off a tee. "Go get Tommy," Gibson told Dodgers batboy Mitch Poole. Arriving, Lasorda met deliverance. "Skip," said Kirk, "I think I can pinch-hit." "Okay," gaped Major Tom, "but you hang back, sit here, don't go in the dugout," build surprise. "If we get to the ninth spot [in the ninth inning], we'll go."

Dennis Eckersley walked Mike Davis. Seeing a monitor, Scully said, "And look who's coming up! All year long they looked to him [Gibson] to light a fire and all year he answered the demands, until he was physically unable to start tonight with two bad legs. . . . And with two out, you talk about a roll of the dice, this is it! Four–three, A's, ninth inning. Not a bad opening act."

Limping, barely able to reach the plate, Kirk Gibson appeared scarcely able to swing. "Fouled away . . . oh and one," Vin said. "Fouled away again. . . . Little nubber foul, and it had to be an effort to run *that* far. . . . So the Dodgers trying to capture lightning right now." Few anywhere had an inkling of the thunderbolt about to strike.

In 1940, after France capitulated, Britain stood alone against Hitler. Churchill vowed, "If the British Empire and its Commonwealth last for a thousand years men will still say, 'This was their finest hour.'" Enter Scully's. "Three and two. [Steve] Sax waiting on deck, but the game right now is at the plate. . . . High fly ball into right field! She is *gone!*" Neither viewers, gaping, nor Vin, speaking, grasped what they were seeing. Sixty-seven seconds later: "In a year that has been so improbable, the impossible has happened!"

Later Scully asked, "Where did *that* come from?" of "improbable . . . impossible." Lasorda levitated. Gibson pumped fists like pistons, slow-walking around the bases. Vin closed in orange shirt, white collar, red tie, and flushed face. "And I think we've got a leading man, and many of 'em, between now and the end of this great 1988 World Series." It was not a great World Series: the Dodgers in five. It was, however, as grand as baseball gets.

The prairie novelist and photographer Wright Morris wrote, "[Reagan's] special triumph is in the conviction his countrymen share that the mythical world he evokes exists." It did. Loyalty did too. The Gipper worked in 1964 for hapless Goldwater, was the last major Republican to defend Nixon in Watergate, and wrote a public letter in 1994 revealing his Alzheimer's disease. "Let me thank you, the American people, for giving me the great honor of allowing me to serve as your president," his handwritten draft ended. "When the Lord calls me home, whenever that may be, I will face it with the greatest love for this country of ours and eternal optimism for its future. I now begin the journey that will lead me into the sunset of my life. I know that for America there will always be a bright dawn ahead."

Dutch's letter, beautiful in its bravery and simplicity, caused tens of thousands of letters to overwhelm the Reagan Library and Museum. For some it conjured an event three years earlier when the Gipper helped to dedicate the library in Simi Valley, California, on November 4, 1991. From 1862 until Bush's 1989 inauguration, no more than three former presidents had ever been alive at the same time. On this day, for the first time, five U.S. presidents gathered in one place—Nixon, Ford, Carter, Bush, and Reagan—as did their wives: Pat, Betty, Rosalynn, Barbara, and Nancy.

No one who was there will ever forget Dutch confessing, "My optimism comes not just from my strong faith in God, but from my strong and enduring faith in man." At the library dedication the other U.S. presidents spoke generously of Reagan. Grateful as he was, the Gipper was not obsessed with having others cherish him. Rather he was far more intent on cherishing people in places like the Eden he never tired of going back to, if only in memory—Dixon, Illinois.

"[We] may have had little in material terms, but we were emotionally wealthy beyond imagination," Reagan said in the best speech of the day. "I grew up in a town where everyone cared about one another because everyone knew one another. Our neighbors were never embarrassed to kneel in prayer to their maker. Nor were they ever embarrassed to feel a lump in their throat when Old Glory passed by. No one in Dixon, Illinois, ever burned a flag. No one in Dixon would have tolerated it." When Ronald Reagan died in 2004, at ninety-three, Dixon was not embarrassed to emotionally grieve its son.

THIRTEEN

The Baseball Lifer

George H. W. Bush, 1989–1993

From 1989 to 1993 in the White House, then later when both of us had left, I was privileged to be a speechwriter for George Herbert Walker Bush, whose favorite sport was baseball, the president having played, coached, watched, and learned its endless permutations.

Born June 12, 1924, in Milton, Massachusetts, Bush grew up in Connecticut, spending each summer in Kennebunkport, Maine, at the family home at Walker's Point. As a child, he learned modesty and propriety from his mother, a slight woman and steel force. "Now, George," Dorothy Bush would say, referencing the Protestant hymn, "none of this 'How Great Thou Art' business." Father Prescott was a stern, tough, and stately U.S. senator. Each vied tenaciously to will and to win. Both also prized family informality: their eldest son was nicknamed "Poppy" after his grandfather's "Pop."

Poppy inherited a formidable DNA, honor its highest trait. Several of George's friends were killed when the Japanese attacked Pearl Harbor on December 7, 1941. A day later he tried to enlist but was rejected due to age. Instead, Bush got a diploma in 1942 from Phillips Academy at Andover, Massachusetts, enlisted in the navy the day he turned eighteen, received wings and his commission, and became its youngest naval aviator, training in North Carolina. Not even twenty, he was then assigned to the Pacific theater.

In 1944 Bush's Avenger aircraft was shot down at 12,500 feet above water, its pilot rescued by the submarine USS *Finback*. George was brave under tension, facing death with stark resistance. At night he went on deck, stood watch, and sensed "God's therapy." Later, in another world, Bush parachuted from the Avenger's height every fifth year, even at age ninety, to honor his two buddies killed in that original flight, blaming himself for each.

By the time Bush became president in 1989, a friendship of nearly half a century linked him to a hero of the male half of America. Ted Williams had met him in that 1942 war training, each soon fighting here and abroad respectively for nothing less than his nation's life. In February 1988 the Hall of Famer and greatest hitter who ever lived helped save Bush's political life.

The vice president badly trailed Kansas senator Bob Dole in the New Hampshire GOP primary, barely a week away. Having lost the Iowa caucus, the native New Englander would likely withdraw if he lost here too. Arriving at a rally, Bush began scolding an aide, an act so uncommon by itself as to rival the sun moving east.

As Rick Robinson wrote in *All Right Magazine*, out of the blue baseball's most Falstaffian legend suddenly approached Bush from behind. "Any problems, Mr. Vice President?" boomed a voice that instantly would have been recognized by anyone in the baseball world. "Not now," said Poppy, shocked, turning around to see Williams, who unannounced had just flown his own plane from his home in Florida. "Everything's going to be fine now." Bush must have felt as saved as when the *Finback* plucked him from the sea.

For the next two days after Williams's arrival, The Kid—a World War II and Korean War icon; more handsome than any cover photo; an outstanding hunter and fisherman in addition to baseball eminence— campaigned with another Good War paladin, the future forty-first president of the United States—hereafter Bush 41.

As they barnstormed across the Granite State, Poppy joking that he was Williams's hired help, crowds went over the moon. Later three-term New Hampshire governor and future Bush chief of staff John Sununu was asked what pivoted the primary. Dutifully he said, "the

President's campaigning." Then a smile surfaced, Sununu beaming, "The Kid!" George H. W. Bush won easily, making his nomination, then election, possible.

Bush was likely the most nonpartisan president since Dwight Eisenhower in a period that had been nothing if not partisan—sharply, even recklessly. For a clear majority of Americans, Poppy promised a welcome time out, liking to fish, hunt, run, play golf and tennis, and drive his cigarette boat, *Fidelity*, at Walker's Point. He installed a horseshoe pit on the South Lawn of the White House and played to win but didn't demand a mulligan.

The future president liked pork rinds, popcorn, and gospel strains out of Nashville. He was religious but not off-putting; dignified but not starchy; humorous but not risqué. Bush was a fine husband, father, and grandfather. To learn about Poppy's wartime gallantry, you had to hear it from others, as with most members of *The Greatest Generation*, which Tom Brokaw so concisely and exactly named.

These and other qualities tied Bush's upper-class Connecticut lineage to my and many others' middle-class milieu. The mix was vital to his political success: president but regular guy. Another denominator was a game so American that the United States introduced it before and after the war to the nation that we defeated, Japan. Billy Joel sang "A New York State of Mind." For Bush and later Baby Boomers, baseball's "state of mind" enriched our growing up.

In 1982, septuagenarian author Joseph Alsop wrote, "If I feel that there were giants in the Roosevelt years, I claim the right to say so." For Bush, as we will see, Lou Gehrig was *the* giant. Poppy's coming of baseball age included Babe Ruth and Jimmie Foxx, then Stan Musial and Enos Slaughter. Mine tied names like Roberto Clemente, Willie Mays, Mickey Mantle, and Duke Snider. Each expressed our mental picture of the game.

Moreover, both of our baseball marquees—Bush's and mine—would have lit the same name that Brendan C. Boyd and Fred C. Harris did in 1974, writing in *The Great American Card Flipping, Trading, and Bubble Gum Book*: "In 1955, there were 77,263,127 male American human beings, and every one of them in his heart of hearts would have given two arms, a leg, and his collection of Davey Crockett iron-ons to be Teddy Ballgame."

In 1959 a pinched nerve caused Ted to bat a career-low .254, leading him to refuse to sign a 1960 contract until Red Sox owner Tom Yawkey *cut* his salary. The Kid then hit .316. On August 30, 1960, at age nine, I saw my first big-league game on No. 9's forty-second birthday—Red Sox and Tigers, before a full house at Fenway Park.

Four weeks later, September 28, 1960, also at the Fens, Teddy Ballgame exited as only a deity could, with a home run, No. 521, in his last at bat. As explained earlier, Ted declined to tip his cap. Three decades later George H. W. Bush plotted a tip of his own.

In 1990 Bush 41 started the process of giving Ted the Medal of Freedom, America's highest civilian honor. It began more than a year of anticipation—"like waiting for Godot," said a West Wing aide, "except that Godot couldn't hit." As Leigh Montville writes in his fine book *Ted Williams: The Biography of an American Hero*, Williams originally declined. Startled, now chief of staff Sununu called to learn why.

"No thanks," Williams said

"No *thanks*?" said Sununu.

Teddy Ballgame: "I don't want to do it."

Sununu called a longtime Bush family friend, Baseball Commissioner Fay Vincent, to ask Ted to change his mind. Vincent found that Williams didn't want to wear a tuxedo. In turn, wrote Montville, "Sununu said he didn't have to wear a tuxedo, but did have to wear a tie." Ted, who heretofore had likened a necktie to a noose, finally agreed. Stroke and heart surgery delayed the Medal of Freedom event until November 1991.

That June the president concocted another event. Sununu called me not to discuss a United Nations speech, Oval Office talk, or birthday message for the Dalai Lama. *This* was important—a tribute to Ted's and Joe DiMaggio's 1941 magic daybook—the Yankee Clipper's fifty-six-game hitting streak and Williams's colossal .406 average.

"The President wants to celebrate 'em," Sununu said. I was to write Bush's speech and text for each "President's Award."

"*President's* Award?" I said. "When was it last given?"

"Never," said Sununu, a covert Yankees fan, nor has the award been given since.

On July 9 I joined other Teddy-boppers in the Rose Garden to laud a generation—and a year. Bush praised DiMag's "grace and modesty," asked Williams's "help with [his] press relations," and talked about Ted's ninth-inning homer to help the American League beat the National, 7–5, in the 1941 All-Star Game. He then introduced The Kid, who domineered the event.

"I've always realized what a lucky guy I've been in my life," Williams said. "I was born in America. I was a Marine and I served my country, and I'm very, very proud of that. I got to play baseball and have a chance to hit. I owe so very, very much to the game that I love so much. I want to thank you, Mr. President. I think you're doing a tremendous job. And I want you to know you're looking at one of the greatest supporters you'll ever have."

Joe D. then followed. "Thank you, Mr. President, ladies and gentlemen. I'm honored. Thank you. And to you LSU players [who won the NCAA title and were in the audience], congratulations on your championship. I know the feeling. I've been in one or two myself. [His Yankees won nine World Series.] It's nice to be here with you. And thank you again."

Bush then asked Major David Bonwitt, Marine Corps aide to the President, to read each citation.

JOE DIMAGGIO. Graceful afield and sterling at bat, Joe DiMaggio bespoke excellence as few athletes ever have. In 1941, "Joltin' Joe" electrified America by hitting safely in a record 56 straight games. . . . Today, the Nation still turns its eyes to you—No. 5, the Yankee Clipper.

TED WILLIAMS. He was called The Kid, the Splendid Splinter, and in New England, simply Himself. He was an iconoclast and rebel who, half-a-century ago, batted .406—[the] last hitter to eclipse .400. . . . Teddy Ballgame remains John Wayne in baseball woolies—perhaps the greatest hitter of all time.

Nos. 41, 9, and 5—Bush, Williams, and DiMaggio respectively—then took Air Force One to a "summit" in Toronto with Canadian prime minister Brian Mulroney, arranged hurriedly so that Bush and friends could see that night's All-Star Game. "The idea behind the whole thing," Sununu told Montville, "was that we could ride on the plane for an hour and a half and have these two guys to ourselves and listen to them talk. It was wonderful."

A Red Sox–loving president, his Yankees-cleaving aide, and two names synonymous with the twentieth century: who wouldn't listen, in the Rose Garden or on Air Force One, like disciples of Dylan Thomas, leaning forward, wanting *more*? Few presidents have enjoyed baseball as much or stage-managed as much baseball.

A fine example was Poppy's July 7, 1989, speech on the fiftieth anniversary of Little League Baseball to five thousand players, officials, and coaches on the South Lawn of the White House. A day later Bush was to begin a week-long trip to Europe to, among other things, christen Little League baseball in Poland. The president used *The Encyclopedia of Baseball* to reference it in his speech. "At this point," he wrote me, "I will take out my handy baseball ref. book and read a couple of lines on both Stan [Musial] and Yaz [Carl Yastrzemski]," both Polish.

Describing his trip, Bush told the crowd, "Wanna know about Yaz? You gotta have this book!"—as enthused as he had been the prior election night, taking forty states to Democratic nominee Michael Dukakis's ten. "I'm going to be talking about them [Yaz and Stan] all over Poland about two or three days from now." It was clear why. Boston's Yastrzemski entered Cooperstown that month. Stan the Man had hurt his arm in 1940, become a Class C pitcher-turned-outfielder, and made the Hall in 1969. Musial was nicknamed at Ebbets Field, diehards mourning, "Here comes that man again!" He linked seven batting crowns, three MVP awards, and two RBI titles—a career top ten in almost anything there was to measure. Self-made, Stan was the antithesis of self-absorbed. "The key to hitting," he mused, "is to relax, concentrate—and don't hit a fly to center field."

Like Williams, Musial felt that he owed baseball, not that it owed him. At the end of Bush's South Lawn talk, Stan, sixty-eight, strode into the crowd, braving ninety-seven-degree heat to sign autographs for an hour. That mindset, which Poppy shared, led 41 to write the Official 1990 World Series Program cover story, saying, "You never forget your first love. For me, that was and is Barbara, but a close second is baseball." Yearly Bush welcomed the World Series champion to the Rose Garden—from 1989 through 1992, Oakland, Cincinnati, Minnesota, and Toronto respectively. "Usually when I'm told of a meeting with some heavy hitters, it turns out to be the Congressional leadership," he told one team. "Today it's you." He advised another, "When I talk to Mr. Gorbachev about reducing offensive weaponry, I'm going to tell him your bats are not negotiable."

In 1990 a special baseball card was produced by the Topps Baseball Card Company. The idea originated with Bush and Reagan writer Doug Gamble, whose prepared joke welcomed the Athletics: "One of my grandkids told me he wanted to be a baseball player, not a politician," Bush said, "because politicians never get their picture on bubble gum cards." Topps took the story seriously, printing one hundred cards with a picture of Bush, age twenty-four, in his 1948 Yale uniform. *Newsweek* printed a photo, the president was given the card set, and by 2013 a signed card in good condition and clear coated sold for $3,367. Unlike Pete Rose, Bush wouldn't charge you for his name.

In 1981 Ronald Reagan chose James A. Baker III, Bush's campaign manager and friend, as his White House chief of staff. Named secretary of the treasury in 1985, Baker ministered to Reagan's economic and international agenda. He also abetted the Reagan-Bush friendship, kept his old friend aware of decisions large and small, and helped Poppy remain what he had been since age ten at Greenwich Country Day School—the ultimate team player.

As observed, Bush's beau ideal was Lou Gehrig, the Pride of the Yankees, a good and quiet man of whom captain Bill Dickey said: "every day, any day, he just goes out and does his job." From 1923 to 1939 Lou hit 493 home runs, drove in 1,995 runs, and had a .340 batting average. In 1926–38 he led the American League in homers thrice, including a career-best forty-nine in 1934 and 1936; had more than a hundred RBIs in each of a record thirteen straight years, topping the AL five times, including a record 185 in 1931; and won the 1934 batting title, averaging .363. "I remember Lou's continuity," Poppy said of ten Series homers, thirty-five RBIs, and a .361 average. "Gehrig was steadier, less flamboyant, and more dependable than the Babe, steadily achieving excellence"—a telling self-portrait.

After playing a big-league record 2,130 straight games, Gehrig fell in May 1939 to a foe that never made a box score—amyotrophic lateral sclerosis (ALS), now known as Lou Gehrig's Disease. That July 4 the Yanks retired No.4, Lou giving a talk that broke a teenage Poppy's heart, its start and peroration choking words, not tears. Gehrig died in 1941. Three-quarters of a century later Bush termed him his "hero" when he was young, saying that he still was—one first baseman to another. "Lou was a great example in his personal life, and showed courage facing death"—like George, unpretentious, on occasion diffident, more often valiant, and a loyal son and spouse. Such depth underlay Bush's grace and boyish front, seeking oil in Texas or office in the Senate, being a diplomat or Reagan's VP.

To Bush, grief before the war meant Gehrig's death, hurt keen yet distant. Grief *in* war was as near as the closest bullet, as Poppy piloted his Avenger aircraft to destroy the radio transmission center on Chichijima. Japanese flak struck the plane, its engine set afire, yet Bush completed his run, emptied the tonnage, and scored dead-on hits. Each wing burning, he flew out to sea to give two crewmates and himself a better chance to parachute. One mate was trapped aboard; the other's chute didn't open; both died. Bush pulled his rip cord, jumped, braved more fire, and landed near an island he thought Japanese-secured. "It was about as close to death as you can get," said Poppy, for four hours paddling away from land in an inflated raft until spotted by U.S. fighters, which circled above protectively till the lifeguard submarine USS *Finback* pulled Bush aboard—exhausted but alive.

At war's end, feeling gratitude, recalling so many dead, so happy to be alive, he was honorably discharged after fifty-eight combat missions, married Barbara Pierce, and enrolled at Yale University, Dad's alma mater, where Poppy had been accepted prior to prewar training.

Back home, the young man in a hurry began Yale's program to graduate in less than three years, not four, his schedule aping Andover's: president, Delta Kappa Epsilon fraternity; member, Phi Beta Kappa; like Dad, member of the secret society Skull and Bones; and captain, Yale baseball. A photo shows Ruth, dying of throat cancer in 1948 at fifty-three, giving Bush the manuscript copy of his memoir, *The Babe Ruth Story*, for the Yale Library before a game at Yale Field. The yearbook shows Bush, in uniform, with text: "Captain of championship college baseball team [making the first two (1947–48) College World Series finals], while completing school in 2½ years after war service. Phi Beta Kappa—Economics."

The Baseball Quarterly Reviews (BQR), published by the Collegiate Record, has compiled statistics on its famed—"infamous," laughed Bush—no-hit, good-field first baseman. It finds that Bush's batting average was even lower than thought (.212) but that his fielding was even more luminous (a remarkable .992 his senior year). "He was the only [Yale] man to start every game in that 1946–48 [Yale varsity] period and the only Eli player to achieve that 'iron man' distinction," BQR writes. If Gehrig was baseball's "Iron Man," Bush was aptly Yale's.

In 1947 the future president also played a team on which another good-field, no-hit (center) fielder starred: Vin Scully. In a 1990 video Bush reminisced, "Remember a few years back in our baseball-playing days when you were roaming the outfield for Fordham University and I was that heavy-hitting, smooth-fielding first baseman for Yale?" Smiling his lopsided, unflim-flam grin, Poppy noted that each went hitless in three at-bats. It helped him "realize [he]'d never make it in the bigs." "What about you?" he asked Scully. "You still playing in the outfield? . . . Congratulations, old friend."

In 1948 Bush forgot "the bigs," packed his Studebaker, and went to Texas to prove himself. 1951: With neighbor John Overbey he founded the independent Bush-Overbey Oil Development Company, into which he parlayed heart, work, and Wall Street family capital. 1953: it and another indie became Zapata Petroleum, Bush choosing the name of Mexican revolutionary Emiliano Zapata, portrayed in that year's Oscar-winning film *Viva Zapata!* The wildcatting firm transferred Poppy to

California as a salesman, then to Midland, Texas. The family became happy wanderers, by 1989 gauging they had lived in twenty-eight houses. In 1959 Zapata split operations between inland and offshore oil and gas. Bush headed Zapata Offshore, moving to Houston, starting oil drilling as an investor and prospector. "They were can-do, like the age," said J. Roy Goodearle, a postwar oil wildcatter and Bush's first campaign manager in 1963 for Harris County (Houston) GOP chairman. "Background meant less than ability." To others' and perhaps to Bush's own surprise, the Yalie found that ability and friendship could dwarf the lack of a Texas drawl.

Then, in the worst moment of his life, Poppy found how both might not suffice. In early 1953, daughter Robin became ill. "We felt helpless," Bush said about the three-year-old. When she was diagnosed with leukemia, the Bushes had never heard the word. They called doctors in Houston and New York, tried every treatment, held Robin, wept with her. Nothing worked, not even prayer. In 1988, sensing that TV interviewer David Frost felt he had made her sad by referencing the illness, Mrs. Bush said, "I'm not sad. I only cry when I am happy. I think of Robin as a happiness now, so please don't feel uncomfortable." At the time, it was different. Even as a youth Barbara had been independent: swimming, bike riding, reading. As Robin weakened, though, Mrs. Bush yielded to depression—brown hair turning white.

Stoic and protective, Dorothy's son endured the unendurable, sturdy as a rock inside. Barbara told Frost that Poppy "wouldn't let [her] go, saved [her] from a dark hole," adding, "I think we grew closer because of Robin." Unable to save their only daughter, not understanding why "this child of God" had been taken from them, Bush said her death "was inexplicable. . . . Why an innocent child?" At such a time he buried grief, disbelief yielding to belief that "God works in wondrous, mysterious ways." Instantly the tragedy could resurface. More than half a century after Robin's death, describing her, Bush's voice caught, choking, unable to proceed.

In 1953 the Bushes began giving time and millions of dollars toward cancer research, including leukemia. Robin is buried at the Bush Library at Texas A&M University, next to the space reserved for parents who, Barbara said, "loved her more than life."

At least politics allowed a measure of control. Bush was slim, with an athlete's gait; selfless, like most pols are not; had manners that Miss Manners would envy; and drew strangers to him, making them forget his less hardscrabble than chauffeured youth. The effect helps explain why except for Ike, who died in 1969, and Reagan, the GOP's Orion, Bush 41 is the only Republican in post–World War II to become largely *beloved* in the autumn of his life. Often family supplied his cast. Frequently baseball was their subject. "My four boys played baseball. I coached it. And there were tens of thousands of kids in Little League. I think that Barbara car-pooled 'em all," Poppy laughed. George W. Bush later ran the Texas Rangers before trying politics. Dad already had and would.

Bush won a 1966 election for Congress; lost a 1964 and 1970 bid for the U.S. Senate; and was named to a bevy of appointive posts: UN ambassador, U.S. liaison to China, Republican National Committee chairman, and CIA director. In 1975 the New Englander's and the liaison office's favorite team, the Boston Red Sox, played Cincinnati in a World Series that, the *New Yorker* wrote, "was replayed . . . in memory and conversation through the ensuing winter, and even now . . . light[s] up the sky." On October 22, at 12:34 a.m. Eastern Time, Carlton Fisk's twelfth-inning blast off the left-field foul pole at Fenway Park won Game Six, 7–6, tying the Series, three-all. At noon in Beijing, Bush and his staff cheered this keeper of an event, he said, "almost as soon as the homer cleared the wall."

In 1980 and 1984 the Reagan-Bush slate was twice elected. In 1987 Senate Majority Leader Bob Dole, Poppy's imminent presidential foe, attacked the Gipper for disowning a no-nuke weapons plan (proposed at Reykjavik) for a high-tech toy unsure to work (the Strategic Defense Initiative—SDI). Bush had long ago attached his flag to Dutch's staff, "feeling very comfortable with President Reagan's priorities." In 1988 Poppy trailed Dole in the primaries, as noted, and then in the general election. His spectacular comeback against Dukakis—the Republican lagged in polling by 17 percent that August—vied with the A's-Dodgers Series for exposure; thus, California's giant electoral vote swag. Even political junkies obsessed over Kirk Gibson's magic wand and Scully's magic call felt their air of joy a boon to keeping things as they were—

thus, helping Reagan's protégé, who became the last GOP presidential candidate to win that state and perhaps the last who ever will.

By any objective yardstick Bush ran a brilliant—also, reluctantly and atypically for him, ruthless—campaign, fusing foreign policy, an exceptional resume, Reagan's record, and onslaught against liberalism. On January 20, 1989, the Gipper handed off to his successor, whose inaugural address pledged "to make kinder the face of the nation and gentler the face of the world." At one point, Bush turned from the lectern and extended a hand to Speaker of the House Jim Wright and then to Senate Leader George Mitchell. "For this is the thing," he said. "This is the age of the offered hand." Too late he realized that they wanted his head, not hand. Bush smoothed the rough edges of Reaganism. Congress passed child-care and disability legislation. The Left welcomed a Clean Air Act rewrite. The Right liked Supreme Court Justice Clarence Thomas. Both cheered volunteerism: Bush's "Thousand Points of Light." Feint, zig, and zag: this president hated extremes.

When Bush served in New York, Barbara dubbed him "the Perle Mesta of the United Nations"—Washington's Ike-era "hostess with the mostest." Bush similarly knew most members of Congress, had worked with some still serving, liked to kibitz, and was a quick study. As president of the Senate, he had also briefed Reagan regularly and well. Poppy traveled 1.3 million miles, visited all fifty states and sixty-five countries, and attended so many funerals that Secretary of State Baker coined a tongue-in-cheek mot to describe him: "You Die. I Fly." The First Lady bristled at the fuss, saying that they let "[Poppy] . . . forge personal relationships that were important to President Reagan—and later, President Bush." The 1991 Gulf War became Exhibit A.

In 1988 Bush said, "If you're a supportive Vice President, you sublimate your own priorities and your own passion for a team." He had, adding, "Ultimately, I'm not going into this game [of criticizing President Reagan]. It's talking about character, about fundamental honor. These are things that matter with me. Decency. Talk about what I learned from my Dad. Let somebody else play that game. Not me." In today's me-first culture, this was one game from which the former first baseman was delighted to abstain.

Bush's popularity rose and fell with events from the Gulf War stratosphere to the 1992 election, both to be examined. That was not true of Barbara Bush Superstar. Her noblesse oblige populist score buoyed Bush's presidency, its initial note the first open house inaugural reception since the presidency of William Howard Taft. On the morning after her husband's swearing-in, citizens who had waited through the night were greeted by the new first couple and escorted through the mansion. Early in the administration the First Lady founded the Barbara Bush Foundation for Family Literacy, a private group seeking grants from public and private institutions, today chaired by Bush children Jeb and Doro. Soon she began *Mrs. Bush's Story Time*, a national radio program about reading aloud to children.

Mrs. Bush taught that failure to comprehend what you read could mangle every chapter of a life—education, work, parenthood, travel. At the same time she opposed any law making English America's official language due to "racial overtones." Her approach let the First Lady discuss problems like AIDS, teen pregnancy, and homelessness without baggage. She visited the inner-city center "Martha's Table" to provide food for the poor and homeless; noted the need of unmarried mothers for help with children; at "Grandma's House," a pediatric AIDS care center, held a baby infected with the virus and posed for photographers to disprove the impression at the time that the act could spread the disease. She made a difference.

One day Mrs. Bush announced that the family English springer spaniel Millie, who got a biographical entry in Wikipedia, had given birth to puppies, making *Life* magazine's cover. In 1990 *Millie's Book: As Dictated to Barbara Bush* became the *New York Times*' No. 1 nonfiction best seller. Other days, in sneakers and jeans or slippers and housecoat, she walked Millie in Maine and across the White House lawn respectively. Mrs. Bush kept setting precedent: the first First Lady to score a game since Bess Truman now became the first to throw out a ball to open the season. The Bushes had grown up amid the pre-1958 Eastern history of three New York teams. In October 1989 the former New York Giants wrote a postlogue. It began in the White House.

Early that month the president, like any good American wanting to discuss the World Series, summoned a group of leading journalists to the mahogany table of the Roosevelt Room—named, depending on whom you ask, after Theodore Roosevelt, who hated baseball, or Franklin Roosevelt, who loved and saved it. "If you're president," wrote USA TODAY's lead baseball writer Hal Bodley, "the quickest way to find out what's going on in baseball is to summon a dozen baseball journalists to the White House."

For the next forty-five minutes Bush talked a little ball. "I'd rather watch baseball more than anything else," he began. "There are some things I'm sure I'm behind on, but I love sitting there, thinking what would you do next—would I walk this guy or tell a fellow to steal?"

"What about your good field–no hit?" a writer asked.

"Now wait a minute!" the president protested. "Is this an assault by the press?" The press began laughing, Bush's impromptu wit easily his most unreported trait as president.

NBC had that Saturday televised its last *Game of the Week*, the oldest and longest-running series in any sport, more than a thousand games since 1957. In it, DC's adopted Orioles lost a close-run AL Eastern Division title to Toronto. Bush felt the O's great start and bad finish might have led the late Dizzy Dean to say, "Them Birds got off to a hitterish start and then slud back to the cellar"—an accurate and impressive quote.

In 1990 CBS would air baseball. Bush said its just disclosed pygmy regular-season schedule evoked a French Renault he bought in the early 1950s—"by far the world's smallest car." Poppy had asked longtime friend Fay Vincent and cousin Bucky Bush to drive it from Connecticut to Texas. The Renault's best feature was size: "so small, it made great speed." Its worst: "Fay played football, and with Bucky they weighed more than the Renault."

Two weeks later, October 17, Al Michaels began ABC's World Series pre–Game Three show from the Giants' Candlestick Park in San Francisco at 5:04 p.m. PDT: "We're having an earth . . . [7.1 Richter scale]!" Al abruptly bayed, the network feed ending, Michaels falling to the floor. The earthquake caused one span section of the Bay Bridge to hit another. Sixty-seven died. The postponed game and Classic ultimately resumed, the A's sweeping their Bay Area foil.

Given that NBC had telecast the pastime since 1939, the possibility of it losing baseball in a post-1989 TV pact had seemed as inconceivable as Game Three's carnage—or even as implausible as the 1988 Series opener: "In a year that has been so improbable," Scully had said, "the impossible has happened!" Surely any new partner would augment NBC's regular-season coverage. "Who'd kill *Game*?" said NBC's Bob Costas. "Not unless a new network cared only about post-season"— and baseball, as in prostitution, cared only about the cash such a network would bid.

Such a network existed—and baseball was such a prostitute. In late 1988 CBS announced it would pay $1.04 billion for 1990–93 baseball exclusivity. Later even greater shock greeted its coverage: twelve regular-season games yearly aired in twenty-six weeks. "Then an outcry, and they make it sixteen—big deal, still a month goes by without a game," said Costas. No longer would Saturday afternoon hinge, as Scully said, on pulling up *Game*'s chair. "You no longer knew when *Game* was off," said NBC's Marv Albert, "or cared when it came back."

By 1992 CBS's ratings were already less than 40 percent of Scully's weekly *Game*'s. Since then, segueing from national to regional pastime, baseball has relied primarily—now almost totally—on cable to promote its regular season despite the medium's wildly varied exposure, lesser ability to market, and millions of homes sans cable wiring and/or ability to pay. A generation has grown up with baseball almost blacked out on the one free national medium—key to whether it likes or even knows about the sport.

Baseball's withdrawal began with the resignation of Joe Garagiola, a 1972–88 *Game* staple. Analyst Tony Kubek retired, weary less of the pastime than the men who spoil it. *Game*'s core explained the exit's cost. "End[ing] a great American institution is sad," said Scully. "I really and truly feel that. It will leave a vast window [of viewers without access] and I think that's a tragedy." Vin evoked the hypothetical, what might have been. As backup voice, Costas hoped someday to succeed him, "but whatever else . . . would never have left the series." Its passage wrote the Law of Unintended Consequences. Elsewhere, Bob virtually retired the Emmy award.

For a decade baseball rationalized the irrational. More sanely the *Washington Post* blasted what it styled "nothing short of an abomination." In print I scored baseball's Reverse Midas Touch. Finally, Commissioner Peter Ueberroth's public relations domo, Richard Levin, wrote a gracious letter ending, "You were right all along." Today the pastime has virtually disappeared from April-September network television, cashiering much of the game's allure.

Bush's acceptance speech had proclaimed, "Read my lips. *No new taxes!*" As much as anything, the proclamation made him president. In 1990 Democrats told Bush to raise taxes or risk fiscal gridlock, thus freezing interest rates, which might deep-six growth. Trusting Democratic Senate Majority Leader George Mitchell—"We'll cover you politically," he said—Poppy upped taxes to fuel the economy and get the issue off his back. Due to a federal budget deficit deadline, he missed Cincinnati's 1990 World Series first-ball pitch—regrettably, since the area had always supported him. In 2003 when the forty-third president, George W. Bush (a.k.a. Bush 43 to distinguish himself from his father), was unable as scheduled to open Cincinnati's new Great American Ball Park, Dad redeemed himself, pinch-tossing before a fond and forgiving crowd.

"Great Nations, like great men," Bush Sr. had said, "must keep their word." Many felt that the concord with Mitchell made Poppy break his. Tardily, he grasped how sandbagging had trapped him. Some wanted debate to stop at the water's edge. Bush hated it even lapping at the shore. Abroad he could forget politics. What mattered was America's global niche. "We know what works," his inaugural address read. "Freedom works." The premise hymned what the ex-globe-trotting diplomat and vp called "some of the most revolutionary changes that have ever taken place." In China, Tiananmen Square invited caravans of concern. Margaret Thatcher resigned as British prime minister. Mikhail Gorbachev became president of the Soviet Union, conceding its collapse. Lech Walesa was voted Polish president. The rest of Eastern Europe turned from tyranny to democracy. Marveled Bush: "It's amazing the changes that occurred in a blink of history's eye."

At Bush's 1942 prep school graduation, Secretary of War Henry Stimson said the U.S. soldier "should be brave without being brutal, self-confident without boasting." Bush reacted warily when the Berlin Wall fell in 1989. A reporter asked, "Why don't you show the emotion we [the U.S.] feel?" Unsaid: you don't insult people you need. Later Bush said, "I wanted the Soviets' help. I couldn't get it by bragging," never saying, "The Cold War is over" till Germany reunited October 3, 1990. His breeding masked a poker-faced heart. On December 19, 1989, Poppy met writers at the residence to review the first year, leaving at 7 p.m. for a media Christmas party. At 2 a.m. press secretary Marlin Fitzwater reported an invasion of Panama. Meeting Bush, no writer would have known he had just okayed the then gravest decision of his presidency. You would want him on your side playing blind man's bluff.

Bush never bluffed about American leadership. Pre–World War II isolationism taught that letting the globe become a worse place would not make the United States a better place. On August 2, 1990, Saddam Hussein invaded Kuwait and dubbed it Iraq's nineteenth province. Bush quickly formed a UN armada—"Operation Desert Shield"—a coalition of American-led forces to defend nearby Saudi Arabia, even as for 166 days he tried peacefully to remove Hussein from Kuwait. Iraq, the president said, must withdraw "completely, immediately, and without condition"; its "aggression w[ould] not stand." All the ghosts fused from Bush's past: Stimson, duty, scripture. "No one wanted war less than I," he said, "but we will see it through." Some in Congress wildly prophesied one hundred thousand "body bags." Bush pledged, "This will not be another Vietnam."

On January 16, 1991, "Operation Desert Storm," the American-led offensive campaign to remove Hussein, began. Bush announced the first high-tech bombing war, which quickly mesmerized TV viewers. Then, on February 22, he declared the coalition's ground assault had commenced. "Saddam [called] this a religious war," the president later said, "but it is not a Christian or Jewish or Moslem war. It is a Just War . . . in which good will prevail." Headlines blurred: smart bombs and Scuds and Patriot missiles. Hussein's Mother of Battles became the Orphan of Defeats. Wrote the *Times'* Maureen Dowd, "War never leaves a . . . President where it found him." Bush's popularity soared. He knew that whatever else happened, he would always be recalled for this.

What mattered most was country. "By God," he exclaimed, "we've licked the Viet Nam syndrome once and for all!" In early March Bush left for the weekend at Camp David. Staff members and families held hand-lettered signs: "Thank you, Mr. President" and "The Great Liberator." It was surreal, and couldn't last. Yet such a time—America as moral sunshine—deserved a coda and got it at a sacred place. Bush had lost teenage friends at Pearl Harbor on December 7, 1941. "Now look, I have to be careful," he warned preparing a fiftieth anniversary speech aboard the uss *Arizona* memorial site. "I don't want to break down." Much of his staff, though, hoped that others would see the character that *they* saw each day.

"Every fifteen seconds, a drop of oil still rises from the [sunken] *Arizona*," Bush said as light reflected off the Pacific. "As it spreads across the water, we recall the ancient poet: 'In our sleep, pain that cannot forget falls drop by drop upon the heart.' It is as though God Himself were crying."

Bush's church was self-effacement, not spectacle. Yet his peroration linked Battleship Row and its gun turret, still visible, and the flag, flying proudly from a blessed shrine.

"Look into your hearts, and minds. You will see boys who this day became men, and men who became heroes. Look into the water here. One day—in what now seems another lifetime—it wrapped its arms around the finest sons any Nation could ever have, and carried them to another world. God bless them," he said, his voice cracking a third time. "God bless America—the most wondrous land on earth."

Fearing emotion, Bush bared it at Pearl Harbor. The memory jarred during the long free fall ahead.

In March 1991 Gallup gave Bush a 91 percent approval rating—a record. In November 1992 he got barely 37 percent of the vote—a historic fall. In the view of many, the gop's dive into an empty pool arose from playing by the other team's rules. The Democratic Party's mantra was, "It's the economy, stupid." Since much of the media and GOP hierarchy agreed, it became the campaign's. Forgotten was Bush's victory in the Gulf, Gorbachev dissolving the Soviet Union, and how Poppy had changed the globe. Instead, by election day, "It's the economy, stupid" meant two things: (1) unemployment, highest since 1984 and (2) Bush breaking his "No new taxes" pledge. Each kept him from connecting with the economically restless middle class.

TIME's Hugh Sidey, who covered ten presidents from Ike through Bush 43, said Bush 41 "ran the government better than any other modern president." Republican delusion concerned eventual Democratic nominee Bill Clinton, whom it was sure America would never choose since he had written that he "loathed the military," was said to be unfaithful, and had admitted using drugs. When his "time came in Vietnam," commentator Patrick Buchanan said at the 1992 GOP convention, "he sat up in a dormitory room in Oxford, England, and figured out how to dodge the draft." Beating Bill was going to be *so* easy, many Bushies felt, not seeing until too late how culture had changed—to them, more permissive, less religious, more self-absorbed—ergo, America. Democrats thought that attitude sour grapes. Clinton was a policy wonk, political animal, and quality speaker, had a fine mind, and could roughhouse the courtly Bush. Such alloys are rare.

On one hand, the Democratic campaign rested on a wide but shallow 1990–91 recession that had ended before the campaign began. Reagan's 1981–83 black dog and Barack Obama's 2009–12 black hole dwarfed Bush 41's downer. Past recessions had been far longer and deeper. It didn't matter. Like Jimmy Carter's 1979 "Malaise" speech, the memory of which lasted into 1980, the effect of Poppy's downturn lasted into 1992. Clinton, for whom campaigning was an extension of governing, was at least as good on the stump. He undid Bush's 1988 lunch-bucket coalition, won the twenty-something and college vote, and mimed the media's opinion that only things domestic counted. Inexplicably Poppy let the Dems keep foreign policy off stage—41's forte—Clintonistas dictating what *Bush* could say.

If foreign policy was Poppy's ace, the joker was wealthy Texas businessman Ross Perot, who had ears like *Mad* magazine's Alfred E. Newman and a visceral hatred of Bush. Twitting Clinton, he said, "I'm a Rhodes scholar, too. R-O-A-D-S." His theme song was "Crazy," by country music's Patsy Cline—art as life. In the end, Perot's campaign was music to Clinton's ears. Bush and Clinton both endorsed the North American Free Trade Agreement (NAFTA), but the president had signed it, reaping blame. Perot called NAFTA "a giant sucking sound," killing American jobs or outsourcing them abroad. In addition, he sensed voters' fear about internal and external debt, said our children would get the bill, and vowed a plague on both political parties. Each party's voters complied.

On paper, the Perotistas were inherently Republican—overwhelmingly white, traditional, and moderate to conservative backing limited taxes, spending, and size of government. By 1992, however, three in four Americans felt the economy was fair or very bad (distant perspective). Six in ten said their own finances were better or unchanged since 1988 (up-close view). They bought a blame-Bush narrative a year and a half after aides had told the president the economy would boom. Worse for Poppy, after a 1988 Republican law-and-order campaign so brutally graphic that its convention seemed to have occurred in Alcatraz, not New Orleans, any GOP attempt now to renew the issue would be tarred by the media—and was. The upshot was that Perot's Independent Party got on all fifty state ballots, the most successful presidential third party since Theodore Roosevelt's in 1912.

By June 1992, Perot's 39 percent led a Gallup trial run against Bush's 31 percent and Clinton's 25. Perot hurt both, most plainly Bush. After Perot withdrew in July, the president trailed 55 to 31 percent! At the White House denial and incredulity mixed. Where was 91 percent approval? Before Christmas 1991 conservative John Sununu had been forced to resign as chief of staff. Replacing him, the inept Sam Skinner decided to blame the speechwriters, firing half of them barely four months before election day. Even survivors found it wrenching. In the *Washington Post* a Herblock cartoon showed Bush campaigning: "I'm concerned about jobs, jobs, jobs!—My job, [VP] Dan Quayle's job, my speechwriters' jobs—." The shakeup was needless (so late, for what?) and telling (like a bid to dump VP Quayle, missing the point). The point was the message, remaining garbled past election day: What was Bush's for a second term?

One message didn't save his presidency but enriched it nonetheless. Bush may have had more rapport than any Republican president of the last century with black leaders, especially those less partisan who preceded the late 1960s riots and murder of Dr. Martin Luther King Jr. He was a rare GOPer to back the Federal Fair Housing Act of 1968, making private as well as public housing color-blind in theory. Bush's support, intensely unpopular in his almost all-white Houston congressional district, prompted obscene letters, phone calls, and telegrams. Uncowed, as president he later approved the Civil Rights Act of 1991. Forty-one's father, Prescott Bush (R-CT), was doubtless the most liberal U.S. Senate Republican of his time. Each Bush deeply admired Jackie Robinson's courage in ignoring death threats on the field and urging legislation off it.

In the early 1990s two incidents occurred quite alien to those desired by Robinson and Dr. King. In 1991 black motorist Rodney King was beaten by mostly white Los Angeles police who were then tried for brutality. On April 29, 1992, a verdict reared: not guilty. Straightaway South LA burned. Pulled from his vehicle, white truck driver Reginald Denny was beaten by a mob, the assault rebroadcast on TV. Once, visiting Dodger Stadium, Eric Neel, columnist for ESPN's *The Magazine*, wrote, "Every radio was on. The stadium was like your living room, rich with [Vin Scully's] voice. I remember thinking then that it's Vin who unites us—culture, class, and race be damned." Now, giving the lineup for a Dodgers game at Chavez Ravine, Scully saw the fire on a ballpark monitor. Neel had been at "stop lights and in unfriendly bars, restaurants, gas stations, gyms, and liquor stores where Vin's name [was] nothing less than a shibboleth." Even a legend's name could not douse this rage.

Vin "was extremely aware of the obligation I had not only to broadcast the game," he said, "but my obligation to maintain the safety of . . . people at the ballpark or panic. So I said nothing. I really think that my job is to hold on to some degree of normalcy." Bush hoped to restore it. From his White House came conflicting words—on racial tolerance and the rule of law, sensitivity and appeasement, on where the former ended and the latter began. Bush spoke two days later, siding with the law. "What we saw last night and the night before in Los Angeles is not about civil rights," he said. "It's been the brutality of a mob, pure and simple. And let me assure you: I will use whatever force is necessary to restore order. . . . As your president, I guarantee you this violence will end." Many blacks felt that Bush was callous. Among whites his initial wavering hurt. Soon the president visited Los Angeles to show he "care[d]." Polling showed that Angelenos cared about order.

Trying to avoid extremism, while caught in an election swirl, Poppy succeeded only in seeming weak: bitter irony, given his past courage on race. At one end, his party had changed; at the other, the civil rights elect had. The center can be a lonely place.

Amid this Summer of Discontent, an exception was Barcelona's 1992 Summer Olympic Games, where the U.S. team conquered all. On August 11 it arrived in Washington for a South Lawn ceremony. Often enduring middle-age to aging pols, Bush relished the chance to mingle with young jocks. "It's an honor to see you," he told swimmers to marathoners to divers, noting that America had caught Olympic fever. "Last week Barbara asked me to help her rearrange a couple of chairs. I said, 'What's the degree of difficulty?'" One by one, the president told stories of Olympians, letting memory retrieve his time as a teenage athlete.

The 1992 summer American team carpet-bombed the opposition: 108 medals, the most since 1904 for a non-boycotted Olympics. Pablo Morales became the people's choice, a swimmer who missed the 1984 and 1988 teams but came back in 1992 to earn a gold medal at twenty-seven. "Let that be a lesson," Bush said. "Youth and inexperience are no match for maturity and determination!"—foretelling, he hoped, the campaign against Clinton. "Now let's have a picture, then I want to meet each of you." My guess is that aides had to drag him away.

That summer Perot, having formally announced, suddenly withdrew, citing fictive GOP-vowed intrusion at his daughter's wedding. His support fled to Clinton—one outsider to another. Perot later briefly reentered, then exited politics after election day, making Patsy Cline look sane. The GOP convention began August 17 in Houston, Bush behind, 52–35 percent, in a CBS/*New York Times* poll. The economy seen as stalled, Poppy let the social Right draft the platform, set the speaking schedule, and pick as keynote speaker Patrick Buchanan, the 1992 primaries' thorn in Bush's side. Pat fingered the schism that many felt then and now: "There is a . . . cultural war, as critical to the kind of Nation we shall be as the Cold War itself. For this war is for the soul of America." To elites it became a rite of faith that the "Culture War" speech doomed Bush's campaign. Polling data remains more complex, even contradictory.

The Gipper spoke after Buchanan ended. According to the A. C. Nielsen Company, twenty-two million viewers witnessed, as noted, the last major speech of Reagan's career. How many would watch Bush accept his nomination—and how would it affect the race? A pastiche of cheer line, foreign policy review, domestic preview, and attack on Clinton, the speech was a committee job. Thirty-four million people watched—the week's most viewed address. Yet Bush got only a two-point bounce, Clinton leading, 51–36 percent. In 1989–90, said pollster Bob Teeter, most respondents defined Poppy as "tak[ing] firm stands . . . caring very well . . . likeable . . . strong." A majority now said "changes his mind too much . . . uncaring . . . not likeable . . . weak." They were drawing two different people. Clinton could not have beaten the first Bush. He might beat the second.

Bush faced a towering pre-election hurdle: three ninety-minute debates with Clinton and Perot, the first debates where three presidential nominees shared a single stage and to include one "town hall meeting," letting voters participate. Before the second (town hall) debate, ABC's Carole Simpson arbitrarily ruled that no questions would be allowed on the subject of "character"—Clinton's quicksand. In a surreal scene Bush checked his watch, as if he couldn't wait for the debate to end. In another the candidates were asked about the national debt's effect on them personally. Bush replied, haltingly, "I'm not sure I get it. Help me with the question, and I'll try to answer it."

With Poppy on the road, the White House was largely empty each weekend of the campaign's last month. You could walk through the Rose Garden, by the Oval Office, or through the East Wing, where many official portraits of each president and first lady hang. The sense was, if not of desperation, of time running out. For Bush each day meant another final chance to somehow catch Clinton. The Gulf War seemed a long time ago.

"Tonight, in Texas, I will give my last speech ever on my own behalf as a candidate for reelection as President of the United States," Bush said in Houston, introduced by Bob Hope in a state and on an election eve where nostalgia was in vogue. Among friends and family, his talk was home talk. Texas taught character, Bush said. "Character is what you are when no one's looking and what you say when no one is listening." A day later he lost the presidency, conceding early. "Here's the way I see it," he said, "here's the way we see it, and the country should see it—that the people have spoken." He was plain, direct, and true.

In Bush's study hung a painting. *The Peacemakers* showed Lincoln and his generals near the end of the Civil War. Outside battle rages. A rainbow denotes the passing of the storm. Bush was a peacemaker. The storm was an election that confused and then unhorsed him. History will ask how the Bush of Desert Storm was given "the Order of the Boot," as Churchill described *his* dismissal as Britain's prime minister in 1945. The "why" is that Bush was a world statesman but a tepid politician. He hated campaigning's self-disclosure, fake intimacy, and grandstanding. Politics is bloodletting. In 1992 much of the blood was Bush's own.

For a time Bush brooded about his loss. "I couldn't get through. I'd say, 'Good news, the economy is recovering,' and there would be all these people saying, 'Bush is out of touch.'" The president was losing the job for which he had worked almost all his adult life. Less than three weeks after the election he lost the person—"Mum," Poppy called her—who had most forged his *entire* life. "George Bush was shaped and tempered by his mother's nature," Hugh Sidey wrote. "His was a soul finally formed by strata of love and discipline relentlessly laid down. Bush was lucky, so very lucky, to be rooted in a woman like [her]."

Dorothy Bush's death, at ninety-one, was "added anguish in the President's season of political rejection, a burden few men have known," Sidey said. Yet—this is the thing—leaving office, smiling, retrieving names, putting guests at ease at one official Christmas function after another, he never revealed to the outside world the inner turmoil of a broken heart. Poppy went on, never complained, took refuge in what lay ahead.

Bush said of the campaign, "I couldn't jump over the [media's] hurdle" of opposition. Finally, he cleared it to find perspective: "This is great. I don't need new suits for the rest of my life." He got new support in a prominent post-2000 Zogby Poll showing a pronounced rise in personal and presidential approval. In turn Bush lauded liberation/ retirement. He took up golf again, saying, "It's amazing how many people beat me now that I'm not president."

In 1991 Her Majesty Queen Elizabeth and Prince Philip visited President and Mrs. Bush at the White House. Out of office, Poppy was made an Honorary Knight Grand Cross of the Order of the Bath by Her Majesty at Buckingham Palace. Back in Texas, the former president asked Barbara, "How does it feel to be married to a real Knight?" She said, "Sir George, make the coffee."

As a boy, Bush was taught to act knightly. Now, being knighted in a fashion, 41 had a U.S. Navy supercarrier named the USS *George H. W. Bush* commissioned in his honor—and returned to Kuwait to be greeted as a hero, a little boy telling him, "If it wasn't for Desert Storm, I would have no country." He became a close friend to—of all people— his former bane, Bill Clinton. He and Mrs. Bush became easily the presidency's longest-married couple, seventy-three years in January 2018. After 1999 you could often find them behind home plate in the Astros' grand new home, Minute Maid Park (née Enron Field), Poppy greeting visitors, Barbara, hair instantly recognizable on TV.

Mrs. Bush wrote numerous best-selling books after her smash *Millie's Book*, including *Barbara Bush: A Memoir* and *Reflections: Life after the White House*. With 41 she embraced the M. D. Anderson Center, helping to raise money especially for cancer research. In 2004 the center created a clinic in daughter Robin's name. Spurning autobiography, Bush filled the void by penning other books, including *All the Best, George Bush: My Life and Other Writings*, a lifetime of thank-yous, other letters, appraisals of well-known leaders, brutal confessionals, and personal passages. In a video age his old-timey pen-to-page grace glowed.

Bush glowed when a new rule was passed: the young among his now seventeen grandchildren and seven great-grandchildren must "deimperialize the presidential retirement" by giving him a hug. The family divided time between Houston and Kennebunkport, feeling each a site that belonged. On February 15, 2011, Poppy returned to another site, the White House. Having given the Medal of Freedom to, among others, Ronald Reagan and Margaret Thatcher, Bush received it himself, President Obama saying, "[To] those of you who know him, this is a gentleman, inspiring citizens to become points of light." In July 2013 the ex-president and first lady were invited back to the White House to recognize the five thousandth daily Point of Light award: turnabout, fair play.

About three years earlier a form of Parkinson's Disease known as Parkinsonitis, a loss of balance and mobility in the legs, struck Bush, who increasingly relied on a cane or motorized wheelchair, "President of the United States" scripted on the back. On November 23, 2012, Poppy entered Methodist Hospital in Houston for treatment of bronchitis. He was supposed to be home by Christmas, but suffered a persistent fever, mandating a December 23 move to intensive care. Family members flew to Houston, the prognosis grave. In critical condition for several days around Christmas, Bush recovered, saying, "Tell people to put the harps back in the closet."

By December 30, two weeks before his release, family spokesman Jim McGrath reported Poppy singing with his doctors. Hospital officials were moved by people trying to contact him: in person, by phone, via Facebook, even Twitter—strangely apt, since Bush, once so technically challenged that he burlesqued his inability to learn Nintendo from a then ten-year-old grandson, became email and Twitter savvy—his playful email address ending "@flfw.com" for "former leader of the free world."

What Bush did worst in 1992—glad-hand, go for the jugular—is what polls say Americans now disdain. By contrast, his strength—ability and character—is what they allege to prize. America's vision of the man who sired "the vision thing" changed as he aged, as Bush's coin toss in 2017 from his wheelchair showed before a roaring crowd at Super Bowl LI. Said USA TODAY, "Who thought a coin toss could be so emotional?" That October he helped toss the ceremonial first pitch before the spectacular, epochal Game Five of the World Series at Minute Maid: Astros 13, Dodgers 12, in extra innings, Houston ultimately taking its first big-league title.

TIME's Hugh Sidey had predicted the response a generation earlier. "His presidential record was better than anybody in this dismal campaign ever admitted, and better than he could articulate. And there was something more that could never be fitted into the strictures of raucous electronic politics: the sheer decency of the son of Prescott and Dorothy Bush," he wrote in 1992's worst autumn of Bush's life, adding, "History will remember."

In 2013 the George W. Bush Presidential Center opened in Dallas. President Obama and former presidents Clinton, Carter, 41, and 43 gathered to hail the newest presidential library. Each president spoke. The oldest, George H. W. Bush, said simply, "God bless America, and thank you very much." He rose to acknowledge the crowd, whose applause was loud and lasting.

Wrote the *Wall Street Journal*'s Peggy Noonan of America's last president from the Greatest Generation: "That crowd, and the people watching on TV—the person they loved and honored most was him."

FOURTEEN

Our Man Bill

William Jefferson Clinton, 1993–2001

"I t might be! It could be! It is!" went the home run mantra of the man who helped Bill Clinton learn baseball, entrancing for a half century most famously for the Cardinals and the Cubs. In Harry Caray, God broke the mold *before* He made perhaps the most beloved baseball voice of all time. Hail the Maestro of the seventh-inning stretch for restarting "Take Me Out to the Ballgame." Be grateful that Caray's "Holy Cow!" catchphrase endures. Like Clinton, born on the wrong side of the tracks, Harry was forever on the little guy's side— in his case, seemingly a little truant across the land. "I was lucky I came along when I did," he said. "With clubs hiring ex-jocks-turned-announcers, a young man like me couldn't get a job today." His tale is worth recalling, even as Clinton's life is worth reliving.

Before the Dodgers' and Giants' 1957 apostasy, leaving one coast for another, and the Braves' 1966 march from Milwaukee into Georgia, the St. Louis Cardinals were for the better part of a century America's western- and southernmost team. Over booming fifty-thousand-watt KMOX St. Louis, Caray became an Arthur in Webster, Iowa, and Lawton, Oklahoma, and Cleveland, Tennessee.

"In the years when baseball stopped at the Mississippi, KMOX built a network that brought major-league baseball into every little burb," said the father of modern baseball statistics, Bill James. Even with today's Internet, cable, and high-tech's horn of plenty, its network still anchors Cardinals Country, as it did for Clinton, born August 19, 1946, in tiny Hope, Arkansas. For the Ozark tyro, the radio behemoth evoked a faraway world through soft soap and hard sell.

Our age would term the Clinton clan dysfunctional. The future president was born William Jefferson Blythe III to Virginia Dell (née Cassidy) and William Jefferson Blythe Jr., thirty-six, a traveling salesman killed in a car accident three months before Bill's birth. After Virginia moved to New Orleans to study nursing, Bill stayed with her parents, who owned and ran a small grocery store that sold goods on credit to every race, a rarity in then segregated Dixie.

In 1950, after four years away, Virginia returned from nursing school to marry Roger Clinton Sr., who owned a car dealership with his brother and Earl T. Ricks in Hot Springs a.k.a. "the Las Vegas of the South." That year the family moved the ninety miles to live there. At fifteen Bill formally adopted the surname Clinton as a gesture of respect for his stepfather, whom he later called a gambler and an alcoholic who abused his mother and half-brother Roger Clinton Jr., Bill intervening by vowing violence.

Harry Caray was orphaned at three. In a sense, Clinton was too, making his way alone. At three schools, the last Hot Springs High, he built an alternate existence as an active reader, student leader, and musician who joined the chorus and played the tenor saxophone, winning first chair in the state band's saxophone section. Bill decided not to make music his life's work. Yet his sax enabled *another* life. It happened much later—and to quote Lewis Carroll, in a "curiouser and curiouser" way.

In *My Life*, his 2004 autobiography, Clinton wrote of choosing a career: "Sometime in my sixteenth year, I decided I wanted to be in public life as an elected official." Bill loved music and medicine but felt he could excel in neither. "But I knew I could be *great* in public service [author's emphasis]." He never mentioned baseball, for he was barely fair as a player—uncoordinated and not fast. "I knew the game okay, but I knew from the start my enjoyment was as a spectator. And being a Cardinals fan, how could you fail to love the guys who did their games?"

Clinton turned sixteen in 1962, a season the Redbirds placed sixth. Stan Musial turned forty-two, batting .330, an average that defied gravity, common sense, and the calendar, above all. That year the St. Louis Swifties televised twenty road games on Saturdays and Sundays except those from California, line charges too costly. The Cards radio ubiquity bred envy from every other team, their flagship KMOX AM/FM network reaching baseball's largest number of affiliates (120) from Pocahontas, Arkansas, to Galesburg, Illinois, Clinton hearing the last year of arguably the greatest trio to call baseball play-by-play.

As of 1945, Caray conducted each Cardinals game like a bartender singing an aria: hits, runs, and errors rising and falling in rate and intensity. His favorite call was Musial's 1958 career maker/breaker: "Line drive—*There it is!*—into left field! Hit number three thousand!" Harry blared. "A run has scored! MOO-zell around first, on his way to second with a double. *Holy cow!*"

Partner Jack Buck was always ready with a beguiling gesture and winsome word. "The Irish are so relaxed," he said. "If you buy a paper, they say, 'Do you want yesterday's paper or today's?' I say, 'Today's, of course.' They say, 'Then come back tomorrow.'"

The third man in the booth, Joe Garagiola, told stories about lifelong pal Yogi Berra. "A woman came up to Yogi at a party and said, 'Mr. Berra, you look pretty cool in that outfit.' Yogi smiled. 'Thanks,' he said. 'You don't look so hot yourself.'"

In 1962 Joe left to join NBC-TV's *The Today Show*. Buck and Caray carried on through 1969, at which time Harry was fired for an alleged affair with the daughter-in-law of Redbirds owner August Busch. Buck stayed till his death in 2002. Harry briefly joined the A's, then the 1971–81 White Sox, then memorably America's 1982–97 Cubs, his stage cable Superstation WGN-TV, seen in a huge swath of U.S. homes. By then Bill Clinton's interest in public service had narrowed to the law, wrote author David Maraniss, "his budding rhetorical and political skills" evinced in defense of the ancient Roman senator Catiline in a Latin class mock trial. Looking ahead, Clinton saw that a majority and plurality of members of the U.S. Senate and House respectively had legal training.

According to any Arkansas traveler, two events in 1963 sealed Clinton's future. As a Boys Nation senior, Bill visited the White House July 24 to meet President Kennedy, the photo of them at one time or another gracing each president's library. The second was watching Martin Luther King Jr.'s August 28 "I Have a Dream" speech on TV, the counselor-in-the-making so impressed that he memorized it. The scholarship-aided Clinton, brighter than most, as ambitious as any, interned and clerked for Arkansas senator J. William Fulbright, graduated from Georgetown University in 1968, won a Rhodes Scholarship to the University of Oxford, led a 1969 moratorium there against U.S. involvement in the Vietnam War, weathered uproar back home about avoiding the draft, and attended Yale Law School, class of '73.

A year later Clinton returned to Arkansas to teach law at its university and lose as a Democrat for the U.S. House of Representatives. In 1975 Bill married a fellow lawyer and Yalie, Hillary Rodham. In 1976 and 1978 he was elected Arkansas attorney general and governor respectively. Nineteen eighty brought another loss; the "Boy Governor" once more felt too liberal for rural, fundamentalist, increasingly Republican Arkansas—at thirty-four, Clinton joked, now "the youngest ex-governor in the nation's history." He then turned right again, winning in 1982, 1984, 1986, and, after a governor's term became four years, 1990—a decade of education reform, ethics controversy, and Bill having found the Chicago Cubs endearing—the team, to quote longtime announcer Jack Brickhouse, of those "born to suffer."

For this occurrence, blame or credit must reside with Clinton's wife Hillary, originally from suburban Chicago, and an old friend from KMOX Radio. The old friend was Harry Caray. For Hillary, such attribution was a fate to which she had already become accustomed. As a child, Bill liked play-by-play's rhythmic tissue between a team and its public. Hillary did too, hearing such Cubs play-by-play or color voices as Brickhouse, Lou Boudreau, Jack Quinlan, Vince Lloyd, and later Caray. On WGN-TV Harry's audience topped even his Cardinals' peak, beamed by satellite from Alaska to Key West. On the road he saw banners reading or half-drunk patrons baying, "Hey Harry!" or "Holy Cow!" or "It might be! It could be! It is!"

"I'm bigger than ever," Caray said, honestly if immodestly, despite a stroke in his sixties that slowed speech and mangled surnames after a glorious 1950s through '70s Everest. Small matter; as a friend said, Harry at 50 percent was "more entertaining than any other Voice at a hundred." Cable technology flung the old warhorse into every corner of Chicago, then every state of the country. Wrote a newspaper a decade before his death in 1998: "The greatest show, no ifs or buts, is to hear . . . Caray going nuts."

Especially pleased was Arkansas's then First Lady, born into Cubdom, aware of her husband's youth, and seeing Bill accept the Cardinals' bête noire gradually, like adding one religion to another. Unsurprisingly, his approach to baseball was sensory, not statistical. Caray's attraction was one example. Another: his devotion as governor to watching daughter Chelsea, born in 1980, the Clintons' only child, play softball for the Molar Rollers in the Little Rock Hillcrest Softball League. Formed by parents because daughters, unlike sons, lacked organized sports, the league yearly asked Hillary, as the governor's wife, to throw out the first ball. Until 1992, when the presidency turned all-consuming, Bill attended a clear majority of games.

Clinton could normally be found at almost any time talking politics, already his party's strategic seer. According to *The Presidents' Game*, Dad's sole distraction, friends agreed, was Chelsea, playing softball. James "Skip" Rutherford, a longtime friend whose daughter was her teammate, recalled a 1990 game in which he found Clinton behind the backstop screen, the governor studying the field like a Busch Stadium season-ticket holder. Rutherford tried to talk politics, usually as natural to Bill as breath. Implausibly Skip found no taker, Clinton wanting to talk ball.

"We're playing terrible defense," Rutherford recited Clinton's pain. "I asked him . . . again, and he said the same thing—'We're playing terrible defense.' . . . He hadn't even heard me, he was so wrapped up in the game." Finally Clinton said something else, asking Rutherford what he was doing that weekend. "I said, 'I don't know.' And he said,

'Let's have a good practice.'" Rutherford had then to remind him that neither of them was a team coach.

It must have been hard for Clinton to be so dutiful about Chelsea before running for president. He was now a leader among New Democrats, a group tired of losing forty-nine states in 1972 and 1984, choosing nominees like George McGovern and Walter Mondale, and having the party viewed as sympathetic to draft dodgers, flag burners, deadbeats, and "welfare queens," a term coined by Ronald Reagan. The capital's Democratic orthodoxy was killing them at home. Clinton's 1980 reelection humiliation stemmed from being viewed as closer to Tip O'Neill, Jane Fonda, and bicoastal donors than to the people who elected him. He never forgot the lesson.

As governor, Clinton presaged his "Third Way" as president—common sense between extremes. Skeptics hooted. Was it pose or philosophy? Neither, Bill said—instead, reality to fix a state education system then rated worst in America. He let Hillary chair a new education standards committee, waited for brickbats, then called a special legislative session—the longest in state history—that passed reforms: more spending overall for gifted children, vocational education, course variety, teacher salaries, and compulsory teacher competency exams. In time, the state education system ranked among America's elect.

In 1985 Clinton gave his party's response to Reagan's State of the Union Address, then, moving upstairs, served as 1986–87 chair of the National Governors Association. By comparison conflict of interest charges rose about state business and the Rose Law Firm, at which Mrs. Clinton partnered. A U.S. Securities and Exchange Commission probe after the Clintons left Little Rock led to the conviction of associates in the Whitewater Development Corporation, in which Bill and Hillary lost money.

After Clinton announced for the Democratic nomination for president, Hillcrest Softball League officials doubted that Hillary could make Opening Day, but mailed an invitation. To her credit, she came, tossed, and as usual saw many of Chelsea's games in 1992. The PA voice said, "Next year we're going to throw out the first ball on the lawn of the White House." Many people at the White House laughed. They did not laugh last.

At the time the White House seemed as remote a prospect for the Clintons as a computer in a home in Bangor, Maine, being linked to a computer in another home in Bangkok, Thailand. Later Bill called such a connection an "Information Super-Highway." He got that right—the Internet. When he guested in 1992 on the late-night *Arsenio Hall Show*, the would-be hipster bad boy from Hot Springs wearing sun glasses and grooving on his saxophone, I thought it benign but irrelevant, never imagining the program would consolidate support. Around such subjects do we deliberate today's leader of the free world.

That February Clinton lost to George H. W. Bush in a two-way Market Opinion Research matchup, 50 to 38 percent, but had a 43 to 25 percent favorable to unfavorable rating. Losing the Iowa caucus, he finished second in New Hampshire, dubbing himself "the Comeback Kid." Clinton's first national exposure mentioned a woman, Gennifer Flowers, who claimed an alleged affair. The governor denied it on television's *60 Minutes* with Hillary, who said she was unlike singer Tammy Wynette, twanging "Stand by Your Man." Then she did, impugning a "vast right-wing conspiracy." Each spouse scored claims by other women of sexual harassment, Clinton soon flanking the Democratic field. Relaxed, he often played softball with the media—the first Boomer presidential nominee and eventually president: depending on how you view the 1960s, a mirror of creative or toxic culture.

By June 1992 a Gallup Poll showed Clinton behind third-party candidate Ross Perot and Bush. Chapter 13 shows Perot hurting both, especially the president. On July 9 Clinton chose Tennessee senator Al Gore as his running mate. Improbably that week Perot, still leading Gallup's three-way trial, withdrew, saying that staying in the race with a "revitalized Democratic Party" would cause the election to be decided in the House of Representatives! Clinton's nomination acceptance speech vowed to seal a "New Covenant" with America—and to heal the GOP economic gap between the rich and poor. Politically the talk glowed. The biblical term "covenant" lured evangelicals—an anchor of the 1988 Republican victory. The income gap addressed another GOP vulnerability—blue-collar Reagan Democrats. The session in New York spurred a thirty-point convention "bounce," a modern polling high. With Perot momentarily gone, Republicans adrift, and Gore mixing Boomer synergy, Clinton took a 24 percent lead.

From their convention Clinton and Gore began a bus tour around the country, the sound system blaring Fleetwood Mac's "Don't Stop [Thinking about Tomorrow]." For more than a quarter century the Democrats' major flaw had been a perceived or real leftist tilt. Accordingly, Clinton's aim was to seem a candidate Middle America might buy. Proactive, he scored Sister Souljah, a rap musician, for sewer lyrics. The bus tour gave Clinton another chance to appear centrist by backing the death penalty and uniforms in public schools. Officially the Bush campaign said that every major-party nominee got a "bounce" from his convention. Unofficially Bush referenced Clinton's tour and how the nominee conceded he had smoked marijuana—but not inhaled. "People ask me why my opponent keeps saying the things he does," said the president. "Maybe he's been inhaling too many bus fumes."

Behind by double digits, Bush tried in the first three-way presidential debate to knock Clinton out. Instead his strategy hit the ropes. The incumbent attacked Clinton for what he did as a Rhodes Scholar at Oxford University in the late 1960s: organize Vietnam War demonstrations "against [his] own country on foreign land [London]," charged Bush. "When young men are held prisoner in Hanoi or kids out of the ghetto [are] drafted. . . . it's not a question of patriotism, it's a question of character and judgment." Expecting the assault, Clinton responded personally: "When Joe McCarthy went around this country attacking people's patriotism, he was wrong . . . and a Senator from Connecticut stood up to him, named Prescott Bush. . . . Your father was right to stand up to Joe McCarthy. You were wrong to attack my patriotism. I was opposed to the war, but I love my country."

Bush could have blistered Clinton for using his father, dead twenty years ago that month, as a prop. Instead he replied defensively: "I have to correct one thing. I didn't question the man's patriotism," only his character. "What he did in Moscow [Clinton visited there as a student], that's fine. Let him explain it. . . . What I don't accept is demonstrating and organizing demonstrations in a foreign country when your country's at war. I'm sorry. I cannot accept that." Would voters? CNN/USA TO-

DAY found that after the debate 47 percent named the reentered Perot the victor; 30, Clinton; 16, Bush. Four days later the trio traded a lectern for a "town hall" format—the first presidential debate with stools and an open stage, encircled by an audience, the crowd and moderator questioning. The issues were domestic only—Clinton's forte. In the CNN/USA TODAY poll, 58 percent named the governor best while 16 percent named Bush and 15 percent Perot.

The last debate, on October 19, resembled bumper cars along the boards trying to permanently demobilize one another. Perot used psychological projection to charge the GOP with raising "dirty tricks" to a "sick art form." Bush said that Clinton would repeat "what it was like when we had a spending President and a spending Congress and interest rates . . . at 21.5 percent under Carter." Clinton artfully one-upped 41: "I will not raise [middle-class] taxes. . . . Furthermore, I am not going to tell you to 'read my lips.'" In the end "Slick Willie," a name born in Arkansas, returned to "It's the economy, stupid" and Bush's "No new taxes" and a pledge not to fixate on foreign policy. Said Clinton: "In that first debate, Mr. Bush made some news" by announcing that James Baker would oversee domestic policy. "Well, I'll tell you, the person responsible for domestic policy in my administration will be Bill Clinton." Bush: "That's what worries me."

As in the first debate, CNN/USA TODAY gave Perot the nod: 38 percent against 28 percent for both Bush and Clinton. Election day stalked the White House, time—fifteen days—slip-sliding away. By now, the Republican electoral lock, dominant as recently as 1988, seemed as ancient as a daguerreotype. Clinton led by double digits, having New England, the industrial Northeast, the formerly GOP West Coast, and much of the Midwest in the bag. Bush would have to draw his late aide Lee Atwater's "inside straight"—a combination of upset states and historically Republican states that never should have thought of leaving the Grand Old Party. He visited Georgia, the Carolinas, and Kentucky, where Clinton seemed increasingly convincing, and Louisiana, which had a history of backing rogues.

It was hard to define even at the time the clang of noise and dream and caffeine and anguish that is a U.S. presidential campaign. Celebrities enlist for reasons noble or selfish, personal or public, worry about the future or calculus about a career. In Reagan's age in Hollywood some were actually Republican: John Wayne, Ward Bond, Olivia de Havilland, Gabby Hayes, Walter Pidgeon. Today GOP-leaning singers and actors largely cloister in country music. On October 28, 1992, Bruce Willis and the Oak Ridge Boys joined George Bush, who said on election eve, "These Oak Ridge Boys are really great. I wish you could have been with us on the plane—every single one of you. I wish you could have heard these guys singing those beautiful gospel songs. . . . Not a dry eye in the house."

All fall, rabid thirty- and sixty-minute infomercials boosted Perot's support near 20 percent. Bush's frantic campaigning—five states in one day—brought him within single digits. Then on Friday, October 30, Lawrence Walsh—Columbia Law School graduate, Thomas Dewey protégé, ex-GOP deputy attorney general, and American Bar Association head named independent counsel in charge of the 1986 Iran-Contra investigation—sprung a Halloween surprise. Walsh reindicted former defense secretary Caspar Weinberger on one count of "false statements," implicating Bush, though his accusation was irrelevant to the indictment. Clinton administration attorney Lanny Davis later called the decision to indict before, not after, the election "bizarre." Poppy said, "We had momentum—the crowds, the polls, character as the issue"—until Walsh halted his last-week comeback and "put the last nail in our campaign."

By late morning election day, talking to on-site officials, I knew that New Jersey and Ohio—thus the election—were gone. Clinton's final Ohio edge was 90,632; Perot's 1,036,426 total there largely white, conservative, and middle/working class. In ten other mostly Southern, some Northeast and Midwest, states, Perot's vote topped Clinton's margin over Bush. As it was, despite the recession, third party, an inept Bush high command, and GOP strategies changing faster than fortunes on Wall Street, Clinton got only 43 percent of the electorate, or 44,909,806 votes. Bush's 37.4 percent, or 39,104,550 votes, was the lowest total for an incumbent seeking reelection since William Howard Taft's 23.2 percent against TR and Woodrow Wilson in 1912. Inheriting many who refused to vote for either Bush or Clinton, Perot got 18.9 percent, or a third-party record 19,743,821.

According to CNN/USA TODAY polling, Perot drew more support from Bush conservatives than Clinton liberals, the Republican right-center base feeling deserted, as it would in the 2010s, showing its sense of betrayal then by backing Donald Trump. In 1992 Clinton led widely among unmarried men and women and narrowly among married. Two in ten whites favored Perot; the rest tied between Bush and Clinton. Minorities broke Democratic. White Protestants, nearly half the vote, liked Bush, 47–33 percent. Catholics and Jews favored Clinton, whose edge was also strong in age groups 17–29 and 60 and older. Bush led among college graduates. Bill fronted at the poles—among those who had not graduated and those with post-graduate schooling. Independents, moderates, Reagan Democrats—the GOP presidential majority washed away in the Clinton flood.

A political rite endearing even to a casual observer occurs election night: the loser speaks first; the winner, last. Clinton, his smile after Bush's concession call lighting Little Rock, appeared before a crowd that might have been heard in Houston. The president-elect began, "On this day, with high hopes and brave hearts, in massive numbers, the American people have voted to make a new beginning." The victor hailed "a clarion call" to address the economy, implied that he meant more than mere taxes and spending, and promised to "bring our nation together." He noted the thousands of fellow citizens a candidate would meet in a motorcade, before a speech, or in a noontime rally who simply said, "We want our future back." The crowd roared. Clinton paused, then said, "I intend to give it to you." Another roar, louder.

Finally, the youngest president-to-be since JFK thanked Bush for "his lifetime of public service" and "his generous and forthcoming telephone call" of concession. Poppy often said, "The definition of a successful life must include serving others." How that might happen after such a crushing loss was a question not without its mystery.

Within a week of Clinton's election, George Vecsey of the *New York Times* suggested his two priorities: "He [first] should pressure baseball to restore a meaningful commissionership and [second] revive a nationally televised game of the week on Saturday afternoons," killed by money-crazed owners, "or face some questions about baseball's cushy anti-trust exemptions." Sadly the forty-second president did neither. *Game of the Week* briefly revived in the late 1990s and early 2000s, was barely promoted, and died in 2016, regular-season baseball now seen almost as seldom as British soccer on U.S. network television. Meanwhile, its commissioners have almost made William Eckert look good. By contrast, Mrs. Clinton got her chance to throw out a first ball on the White House South Lawn.

The Clinton clan's 1993–2001 baseball schedule flaunted the type of big leaguers whom the president had imagined in his KMOX boyhood mind. On April 5, 1993, he did his first-ball duty at Baltimore's Oriole Park at Camden Yards, tossing from the mound to behind the plate; the Rangers won, 7–4. Clinton loved the park's pastiche of sharp quirk and odd angle; arched façade like old Comiskey Park; ivy backdrop; right-field scoreboard like Wrigley Field; and behind it the Eastern Seaboard's longest building. In 1996 the president returned to Camden's varied wall heights and distances—its *feel* as a "new old" park—to toss a first ball a second time: O's 4, Royals 2.

In 1994 Clinton inaugurated Jacobs (now Progressive) Field in Cleveland: Indians 4, Mariners 3. Perhaps he thought of postwar Tribe icons. Rocky Colavito would have liked the 325-foot left-field porch. Like the Rock, Al Rosen played too soon: left-center field at the new place measured just 368 feet. Pitcher Herb Score would have hailed the mini-Monster: a nineteen-foot-high wall tying the left-field pole and then 410-foot mark near center field. Ultimately Cleveland set an improbable then big-league record of 455 straight sellouts. In 1999 Hillary got her husband to visit Wrigley Field and root for a *new* home team: Cubbies 5, Brewers 4, the Clintons arriving in the fifth inning but early enough to see Sammy Sosa's game-winning belt.

Two years earlier baseball had created a memorial to a black American hero whose memory, like the monument, would last. As related earlier, on April 15, 1997 baseball permanently retired Jack Roosevelt Robinson's No. 42 on the half-century anniversary of his Major League debut. The observance was held before a game between two teams perhaps fated by history to play: the Dodgers and Mets at Shea Stadium; wife Rachel Robinson, her husband, and Acting Commissioner Bud Selig attended. A photo at the ceremony showed Jackie, knees bent, facing the pitcher, ready to dance off first.

When he sold the Dodgers to Walter O'Malley in 1950, owner Branch Rickey, the man who signed, counseled, and loved Robinson like a son, asked, "Comest thou [reporters] here to see the reed driveth in the wind?" Robinson was a rock, not reed. Each year the Dodgers barnstormed from their spring training camp in Vero Beach, Florida, back to Brooklyn, playing games in stops like Greensboro and Winston-Salem, where segregation ruled. Giants prospect Bill White had his bus stoned in rural Virginia. Jackie braved "colored only" restrooms and hotels. Proud of No. 42, black fans packed each park, celebrating.

Robinson felt responsible for himself and his race, said Vin Scully: "He also could not be bullied, a rarity who excelled when he was angry." After a pitcher tried to hit him, Jackie walked, stole second base, third base, and home. Without Rickey there was no Robinson. Without Jackie, there might have been no Rosa Parks. Bill Clinton's attitude toward Robinson differed little from George H. W. Bush's, seeking to give each American an equal chance at the starting line so that initiative and character could determine the finish line. Their presidencies differed in that Clinton's, like Barack Obama's, focused more on domestic than foreign policy. All found the presidency, like baseball, a marathon, as Clinton and the Orioles' Cal Ripken Jr. showed.

On Wednesday, September 6, 1995, ESPN visited Oriole Park for a most important game. Baseball had just emerged from a player-owner strike, needing help from such history as Cal's 2,131st consecutive game played, a number that passed Lou Gehrig's. Usually network ball-and-striker Jon Miller would call the match, but the voice also of the O's declined, calling it a national "game" but a Baltimore "thing." When Jon opted for Birds radio, Chris Berman did ESPN-TV, Miller his guest, wearing a tuxedo since Jon was to host ceremonies on the field.

Clinton was to join Jon on Orioles wireless in the fourth inning. An inning earlier Miller had run to the restroom "just to make sure

I was set." The plan exploded when the Secret Service, also assigned security for vice president Al Gore, blocked him trying to leave the restroom for the booth.

"I'm the broadcaster," Jon said. "I'm going to interview the president next inning."

"I don't think so," the agent said, making clear he was not a straight man for a Miller ad. "This huge night," Jon said, "me and the president and the booth might as well be in Boise."

Blessedly another Secret Service agent, an Orioles fan, then appeared. "Hey, let him through!" he said. "He's going to be interviewing the president." Passing agent number one, Miller tried not to rub it in.

Fourth inning: Clinton goes on the air, the count on Cal goes to 3-0, and Jon makes a little funny. "This night of all nights," he said. "He [Angels pitcher Shawn Boskie] can't be walking Cal, not in this game. Maybe you could send a presidential order down there ordering him to throw Cal a strike."

"I know one thing," the president said. "Cal wants to hit this pitch, but if it's not a strike he'll take the walk for the good of the team because that's the kind of guy he is."

"That's very true," Jon said. "On the other hand, if he [Boskie] grooves one, even on three and oh . . ."

"Oh, well," said Clinton, "then Cal'll hit it a long way."

At that moment Cal swings—and *boom*! Home run! Jon starts describing it, but Clinton, with his own microphone, began yelling, "Go! Go! Yes! Ah-ha!" The president is clapping his hands, shouting into the mic, and helping to call the homer! What does Miller do? He can't grab Clinton's mic away—so Jon becomes background noise, his voice almost disembodied.

"The bad news was that it kinda put me off, because this was a major moment in baseball history," Jon continued, tongue in cheek, "but the good news mattered more. He was the President of the United States. The First Fan. He's reflecting the excitement of the night better than any broadcaster could." Plus, Miller thought, "I could now put on my resume, 'Worked with President Bill Clinton, a very close friend.'"

At the end of the top half of the fifth inning, the game now official, applause rocked the adjacent warehouse. Cal repeatedly tipped his cap, Rafael Palmeiro and Bobby Bonilla finally pulled him from the dugout, and Ripken circled the ballpark, high-fiving and handshaking. Many forget how divisive that age was. Clinton fueled eight years of peace and prosperity, welfare reform, and growing trade, but polarization, an affair-turned-cause-célèbre, and impeachment largely for private conduct judged irresponsible by the nation left an electorate cleaved. Ripken became the perfect player in an imperfect time.

Clinton and Miller fit like missing pieces in completing the jigsaw of Ripken's historic night: at the time each the finest (non-Scully) communicator in his field. Both the president and Jon knew that rhetoric means storytelling. Depending upon the occasion, each could be huckster, reporter, cornball self, or personality in the flesh. Clinton would have been a knockout big-league announcer. Miller loved politics' theater but would have hated its brutality. Clinton's Ripken riff drew wide applause, a precursor of his 1996 reelection, pleasing Jon, a great admirer of the forty-second president and, as we all know, "a very close friend."

On January 22, 1993, the most masterly politician to take the oath since Lyndon Johnson began his term with a bow to his base. Two days after Clinton's inaugural—twenty *years* since the U.S. Supreme Court landmark decision on abortion in *Roe v. Wade*—he reversed restrictions on family planning started by Reagan or Bush. Two weeks later the Arkansan signed the Family and Medical Leave Act of 1993, making large employers give workers unpaid leave for pregnancy or a serious medical condition. Clinton's economic plan cut the deficit, not taxes. A national health care reform plan ensured universal coverage. Directed by Mrs. Clinton, the campaign attacked conservatives, the health insurance industry, and even the American Medical Association before dying in August 1994. Antipodally, liberalism triumphed in Clinton's appointment of Supreme Court justices Ruth Bader Ginsburg and Stephen Breyer in 1993 and 1994 respectively.

"Don't ask, Don't Tell" became a compromise to let gays serve in the armed services if they kept their sexuality a secret—and the military didn't pry. In Washington, as in Little Rock, Clinton hyped a "Third Way"—here, between his party's center and liberal wing, the latter more dominant each year. The president signed the Defense of Marriage Act (DOMA) in 1996, defining marriage as the legal union of one man and one woman, letting states refuse to recognize gay marriages performed in other states—"heading off," Clinton said, "an attempt to send a constitutional amendment banning gay marriage to the states," a possibility he called "highly likely in the context of a very reactionary Congress." Clinton's strategy was astute, reversing himself on gay marriage—against, then for it. His path was identical on DOMA—against, then for, then urging the U.S. Supreme Court to overturn the law, which it did in 2013.

Clinton the free-trader signed NAFTA. The domestic centrist inked the Omnibus Crime Bill to swell the death penalty, yet also signed the Brady Bill to mandate a waiting period on handgun purchases. Clinton the internationalist deployed American peacekeepers to Bosnia and to Somalia on a UN humanitarian mission, where an urban battle killed eighteen U.S. soldiers. The would-be peacemaker tried vainly for eight years as president to capture terrorist Osama bin Laden—also to preserve the union of Palestinian Authority chairman Yasser Arafat and Israel's then prime minister, notably 1999–2001's Ehud Barak, to seek what Clinton called a "just and lasting peace." In his autobiography Clinton blamed Arafat for the collapse of the Arab-Israeli summit after he, Arafat, and Barak convened in 2000 at Camp David.

Even in baseball Clinton tried to emulate Isaiah: "Come, let us reason together." The strike that Ripken did his best to counter had blacked out baseball from August 12, 1994, till April 2, 1995—canceling a World Series for the first time since 1904, aborting each season, and undoing both's records. In 1990, 61 percent of CBS-TV poll respondents said that they cared about baseball; 39 percent did in a similar 1994 poll. Worried about a sport he had enjoyed since youth, Clinton, like former president Carter, offered to mediate between owners and players. Sure they knew best, each side declined, the strike lasting a record 232 days. America took a long time to forgive, attendance and TV ratings falling. Baseball rivaled the Flying Dutchman, seeking Port Common Sense.

For a while some found Clinton's sense lacking too. In 1994 Republicans took both houses of Congress for the first time since 1952—a thumbed nose at the big government of Clinton's first half-term. Moving right, Clinton ran in 1996 against U.S. Senate Majority Leader Bob Dole, a product of a hard-knock youth, military service, and moderate impulse. Severely injured in World War II, an arm shattered by German machine gun fire, Dole valiantly manifested the Greatest Generation. Hipper, newer, Clinton won easily, 49.2–40.7 percent, his "Third Way" effective. The first Democratic president since FDR to be elected more than once looked, if not invincible, at the top of his game.

By this time, wafting through Clinton's opposition and the press, especially but not limited to Little Rock, was a problem of which many had long been at least vaguely aware: the president's casual relationship with self-discipline. Repeated charges of several liaisons before his arrival in the capital went nowhere. In 1992 Gennifer Flowers stated her involvement with him went as far back as 1980. Much of the media found the charges old hat—and if true, the accuser's fault. Three women brought four suits against Clinton for alleged sexual harassment, rape, and groping. They included Paula Jones, who brought a lawsuit in 1994 and whose lawyers in 1998 released court documents claiming a pattern of sexual harassment when Clinton was governor and that his main lawyer, Robert Bennett, dubbed "a pack of lies."

Increasingly America was transfixed, if not transcended, by the possibility of another U.S. president to be impeached after Andrew Johnson, based on charges that Clinton, then forty-nine, had illegally lied and concealed a 1995–96 relationship with White House intern Monica Lewinsky, twenty-two. The GOP-controlled House found that Clinton may have committed perjury in a sworn deposition in Jones's lawsuit and cited a cause: an alleged effort to hide the affair with Lewinsky during and after his deposition. To many, it became Shakespeare's "stain that will not out," like Watergate with Nixon or Vietnam with LBJ.

After the 1998 election the House impeached Clinton, charging him with perjury and obstruction of justice related to the Lewinsky scandal. The Senate voted to acquit, the episode leaving Washington profoundly depressed: by Clinton's behavior; people on the make like

Lewinsky, doing anything to get ahead; and each party's initial reaction, instinctively sliming the other. Clinton deftly survived, having grown up, said friends, as an amalgam of two warring sides: "Saturday Night Bill," hitting Hot Springs's hot spots, and "Sunday Morning Bill," singing hymns and knowing scripture.

Retrieve January 2001. Clinton left office with a 68 percent approval, tying FDR and Reagan as the highest-rated postwar president. Then fast-forward to a postlude to the 1992 campaign that few expected to see. In the decade after leaving office, Clinton published his memoir *My Life*, dedicated the William J. Clinton Presidential Center and Park, and founded the William J. Clinton Foundation to address such "international causes" as AIDS and global warming. After the 2004 Asian tsunami and 2005 Hurricane Katrina, he also joined George H. W. Bush to form the Bush-Clinton Tsunami Fund and Bush-Clinton Katrina Fund. In 2009 Clinton became United Nations Special Envoy. In the wake of Haiti's 2010 earthquake, President Obama named Clinton and Bush to coordinate raising funds. This each was pleased to do since to everyone's amazement but their own, Poppy had become Bill's amigo.

The bulletin of the pair's friendship had initially shocked and even appalled staffers of each former president—more partisan than either. *How could he?* was the question, yielding to *Why not?* Ex-presidents *should* unite, not divide. After a while Clinton spent so much time with the Bushes that Barbara called him "our son," and Bill termed himself "the black sheep in the Bush family." Forty-one delighted in 42's company. Asked about their buddy system, Clinton invoked his predecessor's "capacity for giving and receiving love": "I guess it's surprising because we opposed one another, but George Bush is a man I love"—grace typical of a former president who called Elton John's lovely "Your Song" his *favorite* song. When, braving bronchitis described earlier, George H. W. Bush was hospitalized at eighty-eight, among the callers was his successor.

In 1990, invited to speak at all-women's Wellesley College, Barbara Bush was criticized for defining herself through her husband, not her resume. Adeptly she calmed a student backlash, quipping "I was once twenty myself," discussing family and career, and saying that perhaps one day a member of the audience might follow her path—"and I wish *him* well!" That person—to be called "First Gentleman," who knows?—was almost Bill Clinton. In 2008 his wife contested Barack Obama for the Democratic presidential nod, losing but finding her voice as Joe Six Pack's Joan of Arc. In Kentucky Hillary swilled local whiskey. In West Virginia she became a pitchfork tribune of the working class. But was it *real*? No one knew until 2016, when Mrs. Clinton again ran as the choice of the Democratic Establishment, Obama's heir apparent.

Hillary Clinton will reenter our narrative in 2016's clash with Donald Trump. Certainly, the planets seemed aligned. She had been New York's junior U.S. senator, frequent-flying secretary of state, and a bicoastal favorite. She was said by those who knew her to possess courage, tenacity, and loyalty. Moreover, she was lucky—*had* to be to get Trump as her opponent. He had little grasp of detail, was prone to err, used vulgarity in public, and seemed to some to be a clown without being funny.

Only the most stunning coda in the American political storybook could keep Hillary from becoming president, which is what election night 2016 composed. The verdict is still out about why she lost—Mrs. Clinton has spent ample time explaining it—as well as whether she will run again. Bill Clinton may never be the nation's first "First Gentleman" after all. But after what the Clintons have done, had done to them, and still survived, if there is a political family to which the maxim "Never say never" applies, it must surely be them.

Bill Clinton's birth year, 1946, was among the most unanswerable in the history of his boyhood team, Country Slaughter speeding like a fire truck to score from first base on a double in Game Seven of the World Series to give the Running Redbirds a 4–3 game and title. They had made the Fall Classic by taking baseball's first best-of-three playoff against Brooklyn to win the NL pennant—their ninth as opposed to the seven other NL teams' twelve in the last twenty-one years. By comparison, St. Louis's next flag broke a hiatus of *eighteen* years, in 1964, when the Yale-bound Clinton turned eighteen and Harry Caray aired the Series on NBC TV. "That's some hiatus," a writer mused about the contrast. "Bill should have been born earlier" or a bit later, the Cardinals next winning the pennant and the Classic in 1967.

The Yankees, of course, were baseball's Cadillac throughout—in particular, manager Casey Stengel's 1949–53 Stripes, whose nonpareil five straight World Series titles gilded a time of sixteen teams, two leagues, win your pennant and go to the Classic, or don't and go home. After the mid-1960s they stayed home in October as if Pop had taken the car keys and the Yankees couldn't bum a ride.

In 1996 the Bombers won their first Series since 1978 and only their third since 1962. A year later they might have won again save a rare postseason homer yielded by future Hall of Fame reliever Mariano Rivera against Cleveland in the American League Division Series. The 2000 Yanks extended their *latest* dynasty to four world titles in the last five years by winning a third straight Series, having also triumphed in 1998 and 1999.

In the dugout and on, above, and beyond the field, the Yankees became the *Yankees* again in Clinton's presidency. First the ultimate mid-century player on the ultimate team in America's then ultimate game died—Mickey Mantle. Then a beloved star from Stengel's first dynasty left the Stripes TV booth—Phil Rizzuto. Finally, a man who resembled Clinton in approach and background revived their dynasty as manager—Joe Torre.

In Ike's and JFK's America, Mantle was more idolized than any president, athlete, astronaut, or actor but a few—America's poster boy before the fall. Every October but twice Clinton saw his Yankees in the World Series from 1951 through 1964. Said Stengel of the three-time MVP, "Mantle was better on one leg than anybody else on two."

In 1994 No. 7, a longtime alcoholic, was interviewed by Bob Costas in what was later seen as a sum up and farewell. "If I had known [I would live longer], I would have taken better care of myself," Mantle said. By then he had gone dry, slowed a fast-lane life, and urged, "Kids, please don't be like me." Mick was warm and penitent.

Bob's NBC show pealed love. As his childhood hero talked, Costas thought "of standing holding [his] father's hand in deepest center field at Yankee Stadium and saying to him, 'Is this where Mickey Mantle plays? Is this where he stands? Can Mickey Mantle throw a ball from here all the way to home plate? Can Mickey Mantle hit a ball here?'"

A year later the Achilles Okie was admitted to a Texas hospital, dying of alcoholism August 13, 1995, at sixty-three. Costas spoke at a memorial in Dallas, Mick's home. "We wanted to crease our caps like him, kneel in an imaginary on-deck circle like him, run like him, heads down, elbows up," said Bob, who hadn't known the eulogy would be telecast. "All I wanted was for it to be worthy of the family."

Costas was mobbed by passersby returning to New York, where a former mate of Mantle's had been especially moved by the service's sense of life's final out. It "just hit me," said Phil Rizzuto, the Yanks' 1941–42 and 1946–56 shortstop and 1957–96 broadcaster. Smaller than the game, the 5-foot-6 Phil made baseball seem larger than it was. He was named "Scooter" by a player who said, "Man, you're not runnin', you're scootin.'"

At sixteen, Phil was cut by the Giants and Dodgers, phoned the Yankees, signed, and began at Bassett, Virginia. "Bassett!" he said. "Sounds like I'm swearing at somebody." In 1941 several Stripe vets gave Rizzuto a cold shoulder. Hurt, he approached a Bombers pitcher. "They're not snubbing you," lefthander Lefty Gomez mused, "they just haven't seen you." He became hard to miss, bunting, hitting, or with the glove. "My best pitch," said another pitcher, righty Vic Raschi, "is anything the batter grounds, lines, or pops in his direction."

Released in 1956, Scooter next year joined radio/TV's Mel Allen and Red Barber, thinking himself "a thorn between two roses." By the 1960s the now lead voice might fill an inning, wrote the *New York Times*' George Vecsey, with birthday greetings to "movie reviews, golf tips, war memories, fearsome predictions of . . . thunder" to critiques on allergies and insects. One day a devoted listener, Carmel DiPaolo, ninety, wrote a letter. Phil replied, wanting to do so "before it [was] too late": "She might not be with us the whole game"—going to bed or the great beyond, Phil didn't say.

In 1994 Rizzuto belatedly made Cooperstown as a player. He and wife Cora took a trip to Europe, where at the Vatican, Pope Paul II changed his schedule for an audience—"as close to God," said Phil, "as you can get." It is doubtful that Phil termed the Pope "a huckleberry!"—Scooter's favorite phrase—though he borrowed and venerated Caray's trademark "Holy Cow!" For five decades, bad game, good game, Rizzuto meant a fun game: baseball's *paisan* with pizzazz.

Some people are born to do certain things. Franklin D. Roosevelt was born to be president, Ethel Merman to shatter glass, and Scooter to make us smile. In New York they will tell you that a fellow *paisan* of the Scooter's was born to manage the Yankees. Before winning victory after victory for baseball's most famous franchise, Joe Torre won a more important victory, over himself. Like Bill Clinton, Joe grew up in a dysfunctional family, with a hard father in the home, taunted by weight and bigotry outside it, insecure but dogged.

Take two students. Assume, Torre said, that one got A's and the other C's. Joe felt a kinship with "the kid getting the C's" because "he is probably trying harder." Torre learned to hate strife in boyhood, fear of the world finally dimming after success as a player; failure managing the Braves, Mets, and Cardinals; glory leading the Stripes; and beating prostate cancer. Having risen and fallen and risen again, Torre became baseball's Saint Joe, remaining, he said, "the person I needed to be." Like Clinton, who said, "I feel your pain," Joe felt the pain of others, having felt *his* from the start.

In one unlikelihood, Torre came to Yankee Stadium the year the Scooter retired from its broadcast booth—1996. In another, each, destined to wear pinstriped underwear, was born in Brooklyn! Teams once went directly from a pennant to a World Series. (Joe won six and four respectively.) Today's manager must win three series—a much steeper climb. In 1958 Stengel only had to win ninety-two games in the regular season and four in a seven-game Series. In 1998 Torre won 125 games, including three postseason series—the last, a Classic sweep.

This most unaverage Joe won his last Stripes pennant in 2003. In 2007 corporate suits forced the resignation of arguably the greatest skipper in big-league history, making postseason *all twelve* seasons in the Bronx. After three years managing at Dodger Stadium, Joe himself became a suit in 2011 as baseball's executive vice president of baseball operations, where, for better or worse, he helped author instant replay.

Numbers judge between the lines. Joe's genius went beyond. He massaged George Steinbrenner—the Boss—a mix of P. T. Barnum, Phineas T. Bluster, and a pre-presidential Donald Trump. The ultimate players' manager insulated them from a crazed fandom and 24/7 Apple media. Inducted at Cooperstown, Torre joined such Stripes skippers as Miller Huggins, Joe McCarthy, and Stengel. The Yankees retired his No. 6, prompting debate. Greatest skipper ever? Some say it *is* so, Joe.

Merman was once asked if Broadway had been good to her. "Yes," mused the great singer, "but then I've been good to Broadway." The Yankees were an estimated $50 million in salary good to Torre. He was even better to the Yankees, putting a human face on a haughty franchise, even as Bill Clinton put a human face on an often impersonal, if not haughty, institution.

Envision Torre as president, governing more like Clinton than any other peer. Like a painter or politician, every manager has a unique bloodline. Torre's supernatural ability to relate was almost Clintonian. Similarly, Bill would have echoed Joe as skipper: media-directed; office door open; players free to talk; his temper redolent of Tom Lasorda, tutoring an ump.

A cynic might snipe that Bill Clinton *caused* much of his suffering while Torre *inherited* his. In fact, the former president overcame much, starting in his youth. As Harry Truman proved in 1948, America loves a fighter. "Holy Cow!" No one can deny Clinton that.

FIFTEEN

W.

George W. Bush, 2001–2009

In 1994 George W. Bush, the forty-first president's eldest son of four, was elected governor of Texas, perhaps thinking it a consolation prize. The Texas Rangers co-owner and president would have enjoyed being named baseball commissioner, having called Willie Mays his favorite boyhood player, deemed ESPN's *Baseball Tonight* his favorite television show, and managed an extreme makeover of his 1989–94 franchise. We met in 1990, a decade before his presidency. I was then a speechwriter to his father, knowing that the future Bush 43 had shed alcohol after years of heavy use; that even many cool to W. politically liked what a friend termed his "Everyman kind of vibe"; and that he was said to know ball like an insider—its politics, history, inner workings, and strategy.

The son entered my office in the old Eisenhower Executive Office Building hard by the West Wing wearing a knotted tie, shirt and suit, and cowboy boots. We met to talk a little ball, since I had written about the decidedly erratic condition of baseball's broadcast state. We began with family, as Texans are wont to do, W. rightly hailing his mother's "genius with the media." Barbara Bush's White House staff impressed me with its courtesy and quality—the class we seldom see any more, aping the First Couple's lack of pretense and condescension. I hoped that potential successors were taking notes.

Our next tie was the 1962 expansion Houston Colt .45s (later Astros). As a child in Upstate New York, I heard them over WWL New

Orleans, the Gibraltar of their Colt .45s radio network, feeling like I had reached Timbuktu. Bush grew up equating their and other baseball cards with liturgy. He also caught and pitched for his west Texas Little League and New England prep school teams, could still name the 1958 Cardinals infield, and conceded to having "felt like a man" when told by Poppy that playing catch Dad would no longer throw slow stuff disguised as heat.

In 1989, with $600,000 of his own, the "man" led a group of twenty-six to invest $34,000,000 to acquire 54 percent of the Rangers. As co-owner, he fueled funding for The Ballpark at Arlington, which opened in 1994. He was "protecting his investment," said political guru Karl Rove—also Bush's and millions' final tie—the '50s culture of his youth, where to be a real American meant loving the American game.

"People believed in the American Dream," W. said of the postwar boom. "Folks from other states were all neighbors. We'd go to barbecues, help each other out. The four [Bush] boys played baseball. Dad was involved in coaching." Like Sr., he called Barbara "among the great car-poolers of all time." In the White House she never drove a car.

W. was born July 6, 1945, in New Haven, Connecticut, the eldest of six children. As the reader knows, his younger sister Robin was diagnosed with leukemia in 1953 at the age of three. George was not quite eight. He played with Robin, loved and looked after her, marveled at her bravery. After she died, both parents were devastated, but Dad had work to divert, even own, him; Barbara, a housewife, had memory—and loss.

On his own, George Jr. decided he must shield her, be a salve as well as son. When Barbara learned why W. hadn't left the house to play with friends, she broke down, feeling guilty that she had made her burden his. The surface cutup was protecting a greater investment than even baseball—familial love.

With Dad trekking the oil fields as an independent wildcatter, running for the U.S. Senate as a Republican in Lyndon Johnson's 1964 avalanche, winning a house seat from Houston in 1966 and 1968, and almost sure to run again for the Senate in 1970, W. had a chance, if nothing else, to compare private and public school. He attended Midland, Texas, public school through seventh grade, and the next two grades at Kinkaid Prep School in Houston. Like his father, George Jr. graduated from then all-male Phillips Academy at Andover, Massachusetts, playing baseball, albeit briefly. Unlike Dad, W. was head cheerleader his senior year. He did undergraduate work at Yale, getting a BA in history in 1968, then earned his MBA from Harvard Business School in 1975.

Through the 1970s and 1980s W.'s plunge into Texas Tea created many small independent oil companies, including Bush Exploration. Likely George's best decision was his marriage in 1977 to Laura Welch, also thirty, a schoolteacher and librarian who stabilized him emotionally, calm to his kinetic. In 1978 he lost a congressional election to Democrat Kent Hance, who accused Bush of not grasping rural Texas—increasingly a GOP redoubt. In 1981 the Bushes had fraternal twins, Barbara and Jenna, an event the senior Bushes greeted with unallayed applause.

By contrast, as Rangers boss, W. rarely found early applause at all. The *Fort Worth Star-Telegram*'s Randy Galloway thought him "a total smart-ass who didn't have a clue about baseball." To Rangers GM Tom Grieve, Bush was a "spoiled brat who thinks he runs the world because of his last name." Like politics, baseball bred nicknames. W.'s emerged as "Shrub," a snide derivative of "Bush." Still, George believed it could aid the "kinder, gentler" tone Pop's inaugural address had summoned. Of the businessman/romantic, the *Wall Street Journal* mused, "He does not think that America would be America without baseball."

Arguably, what Bush tongue-in-cheek called his "worst mistake in or out of office" occurred that first year with the Rangers: the 1989 swap of slugger Sammy Sosa to the White Sox. Nine years later Sosa, now a Cub, and the Cardinals' Mark McGwire staged an epic homerthon that even a later revelation of drug use did not erase. It is fair to say that for a time 1998 spectacularly revived the pastime. "What a record-assaulting home run-blasting summer," *Sports Illustrated* wrote. The Great Race against Babe Ruth's and Roger Maris's single-season homer mark of sixty and sixty-one in 154 and 162 games respectively greased a Greater Feud. "Forget other rivalries," Cubs voice Pat Hughes said. "The best is Cardinals-Cubs." The race would have stirred anyway. The rivalry made it throb. "Daily pressure rose," said Hughes about calling number sixty-two. Like Milo Hamilton airing Hank Aaron's number 715, Pat neared the final month determined to be fresh, not scripted.

At 8:18 p.m. Central Time, September 8, at Busch Stadium, St. Louis's then Bunyan lashed the Cubs' Steve Trachsel's first pitch. "Drives one to deep left—this could be—it's a home run! Number 62 for Mark McGwire!" Hughes waxed. "A slice of history and a magical moment in St. Louis. A line drive home run to left for Mark McGwire of the St. Louis Cardinals!" W. was most attractive when he shelved jock-talk sarcasm to recall history like this—or his self-deprecatory golden age at Yale. Down by ten runs late in a game, bullpen battered, the Bulldogs had only one pitcher warming up. Reaching the mound, their skipper saw who it was: Bush! Trying to buy time, he signaled the pen while talking to the umpire about everything else. "Finally, with no choice, the manager makes a decision I hadn't counted on. He calls for the second baseman to come on to pitch. Talk about humiliation," W. laughed.

Bush's interest in the Rangers gave him a new career as the face of a historic franchise, the former Washington Senators moving south and west—the opportunity "perfect for a hail-fellow-met [person]," said the *Washington Post*'s Dana Milbank, "with a barbed, cynical sense of humor. The new [person] needs to be young, able to communicate and focus on a problem, not become diffused by the extraneous and the trend." Granting that baseball had "made [W.] a regular guy—not a president's son from Andover, Yale, and Harvard but someone who spit sunflower seeds while hobnobbing with the on-deck batter," Milbank asked what qualified W. for office. Step one was to show himself to be a leader—Jr.'s version of "the vision thing."

W. helped build the Rangers' first AL Western Division or any title in 1994 (first place at the season-ending players lockout a.k.a. strike), 1996, and 1998–99. "They leave DC in 1960 for Minneapolis," a then staffer said. "A new Senators club arrives, just as bad, and they leave in 1971. What a loser. That changed with George." Most said their rise occurred *under* Bush. Some felt it happened *because* of Bush. Wife Laura felt it showed "the almost mystical way baseball fits overall into American life, how he talked to people in the park, maybe about new players on the field, or the baseball game he and his brothers played while young," with a board, dice, and a fresh pack of seasonally up-dated cards, with which W. played for hours. He felt that competition revealed one's "personality in a pronounced way," saying, "I'm a practical person." For him baseball's consequences were practical, far beyond the sport.

The pre-1989 Rangers had never drawn two million spectators in a year. Bush promptly hit that level yearly, even in lockout-shortened 1994. "We won't be meddlers," he had vowed. "We won't tell the baseball people how baseball should be played." Not a few felt the new Rangers president a rich boy playing poor boy: "Some of my partners are fairly well off, but I'm not—all name and no money." What Bush brought was a sense of how and where baseball should be staged. Think of Yankee Stadium as baseball's most famous park; Wrigley Field, gorgeous; Fenway Park or Ebbets Field, beloved. Oriole Park at Camden Yards, visited by Bill Clinton in chapter 14, is the most *crucial.* "When parks seemed lost," said Bob Costas of the 1960s through '80s, "along Baltimore came to show how baseball thrives." The Yard ditched failure (domes, clones, faux grass, and sameness) for success (idiosyncrasy, closer-is-better, smaller-brighter, tied to the community). Ronald Reagan: "How do you insult a pig by calling it a pig?" W.: "How do you better a perfect park?"

On April 6, 1992, Bush 41 threw out the first ball to open Camden Yards, created by Orioles president Larry Lucchino, followed by more than two dozen "new old" parks trying to outdo the original. If step one in 43's blueprint for higher office was leadership (vision), step two—W. never conceded this—was to build a monument (a ballpark) showing it. "The baseball position, especially building the park, introduced him as a can-do guy," said Karl Rove, "someone who could talk to officials, to politicians, plow through red tape, and pave his way to politics." By 1998 Bush had sold his original percentage of the team for $14.9 million, a twenty-five-fold increase. Meanwhile, the city of Arlington, Texas, had backed a half-cent sales tax hike to raise $135 million to pay for his vision. Another $56 million was added in private cash. Architects were told to integrate a complex of two artificial lakes, an area of shops and eateries, and W.'s legacy in the middle—The Ballpark in Arlington, capacity 49,166.

"Other parks were built in a neighborhood," said Bush. "Our thought was to build the neighborhood around the park," starting four days before Camden Yards opened. The Rangers began by borrowing. Like Wrigley and Tiger Stadium, among others, lengths varied: foul lines were initially 332 and 325 feet from home plate to left and right field respectively; power alleys, 388 and 403, left and right field respectively; and center field, 400 feet. The deepest point was 407 feet, nooks evoking Brooklyn. Right field feted Detroit's columned upper-deck overhang, a giant scoreboard topping its Home Run Porch. Like Flatbush, a sign read, "Hit It Here and Win a Free Suit." As often elsewhere, a hand-operated board framed a (here, left-field) wall. Ex-team head Tom Schieffer mused, "We didn't want to have ivy on the wall *and* a green monster *and* a Porch—a conglomeration. We said, 'Let's think why those things are special in other parks and build on ideas generated.'"

From *outside* The Ballpark in Arlington was high, wide, and handsome because this, after all, was Texas. A visitor off the Nolan Ryan Expressway parked in one of nine color-coded lots named for a figure from Texas's birth in the 1830s and 1840s. Beyond center field a four-story office building of Cajun twist, steel trusses, and wrought iron towered. *Inside*, box seats were a mere pickoff throw from first and third base. "Everything points inward," Bush said. "The place feels smaller than it is," opening April 11, 1994: Brewers, 4–3. Soon Kenny Rogers pitched the fourteenth big-league perfect game—and first by an AL lefty. By August the Rangers' .456 percentage led the Western Division by a game, the lockout killing the rest of the 1994 season and next year's start of play. When play resumed, Arlington hosted the 1995 All-Star Game: National League, 3–2, Texans watching from balconies and bleachers on either side of an outfield incline. The slope pleased hitters (backdrop) and kids (chasing homers on the grass).

Later W. rued, "We have everything but a pennant," his team trying long ball, little ball, and also free agency in a vain bid to buy an AL pennant and a farm system trying to grow one. Eventually Bush had to choose, spending the rest of the 1990s breaking expectations and the Rangers, breaking hearts. In 1996 and 1998–99, Texas took the West but lost each best-of-five Division Series to New York, which each year won the World Series. The Rangers' interest defaulted to regular season: Juan Gonzalez, whose 1996 and 1998 Most Valuable Player statistics totaled 92 home runs, 301 RBIS, and a .317 average; Ivan "Pudge" Rodriguez, the Rangers' third MVP (1999) in four years and "only catcher with thirty homers [35], a hundred ribbies [113], and a hundred runs [116] in a year," said skipper Johnny Oates; Bobby Witt, the first AL hurler to homer in a quarter century; and The Ballpark, housing the first inter-league match, Giants, 4–3, on June 12, 1997, common sense soon asking what took baseball so long.

In 1999 Rafael Palmeiro outdid everyone: 47 homers, 148 RBIS, and a .324 average, only to admit illegal drug use. Each year Texas seemed to mix and match on the mound: Jose Guzman, Rick Helling, Kevin Brown, Tom Henke, even Nolan Ryan, arriving in 1989. Past his prime, Ryan still threw a sixth career no-hitter in 1990. Even *in* it, Nolan could not start daily, and the staff would have been revealed as inadequate come fall. "I am always ready to learn," said Churchill, "though I do not always enjoy being taught." The debate over Rangers owner Tom Hicks concerned his *ability* to learn, buying not a pitcher but Seattle shortstop Alex Rodriguez prior to the 2001 season for $252 million over a decade.

Glib, handsome, fast, sure-gloved, a power- and high-average hitter, at twenty-six A-Rod seemed a sure Hall of Famer until he too took illegal drugs. The 2000–01 Rangers finished last. Their decade-long window of opportunity had closed, long after Bush's opened.

By 1994 Bush had solidified his predicate for political office: enhance the Rangers' on- and off-field health, then build a grand park worthy of the state. Yet which office and when? "Baseball has been arguably the most important thing in Bush's life," Dana Milbank wrote, adding that it let W. continue a family tradition, shed his father's shadow, survive early drinking—"It's Jim Beam or me," Laura said—the loss to Hance, erratic oil start-ups, and a 1968 commission into the Texas National

Guard. The last happened after two years of active-duty training, assignment to Houston and the 147th Reconnaissance Wing, and derision of his choice as a pilot with low aptitude scores and attendance. "The [presidential] retreats say a lot," said journalist Tom DeFrank, knowing each Bush well. "One [Bush 41] went to Kennebunkport, the other [43] to the [Crawford, Texas] ranch"—sites as different as the men. "Forty-one was cerebral, knew the issues. Forty-three didn't lose sleep when he made a decision, everything instinctive. Didn't ask questions, even when he should."

In summer 1993 Bush 41 began a return to public life, partly to help the younger Bushes. A speech routine boded his coming out. Poppy had vowed not to criticize Clinton for a full year after the 1992 election, in one talk saying, "And I've kept my promise." Chuckles. "But, you know, I checked the calendar this morning." More laughter. "Just ninety-eight days to go." For a time conjecture spread of W. running for baseball commissioner, acting commish Bud Selig spurring, then dashing, hope. In late 1993 George and younger brother John Ellis "Jeb" Bush Sr. announced for governor of Texas and Florida respectively. Dad's interest was now less his party than his sons, Pop eager to campaign for both. To generalize, Jeb was Poppy's son, soft-spoken and sensitive. George was Barbara's, as subtle as a right hook. "I have my father's eyes and my mother's mouth," W. said, a fine self-appraisal.

Bush 41 found it harder to be a family member than to be the candidate. "As the front guy, you can slug back," he said. "The family has to take it." Mrs. Bush found it harder to lose, urging W. not to run against a person the family loathed, Texas governor Ann Richards, her acidic 1988 Democratic convention speech still raw: "Poor George, he can't help it. He was born with a silver foot in his mouth." In Florida early election night polls showed Jeb ahead of incumbent Lawton Chiles. His loss later that evening crushed the former president. In Texas W. had campaigned with newfound discipline, veiled for most of his then forty-eight years. George's on-theme message beat the unbeatable Richards by 334,066 votes. "Poor Ann," said a cousin. "What'll she do with the extra foot?" Barbara Bush was pleasantly shocked, her political scale usually on-key.

That winter, readying one priority, his inaugural, W. fretted about another—the chance that baseball's fourth and longest in-season work stoppage in twenty-two years had pushed luck to its limit. Revenue shortfall soon revealed baseball's fragility, almost everyone in the game mad at everyone else. Ironically, joy was in season November 7, 1997, when five presidents—current (Clinton), three past (Bush, Carter, and Ford), and a future (W.)—and their wives, plus Lady Bird Johnson and Nancy Reagan, opened Bush 41's library and museum at Texas A&M University. Guests of honor arrived by train a day before, flags crying, "Welcome to College Station." Fifty thousand people heard Governor Bush say that objective historians would conclude that his father stared tyranny "in the face and never blinked. George Bush was a great President of the United States because he is first and foremost a great man." Once he said of Dad, "I wasn't trying to copy him, although you couldn't get a greater human being if you were."

Earlier in 1997 the International Parachute Association had invited Bush 41 to be guest of honor at an annual meeting. As etched earlier, Bush parachuted from the navy Avenger he piloted in 1944 after the Japanese attacked it, two crewmates killed. "As I recounted these errors, something happened," Bush wrote his five children. "For some reason, I went back to a thought I had way in the back of my mind. It has been there, sleeping like Rip Van Winkle, alive but not alive. Now it was quite clear. I want to make one more parachute jump!" He expected Barbara to put a foot down, but he would convince her it was safe and said, "This is something I have to do, must do." Former secretary of state Colin Powell was incredulous. "Are you planning to jump from a *plane*?" he asked. "It's the talk of the Pentagon. I know you look forty-five, but you're seventy-two. How are your ankles, knees, etc.?" Bush went ahead, honoring his mates.

Eleven days before the jump—J Day—he called each child. All gave consent, including W., though not carefree advice. Finally, that March 25, "caught up in the spirit of it all, totally hyped," wearing his Desert Storm boots, white helmet, and white gloves—Bush Sr. termed it his "White Elvis Suit"—and having learned the jumpers' secret handshake ending with index fingers pointed at each other, a signal to pull the rip cord, Poppy jumped with the U.S. Army's famed Golden Knights, successfully. To him, it was almost surrealistic. "The floating to death took longer than I thought, but I wish it could have gone on twice as long," he observed. "I didn't hit hard, but a gust of wind seemed to pull me back. . . . I was down. It had gone well. I had lived a dream."

Mrs. Bush hugged him. Their children were amazed and perhaps amused—that Dad! Untold millions here and abroad thought this the most endearing Bush since he told America at a 1990 news conference that he hated broccoli and that his mother made him eat it as a kid, but now that he was president he wasn't going to eat it anymore. Like the jump, the media had covered that broadside around the world.

Late in 1997 editing a speech, Bush suddenly stopped to say, "You know, it's the damndest thing. I was worried people would laugh at me. I did it to honor my mates, and to prove that old guys can still do things." He started laughing. "I go abroad, and the first thing foreign leaders ask is, 'Tell me about the jump!'" They were still asking in 2014, when, despite illness, he jumped to mark birthday number ninety.

In 1998, the year after 41's first jump, W. won a landslide reelection for governor. A year later he enacted a $2 billion tax cut and legislation helping Texans obtain permits to carry concealed weapons, reduce domestic violence, and increase renewable energy sources, especially wind. In July 1999 W. traveled to Cooperstown with officials of the franchise he had helped to build—and which had helped him become a millionaire, today's Rangers among the Major Leagues' ten largest revenue teams. With them were Nolan Ryan, George Brett, and Robin Yount, each a five-star honoree, as fine an induction class as any dating to the Hall of Fame's 1939 official debut.

At 5 p.m. in an elegant home on the edge of Cooperstown, another induction—the January 20, 2001, presidential oath of office—was discussed. Present were New York governor George Pataki (who introduced Bush backers, including baseball's Enos Slaughter, Bob Feller, Gaylord Perry, and Paul Blair) and the candidate (a year before the GOP convention would choose its nominee). Bush preached "compassionate conservatism" to the well-heeled crowd—a tipoff that he deemed conservatism insufficient by itself. "I thought conservatism didn't need an adjective," said a donor. Those who did often thought the party didn't need conservatism.

At the start of 2000 Bush 41 wrote and spoke as a fair man and loving father seeking tolerance for the political system and understanding for his son. "I have tried not to criticize my successor—realizing that he has a hard job to do, and that there are plenty of good people in the loyal opposition out there fighting for many of the beliefs that I share," Bush said, his belief in bipartisanship as rare as his humility in the public square. Of more immediate aid to W. was his ability to raise money: first in George's primaries against John McCain (R-AZ), then in the general election with vice president Al Gore, the Democratic nominee.

On January 24, 2000, Jr. won the Iowa caucus. Poppy then introduced him at a New Hampshire primary event by saying, "This boy of ours will not let you down." McCain observed that it took a man to be president, whereupon W. lost the Granite State by nineteen points, after which Pop seldom introduced him again. Instead he appeared, like Barbara, where the campaign wanted, reminding Republicans and then the general electorate after eight years of Bill Clinton what they *liked* about Bush. The South Carolina primary was W.'s pivot, Karl Rove his Lee Atwater. After McCain withdrew, Jr. chose Bush 41 defense secretary Dick Cheney as VP. At the convention the Bush parents sat, beaming, as their eldest son said of Dad, "All my life I have been amazed that a gentle soul could be so strong."

Bush 41, W. said, "was the last President of a great generation. Now the question comes to [its] sons and daughters. . . . What is asked of us?" To some his answer was a Trojan horse of greater spending and larger government. Social engineering didn't defeat Al Gore in November 2000. Not being Gore and Bill Clinton did—barely. In late August I interviewed 41 on TV at his home in Kennebunkport. He was friendly but preoccupied: the campaign was going badly. The following debates swiveled the election, Gore losing more than Bush won: sighing and rolling eyes in one; seeming sedated in another; crowding the Republican physically in the last. The Old Man—W.'s affectionate moniker for his father—viewed every minute. The house Cassandra, Mrs. Bush, couldn't watch.

Election day came, stayed, and wouldn't leave. Early that night the networks gave Florida to Gore and thus, it seemed, the presidency. Jeb, belatedly elected governor in 1998, was aghast, having thought it solid for his brother. The Bush family was in Austin, Poppy feeling like the baseball voice who, airing a bad team, turned fifty in August. "I don't mind that," the announcer said. "It's just that when the season began I was forty-three." As Florida, mocking early polls, seesawed back toward W., then Gore, then George, then "undecided," the former president, seventy-six, told a friend, "I feel twice my age."

Early next morning Florida was declared for Bush—giving him the 270 electoral votes needed to become president. On cue Gore closed the gap. Florida again turned undecided, the networks throwing up their hands. Prince Al led by about five hundred thousand popular votes nationally, but neither candidate had a majority of the electoral college. For thirty-six days neither would, as lawyers on behalf of each side took over, honorary family member James Baker leading 43's team. A recount began and continued until the U.S. Supreme Court's decision in *Bush v. Gore* stopped it. Bush 41 no longer felt 152—seventy-six times two.

The night of the Supreme Court decision, Gore conceded in a gallant speech. Bush Sr., knowing political victory and defeat, called the White House switchboard to congratulate the vice president. He then saw the televised image of his son, about to address the nation from the Texas state legislature. As the camera "focused on George and Laura walking into the chamber," he wrote in *All the Best, George Bush*, his body "was literally wracked with uncontrollable sobs. It just happened. No warning, no thinking that this might be emotional for a mother or dad to get through—just an eruption from deep within me where my body literally shook. Barbara cried too. We held hands."

On January 20, 2001, the new president took the oath of office, gave his inaugural address, and repaired to his office, where he wanted his first visitor to be someone who knew the way. The visitor was already in the family quarters of the White House having a hot bath when he was told, "The President wants to see you." The guest rose, dried, and dressed quickly because he knew that a president's time is precious. He entered the Oval Office, to be greeted by his son.

"He knew how much this would mean to his Dad, and he wanted to share his first moments in this revered office with him," Barbara Bush later described W. setting the scene. He also wanted the world to know that his father had been visitor Number One. For his part, Poppy hoped to show respect for W., erase confusion with his son, and write finis to his political career. Dad said that he would now be called George H. W. Bush, restoring the patrician name he had dropped on entering Texas politics, also Sr. or Bush 41. W. would be known as George W., Jr., or Bush 43. The gymnastics each did to honor the other did honor to each.

The Bushes were America's first father-son presidential combination since John Adams, president in 1797–1801, and John Quincy Adams, president in 1825–29. As intriguing a comparison was likely between 41 and 43. At first they differed on, among other things, the role of foreign versus domestic policy; the value of a balanced budget versus tax cuts; the effect of Donald Rumsfeld, W.'s defense secretary; and whether the Strategic Defense Initiative had largely won the Cold War. (Jr. was more certain than Sr.)

British Prime Minister Edmund Burke once eulogized a peer: "He may live long. He may do much. But here lies the summit. He can never exceed what he does this day." Bush 41's summit was the Gulf War. What would 43's be? Before he climbed it, it was time for a little ball.

Later Bush 43, not usually a sentimental man, recalled with sentiment the start of his presidency—in particular, his own private fantasy camp, where W.'s huge-size baseball interest stoked the creation at the White House of a junior-size baseball field. BUSH TO BUILD FIELD OF DREAMS, headlined the *Washington Post*. On March 30, 2001, the president noted, "We've got a pretty good-sized back yard here," his audience more than forty Hall of Famers. "As much as anything else, baseball is the style of a Willie Mays, or the determination of a Hank Aaron, or the endurance of a Mickey Mantle. . . . In a small way, maybe we can help to preserve the best of baseball right here in the house that Washington built."

Bush's "Field of Dreams Day" salute rivaled Ronald Reagan's 1981 Hall of Fame luncheon, if not Richard Nixon's spectacular 1969 All-Star Gala. It invited largely five-to-eight-year-olds from around the country to the White House field. CNN-TV showed children in caps and pants and shirts and jerseys, trading bats and gloves and playing catch, and a baseball diamond in and outside with T-ball games. It also showed "heroes," said W., worthy "of a kid's devotion," like the Yog.

Born in 1925, raised "a pickoff away" from bud Joe Garagiola in the Italian section of St. Louis, Lawrence Peter "Yogi" Berra learned a salute-to-the-flag, catch-in-the-throat Americanism. He died in 2015, a man possible to think of as living "Only in America"—a phrase Yogi himself used upon learning that the mayor of Dublin was Jewish. W. called him "an inspiration, [leaving] an enduring mark on the English language," passing Shakespeare, as noted earlier, as the person most quoted by American public speakers.

One Berraism suggests: "When you come to a fork in the road, take it." Another: "It's dangerous to make predictions—especially about the future." Try debating *that*. Others: "It ain't over till it's over" and "If you can't imitate him, don't copy him." A favorite: "Always go to other people's funerals. Otherwise they won't come to yours." Even on the field common sense hit .400. Once the three-time MVP, ten-time World Series champion, and Cooperstown Class of 1972 fielded a bunt and tagged a hitter and runner near the plate, saying "I just tagged everybody, including the ump."

Berra was more than "Yogi thinking funny," said Garagiola, "and speaking what he thinks." At nineteen he braved D-Day—June 6, 1944—the water off Normandy deep red. Back home, Berra became baseball's all-time catcher, W. even more wowed by his modesty, kindness, and how some of the press corps fancied that Yogi might be his speechwriter. At the Yogi Berra Museum and Learning Center at Montclair University, Berra liked to "teach kids things like sportsmanship and work," he said. How far did No. 8 go in high school? "Nine blocks," Garagiola had once jibed. By any rule, few American lives went farther.

"Field of Dreams Day" also included a Baseball Hall of Fame White House luncheon aired live by CNN, five decades of baseball "represented here from Bob Feller to Robin Yount to Duke Snider to Dave Winfield," said Bush 43. There and earlier W. waxed about his boyhood Lancelot, of whom Reggie Jackson once said, "You used to think if the score was 5–0, Willie Mays would [come up and] hit a five-run home run."

In the 1950s, said Bush, America's Boomer public cleaved into Mickey and Willie camps. "There were the Mantle Kids, like [Billy] Crystal and [Bob] Costas, and there were the Mays Kids," he recalled of growing up. "You'd think that with Mickey Mantle coming from Oklahoma, which was next door to where I was raised, that I'd have been a Mantle Kid." Pause. "But for some reason I was a Mays Kid," Willie then playing in New York. "And I am really proud of it, by the way." His 1951–73 career studded 3,283 hits, 660 homers, the 1954 and 1965 MVP awards, twelve Gold Gloves, and a record-tying twenty-four All-Star Games.

Major Garrett, then CNN's White House correspondent, now at CBS, interviewed Bush at lunch: "I always thought I was going to be Mays, but couldn't hit the curveball," W. laughed. "I . . . don't know why, but I was living in Midland, Texas, and Willie captured my imagination," the Say Hey Kid's lure color-blind. In New York he played stickball with kids in the streets; cooked up a top-this 1954 of 41 homers, 110 RBIS, and a .345 average; and played center field at Coogan's Bluff as though he took it personally when an extra-base hit dropped in.

With its yawning acreage and pint-sized foul lines, the Polo Grounds could have been designed by No. 24. In his abbreviated 1951–57 New York tenure, he hit as many as fifty-one home runs, thrice led the league in slugging percentage and in triples, and on September 30, 1954, made the World Series' all-time most memorable catch and throw—the ultimate five-tool player. The 1958 move to San Francisco soured him: Willie was a stranger, greeted coldly, seen as from and of the Big Apple, and he reciprocated the response. Bush 43 recalled the player, not the reaction, inheriting Poppy's years-after-the-fact loyalty. He liked to quote Mays's first skipper, Leo Durocher: "If somebody came up to me and hit .450, stole a hundred bases, and performed a miracle in the field every day, I'd still look you in the eye and say Willie was better."

At the "Field of Dreams Day" W. almost levitated about the first big-league game he saw, saying, "Monte Irvin is here [today]. He was standing in the Polo Grounds, I might add, on grass. Monte, you probably didn't see me, because I was up in the stands with my Uncle Buck." Bush nodded toward the Giants great. "And as I recall, Red Schoendienst was there, as well. Well, gentlemen, if you're half as excited to be at the White House as I was that afternoon, I'm really glad to repay the favor," adding the kind of grace note few pols today do.

Network co-anchor Stephen Frazier asked, "Major, are you in just total Nirvana right now?" Garrett: "Oh, yes, this is the best photo-op I've ever seen [working at CNN]."

Slightly more than five months later America entered neither photo-op nor Nirvana—instead entering a place it had never known.

On September 11, 2001, terrorists seized and crashed four planes into New York City, the Pentagon, and rural Pennsylvania, Bush 43 becoming a wartime president. As usual, hundreds of thousands had trooped to work in Lower Manhattan that Tuesday morning. Normally at their desks by 9 a.m., some had stopped at a polling booth to vote in that day's primary. They were late—so, lucky—as two planes intersected New York's Twin Towers. In an airplane high above farmland between Pittsburgh and Washington, a group of Americans, knowing the likely consequence, stormed the terrorists, seized the plane, and by crashing perhaps saved the U.S. capital from incalculable human loss. The Pentagon, epicenter of the world's most powerful defense, was assailed from the air as no enemy had done in war. The fatality total, nearly three thousand, was America's highest-ever single-day figure inflicted by an enemy on U.S. soil.

After Pearl Harbor, FDR's speech declaring war on Japan was heard next day on radio—and seen next week on newsreel. President Kennedy's 1963 assassination was reported on television within an hour of the shooting. The Twin Towers tragedy was felt instantly in New York—and by TV in America. New York's finest kept this date of infamy from becoming a law of the jungle. New Yorkers were magnificent. America was. That night Mayor Rudy Giuliani retreated to his apartment and read Churchill's account of Hitler's attempt to destroy Britain, other European democracies having surrendered to him in spring 1940. Giuliani was inspired by Churchill vowing, "We shall never flag or fail" and "We shall never surrender." He spoke as Germany controlled virtually all of Europe, its forces seventeen miles from England across the Channel.

The enemy then was Nazi fascism; now it was Islamic terrorism. Overnight W.'s America changed. The elder Bushes had left Houston early the morning of September 11 to fly to St. Paul, Minnesota, to speak before returning home at night. Their private plane was diverted to Milwaukee, the Secret Service telling them that George W. and Laura were safe in Florida and DC respectively. That night 41 and Mrs. Bush talked to people at a Milwaukee mall, golf course, and family restaurant. A day later, terrorist strategy still murky, U.S. airspace was still closed. An exception was made for the Bushes, who were flown to Kennebunkport.

Forty-three reacted slowly to 9/11, finding his voice that week on an unforgettable trip to New York. Standing in the Towers' rubble, using a bullhorn, his arm around an elderly firefighter—the kind of blue-collar worker W. liked most and with whom he felt most comfortable—Bush heard another worker shout that he couldn't hear the president. His timing evocative of the Gipper, W. replied, "I can hear you! The rest of the world hears you! And the people . . . who knocked these buildings down will hear all of us soon!" The crowd roared. Electricity rifled through the city. It was not Bush's most *crucial* moment—those lay ahead—but it was his *greatest* moment, unless you count another forthcoming visit to New York.

Tuesday, October 30, Game Three of the 2001 World Series: Arizona's Diamondbacks lead the Yankees, two games to zero. The Stripes' Derek Jeter asks if Bush wants to loosen up before tossing the first pitch—amazingly, the first U.S. president to attend a World Series game at Yankee Stadium. They go under its bowels—to 43, "a decrepit-looking undercarriage of this magnificent ballpark." Junior asks if Jeter wants to play catch. Derek replies, "Are you going to throw the ball off the mound?," adding, "I would if I were you." That is good enough for Bush, saying that whatever the shortstop thinks is fine.

Out of the blue Derek says, "Don't bounce it because if you do, they'll boo," something Bush 41 was forever doing and the crowd forever booing. Minutes elapse. The crowd starts chanting "USA"—to 43, "a very emotional, pulsating experience." That night the 9/11 attack of the prior month still ran rawer in New York than anywhere else. Memory freeze-frames the three-tiered colossus; massive security; and tattered 9/11 flag, carried from the Twin Towers, lapping in the wind—above all the presidency and baseball fused so tightly as to allow no degrees of separation. The Republican Bush was to throw out the pregame ball in this overwhelmingly Democratic city. How would he be greeted? Moreover, how would he do?

The first question instantly answered itself. Bush met a roaring ovation as he left the Yankees dugout, blue and red states vanishing, as they had for the last U.S. president to throw out a first ball at a Series in the Big Apple: Ike at the 1956 opener at Ebbets Field. Somewhere along the way we had ceased to be *Americans*. This night reminded us how wonderful that once had been and, pray God, might be again if only we would let it.

Bush passed the first-base line, wearing a jacket and under it a forty-pound steel vest, then moved toward the mound, as big-league pitchers do—not in front, as most first-ball hurlers do. He readied to throw to a catcher behind home plate—a difficult task, as any practitioner knows. Add the fury in every seat, in every tier, among every Series watcher—the emotion overwhelmed. Needed was someone possessed of inner peace.

W.'s serenity could be a weakness, blinding a need for counsel. Here it helped, blocking out the world. Bush wound up and threw a perfect strike to the Yankees' Jorge Posada, exactly splitting the plate, precisely at the knees, as if 43 had placed the ball lovingly in the catcher's glove. As in the rubble near the Towers, the crowd exploded, its cry for simple justice piercing the cool Bronx air.

Slowly Bush left the field, Gary Cooper in *High Noon*, a hero more than he had ever been or ever would be again. Watching, Dad loved his son and a game so instilled in their lives that as president he kept his first baseman's college mitt in his Oval Office desk.

Bush 43 had planned to be a domestic president—the environment, cell research, and education—working with Democrats to pass legislation. Now he enlisted in the officially undeclared war on terrorism. After 9/11 he gave superb speeches at Washington National Cathedral ("Today we feel what Franklin Roosevelt called 'the warm courage of national unity'") and to a joint session of Congress ("The enemy of America is not our many Muslim friends") that could have been given by FDR himself. "He can run, but he can't hide," Bush, quoting boxing great Joe Louis, said of Osama bin Laden, leader of the terrorist group Al Qaeda, which had planned and implemented the September 11 attack.

W. fingered the Taliban regime and bin Laden's sanctuary in Afghanistan. Eying Saddam Hussein as a force behind Al Qaeda, he included Hussein's Iraq with North Korea and Iran in an "Axis of Evil." Usually Bush Sr. and Donald Rumsfeld treated each other as the price you pay for entering politics. Now they independently reached the same conclusion: Poppy's Antichrist, whom he thought would be overthrown after the Gulf War, would have to be silenced, likely for good.

As W. debated whether to attack or not—to "nation build," having vowed not to in the campaign—the media asked if Dad had advised him on Hussein. In 2002 Bush 41's national security adviser, Brent Scowcroft, wrote a *Wall Street Journal* article suggesting 43 not invade and occupy Iraq. Would he have done so without Sr.'s consent? Would the U.S. inherit a quagmire, without an exit plan, thus violating one of 41's three criteria to invade (the others: What was the goal? How to achieve it?). To journalist Bob Woodward, W. raised as many questions as he answered, not "remember[ing]" what, if any, advice he got from Pop and adding, "There is a higher Father that I appeal to." To most, Bush 43's last sentence made sense. Not consulting 41 about Hussein, Iraq, and the U.S. military did not. After 1991 who knew more about the region?

Ultimately Bush 43 led a far smaller UN coalition—less than half the number of nations and 250,000 troops of the initial invasion force, versus 800,000 troops, including half a million Americans—than his father forged in 1990-91. The rationale for invading—Hussein had weapons of mass destruction—was never proven. The U.S. military victory's "shock and awe" helped W. beat Massachusetts senator John Kerry in 2004, making the Bushes a legitimate "political dynasty," a term Poppy hated—two presidents of three terms, two governors, one U.S. senator, and a U.S. congressman. "I want our kids to be proud, not intimidated, by what came before," said Bush 41. "Just go where their interests are, follow where your hearts lead you, as we did when Bar and I were married."

That October, the Boston Red Sox, a franchise long legendary for snatching defeat from the jaws of victory, went where neither Bush nor untold millions of other Americans expected. On cue, the Olde Towne Team, its last world title 1918, spotted the Yankees a 3-0 game best-of-seven League Championship Series lead. What occurred next sounded, as F. Scott Fitzgerald wrote, like "the tuning fork that had been struck upon a star." Shockingly, Boston won four straight games to take the 2004 LCS. "And the Red Sox have won the American League pennant!" whooped radio voice Joe Castiglione, "their greatest victory in team history!"—the first "significant victory" over AL New York in 104 years. Without it, he noted, what "happened next didn't happen"—to owner John Henry, "the biggest story in New England since the Revolutionary War." Not wishing to contradict, Castiglione smiled. "I think he understated."

On Wednesday, October 27, 2004, at 10:40 p.m. Central Time, at Busch Stadium, the St. Louis Cardinals' Edgar Renteria swung. "A ground ball, stabbed by [Boston pitcher Keith] Foulke!" said Castiglione. "He has it! He underhands to first! And the Boston Red Sox are the world champions for the first time in eighty-six years! The Red Sox have won baseball's world championship! [They also won in 2007 and 2013.] Can you believe it?" The question was rhetorical. That Saturday a Hub rally of seventeen amphibious vehicles rolled through the streets of Boston before entering the Charles River and passing under the Harvard Bridge—more than three million delirious of the devoted and deranged. In November Bush lost most of New England to Kerry. On a frigid March 2, 2005, W. welcomed the Sox to the White House, saying: "There's been a lot of people in this town waiting for this day to come. Some have said it would be a cold day when the Red Sox made it here." Bush then quoted "a guy" from Boston: "Now we just have to wait for the other six signs of the apocalypse."

As president, W. authorized the Bush Doctrine; urged passage of the Patriot Act; committed U.S. troops to war not just in Iraq in 2003 but first to Afghanistan in October 2001; and began a war on terror demanding a global military campaign. At the same time at home Bush inflamed his own party and ignored majority opinion by backing an immigration policy many thought tantamount to amnesty, saying in a non sequitur, "Family values don't stop at the Rio Grande." He signed the No Child Left Behind Act, Partial Birth Abortion Act, Medical Care Prescription Drug Benefits for Seniors Act, AIDS funding, and for political consumption, a constitutional amendment to prohibit same-sex marriage.

Harming the economy and his reputation was the 2008 Great Wall Street Recession. Acting boldly but belatedly, Bush got Congress to pass multiple programs after the banking roof fell in. In more than a dozen speeches he touted federal intervention, virtually each address getting less polling support at its end than at its start. Similarly, government at each level failed in late summer and early fall 2005 to offset Hurricane Katrina in every area from cleanup, transportation, and traffic to electricity, order, and maintenance. Property damage was about $108 billion in numerous Southern states, especially Louisiana and Mississippi. Fatalities totaled between 1,245 and 1,836 in the deadliest U.S. hurricane since 1928's Okeechobee. A photo of an apparently indifferent W. returning to DC aboard Air Force One showed him looking out and declining to land at Katrina's vortex, flooded New Orleans, with thousands homeless, below. Fact: 43 didn't want a presidential trip to complicate recovery. Effect: it changed how many viewed him.

In Bush's parallel world, little dimmed his luster in and around baseball. That same year owners backed his presidential order forbidding the admittance of a Cuban team to the inaugural World Baseball Classic in Puerto Rico. Personally the 2005 season was special for W., the Montreal Expos moving to DC. To know what it meant, you had to hear him talk, impromptu, in dribs and drabs, about how the game had been loved and missed in the capital, the city bypassed time and again, and then the team born anew as the Washington Nationals. Forty-three was as excited as the baseball cheerleader he once had been in school. "I think it's good for baseball to come to the Nation's Capital," said Bush. "I know how exciting baseball can be for a community." Not since Richard Nixon—or Dad—had a president so evangelized. W. had a TV dish in the residence, watched games when possible, and was "honored to . . . [continue] a tradition of presidents throwing out the first pitch for a Washington baseball team."

Never "knowing a day when I didn't want to learn about the game," Bush realized how first ball liturgy brewed the presidential and personal. As noted earlier, the last president to catapult the pitch from his box at or over the heads of a herd of players on the field, each panting for a signature, had been a fellow Texan, using the Johnson Treatment at the park. Nixon, a stickler for formality, restored the ritual to a pre-FDR age of pitch and catch between the president in his seat and a player on the field. Reagan took his act *to* the field, tossing the ball near the home dugout or from the mound to a catcher behind the plate. On cue, each successor has followed the old actor's lead with varying accuracy and panache and—of this they were grateful—without a radar gun to measure speed.

"It's a really great moment," W. said of throwing out the first pitch at the season's opening game on April 14, 2005—Nationals 5, Diamondbacks 3—Washington's first Major League game after an interminable *thirty-four*-year absence. "Especially *this* year," and for largely young to aging males, wandering to RFK Stadium that spring, as groundskeepers planted and ushers cleaned and vendors sold, a time that for those who had despaired of ever seeing a big-league game there again was close to tear-provoking. Bush later held court on the dos and don'ts of the opening ball. "A relationship between the pitcher and man behind the plate is totally different than what you think when you're out there," he said. Once W. tossed out the first ball in Milwaukee, Brewers coach Davey Lopes catching the ball as designated "catcher." When Bush got to the mound, he remembered asking, "'Where is Lopes?' He seemed so far away, he'd might as well be swimming in Lake Michigan."

On March 30, 2008, the only place Bush wanted to be was the Senators' new home, Nationals Park, a 41,339-seat jewel in the capital's Navy Yard neighborhood flanking the Anacostia River, which W. inaugurated with his final first pitch as president and which ended with a game-winning Nats home run, 3–2, over Atlanta by the player who still defines the Washington National League franchise, veteran Ryan Zimmerman. A year later the place he returned to was Texas, as Dad had in 1993, to a state defiantly proud of each.

In 2001 Bush had reminisced about baseball watching: "I used to sit in the cheap seats. It's probably not practical now." Now, he threw out a pitch at a 2009 Rangers game, following a drive from home that "brought back a lot of memories." Owner Tom Hicks was glad 43 "was reconnected with the team," just as baseball had always connected Bush's clan. Asked what he liked most about baseball, 41 once told me, "Baseball has everything." It was a thought, he said, that came to him not long after he first picked up a bat.

Covering Bush 41 in Kennebunkport meant "lobster every day, civilized and sophisticated, old-line money; [that was] Bush's Brahmin and patrician, which is not to say elitist, side," said Tom DeFrank, who also covered Jimmy Carter in Plains, Georgia. The traveling media dubbed Plains's nearest hotel, a Best Western, the Worst Western. DeFrank was from small-town Texas—no elitist here—yet felt that Crawford, the site of Bush 43's ranch, had "such an utter lack of civilization that it looked like a grasshopper plague," making "Plains look like Kennebunkport."

There was a certain Old West quality to W. that many critics and even patrons never bothered to or could culturally grasp. You took Bush straight: not on policy, where he could be malleable, but on personality, where he declined to change. You took him on his terms: as he was, or not at all. He snubbed his nose at the best and brightest: the Hamptons and Malibu, the newest garb and style, who was in and out. He didn't care and was glad to make that clear. Millions loved or hated him. It was his misfortune that the latter had access to printer's ink and a radio/TV mic.

In 2004 Bush gave his State of the Union address, devoting about forty seconds in a fifty-four-minute speech to a way Americans were killing themselves: the evil of steroids. Senator John McCain, a once bitter foe, straightaway agreed. Bush did not say whether drug user Mark McGwire should be elected to the Hall of Fame. He spoke the unspeakable, called people to account, expected pushback, and got it. Steroids were too base to discuss, some said, or unstoppable, said others. W. shrugged, knowing his responsibility to fight illegal drugs and have citizens tell a game they loved or had, "Baseball, heal thyself." Bush moved it in a direction the sport might otherwise not have gone.

W.'s sense of duty suggested his father's January 28, 1991, "Just War" speech, where clerics, educators, and policy experts considered how force could be used and "still uphold," text said, "moral values like tolerance, compassion, faith, and courage." The address quoted the clergyman Richard Cecil: "There are two classes of the wise: the men who serve God because they have found him, and the men who seek him because they have not found him yet." At one time or another W. had qualified as each—having not found Him yet, then finding Him to "serve and seek wisely."

Saddam Hussein had cast the first Gulf clash as a religious war. It was not, said Sr.—rather, "a Just War . . . in which good will prevail." Bush Jr. shared that belief, forged by reading the Bible daily in the White House, such classical Greek and Roman philosophers as Plato and Cicero, and later Christian theologians like Ambrose, Augustine, and Thomas Aquinas. He was determined to be seen as his own man. "I was married late," W. said, trying to show that he would not *imitate* his Dad, wed at twenty and still married to his "first love" at ninety-three. That was true, although all his life George tried to *emulate* his Dad.

As noted, the George W. Bush Presidential Center, including the presidential library and museum, Bush Policy Institute, and Bush Foundation, opened in 2013, between the release of 43's first two best-selling books: a memoir, *Decision Points*, and *41: A Portrait of My Father*. In 2017, *Portraits of Courage* hailed America's military warriors, vaunting W.'s new career as—to some—a shockingly fine impressionist painter. That year father and son helped forge *The Last Republicans*, a critique of Donald Trump as—to the Bushies—a shockingly un-Republican and perhaps unworthy president.

The Bush Center, at University Park, near Dallas, lies on the campus of Southern Methodist University. To a visitor exploring the second largest only to Ronald Reagan's among all thirteen current presidential sites, two themes emerge, each indispensable to the other. As president, George W. Bush kept us strong. He also kept us free. Retrieve October 30, 2001, seven weeks to the day after 9/11, Bush taking the mound in the Big Ballpark in the Bronx and firing a perfect pitch—America's signpost to the world.

SIXTEEN

The Pioneer

Barack Obama, 2009–2017

O n January 20, 2009, George W. Bush was succeeded by Barack
H. Obama—the first president to be an African American,
call Chicago's South Side home, and wear the exquisite White
Sox Olde English jacket in the White House. As a U.S. senator, he had
pledged Pale Hose fealty by throwing out the first pitch of the second
game of the 2005 American League Championship Series at U.S. Cellular Field in Chicago. In 2009 he encored for the All-Star Game in St.
Louis. That July 23 Obama phoned Mark Buehrle after the lefty threw
baseball's eighteenth perfect game in its 140-year history. "I mean,"
he told the White Sox ace, "a perfect game—that's something!" For
many the exclamatory "something!" seemed to define the presidents'
and pastime's tie.

Baseball's relationship with Obama's presidency-to-be began a week
before the 2008 election, his campaign asking fifteen minutes of network television time for a "long-form" speech, a length few campaigns
still use. Told that an 8:00–8:15 p.m. ad would preempt Fox's World Series pre-Game Six show, the Republican National Committee hit the
roof. "Not only is Obama putting politics before principles," a spokesman said, "he's putting it before baseball." The ad ran, nothing in either party being put before profit.

In the forty-fourth president's (hereafter, 44) first year in office
the Class-A Minor League Brooklyn Cyclones renamed themselves

"Baracklyn" for a game. In 2010 he graced his only Opening Day in office, visiting Philadelphia routing Washington, 11–1. That June he again visited Nationals Park, admiring its four seating levels, superb sight lines, and view of the Capitol and Washington Monument from the first-base upper deck. Above all, pitching whiz Stephen Strasburg lost, 2–1, to Obama's Sox. Quickly Barack grasped baseball's need to lure the young, where its appeal is weak, and protect its lineage, which is unsurpassed.

Obama was the first technology president, as if Mr. Wizard had been elected, with whom Millennials and younger people found kinship as a pioneer. He was not only a racial but a high-tech trailblazer immersed in "stuff"—arguably his favorite word. In 1955 future president Ronald Reagan hosted an ABC special, "Tomorrowland," to debut Disneyland theme park in Southern California. Founder and co-host Walt Disney would have twitched his mustache in wonderment had he foreseen *baseball's* tomorrow, a universe not of two-camera black and white but of gaudy-graphic color. XM Satellite Radio now airs each game, for a fee accessing team and/or announcer archives. MLB.com's Gameday Audio, Fox, DirecTV, and other packages sculpt a smaller world. Once, Jon Miller said, a local-team announcer would be known in "his particular area." Today, "There *is* no area."

One afternoon in 2014, motoring to a fundraiser, Obama briefly shelved his beloved Blackberry to stop unannounced at a scene that could have come from an urban Andrew Wyeth—a Little League game at Friendship Park in northwest Washington, players turning widemouthed upon spotting him. The president threw a ceremonial first pitch, perhaps hooking baseball converts. In that week's regular radio and Internet address, 44 said he would go to Cooperstown, home of the Hall of Fame, "to stress how tourism can produce jobs"—and why Congress should modernize U.S. bridges, roads, and ports. "A first-class infrastructure lures first-class jobs."

On May 22 Obama became the first president in office to visit Cooperstown since Martin Van Buren in 1839 and the first in office to enter baseball's Hermitage since its debut in 1939. He began by saying that the day's "timing could not be better"—the Hall's seventy-fifth birthday—and that he had kept his pledge to all-time White Sox home run leader Frank Thomas that he would "check the place out before he [was] inducted in July." Obama liked the "Sox locker of memorabilia" and getting to "bask in the glory of the 2005 World Series win [against Houston]"—the first Hose title since 1917. (Crowd applause.) To paraphrase his "Yes, we can!" 2008 campaign mantra, "Yes!" he said. The Sox had.

At the Hall's request, Obama donated his 2009 White Sox jacket, worn at that year's All-Star Game but forgot in the attention given his "mom jeans." The president said: "The media had a lot of interest in the jeans I wore. [Crowd laughter.] Don't worry, you won't be seeing them again. [Wife] Michelle retired those jeans quite a while back." Obama left for Washington struck by the region's beauty—and baseball's status in the Empire State.

The pastime's primacy there stemmed from tradition, the Hall's existence, New York having among the most organized professional baseball teams of any state, and the still surpassing presence of the Yankees—especially radio and TV. Growing up, a Baby Boomer in New York could not frequent a beach, zoo, or picnic without hearing Mel Allen—The Voice long before any TV show of the same name aired contestants.

Even now, Yankees video and wireless knit the nearest high-tech hub and sports bar and manufacturing site. In 2004 a *Sports Illustrated* poll showed that New Yorkers overwhelmingly chose a baseball team as their favorite club. In this sense, at least, making America more like New York State might be a great thing to do.

In Ecclesiastes, we read of "a time for every season." In a White House Historical Association event, the Senators, hosted by Calvin Coolidge, were the first team photographed in the building September 25, 1925. Obama lacked Woodrow Wilson's academic baseball vitae, George W. Bush's knowledge of its inner politics, and Richard Nixon's grasp of the game. Yet his hometown baseball defiance enjoyed a season too.

In 2009, citing scheduling, Obama spurned invites to throw out the first ball by the Senators, Reds, and ironically White Sox before picking the All-Star Game. The host Cardinals wanted the new president to wear the classic Redbirds cap and jacket. Instead 44 appeared clad in an unretired shirt, socks, jeans, Chicago AL jacket, and well-loved Sox cap. Somehow the Hall talked the Pale Hose into putting on temporary display the cap of what a team spokesman called "the most popular man on the planet. That's pretty powerful stuff!" At about this time, another White Sox official suggested that they manufacture a duplicate! The plan failed because, I prefer to think, Obama, like Oscar Wilde, loathed those who knew "the price of everything and the value of nothing."

The Pioneer's elan gave edge to the yearly visit of the World Series victor to what Ronald Reagan styled the "world's most famous public housing." On May 15, 2009, the White House dripped Quakers red and white to hail the 2008 Philadelphia Phillies' first title since 1980. Daily Ryan Howard's bat seemed to find new corners of Citizens Bank Park: witness 46 home runs and 146 runs batted in. Second baseman Chase Utley added 33 and 104 respectively. The Phils celebrated outfielder Shane Victorino a.k.a. "The Flyin' Hawaiian" Day with Victorino hula figurines. He and shortstop Jimmy Rollins won a Gold Glove for fielding. Obama campaign manager David Plouffe and others filled the South Lawn as 44 razzed players and officials, enjoying himself as usual, at such a time, as much or more than they did. "I'm not sure whether he [Plouffe] cared more about my victory or the Phillies' victory," said the president. "It was a close call."

Rain and cold had suspended Game Five of the 2008 Series against Tampa Bay for two days, more evocative of hockey than baseball weather. Recalling a campaign event, Obama told his staff that if baseball could improvise "and stop the Series in the middle [sixth inning] of a game, the least you [could have done] is find an indoor location for my speech." Instead he joked about being "the coldest [he] may have ever been. But thousands of Philadelphians showed up to brave the rain, just like fans braved the rain to cheer the Phils." As noted, the 2010 Phils were the Nats' unbrotherly first-day guest. On the centennial of W. H. Taft's initial first-ball pitch, Obama was asked to wear the Nats cap while throwing. Instead he hid his cap in a glove, whipped the hat out when set to throw, put on his Sox chapeau, and arced a speed-challenged toss.

Before long the third lefthander among the last four presidents welcomed the Stripes for their 2009 title. "It's been nine years since your last title, which must have felt like an eternity for Yankees fans," Obama told the Bombers. "I think other teams would have been just fine with a spell like that—the Cubs, for example." Rimshot and touché. He invoked the Yanks "Core Four"—Derek Jeter, Andy Pettitte, Jorge Posada, and Mariano Rivera—from their 1996–2009 roster. Jeter was "a classic." "Keep throwing the cutter!" he said of Rivera's one-pitch-fit-all. Curtis Granderson, having manned Obama phones in 2008, vowed support for Michelle's popular campaign against childhood obesity. It was hard to leave such an event unimpressed by the president's homework, wit, and ease.

The Yankees have been a national team preceding the memory of any conscious American. The Giants have been bicoastal—in New York until 1958; in San Francisco since—and a dynasty between 2010 and 2014, winning a World Series every even year. On July 25, 2011, the first Giants title team in fifty-six years convened in the East Room, including the favorite player of Obama's predecessor. First 44 recalled Game One of the 1954 Fall Classic at Coogan's Bluff, Willie Mays making his famous catch, off Vic Wertz, over a shoulder, back toward the plate, to start a Giants sweep of Cleveland. In 2011 Willie took the franchise's newest Series trophy back to northern Manhattan, where the Polo Grounds had stood, visiting students at Public School No. 46. "There Mays told students the stories of his playing stickball in the streets," the president said, "remembering their [Giants] roots, especially when those roots [ran] deep."

A month later Obama honored Jewish American Heritage Month with guests including rabbis and scholars and "jurists . . . and Sandy Koufax," prompting the audience to applaud perhaps baseball's greatest mid-1960s pitcher. In 1965 Koufax compiled a 26-8 record and brilliant 2.04 ERA. Plainly, Dodgers manager Walter Alston wanted to start him in the Series opener at Minnesota, but Koufax felt obliged to abstain because it fell on Yom Kippur, the holiest day on the Jewish calendar. Such fidelity made Sandy a hero to his faith—the reason he was the only guest the president cited by name. "Sandy and I actually have something in common," reasoned Obama. "We are both lefties. He can't pitch on Yom Kippur. I can't pitch." Laughter and applause. Coda: On two days' rest, Koufax, curve gone, left with his fast ball and heart, pitched Game Seven against the Twins, winning, 2–0, the Dodgers' third world title since 1959.

Another force of nature died in January 2013. "The President was saddened to learn of the passing of baseball legend Stan Musial," the White House said. For twenty-three seasons Musial used a coiled stance to crush a baseball, yet made his uniform No. 6 a symbol of gentle class. Possibly no place ever loved an athlete as St. Louis did the Man—modest, courteous, and a glorious humanitarian. Few hit as well as he did, with power to every field, buoying a summer series, out-of-staters from Middle America jamming each parking space, or a September struggle, the Redbirds filling an aviary of interest, dads pointing sons to Musial and saying, "I hope you turn out like him." In 2010 Obama gave Musial the Medal of Freedom "for his unrivaled passion for the sport and the example he set for all young Americans."

To Obama the Hall of Fame, of which Koufax, Stan the Man, the Say Hey Kid, Jeter, and Rivera are or will be members, taught "some eternal, timeless values of grit and determination and hard work and community. Those are American values—just like baseball," he said, "always with us." Among those values is mutual respect. Obama said he hoped that as Americans we would talk to one another. In retrospect, the issue is how we can learn not to scream at one another.

Forty-four was born Barack Hussein Obama II in Honolulu, Hawaii, on August 4, 1961, though conspiracy theorists made a cottage industry of claiming his birth certificate was specious—thus making him ineligible for the presidency. His background was unlike any president's in American history—foreign and alien to millions of voters, fresh and very cosmopolitan to millions of others. The first president born in Hawaii had a mother, Ann Dunham, born in Wichita, Kansas, of English ancestry, who was white. His father, Barack Obama Sr., was a

Luo from Nyang'oma Kogelo, Kenya, and was black. Mother and father married and separated in 1961 and were divorced in 1964. Obama Sr. returned to Kenya that year, remarried, visited Barack in Hawaii only once in 1971, and died in a car accident in 1982.

In 1965 Obama's mother moved with Barack to Washington to attend college, got remarried, then two years later moved to Indonesia, site of her new husband's home. In 1971 Barack, ten, moved back to Honolulu to be with his maternal grandparents, staying there until his 1979 high school graduation. "That my father looked nothing like the people around me—that he was black as pitch, my mother white as milk—barely registered in my mind," he later wrote, diversity a part of Hawaii long before it hit the mainland. Obama used alcohol, marijuana, and cocaine to "push questions of who I was out of my mind." He entered Occidental College, transferred to Columbia College, and graduated with a BA degree in political science with a specialty in international relations in 1983. By now Barack thought of himself as much a citizen of the globe as of America.

After graduation Obama worked a year at the Business International Corporation, then at the New York Public Interest Research Group. In 1985 he was hired in Chicago as "community organizer" to direct the Developing Communities Project, a church-based group originally including eight Catholic parishes in communities on the city's South Side. In three years Obama created job training and college preparatory tutoring programs—also a tenants rights group, organizing residents of a public housing project to pressure city hall. Later, he said of its bureaucracy, "I [learned] I just can't get things done here without a law degree." So the future president entered Harvard Law School, was chosen editor of the *Harvard Law Review* his first year and president of the journal his second, and became research assistant to the constitutional scholar Laurence Tribe.

In 1991 Obama left Harvard with a JD degree magna cum laude to return to Chicago, where a year later he married Michelle Robinson, a native South Sider, lawyer, and whose Gallup Poll approval rating, like many First Ladies, would regularly top her husband's. In 1992 Barack parlayed the *Law Review's* first black presidency into a publishing contract and advance for a book about race relations. Shrewdly, he converted it into a personal memoir—an autobiography in his early thirties!—released in mid-1995 under the title *Dreams from My Father*. Obama got a two-year position as Visiting Law and Government Fellow at the University of Chicago Law School to write the book, eventually teaching there as lecturer and then senior lecturer through 2004, academe his seeming home.

Later, as U.S president, Obama denounced business with satisfying regularity, yet about this time began to augment his teaching job as counsel of varied law firms and member of numerous boards of businesses and nonprofits. To accommodate their growing family, daughters Malia Ann and Natasha ("Sasha") born in 1998 and 2001 respectively, the Obamas left their Hyde Park condominium in 2005 for a $1.6 million house in neighboring Kenwood, paid for with proceeds from Obama's second book, *The Audacity of Hope*, released in 2006. By then he had added the public world of politics, with its many private costs, to the quiet campus life.

In 1996 Obama ran for the Illinois Senate from its thirteenth district on Chicago's South Side with support from incumbent Alice Palmer, who had decided to run for Congress. Her effort lagged, whereupon she reconsidered, wanting to keep her job. Obama declined to withdraw, helped keep her off the ballot, and coasted to a state Senate victory, then was reelected in 1998 and 2002, despite losing a 2000 Democratic primary for Illinois's first U.S. House congressional district. As chair of the state Senate's health and human services committee, he birthed a bill to make police record the race of drivers they detained and require videotaped homicide inquiry, acts prophetic of his presidency, when many police thought him hostile. He opposed a congressional resolution okaying the use of U.S. armed forces in Iraq in 2002, enlisted for the U.S. Senate in 2003, and a year later was elected.

Obama played to his strength at the 2004 Democratic National Convention, in Boston. "I've always had the gift," he would tell U.S. Senate majority leader Harry Reid—the ability to talk convincingly and compellingly about almost anything at any time. His convention keynote speech was a springboard—to the White House. The law professor's act, heretofore local, turned national as one judge/voter after another gave him a near-perfect grade. "There's not a liberal America and a conservative America," Obama insisted. "There's the United States of America." Much of the nation rose, panting for a trace of such elusive unity. Later came the question of how much and what he meant. Yes, he would—spend 2005–06 in the Senate preparing for the presidency and 2007–08 on the stump readying to win it.

From the texts of stray Obama speeches and press releases as a U.S. Senate candidate and officeholder, two themes emerge. First was the centrality of Jackie Robinson, for reasons detailed. "As much as any figure in American history, he [Robinson] made it impossible for millions of white Americans to justify the absurdity of segregation," wrote the Syracuse *Post-Standard*'s Sean Kirst. "For decades, he was the unrivaled model, the historic template, for American diversity. In 1972, when he died, no black candidate had a chance, even remotely, to become president." Robinson changed that. A favorite saying of Kirst's engraved Jackie's tombstone: "A life is not important except in the impact it has on other lives." No. 42's impact was massive. Before Jackie died, he and his wife, baseball's first lady, Rachel Robinson, knew so too.

The second theme was the centrality of neighborhood—Tip O'Neill's "All politics is local." Obama's support of the White Sox showed a knowledge that most Chicago South Siders loved them. After their 2005 Series sweep of Houston, he rose in the U.S. Senate to speak. "It [victory] has been a long time coming," Obama began, noting that four games were won by a total of six runs. "Win by the skin of our teeth. Win or die trying, that's been our motto this year." Obama attended the Series opener. "The fans in and around the park were a cross-section of the city. Plenty of folks who remember the '59 team. Almost everyone remembered the 2000 team that made the playoffs. A few were even alive in 1917," only to find that 1919 almost killed them.

Below is an ode to Sox long-sufferers of every age, including the White House resident from 2009 to 2017. Certain points in a life open a window on its future. The 1959 White Sox taking the AL pennant, then passing *Go* to the World Series against the Dodgers, opened my window on the Major Leagues at age eight. As noted, Upstate New York was Yankees country—and by 1959 that country overflowed, the Stripes having won nine of the last ten pennants. That spring *Sports Illustrated* wrote: "Even in an inflationary economy there is no safer and better return on your money than the 40 cent profit you get in the fall from the dollar you bet in the spring that the Yankees will win the pennant. New York will win again in 1959." The idea that the White Sox would topple them seemed as absurd as if "Albania had licked NATO," columnist Larry Merchant wrote in a different context. The Bible describes forty years in the wilderness. By 1959 the Pale Hose had wandered pennantless since the darkest of all teams—the 1919 Black Sox.

Obama was born two years after the wandering ended, after which decades later it resumed. For those alive from the year of the Go-Go White Sox, the Go-Go has never gone. For one thing, it occurred in the cradle of baseball radio/television. The Hose were ferried over WCFL Radio, Bob Elson voicing. As a boy, he sang in Chicago's famed Paulist Choirister Choir, later became a gin rummy whiz, and debuted on the wireless with the 1929 Sox and Cubs. Before long Elson became baseball's prewar network prism, airing the first on-field interview, All-Star Game in 1933, and World Series highlight film from 1943 to 1948. "He had an excitement," Jack Brickhouse said. "His voice cut through the air." In 1943 "the Old Commander," named for wartime service at the U.S. Great Lakes Training Center, got leave to call the Series. "Franklin Roosevelt asked that he announce," said Jack. "The only time that a president pulled rank to get a uniformed baseball guy home."

In 1946 Elson returned to radio, his trademark call, "*He's* out!" Brickhouse, a big, ruddy personality who preferred "Hey-Hey!," came home to television, Chicago having more than one in ten U.S. sets. In 1948 WGN Channel 9 made him, like Bob, a big-league explorer. Jack's video firsts included becoming a daily voice (each Sox and Cubs game from Comiskey and Wrigley Field respectively), mic man (boxing), and chronicler of baseball's center-field camera shot (1951). Jack aired four political conventions, Churchill's funeral, one-on-ones with seven U.S. presidents, and interviews with Pope Paul VI and motormouth Leo Durocher—alas, a writer said, not simultaneously. In March 1959 a different name entered Sox dialogue: new owner Bill Veeck, buying Charles Comiskey's granddaughter's interest. For the first time in fifty years, a non-Comiskey owned the park. Veeck shocked many merely by his presence.

At one time or another, *Veeck—As in Wreck*, his memoir title, had signed ancient pitcher Satchel Paige, brought three-foot-seven Eddie Gaedel to bat, and planted ivy at Wrigley. Before a May 1959 game he ordered a helicopter to land behind second base. Four people dressed as spacemen—Gaedel and three others as small—gave diminutive Nellie Fox and Luis Aparicio a tandem ray gun. Fox hit an MVP .306. "Little Looie" stole fifty-six bases. Sherm Lollar had a team-best twenty-two homers. Early Wynn finished 22-10. "It was our pitching," said manager Al Lopez. "A rally meant a single, steal, sacrifice, and error." The Yankees had won four straight pennants and seemed unlikely to be awed. The season began in Detroit: Sox, 9–7, on Fox's fourteenth-inning homer. One day Chicago scored eleven runs in an inning on one hit, ten walks, a hit batsman, and an error, winning, 20–6. The South Siders nabbed first place for good on July 28. Later a Comiskey-high 45,510 saw eventual Cy Younger Wynn unhorse the Tribe, the '59ers setting an attendance mark (1,423,144). On September 22 Chicago clinched the pennant, 4–2, at Cleveland. "The Sox are champions!" Elson rasped of Indian Vic Power's game-ending double play. To celebrate, Mayor Richard Daley activated Chicago's air sirens, terrifying much of the city.

WGN broadcast from a United Airlines charter returning from Ohio, Brickhouse asking if Fox ever swallowed his chewing tobacco. "Remember it!" said the Mighty Mite. "I thought I'd swallowed a volcano!" At Midway Airport fifty thousand howled as the plane arrived after 2 a.m. "Whatever happened to the Yankees?" outfielder Jim Rivera taunted, New York placing worse than second (third) for the first time since 1948. From 1947 through 1965 the commissioner, NBC-TV, and sponsor Gillette chose World Series voices. "They'd pick a guy from each team," said Veeck, knowing that Mel Allen, usually doing Series TV, couldn't because the Yankees hadn't made it. (He aired NBC Radio.) Elson was not considered, having grown up on the same block as NBC sports director Tom Gallery, who detested him.

By default, Brickhouse joined the Dodgers' Vin Scully on NBC-TV to air the then largest-ever-watched Rounders Championship of North America. Chicago exulted as did Bill Veeck on the pennant-clinching play, the Sox owner saying, "The magic number is *none!*"

No TV play-by-play preserves the 1959 Fall Classic. "To record, you had to fuzzily shoot the screen," said Brickhouse, etching a process called kinescope. "Even if you did, it was bulky to store." Only audio recalls a World Series viewed by 120 million people, including the final game's still-record 90 million. To make the Series, the Dodgers had to beat Milwaukee in a best-of-three playoff before moving to Comiskey Park.

"And so the scene is set," Allen said of the opener. Chicago soon led, 3–0, as Ted Kluszewski batted in its one-out and one-on third inning. "Klu hits a long fly to right!" cried the Phillies' Byrum Saam. "Norm Larker goes back, back! It . . . goes in for a home run!"—Pale Hose, 5–0. Later the Dodgers' Charlie Neal tried to nab Al Smith at the plate. "There's a bounding ball to the second baseman. They're coming to the plate. [John] Roseboro lets it get by! . . . Another run scores!" The Sox led, 8–0, except that eight was not enough.

Thrice hitting forty or more homers, Kluszewski was baseball's Christian Dior. "We had these heavy woolies. I'd feel cramped," Ted explained, cutting sleeves at the shoulder. In the fourth inning Nature Boy hit again. "Klu lets go another long salvo to right field! It's a home run into the upper deck!" bayed Saam. The Sox led, 11–0. Allen remarked, "This is quite surprising," given the light-hitting Hose reputation. Saam replied prophetically: "Maybe the Sox should have saved some runs."

Readying to run for president, John F. Kennedy sat in Mayor Daley's box for Game Two. Chicago's creative vote-counting would affect the 1960 election. For now, Daley, a true Sox fanatic, and his guest fixated on the field. "Lollar smacks the ball just out of Neal's reach for a single," said Scully, voicing the Series highlight film, "and Jim Landis scores to give the Sox a quick 2–0 lead." Neal later drove to left. "Unintentionally, an eager fan knocks over his drink. And in front of forty thousand, Al Smith takes a bath in left field." The photo of beer falling on Smitty's head won an Associated Press award.

In the seventh inning Chicago lost its lead on Chuck Essegian's two-all pinch homer. Neal then "rip[ped] into the ball again," said Scully, "for a long drive to deep center" that landed in the Sox bullpen in pitcher Billy Pierce's glove. Suddenly the Dodgers led, 4–2. In the home eighth inning the Sox put two men on base, Al Smith up. "He gets ahold of one and drills it into deep left-center field!" said Vin. "It's going to the wall for a double. [Earl] Torgeson scores. [Wally] Moon plays the rebound to Maury Wills. His relay to Roseboro cuts Lollar down at the plate by a big margin." Sox lose, 4–3. "The World Series is all even!" said Allen. Actually it was all over, having pivoted on Wills's relay throw.

Game Three moved the Series to a place it had never been: the Los Angeles Memorial Coliseum, with a 251-foot left-field pole, bleachers one-eighth of a mile from the plate, and a grandstand in Orange County. The Sox stranded thirteen runners, losing, 3–1. A day later, the Dodgers again won by one run, 5–4, ahead, three games to one. "Will the Series be ended or will we move back to Comiskey Park?" Allen said before Game Five. Fox scored on a double play. In the seventh the Dodgers trailed, 1–0, two out and two on: "And it's swung on [by Neal]. There's a drive to deep right-center!" Mel roared. "Landis digging hard! And the ball is caught by Rivera! A tremendous catch by Jim Rivera as he raced over to right field!" The Sox still lived, 1–0, before a record Series crowd of 92,706, having merely postponed extinction. Back home for Game Six, Early Wynn was shelled, 9–3.

Chicagoans blamed Dodgers reliever Larry Sherry's twelve and two-thirds innings, two wins, and 0.71 ERA. Aparicio knocked "the white shirts, noise, the crazy dimensions [of the Coliseum]." Said Fox, "It was a great year." The Hose left forty-three on base in the Series. Key hits would have made it greater. In 1960 Brickhouse, among others, foresaw a slew of flags. "Fox, Aparicio, I couldn't wait." He was still waiting upon his death in 1998. South Siders older than Obama recall Little Looie and skipper Lopez and the Mighty Mite—also Elson's "*He's* out!" and Jack's "Hey-Hey!" The poet Sophocles said, "One must wait until the evening to see how splendid the day has been." To his credit, Obama always knew why one year's day remains splendid.

After the British victory at Tobruk in November 1942, Winston Churchill pronounced, "Now, this is not the end. It is not even the beginning of the end. But it is perhaps the end of the beginning." The beginning of Obama's presidency was rocky, from a non-shovel-ready stimulus program to fury over Churchill's bust being booted from the Oval Office. The presidency is a bad place to make a bad first impression. (Ask Obama's successor, Donald Trump.) The flip side is that one or two four-year terms leave ample time to rally.

The late Mario Cuomo said, "Campaigning is poetry. Government is prose." As candidate, then president, Barack Obama employed both. Before his election undecideds worried about Obama's average-guy rapport. Afterward many fretted about a liberal trying to lead a center-right nation. In 2008 the Illinoisan upset Hillary Clinton for the Democratic nomination. Next he faced Republican nominee John McCain, aided by the Great Recession of 2008. Cannily Barack made George W. Bush the cause of the financial fall—paraphrasing *The Music Man*, W. the villain of every trouble in every River City of his presidency. Obama routed McCain, 365 to 173 electoral votes and 52.9 to 45.7 percent of the popular vote.

Being the first African American president gave him great self-possession: the Pioneer had written history even before taking office. The candidate campaigned in poetry. His less poetic than prose first inaugural address befit a president. It addressed those who opposed, not just supported, him. "These things [values] are true," Obama said, recalling scripture and Washington at Valley Forge. The forty-fourth president seemed able to absorb dueling data, acting cerebrally, a supposed change from Bush 43. Moreover, it had been a while since an era of good feeling so suffused the land. His persona tied a picaresque youth; informality; basketball; the search for a White House puppy; and two young daughters, their father hoping to keep them "courteous, sweet, and disciplined," wooing those who mourned the desperate need in a dysfunctional age of setting a good parental example for those who had none at home. In what became two terms, policy was the rub.

A 2014 Gallup Poll reported that Americans by 53 to 41 percent did not believe foreign leaders respected their president. Obama ended military involvement in the Iraq War, letting Islamic State in Iraq and Syria (ISIS) terrorists fill a void left by the U.S. exit and voiding his pledge for "a stable, democratic, united Iraq." To avoid defeat, 44 then *returned* troops to regain hard-won land. In Afghanistan he added 47,000 troops, found his strategy checked, and held out till leaving office. Obama cut army size to a post–World War II low of 450,000; traded five Al Qaeda terrorists for U.S. POW deserter Bowe Bergdahl; fought a probe about the terrorist murder of four officials and soldiers at the U.S. Embassy at Benghazi; and made a deal that helped make Iran a nuclear power, improved relations as claimed with its regime, or both. In the Senate, Obama had served on the Foreign Relations Committee, traveling to Europe, the Middle East, Asia, and Africa. As president, after meetings with Pope Francis as an intermediary he visited Cuba to end more than half a century of estrangement. By contrast, Obama also ordered the murder of Al Qaeda's leader, Osama bin Laden—a feat that had eluded two predecessors and his one foreign policy act to gain universal acclaim.

At home Obama kept two promises: reversing a Bush funding limit on embryonic stem cell research and naming justices Sonia Sotomayor and Elena Kagan to the Supreme Court. He got a bonus in 2009, named a Nobel Peace Prize laureate. For a long while the Great Recession was not as disposed to success. Obama's first full year began a long, slow recovery. In 2008, 2.6 million jobs disappeared. In 2009 Congress passed the $787 billion American Recovery and Reinvestment Act, reserving only $26 billion for jobs in the first fiscal year. The Congressional Budget Office said just 18 percent of new spending would help two fields with a high jobless rate, manufacturing and construction.

Obama campaigned brilliantly as a moderate Democrat. Elected, he governed as a "progressive." The president proposed the Dodd-Frank Wall Street Reform and Consumer Protection Act; urged background checks on all gun sales; slowed coal production; touted wind and solar energy; spurned oil production, including fracking; and signed a proviso prodding children from south of our southern border to try to become illegal immigrants. He used Uncle Sam to stop the hemorrhage of the auto industry, including a temporary 60 percent government equity stake in General Motors. It largely worked, but the president was already so tarred by stimulus disillusion that he got little credit. Above all Congress passed the Affordable Care Act—Obamacare— vowing universal coverage, lower costs, better quality, and greater options regardless of premiums.

Time and again Obama vowed, "If you like your doctor [and/or] health care," you could keep them. Both claims were false. Obamacare helped the GOP win the House and Senate in 2010 and 2014 respectively, and the presidency in 2016. For Democrats politically, the apotheosis of Big Government was not what the doctor ordered.

Obama's New Age persona was cool, hip, and au courant, yet mattered far less than the state of the economy. In 2014, 33 percent in a Quinnipiac University national poll deemed Barack the worst president dating to the end of World War II, trailed closely by W.'s 28 percent. Others lagged far behind. Where were all the jobs? Midway through his second term, an incident happened far closer to his wheelhouse.

On a June 2015 night in Charleston, South Carolina, historically reserved for Bible study, the faithful gathered in Charleston's famed Mother Emanuel AME Church. After an hour an unknown visitor took out a gun and cold-bloodedly killed nine people—the kind of evil act about which the Gospel writes. A few days later relatives of the victims responded at the alleged murderer's bail hearing in a way equally biblical. One by one they showed amazing grace, preaching the essence of Christianity: mercy and forgiveness. It was riveting, and it was real.

Nadine Collier's seventy-year-old mother had been murdered. "You took something very precious to me," she told the alleged killer. "But if God forgives you, I forgive you." She inspired Alana Simmons, whose grandfather, a reverend, was also killed, to speak: "We are here to combat hate-filled actions with love-filled actions." Bethane Middleton-Brown said of her murdered sister, "She taught me that . . . we have no room for hating, so we have to forgive." As Governor Nikki Haley said, "[The victims' relatives'] expression of faith and forgiveness took our breath away."

That week President Obama delivered an elegant eulogy to the AME church, the Reverend Clementa C. Pinckney among the nine killed. The speech began: "The church is, and has always been, the center of African American life," which is irrefutable. At home as much there as in the salons of Georgetown, Obama suggested the alleged murderer "didn't know he was being used by God" to show Charleston's love. "God does work in mysterious ways." The eulogy contained grace notes about Reverend Pinckney's life, recalling the man who pledged to transcend red and blue states for the *United* States of America. To a friend who had been there, it was reminiscent of Obama and Bush 41 talking easily in 2009 about domestic policy.

Poppy had touted a kinder, gentler Reaganism. Obama named two GOP Cabinet members, put evangelist Rick Warren in his inaugural, and touted tax cuts for stimulus. Each then agreed the presidency meant example, needing bipartisanship. Somehow the message of each got clouded in the rendering. A weak economy beat Bush 41 in 1992. The forty-fourth president faced two hurdles by 2012. First, the electorate's job one was the economy. Second, Obama didn't reach his initial goal of 5.4 percent unemployment until year *seven*. The incumbent might not want to take responsibility, but voters might insist.

Four straight budgets showed a $1 trillion deficit. Food stamp recipients had soared from thirty-two million to more than fifty. Given that, the temptation would be to demonize, not defend, which Obama did in 2012, casting GOP nominee Mitt Romney as a corporate jackal of all money and no soul. The economy rose just enough to reelect 44 in a race still debated: did the Democrat win, or Republican lose? As the president neared the end of a second term, Donald Trump was elected. Antithetically, Obama left office with unemployment at 4.7 percent, far *better* than his original goal.

Clearly, Obama meant to make his *last* impression as president better than the *first*. The number of monthly jobs grew, even as people not looking for work did also. The percentage of people supporting Obamacare began to rise, more fearing repeal. The White House rightly observed that Obama remained popular, his personal as opposed to job approval topping 60 percent. Policy remained stickier. Most governors, state legislators, and federal legislators were now Republican, the other party having shrunk since 2009. Trump would try to reverse a two-term Obama first: not one year of at least 2 percent growth. He took the oath as economic redistribution eclipsed economic expansion—perhaps what his predecessor had in mind all along.

Certain moments can reveal a candidate. The 2016 GOP nominee showed insight into Middle America's grievances and fears. Donald Trump then went an insult or two too far against women and minorities including gays, Muslims, and the disabled, among others. Each time many of his supporters defended him by "explaining" him. Similarly, in 2008 president-to-be Obama traveled to San Francisco—"elitism's epicenter," said a supporter, the *New York Times*' Maureen Dowd—where he told donors why the working class mistrusted him. Small-town America felt angst, whereupon it became "bitter . . . cling[ing] to guns or religion or antipathy to people who aren't like them or anti-immigration sentiment or anti-trade sentiment as a way to explain their frustrations." In Obama's telling the citizenry of small-town America, having sired the vast majority of U.S. presidents, had devolved overnight into gun-obsessed, religion-crazed rubes.

The future president soon said he had been misinterpreted, presaging Trump's explanation of the week, which, in turn, was reminiscent of Spiro Agnew's introduction as a gaffe-prone candidate for VP in 1968. "Apologize now," an opposition sign at an Agnew rally read. "It will save time later." In 2008 Hillary Clinton, opposing Obama for the Democratic nomination, had championed that working class, charging him with disdain for all things bourgeois: "We don't want a President who looks down at us. We want a President who stands up for us." In 2016, running as a down-the-line liberal, would she have thought about saying the above?

Obama was a shrewd politician—he would otherwise never have been president—who grasped that much of his appeal lay in not seeming to be a pol. Politicians get into trouble when they appear to favor one group over another. Obama's 2008 election was magical because it seemed to stir opportunity for every race, sex, and creed. Like any president, he cares about his legacy—especially that of representing and treating all Americans alike. Late in his second term a *New York Times*/CBS poll reported that "69 percent of Americans say that race relations are generally bad," the highest since the 1992 Los Angeles riot. Obama should address that rise, now out of office. He might also help unlock the puzzle of why many blacks don't play or follow baseball—and suggest personnel for its front office and radio/TV. He hopes to shape policy, advising and tutoring potential Democratic candidates, and has already commented on his successor, a break from tradition. Yet he is unlikely to leave the Second City behind.

As Obama primed to leave office, an otherworldly event for any Chicagoan, even a White Sox fan, occurred. At 12:46 a.m., November 3, 2016, baseball's longest-running symbol of wait till next year vanished. The Chicago Cubs won a Game Seven 8–7 ten-inning victory over Cleveland: their first title since beating the Tigers in the World Series of 1908. The "drought, as all eventually do, ended with help from above," wrote *Sports Illustrated's* Tom Verducci of how, after nine innings, the score being tied at 6, "rain, glorious cool rain . . . fell on Progressive Field in Cleveland just as the Cubs were about to flush away their 108th consecutive season without a World Series title." A seventeen-minute rain delay prompted a players meeting that staunched an Indians comeback and renewed Cubs confidence—"a 17-minute interlude that changed history," *SI* mused.

On January 16, 2017, four days before Obama's farewell, the Cubbies graced his last official event at the White House. "Throughout our history, sports has had this power to bring us together, even when the country is divided," said the president, referencing the recent Clinton-Trump election, or was it Chicago's two big-league teams? His grin signaled a dig was coming: "Now, listen, I made a lot of promises in 2008. But even I was not crazy enough to suggest that during these eight years we would see the Cubs win the World Series." Cubs president Theo Epstein gave Obama a "midnight pardon" for his "indiscretions as a baseball [White Sox] fan," a lifetime admission to Wrigley Field, a

No. "44" panel from its manual center-field scoreboard, and two Cubs baseball jerseys—home and away—with the No. 44. First baseman Anthony Rizzo also wore it, the president styling him "my fellow 44." He conceded it might be hard psychologically for him to wear, then added, "Do know that among Sox fans I am the Cubs number-one fan?"

In his household, Obama ranked second in Cubdom to "FLOTUS [First Lady of the United States], a lifelong Cubs fan," the president said. He told the East Room event of hosting more than fifty teams in eight years, yet "Michelle [who had to leave before speeches began] never came to a single event celebrating a champion until today!" Talking with Cubs execs, she confessed "what it meant for her to be able to see them win," because the First Lady recalled returning from school, her dad watching the Cubs on TV, "and the bond and the family, the meaning that the Cubs had for her in terms of connecting with her father and why it meant so much for her." Hearing her, said Obama, "I almost choked up."

Before Michelle left, 44 told the crowd, she related how her favorite player, 1972–77 Cub Jose Cardenal, had "had a big Afro [hair style]" and as a teen she "[wore] her hat over her Afro the same way Jose did." Even then, "baseball [was] personal." Obama recalled pilgrims in 2016 trekking to "their dads' gravesites" to hear games on radio; wearing their "moms' old jerseys" to the Friendly Confines; and covering its "brick walls with love notes" in chalk to their departed—a communion with generations who hadn't lived to see a title. With the final out, "suddenly everything . . . changed"—"our hometown [became] the very definition of joy."

That same month Obama leased a home in the exclusive Kalorama part of Washington, like Chicago a Democratic hub, which hopes the Nationals will join the White Sox as his new home team. Obama will write books, including his memoir, because as a fine writer he grasps the art of putting pen to paper, or finger to computer key. The Barack Obama Presidential Center in Chicago, partnered with the University of Chicago, is expected to be completed by 2020 or 2021. Professor Obama will likely spend time teaching, at which he is likely to excel. Another gift from the Cubs may be there: a flag with a "W" for "win" like that flown over Wrigley to signal a home team victory, signed by the players, Epstein suggesting that it be flown when the center opens.

Even as I cheered the Yankees at age eight, a window on my future involved that *other* Chicago team of White Sox pinstriped garb and "Pale Hose" moniker of quaint childhood usage. Who wouldn't want to troop out to Comiskey Park—forget today's corporate imposter of a name—and find that 1971–81 voice Harry Caray still lives, or at Wrigley Field, where Caray reigned from 1982 through 1997? Quoting him, Obama said, "You can't beat fun at the old ball park," becoming an ex-president at fifty-five, with grace a long life ahead.

I have always opposed the Twenty-Second Amendment, which keeps anyone from serving more than two consecutive terms as president. Five minutes of some presidents are too much. Four terms of Franklin Roosevelt were not enough. Having made history for himself, Obama could make it for others, backing the amendment's repeal for future presidents. "Yes, [he] can" can help undo this undemocratic amendment, saving the Pioneer's best deed for last.

SEVENTEEN

The Donald and the Game

Donald Trump, 2017–

On January 20, 2017, Donald John Trump became the forty-fifth of America's presidents, a majority of whom had served since baseball turned professional in the last third of the nineteenth century. No team sport equals baseball's longevity, dating to its amateur genesis. None summons its mélange of presidential memory. Film captured Franklin Roosevelt's buoyant overhand delivery. Ronald Reagan portraying Grover Cleveland Alexander was a peak of his career. Throwing out the first ball unlike anyone is likely to, Harry Truman gave "ambidextrous" new meaning. George W. Bush's first-pitch strike from the mound at Yankee Stadium after 9/11 wrote another definition: Hemingway's "grace under pressure."

At Hyde Park you can see a remarkable letter from one navy man to another ending with Longfellow's poem, "Sail On, Oh Ship of State." FDR had sent it to Churchill, who read it on the air and vowed, "Give us the tools, and we will finish the job," cementing the "Special Relationship" between America and Great Britain. In 1942 actor William Frawley showed another special relationship between the media and baseball, so liking the pastime that he hoped to do Yankees radio. Minus: Most acting would have had to go, baseball's schedule precluding film. Plus: He would have aired ball daily. Frawley stuck to the moving image, living a curmudgeon's dream as TV's Fred Mertz on *I Love*

Lucy, his contract providing ten days off each October to attend the World Series, drinking and talking ball.

Donald Trump's background accented the special relationship peculiar to this book: baseball and the presidency. In 2016 he won the latter, having grown up with the former. Trump was raised on the Yankees, was later approached by two teams about trying for the Majors, and made "big league" his favorite adjective. George Bernard Shaw famously called America and Great Britain "two countries separated by a common language." Trump took office in an America in which *its* two countries—red and blue states, right and left, liberal and conservative—seemed separated by a warring language. All some could *agree* upon was baseball.

The presidency is personal; depending on your view, a president may mirror duty, ignominy, old-fashioned heroism, and/or even new-age narcissism. Baseball too: save the catcher, no player is masked by a face guard or padding. Each stands alone, exposed. A look at Trump's life may tell how he staged what the website Bloomberg Politics called "the most stunning political upset in American history." It came out of nowhere, but came deep from somewhere.

Born June 14, 1946, the fourth of five children and second son of Fred Trump and Mary Anne MacLeod, the upper-class Donald grew up in middle-class Jamaica in Queens, New York, his father a developer and mother a housewife. At sixteen Fred had begun his career. First, he built a two-car garage; in time, thousands of rental properties, larger homes, and larger properties; and for his family, the colonial revival, a mansion of twenty-three rooms, nine bathrooms, and room for a live-in maid and chauffeur.

Trump Sr. also ensured that what Donald demanded, he didn't necessarily get. In 1958 many young baseball players yearned for new mitts with intricate webbing that the Rawlings Company had begun to sell. A friend of Donald's, Peter Brant, persuaded his father to buy him the $30 glove. Trump failed with his father. Yet $30 translates to $246 now, so when Fred Trump agreed to a slightly cheaper glove, the twelve-year-old wasn't slumming. Even then "The Donald," a name coined by first wife Ivana, could make a deal.

"We never thought of ourselves as rich kids," said Trump, if on occasion he seemed to expect the world to fly his carpet. In second grade Donald alleged to having given his music teacher a black eye because he "didn't think he knew anything about music." He taunted older brother Freddy, who died at forty-three of alcoholism, about "wasting [his] time" as an airline pilot. Fred Trump insisted on Donald doing summer jobs and paper routes, but playing nice didn't take. "[I] was a very assertive, aggressive kid," he conceded. "I liked to stir things up, liked to test people." Conflict appeared inevitable. It happened when he went away to school.

Later Trump credited two people for creating the man who became president. One was Dad, who any day might oversee a work site, bargain with suppliers, and negotiate with builders. Everywhere, said his son, Fred taught "toughness in a very tough business," an "unbelievably demanding taskmaster [who] would just pound and pound and pound." The other man surfaced because, to friends, "Donald Trump" had become a.k.a. "DT," for "detention," verging on junior high school delinquency. In 1959, Trump, thirteen, left the Kew-Forest School and enrolled in the New York Military Academy at Cornwall-on-Hudson, north of New York City. Here he finished eighth grade and high school, graduating in 1964 after learning self-discipline from academy sports coach and former army drill sergeant Ted Dobias, who had been appalled by what he saw in Donald.

"He didn't know how to make a bed," Ted said to National Public Radio. "He had a problem, you know, with being a cadet." The World War II veteran was especially hard on the sons of the privileged—until he had dinner with Fred, visiting the academy, who showed "how really tough he was on the kid," Colonel Dobias told Michael D'Antonio, author of 2015's *Never Enough: Donald Trump and the Pursuit of Success*. "He was very German." When students misbehaved, Donald said, "Dobias smacked you and smacked you hard." Some students fought back physically. Others turned the other cheek, earning his contempt. Trump respected him but refused to be cowed. It helped that he could play. Donald tried other sports, but baseball was his best sport and Dobias's favorite. "Good hitter, good fielder, good attitude," the coach said. "He was a good athlete. I'd give him an eight and a half out of 10." By ninth grade, Trump had become a model cadet. As a senior, he was cadet captain and star first baseman.

To *Rolling Stone* Ted called him "good-hit *and* good-field. We had . . . Phillies [scouts] to watch him, but he wanted to go to college." As usual Trump was his own best booster, "always the best player," he termed himself. "I always knew I was good, the best baseball player in New York when I was young. Not only baseball, but every sport." Former classmate Ted Levine agreed in *Business Insider*: "He was just the best . . . a great athlete. He could have probably played pro ball as a pitcher. I think he threw 80 miles an hour. . . . He could do anything he wanted." What he wanted was to make "real money." Trump wanted to enter sports but "also knew that was very limited because in those days"— it seems hilarious now—"you couldn't even make any money being a great baseball player." Too bad. It would have been a show.

Trump resembled Pete Rose via Dustin Pedroia by way of Enos Slaughter—the most never-say-die kid in town. The *Washington Post* wrote, "Trump's uniform was often the dirtiest on the field, and he shrugged off foul balls clanging off his mask." Added MSNBC: "Even as a catcher, he was unbothered by balls to the face." A baseball phrase, "red-a--," references someone whose temper wins a batting title. Even a young Trump's did. According to two boyhood neighbors, the *Post* continued, when making an out he could erupt, hitting another boy or smashing a baseball bat, without apology. By sixth grade Trump was such a feared right-hand pull hitter that rival teams shifted to left field. "If he had hit the ball to right, he could've had a home run because no one was there," said schoolmate Nicholas Kass. "But he always wanted to hit the ball through people. He wanted to overpower them."

All the traits that in 2016 made Trump loved or loathed loomed early: defiance, work, study, rage. So did his love of ball. In sixth grade he wrote a poem, published in his yearbook:

I like to hear the crowd give cheers,
so loud and noisy to my ears.
When the score is 5–5, I feel like I could cry.

And when they get another run, I feel like I could die.
Then the catcher makes an error,
not a bit like Yogi Berra.
The game is over and we say
tomorrow is another day.

Rhyming "error" with "Berra" suggests that Trump preferred action to reflection, an attitude that by 2016 made his net worth between $10 billion (his estimate) and $3.0 billion (Bloomberg's). In 1987 Trump released his first book, *The Art of the Deal*, which topped the best-seller list, built name recognition, and became the philosophy that led to the White House door.

In 1964 the Red Sox visited the New York Military Academy to talk with Trump about delaying college. Again he chose "real money" over baseball money, spending the next two years at Fordham University in the Bronx. In 1966 Donald transferred to the Wharton School of the University of Pennsylvania in Philadelphia, then among the few schools in America with a real estate studies department. In 1968 Trump graduated with a BS degree in economics, working concurrently at the family real estate firm, Elizabeth Trump & Son. In 1971 he took over, creating the Trump Organization, avoiding Vietnam War service through a medical deferment.

Trump spent the next five decades mixing brass, guile, timing, intelligence, hyperbole, a sizable inherited sum, and a much larger fortune he made into a unique niche as barker, playboy, TV personality, prolific builder, boffo marketer, and—dare we say—commander in chief and leader of the free world. Among others, he bought the Miss USA and Miss Universe Pageants, the short-lived U.S. Football League's New Jersey Generals, and nearly twenty golf courses. The Trump Taj Mahal Casino, Trump Shuttle, and Trump University, among others, went or already were going belly up. By contrast, he built successful Trump Tower, Trump's International Hotel in Chicago, and a Trump Hotel near the White House, an extremely partial list. "I build," Trump said. "It's what I do."

By 2017, 268 of the 515 businesses with which Trump was associated bore his name. The brand, valued by the Donald that year at $3.3 billion, profited from NBC-TV's smash reality show *The Apprentice*, of which Trump was host and executive producer in 2003–15. TV encourages excess, which can midwife falsehood. Trump breathes the first and is thought to tolerate the second. Depending on your view, an example of one or the other was his claim that film footage showed thousands of Muslims celebrating in New Jersey after the September 11, 2001, terrorist attack. This conduct began before Trump became a candidate and has not been fatal on the sound assumption, one supposes, that all politicians lie.

In 1977 Trump was married for the first time to Czech model Ivana Zelnickova. An affair with actress Marla Maples ended the marriage, Trump wedding Maples in 1993. That too ended six years later, Trump later saying that work caused each failure. In 2005 he married Melania Knauss, a former supermodel and Slovenian immigrant who became a naturalized citizen a year after their wedding. She spoke five languages, was said to be a fine mother and lovely woman, and inherited her husband's press, then and as First Lady.

For more than half a century DEWEY DEFEATS TRUMAN—the *Chicago Tribune*'s epic miscall of Harry Truman's defeat of Thomas E. Dewey in 1948—remained the shorthand for political or any other kind of unexpected result. No more. Like it or not—and many discerning voters felt both at one time or another—Trump's victory in 2016 became America's most spectacular personal upset ever. Truman was thought to have a chance, however miniscule, due to organized labor's support. Trump was felt to have *nothing*—except the animus of virtually every institution in the republic. Instead he wrote a most astonishing tale, which put him in the White House at the cynosure of scrutiny. If he succeeded, his admirers would never forget him. If he failed, they would never forgive him.

Most had first eyed the Donald descending the Trump Tower escalator, Melania in arm, to announce he would seek the 2016 GOP nomination. He was thought an asterisk, an unreality show, a joke. Moreover, the Republican field was abloom—seventeen candidates in all, including Florida's telegenic U.S. senator Marco Rubio, who was young, schooled in foreign policy, the best Republican speaker since Ronald Reagan, crucial to a growing demographic, and the GOP candidate most feared by the likely Democratic nominee, former secretary of state Hillary Clinton.

Rubio won or contended in each early debate. Trump won or contended in each early primary, mocking "Little Marco" and Bush 41's youngest son, "Low-Energy" Jeb. Bush's fall was humiliating. Rubio was hurt when tag-teamed in a debate by Trump and the corpulent New Jersey governor Chris Christie. More than any rival, Trump grasped his base. His vows were clear: make trade fair; rebuild manufacturing; curb illegal immigration through a border wall; "Make America Great Again." His rallies were the largest for a populist or conservative since Ronald Reagan sought the presidency: their tone, messianic, and cast, resolutely middle and working class.

At one time or another Trump seemed to malign every liberal interest group against which it seemed possible to be malignant. He lacked a campaign structure, was despised by the GOP elect, and had nothing but contempt for *it*—"losers" who in his view had betrayed people like his father. Most Republicans cheered, loathing the same elite. Chosen in a peaceful coup d'etat, he went forth against Clinton, two nominees with the Gallup Poll's worst-ever modern major-party approval rating: Clinton, 55 percent disapproval; Trump, 65. In 1972 nominees Richard Nixon and George McGovern had sharply clashed, reconciling even before the Democrat attended the 1993 funeral of Nixon's wife Pat. "There has to be a place for kindness in politics," McGovern later told me. It didn't exist in 2016. One nominee had to win. But which nominee, and how?

Clinton wanted Trump to be the issue. Foundations, think tanks, and corporations disliked him. So did most clergy, faculty, and especially the media. Trump wanted Hillary to be the issue since only 27 percent in an NBC/*Wall Street Journal* poll dubbed her "honest." Clinton had money, staff, experience abroad, an economy recovered from most of a multiyear recession, and above all the fact that she wasn't Trump, who, among other gaffes, claimed that Vietnam

War POW John McCain was "not a hero" since he "had been captured." Trump benefited from addressing issues that moved the working middle: terrorism, border safety, political correctness. Would it be enough? "No," polling said.

Cornelius Ryan titled his classic D-Day novel *The Longest Day*. The rhythms of election day and night began soothingly, for the outcome seemed sure: a Clinton victory, only its size in doubt, her aces the states of Florida, North Carolina, Ohio, Michigan, Wisconsin, and Pennsylvania, the last a redoubt. Hillary took a lead, topped two hundred electoral votes—and stalled. In one state after another the same schism loomed: rural against urban, old against new, religious against secular; traditional against nontraditional. The only certainty seemed that to win, Trump would have to carry every key battleground state—run the table, impossible for even an artist of the deal.

At a little after midnight North Carolina's GOP moorings kicked in. A Rust Belt tide began lapping at states from Ohio to Wisconsin. "Voters showed up in an astounding number," stated analyst Mike Barnicle, terming it "an avalanche" of working-class voters leaving the party of FDR. Facing a massive Philadelphia deficit, Trump swept the rest of Pennsylvania—largely rural, often Democratic—much of it part of the stretch of upland named "Appalachia" starting in New York State and ending in Alabama. "We've got to reconnect with working-class Democrats, patriotic, religious," said VP Joe Biden. Feeling ignored for the last eight years, they connected with the one nominee who simply treated them with respect.

By 2:44 a.m. Trump *had* run the table, an inside straight of blue-collar, live-by-your-hands, non-boutique, mostly Midwest states. Clinton bravely called to congratulate. (Losing the popular vote, Trump won in electoral votes, 302–227.) Without Obama the coalition of minorities, youth, women, and affluent whites waned. Trump won the 70 percent white voting majority by 21 percentage points and working-class whites by 41. The result hung on the erosion of the Democratic New Deal base—many of whom had supported Trump and whom Hillary had termed "the basket of deplorables," saying of coal miners, "We'll put you out of business." The last word was theirs.

Given the Donald's flaws and errors, his victory merited being called "a miracle," as JFK dubbed *his* election in 1960, especially given Trump's opposition. On his side were instincts and a friend, he said, "who will never be forgotten again." Wealthy, a young Trump never knew "the Forgotten American," who years later had now elected him. FDR coined the term for those who felt alone and voiceless, even stigmatized, from a small town, an inner city, more often a farm. Think actress Jane Darwell as Ma Joad in film's magnificent *The Grapes of Wrath*, saying, "'Cause we're the people." Those people won the election of 2016.

Trump's January 20, 2017, inaugural received a mixed response, not surprising given the election's split verdict. He had a rocky start, hit some bumps, buoyed the economy, tweeted to his admirers' glee and likely to his own harm, and then tripped, skipping the capital's traditional presidential Opening Day on April 3 at Nationals Park: Nationals 4, Miami Marlins 2. Obama had opened a season only in his second year. Given his baseball lineage, more was expected of Trump.

The White House cited a scheduling conflict. Others suggested another cause. Had Trump been introduced, the new president correctly expected to be loudly and thoroughly booed. This is not an exception, but a universal: almost all presidents are booed at baseball parks, especially Republicans in Washington, to many a *foreign* capital, where in 2016 Trump got *four* percent of the vote versus Clinton. Bush 41 was harshly booed when the economy dove. His composure seldom fled. After Iraq, Bush 43 was heckled. He never hid. Reagan met booing with a quip and his All-American smile. Trump's riposte to its threat was to play more golf in 2017 than his friend Tiger Woods, hurt much of the year.

Several ironies of Trump's early time in office have been downplayed or gone unmentioned. One was that the Donald truly likes baseball. Before the White House, he tossed out the first ball with gusto at Wrigley Field, Fenway Park, and Yankee Stadium; sang "Take Me Out to the Ballgame" at the Friendly Confines; and even in the early 2010s blew up Twitter, saying that Alex Rodriguez "simply can't perform well without drugs"; that "It's time to let Pete [Rose] into the Hall of Fame!";

and more irrefutably, that Mariano Rivera "is the greatest closer of all time." A review of Trump's tweeting shows a man for whom shock talk was as natural as great hair.

The Donald had been in office only five months when sixty-six-year-old James Hodgkinson drove from home in Illinois to an Alexandria, Virginia, baseball field, where Republican members of Congress were practicing for the next night's annual charity GOP-Democratic Congressional game. On June 14 Hodgkinson asked a bystander if the players were Democrat or Republican. Told, he began firing assault rifle bullets, injuring five, including two Capitol Hill police officers, and bringing House Minority Whip Steve Scalise "within imminent risk of death," his doctor said. The police saved many lives, Trump observed, only the killer dying. Few noted a second irony: violence on baseball's pacific field. Two weeks later, several of the 2016 champion Cubs that Obama so uproariously welcomed in January returned to see Trump: Cubs chairman and Trump donor Tom Ricketts, skipper Joe Maddon, sluggers Anthony Rizzo and Kris Bryant, and pitchers John Lackey and Jon Lester. "Your team's doing okay," the president said of the then struggling '17ers, in town to play the Nats, "but you're to do great starting now, okay?"

At a time like this, the Donald could affect a rough blue-collar charm appealing to the people who elected him, largely tired of and embittered by being ignored by institutions, especially government. Yet the last irony of his no-first-year first pitch is that it affirmed a similar angst already epidemic among those who follow another institution, baseball, their voices judged unworthy of being heard as the pastime itself has ebbed. For a quarter century and more baseball has often been in eclipse, especially on network television. At best "baseball's place in society is not nearly what it should be," says Bob Costas, the 2018 newest Hall of Fame Ford C. Frick inductee for broadcast excellence. At worst the game has been in cultural freefall, especially among the young.

In a 1964 Gallup Poll baseball routed football, 45–23 percent, as America's "favorite game." By 2015 baseball trailed a similar Gallup survey by 43–11 percent, behind in *every* category of voters: white, black, brown, rich, poor, middle class, small town, suburban, and city. Says

Sports Illustrated, "In every metric, the stance [of football] as America's game is undisputed." In 1985 a Harris Poll showed football and baseball virtually tied as America's "favorite sport," 24 and 23 percent respectively. By 2014 the NFL led, 35–14 percent, baseball's decline the largest of any sport, faring worst among young people—Millennials—and, ironically, given Jackie Robinson, blacks. Football's 2017 contretemps over players kneeling during the National Anthem to protest ills of one type or another has seemed to only slightly dim its appeal.

Baseball's plunge has been steepest on TV. In 1952 each World Series telecast averaged one in two Americans; in 1980, one in five; in 2010, one in sixteen. By contrast, the 2018 Super Bowl lured nearly one in three, or 103.4 million viewers, among the all-time most watched programs. In 2017 football forged TV's twenty top-rated sports events, the NFL Pro Bowl out-rating baseball's All-Star Game. The day when 1969–84 baseball commissioner Bowie Kuhn called the All-Star Game and postseason "baseball's jewels" seems an eon ago.

The man ultimately accountable for much of this hemorrhage, Bud Selig, acting, then official, commissioner from 1992 to 2015, yearly opined, "Our game has never been near this popular." This is true only if fact is ruled unconstitutional. Fact: football routs baseball in yearly video game sales, licensed garb, unique Internet users, and "marketable athletes." Fact: Hollywood once meant baseball's *The Natural* and *Field of Dreams*. In 2009 football's *The Blind Side* became sport's all-time highest-grossing film. Fact: in ESPN's summer 2013 Kids in Sports focus, only 25 percent of U.S. adolescents age six to seventeen played baseball against basketball's and football's 40 percent each.

Fact: in a 2017 survey conducted by Q Scores Company measuring the appeal and recognition of celebrities among sports fans ages thirteen to sixty-four, baseball's highest-ranked active player was the Cubs' Kris Bryant, in thirty-third place. The Dodgers' Clayton Kershaw placed 167th and the National's Bryce Harper 253rd. Pro basketball's LeBron James ranked fourteenth. Hoops and pro football trounced the pastime. "Facts," John Adams said, "are stubborn things." Fortunately, Selig's successor as commissioner, Rob Manfred, seems aware of baseball's state. The immediate past teaches lessons the game must not ignore.

First, baseball must hire broadcasters who enliven. Baby Boomers were weaned on Vin Scully, Mel Allen, Dizzy Dean, and Harry Caray, among other artists, who employed language to entertain. Today, robotic and alike, many forget that, as Caray once told me, "For God's sake, don't guys now know what it's all about? 'Let me entertain you'!"

Second, baseball needs network TV. Put another way, how *has* British soccer nearly tied its network regular-season coverage? Since 2009 baseball has fixated on cable's MLB Network, a fetching display luring those *already* interested in the sport. Meantime, it has virtually deserted national, as opposed to cable or local, TV, airing nothing like a *Game of the Week* to *grow* interest. Its sole network, Fox, got baseball essentially to fill Saturday programming on remote low-rated outlets: refuse for a cable dump. Such cynicism fills owners' pockets while giving baseball zero buzz. Historically a tiny regular-season network niche sires a peewee October audience. F. Scott Fitzgerald helped to popularize "the Lost Generation." How many generations of children does baseball intend to lose?

Third, baseball should restore TV camera intimacy. Legendary NBC director Harry Coyle hailed Fenway Park's "great" coverage, its major camera shot from behind the plate low yet *above* a wire backstop. Contrast that up-close coverage to San Francisco's, Detroit's, and others, their home plate camera so high the field seems to be in Japan. Many new parks put the TV booth above swanky suites, players resembling ants. Worse, mesh screens obstruct the camera, like watching through prison bars. What a recipe: a picture where little happens and we can't see what does. Incredibly, today's "new old" parks provide more TV-unfriendly coverage than cookie-cutter stadia of the 1970s and '80s. Fenway's "great" coverage rose from Boston's decision to build a TV catwalk above an angled backstop to benefit the viewer. Each team should move the home plate camera—a fan's picture window—as close as possible to the field.

Fourth, baseball should solve problems (suggested here) that trouble Joe Fan, not those that don't (e.g., umpire fallibility). Selig said that instant replay would shorten games. Naturally it lengthened them. Worse, it bleached baseball's color and human element, axing them for baseball execs' "imperfect way of getting umpires close to perfect," said the *Wall Street Journal*. Brass pined for nearly three thousand calls to be reviewed in 2016–17 as ear-phoned umpires, linked to New York, waited on the field two, three—in some cases more—minutes while the game literally *stopped*—a slow sport made unwatchable. Baseball's excuse is that bad calls need correcting. Skipping the obvious—if the umpiring stinks, hire better umpires—instant replay slights great characters on the field. It makes the man in blue a mere mannequin for a wire between the park and New York, not a co-star in florid flare-ups with Billy Martin. Meanwhile, the manager busies himself consulting with replay aides, who decide whether to challenge a call—gaming the system as viewers snore. What a loss—at what a cost.

Fifth, in that sense, baseball must quicken a pace even an octogenarian finds slow. Game Seven of the 1960 World Series scored nineteen runs in two hours and thirty-six minutes. Today a 1–0 game can take three or more hours. In 2015 baseball vowed to shorten an average game. It dropped from 3:02 to 2:56, then reverted to three hours in 2016 and a comical 3:05 in 2007—more glacial than at the "speed-up's" start. Manfred admits to "not being pleased." So please the public by *doing* something. If America could storm Normandy, split the atom, and reach the moon, baseball can enforce laws already written. Uphold the strike zone, keep a batter in the box, and ensure a bases-empty pitch every twenty seconds, even using a "pitch clock" as the commissioner implies. As culture turns less patient, pray God, let baseball be less inert.

Sixth, baseball must change the time some coverage starts. In 1985 it began an all-prime-time World Series, hoping to swell viewership, which shrank. Almost all network post- and regular-season TV is now nighttime, for cash. As children sleep, even adults nod off, cool to the slow pace and late hour. At the 1969 All-Star Gala, Nixon recalled the 1929 A's scoring ten runs in the seventh inning to overcome an 8–0 Series deficit. "I stay all the way every game after that experience!" he said, a vow most recently relevant to earlier noted Game Five of the 2017 Fall Classic—a big-league jai alai of seven homers and four half-innings of three or more runs. Covering the Series since 1975, the *Washington*

Post's Thomas Boswell pronounced the Astros' 13–12 victory in Houston the "most insanely entertaining" game he had seen. He may have liked the affair even more had it ended before 1:37 a.m. Eastern Time.

Almost midway through the score was tied at four, millions already in bed, not aware what lay ahead. In the fifth inning, the Dodgers' Cody Bellinger's belt put a brief mute button on the Minute Maid Park crowd: LA, 7–4. Five-foot-six 'Stros strong man Jose Altuve went deep to the center-field balcony: 7-each. In the seventh, Houston outfielder George Springer misplayed a ball for a run, then hit a game-tying orb onto the railroad tracks: 8-apiece. Doing if not believing, Carlos Correa homered for an 11–8 Houston lead, LA bunched three ninth-inning 12-all runs, and Alex Bregman singled in the tenth, ending a five-hour and seventeen-minute madhouse that mesmerized twenty-three million viewers. How many *more* would have marveled had the first pitch arced at 4:20 p.m. Eastern Time on Sunday instead of 8:20? Envision the interest tomorrow born from youth today.

Retrieving that night, baseball should address the future as viewed by the mass, not just elect, and inhale film mogul Adolph Zukor's truism that "The public is never wrong." It should solve a horse-and-buggy pace, an October of drowsy adults and slumbering kids, and network invisibility from April through September. It should build on the storybook wonder of the 2016 Cubs and 2017 Astros. Beyond cable—"MLB: All Baseball, All the Time," reaching the already devout—it needs another over-the-air free *network* like NBC or CBS to complement Fox and use the sole vehicle to reach each living room. The pastime deserves better after the joy it has endowed.

"Baseball," remarked the writer and historian Doris Kearns Goodwin, "is the most timeless of sports." In a sense, this book started with two presidents who cherished it: Republican William Howard Taft and Democrat Woodrow Wilson, each their party's first to throw out a first ball. It ends with other presidents who have loved the pastime too. Baseball must do what Franklin Roosevelt urged in a speech he was writing when he died—"move forward with strong and active faith"—so that years from now an American child will feel on Opening Day what we as children did: there is no place on earth you would rather be.

BIBLIOGRAPHY

Addie, Bob. "Presidential Pitch Began with Taft." *The Sporting News*, April 15, 1967.

Allen, Charles F., and Jonathan Portis. *The Life and Career of Bill Clinton, the Comeback Kid*. New York: Birch Lane Press, 1992.

Allen, Mel, and Frank Graham Jr. *It Takes Heart*. New York: Harper and Brothers, 1959.

Alsop, Joseph. *FDR: A Centenary Remembrance*. New York: Viking, 1982.

Ambrose, Stephen E. *Eisenhower: Soldier and President*. New York: Simon and Schuster, 1990.

———. *Nixon*, 3 vols. New York: Simon and Schuster, 1987.

Asinof, Eliot. *Eight Men Out*. New York: Ace Books, 1963.

Baker, James, with Thomas M. DeFrank. *The Politics of Diplomacy: Revolution, War, and Peace, 1989–1992*. New York: G. P. Putman's Sons, 1995.

Barber, Red. *1947—When All Hell Broke Loose in Baseball*. New York: Doubleday, 1982.

Bartlett, Arthur. *Baseball and Mr. Spalding*. New York: Farrar, Strauss, and Young, 1951.

Bealle, Morris A. *The Washington Senators*. Washington DC: Columbia Publishing, 1947.

Black, Conrad. *Richard M. Nixon: A Life in Full*. New York: Public Affairs, 2007.

Boswell, Tom. "A President's Passion for Baseball." *Washington Post*, March 31, 1989.

Brady, Dave. "JFK Goes All the Way with Nats—as Laotian Prince Cools Heels." *The Sporting News*, April 18, 1962.

Busch, Andrew E. *Reagan's Victory: The Presidential Election of 1980 and the Rise of the Right*. Lawrence: University Press of Kansas, 2005.

Bush, C. Fred. Edited slightly by Barbara Bush. *C. Fred's Story: A Dog's Life*. Garden City NY: Doubleday, 1984.

Bush, George. *All the Best, George Bush: My Life in Letters and Other Writings*. New York: Scribner, 1999.

Bush, George, and Brent Scowcroft. *A World Transformed*. New York: Knopf, 1998.

Bush, George, with Vic Gold. *Looking Forward: An Autobiography*. New York: Bantam, 1988.

Cannon, Lou. *President Reagan: The Role of a Lifetime*. New York: Simon and Schuster, 1991.

Caro, Robert. *The Years of Lyndon Johnson: Master of the Senate*. New York: Knopf, 2002.

Carter, Jimmy. *Sharing Good Times*. New York: Simon and Schuster, 2004.

————. *Why Not the Best?* Nashville: Broadman Press, 1975.

Cassuto, Leonard, and Stephen Partridge, eds. *The Cambridge Companion to Baseball*. Cambridge: Cambridge University Press, 2011.

Cater, S. Douglass. *The Fourth Branch of Government*. New York: Knopf, 1959

Clinton, Bill. *My Life*. New York: Knopf Publishing Group (Random House), 2004.

Coffin, Tristram Potter. *The Old Ball Game: Baseball in Folklore and Fiction*. New York: Herder and Herder, 1971.

Cohen, Richard M., David S. Neft, and Roland T. Johnson. *The World Series*. New York: Dial Press, 1976.

Connally, John, with Mickey Herskowitz. *In History's Shadow: An American Odyssey*. New York: Hyperion, 1993.

Creamer, Robert W. *Babe: The Legend Comes to Life*. New York: Simon and Schuster, 1974.

————. "The Great American Game." *Sports Illustrated*, April 12, 1956.

Daniel, Daniel M. "Roosevelt Saved Baseball with His 1942 Letter to Judge Landis." *Baseball Magazine*, June 1945.

Darman, Richard. *Who's In Control?: Polar Politics and the Sensible Center*. New York: Simon and Schuster, 1996.

Dickson, Paul. *Baseball's Greatest Quotations*. New York: HarperCollins, 1991.

————. *The Dickson Baseball Dictionary*. New York: Facts on File, 1989.

Falls, Joe. *Baseball's Greatest Teams: Detroit Tigers*. New York: Macmillan, 1975

Ford, Gerald. *A Time to Heal: The Autobiography of Gerald R. Ford*. New York: Harper and Row, 1979.

Garagiola, Joe. *Baseball Is a Funny Game*. New York: Bantam Books, 1962.

Gates, Robert M. *From the Shadows: The Ultimate Insiders' Story of Five Presidents and How They Won the Cold War*. New York: Simon and Schuster, 1996.

Gavin, William. *Speechwright: An Insider's Take on Political Rhetoric*. East Lansing: Michigan State University Press, 2011.

Green, Fitzhugh. *George Bush: An Intimate Portrait*. New York: Hippocrene Books, 1989.

Griffith, Clark, as told to A. E. Hotcher. "Presidents Who Have Pitched for Me." *This Week*, April 10, 1955.

Haldeman, H. R. *The Haldeman Diaries: Inside the Nixon White House*. New York: G. P. Putman's Sons, 1994.

Hano, Arnold. *A Day in the Bleachers*. New York: Crowell, 1955.

Henle, Raymond. *A Conversation with Herbert Hoover.* New York: NBC Television, 1955.

Henry, William A., III. *Visions of America: How We Saw the 1984 Election.* New York: Atlantic Monthly Press, 1985.

Hollander, Zander. *Presidents in Sport.* New York: Associated Features, 1962.

Hoover, Herbert. *The Memoirs of Herbert Hoover,* 3 vols. New York: Macmillan, 1951–1952.

Hynd, Noel. *The Giants of the Polo Grounds.* New York: Doubleday, 1988.

Johnson, Boris. *The Churchill Factor: How One Man Made History.* New York: Riverhead Books, 2014.

Johnson, Lyndon B. *The Vantage Point.* New York: Holt, Rinehart, and Winston, 1971.

King, Nicolas. *George Bush: A Biography.* New York: Dodd, Mead, 1980.

Kissinger, Henry A. *White House Years.* Boston: Little, Brown, 1979.

Koch, Doro Bush. *My Father, My President: A Personal Account of the Life of George H. W. Bush.* New York: Warner Books, 2006.

Koppett, Leonard. *Koppett's Concise History of Major League Baseball.* Philadelphia: Temple University Press, 2015.

Kuhn, Bowie. *Hardball.* New York: Times Books, 1987.

Lash, Joseph P. *Eleanor and Franklin.* New York: Norton, 1971.

Leuchtenburg, William E. *The LIFE History of the United States.* New York: TIME-LIFE Books, 1976.

Lieb, Frederick G. *Baseball as I Have Known It.* New York: Tempo, 1977.

Lindberg, Richard. *Who's on Third? The Chicago White Sox Story.* South Bend: Icarus Press, 1983.

Lowry, Phillip J. *Green Cathedrals.* Cooperstown: Society for American Baseball Research, 1986.

Macht, Norman L. "Presidents Made a Pitch for Popularity at Games." *USA TODAY Baseball Weekly,* June 29, 1992.

Manchester, William. *One Brief Shining Moment.* Boston: Little, Brown, 1983.

Maraniss, David. *First in the Class: A Biography of Bill Clinton.* New York: Simon and Schuster, 1995.

Matthews, Christopher. *Kennedy and Nixon: The Rivalry That Shaped Postwar America.* New York: Simon and Schuster, 1996.

McCoy, Donald. *Calvin Coolidge: The Quiet President.* New York: Macmillan, 1967.

McCullough, David. *Truman.* New York: Simon and Schuster, 1992.

Mead, William B. *Baseball Goes to War.* Washington DC: Farragut Publishing, 1985.

Mead, William B., and Paul Dickson. *Baseball: The Presidents' Game.* Washington DC: Farragut Publishing, 1993.

Miller, Doug, and Marion Nowak. *The Fifties: The Way We Really Were.* New York: Doubleday, 1975.

Montville, Leigh. *Ted Williams: The Biography of an American Hero.* New York: Doubleday, 2005.

Morgan, Ted. *FDR: A Biography*. New York: Simon and Schuster, 1986.

Morris, Willie. *North Toward Home*. Boston: Houghton Mifflin, 1967.

Morris, Wright. *God's Country and My People*. Lincoln: University of Nebraska Press, 1981.

Naftali, Timothy. *George H. W. Bush*. New York: Henry Holt, 2007.

Nevins, Allan. Afterword to *The Deerslayer*, by James Fenimore Cooper, 535–41. New York: New American Library, 1963.

Nixon, Richard. *The Memoirs of Richard Nixon*. New York: Grosset and Dunlap, 1978.

———. *Richard Nixon in the Arena: A Memoir of Victory, Defeat, and Renewal*. New York: Simon and Schuster, 1990.

———. *Six Crises*. New York: Simon and Schuster, 1990.

Noll, Mark. *America's God: From Jonathan Edwards to Abraham Lincoln*. New York: Oxford University Press, 2002.

Novak, Robert D. *The Prince of Darkness: 50 Years of Reporting in Washington*. New York: Crown Forum, 2007.

Okrent, Daniel, and Harris Lewine. *The Ultimate Baseball Book*. Boston: Houghton Mifflin, 1979.

O'Neill, Thomas P., Jr., with William Novak. *Man of the House: The Life and Political Memoirs of Speaker Tip O'Neill*. New York: Random House, 1987.

Parmet, Herbert S. *George Bush: The Life of a Lone Star Yankee*. New York: Scribner, 1997.

———. *Richard Nixon and His America*. Boston: Little, Brown, 1990.

Perelman, Josh, ed. *Choosing Dreams: Baseball and Becoming American*. Philadelphia: National Museum of American Jewish History, 2015.

Plimpton, George. *One for the Record: The Inside Story of Hank Aaron's Chase for the Home Run Record*. New York Hachette Book Group USA, 2016.

———. "A Sportsman Born and Bred." *Sports Illustrated*, December 26, 1989.

Porter, Sylvia. *Sylvia Porter's Your Finances in the 1980s*. New York: Macmillan, 1990.

Price, Raymond. *With Nixon*. New York: Viking Press, 1977.

Reagan, Ronald. *An American Life*. New York: Simon and Schuster, 1990.

———. *The Reagan Diaries*. Edited by Douglas Brinkley. New York: HarperCollins, 2007.

———. *Where's the Rest of Me?* New York: Karz Publishers, 1981.

Reeves, Richard. *President Kennedy: Profile of Power*. New York: Simon and Schuster, 1993.

———. *President Nixon: Alone in the White House*. New York: Simon and Schuster, 2001.

Rickey, Branch, with Robert Riger. *The American Diamond: A Documentary of the Game of Baseball*. New York: Simon and Schuster, 1965.

Ritter, Lawrence S. *The Glory of Their Times*. New York: Macmillan, 1966.

Robinson, Jackie, with Alfred Duckett. *I Never Had It Made*. New York: Putnam, 1972.

Roosevelt, Franklin D. Keynote speech, laying of cornerstone for FDR Presidential Library and Museum. Hyde Park NY, November 19, 1939.

Rosenman, Samuel. *Working with Roosevelt*. New York: Da Capo Press, 1972.

Ruth, George Herman, with Bob Considine. *The Babe Ruth Story*. New York: Dutton, 1948.

Schlesinger, Arthur M., Jr. *A Thousand Days: John F. Kennedy in the White House*. Cambridge MA: Houghton Mifflin, 1965.

Schlesinger, Robert. *White House Ghosts: Presidents and Their Speechwriters*. New York: Simon and Schuster, 2012.

Schweizer, Peter, and Rochelle Schweizer. *The Bushes: Portrait of a Dynasty*. New York: Doubleday, 2004.

Seymour, Harold. *Baseball: The Early Years*. New York: Oxford University Press, 1960.

Sheed, Wilfred, and Jacques Lowe. *The Kennedy Legacy: A Generation Later*. New York: Viking Penguin, 1988.

Smith, Curt. *George H. W. Bush: Character at the Core*. Lincoln: Potomac Books/University of Nebraska Press, 2015.

———. *Pull Up a Chair: The Vin Scully Story*. Washington DC: Potomac Books, 2009.

———. *Storied Stadiums*. New York: Carroll and Graf, 2001.

Smith, Richard Norton. *Thomas E. Dewey and His Times*. New York: Simon and Schuster, 1982.

Smithsonian Institution Books. *Every Four Years*. New York: Norton, 1980.

Swift, Will. *Pat and Dick: The Nixons: An Intimate Portrait of a Marriage*. New York: Simon and Schuster, 2014.

Truman, Harry S. *Memoirs*. Garden City NY: Doubleday, 1955–1956.

Turner, Frederick, W. *When the Boys Came Back: Baseball and 1946*. New York: Henry Holt, 1996.

Uecker, Bob, with Mickey Herksowitz. *Catcher in the Wry*. New York: Jove, 1982.

Underwood, John. "Progress Report on the Unknown Soldier," *Sports Illustrated*, April 4, 1966.

Valenti, Jack. *A Very Human President: A First-Hand Report*. New York: Norton, 1975.

Veeck, Bill. *Veeck—As in Wreck*. New York: New American Library, 1962.

Wallop, Douglass. *The Year the Yankees Lost the Pennant*. New York: Norton, 1954.

White, Theodore H. *In Search of History*. New York: Harper and Row, 1978.

———. *The Making of the President 1960*. New York: Atheneum, 1961.

Wicker, Tom. *George Herbert Walker Bush*. New York: Viking, 2004.

INDEX

All-Star Games: in Arlington, 364; Barack Obama at, 384, 386–87; Bess Truman's ballot for, 114; at Briggs Stadium, 246; broadcasts of, 115, 140, 193, 293, 393, 415; at Candlestick Park, 170; at DC Stadium, 190; in Detroit, 247, 251; at Griffith Stadium, 80, 137; Mark Fidrych in, 255–56; Mickey Mantle in, 133; Richard Nixon at, 211–13, 215, 220; Ronald Reagan at, 294, 295; Ted Williams in, 313; in Toronto, 314; Willie Mays in, 373; at Yankee Stadium, 91
All the Best, George Bush (Bush), 370
Alomar, Roberto, 229
Alou, Felipe, 146, 170
Alou, Matty, 170
Alston, Walter, 228, 229, 388
Altuve, Jose, 418
Ambrose, Stephen, 129, 157
American Association, 5–6, 13
American Enterprise, 257
American Enterprise Institute, 258
American Federation of Labor, 58
American League: 1968 batting title in, 192; in 1970s, 220–21, 251; in 1983 All-Star Game, 294; Angels winning, division (1979), 238; ballparks in, 77, 119, 151, 166; Championship Series (1972), 230–31; Championship Series (2005), 384; Cleveland Indians in, 132; creation and leadership of, 13, 26, 116, 185, 199, 243; divisions in, 218, 362, 364–65; expansion of, 147–49, 172; honoring of FDR, 98; Minnesota Twins in, 204; pennant race (1949), 122; presidents at games of, 24; records in, 79, 137, 155, 244; Red Sox winning, 378; Richard Nixon's All-Star team in, 225–30; Richard Russell as fan of, 197; team names, 14; teams in Washington, 23; Ted Williams in, 313; Tigers winning, 245, 246, 259; on wartime baseball,

37; Washington Senators' standing in (1924), 52; White Sox as, pennant winner (1919), 28; under William Harridge, 78; Yankees winning, 355
American League Park, 23
American League Park II, 23, 24. *See also* Griffith Stadium
American Recovery and Reinvestment Act (2009), 398
Amoros, Sandy, 141
Ampex, 131
amyotrophic lateral sclerosis, 90, 217, 316
Anaheim CA, 220, 295
Anaheim Convention Center, 212
Anderson, Jack, 242
Anderson, Sparky, 231, 259
Andy Griffith Show, 155–56
Angell, Roger, 221
Angels in the Outfield, 130
Annapolis. *See* U.S. Naval Academy
Anson, Cap, 7, 8
Aparicio, Luis, 146, 216–17, 227, 229, 394, 396
Apollo 11, 206, 216
Appling, Luke, 169, 226
The Apprentice, 410
Arafat, Yasser, 351
Argus (Caledonia OH), 45
Argus (Princeton NJ student newspaper), 31
Arizona, 35, 122, 232
Arizona, USS, 326
Arizona Diamondbacks, 375–76, 380
Arkansas, 87, 336–38, 339, 344
Arlington Cemetery, 174
Arlington Stadium, 255
Arlington TX, 255, 363
Armed Forces Radio Network, 87, 256
Armstrong, Neil, 206
Army-Navy game, 162, 183. *See also* U.S. Army; U.S. Naval Academy; West Point
Arroyo, Luis, 175
Arthur, Chester A., 7, 9

baseball (*continued*)
administration, 346–47, 351; in Cuba, 281; decline of popularity of, 191, 224–25, 236–37, 323–24, 351, 385, 414–18; drug use in, 361, 365, 381–82, 413; Dwight Eisenhower's pay for playing, 134–35; origins of, 1–3, 405; rules of, 2, 5, 12, 131, 192, 221, 357, 417; tradition in, 26–27, 87, 212, 298, 336; during wartime, 36–38, 76, 82–85, 96–102, 393
"Baseball as America" exhibition, 27
baseball cards, 315, 360, 363
baseball games: for charity, 36, 85, 86; congressional, 36, 82, 414; effects on attendance at, 89, 146–47; first postwar, 106–7; first professional, in Washington, 6; at night, 77, 86, 193, 197, 247, 417, 418; pace and timing of, 416–18; presidential attendance at, 5, 8, 9, 32, 93–94, 216, 265; presidential passes to, 17, 33, 106; presidents booed at, 66–67, 118, 413
Baseball Magazine, 11, 37, 53, 76, 85
baseball parks: of American League, 13; artificial grass in, 201–2; in Atlanta, 270–71, 280–81, 283; atmosphere at, 24, 77, 165–66, 170, 172, 192, 259, 347; Babe Ruth at, 186; in Boston, 180–81; in California, 153–54; in Chicago, 48; in Detroit, 241–44, 257, 259–60; in New York, 43–44, 149–52, 168; opening of, 25; for professional teams, 12; Teddy Roosevelt's pass for, 17; television coverage at, 416; in Texas, 200–202, 363–64; in Washington DC, 23–24, 166–67, 169–73
baseball players: in armed services, 10, 81, 84–88; G. H. W. Bush's honoring of, 312–15; G. W. Bush's honoring of, 371–74; as Hall of Fame inductees, 97; payment of, 13, 28–29, 38, 43, 64–65, 69–70, 211, 230, 312; popularity of, 311–12; Richard Nixon's All-Star team of, 212, 225–30;

during wartime, 37, 85–88, 247. *See also under* labor issues: in baseball
baseball teams: amateur, 3, 12; at Bush 41 White House, 315; first professional, 12; geographic distribution of, 147, 168; at Obama White House, 387–88, 402–3; professional leagues of, 13; in Southeast, 272
Baseball: The Presidents' Game (Mead and Dickson), 2, 17, 112, 263
Baseball Tonight, 359. *See also* ESPN
baseball uniforms: of Braves, 280; of Tigers, 259, 260; of Donald Trump, 408; of Joe Torre, 358; of Knickerbockers, 12; of Lou Gehrig, 316; of Mets, 168; numbers on, 68, 109; of Ted Williams, 179
Baseball Writers' Association of America, 70, 97, 199–200, 214
Bashian, Aram, 300
basketball, 215, 220, 415
Bauer, Hank, 132
Bay of Pigs, 162, 188
Becquer, Julio, 137
Begin, Menachem, 274–75
Beirut, 289, 301
Bell, John, 4
Bellinger, Cody, 418
Bench, Johnny, 222, 227, 229, 231, 232, 251
Bennett, Charles G., 23, 243
Bennett, Robert, 352
Bennett Park, 243–44
Berardino, Johnny, 291
Berlin, 162, 300, 325
Berman, Chris, 348
Berra, Yogi: in Donald Trump's poem, 408–9; G. W. Bush on, 372; honoring of, 68–69, 227; on Mickey Mantle's batting, 133; stories about, 338; in World Series, 132, 138, 141, 144, 145, 156
Berry, Charlie, 167
Bessmertnykh, Alexander, 301
Bethesda MD, 34

China: communism in, 117–18; G. H. W. Bush in, 319, 324; and Jimmy Carter, 274; mining interests of, 62; Richard Nixon in, 206, 224, 233, 274–75

Christie, Chris, 411

Churchill, Winston: on Clement Attlee, 128; correspondence of, 405; on courage, 183, 375; dismissal of, as prime minister, 332; FDR on, 94; funeral of, 393; on Iron Curtain, 105, 110; on learning, 365; and Obama administration, 397; poker playing by, 106; on salvation of Western civilization, 104; vocabulary of, 174; on World War II, 81, 306

Cicotte, Eddie, 28, 29

Cigar, Lou, 14

Cincinnati OH, 21, 223, 234, 292

Cincinnati Reds: 1995 season of, 280; and Barack Obama, 386; and Black Sox scandal, 28–29; Bob Allen with, 42; Carters at games of, 264, 265; and Continental League, 168; in first night game, 77; home fields of, 61, 172, 324; Jake Daubert with, 42; Larry MacPhail with, 89; Opening Days of, 78, 253; Ronald Reagan at game of, 292; Sparky Anderson with, 258; on video, 89; William Howard Taft at game of, 24; in World Series, 221, 231–32, 246, 315, 319, 324

Cincinnati Red Stockings, 6, 8, 12, 25, 26, 27

Citi Field, 151, 172

Citizen's Bank Park, 387

civil rights, 32, 129, 329, 330

Civil Rights Act (1991), 329

Civil War, 3, 6, 30, 332

Clark, Champ, 36

Clark, Edward T., 54

Clark, Stephen C., 97, 98

Clark, Tom, 106

Clark, Will, 230

Clatfelter, Harry, 54

Clayton Antitrust Act, 32

Clean Air Act, 320

Clemens, Roger, 230

Clemens, Samuel. *See* Twain, Mark

Clemente, Roberto: in All-Star Game, 251; at Candlestick Park, 170; career of, 146; death of, 222–23; image of, 10, 311; on Richard Nixon's All-Star team, 227, 229; in World Series, 155, 221, 222

Clendenon, Donn, 218

Cleveland, Grover, 7–9

Cleveland Blues, 7

Cleveland Browns, 24

Cleveland Indians: Bill Clinton at game of, 347; at DC Stadium, 167; and Jimmy Dudley, 34; Joe DiMaggio vs., 91; racial integration of, 136; Rick Sutcliffe with, 297; Ted Williams vs., 177; uniforms of, 68; White Sox vs., 394; in World Series, 132, 280, 388, 402; Yankees vs., 355. *See also* Cleveland Naps

Cleveland Municipal Stadium, 166

Cleveland Naps, 18. *See also* Cleveland Indians

Cleveland OH, 13, 243

Clevenger, Truman "Tex," 137

Clifford, Clark, 106, 303

Clinton, Bill: on *Arsenio Hall Show*, 342; as baseball fan, 336, 337, 348–51; criticisms of, 342, 350, 352–53; effect in 2000 election, 369; as "First Gentleman," 354; first pitch by, 347; and G. H. W. Bush, 327, 328, 330–33, 335, 353, 366, 367; image of, 21, 342; impeachment of, 352; policies of, 339, 341, 348, 350, 351, 352; political career of, 337–39; presidential campaign of, 341–46; at softball games, 340–41; Yankees during administration of, 355, 357–58

Clinton, Chelsea, 340–41

Clinton, Hillary Rodham: on education, 341; first pitches by, 340, 341, 347; on health care, 350; at library dedication,

Great Britain: aid to Greece and Turkey from, 110; baseball signed by king of, 40; Calvin Coolidge's heritage in, 57; Dwight Eisenhower in, 130–31; games in, 2, 9–10; JFK in, 180; Joseph Kennedy in, 160; Margaret Thatcher in, 324; navy of, 48; and United States, 405, 406; Winston Churchill in, 332, 397, 405; in World War I, 35; in World War II, 76, 81, 306, 375

Great Depression, 63–64, 66–68, 73, 76, 79, 89, 159. *See also* economy

Greatest Generation, 311, 335, 352

Greenberg, Hank: and 1934 All-Star team, 245; 1937 season of, 246; honoring of, 226, 259; image of, 10; vs. Senators, 115; at Tiger Stadium, 242

Greenfield, Meg, 207, 237

"Green Light Letter," 83–85, 94, 97, 100–101, 149

Grenada, 289

Grey, Sir Edward, 20

Grich, Bobby, 228

Grieve, Tom, 361

Griffey, Ken, Jr., 229

Griffith, Calvin, 130, 136, 146, 147, 152, 153

Griffith, Clark: and Bob Wolff, 116, 117; on Calvin Coolidge, 52; at charity game, 36; death of, 26, 185; and FDR, 78, 82, 98; and first pitches, 25, 26, 112–13; and Grace Coolidge, 54; and Harry Truman, 106, 107, 112, 116; and home run mark, 132; monument to, 137, 167; and racial integration, 136; and wartime baseball, 83, 86; in Washington DC, 147; at White House, 18; and Woodrow Wilson, 39, 40

Griffith Stadium: All-Star Game at, 80, 137; Bess Truman at, 114; Bob Wolff at, 115–16; Bowie Kuhn at, 213; declining attendance at, 146–48, 163; design of, 25, 77, 146, 147, 167, 185–86; FDR at, 82, 94; first pitches at, 105; flag ceremony at, 36;

Grace Coolidge at, 54; Harry Truman at, 106–7, 113, 118; Herbert Hoover at, 64; history of, 184–86; JFK at, 163; LBJ at, 190; naming of, 24; Richard Nixon at, 210–11, 219, 225; tape-measure home run at, 116–17, 132; Walter Johnson at, 34; Warren Harding at, 44; Woodrow Wilson at, 33, 39, 40; World Series at, 55–56. *See also* American League Park II

Grillo, J. B., 24

Grimes, Burleigh, 66, 113, 226

Grimm, Charlie, 49, 286

Groat, Dick, 155, 227

Gross, Edwin K., 51

Grove, Lefty, 66, 136, 180, 214, 226, 228

Gulf War, 321, 325–26, 327, 371, 382

gun laws, 351, 368, 398, 401

Guzman, Jose, 365

Gwynn, Tony, 230

Hack, Stan, 245

Haddix, Harvey, 138

Haefner, Mickey, 117

Haig, Alexander, 288

"Hail to the Chief," 159, 274

Haiti, 276, 353

Haley, Nikki, 399–400

Hamilton, Milo, 253, 271, 362

Hance, Kent, 361, 365

Hannegan, Robert E., 83

Harding, Florence Kling, 46, 47, 50

Harding, George (Tryon), 45

Harding, Phoebe, 45

Harding, Warren G.: in baseball documentary, 186; and Calvin Coolidge, 58; career of, 45–48; drinking of, 44; election of, 39, 41; first pitches by, 44, 186; "front-porch" campaign of, 47, 50; and Herbert Hoover, 62; illness and death of, 45, 50, 59; and love of baseball, 42–44, 48; presidency of, 47–48, 50–52, 57; as team owner, 42; on Yankee Stadium, 44

Theodore White on, 103; and Vietnam War, 189; and Washington ballpark, 171–73; World Series during presidency of, 194, 395

Kennedy, John F., Jr., 159, 173, 174, 181

Kennedy, Joseph, Jr., 160

Kennedy, Joseph P., Sr., 160, 175, 207–8

Kennedy, Robert F., 169, 194, 249

Kent State University, 206

Kentucky, 98, 108, 344, 354

Kerr, Paul S., 97, 98

Kerry, John, 378

Kershaw, Clayton, 415

Khachigian, Ken, 300

Khomeini, Ayatollah, 275

Khrushchev, Nikita, 162, 163

Killebrew, Harmon, 137–38, 147, 227, 228, 251

Kinard, Frank (Bruiser), 224

Kiner, Ralph, 168, 223

King, Larry, 107, 193

King, Leslie Lynch, Jr. *See* Ford, Gerald

King, Martin Luther, Jr., 191, 249, 329, 339

King, Rodney, 329–30

Kingdome, 172

Kirst, Sean, 392

Klein, Chuck, 227

Klein, Herbert, 220

Kluszewski, Ted, 395

KMOX radio, 336–39

Knoblauch, Chuck, 279

Knothole Gang, 115–16

Knotts, Don, 156

Knute Rockne All American, 287

Koenig, Bill, 257

Koppett, Leonard, 141

Korea, 276, 377

Korean War, 117, 118, 140, 177, 310

Koufax, Sandy, 171, 191, 204, 225, 227, 229, 388–89

Krichell, Paul, 89

Kubek, Tony, 323

Kuhn, Bowie, 192, 213–15, 237, 264, 267, 415

Kurowski, Whitey, 88

Kuwait, 325, 333

Labine, Clem, 145

labor issues: in baseball, 281–83, 351, 362, 363, 364, 367; Calvin Coolidge on, 58; Harry Truman on, 111, 112; in Michigan, 248; postwar, 105; Ronald Reagan on, 289; Warren Harding on, 48; Woodrow Wilson on, 32

Lackey, John, 414

LaFollette, Robert, 56

LaGrow, Lerrin, 231

La Guardia, Fiorello H., 82–83

Lajoie, Napoleon, 18

Lake Front Park, 48

Lake Front Park II, 48

Landis, Jim, 395, 396

Landis, Kenesaw Mountain: on Black Sox scandal, 29–30; and Calvin Coolidge, 56; as commissioner, 39, 101; at dedication of museum, 3; political position of, 101–2; on vulgarities in World Series, 65, 286; on wartime baseball, 83–85, 97, 98

Laos, 167, 235

Lardner, Ring, 68

Larker, Norm, 395

Larsen, Don, 115, 144, 145, 155, 170, 218

LaRussa, Tony, 230

Lary, Frank, 242, 248, 257

Lasorda, Tommy, 230, 267, 305, 306, 307, 358

The Last Out, 184–86

The Last Republicans (Updegrove), 382–83

Latin America, 21, 105, 120, 136–37, 146, 222, 223. *See also* Cuba; Mexico; Nicaragua; Puerto Rico; Venezuelans

Lavagetto, Cookie, 108

Lazzeri, Tony, 67, 292

LBJ Ranch, 187, 204

National Association of Professional Baseball Leagues, 17, 82

National Baseball Hall of Fame and Library Old-Timers Committee, 97–102

National Baseball Hall of Fame and Museum: Abner Doubleday honored at, 11; Al Kaline in, 242; American values at, 389; Barack Obama at, 385–87; dedication of, 3; FDR as candidate for, 96–101; gavel in, 282; George Brett in, 276; G. W. Bush at, 368; inductees at Pirates' bicentennial, 211; inductees at White House, 212, 290–92, 371–74; Joe Torre in, 358; and Mark McGwire, 382; and Pete Rose, 282–83, 413; Polish players in, 314; postage stamp dedicated to, 77; research at, 2, 6, 12; Richard Nixon on induction into, 237; Roberto Clemente in, 223; Ted Williams in, 178. *See also* Cooperstown NY

National Broadcasting Company (NBC): in 1960s, 206; baseball programming on, 196, 250, 296–97, 322, 323, 416; and center-field shot, 131–32; documentary on, 184; Donald Trump on, 410; FDR's speeches on, 73; football on, 152; Gerald Ford on, 256; Joe Garagiola with, 338; Mickey Mantle on, 355–56; news program on, 233; Singing Senators on, 137; Vin Scully on, 293; World Series on, 79, 141, 144, 154–56, 171, 193, 194, 218–19, 232, 250–51, 305–6, 354–55, 394–95

National Collegiate Athletic Association (NCAA), 134, 241

National Football League, 152, 153, 185, 224, 271, 415. *See also* football

National Governors Association, 341

National Guard, 124, 191, 365–66

National League: 1935 MVP of, 286; in 1950 pennant race, 122, 124–25; in 1970s, 220, 231, 271–72; in All-Star Games, 80, 170, 216, 364; attendance records in, 69; ballparks in, 151; batting title in,

155; Bob Allen in, 42; competition of, 13; divisions in, 218; expansion of, 153; founder of, 9; franchises in, 5, 14, 23, 28, 168, 171–72, 200, 272, 277, 278, 354; game in Astrodome, 201; Jake Daubert in, 42; presidents at games of, 24; professionalization of, 13; records in, 79; Richard Nixon's All-Star team in, 225–30; television earnings of, 150; on wartime baseball, 37; in World Series, 14

National League Park, 24

National Park and Boundary Field, 22

Nationals Park, 25, 28, 381, 385, 413

The Natural, 8

The Naval War of 1812 (Roosevelt), 15

Navin, Frank, 244, 245, 246

Navin Field. *See* Tiger Stadium

Nazis, 81, 95, 375. *See also* Hitler, Adolf

NBC. *See* National Broadcasting Company (NBC)

Neal, Bob, 151

Neal, Charlie, 395, 396

Neel, Eric, 329

Negro League, 119

Nehru, Jawaharlal, 68–69

Nelson, Lindsey, 69, 139, 168, 196, 202, 219

Nelson, Rocky, 156

Never Enough (D'Antonio), 407

Newcombe, Don, 138, 145–46

New Deal, 74–76, 117, 289

New Hampshire, 35, 269, 310, 342, 369

Newhouser, Hal, 242, 246, 259

New Jersey, 31–32, 238, 345, 410

New Jersey Generals, 409

Newman, Wallace "Chief," 212

New Orleans, 337, 379

Newsday, 195, 266–67

Newsom, Bobo, 214, 226, 228

Newsweek, 111, 200, 234, 253, 315

New York: 1992 election in, 342–43; in 2016 election, 412; advertising firm in, 236; Al Smith from, 62, 63;

baseball rivalry in, 125–26; baseball tradition in, 2, 3, 147, 152, 321–22, 386, 393; Bob Wolff in, 115; Charles Evans Hughes as governor of, 35; expansion team in, 168; FDR's political career in, 74; George Pataki in, 368; Hillary Clinton in, 354; history of major league baseball in, 11; Lou Gehrig in, 90; Max Jacobson's license in, 194; Nixons in, 205, 238; stadium construction in, 168; Teddy Roosevelt's political career in, 15; television stations in, 131, 152; Thomas Dewey as governor of, 110; umpires' calls to, 417

New York City: baseball parks in, 43–44, 150–51; Brooklyn as part of, 70; Eleanor Roosevelt in, 102; John Rocker on, 281; Lou Gehrig's employment with, 90; September 11 in, 374–76; Teddy Roosevelt in, 14; Trump property in, 409

New York City Parks Commission, 149–50

New York City Police Commissioners, 15

New York Daily News, 150, 212

New Yorker, 168–69, 319

New York Giants football team, 152

New York Giants: in California, 87, 147, 149–53; Dodgers vs. (1951), 125–26; Dwight Eisenhower at game of, 134; G. W. Bush's memories of, 374; home field of, 43–44, 152, 170; influence of, on Mets, 168; and Jackie Robinson, 146; under John McGraw, 42; Phil Rizzuto, cut by, 356; radio ban by, 89; success of, 388; Ulysses Grant's following of, 6; William Howard Taft at game of, 27; Willie Mays with, 373; in World Series, 14, 28, 54–56, 78–80, 184–85, 388. *See also* San Francisco Giants

New York Highlanders, 18. *See also* New York Yankees

New York Knickerbockers, 12

New York Mets: 1969 season of, 217–19, 222, 272; at Astrodome, 202; Atlanta Braves vs., 277; expansion team of, 168–69; home field of, 12, 150, 151, 172; and honoring of Jackie Robinson, 348; Joe Torre with, 357; radio voice of, 69; and Richard Nixon, 237, 239

New York Military Academy, 407, 409

New York Post, 150, 207, 295

New York Times: on 1955 World Series, 142; on 1956 World Series, 145–46; on 1992 election, 331; on Barack Obama, 401; on broadcasters, 293; on Clinton administration, 346–47; on Dwight Eisenhower, 134; on football, 16; on Gulf War, 326; and Kenesaw Mountain Landis's job, 29; on LBJ, 198, 203; on origins of baseball, 3; on Phil Rizzuto, 356; and Richard Nixon, 213, 235; on Ulysses Grant, 6; on wartime baseball, 83, 85

New York Yankees: 1924 season of, 52; 1933 season of, 79; 1959 season of, 394; 1960s teams of, 195–96, 199, 213, 221; in All-Star Game, 91; at Astrodome, 202–3; Babe Ruth purchased by, 43; Boston Pilgrims vs., 14; Boston Red Sox vs., 378; with Calvin Coolidge, 54–55; Carters as fans of, 269; Casey Stengel with, 123; competition of, 153; Donald Trump as fan of, 406; farm team of, 119; and FDR, 78, 97; and firing of Mel Allen, 194–95; Gabe Paul with, 212; George Steinbrenner with, 238; at Griffith Stadium, 163; Harry Truman at game of, 113; and Herbert Hoover, 62, 67; home field of, 43–44; in Japan, 142; JFK at game of, 175; Joe Torre with, 355, 357–58; Lou Gehrig with, 89–91, 315–16; Mark Koenig with, 49; media coverage of, 87, 89, 131–32, 140, 239, 356; Mickey Mantle's retirement from, 217; in movies, 292; players traded to,

Chicago Cubs, 402–4, 414; criticisms of, 397; in Cuba, 281; economy under, 327, 397, 398, 399, 401; first pitches by, 384–88; and G. H. W. Bush, 334, 335, 353; Hillary Clinton vs., 354; image of, 21, 388, 397, 399, 401; inaugural parade for, 164; policies of, 348, 385, 390, 391, 397–402; political career of, 391; public opinion of, 390, 398–402; speeches of, 384, 391, 392, 397, 400; and technology, 385; voting base of, 412; Washington Senators during presidency of, 80

Obama, Malia Ann, 391

Obama, Michelle Robinson, 386, 388, 390, 403

Obama, Natasha (Sasha), 391

Obamacare. *See* Affordable Health Care Act

O'Brien, Larry, 199

O'Connor, Leslie M., 97–98

Odom, John "Blue Moon," 120, 231

Ohio, 41, 45–47, 266, 345, 412

Ohio Historical Society, 51

Ohio State League, 42

Oklahoma, 65, 87, 336, 373

Oklahoma Outlaws, 286

Old Man and the Sea (Hemingway), 123

Old Timers' Days, 70

Oliva, Tony, 227

Olympics, 134, 135, 275, 280, 299, 330

Olympic Stadium, 172

O'Malley, Peter, 267

O'Malley, Walter, 69, 138, 149–54, 168, 348

Omnibus Crime Bill, 351

One Flew Over the Cuckoo's Nest, 193

One for the Book (Plimpton), 253

O'Neill, Paul, 280

O'Neill, Thomas P. "Tip," 7, 8, 265, 341, 392

"one old cat," 1–2

Opening Days: Barack Obama at, 385, 413; Bob Wolff's broadcasting of, 114; and Donald Trump, 413; Dwight Eisenhower at, 136; first pitches at, 25, 27;

first two of season, 78; Hank Aaron's home run on (1974), 253; Harry Truman at, 105–7, 112–13, 120; Jackie Robinson's first, 266; JFK at, 163–65, 167, 174; LBJ at, 198, 199; Richard Nixon at, 211, 213, 220; of Senators, 147, 166, 191; U.S. senators at, 197; Warren Harding at, 44; William Howard Taft at, 39–40; Woodrow Wilson at, 33

Operation Desert Shield, 325

Operation Desert Storm, 325–26, 333

Oriole Park at Camden Yards, 10, 25, 259, 347–50, 363, 364

Orlando, Johnny, 93

Oswald, Lee Harvey, 174, 251

Ott, Mel, 79–80, 134, 226, 228, 242

Overbey, John, 317

Oxford University, 327, 339, 343

Oyler, Ray, 250

Pacific Coast League, 82, 153, 210, 295

Pacific Palisades CA, 196–97, 294

Paige, Satchel, 178, 226, 228, 394

Palmeiro, Rafael, 350, 365

Palmer, Alice, 391

Palmer, Jim, 229

Panama Canal, 16, 21, 50, 274, 325

Paris, 16, 173–74

Paris Peace Accords, 233

Parker, Salty, 198

Parrish, Lance, 258

Pascual, Camilo, 136, 147

Pataki, George, 368

Patterson, Arthur (Red), 132

Patton, George, 94, 152

Paul, Gabe, 212

Paula, Carlos, 137, 146

Paul II, Pope, 356–57

Paul VI, Pope, 393

PBS, 47, 206, 208, 300

Peanut Classic Softball Tournament, 263

Pearl Harbor, 81, 122, 185, 309, 326, 374

Pearlman, Jeff, 281
Pearson, Albie, 137
Peckinpaugh, Roger, 57
Pedroia, Dustin, 408
Pendergast, Tom, 104
Pendleton, Terry, 279
Pennock, Herb, 226
Pennsylvania, 374, 412
Pentagon, 235, 374
Perot, Ross, 328, 330–31, 342–44, 346
Perry, Gaylord, 368
Pershing, John J. "Black Jack," 35, 46
Personal Memoirs of Ulysses S. Grant (Grant), 6
Pesky, Johnny, 85, 88
Petrocelli, Rico, 181, 183
Petroskey, Dale, 251
Pettitte, Andy, 388
Philadelphia Athletics: in 1910s, 42; at American League Park II, 24; Andrew Johnson's following of, 5; Benjamin Harrison at game of, 8; and FDR, 78, 97; during Herbert Hoover's presidency, 64–67, 69; home run record of, 69; Joe DiMaggio vs., 91; to Kansas City, 119; William Howard Taft at games of, 23, 25; in World Series, 214, 417
Philadelphia PA: 2016 election in, 412; All-Star Game in, 255–56; baseball fans in, 172; baseball field in, 13; Donald Trump in, 409; Enterprise Baseball Club of, 5; night game in, 247; proximity to Washington, 64; stadium in, 183; World Series in, 232
Philadelphia Phillies: 1950 season of, 124–25; announcer for, 395; at Astrodome, 201; Atlanta Braves vs., 279; Barack Obama at games of, 385, 387–88; Bill White with, 192; Bob Allen with, 42; and Continental League, 168; and Donald Trump, 408; Gerald Ford at games of, 256; home field of, 172;

Hugh Mulcahy with, 81; Jackie Robinson vs., 266; Jim Bunning with, 211; Pete Rose with, 282; at White House, 387; Woodrow Wilson at game of, 36
Phillips, Carrie Fulton, 51
Pierce, Billy, 396
Piersall, Jim, 136
Pidgeon, Walter, 345
Pinckney, Rev. Clementa C., 400
Pinelli, Babe, 145
pitches, first: at Astrodome, 202; by Barbara Bush, 321; in baseball documentary, 186; by Edward Kennedy, 183; by Hillary Clinton, 340, 341, 347; by Hubert Humphrey, 191; by John "Honey Fitz" Fitzgerald, 160; by Lillian Carter, 267, 275; by Nancy Reagan, 305; by Pat Nixon, 219; styles of, 23, 112–13, 380; tradition of, 25, 26, 183, 185. *See also under individual presidents*
Pittsburgh PA, 11, 26–27, 41, 130, 260, 297
Pittsburgh Pirates: Atlanta Braves vs., 271, 279; bicentennial of, 211; Carters at games of, 264; and Continental League, 168; Harvey Haddix with, 138; home field of, 130, 281; and mourning of Roberto Clemente, 222–23; in National League playoff, 231; ownership of, 212; Pat Nixon at game of, 219; Paul Waner with, 76; "Pud" Galvin with, 7; Richie Hebner with, 166; Wilbur Cooper with, 42; Willie Stargell with, 294; in World Series, 13–14, 56–57, 69, 155–56, 185, 222, 265–66
Pitzer, David, 220
Plains GA, 61, 262–64, 268, 269, 381
Pledge of Allegiance, 138
Plews, Herbie, 136
Plimpton, George, 253
Plouffe, David, 387
PNC Park, 260
Podres, Johnny, 141, 171

radio (*continued*)

59, 60, 75, 93, 157, 284–85, 374, 385; Richard Nixon on, 210–11; Ronald Reagan on, 196–97, 284–86, 292, 294, 295, 304; St. Louis Cardinals on, 336–38; Vin Scully on, 196–97, 295; during World War II, 86. *See also* Fireside Chats; media; *specific stations*

Radio Act (1927), 60

railroads: baseball parks near, 12; Harry Truman's campaign on, 122; legislation regarding, 32; between Philadelphia and Washington, 64; role in U.S. economy, 11; St. Louis Cardinals on, 68; Teddy Roosevelt's policies on, 16; Warren Harding on, 48, 50; to Washington Senators' games, 33, 34; Woodrow Wilson on, 38; during World War I, 35

Raissman, Bob, 150

Ramos, Pedro, 137, 216

Randolph, Jay, 82

Randolph, Jennings, 82

Raschi, Vic, 131, 141, 356

Rawlings Company, 406

Rayburn, Sam, 94, 103, 105

Reagan, Nancy Davis, 288, 290–91, 304, 307, 367

Reagan, Nelle, 285

Reagan, Ronald: 1984 campaign of, 298–99; and 2016 election, 411; age of, 298–99, 304; aides of, 251, 300; on America, 131; approach of, to politics, 285; assassination attempt on, 288–89, 292; as athlete, 8, 285–86; and baseball, 285–86, 290–94, 372, 405; booing of, 413; boyhood home of, 61; as broadcaster, 284–86, 294, 295; on Calvin Coolidge, 60; as communicator, 75, 284, 287–88, 299–300, 304, 305, 363; Democrats for, 342, 346; description of, 21; economy under, 289, 296, 302, 315, 327; and FDR, 129; first pitches

by, 292–95, 380; and Gerald Ford, 256, 258; at GOP convention, 331; Hollywood supporters of, 345; honoring of, 334; as host of television program, 385; illness and death of, 284, 285, 307; and image of America, 300–301; and James Baker, 315; and Jimmy Carter, 273, 276; library of, 307, 383; policies of, 57, 287, 289, 296, 302, 320, 350; political career of, 26, 290–91; on presidency, 290; public opinion of, 302–4, 319, 353; religious background of, 285, 304; and Richard Nixon, 236, 299, 307; running mate of, 319; and Silent Majority, 252; at Statue of Liberty centennial, 301; State of the Union address by, 341; and Vin Scully, 196–97; on White House, 387; and Zero Option, 289

Reagan Presidential Library and Museum, 307, 383

Red Cross, 36, 85, 86, 198

Redding, Jack, 2, 12

Reed, Jack, 248

Reese, Harold "Pee Wee," 69–70, 108, 109, 124, 131, 141, 142, 144

Reeves, Richard, 289; *President Kennedy: Profile of Power*, 194

Reichler, Joseph, 237

Reid, Harry, 391

Reilly, Rick, 196–97

Renteria, Edgar, 378

Republican National Committee, 235–36, 319, 384

Republican National Convention, 46, 47, 64, 70, 129, 233, 238, 297, 305

Republican Party: in 1984 election, 297; in 1992 election, 326–31, 342–46; in 2000 election, 369; in 2008 election, 397; in 2016 election, 401, 406, 410–12; Abe Lincoln nominated by, 4; and Affordable Care Act, 399; in Arkansas, 339; in California, 319–20; celebrity

Roosevelt, Franklin Delano (*continued*)
83–85; description of, 21; dog of, 73–74;
first pitches by, 23, 36, 78, 81–82, 405;
on "Forgotten Americans," 413; G. W.
Bush's reference to, 377; Harry Truman
compared with, 103–4; and Herbert
Hoover, 122; honoring of, 96–100, 129;
illness and death of, 73, 74, 86, 94–96;
LBJ on, 187; library and museum
of, 72, 73; and love of baseball, 65,
76–78, 93–94, 96–101, 135–36, 149,
157, 213, 294, 322; and love of driving,
31; as nominee, 63–64; Opening Day
photographs of, 112; policies of, 74–76,
83, 101, 117, 289; popularity of, 254,
353; presidency of, 41, 73–87, 236, 352;
and Ronald Reagan, 287; season pass
of, 112; speeches of, 50, 72–77, 93, 157,
284, 374, 418; street named for, 131; and
World Series, 49, 79–80, 138, 194, 393
Roosevelt, Kermit, 18
Roosevelt, Martha Stewart "Mittie"
Bulloch, 14
Roosevelt, Quentin, 18
Roosevelt, Sara, 73
Roosevelt, Theodore "Teddy": attitude
of, toward baseball, 16–18, 266, 322; as
conservationist, 60; first pitch by, 22;
G. W. Bush on, 129; life and career of,
14–19; in "Presidential" race, 28; and
San Juan Hill, 15; third party of, 18, 32,
328; and William Howard Taft, 21, 22,
26, 32, 58, 345; on World War I, 35
Root, Charlie, 49, 214
Rose, Pete, 220, 229, 232, 282–83, 315,
408, 413
Roseboro, John, 171, 395, 396
Rose Law Firm, 341
Rosen, Al, 347
Rothstein, Arnold, 29
Rough Riders, 15. *See also* U.S. Army
rounders, 2, 9–10

Roush, Edd, 28, 227
Rove, Karl, 360, 363, 369
Rowe, Lynwood, 245
Royal Rooters, 13, 160
Rozelle, Pete, 152, 192
Rubio, Marco, 411
Ruby, Jack, 174
Rudi, Joe, 231, 232
Ruel, Muddy, 55–56, 185
Ruffing, Red, 70, 226
Rumsfeld, Donald, 371, 377
Ruppert, Jacob, 90
Ruppert Stadium, 119
Russell, Richard, 197–98
Russia. *See* Soviet Union
Rustand, Warren, 242
Ruth, George Herman (Babe): in 1920s,
43; for Al Smith, 62; with Calvin
Coolidge, 54–55; Carters at game of,
265; drinking of, 44, 69; at Griffith
Stadium, 185–86; in Hall of Fame, 223;
home run record of, 170, 246, 248, 252,
253, 265, 270, 361; illness of, 109–10, 317;
popularity of, 30, 311, 316; retirement
of, 185; and Richard Nixon, 216, 226,
228; salary of, 63; success of, 69; and Ty
Cobb, 245; uniform number of, 68; and
Warren Harding, 45; in World Series,
49, 67; at Yankee Stadium, 44, 193
Rutherford, James "Skip," 340–41
Ryan, Nolan, 230, 365, 368

Saam, Byrum, 395
Saberhagen, Bret, 230
Sadat, Anwar, 274–75
Sale, Kirk, 5
San Clemente CA, 219, 237
Sandberg, Ryne, 230, 296–97
Sandburg, Carl, 28
San Diego Padres, 156, 221, 259, 267, 277, 298
San Francisco CA: ballparks in, 259;
Barack Obama in, 401; earthquake

Taft, William Howard: death of, 26; first pitches by, 22–25, 27, 199, 387, 418; G. H. W. Bush compared to, 345; inaugural reception of, 321; and love of baseball, 21, 24, 27, 39–40, 60, 264; political position of, 17–18; presidency of, 21–27, 58; in "Presidential" race, 28; and Republican Party split, 32; and seventh-inning stretch, 26–27; and Warren Harding, 46; Woodrow Wilson compared to, 20

Taft-Hartley Act, 111

"Take Me Out to the Ballgame," 25, 27, 336, 413

Tasby, Willie, 167, 168–69

taxes: amendment authorizing income, 21; Barack Obama on, 400; Bill Clinton on, 344, 350; G. H. W. Bush on, 324, 327, 328, 344, 371; G. W. Bush on, 368; JFK on, 173; Jimmy Carter on, 274; Ronald Reagan on, 289, 292, 299; Warren Harding on, 48; Woodrow Wilson on, 32. *See also* economy

Taylor, Charles, 14

Taylor, John, 14

Taylor, Robert, 286

Taylor, Tony, 201

Teapot Dome scandal, 51

Teeter, Bob, 331

Tehran, 262, 275

television: in 1960s, 206; Barack Obama on, 384; baseball coverage on, 114, 120, 125, 138–40, 143, 193, 196, 200, 219, 239, 258, 277–78, 281, 293, 322–24, 338, 347, 351, 380, 384, 386, 393, 414–18; baseball documentary on, 184–85; African Americans on, 402; Bob Wolff on, 115; Braves on, 271, 277, 279; Cal Ripken on, 348; Cardinals on, 338; Carters' watching of, 269, 283; Cubs on, 297, 339–40, 403; Dizzy Dean on, 139, 196; Donald Trump on, 410; Dwight

Eisenhower's watching of, 130; effect of, on game attendance, 132, 139, 150, 151, 277; football on, 152; Gerald Ford on, 251–52, 256–57; G. H. W. Bush on, 369; Herbert Hoover's watching of, 69; innovations in, 131–32, 145, 267, 272–73, 358, 385, 395, 416–17; JFK on, 163; Jimmy Carter on, 281; LA riots on, 329; LBJ on, 203; Martin Luther King Jr. on, 339; Mel Allen on, 195, 356; Mickey Mantle's eulogy on, 356; political ads on, 345; popularity of, 131, 139, 161, 180, 393; presidential speeches on, 75, 129; Richard Nixon on, 161, 207; Ronald Reagan on, 287, 294, 296, 299–300, 385; September 11 on, 374; at Turner Field, 281; wars on, 117, 188–89, 254, 325; White Sox on, 393; World Series on, 144, 154–56, 171, 395, 415; Yankees on, 195, 255, 355. *See also* media; *specific stations*

Tenace, Gene, 231, 232

Tener, John, 37

Tennessee, 42, 87, 198, 271, 336, 342

terrorism, 377, 379, 398, 412

Terry, Bill, 79, 80, 93, 226

Terry, Ralph, 120, 156

Texas: ballparks in, 200–202, 364; ceremony for LBJ in, 204; Dwight Eisenhower in, 127, 131; first pitches in, 22; Ford and Carter campaigns in, 255; G. H. W. Bush in, 317–18, 332, 370; G. W. Bush in, 287–88, 359–61, 366, 370, 373, 381; JFK in, 173, 288; Joe DiMaggio in, 123; Kennedy-Nixon election in, 208; LBJ in, 186, 187, 189, 190; as Mexican territory, 35; Mickey Mantle in, 356; presidents from, 380; Richard Nixon in, 230; Ross Perot in, 328

Texas A&M University, 318, 367

Texas Hill Country, 61, 187, 189

Texas League, 153, 200

Twenty-Fifth Amendment, 39
Twenty-Third Street Grounds, 48

Ueberroth, Peter, 294, 305, 324
Uecker, Bob, 238
umpires, 191, 214, 416–17
Union Grounds, 12
Unitas, Johnny, 152
United Nations: Bill Clinton as envoy
    for, 353; in Bosnia and Somalia, 351;
    Douglas MacArthur's command of,
    118; FDR's role in, 94; G. H. W. Bush
    with, 319, 320; in Gulf War, 325; prede-
    cessor of, 39; in war on terror, 377–78
United States: in 1960s, 205–6; in Barce-
    lona Olympics, 330; culture in, 327, 331;
    "Forgotten Americans" in, 413; and
    Great Britain, 405, 406; lagging behind
    Russians, 140, 146; political tone in,
    401; Ronald Reagan's image of, 300–
    301; unity in, 392, 400, 402; in World
    War II, 81. *See also under* baseball: as
    American game
University of Michigan, 133, 241, 246, 258
U.S. Air Force, 178, 190. *See also* U.S.
    military
U.S. Army: baseball fans in, 83; African
    Americans in, 32; broadcasts followed
    by, 114; conscription for, 37; Dwight
    Eisenhower in, 127–29; football game,
    162, 183; Golden Knights of, 368; Ted-
    dy Roosevelt with, 15. *See also* Rough
    Riders; U.S. military; West Point
USA *Today*, 282, 322, 335, 343–44, 346
U.S. Cellular Field, 384
U.S. Congress: and Barack Obama, 385,
    398, 399; baseball game of, 36, 82,
    414; at baseball games, 9, 197; Calvin
    Coolidge's address to, 45, 59; censure of
    Andrew Johnson by, 5; confirmation of
    Gerald Ford by, 252–53; and Contras,
    302; on energy crisis, 274; FDR's post-

war report to, 94; on financial issues,
    32, 75, 148, 150; and G. H. W. Bush, 320;
    and G. W. Bush, 361, 377, 379; and Har-
    ry Truman, 117–18, 121; on labor issues,
    111; Lyndon Johnson's speech to, 186–
    87; on nuclear test ban, 173; Republican
    majority in, 39; and Richard Nixon,
    234; and Ronald Reagan, 289; on seg-
    regation, 187; and support of Western
    governments, 110; and wars, 38, 81, 188,
    325; and World Series, 54. *See also* U.S.
    House of Representatives; U.S. Senate
U.S. Constitution, 21, 38–39, 50–51, 404.
    See also Nineteenth Amendment;
    Prohibition
U.S. Football League, 409
U.S. House of Representatives: and
    Affordable Care Act, 399; and Bill
    Clinton, 339, 352; and election of Ruth-
    erford Hayes, 6; George H. W. Bush in,
    240; Gerald Ford in, 247–48, 251–52,
    262; Geraldine Ferraro in, 297; JFK
    in, 160; members' qualifications, 338;
    Richard Nixon in, 207; on World War
    II, 81. *See also* U.S. Congress
U.S. Marine Corps, 93. *See also* U.S.
    military
U.S. military: and Barack Obama, 391,
    398; baseball players in, 10, 81, 84, 86,
    247; and Bill Clinton, 327, 339, 350–51;
    Bob Elson in, 393; crowd control by,
    191; desegregation of, 107; G. H. W.
    Bush on, 326; and Iranian hostages, 275;
    JFK in, 128; at NFL game, 185; portraits
    of, 382; under Richard Nixon, 224, 234;
    under Ronald Reagan, 289–90, 296; in
    Vietnam, 188, 234, 254, 274; in war on
    terror, 377–79; on wartime baseball, 83,
    102. *See also* U.S. Air Force; U.S. Army;
    U.S. Marine Corps; U.S. Navy
U.S. Naval Academy, 263, 268–69. *See
    also* Army-Navy game

U.S. Navy: Bob Wolff in, 114, 115; Charles Lindbergh on ship of, 60; and FDR, 36, 74, 76; football game, 162, 183; Gerald Ford in, 247; G. H. W. Bush in, 309, 316, 333, 367; JFK in, 162; and Teddy Roosevelt, 15, 16; Warren Harding's limiting of, 48. *See also* U.S. military

U.S. Senate: and Affordable Care Act, 399; Andrew Johnson in, 13; on antitrust, 155; Barack Obama in, 384, 391–92, 398; on Bill Clinton, 352; commissioner from, 98; Everett Dirksen in, 251–52; G. H. W. Bush in, 319, 320, 360; Harry Truman in, 94, 104, 121; JFK in, 160, 177; LBJ in, 187, 188, 190; members' qualifications, 338; Prescott Bush in, 309, 329; Richard Russell in, 197–98; on Treaty of Versailles, 38, 39, 48; Walter Mondale in, 297; Warren Harding in, 46. *See also* U.S. Congress

U.S. Supreme Court: on 2000 election, 370; on abortion, 350; under Barack Obama, 398; on baseball strike, 281–82; under Bill Clinton, 350, 351; Calvin Coolidge sworn into office by, 59; Charles Evans Hughes on, 47; under FDR, 76; G. H. W. Bush's appointment to, 320; on prayer, 190; and Richard Nixon, 149, 220; on segregation, 146; and William Howard Taft, 21, 27

Utley, Chase, 387

Valdivielso, Jose, 137
Valenti, Jack, 189
Van Brocklin, Norm, 224
Van Buren, Martin, 3, 10, 385
Vandenberg, Arthur, 110
Vaughan, Arky, 226
Vecsey, George, 16, 145–46, 346–47, 356
Veeck, Bill, 49, 87, 394, 395
Venezuelans, 105, 120, 146. *See also* Latin America

Verducci, Tom, 402
Vernon, Mickey, 137, 199
Veterans Committee. *See* National Baseball Hall of Fame and Library Old-Timers Committee
Veterans Stadium, 172
Victorino, Shane, 387
Victura (sloop), 177
videotape, 131. *See also* motion pictures
Vietnam War: aftermath of, 254; Bill Clinton during, 327, 339, 343; Donald Trump during, 409; effect of, on America, 181; Gerald Ford on, 252; Gulf War compared with, 325, 326; and Jimmy Carter, 274; under LBJ, 188–89, 199, 204, 352; Pentagon study of, 235; players' visits to, 199; prisoners of war in, 220, 234; under Richard Nixon, 205–6, 208, 224, 233–34
Vincent, Fay, 312, 322
Virginia, 71, 199, 348, 356, 414

Wagner, Honus, 13–14, 57, 136, 223
Wagner, Robert, 138
Waitkus, Eddie, 124
Walberg, Rube, 214
Walesa, Lech, 324
Walker, Harry, 88
Walker, Levi, Jr., 271
Wallace, Henry, 103, 105
Wall Street Journal, 190, 298–99, 335, 361, 377, 411, 417
Walsh, Lawrence, 345
Walter Johnson Day, 33
Walters, Bucky, 226
Waner, Paul, 76, 226
Ward, John Montgomery, 6
Ward, Willis, 241
Warner Brothers Studios, 286, 304
Warren, Earl, 251
Warren, Rick, 400
Warren Commission, 251

Washington, Booker T., 16
Washington DC: in 1984 election, 299; All-Star Game in, 212–16; amateur baseball in, 3; baseball field in, 13; Charles Lindbergh in, 60; commissioner from, 192; FDR at games in, 78; FDR's body in, 95–96; first pitches in, 234; Gerald Ford's funeral in, 261; G. W. Bush's post-9/11 speeches in, 377; Harry Truman's birthday in, 121; Jimmy Carter in, 268; Little League Baseball in, 385; Obama family in, 390, 403; professional games in, 6, 169; Republican presidents in, 413; rioting in, 191, 221; Ronald Reagan's shooting in, 288; September 11 in, 374, 375; stadiums in, 166; teams in, 5–6, 147, 148, 220, 224–25, 294, 322, 362, 379–80; Trump property in, 409; Woodrow Wilson's home in, 39, 40; World Series in, 79
Washington, George, 2, 21, 28
Washington Monument, 3
Washington Nationals: Andrew Johnson's following of, 5; Barack Obama at games of, 385, 387–88; Cincinnati Red Stockings vs. (1869), 6; history of, 5, 169–70; Montreal Expos as, 221, 379–80. *See also* Washington Senators
Washington Naval Conference, 48
Washington Olympians, 5
Washington Post: on 1984 Cubs, 298; on 1992 election, 328; on baseball coverage, 324; on Calvin Coolidge, 55; on DC Stadium, 166; on delayed Opening Day, 25; on Donald Trump, 408; on Griffith Stadium, 184; on G. W. Bush, 362, 371–72; on Jimmy Carter, 276; on Margaret Truman, 118; Morris Siegel with, 8, 24; photo of FDR's pitch, 81–82; on Richard Nixon, 111, 207, 213, 224, 235; on Ronald Reagan, 304; on Senators' ineptness, 169; Shirley Povich

with, 5, 167, 183; on William Howard Taft, 22, 24; on Woodrow Wilson, 36; World Series coverage in, 417–18
Washington Redskins, 167, 185, 209, 224
Washington Senators: 1924 season of, 52–54; 1925 season of, 56–57; of 1950s, 136–38, 146–47; at American League Park II, 24; and Barack Obama, 386; Benjamin Harrison at game of, 8; Bess Truman's following of, 113–14; Carters at games of, 264; Clark Griffith with, 18; at Coolidge White House, 386; departure from Washington by, 148–49; and Dwight Eisenhower, 130, 136, 138; expansion team of, 168, 169; FDR at games of, 78; first pitches at games of, 183; Gil Hodges with, 169; Harry Truman at games of, 106, 112, 118; Herbert Hoover at games of, 65; home fields of, 6, 23, 26, 171, 184, 381; Hubert Humphrey at games of, 191; and LBJ, 190, 198, 199; league records of, 79; Lynwood Rowe vs., 245; New York Yankees vs., 69; Opening Days of, 78, 147, 164–65; in Oval Office, 9; parade for, 116; Pat Nixon at games of, 219; Pedro Ramos with, 216; popularity of, 415; postwar, 105; racial integration of, 136–37; radio and television coverage of, 87, 114–15, 213; Richard Nixon at games of, 210–11, 217; Richard Russell as fan of, 197; tape-measure home run against, 132; Walter Johnson with, 33–34; Warren Harding at games of, 44; in Washington DC, 220–21, 362; William Howard Taft at games of, 22, 23, 25–26; William McKinley at game of, 9; Woodrow Wilson at games of, 33, 36, 39, 48; in World Series, 54–56, 79–80, 184, 185. *See also* Washington Nationals
The Washington Senators (Bealle), 22
Washington Unions, 5

31901063258943